Also by Samuel Flagg Bemis:

Jay's Treaty, a Study in Commerce and Diplomacy (New York: The Macmillan Co.; 1923).

Pinckney's Treaty, a Study of America's Advantage from Europe's Distress (Baltimore: The Johns Hopkins Press; 1926).

American Secretaries of State and Their Diplomacy, editor and contributor (10 volumes; New York: Alfred A. Knopf; 1927–9).

The Hussey-Cumberland Mission and American Independence (Princeton: The Princeton Press; 1931).

The Diplomacy of the American Revolution (New York: D. Appleton-Century Co.; printed for the American Historical Association; 1935; second edition, 1937).

Guide to the Diplomatic History of the United States, 1775–1921, with Grace Gardner Griffin (Washington: Government Printing Office; published for the Library of Congress; 1935).

Diplomatic History of the United States (New York: Henry Holt and Co.; 1936; revised edition, 1942).

The Rayneval Memoranda of 1782 (Worcester: American Antiquarian Society; 1938).

La Política Internacional de los Estados Unidos. Interpretaciones (Lancaster, Pa.: printed for the Carnegie Endowment for International Peace; 1939).

Early Diplomatic Missions from Buenos Aires to the United States, 1811–1824 (Worcester: American Antiquarian Society; 1949).

The Latin American Policy of the United States, an Historical Interpretation (New York: published for the Yale Institute of International Studies by Harcourt, Brace and Co.; 1943; Spanish translation: Fondo de Cultura Económica; Mexico, 1943).

JOHN QUINCY ADAMS

AND THE FOUNDATIONS OF

AMERICAN FOREIGN POLICY

JOHN QUINCY ADAMS

AS SECRETARY OF STATE AND PRESIDENT

PORTRAIT BY GILBERT STUART, PAINTED IN QUINCY, 1825–8
BODY BY THOMAS SULLY, 1830. OWNED BY HARVARD COLLEGE

JOHN QUINCY ADAMS

AND THE FOUNDATIONS OF

American Foreign Policy

BY

SAMUEL FLAGG BEMIS

NEW YORK ALFRED A. KNOPF
1949

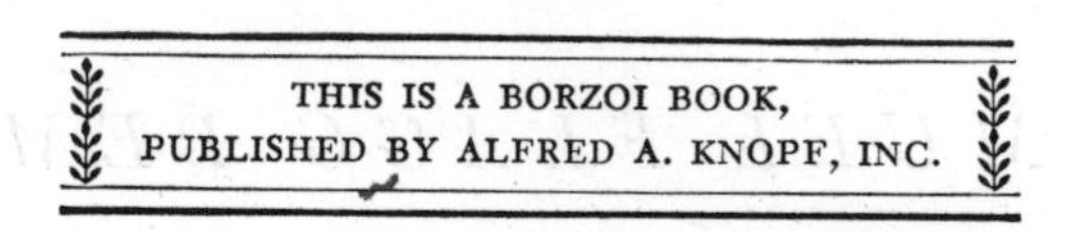

FIRST EDITION

Manufactured in the United States of America

TO THE MEMORY OF

WORTHINGTON CHAUNCEY FORD

FRIEND, AND PRINCE OF EDITORS

For the Lord thy God bringeth thee into a good land, a land of brooks of water, of fountains and depths that spring out of valleys and hills;

A land of wheat, and barley, and vines, and fig trees, and pomegranates; a land of oil olive, and honey;

A land wherein thou shalt eat bread without scarceness, thou shalt not lack any thing in it; a land whose stones are iron, and out of whose hills thou mayest dig brass.

DEUTERONOMY, VIII, 7–9

Preface

IN ONE LIFETIME John Quincy Adams had two notable careers, separated by an interlude as President of the United States. The first career was that of diplomatist and continentalist, the second a crusader in the House of Representatives against the expansion of slavery. The present book tells the story of his life during his first career. I have taken him through the Presidency only in so far as necessary to round out his career as diplomatist. So closely identified was his whole life before he became President with the foundations of American foreign policy during the first half-century of our independence that it is possible to submit this work as an endeavor that stands by itself and yet may be the first volume of a complete biography.

Here you have a diplomatic biography—if such a thing there can be—a biography of the man from boyhood to Presidency against the background of American foreign policy, or a study of the foundations of American foreign policy against the background of John Quincy Adams. One may look for more of the man and less of the diplomatist in his second career, which remains a subject of further treatment. But I hope that the reader will agree there is a lot of the man in the foundations of American foreign policy as here set down.

Some years ago I projected a study of the Foundations of American Foreign Policy in three volumes, the first of which appeared in 1935: *The Diplomacy of the American Revolution.* A variety of circumstances, including the appearance of excellent books on the diplomatic history of the United States during the period 1783–1826, have impelled me to take the present biographical device to acquit myself of my earlier project. The rich accumulation of special studies in diplomatic history touching, through archival investigation, nearly every important topic of American foreign relations during this period,[1] was not available to John T. Morse, Jr., when he wrote his short biography of John Quincy Adams for the American Statesmen series (1882), not to mention earlier, uncritical volumes by William H. Seward (1849), and Josiah Quincy (1858). Professor Dexter Perkins had much of the new literature ready to his expert hand when he wrote his scholarly sketch in *The American Secretaries of State and Their Diplomacy* (New York: Alfred A. Knopf; 1928), but he was cruelly cramped for space; his excellent account of Adams's diplomacy is therefore very summary. Senator Bennett Champ Clark's fine piece of writing makes *John Quincy Adams, Old Man Eloquent* (Boston:

[1] See the relevant sections of Samuel Flagg Bemis and Grace Gardner Griffin: *Guide to the Diplomatic History of the United States, 1775–1921* (Washington: Library of Congress; 1935). Later studies are indicated in my notes.

Little, Brown & Company; 1933) live as a man of his age, but pays more attention to his life as a politician and a crusader than to his career as a diplomatist and his role in laying the foundations of American foreign policy. Of the above writers Morse was the only one who seems to have used the rich collection of personal papers of John Quincy Adams, and he very cursorily. Thus no full biography of this major personality in American history has been previously attempted.

The two principal printed sources for the life of John Quincy Adams are the well known *Memoirs of John Quincy Adams, Comprising Portions of His Diary from 1795 to 1848,* edited by Charles Francis Adams (12 volumes; Philadelphia, 1874–7), and Worthington C. Ford's edition of *The Writings of John Quincy Adams* (7 volumes; New York: The Macmillan Company; 1913–17). Both publications are selections of documents from a much more voluminous collection. The original manuscript Diary of John Quincy Adams, certainly the most important personal memoir in American history, is perhaps half as long again as the selections published in the twelve meaty volumes of *Memoirs.* Charles Francis Adams printed only those passages which he deemed to be of historical value and omitted what he considered to be personal matter or trivia. Whenever there was any doubt in either case, he printed, so copiously that some of the descendants have felt that he went too far. Constant searching behind the *Memoirs* into the Diary, with the uninhibited and indefatigable assistance of Mr. Henry Adams, 2d, has yielded little new historical matter.

The first question that presents itself to the student of the *Memoirs* and of the Diary is how reliable they are as historical sources for the life of the man who wrote them. I am persuaded that John Quincy Adams did not write this Diary for publication: if he had done so, he would have polished its style and structure. He kept the Diary first and foremost for his own reference as a record of facts and dates in what he intended to be a long and important public service, secondly as a secret tuning-fork for his pent-up emotions, thirdly as a process of self-discipline and introspection, and finally as a family monument for the perusal of his children, doubtless with the hope that one of them someday would use it in the preparation of his biography. For facts and dates, for the record of conversations, the Diary is generally a trustworthy source, often even a corrective. I have felt justified in taking many a passage of dialogue verbatim from its pages, stiff and awkward though the hasty phraseology sometimes is, and reproducing it in direct discourse in my narrative. But whenever the diarist's opinion enters into the record of men or of measures, particularly of men, colored as it is by his own emotions and points of view, the more stubbornly and hotly as he advanced in life, what he wrote down must be held strictly to the canons of historical criticism, as must all personal documents. Certainly the world of scholarship owes a continuing debt to the conscientious labor of John Quincy Adams's distinguished son for making convenient public property of the historically significant passages of the immortal Diary.

Mr. Ford's selections of the *Writings of John Quincy Adams* contain a smaller portion of his letters than the *Memoirs* do of the Diary, and a still smaller part of the articles from Adams's pen — the latter being mostly published already. At a guess, the letters published by Ford for the years covered in his volumes are not more than a third of the whole; but the selections are made mostly to reveal rather than to conceal, and the limitations are principally those of space; even so, this publishing enterprise was cut off unaccountably at the end of the seventh volume, in the middle of the most important year 1823, when the work was only half completed. Nevertheless, the published volumes are a most useful record. The reader will observe from my citations to Adams MSS. that I have found much material, important to the subject of this book, which is not printed in Ford's noteworthy collection.

The *Memoirs* and the *Writings* (so cited by short titles in the following pages) of John Quincy Adams, the monographs and the special studies, and biographies of contemporary statesmen at home and abroad, greatly lighten the burden of the biographer and historian of foreign policy in digesting the original multi-archival record, both personal and official. There are upwards of a hundred large volumes of manuscripts in the Department of State Records in the National Archives at Washington which deal directly with the diplomacy of John Quincy Adams before he became President, and the investigator would have to look through as many more tomes in the official archives of such countries as Great Britain, Prussia, the Netherlands, France, Spain, Mexico, Cuba, Argentina, and Chile. Although I have made excursions into all of these repositories, I have relied on the works of many competent scholars to assist such a vast tour of duty; but I have drawn upon my own visits to the foreign archives for at least a feeling of the subject and for occasional documents not otherwise available. I have also toured the spacious scenes of John Quincy Adams's continental diplomacy in so far as an automobile will take one there, scenes he never saw himself.

Most particularly have I profited from an intensive study of John Quincy Adams's own papers — his Diary, his personal and official letter-books, all fortunately preserved and in good order, and his incoming correspondence through the years, together with his drafts of diplomatic dispatches and instructions and other state papers, now stored in the Massachusetts Historical Society under the custody of the Adams Manuscripts Trust. The study of this record has been a long and arduous task made possible only by the patient and discerning assistance of the sixth President's great-grandson, Mr. Henry Adams, 2d, who devoted many months of labor to helping me get thoroughly behind the printed record. Without this sympathetic help from a real and modest friend of historical truth my own work, of course, would have been impossible. The photographs of portraits here reproduced are the contribution of Mr. Adams with permission of the owners.

Courtesies and aids, traditional and very real in the republic of letters, have been so numerous and widespread during the years in which this volume has been in gestation and preparation that, having kept no journal, I fear the embarrassment of overlooking some of the obliging institutions and kind people to whom I am indebted.

I wish to express my thanks to the following libraries and archives and their staffs: Archivo General de la Nación (Buenos Aires); Archivo General de la Nación and Archivo de Relaciones Exteriores (Mexico, D.F.); Archivo Histórico Nacional (Madrid) and Archivo General de Indias (Seville); Archivo Nacional (Santiago de Chile); Archivo Nacional de Cuba; Archives du Ministère des Affaires Etrangères (Paris); British Museum and British Record Office (London); Public Archives (Ottawa); Preussiches geheimes Staatsarchiv; American Antiquarian Society; Boston Public Library; District of Columbia Public Library; Harvard University Archives, and Widener and Houghton Libraries; Library of Congress; National Archives; Massachusetts Historical Society; New York Historical Society; New York Public Library; Pennsylvania Historical Society; Sterling Memorial Library of Yale University.

My learned colleagues Professors Walter Prichard Eaton [2] and Harry R. Rudin and my erudite counselor Mrs. Natalie Summers, for many years a living guide and encyclopedia of the records of the Department of State, and Mr. Alfred A. Knopf, my publisher, all have read laboriously and patiently every page of manuscript. These friends have prevented me from going even more astray in numerous places in matters of style, fact, and documentation. Dr. Harris E. Starr also read more than half the work, and I greatly profited from his suggestions. Others who have perused one or more chapters, and to whom I am grateful, are: my wife Ruth S. Bemis, Dr. Maury D. Baker, Jr., Dr. Harold Bierck, Jr., Miss Helen Boatfield, Dr. Philip C. Brooks, Professor Charles Everett, Professor A. Whitney Griswold, Miss Grace Gardner Griffin, the accomplished bibliographer of American history; Professor Charles W. Hackett, Dr. William W. Kaufmann, Professor Thomas C. Mendenhall, Dr. Hunter Miller, Professor Norman H. Pearson, Dr. Vernon G. Setser, Professor George Vernadsky. Mr. Richard D. Johnson, of the class of 1949, Yale College, helped me, as "bursary assistant," with numerous mechanical and other tasks, including proofreading. Mrs. Geneva M. Walsh has been of invaluable assistance in the typing and retypings of this book. Mr. Robert H. Ferrell has greatly assisted me in reading proof.

[2] Mr. Eaton has the artist's sensitivity to an annoying clutter of footnotes. Under his influence I have greatly reduced the volume of such matter, but have kept the remaining mass at the bottom of the respective pages rather than at the back of the book, so that the reader who wishes to trace my tracks will not have the exasperation of flipping the pages back and forth to find the notes.

I should like to attest my obligation to the American Council of Learned Societies and the Library of Congress American Studies Project for grants-in-aid that have assisted me with typing and other clerical help. By courtesy of Harcourt, Brace & Company I have introduced in Chapters XV, XVII, XVIII, and XIX occasional passages from my *Latin American Policy of the United States* (New York, 1943). Maps 3 and 5 are based in part, by courtesy of Henry Holt & Company, on Maps 8 and 27 of my *Diplomatic History of the United States* (New York, 1942). All maps were designed by Mr. S. Whittemore Boggs and drafted by Mr. Guy P. Meredith and Mr. William J. Luedtke.

S. F. B.

New Haven, Conn.
May 11, 1949

CONTENTS

ILLUSTRATIONS

MAPS

JOHN QUINCY ADAMS

AND THE FOUNDATIONS OF

AMERICAN FOREIGN POLICY

Abbreviations used in footnotes

AHA	American Historical Association
AHR	*American Historical Review*
ASPFR	*American State Papers. Class I. Foreign Relations* (6 vols., Washington, 1832–59)
DS	Department of State Records, in the National Archives, Washington, D.C.
HAHR	*Hispanic American Historical Review*
LC	Library of Congress
Memoirs	*Memoirs of John Quincy Adams, Comprising Portions of His Diary from 1795 to 1848.* Edited by Charles Francis Adams (12 vols., Philadelphia, 1874–7)
Diary	Diary of John Quincy Adams (MS)
MHS	Massachusetts Historical Society
Miller: *Treaties*	*Treaties and Other International Acts of the United States of America.* Edited by Hunter Miller (8 vols., Washington, 1931–48)
PRO	Public Record Office, London (Library of Congress Photostats)
Writings	*Writings of John Quincy Adams.* Edited by Worthington C. Ford (7 vols., New York, 1913–17)
WRC	William Robertson Coe Collection, Sterling Memorial Library, Yale University
AA	Abigail Adams
CFA	Charles Francis Adams
GWA	George Washington Adams
JA	John Adams
JQA	John Quincy Adams
TBA	Thomas Boylston Adams

CHAPTER I
Son of the American Revolution
(1767–1793)

La mollesse est douce et sa suite est cruelle.

QUOTATION FROM VOLTAIRE
AT THE BEGINNING OF JOHN QUINCY ADAMS'S DIARY

JOHN QUINCY ADAMS's lifetime spanned the American Revolution, the achievement of independence, the establishment of a successful national government, the grounding of the Continental Republic. He grew to manhood during the heroic period of the foundations of American nationality, so conspicuous a chapter of the Age of Emancipation. It was the epoch also of the French Revolution and the Napoleonic Wars and their aftermath in the Old World and the New, to which the United States owes in great measure survival of its nationality and the fullness of its Manifest Destiny. In those years the foreign policy of the United States took clear and classical form at the hands of natural statesmen. It was also the time of the rise of the slave power and development of the ominous sectional conflict. To all this history Adams was close witness. In much of it he was an active and guiding participant. More than any other one man he helped to shape the foundations of American foreign policy and the future of the United States as a Continental Republic.

It would be difficult to suggest background, education, and experience better designed for a statesman destined to become one of America's greatest diplomatists. These were: Adams's New England Puritan ancestry; the formative influence of illustrious patriot parents; vivid and ineffaceable childhood memories of the first battles and hardships of the Revolution; extensive trans-Atlantic travels with his father after the conflict spread to Europe; schooling in France and in Holland; diplomatic apprenticeship at the age of fifteen on the first American mission to Russia; Harvard College during the "critical period" of the Confederation; and, finally, conscientious self-education for the law and a struggle for practice in Boston during General Washington's first Administration.

The first chapter of any diplomatic biography of John Quincy Adams therefore must begin with his remarkable parentage, youth, and training, particularly the influence of his father and of his mother.

1

On both sides of the family Adams's forebears had lived among the low hills south of Boston Harbor ever since the founding of the Bay Colony a century and a half before his birth. According to a memorandum [1] that he wrote out in his later years, the first Adams to come to Massachusetts was Henry Adams, a maltster from Bristol, England, who settled in Braintree some time before 1640. There the family lived by the side of the sea, hard-working farmer folk, until the American Revolution. Their descendants still live there in the vastly altered circumstances of our times.

John Quincy Adams's father, John Adams, describes the inheritance left him by his father, Deacon John Adams, in 1761, as a "pretty property." It was a farm of one hundred and forty acres at the foot of Penn's Hill in Braintree, now Quincy, with two typical New England farmhouses, which may still be seen, squarish two-storied clapboarded structures with lean-to backs, the familiar dwelling-house of colonial times, with simple proportions, so satisfying to the eye. Under one of the modest shingled roofs was born John Adams, second President of the United States. Under the other his eldest son first saw the light of day on July 11, 1767. He came into the world just as one of his maternal great-grandfathers, John Quincy, respected member of the colonial legislature, was leaving it. So the child received the name of John Quincy Adams.

The patriot father, John Adams, was a prosperous lawyer with well-to-do clients in Boston. When his first son was seven years old the British Intolerable Acts shut up the courts of law in the colony and cut off his flourishing practice. From then on, John Adams pursued his career as patriot and public servant, one of the fathers of American independence and nationhood. He retired from public life in 1801, defeated by his old friend, Thomas Jefferson, for re-election to the Presidency, and settled down in his home town, where he lived in quiet retirement for the remainder of a long life in the big house he bought there. The Sage of Quincy died in the "Adams Mansion" [2] on July 4, 1826. At that moment the village church bells were pealing out the fiftieth anniversary of the Declaration of Independence. The townsmen were shouting a toast that the venerable patriot had given a few days before to a delegation to take to the celebration: "Independence forever!"

John Adams's last faint memorable words were: "Thomas Jefferson

[1] Henry Adams, 2d, has described *The Birthplaces of Presidents John and John Quincy Adams in Quincy, Massachusetts* (printed for the Adams Memorial Society, Quincy, Mass., 1936).

[2] Henry Adams, 2d, gives historical details about *The Adams Mansion, the Home of John Adams and John Quincy Adams, Presidents of the United States* (printed for the Adams Memorial Society, Quincy, Mass., 1935). The old farmhouses are now owned by the city of Quincy and are preserved as a national historical monument. The Adams Mansion, at 135 Adams Street, is owned by the United States Government and kept as a national historic site by the National Park Service.

survives. . . ."[3] Only an hour before, the author of the Declaration of Independence had died in Virginia, at his home at Monticello, on that same notable Independence Day. In the White House at Washington John Quincy Adams was then sixth President of the United States.

His mother, Abigail Adams, was one of the most remarkable women of the Revolutionary period. She was a daughter of William Smith, well known as minister at Weymouth, in days when the minister was usually the most eminent and influential man in the community. Her father and mother were descendants of other notable Massachusetts ministers. Without formal schooling she became one of the best-educated women of her time in New England, perhaps in all the thirteen colonies. She did not need to be told the old truth that education is self-education. It was the only education possible for women in Massachusetts then, aside from the three R's and in some cases, like hers, decorous little lessons in singing and dancing. Her fully nurtured New England mind fed itself on the best English classics and translations, which were available to her in the homes of her grandfather, father, and husband. Abigail Smith Adams's strong character and patriotic fervor are reflected in her myriad letters to family and friends.[4]

Difficult as it is to distinguish between the formative influences exerted by both admirable parents on their unusual son, it can be said that the mother was as close to the counsels of his heart and conduct as the father was to the shaping of his mind. Together they worked to mold his character. They stimulated his ambition. They prescribed his education to a degree that would stagger a modern psychologist, but which proved wholly agreeable to him. He loved and admired his parents and instinctively agreed with them both. They dominated his youth. His mother taught him to emulate his father. His father kept the boy's affections ever fixed on his mother.

While John Adams was absent in attendance at the Continental Congress, the boy grew up at his mother's side, memorizing heroic poems of patriotic virtues, later listening to his father's historic letters from Philadelphia, reading aloud from serious books like Rollin's *Ancient History*, and helping to take care of his younger brothers and sister. At ten years of age "Master John" was a "post rider" to take the family mail on horseback from Braintree to Boston, nine miles away, and back.[5] There his patriot kinsman, Sam Adams, would take the boy out on the Common to

[3] *Memoirs*, VII, 133.

[4] See the representative selection of *Letters of Mrs. Adams, the Wife of John Adams, with an Introductory Memoir by Her Grandson, Charles Francis Adams. Fourth Edition, Revised and Enlarged, with an Appendix Containing the Letters Addressed by John Q. Adams to His Son on the Study of the Bible* (Boston, 1848). Janet Whitney has written the most recent and best of the popular biographies of *Abigail Adams* (Boston, 1947), based on her letters, unpublished as well as published, rather loosely used to reconstruct conversations.

[5] *Letters of Mrs. Adams*, p. 83.

see with detestation the British troops and alternately to observe with pleasure the Boston militia.[6] In Braintree a company of militia on its way to Lexington stopped overnight at the Adams farmstead. Eight-year-old Johnny stood up with a big musket and went through the manual of arms by word of command from one of the patriot soldiers.[7]

This was the birth-time of the nation. From the beginning the boy was steeped in the spirit of the American Revolution and the essence of independence. Tugging at his mother's hand he climbed Penn's Hill on June 17, 1775 and saw the cannons flash on Bunker Hill. The distant detonations came back to him in Braintree as he watched the smoke drift over the Back Bay from burning Charlestown across the river's estuary. The sound and its awful significance echoed and re-echoed in his mind and heart his whole life long.[8]

After mother and child came down the hill from that fateful view, news reached them of Dr. Joseph Warren's gallant death in battle. Hot tears came to their eyes, for the noble Warren had been a close friend of all the Adamses. Only a few days before he had put a splint on Johnny's badly fractured forefinger, saving it from amputation and perhaps making it possible for him in later life to write in his own hand his many state papers and the long and matchless Diary.

In the farmhouse at Braintree, Johnny and his mother labored to feed and tend patriot refugees streaming south from Boston, while the smaller children looked on anxiously and tried to help. From the hill they could see boatloads of British soldiers rowing out to burn haystacks and barns on the islands offshore, and local militia running up to defend Braintree, if necessary, against landings and burnings in the village. Later they heard the guns thunder dreadfully from Dorchester Heights, a few miles to the north, and learned soon afterward that General Washington had driven the British from Boston Harbor, their ships loaded down with Tories. Abigail Adams had been over to Cambridge to meet the General himself.

Then came news from Philadelphia in John Adams's letters of the 3rd of July 1776, about the resolution for independence that Congress had voted the previous day. Husband and wife had been discussing such a step most earnestly in their letters back and forth. Now the husband was sitting with old Dr. Franklin and young Mr. Jefferson and other patriots on a committee to draw up a declaration to justify the momentous step in the eyes of God and man. Soon people would have the document in Boston and Braintree. "The second day of July, 1776," wrote John Adams, "will be the most memorable epoch in the history of America. I am apt

[6] JA to Samuel Adams, Auteuil, April 27, 1785. *Works of John Adams . . . with a Life of the Author,* Charles Francis Adams, editor (10 vols., Boston, 1854), IX, 532.

[7] *Memoirs,* VII, 325.

[8] *Memoirs,* I, 5.

to believe that it will be celebrated by succeeding generations as the great anniversary Festival. It ought to be commemorated, as the day of deliverance, by solemn acts of devotion to God Almighty. It ought to be solemnized with pomp and parade, with shows, games, sports, guns, bells, bonfires and illuminations, from one end of this continent to the other, from this time forward, forevermore." [9] Actually it was the Fourth of July, the day of the Declaration of Independence that Congress adopted almost word for word as Thomas Jefferson had written it down, that became the national holiday.

This was a childhood worth remembering. By the time that Johnny had grown up to be a man, and President, such Fourths of July had become true in the widest sense of the word. The United States then stretched from sea to shining sea, thanks in large degree to John Quincy Adams's diplomacy.

The Adamses were firmly but not ostentatiously religious people. Their belief in God was a reasoned conviction fashioned out of Puritan backgrounds. Puritan theology had lost much of its extreme doctrine by the end of the eighteenth century. John Adams the father was one of New England's first Unitarians. The son John Quincy Adams, growing up as an independent Congregationalist, came to believe in the existence of one God, Creator and Governor of the universe, particularly of mankind; the immortality of the soul; and the further Christian belief in a future life of rewards and punishments, as taught by Jesus Christ. He felt that man was essentially good, not depraved, and that he was meant to enjoy rather than to shrink from the good things of life.[10] He held that the Bible, despite numerous allegorical passages, was in essence divine revelation. He was not certain about the divinity of Christ nor sure about the virgin birth or miracles. The most important lessons of the Bible, declared the mature John Quincy Adams, were the Golden Rule and the Sermon on the Mount. And the Bible taught obedience to the will of God, sometimes inscrutable, always good. The Christian religion thus offered to him the consolation that rational philosophy could not bring. He believed that he would meet the dear ones, lost by death, in a future existence clean and pure, a blessed and blissful change.[11] He was a steady churchgoer, usually twice each Sunday, to churches of various denominations according to how he liked the minister, and he had a habit of noting down the text of the sermon each time in his Diary, with occasional dissertations of his

[9] *Letters of John Adams, Addressed to His Wife,* edited by his grandson, Charles Francis Adams (2 vols., Boston, 1841), I, 128–9. See also E. C. Burnett: *Letters of Members of the Continental Congress* (2 vols., Carnegie Institution of Washington, 1923–36), I, 519–38.

[10] *Memoirs,* VII, 269, 286.

[11] JQA to JA, Nos. 18, 25, 28, St. Petersburg, October 4, 1812, August 10, November 13, 1813; to AA, Nos. 30, 37, 38, 53, St. Petersburg, February 8, September 27, October 24, 1812, November 19, 1813. Adams MSS.

own. There was always a "smack of orthodoxy" about him, but after the death of his father he belatedly joined the Unitarian church in Quincy.[12]

The boy John Quincy Adams learned these tenets at his mother's knee. We may be sure the family heard them preached in the village church. After he left home for France, as presently we shall see him do, his mother's first letter to him said: "Adhere to those religious sentiments and principles which were early instilled into your mind, and remember that you are accountable to your Maker for all your words and actions." In a letter directed to his son in distant St. Petersburg in 1782 John Adams wrote: "Your conscience is the minister plenipotentiary of God Almighty in your breast. See to it that this minister never negotiates in vain. Attend to him in opposition to all the courts in the world."

These principles are what John Quincy Adams the man in turn taught his own children. He once reminded his eldest son that Jesus said to his disciples: "Learn of me, for I am *meek* and *lowly in heart,* and ye shall find rest unto your souls." "But," he hastened to ask – this was during the War of 1812 – "where did he ever say to them, 'learn of me, for I am *tame* and *abject*'?" Doubtless he remembered the counsel of his own mother, Abigail, who had once written to him when a boy to carry himself modestly and diffidently, to curb his temper, to exercise self-control in the face of provocation. "I do not mean, however," she said, "to have you insensible to real injuries. He who will never turn when he is trodden upon is deficient in point of spirit. . . ."

No Adams would ever bow to an Intolerable Act, or advise yielding to a press captain, but any Adams would and did champion the meek and lowly.[13]

All his life John Quincy Adams read the Bible regularly. During a long period it was his practice to read it through once a year. Every morning he read it for an hour after rising, four or five chapters, when his mind was freshest for the Book.[14] In his mature life he read it in French and German translations as well as in the King James version, and regretted he did not know Hebrew so as to "seek the fountain" in the original words of the Old Testament.[15] He thought the German text the clearest. None of America's statesmen has been better schooled in the Bible than the Adamses.

The boy never went to school in Braintree. The town closed the grammar school to save money for the war, and the schoolteacher enlisted in the army. But Johnny learned more at home than did the boys in school. He must have known how to read and write before he was big enough to walk about the farm and to ride horseback. We know that he began to

[12] JQA to JA, Little Boston, Ealing, January 14, 1817. Adams MSS. JQA to AA, Ealing, December 5, 1815. *Writings,* V, 431. *Memoirs,* XI, 340–1.

[13] Quotations from *Letters of Mrs. Adams,* pp. 95, 116, 427, 467.

[14] Ibid., p. 428.

[15] JQA to JA, No. 32, Ghent, July 7, 1814. Adams MSS.

study systematically under the tutelage of his father's law clerk, John Thaxter. By the time he was ten he had read with delight much of Shakespeare and Pope, and Thomson's *Seasons*, but got stuck until he was nearly thirty years old in the middle of Milton's *Paradise Lost*.[16]

His ambitious parents were hopeful that one day the government would rest upon the shoulder of their eldest son. At an early age they marked him for future leadership "in the cabinet or the field." These were his mother's words. She reminded him that he was destined to be a "guardian of his country's laws and liberties." Father and mother determined to give the boy every chance within their power to improve his natural talents, even at the cost of personal danger. Fortunately a wonderful opportunity came to hand when the Continental Congress appointed John Adams one of the diplomatic commission to France, to take the place of Silas Deane of Connecticut, withdrawn.

2

On a cold winter day in February 1778 father and son stepped into a ship's boat in front of Uncle Norton Quincy's house at Mount Wollaston,[17] on Braintree's pebbled shore. Sailors rowed the passengers, wrapped in blankets, their feet deep in hay, out to the frigate *Boston*, swinging to the tide in Nantasket roadstead. John Quincy was then ten years old, going on eleven. His father soon had reason to regret, at least temporarily, that he had taken his son along, for the voyage proved to be a rough experience, even for a boy who had watched the Battle of Bunker Hill.

After they left Massachusetts Bay, a squadron of British warships pursued the frigate for two days. All across the Atlantic it was chase and be chased. Then the *Boston* sailed into a frightful storm, which worked havoc on everything aboard. The ship's cockpit became a sink of devastation and putrefaction. At midnight a bolt of lightning struck a mast and knocked out three sailors, injuring to a less extent a score of the crew. Then came combat with a British privateer. A cannon ball whizzed over John Adams's head and carried away the ship's spanker yard. Nevertheless the frigate made a rich capture and sent her in to Boston with a prize crew. Shortly thereafter John Adams held the first lieutenant while the surgeon amputated a leg shattered by the explosion of a signal gun. Two weeks later they buried the officer at sea. Through all these exciting and somber scenes the small boy bore himself steadily.

Father and son and their companions reached Bordeaux and Paris safely. "Mr. Johnny" immediately went into a private boarding-school at

[16] Henry Adams, 2d: *A Catalogue of the Books of John Quincy Adams Deposited in the Boston Athenæum with Notes on Books, Adams Seals and Book-Plates,* with an introduction by Worthington Chauncey Ford. Printed for the Athenæum (Boston, 1938), p. 68. JQA to Elizabeth Peabody, of Atkinson, N.H., St. Petersburg, July 29, 1812. Adams MSS.

[17] *Memoirs,* XII, 276–7.

Passy, the suburb where Dr. Franklin lived, near the Bois de Boulogne. For a greater part of a year he studied French and Latin and also fencing, dancing, music, and drawing under Monsieur Le Cœur, the master. There were four other American boys among his schoolmates: two grandsons of Dr. Franklin, William Temple Franklin and Benjamin Franklin Bache, Silas Deane's son Jesse, and Charles Cochran of South Carolina.[18] Benny Bache later became John Quincy Adams's first political enemy. It was at this residence that John conducted his first negotiations: for playdays, and for excuses from attending Mass on Sundays at the Church of the Minimes on the brow of the hill. It was here that he first sealed his devotion to the theater, at the Théâtre des Petits Comédiens in the Bois, where a company of children played simple French classics three times a week.[19]

John Adams found that the diplomatic Commission already had accomplished its principal purpose before he reached his post: the treaties of commerce and alliance, of February 6, 1778, with France. There was no longer need for more than one representative to the court of Louis XVI. Congress appointed Franklin as sole Minister of the United States. No word came from Philadelphia as to what Adams was to do now, so he resolved to take French leave and go home. He and his son got back to Boston August 2, 1779. To John Quincy the trip had been an opportunity to see France and to learn the language; in other respects his father felt that it had interfered somewhat with his education.[20] To his mother it had been a fearful anxiety to be assumed resolutely and borne patriotically.

The travelers had been home for only a few weeks when Congress ordered John Adams back to Europe. Spain had offered to mediate in the war between France and England, and the Comte de Vergennes, French Minister of Foreign Affairs, had suggested that the United States had better have a plenipotentiary ready on the ground in case there should be a general peace conference. So Congress appointed John Adams to conclude a peace of independence. The particular peace conference originally anticipated did not occur, nor did several others that were in the wind of Vergennes's subtle European diplomacy, but John Adams stayed on in Europe, as peace plenipotentiary, and as Minister to the Netherlands, and, after the war, as Minister to Great Britain, until 1788.

Johnny did not want to go back to France even though his younger

[18] *Memoirs,* VI, 418. JQA to Charles Cochran, Charleston, Ghent, July 18, 1814. *AHR,* XV (No. 3, April 1910), 572–4.

[19] "JQA Loquitur." Adams MSS.

[20] John Adams's Diary and his official letters, both printed in *Works* of JA, Vols. III, VII, give details of their first trip to Europe. The MS. log of the *Boston,* Captain Samuel Tucker, February 11, 1778–Monday, September 6, 1779, is preserved in the Adams MSS. under the title of "Journal, Mr. Tucker, 1778. J.Q.A." See also official dispatches in Francis Wharton: *Revolutionary Diplomatic Correspondence of the United States* (8 vols., Washington, 1889), Vols. II, III.

brother Charles, nine years old, went along this time. He wanted to attend Andover Academy, as the family had planned, and prepare for college. He had his heart set on entering Harvard. One Sunday evening after church his mother took him aside to her chamber. In the solemn shadows she talked to him alone. Tenderly and persuasively she urged him to go with his father. "In all human probability," she said, "it will do more for your education to go back to France with your father than to prepare for college at Andover." He yielded to her Spartan advice and asked his father to let him go back with him to France. John Adams immediately consented.[21]

"These are times in which a genius would wish to live," his mother wrote to him with aching heart after the ship sailed forth with husband and children. "It is not in the still calm of life, or the repose of a pacific station, that great characters are formed. . . . Great necessities call out great virtues. When a mind is raised and animated by scenes that engage the heart, then those qualities, which would otherwise lie dormant, wake into life and form the character of the hero and the statesman." [22]

The second voyage to Europe, in the *Sensible,* the same French frigate that had brought them home, was as exciting and dangerous as the first crossing in the *Boston.* John wrote a full letter home to his mother about the terrific storm a few days after they sailed.[23] There was a hole in the ship's bottom, the captain said, as big as a man's head. It finally forced them to make for the nearest port, Ferrol.

The two brothers and their father, with a couple of other boys sent to France in Mr. Adams's care for an education, including John's agreeable friend Master Sammy Cooper,[24] landed in Spain, December 18, 1779. They made their painful way overland as best they could to France, studying a Spanish grammar on the road. As soon as they got to Paris they found themselves in the elder brother's old boarding-school at Passy, John now studying Greek, and Charles Latin. They were also copying passages from English historians and essayists into their notebooks. Beginning in 1780, when John Adams went to the Netherlands as Minister, they attended the public Latin School at Amsterdam, later they listened to lectures at the ancient University of Leiden. They made friends with Benjamin Waterhouse, of Newport, Rhode Island, who was studying medicine in Holland. They learned Dutch. Little Charles got more and more homesick the longer he stayed in Europe. Toward the end of 1781 his father had to send him back to Massachusetts to cure his unhappiness.

About this same time Congress decided to dispatch Francis Dana, who

[21] JQA to Rev. Henry Coleman, Salem, August 25, 1826. Adams MSS.

[22] *Letters of Mrs. Adams,* p. 111.

[23] *Memoirs,* I, 10. Mr. Henry Adams, 2d, called my attention to this letter of February 17, 1780, and some other unprinted letters about the trip and the first months in Europe again.

[24] JQA to AA, on board the *Sensible,* November 20, 1779. JA to AA, Ferrol, Spain, December 11, 1779. Adams MSS.

was an old friend of the Adams family, to St. Petersburg, to see if the Empress Catherine the Great would receive the United States into the Armed Neutrality of 1780 by a formal treaty. This would have meant recognition of the new Republic as an independent nation by nearly all the great powers of Europe. But Catherine had no intention, any more than had the King of Spain, who by now had gone to war with England to reconquer Gibraltar, of recognizing the independence of the United States before King George III should do so. She put off Dana's importunities until Congress called him home in 1783.

Dana, a fellow Bostonian, needed someone to interpret French for him and to translate and copy official letters. At John Adams's suggestion he took John junior on the long journey across Germany and the Baltic Provinces to the court of the Czars. John was in the Russian capital for fourteen months. He learned something about the country, both from Voltaire's history and other books and from first-hand observation. He also acquired a little of the German language during this mission, and thus became perhaps the first American to have an appreciation of German belles-lettres, at the very time when the King of Prussia, Frederick the Great, would have none of them. After a year had passed, John Adams felt that too long a sojourn in Russia would interrupt his son's education. He called him back to Paris, where the father, as one of another diplomatic commission, was negotiating the final Treaty of Peace and Independence. John came back traveling in the company of a returning Italian nobleman – through Finland and Sweden, with an instructive and amusing stop in winter at Stockholm, then by way of Göteborg, Copenhagen, Hamburg, Bremen, and Amsterdam to The Hague – a long and arduous trip of many weeks.[25]

By the time John Quincy Adams got back to Paris from Russia, the diplomacy of the American Revolution had ended in perfect triumph for the Franco-American alliance. His father and colleagues had signed the preliminary and conditional articles of peace with Great Britain, – conditional for their effect upon signature of preliminaries also by France, which in turn had taken place on January 2, 1783, after agreement between France and her ally Spain. The war had ended. American independence was recognized. The Peace Commission had got from Great Britain broad boundaries for the new nation: on the north the St. Lawrence River and the Great Lakes; on the west the Mississippi. Thanks to John Adams they had saved a liberty for American fishermen to pursue their customary calling in the inshore fisheries of British North America. All this they had won at a time when Congress would have been not unwilling to accept the Alleghenies as a western boundary. They had made a magnificent start toward a Continental Republic.

The glory of that great diplomatic victory has overshadowed in history the anxieties and trials of the alliance during the darkest years of the war.

[25] *Writings,* I, 1–13. "JQA Loquitur." Adams MSS.

So desperate had been the military situation in the years 1780 and 1781 that Vergennes, who had signed the treaty pledging "absolute and unlimited" independence of the United States, to be secured "formally or tacitly," had brought himself to the point where he was ready to consider a compromise peace, to be prearranged at the hands of mediators, a peace that would have stopped short of absolute and unlimited independence and left the enemy in possession of such areas of territory as he occupied, according to the contemporary war map.

John Adams was not wholly aware of all this secret European diplomacy of the French ally when he served as sole peace commissioner. But he had insisted that he could not attend any peace conference unless he were first recognized as representative of the independent United States. His insistence, and the plenipotentiary's unbending and forthright attitude toward Vergennes, had persuaded that Minister that Adams was too independently minded to be amenable to French policy and direction. So the French statesman had prevailed on Congress to group its single plenipotentiary in a commission of five, that included Benjamin Franklin, and John Jay, minister designate to Spain; and to instruct them not to sign anything without the approval of France.

Although Franklin and Jay had reached an advanced stage in the negotiations for peace, in 1782, by the time John Adams arrived in Paris from Holland, the New Englander lent an eager hand to their work. He emphatically agreed with his colleagues that they should sign the preliminary and *conditional* articles, providing for absolute independence and expansive boundaries, without consulting Vergennes. He felt that it had been a serious mistake for Congress to put the fate and freedom of the United States completely in the hands of a foreign power, even an ally, for he knew that the ally was looking after its own interests first.

The historian, who now can read documents that John Adams could only suspect to exist, must confirm that diplomat's suspicions and those of his colleagues. Recent historical investigation also has established that the astute Vergennes was really quite content with the separate but conditional signature; in fact, he was subtly egging on the American Commissioners to take that very step. He did this to constrain his other ally, Spain, to make peace promptly without futilely prolonging the war to fulfill France's pledge to her for the recovery of Gibraltar.

Of all these inner problems of the peace negotiations young John Quincy Adams knew nothing at that time. When later he learned about them, from reading the confidential diplomatic record, he saw his father – then Vice President of the United States – as a greater statesman than ever. It was to be his life-work to defend and extend what his father and colleagues had won in 1782 and 1783.

3

The bright years in Paris, 1783 to 1785, when John Quincy Adams served as his father's private secretary, were the most carefree and light-hearted of his long and not unhappy life. Congress had set up still another diplomatic commission in the French capital, consisting of Dr. Franklin, John Adams, and Thomas Jefferson, to negotiate treaties of friendship and commerce one at a time with as many European nations as possible. This greatly expanded the scope of John Adams's activities and personal contacts.

The son was now old enough to mingle with his father's colleagues and associates as an adult. He came to know intimately Franklin and Jefferson, with whom he visited often. At that youthful time of his life he and Jefferson proved to be particularly congenial spirits. Perhaps the Virginian found some consolation for recent bereavements of wife and daughter in being friendly to this bright-minded youth. "He appeared to me to be almost as much your boy as mine," John Adams recollected to his old friend on January 22, 1825, when the elder statesmen were approaching the end of their days and "our John" – Adams's and Jefferson's – was a candidate for the Presidency.[26]

What could be more inspiring in the training of a future American statesman than to spend whole afternoons and evenings alone with Thomas Jefferson, talking about science and politics and governments, history, men, and measures! "Mr. Jefferson is a man of universal learning," the youth noted in his freshly started Diary. "Spent the evening with Mr. Jefferson whom I love to be with." Thomas Jefferson was to have much influence, directly and indirectly, on the career of John Quincy Adams.

John Quincy attended the round of diplomatic dinners and soirées to which his father was invited. He delighted in the Paris theater and opera, the best the world afforded. He could hold his own in any conversation about history. John Adams the Minister was proud of the poise and ease and modesty with which the boy carried himself. He treasured the compliments and inquiries received about his charming and able son. Among other rounds of social activities the youth frequently sat in at the dinners that Lafayette gave every Monday evening to the American group. He heard his host make fun of the French nobility for being ignorant and foolish.

In later years, during the wars of the French Revolution, when John Quincy Adams was holding his first diplomatic commission as Minister Resident at The Hague, he was able to return in a slight way some of the old kindnesses formerly extended to himself and parents by the French hero of the American Revolution. He advanced official funds for the relief of Madame de Lafayette while her husband languished in Prussian and Austrian captivity. Still later, when Minister to Russia in 1812, he

[26] *Works* of JA, X, 414.

secured from Czar Alexander I the parole of Lafayette's son-in-law, the Comte de Tracy, as a prisoner of war under the Minister's personal recognizance.[27] He received friendly letters from the General in later life and as Secretary of State and President had the pleasure of entertaining him in Washington in 1824–5, when the chivalrous friend of American independence came back to the United States as the guest of the nation.

In Paris the youth met most of the diplomatic corps and learned as if by second nature the amenities, formalities, and protocol of their official and unofficial life. He came to understand the peculiar ceremonies and extravagances of Versailles, weighted as they were with centuries of tradition and superstition, curiosities certain to strike an uninitiated visitor from the fresh republican New World as puzzling and absurd. The more he saw of court life whether in St. Petersburg, or Versailles, or London, or even at the capital of Their High Mightinesses the Estates General of the Netherlands, the more ardent republican he became. Such reasoned conclusions were instructive for one who was to be a champion of freedom in the New World.

During these years John Quincy Adams made trips back and forth to the Netherlands, where his father had to take leave as Minister, and to England for the first time on a visit with John Adams in 1783, and again in 1784 to meet his mother and sister, who came out from Massachusetts to join husband and father; and to arrange for reunion of all in Paris.

In London he visited historical places and spent hours listening to debates in the House of Commons. He heard the heaven-born Pitt and the emotional Charles James Fox and faithfully carried out the pedagogical request of his father to size up the oratorical powers of all principal speakers.

"Mr. Pitt," he reported, "is upon the whole the best and most pleasing speaker of them all. He has much grace in speaking and has an admirable choice of words. He speaks very fluently, so distinctly that I did not lose a word of what he said, and he was not once embarrassed to express his ideas. Mr. Fox on the contrary speaks with such an amazing heat and rapidity that he often gets embarrassed and stammers some time before he can express himself. His ideas are all striking, but they flow upon him in such numbers that he cannot communicate them without difficulty. . . . Lord North is very cool. . . . Mr. Sheridan speaks extremely fast, and has a wonderful facility of expression. . . ."[28]

[27] In 1795 he sent 300 louis ($1333.20) to her, upon urgent appeal, recouping himself two years later, presumably out of the $24,424 that Congress appropriated for the relief of Lafayette and his family. *Writings,* I, 297, 298; JQA to Secretary of State, Nos. 45, 71, The Hague, July 3, 1795, July 1, 1796. DS, *Despatches, Netherlands,* I. Timothy Pickering to JQA, Department of State, November 26, 1796. DS, *Instructions, U.S. Ministers,* III, 298. JQA drew the bill of exchange to the "Chevalier de la Gloire," JQA to Lafayette, Quincy, November 30, 1801, and Lafayette to JQA, La Grange, June 24, 1802. Adams MSS. For Tracy, *Memoirs,* II, 490–5.

[28] *Writings,* I, 14–16.

Pitt was then his favorite orator,[29] and a model. Listening to these great parliamentarians was a profitable experience for a future orator in the Congress of the United States.

From inscriptions and bookplates in surviving volumes of John Quincy Adams's library and from notes in diaries and letters we get glimpses of his persistent reading at this time, between his fifteenth and eighteenth years. Before he left Europe he knew French and Dutch and he could read a simple Spanish text. He had seen some of the best pictures in Europe. He had tapped the wellsprings of English literature and history. He was versed in French literature: Voltaire, Molière, Beaumarchais, Rousseau, Rabelais, La Fontaine, Laplace, Le Sage's *Gil Blas* (in a Dutch translation – he had learned it by heart from the original French at the age of twelve). He had seen and heard the offerings of the Paris stage and opera. It would have been a misadventure for an unscholarly person to argue with him on a point of Greek or Roman history, as rich and foppish William Bingham, from Philadelphia, once tried to do at the theater in Paris. He could cite not only his childhood text, Rollin, but also "the original historians" like Suetonius, Livy, and Herodotus. Although he still spoke Latin awkwardly, he had read Cæsar's *Commentaries,* Cicero's *Orations,* Cornelius Nepos, Juvenal, Ovid, and Phædrus. He wrote out careful translations of Virgil's *Æneid,* of Suetonius, Sallust, Tacitus's *Agricola* and *Germania,* and *Annals,* and a great part of Horace, Ovid, and Tully. In Greek he had studied Aristotle's *Poetica,* Plutarch's *Lives,* Xenophon, and the *Iliad.* On the way home from Russia in 1783 he had sojourned three months at The Hague, reading Virgil, a hundred verses a day, with the learned coadjutor to the American Legation there, Charles William Frederick Dumas.[30] He went back there for two three-months periods during the next year to live with Dumas and his family, studying the classics and listening to the musical exercises of his preceptor's bright-eyed daughter.[31]

Familiar knowledge of the classics and ready ability to cite and quote them were great aids to easy diplomatic intercourse in the Age of Enlightenment. They put one instantly on a plane of equality and broke down the formality of even an Englishman. The classics always stood John Quincy Adams in good stead in politics as well as in his ever widening scholarship. He read them as long as he lived. An appealing feature of the remarkable correspondence of his mature life between him and his venerated father, the elder statesman of Quincy, was their constant ex-

[29] "Your favourite orator and the favourite, of all men of taste, Mr. Pitt, is greater, I think, than ever." William Vans Murray to JQA, London, August 2, 1785. Adams MSS.

[30] *Memoirs,* II, 649. Adams renewed his friendship with Dumas, a pensioner of the United States, and with the family of Dumas's daughter, Mrs. Vreman Saint-Cerf, when he returned to The Hague in 1794. Dumas died, an unregenerate Jacobin, August 11, 1796.

[31] William Vans Murray to JQA, London, December 10, 1784. Adams MSS.

change of reflections upon classic writers, ancient and modern, Greek, Latin, French, and English, and the Bible.[32]

John Adams spent his Paris evenings teaching the youth algebra, plane and solid geometry, and trigonometry, instead of playing cards like the fashionable world. They even took a flight together — not very high — into differential calculus, so anxious was the Peace Commissioner to get his son ready for Harvard College.[33]

No youth was ever better prepared for Harvard. Yet, looking back from mature manhood upon these early years of reading, John Quincy Adams felt that his education, thanks to his wanderings about the world, had been unsystematic and desultory. "Hence it has happened," he affirmed at the age of forty-two, "that, though I was always of a studious turn and addicted to books beyond bounds of moderation, yet my acquirements in literature and science have been all superficial, and I never attained a profound knowledge of anything."[34]

Even then it was in the nature of an Adams to bemoan the inadequacies of his education.

It was on January 1, 1785, the last of the youthful Paris years, that John Quincy Adams began his famous Diary, since published most extensively by his grandson, Charles Francis Adams,[35] as a monumental source for American historiography, the best of all records for the famous author's life and times. In it he carried out his father's two admonitions: not to waste time, and always and unfailingly to write a clear hand.[36] A quotation from Voltaire on the title page of the beginning volume of the Diary reflects the first admonition, which ruled John Quincy Adams's life: *"La mollesse est douce et sa suite est cruelle."* It has been remarked: "He never had an idle moment."[37]

Adams reviewing his life would have been first to declaim against such

[32] Illustrated, among many unprinted letters, in JQA to JA (on buying books), No. 31, Reval, May 8, 1814, and Ghent, July 7, 1814 (on the Bible). Adams MSS.

[33] JA to Professor Benjamin Waterhouse, Auteuil, near Paris, April 23, 1785. *Catalogue of the Books of John Quincy Adams*, p. 43.

[34] Autobiographical letter to Skelton Jones, Boston, April 17, 1809. *Writings*, III, 298.

[35] *Memoirs of John Quincy Adams, Comprising Portions of His Diary from 1795–1848.* Edited by Charles Francis Adams (12 vols., Philadelphia, 1874–6). The publication begins with the year 1794, when the author became Minister to the Netherlands. Charles Francis Adams, Jr., brother of the historian Henry Adams and also an eminent historical scholar, printed portions from the earliest years of the Diary, *Life in a New England Town: 1787, 1788. Diary of John Quincy Adams while a Student in the Office of Theophilus Parsons at Newburyport* (Boston, 1903) — hereinafter referred to as *Life in a N.E. Town.* Henry Adams, 2d, utilized unprinted portions of the Diary for the years 1785–94 in his *Catalogue of the Books of John Quincy Adams; Birthplaces of Presidents John and John Quincy Adams; The Adams Mansion.*

[36] JA to JQA, in St. Petersburg, December 14, 15, 1781. *Letters of Mrs. Adams*, pp. 423–4.

[37] Worthington C. Ford's prefatory Note to the *Writings.*

a statement, but it was true as much as it can be true of any man. The Diary itself is proof enough. From January 1, 1795 until at least the year 1816 [38] he kept his journal without the intermission of a single day, and after that, despite interruptions, quite steadily until the end of his life. Sixty-three years of handwriting reflect the second admonition, which ruled the Diary. Page after page, day after day, week after week, month after month, year after year, decade after decade, century into century, the clear, clean roundish slant flows on and on, for many years unwearied, unhesitant, and unblemished, but growing square and shaky as time went on, into the final tremulous and difficult legibility of advanced old age. It is the same in the scores of volumes of letters and state papers. He wrote them all in his own hand. Any child can read them today. Old John Adams taught well his children and grandchildren how to write a neat and honest open script.

Linked to great associations in the shadow of historic events, which he must have come to regard as quite natural in his family, John Quincy Adams so far had preserved a bright, normal, and healthy youth. If there had been little time for disciplined sport at the farm in Braintree on the eve of the Revolution, he had learned to ride a horse, to swim, to use a pistol or a fowling-piece as easily as he learned to read and to recite epic poetry. Already amidst his studies in Paris he had fallen discreetly in love – with an actress! Many years later, a quarter-century after his marriage, when he had become Secretary of State, he described the whole affair to his wife, who had written him a sprightly letter from Massachusetts to ask why he was attending the theater so much in Washington.

"The stage has been to me a source of much amusement for more than forty years. But I have always enjoyed it with discretion; first, with reference to expense, but secondly and chiefly, with respect to morals. To which end I have made it a rule to make no acquaintance with *actresses.* The first woman I ever loved was an actress, but I never spoke to her, and I think I never saw her off the stage. She belonged to a company of children who performed at the Bois de Boulogne near Passy, when I lived there with Dr. Franklin and my father. She remains upon my memory as the most lovely and delightful actress that I ever saw; but I have not seen her since I was fourteen. She was then about the same age. Of all the ungratified longings that I ever suffered, that of being acquainted with her, merely to tell her how much I adored her, was the most intense. I was tortured with the desire for nearly two years, but never had the wit to compass it. I used to dream of her for at least seven years after. But how many times I have since blessed my stars and my stupidity that I never did get the opportunity of making my declaration. I learnt from her that lesson of never forming an acquaintance with an actress to which I have since invariably adhered, and which I would lay as an injunction upon all my sons." [39]

[38] *Memoirs,* III, 407–8. [39] *Writings,* VII, 298–9.

4

It was time in 1785 for the boy to go back to Boston before he became a man. John Quincy Adams had never lost his passion for a Harvard degree. Both parents feared that if he lingered on too long abroad he might succumb finally to the enervating refinements of European luxuries and pleasures to which he was constantly exposed.[40] They left it to him to decide whether he would return to finish his education at his father's alma mater, "that darling child of New England Puritanism." There he would meet a cramped environment and narrowed curriculum, followed inevitably by the "dry and tedious study of the law," but there he would renew the ties of his native land before it was too late.

This was a dreary prospect when compared with the wide world of European culture that had opened up so expansively and delightfully before him. But the young patriot did not want forever to be a charge on his father's limited means. He desired to strike out for himself, to be independent. Before him in Paris was the horrible example of Dr. Franklin's grandson, William Temple Franklin. He had come as a boy with the Doctor to France and had been there so long as to become dandified, to lead a cat around by a ribbon, and be good for nothing. Young Franklin did not care whether he ever went home. This disgusted John Quincy. "At least in America," he noted in his Diary, "I can live *independent* and *free,* and rather than live otherwise I would wish to die." He decided to go back. As long as he lived he never regretted his decision.

He said farewell again to his parents in the late spring of 1785 and sailed back home. It seems strange that a young man of such precocious erudition would think it necessary to study up any more to enter Harvard; but he was resolved to get advanced standing and thus save time; and study up he did, particularly in Latin and Greek, for several months at Haverhill, where he lived with his Aunt Elizabeth (Abigail Adams's sister) and her husband, the Reverend John Shaw. After a rather perfunctory examination President Willard admitted the young man to the junior class, in March 1786. His brother Charles already was enrolled in one of the lower classes. Harvard was glad to have the Adams boys, sons of the Minister to the Court of St. James's. In recognition of his father's public service the college authorities voted not to accept tuition fees for John Quincy Adams.[41]

The college courses, though easy, were not unprofitable for a student of Adams's self-discipline. He seized the opportunity to deepen further his

[40] "If you or my father had known the *moral* dangers through which I passed, and from which by the mercy of Providence I escaped, I think neither of you would have had the courage to expose me to them." JQA to AA, Ealing, No. 77, October 1, 1815. Adams MSS.

[41] Minutes of the Meeting of the President, Professors, and Tutors, March 15, 1786. Archives of Harvard College.

knowledge of the classics. His habitual reading took him far beyond the requirements of the curriculum, to works like Gibbon's *History of the Decline and Fall of the Roman Empire* and Montesquieu's *Esprit des lois.*

Going to college at Harvard really was coming back home. It was the happiest day of his life, he noted, when again he stepped into his father's house at Braintree and gazed at old books and familiar objects in the empty rooms awaiting the return of the statesman. In Massachusetts he was back on the soil of his native land, where he wanted to dedicate his life to the service of his country.

It cannot be said that John Quincy Adams made life at Harvard more colorful. He sought quiet company and stuck closely to his studies. "A person who wishes to make any figure as a scholar at this University, must not spend much time either in visiting or being visited."[42] One incident illustrates characteristically his poignant, almost morbid youthful sensibilities. On the 17th of June 1786, when a bridge between Boston and Charlestown was to be dedicated, the Harvard students arranged to parade over to Bunker Hill for the holiday and to attend a big barbecue and public dinner there. Young Adams heard that the head of the table was to be placed on the very spot where the immortal Warren fell. That recalled the day when he and his mother had watched the battle from Penn's Hill eleven years before. "I think," noted the solemn youth in his Diary, "that the ground which has been the scene of such an awful Day should not be the scene of Revels and Feasting. What must be the feelings of a man of Sensibility, who would naturally say to himself, 'Perhaps I am now seated on the Grave of my dearest Friend, perhaps this is the spot where he drew his last gasp, and I may now be treading on his bones.'"[43] So he stayed behind at the college while the other boys went to celebrate Bunker Hill Day, and ate his meal alone in the nearly empty commons. Many years later as a Harvard professor and distinguished citizen of Boston he partook with perfect equanimity and patriotic enthusiasm of a Fourth-of-July luncheon spread on Bunker Hill battlefield in the year 1809. The noble Warren's spirit rested undisturbed.

Thus passed two short years at Harvard College.[44] John Quincy

[42] JQA to JA, Cambridge, May 21, 1786. *Writings,* I, 25.

[43] *Birthplaces of Presidents John and John Quincy Adams,* pp. 19–20.

[44] See the essay on "Harvard College, 1786–1787," by Henry Adams, the historian, who published copious extracts from JQA's Diary as a Harvard student, in *Historical Essays* (New York, 1891), pp. 81–121.

He lived in Hollis Hall: during junior year in a room on the third floor on the south side of the entry next to Harvard Hall, during senior year on the second floor, No. 6. During the fuel famine of the winter of 1786–7, when the college could not be heated for eight weeks, he lived with two other students at Professor Wigglesworth's house. Henry Adams, 2d: "John Quincy Adams's Room at Harvard," unprinted.

Adams's only regret was that he had not entered the university a year and a half earlier. Unlike his famous grandson, Henry Adams, he always felt that he had benefited from Harvard. For one thing, he had come for the first time to know "amiable and respectable characters" of his own age and disposition. He further noted in his Diary that Harvard had reduced his opinion of himself, his acquirements, and his future prospects, nearer to the level of truth and reality. Harvard always has had a way of doing that.

He graduated on July 16, 1787, a member of Phi Beta Kappa since the end of his junior year. His senior oration was on "The Importance and Necessity of Public Faith to the Well Being of a Nation." It attracted the attention of distinguished visitors at the Harvard commencement exercises.[45] Dr. Jeremy Belknap published it in the *Columbian Magazine* of Philadelphia in September 1787.[46]

The oration reflects the distresses through which the Commonwealth of Massachusetts had just been passing. Shays's Rebellion of 1786–7 had made a profound impression on the youth as he neared graduation. The disorder alarmed him. He was irritated at the opprobrium unjustly heaped upon the profession or "order" of lawyers, which he was preparing to enter. With dismay he beheld the decay of constructive patriotism so soon after the glorious conclusion of the Revolution. He saw the local rebellion as a symptom of national disunity. His European and diplomatic background made him realize how such an event would sap the prestige of the United States abroad. He could imagine what a disastrous effect it would have upon his father's contemporary efforts to negotiate a treaty of amity and commerce with Great Britain. Indeed, it was a plausible demonstration of the truth of what Englishmen like Lord Sheffield were then writing: that the United States constituted no more of a nation to deal with diplomatically than the states of German Europe; the Thirteen States in America could not stand together in any arrangements or engagements nation to nation. The youthful orator's remarks at commencement, delivered, he professed, with involuntary palpitations and a consciousness of his own insufficiency, show his bookish studies of history and politics brought to bear for the first time on the political situation of his own day in his own country.

The commotions in Massachusetts he attributed to a lack of sound circulating money medium, due to collapse of *national* credit. It involved a

[45] "I was present at the commencement in your University of Cambridge, and highly delighted with most of the academic exercises, in particular young Mr. Adams distinguished himself by a manly and dignified oration on public credit." Henry Knox, Secretary of War, to Colonel Humphries, Hartford, July 27, 1787. Knox MSS., in MHS.

[46] Lawrence Shaw Mayo published, with interesting comments, the relevant correspondence between "Jeremy Belknap and JQA, 1787," in MHS *Proceedings,* LIX (October 1925–June 1926).

sacred debt of honor: the money that his country had borrowed from the King of France, and from Dutch bankers, in the times that tried men's souls, to help win its independence. He introduced examples from the history of Greece, Rome, and even Britain to show that when a nation observed its plighted faith it prospered, when it disregarded its pledged word it declined:

> To every reflecting mind [said the orator], the situation of this commonwealth for some months past, must have appeared truly alarming: on whatever side we turn our anxious eyes, the prospect of public affairs is dark and gloomy: the distressing scarcity of a circulating medium, has been constantly increasing: the violent gust of rebellion is scarcely dissipated, and threatening clouds of sullen discontent are still lowering round the horizon; luxury and dissipation, like baneful weeds, have obstructed the growth of all of our useful virtues; and although the hand of patriotism has of late been stretched forth to crop the noxious plant, yet, the fatal root still lies lurking beneath the surface; the bonds of union, which connected us with our sister states, have been shamefully relaxed by a selfish and contracted principle, and the sails of commerce furled within our ports, witness the lamentable declension of our trade.

We could wish that the Harvard senior had gone farther down into the soil where the fatal roots were lurking and working their baleful effects and found there the real reason for the collapse of national honor and credit: the lack of adequate national powers for international dealing, in the existing weak Confederation of the Thirteen States. If he realized this, the vital political problem of his graduating day, the son of His Excellency John Adams, LL.D., American Minister at the Court of London,[47] did not mention it to his commencement audience. The oration nevertheless was a striking performance. It was a suggestion of his forming political outlook.

5

The three years after graduation he spent diligently studying law in the office of Theophilus Parsons at Newburyport. There he continued to read widely in history, science, and literature — Gibbon, Hume, Voltaire, Buffon, Rousseau, Fielding, Shakespeare — and even found time to learn shorthand, by Biron's system.[48] Lawyer Parsons, a law library

[47] "An Oration Delivered at the Public Commencement, in the University at Cambridge, in New England, July 18, 1787, by Mr. John Quincy Adams, Son of His Excellency John Adams, LL.D., the American Minister at the Court of London," *Columbia Magazine or Monthly Miscellany,* September 1787.

[48] JQA to TBA, St. Petersburg, March 17, 1813. While without a private secretary from May to September 1814 on the way to Ghent and during the first months of the negotiations there, Adams entered his private letters in shorthand in his private

in himself, would talk with his pupils more about literature than law. He kept an old rocking-chair in his office. He would tip back in it and cut off a quid of chewing tobacco. Then he would discourse to the young men. "Lord Bacon," he would say, "observes that 'reading makes a full man, conversation a ready man, and writing a correct man.' Now, gentlemen, I would have you full, ready, and correct." [49]

The law student had been studying only a month when he came on this passage in Blackstone:

"It is a principle of *universal law* that the natural-born subject of one prince, cannot by any act of his own, no, not by swearing allegiance to another, put off or discharge his natural allegiance to the former: for this natural allegiance was intrinsic and primitive, and antecedent to the other, and cannot be divested without the concurrent act of that prince to whom it was first due."

It did not seem right to a natural-born son of the American Revolution that a man must be obliged to serve and assist his sovereign, however cruel, tyrannical, and unjust he might be. He took the subject to his preceptor as his first question.

"If it read *common law* instead of universal law," answered Judge Parsons, "the assertion would be just; but in my opinion every man has a right by the law of nature to put off his natural allegiance, for good cause." [50]

It was John Quincy's first introduction to that Anglo-American collision of principles which would take up his attention and energy through so many years of his diplomatic career: the British assertion of inalienable allegiance – once a Britisher always a Britisher – against the American right of expatriation and naturalization. It was the heart of the later vital impressment issue. What with Blackstone, Parsons, and the American Revolution, young John Quincy was getting a proper grounding in fundamental principles.

Preceptor and pupil remained friends until the older man's death, though in later years they came to differ bitterly in politics.

The years at Newburyport were not devoted wholly to *Coke on Littleton,* and Blackstone. Despite long hours at his books – to the actual endangering of his health – the diligent reader of law led a convivial life. His Diary is filled with the social activities of life in a New England town by young people of his age: the doings of a young men's social club, with the table loaded with big-bellied bottles, that made it hard to study lawbooks next morning; all-night serenades to the young ladies; dinners, dances, sailing parties in summer, sleigh-rides in winter. "The art of making love," John Quincy Adams reminisced in his sedate sixties,

letterbook. Fortunately for the biographer, most of these were to his wife and parents and the originals have been preserved.

[49] JQA to CFA, Washington, November 7, 1827. Adams MSS.

[50] *Life in a N.E. Town,* pp. 42–3.

"muffled up in furs, in the open air, with the thermometer at Zero, is a Yankee invention, which requires a Yankee poet to describe." [51]

The young man's interest in the opposite sex was strong but disciplined, unhappily disciplined. His Diary for those years abounds in discriminating if not highly objective appraisals of the charms or lack of charms of the girls of Newburyport. He found their persons comely but their conversation insipid. "Miss Sally Jenkins . . . is of the middling female size and has a fine form. . . . She conversed not much, and indeed in the state of female education there are very few young ladies who talk and yet preserve our admiration." [52]

Soon he found himself in a struggle between his "sentiments" and his "opinions," between love and a career. The amorous youth feared lest his ambition be lulled with soft inglorious dreams that would make him forget the themes of patriots and sages. To his friend and cousin William Cranch he recited feelingly the poet's lines:

> I feel diviner fires my breast inflame
> To active Science and ingenuous Fame,
> Resume the path my earliest choice began
> And lose with pride the Lover in the Man.

He descanted with delicious fearsomeness upon the "danger" in which he stood. He found "no hardship" in the peril. He almost succumbed.[53]

Toward the end of his stay in Newburyport the young Yankee law student fell completely and idyllically in love with Mary Frazier, daughter of the patriot selectman Moses Frazier. Contemporary letters and later correspondence make it clear that the couple were deeply attached. "You may know (though it is known to very few)," he wrote to his old college chum James Bridge, "that all my hopes of future happiness in this life, center in the possession of that girl." [54]

He was then twenty-two and she eighteen. Both realized that he could not support a family. So did their parents. Therefore, for "prudential and family reasons," they broke off the attachment, with this frostily romantic understanding: that neither would marry a person less worthy than his first love. John Quincy poured cold water on the glowing embers, but the spark of tender remembrance never died out entirely. These "troubles of the heart" were "deep and distressing." So President John Quincy Adams wrote from the White House to his youngest son forty years afterward.[55]

[51] JQA to Dr. Benjamin Waterhouse, Washington, December 15, 1832. Adams MSS.

[52] *Life in a N.E. Town,* p. 80.

[53] JQA to William Cranch, Newbury-Port, April 7, 1790. Cranch Papers, LC.

[54] James Bridge in a letter to JQA of September 28, 1790, from Hallowell, Maine, quotes this passage from one of JQA's letters to him of September 5, 1790, not extant. Adams MSS.

[55] JQA to CFA, Washington, March 15, 1828. Adams MSS.

The sad frustration of the first and most intense love of his life had a profound effect. It took away some of the spontaneity and sparkle that had come down to him from John and Abigail Adams. Henceforth he was as determined never to connect a woman to desperate fortunes as he was never to be indebted to a woman for wealth.[56] At the age of twenty-three the young lawyer opened a law office in Boston, safely distant from the temptations of Newburyport.[57]

6

Clients were few. Time hung on his hands. He read – Cicero, Tacitus, Burke, Clarendon, Hume. He meditated much. He wrote.[58] John Adams, now Vice President of the United States, urged the young Boston lawyer to interest himself in politics.

So disheartened was John Quincy at the slow progress of his business that it seemed hard to take an interest in anything, even politics, which had so engrossed his studies. "The prospect is really glorious," he wrote to his father, looking to the future of the new Government, "but it is perhaps impossible, at least for a man whose future is not tinctured with more heroism than mine, to consider the general prosperity with such peculiar pleasure, when he is not one of the individuals who derive any immediate advantage from it, as when the fabric of patriotic endeavor is supported by the firm pillars of private interest."[59]

This mood of discouragement eventually passed. He began to pick up a little practice. And he could not shut off his interest in politics, even if he tried.

Meanwhile Harvard College kept her attachments to him. The year after graduation Phi Beta Kappa invited him to Cambridge to deliver an oration to the society.[60] He spoke on the prospects of youth for fame and fortune in the unseeable future.[61] The address reflected a young man determined not to live unknowing and unknown.[62]

[56] JQA to AA, Boston, August 29, 1790. Adams MSS.

[57] "The *temptations* which you mention, I do not very well know. What should I be afraid of here? The only temptations that can be dangerous to me are such as would lead me away: but I am proof against everything." JQA to William Cranch, Boston, August 1, 1791. Cranch Papers, LC.

[58] JQA to GWA, Washington, March 12, 1826. JQA to CFA, March 26, 1826. Adams MSS.

[59] October 19, 1790. Adams MSS. See also AA to Mary Cranch, Bush Hill, March 12, 1791. *New Letters of Abigail Adams,* Stewart Mitchell, editor (Boston, 1947), p. 70.

[60] Samuel Shapleigh, secretary of the society, to JQA, Cambridge, June 25, 1788. Adams MSS. *Life in a N.E. Town,* p. 166.

[61] The address, without title, is copied into his Diary under date of the ceremony, September 5, 1788.

[62] *Life in a N.E. Town,* pp. 65, 88.

At the invitation of President Willard[63] he came back to Harvard commencement in 1790 and participated in a "forensic disputation" with Samuel Putnam, a classmate at Harvard and former fellow student in Judge Parsons's law office. Little did he then realize that one day he would again return to Harvard as a professor of rhetoric and oratory, nor could he have foreseen that his young colleague on the platform would later be Chief Justice of Massachusetts for twenty-eight years.

During these Boston years John Quincy Adams led the life of a young lawyer with lively companions who gathered together for congenial evenings as young professional and businessmen have done in Boston throughout its history since Revolutionary times. They organized the Crackbrain Club. It was what we would call today an interest club, but it did not neglect the tavern-keepers of the city. Among the members were: Walter Burling, John Callendar, Thomas Crafts, "the delight of his friends," who died in 1797; Nathan Frazier, brother of Mary Frazier; Nathaniel Freeman, and John Gardner, all Harvard graduates of John Quincy's time; Daniel Sargeant, who married Mary Frazier in 1802, and his brother John Thomas, and Thomas Handasyd Perkins. They were the warm friends of his younger years, some of them to be bitter political opponents of his later manhood. The Crackbrains did not survive as an organization many months after Adams's departure from Boston in 1794. He entertained some of the members in London in 1796 and continued an affectionate correspondence from The Hague and Berlin with others, exchanging comments on the inexhaustible fund of European international politics for gossipy bits about the young men and women of the "good Yankee town of Boston." Finally the correspondence broke down under a weight of political commentary.

7

The lawyer's entrance into political discussion was through the columns of the press under protective cover of pseudonymity. This was then a favorite device for an ambitious young man who wished to test his powers and popularity; if the public response was not sufficiently promising he could withhold his identity from his friends and try another cause with a new pseudonym. John Quincy's first trial of this kind was the *Letters of Publicola,* printed in the *Columbian Centinel* of Boston in the summer of 1791 and reprinted throughout the land.

The *Letters* were a critique of Tom Paine's *Rights of Man,* in which the famous propagandist had urged the British people to follow French example, overthrow their Government, and draw up a new constitution, with a national assembly, like that of France; whatever the people did in their "original character," he vouched, would be right. "Publicola" argued that the British people indeed might have the power but they

[63] Joseph Willard to JQA, Cambridge, June 21, 1790. Adams MSS.

did not have the moral right to overthrow their unwritten Constitution unless there were no other redress from intolerable tyranny. Under the British Constitution, he contended, Parliament had power to make such constitutional reforms as might be necessary; therefore revolution was neither desirable, nor expedient, nor right. The real motive of "Publicola," however, was to defend his father against the implication of political heresy launched by their old friend Thomas Jefferson in a prefatory letter to the American edition of Paine's tract.

At first everybody, including Secretary of State Jefferson, thought that "Publicola" was the Vice President; but after the editor of the *Centinel* had denied the fact categorically, James Madison pointed out to Jefferson that it was probably the son editing his father's doctrine. "There is more method also in the arguments," added Madison, "and much less of clumsiness and heaviness in the style than characterizes his [John Adams's] writings." There remains no written evidence of collaboration between father and son, and "Publicola" in his last paper stated that the Vice President "neither wrote nor corrected them"; but the two Adamses must have talked the papers over a great deal, for John Adams was on a vacation visit to Braintree that summer.

The affair brought on the first rift in the long-standing and never completely broken friendship between John Adams and Thomas Jefferson. They now found themselves on diverging paths of political principles: Jefferson, the great American apologist for the French Revolution, even its extremes in the name of liberty, Jefferson the breaker of entails, believer in an aristocracy only of education, open to every man; Adams, who condoned a "natural" aristocracy — not so much different, really, from Jefferson's aristocracy of education — and who saw social values in "paternal estates," who admired the ancient British Constitution, with its stabilizing *balance* of king, lords, and commons; John Adams who was a moral friend of republicanism,[64] but who trembled at the excesses developed by "elective" democracy, as illustrated in the French Revolution.[65] Except for the vital hereditary feature, the elder Adams saw little difference between the British and American Constitutions; both were republican in fundamental character, and he would have amended the new Constitution of the United States so as to give the President powers more nearly like those of the King of Great Britain.[66]

[64] Letters to John Taylor. *Works* of JA, VI, 477–84.

[65] JA to Sir Francis d'Ivernois, Philadelphia, December 11, 1795. *Revue historique de la Révolution française,* V (1914), 346–48.

[66] John Adams set forth his political theories in his *Defence of the Constitutions of Government of the United States of America* (3 vols., London, 1787–8), and his *Discourses on Davila,* printed in the *Gazette of the United States* at Philadelphia, as a sequel to the *Defence,* in 1790. See also Charles Francis Adams's informing notes in *Works* of JA, Vols. IV, V, VI, notably VI, 448–51.

John Adams desired the following amendments to the Constitution of the United States: (1) absolute veto power for the President on all legislation by Congress; (2)

The *Letters of Publicola* reveal John Quincy Adams, on his part, as a conservative republican, admirer of the British Constitution, as distinct from the corrupt British Government, and like his father an early skeptic with respect to the French Revolution. At least four different reprints of the letters appeared soon in London, one in Glasgow, one in Edinburgh, two in Dublin, and a Dutch translation at Dordrecht. If the *Letters* were meant as a trial balloon for a start in politics, they failed. They pleased the father immensely, but they did him more harm than good. On the eve of the national election of 1792 they provoked a debate in the press that gave unfavorable publicity to the Vice President's highly theoretical political writings. John Adams, however, survived it.

John Quincy Adams presently turned his attention to more local matters. He became a member of a committee of citizens appointed in town meeting to reform the Boston police, which, even as early as 1791, seem to have been in urgent need of regeneration. Dr. Charles Jarvis nominated him to this, his first public office, because the doctor felt that the country was under such obligations to John Adams's public service that some notice should be taken of his son. John Quincy's experience with this duty, and the rejection of the committee's proposals after rabble-rousing speeches of opposition politicians in town meeting, confirmed his "abhorrence and contempt of simple democracy as a Government." [67]

The budding lawyer next championed, under the pen of "Menander," opposition to Boston's "blue law" prohibiting theatrical exhibitions. "Publicola" would not wish to have been seen in public with "Menander," who represented another, nonpolitical, but equally passionate interest of the same author, the stage. Young John Quincy Adams was one of the original stockholders in the ill-fated Boston Theatre, which opened on February 3, 1794, went bankrupt after one season, and burned down in 1798.[68]

These efforts of the pen so far yielded no political fruit. The new citizen of Boston meanwhile was chafing at the "useless and disgraceful insignificancy" [69] of his life. It was a time when young men were playing big roles on the stage of politics. Jefferson had been thirty-three when he wrote the Declaration of Independence. Alexander Hamilton had become a public figure in his early twenties. William Pitt, the

---

abolition of the Senate's confirming power on presidential appointments; (3) abolition of the Senate's treaty-making power; (4) removal of Congress's negative on war. See his exchange of letters with Roger Sherman, July 1789, ibid., VI, 427–42. Ford's notes to the *Writings,* I, 65–6, 110, with pertinent references to the personal relationships and political controversy stirred up by "Publicola's" letters.

[67] *Writings,* I, 110–15.

[68] JQA to John Gardner, The Hague, May 28, 1795. Adams MSS. See Justin Winsor, ed., *Memorial History of Boston* (4 vols., Boston, 1880–1), IV, 362–4.

[69] John T. Morse, Jr.: *John Quincy Adams* (Boston, 1882), p. 19, quoting unpublished portions of the Diary.

younger, was Chancellor of the Exchequer at twenty-three, Prime Minister at twenty-four; he was only twenty-four when John Quincy Adams had admired him in the House of Commons. Charles James Fox, to whose tumbling eloquence the youthful Adams also had listened, had entered Parliament in his twentieth year.

It was the impact on the United States of the French Revolution—the same revolution that had put twenty-six-year-old General Napoleon Bonaparte in command of the best army Europe had yet seen—that gave to John Quincy Adams the first profitable topic for his scholarly pen. This in turn led to an appointment on his twenty-eighth birthday that enabled him to follow in his father's footsteps, first in the courts of Europe, then at home in Washington. Now the curtain rises on the dramatic international setting which France's tremendous political upheaval had placed before the world, including the United States of America, newly organized as a nation under its Constitution of 1787.

CHAPTER II

The French Revolution and Jay's Treaty with Great Britain (1793–1794)

Of all the dangers which encompass the liberties of a republican State, the intrusion of a foreign influence into the administration of their affairs, is the most alarming.

JOHN QUINCY ADAMS: *Letters of Columbus,* 1793

Two events of lasting significance in American history occurred in the spring of 1789. One was the inauguration of the National Government under the Constitution of 1787, with General Washington as President. The other was the outbreak of the French Revolution. Both were of controlling influence in John Quincy Adams's career. Both were of paramount importance to the foundations of American foreign policy.

Under the Constitution the Federal Government at last had powers adequate to the direction of foreign policy. President Washington referred to it as a National, rather than a Federal, Government; so did John Quincy Adams. Under George Washington's leadership the ablest men in the country took their stations at the nation's helm: John Adams, Vice President; John Jay, Chief Justice; Thomas Jefferson, Secretary of State; Alexander Hamilton, Secretary of the Treasury. All of these fathers of American nationality had conspicuous international reputations. All of them were schooled in foreign affairs. All of them were natural statesmen of the first water. With these constitutional powers and these natural statesmen the new Government was able to give direction, tone, and character, if not force, to its diplomacy.

The French Revolution was to present American diplomacy with grave dangers and great opportunities. The dangers flowing from the European upheaval and the Franco-American alliance would appear in an attempted intrusion into American domestic politics, after the manner of French intervention in the neutral states of Europe. The opportunities would come from the train of international wars and disputes touched off first by the Revolution and later by its imperial torch-bearer, Napoleon Bonaparte. Those wars put a premium on American neutrality and friendship at the very time when American national power was first taking shape.

1

Looking back upon these events with the aid of history, it is easier for us to understand the scene in which John Quincy Adams was about to begin his public career than it was for him, engrossed as he had been with the small world of Cambridge and Newburyport. At first he did not catch the signals of national forces that would shape and govern his whole life and career. For example, he had nothing to remark about the Philadelphia Convention during the summer of 1787; at least there is no reference in his papers to the demand for a new national constitution. When the Federal Constitution of 1787 came to Massachusetts for ratification, he actually expressed a "fear" that the "new continental form of government" would be adopted.[1]

Judge Parsons approved the new scheme of government, and told his pupil so.

"Nor do I wonder at all that he should approve of it," wrote the young man in his Diary, "as it is calculated to increase the power, influence, and wealth of those who have any already. . . . There are to be no titles of nobility; but there will be great distinctions, and those distinctions will soon be hereditary, and we shall consequently have nobles, but no titles. For my own part I am willing to take my chance under any government whatever; but it is hard to give up a system which I have always been taught to cherish, and to confess that a free government is inconsistent with human nature."[2]

When one is twenty, one has high hopes of human nature! At sixty, reading over some letters he had written forty years before, John Quincy Adams, President of the United States, looked back upon his opinions of 1787 as "monumental errors."[3]

He did not have to wait till sixty to know it. Soon his own State of Massachusetts, after a display of proposed amendments of the Jeffersonian type, ratified the fundamental charter of government. "I am now converted but not convinced," wrote the young law student in Newburyport. "In our government opposition to the acts of a majority of the people is rebellion to all intents and purposes; and I should view a man who would now endeavor to excite commotions against this plan, as no better than an insurgent who took arms last winter against the courts of justice."[4]

His father approved the Constitution though he desired amendments

[1] *Writings,* I, 39.

[2] *Life in a N.E. Town,* p. 46.

[3] *Memoirs,* VII, 307.

[4] *Life in a N.E. Town,* p. 94. The reference is to Shays's Rebellion in Massachusetts.

of a kind quite different from Jefferson's, to make it more like the British system. John Adams, home from his fruitless mission in London, accepted the Vice-Presidency of the new Government. Jefferson, boyhood mentor of John Quincy Adams, returned from France to serve as Secretary of State. "I am glad to find I was mistaken," acknowledged young Adams after reading the concluding letter of John Adams's *Defence of the American Constitutions,* which spoke very favorably of the new system.[5] Thenceforth John Quincy regarded opposition to the national system as "petty," "selfish," "cavilling," "hostile." He became a nationalist.

As soon as the Government had been set up in New York City, he visited his father and mother there. He met the renowned Washington,[6] who remarked to Abigail Adams that he was told that her son was more attentive to books than to the ladies.[7] Somebody must have misinformed the General on this point.

When the President came to Massachusetts on his northern tour, it was John Quincy Adams who drafted the welcoming address of the citizens of Newburyport.[8] He was on hand at all functions which the General attended in that community. Washington remembered the young law student, son of the Vice President, and never lost sight of him.

2

The French Revolution and the establishment of a limited constitutional monarchy — Lafayette's idea for France's government — awakened lively sympathy in the United States. When the French people followed the example of their trans-Atlantic ally and proclaimed a republic, expressions of revolutionary fervor multiplied on this side of the ocean. The glow of freedom and democracy from flaming France everywhere warmed the public heart. Citizens up and down the land formed democratic societies like the Liberty Boys of 1776. They held civic feasts, civic meetings, civic ceremonies; they indulged in civic salutations as Citizen and even Citizeness. They felt a natural friendship for the new Jacobin clubs of Revolutionary France and for the cause of the French Republic and for the Rights of Man.

When the armies of the European monarchs invaded France to stamp out republicanism, the sympathies of the American people were all on the side of their old ally. The townspeople rang their church bells as if they had been celebrating a victory of their own Revolution, as French citizen armies repelled the invading autocrats at Valmy and Jemappes. But the execution of Louis XVI, personal symbol of the Franco-Ameri-

[5] Ibid., p. 106.

[6] Presumably the first meeting. We have no evidence to show whether Abigail Adams had taken her small son over to Cambridge with her in 1776 when she went there to meet the General.

[7] Abigail A. Smith to JQA, Richmond Hill, December 27, 1789. Adams MSS.

[8] *Writings,* I, 43.

can alliance, and the ensuing Reign of Terror, shocked all conservatives and dampened the earlier enthusiasm of many other patriots. The tide of Franco-American affinity receded before the bloody spectacle of Revolutionary atrocities. It took philosophers like Thomas Jefferson, friend of John Quincy Adams's boyhood in France, to reconcile liberty with bloodshed and terror. "My own affections have been deeply wounded," he wrote impulsively, "by some of the martyrs to this cause, but rather than it should have failed I would have seen half the earth desolated. Were there but an Adam and Eve left in every country, and left free, it would be better than it now is."

France's declaration of war on England and the Netherlands took America by surprise. As long as hostilities had been limited to land operations on the Continent of Europe, the United States had little concern with them. A maritime war, a contest of sea power between France and England, was another matter. Commerce and shipping were vital to the new Republic of the Western World. For the revenue that supported the credit of the National Government, which had assumed payment of state debts, came almost wholly from tariff duties on goods imported from England, mostly in English ships.

There was also a direct diplomatic liability to confront. In the French alliance of 1778 the United States had guaranteed "forever against all other powers" His Most Christian Majesty's American possessions,[9] just as His Most Christian Majesty reciprocally had guaranteed the independence of the United States and its territorial integrity. To go to war on the side of France against England in 1793 would have destroyed American commerce, wiped out American revenue, "cut up credit by the roots," as Alexander Hamilton put it. It would have shaken if not demolished the new national structure raised on the Constitution of 1787. It might have extinguished independence itself. All of Washington's advisers, including Jefferson, counseled neutrality.

Fortunately Revolutionary France at first preferred American neutrality to American belligerency. She did not invoke the alliance. So the United States did not violate the French treaty by keeping out of the European war. To France her American ally could be more valuable as a neutral than as a fighting partner if its territory could be turned into a base of belligerent operations and if at the same time it could remain a neutral provider of foodstuffs and naval stores paid for out of the funded Revolutionary War debt still owed to France. French diplomatists hoped that the principles[10] of the Freedom of the Seas, pledged in the Franco-American Treaty of Commerce and Amity of 1778, but never accepted by England in any treaty with the United States, would protect these cargoes en route to France under American

[9] Actually these consisted at this time of the French islands in the West Indies plus the two small islands of St. Pierre and Miquelon in the Gulf of St. Lawrence.

[10] See below, p. 43.

colors. If such maxims could prevail against the British Navy, French purchases of American foodstuffs and naval stores might sail right across the Atlantic under a neutral flag into French arsenals. France could use the supplies to feed her citizen armies and to build up a navy big enough to defeat the British Navy and win the war. These advantages of American neutrality would outweigh any feeble military power the United States might muster to guarantee France's possessions in the West Indies.

To convert the United States into a neutral base of belligerent operations the French Republic sent Citizen Genet to Philadelphia as its new Minister Plenipotentiary. The purpose of his mission was to organize purchases and shipments of foodstuffs and naval stores under the American flag; to set on foot filibustering expeditions against Spanish Louisiana and British Canada; to fit out French privateers manned with American citizens and officers; to set up consular prize courts on American soil for the condemnation and sale of prizes in order to provide more funds for more privateers for more prizes. All of these purposes, except purchase and shipment of foodstuffs and naval stores, were in violation of neutrality in international law.

President Washington decided after much debate in the Cabinet to receive the Citizen Genet as Minister of the French Republic, thus recognizing the new Revolutionary Government and the old treaty obligations, but he refused to countenance Genet's violations of neutrality. There was nothing in the Franco-American treaty to justify them.[11] When Genet persisted, and appealed to the American people over the heads of their Government, Washington demanded his recall. The French Government rebuked its envoy and ordered him home. He did not go home for fear a new regime would chop off his head. Instead he settled down in New York State, married the daughter of Governor Clinton, died in the United States in 1834, and won himself in the twentieth century a spacious place in the *Dictionary of American Biography*.[12] His illegal projects of 1794 soon collapsed; but in the six months that intervened before his recall reached Philadelphia in January 1794, he carried on as impudently as ever in his efforts, with the aid of new-blown popular democratic societies, to overturn Washington's Administration.[13] At first, public opinion wavered before the force of his appeals, but as discussion clarified the diplomatic and technical issues in the

[11] Under the Franco-American Treaty of Commerce and Amity neither party, neutral, could allow an enemy of the other party, belligerent, to fit out privateers within its neutral ports, or to send prizes into its ports. France insisted that because the treaty prohibited her enemies to fit out privateers or send in prizes it therefore allowed France to do both. This contention did not have a legal leg to stand on.

[12] Genet's name is here spelled, without accent, as in D.A.B.

[13] Meade Minnigerode's *Jefferson, Friend of France* (New York, 1928) is really a history of Edmond Genet's diplomatic activities as revealed by his private papers and public correspondence. Eugene Perry Link has written an even more sympathetic account of the *Democratic-Republican Societies, 1790–1800* (New York, 1942).

columns of the press, the people came to realize more and more that George Washington was right, as usual. It became clear to them that the United States had nothing to do with the war in Europe and should steer clear of it. They supported their Government in its first great trial. American neutrality was a significant triumph for President Washington.

3

John Quincy Adams, the young Boston lawyer, was one of the writers who did most to marshal opinion behind the President in this first crisis of foreign affairs. Already we have seen him developing as an opponent of pure democracy, a respondent to Tom Paine, a defender in theory of the British Constitution. As party lines revealed themselves more clearly under the impact of foreign relations, he became in fact a Federalist, opposed to Republicanism or Jeffersonian democracy. In the heyday of enthusiasm for the French Revolution he refused to join any of the new democratic societies or to attend one of their civic feasts — "anarchical dinner" — in Boston.[14]

Looking back across the Atlantic in the light of the French Revolution, John Quincy Adams came to the conclusion that self-government had got out of self-control in France and that the Jacobin societies would be the instrument of its destruction. He was convinced that the French Revolutionary leaders had gone wrong in seeking to overthrow other governments in a war of propaganda, particularly in declaring war on England, thus lining up all Europe against France. He felt that it would be a moral and political mistake of the first magnitude for the United States to desert neutrality and take the side of Jacobinism against the world. Impelled by these thoughts, he expressed himself again in public print, this time under the pseudonym of "Marcellus." Not to impeach his patriotic motives, we may suspect that his eyes were open to political possibilities for himself in a public discussion of American policy toward the European war.

President Washington's proclamation of neutrality was not yet known in Boston when "Marcellus," in his first letter to the *Columbian Centinel*, warned his countrymen against privateering under a belligerent flag. He condemned it on moral as well as on legal[15] grounds, and declared that if American citizens engaged in it they would be liable to punishment

[14] *Writings*, I, 134.

[15] He pointed out that the Constitution had made treaties "the supreme law of the land." Treaties with France (1778), Holland (1782), and Prussia (1785) specifically required the neutral United States to prevent its citizens from taking out letters of marque or arming privateers with commissions under either of the powers against either of the others. "There can be no doubt but that a similar act of hostility against any subject of the King of Great Britain, would be a direct violation of the 7th article of the treaty of peace." (This was the article that proclaimed a "firm and perpetual peace." It also required British forces to evacuate American soil with "all convenient speed.")

as pirates. He held up before them, as an example of enlightened neutral policy, the articles of the Prussian-American treaty that his father, John Adams, had signed along with Franklin and Jefferson in 1785. That treaty had abolished privateering altogether, at least in case of a war between the two parties. The letters of "Marcellus" were John Quincy Adams's first expression of aversion and opposition to the institution of privateering, so popular in his own State of Massachusetts.

In two sequent contributions, written after reading Washington's proclamation, "Marcellus" extolled "impartial and unequivocal neutrality" for reasons of morality, interest, and policy. One passage may be marked now for later quotation when examining the inspiration of Washington's Farewell Address and the authorship of the Monroe Doctrine: "As the citizens of a nation at a vast distance from the continent of Europe; of a nation whose happiness consists in a real independence, *disconnected from all European interests and European politics,*[16] it is our duty to remain, the peaceable and silent, though sorrowful spectators of the sanguinary scene."

No British proclivities marked John Quincy Adams's neutrality as they did that of Alexander Hamilton. Adams was a peaceful, silent, and sorrowful spectator, partial neither to France nor to England. But he argued, as Hamilton had contended against Jefferson in Washington's Cabinet, that the old alliance with His Most Christian Majesty need not hold with the executioners of Louis XVI, even if the treaties were construed, as Jefferson construed them in the Cabinet, to bind nation to nation in international law. No treaty stipulation, young Adams declared, could oblige one nation to adopt or support the folly or injustice of another. There was, for example, Revolutionary France's tyrannical administration of her West Indian island colonies. It had led them to revolt and to seek and secure the protection of Great Britain as trustee for His Most Christian Majesty. "Surely," said "Marcellus," "there would be something singularly absurd and iniquitous, to see the United States support the French in a plan of oppressive administration over their colonies, as a reward for rescuing them from the oppression of Great Britain."

John Quincy Adams's friends easily discovered the identity of "Marcellus." The newspaper articles quickly brought him a small but pleasing distinction. The "inhabitants of Boston" requested him to deliver the Fourth-of-July address in 1793. His patriotic oration steered carefully between the Scylla and Charybdis of public opinion without offending either side in the agitation then raging over the policy of the United States toward the French Republic.[17] The lively plaudits of his fellow

[16] Italics inserted.

[17] *An Oration pronounced July 4th., 1793, at the Request of the Inhabitants of the Town of Boston; in Commemoration of the Anniversary of American Independence,* by John Quincy Adams (Boston: Benjamin Edes & Son; 1793). See Charles Adams to JQA, July 29 [1793], *Writings,* I, 146.

townsmen gave him cheering encouragement on the threshold of his public career.[18]

Genet still went about the land unrestrained, stirring up the popular democratic societies, trying to swing the United States over to France's brand of neutrality for America. Nobody yet knew whether his Government would really recall him. When Washington revoked the exequatur of the French vice consul in New England, Antoine Duplaine, for having caused an illegal French privateer to be released by force from the custody of an American court officer, Genet impudently denied that the Constitution gave the President power to revoke an exequatur.

Under the pseudonym of "Columbus," in letters published in the *Centinel,* John Quincy Adams showed that the President's power to revoke an exequatur or dismiss a foreign minister was a necessary part of his executive functions under the "National" Constitution, indispensable to the continuing existence of the "National" Union. He branded Genet's activities as incitement to insurrection. In words that were to echo three years later in George Washington's Farewell Address, "Columbus" warned his fellow citizens against the insidious wiles of foreign intrigue. "Of all the dangers which encompass the liberties of a republican State, the intrusion of a foreign influence into the administration of their affairs, is the most alarming, and requires the opposition of the severest caution. . . . The interference of foreigners upon any pretense whatever, in the dissensions of fellow-citizens, must be as inevitably fatal to the liberties of the State, as the admission of strangers to arbitrate upon the domestic differences of man and wife is destructive to the happiness of a private family. . . . If we inquire what is the cause which has been within a quarter of a century, fatal to the Liberties of *Sweden,* of *Geneva,* of *Holland,* and of *Poland,* the answer will be one and the same. It was the association of internal faction, and external power; it was the interference of other nations in their domestic divisions. . . ."[19]

The partisans of the French Revolution, and backers of Genet's diplomacy, produced an adversary to "Columbus" by the name of "Americanus," who responded in the columns of the *Independent Chronicle.* Good American doctrine, declared he, the very principles of the American Revolution – and he quoted John Quincy Adams's Fourth-of-July address of 1793 to define them – rested sovereignty in the people, not in their creature, the Government. All powers not expressly delegated in the Constitution by the sovereign people, stressed "Americanus," in language soon to become familiar in American history as one state or section of the Union after another felt its toes stepped on by the new Federal Government of the United States, were reserved to the people. The only organ of the Government, he said, that might be construed to

[18] JQA to CFA, July 14, 1828. Adams MSS.

[19] The letters of "Marcellus," and of "Columbus," are in the *Writings,* I, 135–76.

have a delegated power to revoke an exequatur was the Congress, which had the power to *declare war!* This argument fitted perfectly into Genet's revolutionary diplomacy and his threats.

John Quincy Adams under a new pseudonym, "Barneveldt," defended the strictures of John Quincy Adams, "Columbus." By the Constitution, he declared, the people had delegated a limited portion of their sovereignty to their National Government. Inherent in that sovereignty was the power of the executive branch of the Government, administered by the President, to receive and dismiss foreign ministers and consuls. Thus the younger Adams was one of the first American publicists to uphold the doctrine of implied powers for purposes necessary to *national* life and existence.[20] These early expositions of the Constitution lay at the basis of his whole political thought on American government and politics: national power was essential to the existence of the Union.

At most John Quincy Adams had hoped that the letters would operate upon the public mind, gratify his father, and give himself some reputation among his fellow townsmen.[21] Actually he made himself felt all over the nation. In Boston the "Jacobin anti-federal faction," to use John Quincy Adams's description, tried to stage a second civic festival, but had to give it up. In Philadelphia, President Washington was much pleased and took pains to find out the author. This was not too difficult, with the Vice President at hand.

A few months later a vacancy appeared in the diplomatic service. William Short, American diplomacy's first "career man," who had been Jefferson's private secretary in Paris, afterward Minister of the United States in the Netherlands, had been sent to Madrid to negotiate the Mississippi Question with Spain. His prolonged sojourn there required a new minister to represent the United States at The Hague. John Quincy Adams knew Holland. He also knew Europe and its courts. He had fluent command of French and Latin. He could read Dutch. Although he had got rusty in his speaking knowledge of Dutch, he could soon retrieve it. He was deeply versed in the literature of history and politics, as well as in polite letters. He was now a trained lawyer. International law was his specialty. He had shown a firm grasp of the essentials of American foreign policy as understood by the Administration. He had an ideal training for diplomacy. And — what was most important — he *thought* the way Washington did. On May 29, 1794 the President on his own initiative sent this short message to the Senate: "I nominate John Quincy Adams to be Minister Resident to the Netherlands." The Senate confirmed the nomination unanimously the following day.

[20] The letters of "Americanus" began to appear in the *Independent Chronicle* of Boston, December 16, 1793. "Barneveldt's" first response was in the same journal on December 26, 1793. The controversy continued between the two adversaries up to January 16, 1794.

[21] JQA to CFA, Washington, March 16, 1828. Adams MSS.

Quickly John Adams wrote his son the big news. "The nomination, which is the result of the President's own observations and reflections, is as politic, as it is unexpected. It will be a proof that sound principles in morals and government are cherished by the executive of the United States, and that study, science and literature are recommendations which will not be overlooked. It will, or at least it ought to have in England and Holland more effect than anything that has been done, except perhaps the appointment of Mr. Jay. It is a pledge given by the American Cabinet, that they are not enemies to a rational form of government, and that they are not hurried away by a wild enthusiasm for every unmeaning cry of Liberty, Republicanism and Equality." [22] It is easy to see that the Vice President was greatly pleased.

Here was a splendid start in public life, the beginning of that career of service "in the cabinet or the field" for which John and Abigail Adams long since had marked and groomed their first-born son. The Vice President unhesitatingly urged him to accept. "A few years spent in the present Grade," he wrote, "will recommend [you] to advancement to higher and larger spheres."

Like a Polonius, John Adams proceeded to advise his son on the duties and requirements of the trust. He must pursue researches into international law and diplomacy. He must observe the views and motions of the belligerent powers. He must attend to his dress and person — "no man alive is more attentive to these things than the President — neat at least and handsome." John Quincy must dress as handsomely as any of them, but economically! He must employ all the art and elegance of his pen in writing his dispatches. He must be very cautious in what he said in them, particularly about nations, sovereigns, and even courts and parties, notably those in Holland. "You must make yourself master of all our disputes with England, Spain, France, etc. You must study the lines and boundaries of the United States. You will have to watch the English Ambassador and all the Anglomani[ac]s. . . . It is a serious trust that is about to be committed to you. I hope you will reflect upon it with due attention, collect yourself, let no little weakness escape you, and devote yourself to the service of your Country, and may the blessing of Heaven attend you. So prays your affectionate father, John Adams." [23]

The Doge of Genoa was not more surprised to find himself suddenly at Versailles than John Quincy Adams to view himself as a Minister of the United States to one of the European courts where he had lived with his father ten years before.[24] It meant a serious change in his life. Though his law practice had not yet become affluent, he had already

[22] *Writings*, I, 190, n. 2.

[23] JA to JQA, Philadelphia, May 26, 29 (two letters of this date, the second partly in *Writings*, I, 190, n. 2), May 30 (two letters), 1794. Adams MSS.

[24] JQA to CFA, Washington, March 26, 1828. Adams MSS.

acquired the means of maintaining himself.[25] He could see prosperous days ahead in Boston, a competence, personal independence, then a political career. This had been his aim and his ambition. But here perhaps was a quicker way to distinguished public service, though not with the financial independence he was working for. He decided to give diplomacy at least a three years' trial, not too long to loosen the ties that bound him to his native land. It might lead soon to some appointment outside of insignificant Holland; if not, then he would resume his law practice in time to catch up with contemporaries who would have outdistanced him during his absence.[26]

The newly appointed Minister was able to take his brother Thomas Boylston Adams to Holland with him as his secretary. He was the "Tommy" who had stayed at home during the American Revolution.

As soon as possible he arranged his affairs and set forth for Philadelphia, to receive instructions from the Secretary of State, Edmund Randolph, Jefferson's successor since January 1, 1794; to consult the Department's pertinent papers; and to acquaint himself with all details of his new duty. Really there was not much to do on that score. The Resident in Holland had little more responsibility, so it seemed, than to maintain unimpaired friendly relations that had always existed with that Republic, and to conduct for the United States Government its longstanding financial business, then in extremely good order, with Dutch bankers; this last required some conferences with Alexander Hamilton, Secretary of the Treasury.

In the archives of the Department of State the young appointee saw the diplomatic correspondence of his father. He followed that interesting trail from Dutch documents into the files of French relations. These he read avidly, even furtively, fearful lest the disproportionate time he spent over those historical sources might arouse suspicions of the Secretary of State. The more he read, the more he admired the way in which his father had seen through the stratagems of the French Foreign Minister Vergennes during the American Revolution.

"So long as these books exist," he wrote to his father, the Vice President, after perusing the files, "they will be the highest eulogium that can be past upon your conduct in Europe; but whenever they shall be made public they will make breaches of a very serious nature in the artificial reputation of some other diplomatic characters. The contemptuous insolence of V[ergennes] towards you, and his base malignity as well as his fear of you, and his perfidy to this Country, will at some

[25] "From the month of July, 1790, when I commenced my career as a man, until the close of 1793, I was enabled to accomplish this purpose [living within his income] only by the assistance of small supplies from my father. I had then [1793] acquired the means of maintaining myself." *Memoirs*, II, 136.

[26] *Writings*, I, 192–8.

future period appear in the full face of day, as well as the miserable dupery, if it was not something worse, of 'Papa F[ranklin].'"[27]

John Quincy Adams's understanding of the self-interested character of French intervention in the War of American Independence was of great assistance to him in appraising French interventions in Europe in 1794 and thereafter, notably in the Netherlands. The new Minister left for Europe fortified not only by the instructions of the Secretary of State, who knew little of the brief history of American diplomacy, and of the Secretary of the Treasury, who knew like a wizard everything about American finances and foreign loans, but also by a belief in the unequaled diplomatic achievements of his father, his exemplar, who, at least in the son's estimation, knew more about American diplomacy and foreign policy than any other living man. John Quincy Adams's personal letters to John Adams, the Vice President and then President of the United States, from The Hague, London, and Berlin, were to be more significant than his formal dispatches to his nominal superiors, the successive Secretaries of State.

By the time Adams and his brother sailed from Boston, September 15, 1794, for England en route to his post at The Hague, Chief Justice John Jay already had arrived in London and was well advanced in his famous negotiations for the preservation of peace with England. Because John Quincy Adams was to participate in diplomatic discussions on Jay's famous treaty, both before and after its ratification, and because Jay's memorable mission was such a vital element in American diplomacy, it is well to review at this point the acute crisis in Anglo-American relations that had sent the Chief Justice to the Court of St. James's as Minister Plenipotentiary and Envoy Extraordinary of the United States. It involved the long-standing territorial disputes and other controversies arising out of the Treaty of Peace of 1783, and particularly that continuing problem of American diplomacy with which Adams would have to deal, without crowning success, throughout his whole official life: the Freedom of the Seas.

[27] JQA (Philadelphia) to JA (in Braintree), July 16, 1794. Adams MSS.

The whole American record has long since been public property, ever since Jared Sparks's full but inaccurate edition of *The Diplomatic Correspondence of the American Revolution* (1829–30). The French Government's publication of Henri Doniol's monumental work *La Participation de la France à l'établissement des États-Unis* (1886–92) does not present the documents with complete fullness, nor did that scholar in every instance make his selections objectively. Historians for over a generation now have had before them the entire multi-archival spread for the diplomacy of the American Revolution, including the Spanish and Dutch archives as well as those of England and the United States. As a result John Adams's reputation has fared increasingly well at the expense of Vergennes, although not of Benjamin Franklin.

4

Freedom of the Seas meant, of course, freedom for neutral navigation and commerce *in time of war.* The high seas always have been legally free in time of peace, certainly ever since the independence of the United States. In the eighteenth century, in fact until the Declaration of Paris of 1856, there was no general agreement among the maritime nations of the world on principles defining this freedom. States observed it according to their interests as large or small naval powers. Small-navy nations tried to write their assertions of neutral rights into formal treaties. Big-navy nations endeavored to avoid any recognition of such assertions. The small-navy nations were more numerous than the big-navy nations; hence the tendency was for more and more treaties to lay down principles of neutral rights to govern the contracting parties when one was belligerent, the other neutral. Between 1650 and 1780 thirty-six European treaties recognized free ships free goods, basic principle of the Freedom of the Seas, while only fifteen acknowledged the opposite principle derived from the ancient code of the *Consolato del Mare.* If one counts only the number of nations that pledged themselves in bilateral treaties to the Freedom of the Seas and does not take into consideration the measure of their sea power, it would seem that the drift of the times was to evoke a broader definition of neutral rights. This tendency perhaps gave prestige to those principles, but certainly did not give them strength to prevail. To make them international law required universal agreement, including that of the great sea powers. Great Britain, consistently the strongest naval power of all, would accept such dicta only in special instances in return for particular equivalents; these concessions she always considered as exceptions to the prevailing law of nations, binding only between the parties to the novel bargain.

The United States from the beginning naturally followed the small-navy definitions of mooted neutral rights. Back in 1776 John Adams had sat in a committee of the Continental Congress, which included Benjamin Franklin, appointed to draw up a model plan of articles for treaties with foreign powers. John Adams, the real student of this committee, incorporated in its report the famous Plan of 1776, the small-navy definitions of neutral rights as he had extracted them from the treaties of Ryswick (1697) and Utrecht (1713). American diplomacy introduced them into all treaties of friendship and commerce with European powers before 1793; with France, 1778; the Netherlands, 1782; Sweden, 1783; Prussia, 1785. During the American Revolution the neutral nations of Europe also subscribed to the same dicta – and to an additional article defining blockade – in the Armed Neutrality of 1780; and all the belligerents except Great Britain accepted the principles for the conduct of that war.

After the war, in 1784, Congress advanced a supplementary plan which adopted the Armed Neutrality's definition of blockade and proposed certain innovations like the abolition of privateering and the immunity of all private property, belligerent as well as neutral, at sea. One treaty, that with Prussia of 1785, negotiated by John Adams, Thomas Jefferson, and Benjamin Franklin, actually did away with confiscation of contraband; it could be detained, but had to be paid for, said this ten-year treaty. The same agreement abolished privateering and the capture of enemy private property in case of war *between the signatories.* It was the most "advanced" treaty of the century – indeed, of any century so far as enlargement of neutral rights was concerned.

These, then, were the still-disputed dicta of the Freedom of the Seas, dating from the last war, as they stood at the time of the Anglo-American war crisis of 1794:

1. Free (neutral) ships make free goods (i.e., immune from capture), always excepting contraband of war.

2. Conversely, unfree (belligerent) ships make unfree goods. That is, neutral goods on an enemy ship are subject to capture as if they belonged to the enemy.

3. Neutral ships may carry freely noncontraband goods to belligerent ports and between port and port of a belligerent. This included traffic between home ports of a belligerent (*petit cabotage*), and between home and colonial ports of a belligerent (*grand cabotage*).

4. Contraband of war consists only of "warlike instruments," as listed in treaties, specifically excluding foodstuffs and naval stores, both of which were necessary to civilian life.

To these first four principles, which were articles in all American treaties of friendship and commerce with European powers in 1793, may be added the fifth principle, out of the Armed Neutrality of 1780 and the supplementary Plan of 1784, defining a legal blockade: [28]

5. A blockade shall apply only to a place or port where the attacking power has stationed its vessels sufficiently near and in such a way as to render access thereto clearly dangerous.

When the maritime war began in 1793, Great Britain announced to the United States her intention to capture enemy property wherever she could find it on the high seas, even on board neutral ships, and to include foodstuffs and naval stores in the category of contraband to be captured when destined for the enemy even though they were neutral property not yet delivered; but she promised to pay for the foodstuffs. She further proclaimed the Rule of the War of 1756: not to allow neutral ships to engage in belligerent colonial carrying trade when that trade had been denied to them in time of peace. This putative rule was itself an innovation (since 1756) by a power that denied the validity of in-

[28] A legal blockade entitled the blockading power to intercept all commerce with the blockaded port and to confiscate ships and cargoes of whatever description attempting to breach the blockade.

novations until they were universally accepted. Two of the erstwhile armed neutrals of 1780, Russia and Prussia, made treaties with Great Britain agreeing to British naval measures against France. So did Spain, who as a belligerent in the preceding war had followed, half-heartedly, the Armed Neutrality. Only the United States, Sweden, and Norway-Denmark remained champions of the system of neutral rights invoked against Great Britain during the War of American Independence. Even France, bound by treaty with the United States to respect the latter's neutral rights, herself resorted in 1793 to naval measures similar to those of England, actually before England employed them.

Armed secretly with new orders in council [29] for the capture of neutral ships, British cruisers reached the West Indian cruising waters and swept in over two hundred and fifty unsuspecting neutral American prizes innocently trading to French islands there. They also took, on the open Atlantic, American ships loaded with foodstuffs for French ports. Britain's contempt of American concepts of neutral rights did not violate any treaty with the United States as did French captures. But the French spoliations were not noticeable at first. They occurred mostly in distant European waters, because France was the weaker sea power in this war. Consequently grievances against France were slower to pile up and have diplomatic effect, although in the end they totaled as heavily as the British spoliations. They were even more heinous because, unlike the British captures, they were in violation of solemn treaty obligations to the neutral United States.

[29] These were the orders in council (i.e., British executive decrees) fixing British naval policy in 1793 and 1794:

The so-called "provision order" of June 8, 1793 instructed British naval commanders to bring in all neutral ships bound for French ports with cargoes of corn, flour, or meal, for purchase of their cargoes, with allowance for freight and detention. This was designed to starve out the French "armed nation."

The order of November 6, 1793 directed British naval commanders to bring in all ships (including neutrals) laden with goods the produce of any colony belonging to France or carrying provisions or other supplies for the use of such colonies. The purpose of this was to prevent neutrals from taking over the French colonial carrying trade (i.e., between the United States and five principal French West Indian ports), which had been open before the war to the United States. It thus went beyond the arbitrary Rule of the War of 1756, because France before the war had allowed American ships to trade directly with her West Indian free ports, though not admitting them to the colonial carrying trade between the West Indies and French home ports.

The order of January 8, 1794 modified the extreme November order so as to put it in conformance with the British Rule of the War of 1756 and the principle of capturing enemy goods from enemy ships; but it further ordered the capture of *all* ships laden in whole or in part with military or naval stores (without defining what constituted such) bound for French colonies, and *all* ships bound *for a blockaded French port* (leaving, tacitly, the definition of what constituted a blockade to the British Admiralty). This achieved the same effect of cutting off neutral trade with the French West Indies.

If the more sudden and spectacular British action did not violate a treaty, the same cannot be said of continued British possession of the military posts on American soil along the northern frontier; that was deliberately and with premeditation a long-standing violation of the Treaty of Peace of 1783. News of the Caribbean captures reached Philadelphia in March 1794 simultaneously with publication of a bellicose speech at Quebec by the Governor General of British North America, Lord Dorchester, to a visiting delegation of Indians from the Northwest Territory. That responsible British official told the savages that soon they and the King's warriors would be fighting side by side against the United States and that after the war they could draw a new boundary to suit themselves. Dorchester's hostile words, and occupation by British forces of a new post in American territory (near present Toledo, Ohio), together with the maritime grievances produced a serious war crisis between the United States and Great Britain.

Already there had been in Congress a movement, led by James Madison and enjoying the sympathy of Thomas Jefferson, Secretary of State, for discriminatory taxes on British ships and goods coming into the United States, as reprisal for Britain's refusal to make a treaty of commerce and for her exclusion of American ships from her colonial ports in the New World. Only the arrival of a British Minister to talk about a treaty had prevented discrimination in 1791. The Anglo-American war crisis of 1794 revived these demands for anti-British legislation and stimulated additional proposals for the sequestration of all private debts owed to British subjects, for suspension of all commercial intercourse with Great Britain, for military and naval armament, and for an embargo on all shipping in American harbors. The last measure was designed to injure the British West Indies, which since the outbreak of war had come to depend on American foodstuffs. Congress actually voted an embargo for one month, but the Administration headed off further hostile legislation by sending the Chief Justice, John Jay, to England as a last resort for peace.

Even after Jay's nomination, the proposed nonintercourse bill against Great Britain failed of passage only by the casting vote of Vice President John Adams against it in the Senate. So greatly did the Government rely for its life-giving revenue upon tariffs on British goods, so dependent on sound finances was the new national political structure, that Alexander Hamilton and his Federalist followers quite convinced Washington that the United States must go to great extremes to avoid war with England. Hamilton was ready to give up the Freedom of the Seas, if necessary in order to preserve peace, providing Great Britain would surrender the frontier posts occupied since the treaty of peace. Jefferson would not go that far. Disgusted at the increasing influence of Hamilton and "the party of the British interest" in national councils, he had resigned on December 31, 1793 and retired to Monticello. Hamilton's influence now became supreme in the Cabinet of President Washington.

Jay's Treaty, signed November 19, 1794, was really Hamilton's treaty. It was the price that the Federalists paid for peace with Great Britain at a vitally critical period of American foreign and domestic relations. On Great Britain's part it represented a desire for continued peace with her greatest single foreign customer at a time when the British Navy could not safely be diverted further from its tremendous tasks in European and West Indian waters. By that celebrated treaty the United States gave up the Freedom of the Seas for the duration of the European war. Great Britain in return pledged herself to evacuate the frontier posts by June 1, 1796, and the United States Government agreed to pay all private pre-war debts of American debtors to British creditors in sterling money after their total amount should be established by a mixed commission. Great Britain further agreed to submit to a mixed commission American claims for damages for maritime spoliations arising "under color" of British orders in council, without repudiating the orders themselves. The treaty engaged to submit boundary disputes in the northeast and northwest corners of the United States to the decision of mixed commissions. It also declared that the river Mississippi, no part of which any longer touched British territory anywhere, should be "entirely open to both parties" according to the Treaty of Peace of 1783. The United States further pledged itself not to allow Great Britain's enemies to fit out privateers in American ports or to send in prizes to those same havens; in fact, it agreed to indemnify the owners of prizes already captured by French privateers fitted out illegally in the United States. Finally, the two parties agreed, in case of any future national differences or war between themselves, not to confiscate private debts and to respect innocent enemy aliens and their private property.

Thus did George Washington in his time pluck the flower of national safety from the nettle of European danger. Technically Jay's Treaty was not a violation of the Franco-American Treaty of Amity and Commerce of 1778, any more than American neutrality itself had been a violation of the Franco-American Treaty of Alliance of the same date. This Anglo-American treaty of 1794 represented an articulation of American neutrality to such international law as was then universally accepted, rather than to the novel Plan of 1776, by which the United States had begun to build up a treaty structure that would mold international law to its own interest as a small-navy power. Naturally France, which had signed a treaty of the latter variety in 1778, bitterly resented Jay's Treaty. It led to grave consequences between the allies of the American Revolution. It was on the threshold of these events that John Quincy Adams entered upon his diplomatic career.

5

On the way to his first post at The Hague, Adams passed through London in October 1794 in order to deliver dispatches to Jay and to Thomas Pinckney, the regular Minister of the United States to Great Britain.

For a fortnight the two Adams brothers "whirled round in the fling of London." [30] "There is something so fascinating in the women I meet in this Country," the young Minister noted, "that it is not well for me. I am obliged immediately to leave it." [31] He left without seeing the woman who was to prove most fascinating to him of them all, Louisa Catherine Johnson, second daughter of the American Consul.[32]

The young Minister found Chief Justice John Jay close to the conclusion of his negotiations with Lord Grenville, British Secretary of State for Foreign Affairs during the entire first phase of the wars of the French Revolution. Adams was privileged to sit in with Jay and Pinckney in a detailed study of the proposed treaty and at Jay's request to pass judgment on one of the most important diplomatic instruments of American history. Now practically in its final form, the treaty draft was far from satisfactory to either Jay or Pinckney, but in their opinion it was preferable to war. Adams thought it was below the standard that would be advantageous to the United States, but he agreed with his older colleagues that it was better than war. On the score of spoliations, reparation after adjudication was all that could be expected. It was not much good as a treaty of commerce, he felt, but nothing better could be had as long as England persisted in her navigation laws. There was at least something in the concession that admitted American ships of less than seventy tons [33] burden into the ports of the British West

[30] JQA to Charles Adams, Amsterdam, November 24, 1794. Adams MSS.

[31] Diary, October 27, 1794. Adams MSS.

[32] Thomas Boylston Adams's Diary shows that he took dinner with Joshua Johnson and family on October 23, 1794, but JQA did not; he dined with an old college chum, Thomas Crafts, and other friends the same evening (JQA's Diary). There is no reference to the Johnson family in JQA's Diary during the time of this visit to England. The point is of some importance, in connection with the diplomatic assignment related in Chapter IV hereafter, in that it establishes that JQA's reason for deciding to go to England in 1795 had nothing to do with his private life.

[33] The limitation on tonnage was to discourage such American ships from engaging in the trans-Atlantic carrying trade. For the same purpose the treaty in its original form obliged the United States not to allow the exportation of five West Indian commodities: molasses, sugar, coffee, cocoa, and cotton. In advising and consenting to ratification of the treaty, the United States Senate did so upon condition of deletion of this, the twelfth article. Thanks to proclamations of the local island governors opening the British West Indies to the American flag for the emergency of the war, the United States enjoyed the trade anyway, and it would have been inexpedient to burden it with restrictions, which, incidentally, would have stifled the future lucrative

Indies. Conceivably that might serve as indemnification for deprivation of the fur trade during the period of British occupation of the Western posts, now belatedly to be given up. As to the satisfaction that the United States agreed to make on its part for noncompliance with the Treaty of 1783, he thought that this was no more than in justice was due: [34] so spoke the author of the Harvard commencement oration on the importance and necessity of public faith to the well-being of a community. He made no specific comment on his Government's concessions on the Freedom of the Seas, particularly in admitting that enemy property not contraband of war was subject to capture from neutral ships. Presumably this shortcoming, a negation of the American principle of free ships free goods, was what the youthful diplomat had in mind when he pronounced Jay's Treaty to be below a standard of advantage for the United States.

Knowledge of the treaty's terms, still secret pending ratification, was invaluable to Adams, as a new definition of American neutral policy, when he arrived in the Netherlands, reluctant battleground of French and British power in the midst of European turmoil and strife.

It was the wars of the French Revolution and the distresses of Great Britain in the Old World that had induced that nation to make Jay's Treaty with the United States. It was the same European conflagration, plus Jay's Treaty, that next impelled Spain to capitulate to American terms in Pinckney's Treaty of 1795 – that is, to acknowledge the boundaries of the United States as fixed in the Anglo-American Treaty of Peace and Independence of 1783, and the right of American citizens as well as Spanish subjects to navigate the Mississippi River from its source to the sea, with a right of deposit of their goods at Spanish New Orleans or vicinity for transshipment to ocean-going ships. A most important article of Pinckney's Treaty was Spain's guaranty, and that of the United States reciprocally, to force the Indians dwelling on her side of the Florida boundary to keep the peace, and not to attack citizens of the United States. The two signatories further pledged themselves, in their future treatment of each other, to the principles of the Freedom of the Seas, which the United States had just forgone in Jay's Treaty. This embarrassing inconsistency soon became evident as the wars of the French Revolution progressed.

One of John Quincy Adams's first diplomatic labors was to help reorient American neutrality to Jay's Treaty rather than Pinckney's. Long

---

cotton exports of the United States, although the later importance of that export could not have been foreseen in 1795.

JQA obviously had neglected to consult his Diary when he wrote to Sylvanus Bourne, October 10, 1795 (*Writings,* I, 418, n. 1), that he had not known, before the treaty was made public, of the obnoxious clause suspended by the Senate – i.e., the West Indian commerce article.

[34] *Memoirs,* I, 48–9. JQA to JA, London, October 23, 1794. *Writings,* I, 201–9.

afterward one of his tasks as Secretary of State would be to try to put the Freedom of the Seas back where it stood in the treaty structure of the United States before Jay's Treaty, and where it stood in Pinckney's Treaty — namely, resting firmly on the principles of the Plan of 1776. Another duty would be to take advantage of the territorial articles of Pinckney's Treaty in the negotiation of his famous Transcontinental Treaty with Spain of 1819.

In a continental sense Jay's Treaty and Pinckney's Treaty [35] represented America's advantage from Europe's distress in a vitally critical period of the young Republic's history. They cleared the West of foreign troops. They were first steps, after the Treaty of Independence itself, for that march of Manifest Destiny which, following Pinckney's Treaty and Jefferson's Louisiana Purchase, John Quincy Adams later as Secretary of State was to lead across the mountains to the Pacific Coast.

It was to be still a long while before Adams would try on these transcontinental boots, after two long and separate periods of diplomatic experience in the Old World. The first of these was from 1794 to 1801, during the wars of the French Revolution, at The Hague and in Berlin, as American watchman of the European conflagration. We must now turn to these chapters of his diplomatic apprenticeship.

[35] I have narrated the diplomatic history of these two treaties in *Jay's Treaty, a Study in Commerce and Diplomacy* (New York, 1923), and *Pinckney's Treaty, a Study of America's Advantage from Europe's Distress* (Baltimore, 1926, 1941).

CHAPTER III
At the Hague Listening-Post (1794–1795)

Above all I wish that we may never have any occasion for any political connections with Europe.

JOHN QUINCY ADAMS TO JOHN ADAMS,
THE HAGUE, MAY 22, 1795

OF the five diplomatic appointments of the United States abroad,[1] that to the Netherlands was one of the least significant politically. The Secretary of State, Edmund Randolph, made it clear to John Quincy Adams that his principal duty would be to tend the Treasury loans borrowed during the Revolution by John Adams from Dutch bankers and now in a process of scheduled pay-off under Alexander Hamilton's funding arrangements. Randolph warned the fledgling publicist that the Department could dispense with communications on the general history of the Netherlands, but he directed him to report promptly and carefully any sudden change of policy, any symptom of increasing liberty, any dissatisfaction of the Dutch Government with any of the combined powers of Europe, or any inclination on the part of the United Provinces to make peace with the French Republic. Vice President John Adams made somewhat more of his son's post than that. It was a station in which he could watch and penetrate the whirling secrets of European diplomacy. "You will see Europe," he wrote, "at the most interesting period of its history."[2] It was indeed a wonderful opportunity to observe at close range the wars of the French Revolution.

Suddenly The Hague became a place of extraordinary significance, particularly for an American diplomat. It was a listening-post in the resounding amphitheater of European power politics. It was a perfect testing-ground for any ally of the new French Republic with its revolu-

[1] The five regular diplomatic representations of the United States in 1794 were: in Great Britain, Minister Plenipotentiary, Thomas Pinckney, salary $9,000; in France, Minister Plenipotentiary, James Monroe, salary $9,000; in Spain, Minister Resident, William Short, salary $4,500; in Portugal, Minister Resident, David Humphreys, salary $4,500; in the Netherlands, Minister Resident, John Quincy Adams, salary $4,500.

[2] JA to JQA, Quincy, August 24, 1794, and Philadelphia, December 2, 1794. Adams MSS.

tionary program and propaganda and interventions to "liberate" peoples from their governments. John Quincy Adams's reports helped to correct the partisan impressions and advice of James Monroe from Paris and to strengthen the resolution of the first President, in a very critical period of American foreign relations, not to allow the United States to become, like the Netherlands, a tool of French diplomacy for the purposes of purely European polity, now that the French Revolution had swept beyond the bounds of its first great goals of human liberty.

1

The wars of the French Revolution, like the titanic conflicts of our times, widened the gulf between human aspirations and historical realities. In the full flush of their high ideals the men of 1789 resolved on nothing less than the abolition of war. In words that echo down through two centuries to the Kellogg-Briand Pact of 1928 the French National Assembly wrote into the Constitution of 1791 a noble pledge: "The French nation renounces all wars of conquest, and will never use its forces against the liberty of another people." This exalted self-denial, like the loftier pact of the twentieth century, was utterly at variance with current international practice. It was also opposed to the spirit and genius of the French people and to the whole dialectic of French history.[3] Electrified by a new and universal force that the convulsive domestic politics of the Revolution threw into motion, the nation pushed forward instinctively to secure those "natural boundaries" for which Richelieu, Mazarin, and Louis XIV had fought without complete success through two previous centuries of bloody European strife: the Rhine, the Alps, the Pyrenees. A revolution for the rights of man thus threw Europe into a quarter-century of international war.

When John Quincy Adams arrived at The Hague in December 1794, the unfortunate Netherlands, caught in the conflict between France and Great Britain, was the sinking prey of foreign powers. In those portions of the state still defended by unpopular British troops the pro-French "Patriots" were secretly shaping their ranks as fifth-columnists (to use a modern phrase) in support of the French invasion. No real Dutch patriots rose to defend the sovereignty and independence of the United Provinces. Seeking their own selfish desires first, the rival political factions and their leaders perfectly served the purposes of foreign intrigue, hegemony, and, ultimately, annexation and complete loss of independence. As French armies burst beyond the ancient boundaries of their own country, neighboring peoples rose in revolt against their potentates, lay or ecclesiastical. In Paris the National Convention studied the agreeable problem of whether to annex them outright or recognize

[3] Albert Sorel: *L'Europe et la Révolution française* (first edition, Paris, 1885–1904). See particularly Vol. II. I have used one of many later imprints.

their separate identities as independent satellite republics, and how to collect from them the costs of war. The French Revolution was rapidly changing from a force of liberty to a power of conquest.

From his legation in The Hague the American Minister accurately described in dispatches to the Secretary of State and in still more revealing confidential letters to his father, the Vice President, how the French forces expelled the British troops and the Stadtholder's Government and occupied the whole Netherlands. He told how, in the wake of the invading revolution and army, democratic societies on Jacobin models sprang up like tulips all over the Low Countries. Scarcely a village in the seven provinces but now had its political club and sent delegates to a central assembly.[4] Small groups of revolutionaries, working behind the scenes, were using such organizations as instruments of revolution to supplant the old regime with the new Batavian Republic, set up on French models. These cells were the "unseen spring," Adams reported to the Secretary of State, which gave all visible motion to the Revolution without the people knowing how it came about.[5] They resembled the democratic societies that were flourishing in America under the impulse of the French Revolution. Today we would call them political-action committees. In the Netherlands in 1794 they had French armies behind them.

Quickly the revolutionized Batavian Republic accepted a peace and alliance with the French Republic and changed sides in the war. From her new ally France extracted an indemnity of 100,000,000 florins and territorial rectifications, including the cession of Dutch Flanders; provided a potential naval base for France at Flushing; obliged the Dutch to contribute twelve ships of the line and eighteen frigates for the next invasion campaign against England; and required them to support a French army of occupation of 25,000 men. In secret articles France engaged to restore to the Batavian Republic, in the general peace, all Dutch colonies that the British might capture.[6]

The American Minister Resident soon perceived that the correct conduct of the armies of invasion was no assurance of benevolence. "Correctness" masked implacable exploitation. The French were there as conquerors, and the substance of independence was not so scrupulously preserved as its forms.[7] Nominal independence and republican fraternity did not prevent the usual consequences of conquest: billeting of troops, requisition of clothing, fuel, and food, the continued support of an army of foreigners, the forced circulation of depreciated assignats.

[4] JQA to Secretary of State, Edmund Randolph, Nos. 47, 48, July 22 and 25, 1795. DS, *Despatches, Netherlands,* I, 1794–6.

[5] JQA to the Secretary of State, No. 25, The Hague, February 15, 1795. *Writings,* I, 285–91.

[6] Raymond Guyot: *Le Directoire et la paix de l'Europe, 1795–1799* (Paris, 1912), p. 10.

[7] No. 30 of March 17, 1795 from The Hague. DS, *Despatches, Netherlands,* I.

Toward the end of his service at The Hague in 1797 Adams reported the net result for unhappy Dutchmen of France's revolutionizing of their country. Two years of "liberation" had cost them nearly twenty per cent upon the whole capital of every individual in forced loans, the suspension of almost all their commerce, the loss of their colonies, and the general depreciation by one half of almost all their other property. Before them lay the melancholy prospect of being the victim of both contending belligerents in the final peace.[8]

2

There were a few diplomatic problems at The Hague on which young Adams could cut his eye teeth on this his first responsible diplomatic mission: (1) the question of recognition of the new Batavian Republic by the United States; (2) minor disputes arising out of application of the articles of the Dutch-American Treaty of Amity and Commerce negotiated in 1782 by Adams's father according to the Plan of 1776; (3) the dislocations of international payments and transportation for the service of the American debt to Dutch and Belgian bankers. These were the labors of his diplomatic apprenticeship.

Revolutionary transition from the old Government of the United Provinces of the Netherlands to the new Batavian Republic presented a nice diplomatic question for the American Minister. Should he recognize the new Dutch Government and do business with it, without further instructions from his own Government?

As the French military authorities occupied the capital the diplomatic corps fled the country, except for Adams and the few neutral representatives.[9] Adams's perfect knowledge of the French language and easy familiarity with the French theater were a great help to him in dealing with Generals Pichegru and Moreau and securing respect for the persons and property of neutral American citizens.[10] For a few months the Batavian Republic retained the old designation of States General for the new legislative body and preserved the title of Their High Mightinesses. This was in order that foreign representatives, should they so desire, could continue uninterruptedly their communications with the old offices to which they were originally accredited.[11] The new officials who took over those functions were quite satisfied with Adams's original powers and credentials, and he continued to deal with them. Thus the question of recognition was avoided for the time being.

[8] JQA to the Secretary of State, No. 94, February 17, 1797. DS, *Despatches, Netherlands,* II.

[9] Denmark, Sweden, the United States. The Minister of belligerent Portugal, the Chevalier d'Arujo, also remained, undisturbed.

[10] "JQA Loquitur." Adams MSS.

[11] JQA to Secretary of State, No. 41, The Hague, June 6, 1795. DS, *Despatches, Netherlands,* I, 1794–6.

In this decision Adams acted contrary to the personal advice of Chief Justice Jay, who was already on the way of becoming an American elder statesman.[12] It proved that the younger diplomat correctly anticipated the policy of his Government as set forth by instructions from Secretary of State Edmund Randolph.[13] When finally Their High Mightinesses gave way to a new republican constitution and officials, the United States still continued in formal diplomatic relations.[14] Thus the old Treaty of 1782 continued to govern relations between the two republics.

Such questions as came up under the Dutch-American treaty of 1782 were not very grave. During the war between the United Provinces and France from 1793 to 1795, when Holland was the ally of Great Britain and its navy roamed the seas, a privateer with a Dutch commission out of St. Martin's Island in the West Indies had captured an American merchant ship, the *Wilmington Packet,* on a voyage between Bordeaux and St. Thomas in the West Indies. Condemnation of the ship at St. Martin's on the ground that it carried enemy property was outright violation of the Dutch-American Treaty of 1782, which had stipulated free ships free goods. Under his original instructions John Quincy Adams protested [15] the case and kept it alive during his presence at The Hague, with little satisfaction. In the confusion of the time, occasioned by changing sides in the war and the succession of a new Government, the Dutch executive authorities were able to put off the issue. Adams's successor, William Vans Murray, finally closed the case in 1799 by accepting a compromise payment of 20,000 florins for the claimants.[16]

[12] When Adams passed through London in October 1794, John Jay had vouchsafed some advice on just this point. His opinion was that the Minister's functions would cease in case of a revolution in the Dutch Government, though he might stay on at his post and await instructions. *Memoirs,* I, 56.

[13] *Writings,* I, 379, n. 1.

[14] The transition occurred during JQA's absence in London. Secretary of State to TBA, July 23, 1796. DS, *Instructions, U.S. Ministers,* II.

[15] Adams's instructions directed him not to forgo his right to correspond in his own language with the Ministry of the Government near which he resided. Accordingly in December 1794 he addressed his first memorial, on the *Wilmington Packet* case, to Their High Mightinesses in English. The President of the Estates General received the document, but the Secretary of the Committee on Foreign Affairs returned it to Adams, explaining that established custom required any document submitted to that assembly to be in Dutch, Latin, or French. After some friendly expostulation Adams provided a French copy, pending further instructions from his Government. Randolph approved this deviation from instructions and authorized him henceforth to make representations in the accustomed form. JQA to the Secretary of State, No. 12, The Hague, December 13, 1794. *Despatches, Netherlands,* I. Randolph to JQA, February 25, 1795. *Writings,* I, 218. The matter is worth mentioning only because it illustrates Adams's caution and discretion in this the first item of business that he performed as Minister.

[16] Miller: *Treaties,* V, 1075–1103, has a complete documentary history of the case.

The last occasion Adams had to discuss the *Wilmington Packet* episode presented him with the opportunity for his first little triumph in diplomatic disputation. In a belated reply (October 1796) to his original memorial the Batavian Government, after justifying condemnation on the ground that the ship really carried enemy property (quite protected, by the way, under the Treaty of 1782), turned around and complained, with perfect inconsistency, that the United States since Jay's Treaty was tolerating British captures of enemy property from American ships, contrary to the principle of the Dutch-American treaty (which the Netherlands Government itself had violated in the case at issue).

Adams patiently explained that the United States, determined to stay neutral as long as it honorably could do so, had not felt impelled to go to war in an impossible attempt to compel Great Britain to enforce free ships free goods. No treaty obligated Britain to observe that novel principle toward the United States, as France was obliged to do. Consequently the American Government had made Jay's Treaty. What else could it have done?

"The United States," Adams explained, "are very sincerely desirous of establishing the principle, and I have no doubt will readily use all pacific means to promote it. . . . They could contribute little towards putting it into execution. They might in a war obtain possession of Canada, but it would afford no gain at all to them, and a very trifling loss to Great Britain. Since the delivery of the posts, the British government probably set no great value themselves upon these possessions. . . . But at sea what assistance could we give you without a navy?"

"Why, that is true," acknowledged the Secretary, Van Leyden, "but I am surprised that the United States do not turn their attention to their marine; they have certainly the means of a naval power, and," he added, "they must feel the necessity of having one for the protection of their commerce."

"The object is not forgotten," replied Adams adroitly, "but the obligations contracted in the war which secured the independence of the United States are in their eyes the first and most imperious. In the course of that they necessarily contracted a very heavy debt, the punctual payments of which absorb all the revenues which can be raised upon the convenience of the people."

Here spoke the author of the Harvard commencement address on the good faith of national credit.

"But," argued Van Leyden, "they have paid part of the capital of that debt, so that the burthen is reduced."

"Part of the capital is paid," replied Adams, "but larger sums of it become payable every year, so that the *present burthen* continues to increase, although every payment serves to diminish the whole mass of the weight. For instance, a very large proportion of this debt is due in this country, and being paid with constant punctuality, your citizens receive at this day several millions annually paid by the government of the United States . . . you are sensible that they [the United States] cannot think of diverting the sums destined for the punctual performance of these engagements to any other object, however desirable. They think it better, therefore, even to postpone that of a marine."

The Secretary could hardly protest against the determination of the United States to pay its just debts, particularly those to Dutch bankers. "To be sure," he admitted readily enough, "the sums appropriated to the discharge of debts could not properly be employed to another use, but I do wish," he sighed, "that Great Britain might be compelled to consent to making a peace, which would restore to this Republic all the possessions she had taken from it."[17]

In these Dutch protests against Jay's Treaty, Adams recognized easily enough the French hand that held the Batavian diplomatic pen. To the Secretary of State he explained that one of the members of the Committee on Foreign Relations confidentially had told him to expect some such perfunctory protest – they couldn't help themselves, said this gentleman. Pickering imprudently published Adams's correspondence on the subject after the rupture between the United States and France over Jay's Treaty. The Secretary of State considered it an impressive revelation to the American people of the overweening officiousness of the French Republic toward its allies. Fortunately Adams had left The Hague by the time his Dutch informant experienced much lively embarrassment, and even some personal danger, as a result of the disclosure.[18]

Another question involving the Dutch-American treaty of 1782 concerned the liberty of each party to maintain consuls in the ports of the other, their functions to be regulated by particular agreement. Dutch colonial authorities had refused to give exequaturs to American consuls in the West Indies. Adams had orders to press the Hague Government on that point. It was an unheard-of thing, replied the Dutch Secretary, for the Netherlands to admit foreign consuls into colonial dominions. Adams pointed out that the treaty itself made no distinction between consuls in Dutch home territory and consuls in the Dutch West Indies. Then the Batavian Government fell back on the clause requiring particular agreement as to the functions of consuls. Until such an agreement had been made, argued the Secretary, the colonial officials had acted quite properly in refusing to recognize United States consuls. Meanwhile the war with England had broken out and the Dutch were no longer

[17] JQA to the Secretary of State, No. 86, The Hague, November 4, 1796. *Writings*, II, 38–9.

[18] For documents relating to the *Wilmington Packet*, and the perfunctory Batavian protest to Jay's Treaty, see JQA to the Secretary of State, No. 85, The Hague, November 1, 1796, with enclosures, in DS, *Despatches, Netherlands*, I; Timothy Pickering to JQA, November 25, 26, 1796, *Instructions U.S. Ministers*, III; and *ASPFR*, II, 13–14.

masters of their own colonies. Under these conditions both parties were content to let the dispute rest until more settled times. It was Adams's first introduction in practice to the problem of colonial monopoly.

Tending the Dutch loans was a long and vexatious chore amid the shifting circumstances of war-torn Europe.[19] Instructions [20] issued to John Quincy Adams by the Secretary of the Treasury to govern this duty, with accompanying documents, recited the powers and conditions under which the various loans had been contracted in Amsterdam and Antwerp since 1790, and directed him to consolidate the debt of the United States at home and abroad, including the old loans of the Revolution made by John Adams from Dutch bankers. Congress also authorized an additional loan of one million dollars on March 20, 1794 to meet "contingencies in the foreign service," a polite term for the blackmail that it expected would have to be paid in a treaty then being negotiated with the piratical Bey of Algiers.

When Adams reached Amsterdam, not five years had passed since the first of the new loans had been placed, and the credit of the United States stood high enough; but the situation of Holland had changed by 1794. The money market, then as now a most sensitive barometer of international politics, reflected alarms and disturbances in the Netherlands. The hopes of the Patriots and the fears of the followers of the Stadtholder's Government, as they ebbed and flowed, could be measured by the rise and fall in the stocks (i.e., bonds) of foreign governments on the Dutch bourses. Actual occupation of the country by French armies closed all possibilities of another practicable loan to the United States. The American Minister's duties were consequently limited to coping with the blockades and delays of foreign exchange in his endeavor to transmit remittances of the United States to serve the existing loans, particularly the payments that fell due on June 1, 1795 and June 1, 1796. All remittances had to come from the United States to Holland by way of London, now capital of an enemy country.[21] Adams had particular difficulties in taking care of the small Antwerp loan and met only grudging co-opera-

[19] In preparing these paragraphs on the service of the debt to Dutch bankers I was assisted by an unfinished memorandum by the late Worthington C. Ford when editing the *Writings* of JQA, but never used by him; and by an unpublished thesis by Dr. Robert L. LaFollette of Ball State Teachers College, Muncie, Indiana, on "The Liquidation of the American Revolutionary Foreign Debt" (George Washington University, 1930). Ford bases his memorandum on Adams's unprinted correspondence with the Secretaries of the Treasury, Alexander Hamilton and Oliver Wolcott. LaFollette utilized the archives of the Departments of State and Treasury.

[20] Instructions of Alexander Hamilton, Secretary of the Treasury, to John Quincy Adams, Minister Resident to the United Provinces of the Netherlands, August 8, 1794. Adams MSS.

[21] Fluctuations of exchange between Amsterdam and London were so violent that Adams lost $520 while meeting traveling expenditures caused by his mission to London in 1795–6, a claim for reimbursement that the Secretary of State subsequently sanctioned.

tion from the United States' bankers in Amsterdam in remitting moneys to their rivals on the Scheldt.

Congress endeavored to solve the problem of servicing foreign loans by refunding them into an issue of United States 5 per cent bonds exchangeable for the 4½ per cent foreign loans outstanding (Act of March 3, 1795). This conversion was acceptable to the creditors, principally the American provisioner to France, James Swan,[22] who held the paper for the balance of the Revolutionary debt still due from the United States to the French Government. But the Amsterdam and Antwerp bankers declined the conversion because of their desire for a steady investment income in those unsettled years. In these circumstances the United States Treasury continued, under most exasperating difficulties of exchange, to meet without unreasonable delay the scheduled payments of interest and amortization until the loans were finally paid off in full by 1809, a few months before the French Empire finally swallowed up the Batavian Republic.[23]

The steady stream of cash from the United States to the Netherlands, and even a little to Antwerp, made the French Revolutionary Government increasingly content with the Batavian puppet's continuing relations with the United States. The flow of American funds from Philadelphia to Amsterdam made it easier for the Dutch to keep up their payments on the indemnity to France. So did the prosperous wartime trade between Holland and America. Therefore the French Republic did not require the Dutch to withdraw their representative from Philadelphia when in 1796 France broke off relations with the United States.

All in all, the young Minister's diplomatic labors were not arduous. He had plenty of time to watch the European scene and to study its lessons for the United States.

John Quincy Adams's most important work at The Hague proved to be that of reporting the course of French conquest. In letters to the Secretary of State and to his father, the Vice President, he expressed his hopes and fears for American foreign policy and for the survival of American nationality in a war that he had correctly seen, from the moment of his return to Europe,[24] as a titanic duel between France and England. One by one France was knocking out the continental members of the Coalition: the Netherlands, Prussia, and Spain in 1795; Sardinia

[22] See above, p. 33.

[23] For further information on the Dutch loans and their service and liquidation see P. J. Van Winter: *Het aandeel van den Amsterdamschen handel aan den Opbouw van het Amerikaansche Gemeenebest* (2 vols., 'S-Gravenhage, 1927, 1933).

[24] His very first dispatch contained this statement: "At this moment they [the French] might probably dictate their own terms of Peace to all their enemies except Great Britain, and it is not improbable that at the opening of the ensuing season, these two great rival nations will be the only remaining combatants upon the field." JQA to the Secretary of State, No. 1, London, October 22, 1794. DS, *Despatches, Netherlands,* I, 1794–6.

would soon have to make its separate peace (1796); Austria's defeat was only a matter of time (1797). Then England would stand alone. France would next try to close the Continent, and the United States too, against all trade with England while she mobilized the naval power of the European nations for a final blow against the Mistress of the Seas. The American Minister Resident was the first of his countrymen to discern the outlines of the future Continental System and the relations of the United States to it.

Adams realized that the position of his own country between the two mighty combatants might soon be a matter of life or death, as it had been for the Netherlands. French diplomacy was trying to shape a fifth column in America too.[25] The Revolutionary leaders would overthrow Washington's Government if necessary to accomplish their purpose, to undo Jay's Treaty and American neutrality. They would use the United States as they were using the Netherlands for France's own benefit. They would "hurry us into a war which may hasten their means of making peace." And at the peace they would leave the United States in the lurch. America must steel herself in unity against the dreaded Revolutionary intervention.

Events in America seemed to demonstrate the dangers of French propaganda and intrigue that John Quincy Adams was pointing out from the example of the Netherlands. The dubious relations of Adams's technical chief, Secretary of State Edmund Randolph, with Fauchet, the French Minister in Philadelphia, suggested that there might be a fifth column right inside the American Government. Some dispatches of Fauchet, intercepted by the British Navy and conveyed to Washington's Cabinet, convinced the President that his Secretary of State had advised how to bring success to the Whisky Rebellion against the Federal Government in 1794 by the use of money with a few influential individuals.

Washington believed the insurrection in Pennsylvania to have been the "ripe fruit" of the radical democratic societies,[26] themselves American spawn of the French Revolution. Indeed, the Whisky Rebellion must have looked to French Revolutionary leaders like an instrument ready-made for the implementation of their policy in the United States. After reading the intercepted documents the President quickly and indignantly asked for Randolph's resignation.

John Quincy Adams had known nothing of Randolph's equivocal attitude and susceptibilities to French intrigue, which so resembled those of the Dutch Patriot leaders. Fortunately he had developed no particu-

[25] JQA to Vice President John Adams, May 22, September 12, 1795; to Dr. Welsh, April 26, 1795; to AA, May 16, 1795. *Writings*, I, 339–409.

[26] William Miller has shown that there was no connection between "The Democratic Societies and the Whiskey Insurrection," *Pennsylvania Magazine of History and Biography*, LXII (July 1938), 324–49. Washington's accusation was so hard for the societies to live down that it was a major reason for their decline.

lar confidence with his nominal chief. It was rather for his father, the Vice President, that he reserved his most intimate political analyses and reflections. "I wish," he wrote to John Adams, "that the situation of affairs in America may be such as shall afford a full demonstration, that these are ideas merely visionary, and *above all I wish that we may never have occasion for any political connections in Europe.*" [27]

Randolph's dismissal did not put an end to French intrigue on this side of the Atlantic. Fauchet had got a temporary hold on the American public. Popular indignation flamed up against Jay's Treaty even before its terms leaked out of the Senate. When the francophil *Aurora* of Philadelphia prematurely published the whole text, the public anger seemed to have no bounds. The editor was Benny Bache, Benjamin Franklin's grandson and John Quincy's old school-fellow at Passy. His relations with the French Legation [28] were closer than those of the ruined Secretary of State. Bache personally carried bundles of his newspaper, with its dramatic scoop, as far north as Boston, distributing them at the principal cities en route and calling for public protest. Under his incendiary impulse a Boston town meeting condemned the treaty without ever allowing its text to be read publicly. All the way back from Boston to Philadelphia he worked up mass meetings against Jay's handiwork. In New York the "American Jacobin" enjoyed seeing rioters break up a meeting at which Hamilton tried to address the crowd in defense of the treaty. They stoned the speaker off the platform. In Philadelphia, Bache organized another mob to condemn the treaty, to burn Jay in effigy. Thus lighted and trained by French diplomacy, the fuse of mob protest blazed speedily south and west, to Charleston, South Carolina, and Lexington, Kentucky.

Despite the advice and consent of the Senate to ratify the treaty, petitions against it poured in upon Washington from groups all over the Union. The President nevertheless signed. Then succeeding French Ministers, Fauchet and Adet, worked to frustrate consummation of the accord with England. First they labored with the Senate, where the treaty had obtained a bare two-thirds majority (20 to 10); then they used their influence in the House of Representatives in an effort to prevent the passage of appropriations necessary to carry the agreement into effect. When this failed they decided to go after George Washington himself.

The French Foreign Office looked upon the United States as "the Holland of the New World." "Washington must go," declared the new French Minister of Foreign Affairs under the Directory, the Citizen Delacroix: "A friend of France must succeed him in that eminent office. . . . We must raise up the people and at the same time conceal the lever by which we do so. . . . I propose to the Executive Directory to authorize me to send orders and instructions to our Minister Plenipotentiary at

[27] *Writings,* I, 339–40, 353–63, 409. Italics inserted.

[28] See Bernard Faÿ's *The Two Franklins* (Boston, 1933).

Philadelphia to use all the means in his power to bring about the right kind of revolution and Washington's replacement, which, assuring to the Americans their independence, will break off treaties made with England and maintain those which unite them to the French Republic." [29]

In Paris the partisan American Minister, James Monroe, proved none too loyal to his chief. As Senator he had opposed Jay's mission to England, and Washington had sent him to France as a sympathetic friend of the Revolution to defend strict American neutrality while Jay negotiated a settlement with England. Monroe urged the Directory not to try revolution in America until they should see what happened in the presidential elections of 1796. "Left to ourselves," he slyly hinted to Delacroix, "everything will, I think, be satisfactorily arranged and *perhaps in the course of the present year;* and it is always more grateful to make these arrangements ourselves than to be pressed to it." [30] The Directory took Monroe's advice to await Washington's overthrow in the coming American election. Meanwhile it declared (decree of July 2, 1796) that France would treat American ships precisely as Great Britain did – as if she had not already been perpetrating this very thing since the beginning of the war.

The decree of July 2 was tantamount to a repudiation of the Franco-American Treaty of Amity and Commerce of 1778, by which France had agreed to observe the Freedom of the Seas in the next war if she should be belligerent and the United States neutral. The French Minister, Adet, communicated the text of the decree to the new Secretary of State in Philadelphia, Timothy Pickering, on the eve of the national election. In a burning manifesto (November 19, 1796) full of propaganda he announced the suspension of relations with the United States. Both steps, the new decree and the diplomatic rupture, were designed to scare the American electorate into disowning the Father of His Country. The French Revolutionary Government prepared to do everything in its power to defeat Washington's supposed intention to succeed himself for a third term. A campaign of revilement unequaled in American history descended on him. Propagandists like Tom Paine poured oil on the flames.

But George Washington did not choose to run again in 1796. He did not want any longer to be buffeted ungratefully in the public prints by a "set of infamous scribblers" who misrepresented and tortured every act

[29] *"Rapport au Directoire Exécutif par le Ministre des Rélations Extérieures,"* 27 *Nivôse, An 4. Archives des Affaires Étrangères* [Paris], *Correspondance Politique, États-Unis,* Vol. XLV, doc. 21 (LC photocopies).

[30] Italics inserted. See my article on "Washington's Farewell Address: A Foreign Policy of Independence," in *AHR,* XXXIX (No. 2, January 1934), 250–68, from which documents are quoted in the two preceding paragraphs of above text. Before he left the Presidency, Washington recalled Monroe from Paris for not defending Jay's Treaty with the arguments that Secretary of State Pickering had instructed him to employ. He never knew how far Monroe had gone in disloyal insinuations against himself.

of the Executive with a view to making it appear odious.[31] He did not want a third term. He had not desired a second. Already at the end of his first "Federal cycle" he had yearned to go home to beloved Mount Vernon. It was then, in 1792, that first he had prepared to issue an address to his fellow citizens. Only when convinced that his Presidency was necessary to mold national unity while the Constitution took hold on the people and the nation, and that his retirement might injure negotiations under way with Great Britain and Spain for the redemption of the Western territory, had he consented to serve a second term. Even so he had hoped to resign within a year or two and turn the Government over to the Vice President. Outbreak of the Anglo-French War in 1793 and the problem of neutrality ruined that hope. At last in 1796 he was determined to lay down the burden.

Washington made his decision not to run again the occasion for a popular valedictory that would offset the propaganda of the French Legation. He brought all the weight of his leadership and character into a warning to his fellow citizens against the insidious wiles of foreign intrigue.

Outlined and strictly held to the outline by Washington but phrased principally by Alexander Hamilton, whose mind moved in unison with the President's in these matters of statecraft, the Farewell Address invoked the spirit of national unity against the divisions of political factions and the opportunity that factions opened to foreign intrigue and interference, presenting a danger to independence itself. From this it proceeded to lay down the Great Rule of conduct for foreign policy: abstention from the *ordinary* vicissitudes of European politics and the *ordinary* combinations and collisions of European friendships and enmities; in brief, as little political connection as possible with foreign nations.

> Our detached and distant position [Washington reminded his fellow countrymen out of his vast experience with foreign affairs] invites us and enables us to pursue a different course [from that of the European nations]. If we remain one people, under an efficient government, the period is not far off, when we may defy material injury from external annoyance; when we may take such an attitude as will cause the neutrality, we may at any time resolve upon, to be scrupulously respected; when belligerent nations, under the impossibility of making acquisitions upon us, will not lightly hazard the giving us provocation; ***when we may choose peace or war, as our interest, guided by justice, shall counsel.***[32]

It can be said that John Quincy Adams's contributions to the American press and his subsequent letters from The Hague to his father had

[31] Washington to Hamilton, Mount Vernon, June 26, 1796. *Writings of Washington,* Bicentennial Edition, XXXV, 101–4.

[32] Italics inserted.

an appreciable influence upon the mind of the President as he thought over what he desired to say in the Address. The President had read and commended the earlier letters of "Marcellus" and "Columbus." They had led to the younger Adams's appointment in 1794 to the foreign service. The Vice President passed on to Washington his son's private letters from The Hague.[33] In acknowledging four of them received from Quincy in August 1795 the President wrote: "They contain a great deal of interesting matter, and No. 9 (May 22, 1795) discloses much important information and political insight.[34] Mr. J. Adams, your son, must not think of retiring from the walk of life he is in. His prospects, if he continues in it are fair, and I shall be much mistaken if, in as short a period as can well be expected, he is not found at the head of the diplomatic corps, let the government be administered by whomsoever the people may choose."[35]

And again, a few weeks after the Farewell Address, when the President and the Vice President one evening after dinner were going over a new batch of the letters of John Quincy Adams to his father, Washington said: "Things appear to me exactly as they do to your son."[36]

Without pausing at this place to comment on this highly authoritative appraisal of John Quincy Adams's abilities and future prospects, it is worth noting the similarity of some of his letters and newspaper publications to the ideas, and indeed some of the words, of Washington's first draft of the Farewell Address.[37] Among the conspicuous admonitions of President Washington's famous valedictory are: (1) to exalt patriotically the *national* words, *America, American, Americans;* (2) to beware of foreign intrigue; (3) to have no political connections with foreign nations. In all three of these features of the immortal document we can discern the thought of John Quincy Adams, occasionally suspicious traces of his phraseology.[38]

[33] JA to JQA, New York, June 23, 1795, Quincy, August 25, September 19, 1795. Adams MSS.

[34] This was the letter in which JQA wrote: "Above all I wish we may never have occasion for any political connections with Europe."

[35] *Writings,* I, 408, n. 1. "Fair" prospects in those days meant most excellent prospects.

[36] JA to JQA, Philadelphia, December 5, 1796, acknowledging receipt of JQA's private Nos. 19, London, April 4, 1796, to 24, The Hague, August 13, 1796. Adams MSS.

[37] Victor Hugo Paltsits has edited *Washington's Farewell Address* in facsimile, with transliterations of all the drafts of Washington, Madison, and Hamilton, together with their correspondence and other supporting documents, and a history of its origin, reception by the nation, rise of the controversy concerning its authorship, and a bibliography (New York Public Library, 1935). Horace Binney long since had settled definitively the question of authorship in *An Inquiry into the Formation of Washington's Farewell Address* (Philadelphia, 1859). Neither of these excellent studies pays any attention to the diplomatic setting of the Address.

[38] I have put John Quincy Adams's expressions in parallel columns with Washington's and with the Farewell Address in an article on "John Quincy Adams and George Washington," printed in MHS *Proceedings,* LXVII (1941–4), 365–85.

Of course, this is not to say that John Quincy Adams was unduly responsible for the ideas of the Farewell Address. Until he heard of its pronouncement he did not even know it was being formulated. He never would have claimed any part in its authorship, even indirectly. Doubtless the Address would have been given out in substantially the same form if Adams had never lived, for these ideas were common to American statesmen and diplomatists of the time. They were the fruit of experience during the diplomacy of the Revolution. Indeed, the United States had just declined two offers of European alliance – one from Sweden and Denmark in 1794 for a new Armed Neutrality, and another from Spain in 1795 for a triple alliance with France to guarantee the territories of all in the New World – and it was by now acutely nervous about its "perpetual" alliance with France. John Quincy Adams shared these principles of foreign policy and had tested them from his observation of the wars of the French Revolution. Thus validated, they reinforced Washington's own opinions.

To the President he had a chance to express himself directly upon the Address when an occasion arose of executing a small personal errand in Europe: [39] "I fervently pray that they [the people] may not only impress all its admonitions upon their hearts, but that *it may serve as the foundation upon which the whole system of their future policy may rise,* the admiration and example of future time; that your warning voice may upon every great emergency recur to their remembrance with an influence equal to the occasion; that it may control the fury of domestic faction and check the encroachments of foreign influence; that it may cement with indissoluble force our national Union, and secure at once our dignity and our peace." [40]

John Quincy Adams had helped a little to shape the warning voice of 1796. His first diplomatic commission, from George Washington, had enabled him to play a small part in laying the foundation of a system of American foreign policy for a century to come. Already he had envisioned an American System, distinct from the sphere of European polity. "The American [System] will infallibly triumph over the European system eventually, provided it can be pursued with as much perseverance.[41]

Before President Washington had proclaimed to the world the Ameri-

[39] This concerned investigation into the source of the donation of a sword that had come into Washington's hands from someone in the town of Sollingen. See *Writings of Washington,* Bicentennial Edition, XXXV, 207.

[40] February 11, 1797. *Writings,* II, 119. Italics inserted. Washington wrote to Adams a graceful acknowledgment from Mount Vernon, June 25, 1797: "The approbation of good and Virtuous Men, is the most pleasing reward my mind is susceptible of, for any Service it has been in my power to render my Country." Ibid., XXXV, 476. Adams and his brother saw that a correct translation of the Farewell Address was published in the Leiden *Gazette.* TBA to JA, The Hague, November 26, 1796. TBA photostats, LC.

[41] JQA to Timothy Pickering, private, London, December 2, 1795. *Writings,* I, 465.

can System of foreign policy, as laid down in his Farewell Address of 1796, he had interrupted John Quincy Adams's diplomatic reporting from The Hague to send him on a special mission to London, which presents a curious interlude in his public career and a more enduring association in his private life.

CHAPTER IV
London Interlude
(1795–1796)

You will prove yourself the genuine scion of the stock from which you spring.

ABIGAIL ADAMS TO JOHN QUINCY ADAMS,
SEPTEMBER 15, 1795

JOHN QUINCY ADAMS had some wholly unnecessary associations with the final exchange of ratifications of Jay's Treaty in London in 1795. His superfluous mission to the British capital for that purpose and his clumsy protocol at the Court of St. James's make an unflattering contrast to his excellent beginnings in Holland. The London interlude is nevertheless an essential chapter of his career. It shows a diplomat still young, brimful of Americanism, eager to be another patriotic Adams at the court of George III as important as his father before him, but inexperienced [1] in dealing with top-flight statesmen of the Old World. It had a certain effect in fixing his feelings about British officialdom as contrasted with the British nation and constitution. To understand the new assignment it is necessary to turn back to some of the legal and diplomatic complications and details raised by the vexatious orders in council that had produced the Anglo-American war crisis of 1794 and by Jay's Treaty, which ended it.

1

To ease the negotiation with Jay in the critical summer of 1794, Lord Grenville had suspended the obnoxious "provision order" of June 8, 1793,[2] which had directed British naval officers to seize neutral vessels loaded with grain and foodstuffs and bring them into prize courts for pre-emption of their cargoes as contraband of war. Grenville's action was characteristic British practice of affording temporary appeasements in fact

[1] "I have been accustomed all my life to plain dealing and candor, and am not sufficiently versed in the art of political swindling to be prepared for negotiating with an European Minister of State. In other words, besides numerous other deficiencies of which on this occasion I am strongly sensible, I have not the *experience* which the proper performance of the duty would require." JQA to JA, London, December 29, 1795. *Writings*, I, 471.

[2] See above, p. 44, n. 29.

while holding ground stubbornly in principle. In the final treaty Pitt's Government had its way. Article 18 declared that in view of "the difficulty of agreeing on the precise Cases in which alone Provisions and other articles not generally contraband may be regarded as such," and in order to obviate misunderstandings on that score, it was agreed "that whenever any such articles so becoming Contraband, according to the existing Law of Nations, shall for that reason be seized, the same shall not be confiscated, but the owners thereof shall be speedily and completely indemnified," with allowances also for freight and demurrage to the detained carrier.

Such a statement left the legal status of foodstuffs as uncertain as ever, still subject to the interpretation of either party. The British Government was determined not to let cargoes of provisions get to France under any ownership or any flag. It would stop them, by treaty if possible, but stop them anyway. After allowing sufficient time to pass for Jay's Treaty to have been acted on, one way or another, in Philadelphia, the Admiralty started taking neutral vessels again when found loaded with grain and destined to French ports or ports under French control. The latest seizures rested on a secret order in council of April 25, 1795. Although nobody in America ever saw the text, it was assumed that it renewed the suspended provision order of June 8, 1793.

News of the most recent British captures did not reach the United States until after the Senate had advised and consented to ratification of Jay's Treaty (subject to the excision of Article XII, opening up a limited trade with the British West Indies). Had the Senate known about the most recent order it is almost certain that it would have rejected the treaty altogether. In the popular agitation against that instrument opponents made much of what looked like a diplomatic deception. The apparent British finesse so exasperated President Washington that he delayed signing the document for several weeks after the Senate's approval.

Washington's first thought was not to ratify the treaty finally unless Great Britain withdrew the new order.[3] Such was the counsel of Secretary of State Randolph. Hamilton himself seems to have favored such a condition. Only when disclosure of Randolph's equivocal loyalty to the Administration reinforced the President's conviction of the grave danger of French intermeddling in American affairs, and the likelihood thereby of being drawn into the European war if the treaty failed, did he sign

[3] I wish to acknowledge my indebtedness to the late Dr. Josiah T. Newcomb of Poughkeepsie, N. Y., for allowing me to read and be instructed by his scholarly monograph on *Jay's Treaty: Ratification and Execution of its Provisions,* while still in manuscript form, which has analyzed freshly, with the aid of some new material, the standard sources and secondary works such as Randolph's *Vindication,* Gibbs's *Memoirs of the Administration of Washington and John Adams,* Conway's *Randolph,* Anderson's *Randolph,* and Faÿ's *Two Franklins.*

the document and proceed with the exchange of ratifications. Even then he resolved to attach, at the moment of final exchange, at least an oral protest to the obnoxious British order.

Once President Washington had decided to go ahead with the new British treaty, he was anxious to present the completed instrument as early as possible to the next session of Congress, scheduled to convene in December 1795. He wished to have the necessary legislation promptly enacted for executing the treaty so that there would be no pretext on Britain's part for not delivering over the frontier posts on the date stipulated, June 1, 1796. This required prompt diplomatic action in London. There was also the possibility of supplementary negotiations on West Indian commerce and on other points not covered by the treaty.

Because John Jay had left London for home, and Thomas Pinckney, the regular United States Minister there, had gone to Spain, a problem arose into whose hands to put the exchange of ratifications and ensuing negotiations. The only person left with any authority in the London Legation was William Allen Deas, Pinckney's private secretary, chargé ad interim. Washington preferred to entrust the business to John Quincy Adams, an officer of higher rank, providing he could get over to London from The Hague soon enough. Accordingly he sent him a letter of credence to George III, introducing him as Minister Resident of the United States *at The Hague*, empowered to exchange ratifications of Jay's Treaty with Great Britain. It does not seem to have occurred to the President, or to the Secretary of State, or to John Quincy Adams for that matter, that it would be somewhat anomalous, and even obnoxious, to George III to receive as a special envoy a person described as Minister Resident to another Government with which the British sovereign was in a state of war.[4]

Adams's instructions of August 25, 1795, written by the new Secretary of State, Timothy Pickering, high Federalist and liegeman of Hamilton, covered the subject. Time was important; therefore, in case Adams should not get over to London before the 20th day of October, Deas was directed to assume the responsibility. Adams's, or contingently Deas's, first duty would be to execute the exchange, subject to the excision of Article XII. He was to accompany that act with an oral protest at the new provision order should the latter be found to exist in fact. This trust having been attended to, the special envoy Adams – or Deas, as the case might be – was to urge the British Government immediately to send orders for evacuation and delivery of the frontier posts. He was also to concert with that Government a rate of pay for the commissioners to be employed on each side under various articles of the treaty. Further negotiations to be taken up after the exchange of ratifications, said Pickering,

[4] It is quite possible that the new Secretary of State ad interim, who also held the office of Secretary of War, had not had time to peruse JQA's recent dispatches, including that of May 17, 1795, telling of the signature of the Franco-Dutch alliance.

would be marked out in other instructions.[5] If Pinckney should return to London before the business was completed, then Adams or Deas was to place it in the hands of the regular Minister.

Jay's Treaty was such an unpopular document at home that any ambitious young diplomat might have been well content to leave it alone. Vice President Adams and Abigail feared that their son might quail before his unprofitable assignment. "If I have heard a true whisper," wrote the father, "you have a part to act concerning the treaty. Be of good courage and good cheer. It will not hurt you finally, though it may raise a popular clamour. *Publicola* knows what a popular clamour is." "I hope you have not flinched," he wrote again, as he anxiously awaited news of the treaty.

Abigail too urged her son on to his duty. "You are called to take a part in this important business," she wrote. "You have put your hand to the plow, and I know you too well to believe or even wish you to look back or shrink from your duty however arduous or dangerous the task assigned to you. You will prove yourself the genuine scion of the stock from which you spring. . . ."[6]

As events turned out, it was not really necessary for John Quincy Adams to go to London at all. Pickering's instructions did not reach Holland until October 19, 1795, too late for him to get over to London by October 20.[7] It would have been perfectly proper, therefore, for him to have considered his responsibility completely at end. But some inner urging dictated his return to London. Thus prompted, he rationalized a justification for himself in the line of duty. Had not the Secretary of State's letter referred to the possibility of further negotiations to be undertaken after receiving additional instructions to be awaited in London? "This business is unpleasant and unpromising," Adams recorded in his Diary, "but I have no election."[8]

2

Delayed in getting a direct passage from Holland to England, and held back by head winds in the crossing of the Channel, Adams did not reach the British capital until November 11, 1795. Already Deas had ex-

[5] *Writings,* I, 396–9. In a supplementary letter of September 12, 1795, similarly directed to Adams or Deas, Pickering directed a protest to be made against fresh injuries by the British Navy: impressments from the ship *Anne* within territorial waters of the United States, and again in the port of Jérémie, Hispaniola, where the captain of HMS *Hermione* had stripped upwards of twenty American ships of their crews. DS, *Instructions, U. S. Ministers,* III, 28, concerning Adams and Deas; to Adams separately, August 25, 1795, ibid., 31.

[6] JA to JQA, Quincy, September 19, Philadelphia, December 12, 1795; AA to JQA, Quincy, September 15, 1795. Adams MSS.

[7] The instructions of August 25, 1795 arrived at The Hague on October 19; those of September 12 were delivered in London on November 11.

[8] *Memoirs,* I, 123.

changed ratifications of the treaty, with Article XII excised, accompanied by an oral statement that the President did not consider the exchange to imply any acceptance of the new provision order, whatever its text might be.[9] Lord Grenville had met this unwritten reservation by declaring that a copy of the order had been sent to the President, who would perceive that it did not conflict with the treaty. The treaty and the order in council, the British Minister dryly observed, were quite unconnected, "the treaty being altogether a distinct business." He would hold no further diplomatic discussion with Deas. The stout-hearted chargé had irritated the Minister by the resolute way in which, as directed, he had protested recent violations of American sovereignty by British naval commanders. It was at this point that John Quincy Adams took hold of the business.

The first official whom the American envoy encountered in London was George Hammond, Undersecretary of Foreign Affairs. Adams as a boy had first met Hammond in 1783 in Paris where the Englishman was secretary to the British plenipotentiary, David Hartley, who signed the definitive Treaty of Peace and Independence. Since then Hammond had worked his way up from a précis-writer to be the first British Minister ever sent to the United States, in 1791, at the age of twenty-seven years. Over here he had married a Philadelphia lady, the daughter of Edmund Allen, a conjugal union that failed to increase the groom's American sympathies.

Secretary Jefferson had sadly worsted Hammond in the diplomatic disputation over fulfillment of the Treaty of Peace, but Hammond had made up for this upset by securing Alexander Hamilton and other Federalists as confidants and thus laying a conduit into the inner councils of Washington's Administration. The British Minister knew more about the secrets of American politics than any other foreigner – indeed, more than most Americans. It was he who had turned over to the High Federalist leaders the intercepted dispatches of Fauchet, for the ruin of Secretary of State Randolph.

Hammond's asperities in Philadelphia had done nothing to soften the Anglo-American crisis of 1794, and after it had been settled by the treaty of that year John Jay had suggested to Lord Grenville his recall. The British Foreign Minister complied – at the same time suggesting to Jay that the American Government recall the pro-French James Monroe from his post at Paris – and made Hammond Undersecretary for Foreign

[9] Deas somewhat bungled the exchange. He had been instructed to send home attested copies of the treaty and the instruments of ratification, signed by the King with the great seal of the Kingdom. Instead, in the first dispatches, Deas sent only the form of ratification. The exemplified copies of the treaty did not arrive in Philadelphia until March 4, 1796. Meanwhile the President had given up waiting and sent the treaty to Congress, March 1, on the strength of Deas's imperfect evidence and publication of the ratifications by the President and the King, with full powers of their plenipotentiaries, in a Charleston, S.C., newspaper. Newcomb, op. cit. See also Miller: *Treaties,* II, 269.

Affairs in London. In that post he had just as much to do with American affairs as ever. The returned diplomat had a supercilious regard for Federalist leaders and complete contempt for all Democrats. His one idea was to play them off against each other. He started in right away on Vice President Adams's son.

The Undersecretary told John Quincy Adams how glad he was to see him in London. Indeed, he wished he had arrived earlier. He even desired Mr. Pinckney would go home so that Adams might be appointed in his stead. Then the son could succeed to the station his father once had held! Professing to be an old friend and acquaintance, Hammond complained, with affectation of confidence, about Deas's "violent and fractious" tone.

All this talk did not lead Adams to deprecate his colleague – on the contrary.

Next Hammond tried to bait Adams about the opposition to Washington's Government. He kept referring to Secretary Randolph's resignation, to the machinations of the Democrats.

"I hear the Democrats are cock-a-whoop in America," he said. "They talk very high of impeaching the President."

"There will always be in all countries," Adams retorted, "people who talk very high. You find that in this country as well as elsewhere."

"Have you heard anything," asked Hammond in their next talk, "of the President's intending to resign?"

"No," replied Adams. What sort of soul does this man suppose I have? he asked himself.

"How about the Virginians?" persisted Hammond, "the Southern People, the Democrats? . . . . Next time I see you I will show you Fauchet's intercepted dispatches. They abuse all the Federalists very much, particularly your father. . . ."

"All governments have their opposition," answered Adams. He promptly inquired about the English opposition. Two sedition bills had just been introduced in Parliament to quell radical agitation. Was the Government in great danger? In America, Adams said, opposition was open, constitutional, healthy; in England it was under cover, suppressed. "We have no lurking dissatisfaction that works in secret and is not seen; nothing that rankles in the heart while the face wears a smile."

"I like the sedition bills very much," said Hammond. "They are necessary to preserve this Government; and that is very important to this country, and to yours too. Depend on it, if this Government falls yours will fall too."

It was first mention of a theme that soon captured the High Federalists of New England. Old England was the bulwark, the dike against the revolutionary storm.

Adams did not fall for this line of talk.

"Oh," he exclaimed. "You joke when you talk of a Government so very strong as yours falling." If I stay here any time, the American said to himself, he will learn not to be quite so fond nor yet so impertinent.[10]

So far so good. The younger Adams had not done so badly in his first contacts with British officialdom. He had proved himself to be a chip off the old block – the genuine scion of the stock from which he sprang. The English Undersecretary got nowhere in trying to play on John Quincy Adams's personal feelings or sentiments, any more than George III had been able to work on those of his father ten years earlier.

It is interesting to compare the audiences of the two Adamses, father and son, a decade apart, with their former King. In a well-known report John Adams recorded his exchange with George III when that monarch received him formally as United States Minister in 1785:

"The King then asked me whether I came last from France, and upon my answering in the affirmative, he put on an air of familiarity, and, smiling, or rather laughing, said, 'There is an opinion among some people that you are not the most attached of all your countrymen to the manners of France.' I was surprised at this, because I thought it an indiscretion and a departure from the dignity. I was a little embarrassed, but determined not to deny the truth on one hand, nor leave him to infer from it any attachment to England on the other. I threw off as much gravity as I could, and assumed an air of gayety and a tone of decision as far as was decent, and said, 'That opinion, Sir, is not mistaken; I must avow to your Majesty, I have no attachment but to my own country.' The King replied, as quick as lightning, 'an honest man will never have any other.' "[11]

In his audience with the same sovereign in 1795 John Quincy Adams delivered himself of the following set speech: "Sir. To testify to your Majesty the sincerity of the United States of America in their Negotiations, their President has directed me to take the necessary measures on their part connected with the ratifications of the treaty of Amity, Commerce and Navigation concluded between your Majesty and the United States. He has authorized me to present to your Majesty this letter, and I solicit your Majesty's permission to add the assurances of sincerity on the part of the United States."

Condescendingly George III replied: "To give you my answer, Sir, I am very happy to receive the assurances of their sincerity, for without that, you know, there would be no such thing as dealings among men."

Neither in his official dispatch recounting the interview nor in his Diary does John Quincy Adams comment on the lack of reciprocal assurances of sincerity by the King on his part.[12]

In the perfunctory conversation that followed, the King showed no sign of awareness that Adams was still Minister to the Netherlands rather

[10] *Memoirs*, I, 140–5.

[11] *Works* of JA, VIII, 258.

[12] JQA to Secretary of State, Nos. 4 and 62, London, December 15, 1795. DS, *Despatches, Netherlands*, I.

than to Great Britain. George III's remarks quickly tapered down to thin banalities. From what state did the envoy come? Upon receiving the answer Massachusetts, the sovereign turned to Lord Grenville and said: "All the Adamses belong to Massachusetts?" To which Lord Grenville answered they did. George III then inquired whether John Quincy Adams's father was now Governor of Massachusetts. (It was Samuel Adams who had been Governor recently).

"No, Sir," responded John Quincy, "he is Vice President of the United States."

"Ay," the monarch pondered, "and he cannot hold both offices at the same time?"

"No, Sir."

"Where is your father now?"

"At Philadelphia, I presume, the Congress being now in session."

"And where did you come from last?"

"From Holland, Sir."

"You have been employed there?"

"Yes, Sir, about a year."

"Have you been employed before, and anywhere else?"

"No, Sir."

Later, in the Queen's drawing-room, George III by the Grace of God of Great Britain, France, and Ireland, King, Defender of the Faith, etc., etc., deigned to ask the American Minister Resident from The Hague if the winters in New England were not more severe than those of England.[13]

Discussions with Lord Grenville were on a higher plane, dignified but by no means comfortable to the American visitor. Here the inexperienced diplomat was treating with an Englishman of quite another mark than Hammond, a statesman of the first rank in political experience and ability, a diplomat at ease in any situation, on the whole a frank and kindly person, simple in manner, but an astute connoisseur of human specimens. The discussions with John Quincy Adams in 1795 were minor details of Grenville's daily work of handling foreign affairs of great magnitude with the chancelleries of all Europe during the greatest war in which Britain had ever been engaged.

Adams took up the points in Pickering's instructions that Grenville had not been willing to listen to from Deas. Quickly he reached an understanding regarding the pay of the treaty commissioners. He repeated to Grenville what Deas had already said about the secret provision order: that the President did not regard the exchange of treaty ratifications as sanctioning it.

Grenville retorted incontrovertibly that the treaty made provisions contraband under certain circumstances and had explicitly recognized the right of capturing enemy property from neutral ships. The new order,

[13] *Memoirs,* I, 162–5.

he said, directed captures only when both these circumstances occurred: that was, when the neutral vessels were laden with provisions and when there was suspicion of enemy ownership of the cargo. The Foreign Minister did not reveal the text of the order. He said he would send Adams a copy.

Apparently Grenville did not carry out his promise. Adams's dispatches to the Secretary of State do not cover any transmission of the order in council. His Diary mentions, mistakenly, that it had been revoked. The United States Government never received the text, so far as can be discovered. In London it remained unpublished for a hundred and forty years. Not until after the First World War did an historical investigator discover it where it lay long forgotten in the British archives. Grenville's description of the document was correct, his justification sound. The principle on which it rested was unexceptionable under Jay's Treaty, for the simple reason that this secret order of April 25, 1795,[14] quite in conformity with the treaty, had extended the grounds of capture from contraband to enemy property. But how could anybody know that when the order had not been made public?

There was good practical as well as legal reason for this extension of grounds for detention and pre-emption. In the autumn of 1794 French agents were purchasing provisions in the United States and sending them to France in American ships, really on French account.[15] There was little question that, however labeled, such shipments were actually the prop-

[14] The text of the order of April 25, 1795 is as follows:

Secret Instruction to the Commanders of all Our Ships of War. Given at Our Court at St. James's the Twenty-fifth day of April 1795, in the Thirty-fifth Year of Our Reign.

Whereas information has been received that the persons exercising the powers of Government in France have made large purchases of corn and other provisions, for the purpose of being imported into France, under feigned names and destinations, in order to supply the want of corn and provisions now existing in that country, and to enable them to provide for the support of their military and naval forces in the prosecution of the unjust war which they are carrying on against us and our allies:

We, judging it necessary to counteract the said purposes, and to provide for the interests of our people in this respect, have thought fit to direct that the commanders of our ships of war should, 'till our further order herein, detain all ships laden with corn, or other provisions, that shall be bound to France, or to the ports occupied by the armies of France, or which they shall have reason to believe are proceeding to France, or to the ports occupied by the armies of France, and which they shall also have reason to believe are laden on account of the said persons or of any other [of] His Majesty's enemies; and that they should bring all such ships into such ports of Great Britain as shall be prescribed to them by Instruction from the Lords Commissioners of the Admiralty, in order to be there dealt with as the case shall appear to require.

Josiah T. Newcomb first published the above and threw "New Light on Jay's Treaty," in *American Journal of International Law*, XXVIII (1934), 685–93.

[15] A. Aulard: *"La dette américaine envers la France," Le Revue de Paris*, 32e *Année* (15 Mars, 1 Juin, 1925), 538–49.

erty of Britain's enemies. Therefore their capture was allowable under the terms of Jay's Treaty, doubly so when contraband of war.

"My instructions expressly command me to say," Adams insisted to Grenville, "that the ratification of the treaty must not be construed into an admission of the legality of this order."

"The treaty admits it by implication," was Lord Grenville's only reply.[16]

Adams next remonstrated against Captain Home's aggression in sacking an American coastal passenger ship of the French Minister Fauchet's papers within American territorial waters.

"An order has been issued by the Lords of Admiralty to him for the purpose of hearing what he should have to say in his justification," Grenville responded. "I can assure you that no officer in His Majesty's navy would ever be countenanced in such acts."

There is no record of any censure of Captain Home for his violation of American sovereignty. Doubtless Grenville considered that the act had expiated itself in helping to bring about Randolph's ruin.

According to his instructions, Adams pressed for the immediate evacuation and delivery of the frontier posts. But he discovered a not unnatural disposition in London to wait until the House of Representatives had voted the necessary appropriation for carrying Jay's Treaty into effect. "I am ordered to urge the immediate performance of that engagement," he declared to the Foreign Minister, referring to the treaty article.

"Orders have been made out for that purpose," replied Grenville, "*and I believe they have been sent out.* But it cannot be surprising if, upon seeing in what manner the treaty has been received in America, and the opposition which it has met and still meets there, we should think it necessary to be on our guard. . . ."

"I have not the smallest doubt," asserted Adams bravely but none too confidently, "and I believe your Government has no reason to doubt, but that the United States will faithfully perform all their engagements."

Grenville would not assure him that the orders had actually been sent out. "I *believe* they have been sent out," he repeated ominously.[17]

Adams's heart sank. He realized the virulence of opposition to the treaty at home. If it succeeded, war might follow, his country might be sucked into the European whirlpool, the fatal "vortex."

[16] Grenville pointed out that the treaty declared "that there are cases in which contraband and other articles not generally contraband may become so, and stipulates that until the two countries shall agree on this subject their respective conduct towards each other shall be regulated by the existing law of nations. . . . Besides it is equally clear that vessels may be detained upon *suspicion* of their having on board property belonging to the enemy of the captor, by the treaty and by the law of nations."

[17] For these long conversations, November 27, December 4, 16, 1795, see *Writings,* I, 434–41, 454–61; *Memoirs,* I, 140, 150–60. I have abridged them and rearranged the order of topics, and an occasional order of phrase, in the above dialogue, without alteration of content.

In these conversations the American envoy also took up other maritime issues such as impressment and the law of blockade.

"Impressment," he said, referring to outrages at Hispaniola by the commander of HMS *Hermione,* "is a great evil. It couples insult with injury. The Government of the United States wish that some equitable arrangement on this subject may put an end to complaints."

"I have already had much conversation with Mr. Jay upon it, when he was here," Grenville responded, "and it was then understood to be one of the points reserved for future consideration. The question involved in it was on both sides difficult. For instance, if a sailor belonging to one of the king's ships stationed on the American coast, should desert and run away from his ship, it could not be supposed that he thereby changed his allegiance or acquired a right to the protection of the United States as an American citizen. . . ."

John Quincy Adams must have recalled his first meeting in Judge Parsons's law office with the doctrine of inalienable allegiance when reading Blackstone's *Commentaries.* Here it was in actual practice. He would meet and battle with it throughout his diplomatic career. He did not record his reply to Grenville on this occasion. All he did was to call the attention of the Secretary of State to a comforting newspaper notice, from the Admiralty, that orders had gone out not to impress men "regularly protected" [18] — that is, with certification of American citizenship.

As to the question of blockade, the United States adhered to the definition put forth by the Armed Neutrality in 1780, that a blockade could legally apply only to a place or port where the attacking power had stationed its vessels sufficiently near and in such a way as to render access thereto distinctly dangerous. Great Britain had never accepted this definition. By the simple act of proclaiming a blockade over a general area or coastline the British King pretended to make liable to seizure and confiscation any neutral ship bound for any port he chose to call "blockaded." He could even agree to free ships free goods and a restricted list of contraband but negate it all by a paper blockade.

"It is our idea," Adams suggested, "that the law of nations limits a blockade to such places as may be surrounded in such a manner as to prevent the introduction of all supplies."

"I doubt whether the principle can be admitted in such a latitude," replied Grenville imperturbably. "At least there is no occasion for an immediate discussion of this article."

Adams mentioned the obnoxious Rule of the War of 1756.

"A trade opened by the enemy in favor of neutral navigation *flagrante bello,*" gravely responded the Foreign Minister, "and contrary to the permanent system pursued by that enemy in time of peace, is a mere evasion for the purpose of giving protection to hostile property."

[18] *Writings,* I, 444–9.

The discussions with Grenville illustrate what John Quincy Adams's distinguished son, and editor of his *Memoirs,* called "Mr. Adams's aptitude for the collisions of diplomatic life." The American envoy had asked for trouble and got it, politely. Grenville had easily brushed him off. John Quincy Adams was learning the hard way. He had lost the first round of his lifelong fight for the Freedom of the Seas.

It had already been noted that Adams's credentials to George III described him as Minister Resident of the United States of America *at The Hague.* Lord Grenville, anxious to conciliate Anglo-American relations — on the terms of the Mistress of the Seas — did not stand on form. He insisted on presenting Adams to the King as though he were a diplomatic officer regularly residing near the British court and included him in invitations to official receptions or levees. The royal invitations, the references in the official gazettes, all public allusion to the American visitor referred to him as "Minister Resident of the United States," omitting the words "at The Hague."

This friendly gesture confused and worried Adams. Putting it together with remarks that Hammond had made hoping that he might replace Pinckney, he imagined that the Foreign Office was trying to "construe" him into a minister to Great Britain. It was a snare, he fancied, a trap to be sprung suddenly on him he knew not just how. He sent long dispatches to the Secretary of State about this awful danger.[19] An invitation to attend the King's levee was addressed to him as "Minister Plenipotentiary of the United States." Was this address, a step higher than Minister Resident, still without mention of The Hague, another attempt to cajole him? If it were, he would set the record straight, let the King do what he wanted to about it. Promptly he wrote a formal note to Grenville calling attention to the fact that his invitation to the King's reception mistakenly referred to him as "Minister Plenipotentiary from the United States of America," when really he was Minister Resident of the United States at The Hague. Quite unnecessarily the young diplomat was snarling himself up in a roll of protocol.

Patiently and resourcefully the Foreign Minister assured Adams that it would be all right to attend the levee as "Minister Resident." He continued to hold diplomatic converse with him, even beyond the range of the latter's powers merely to exchange ratifications of a treaty. But the envoy's obstinate emphasis on his precise title seems finally to have worn down the welcome that was evident on his first arrival. At length, at one of the King's receptions, the monarch did not speak to him. Next day the court gazette, for which Hammond prepared official items from the Foreign Office, announced that the American Minister Adams, introduced

[19] See his Nos. 4 and 62, London, December 15, 1795, Nos. 6 and 64, London, January 1, 1796, Nos. 7 and 65, London, January 20, 1796. DS, *Despatches, Netherlands,* I, 1794–6. See also *Writings,* I, 449–53, 472–3.

by Lord Grenville, had taken leave of the King at his levee and was on his way home! [20]

Such a royal snub, and the not very subtle official hint, convinced Adams that his usefulness had ceased at the British court, even if he should receive instructions for further duties. He excused himself from attending the royal drawing-room on the Queen's birthday, and was too unwell to dine with Lord Grenville.[21]

Gouverneur Morris, American favorite at the British court, saw something of Adams during these weeks at London. This famous traveler and American courtier, informer for the British Government, thought his younger countryman vacuous and inane. He noted in his Diary that the youthful Minister had become deeply tinctured with suspicion and saw "design" in everything. "His Mind has received early a Wrong Bias and I think will always go obliquely." Upon learning that Adams had excused himself from the levee, Morris noted: "The jealousy which I marked in his Temper and the suspicious Turn of Mind have already disgusted those whom he had to do business with." At least that is what Hammond put in Morris's ear. The former United States Minister to France and friend of Louis XVI and Marie Antoinette found his fellow countryman a "little critical" of French politics,[22] but in his wrath and indignation at the conduct of the British Government, Adams seemed to Morris absolutely mad: "He breathed nothing but war, and was content to run into it at the hazard of our finances and even of our Constitution. Such sentiments arise in him only for the moment and would not certainly influence his conduct; but such language, if held to those who should repeat it, must do mischief here." [23]

The truth is that the two American diarists at the Court of St. James's were jealous of each other. Morris, who would have liked above all things to have been appointed United States Minister at London, thought Adams envious of his favored social position at the British court. And Adams considered Morris too inquisitive about his diplomatic mission to England.

Adams soon cooled down and recovered his wholesome balance between Great Britain and France. Did he not remember Abigail's advice

[20] *Memoirs,* I, 167.

[21] "Queen's birthday celebrated. Walked with Frazier in the morning to Mr. Pinckney's. Crafts and Gardiner [Boston friends] have arrived and all stopped at Dover. Frazier [another Boston friend] dined with me. Foster. We all walked in the evening to see the illuminations, which were small, and then supped at the London Coffee House. Home unwell. Excused myself from attendance at the Drawing Room, and from dining with Lord Grenville." Diary, January 18, 1796.

[22] I am indebted to Miss Beatrix Cary Davenport for the excerpts referring to John Quincy Adams in London in 1795–1796 in the unpublished portions of Gouverneur Morris's MS. Diary, deposited, under restrictions, in the Library of Congress.

[23] *Diary and Letters of Gouverneur Morris,* Anne Cary Morris, ed. (2 vols., New York, 1888), II, 157.

never to let his passions get the best of him? At any rate, he was enormously relieved when Thomas Pinckney came back to England in January 1796 from his successful mission to Spain to take over the conduct of all business with the British court, and Adams received instructions permitting him to return to The Hague. By then it looked as though the House of Representatives really was going to repudiate Jay's Treaty. In England people were forecasting such an event as proof of American executive imbecility or legislative perfidy. It made him all the more eager to quit the country.[24]

Fearsome that France at last would succeed in involving the United States in the war, Adams gloomily believed that the ensuing conflict would result in a dissolution of the American Union.[25] It was with immense relief that he learned, upon arriving at his own Legation at The Hague, that the House of Representatives on April 30, 1796 had finally passed the appropriations necessary to give effect to the treaty.[26] Delivery of the frontier posts took place under circumstances of good faith and good will on both sides during the summer of 1796. It ended the danger of war, at least of war with England. The Union was safe, at least for the moment.

3

Repeatedly John Adams had suggested to his son that he come back home and "look him up a wife." [27] In London, John Quincy had become a frequent visitor at the home of the American Consul and Mrs. Joshua Johnson and their seven charming daughters, three of whom were of marriageable age. Joshua Johnson was a Marylander by birth, brother to a distinguished patriot, Governor Thomas Johnson. He had gone out to England before the American Revolution as London factor for an Annapolis firm. There he had married a middle-class Englishwoman, Catherine Nuth. During the Revolution the Johnsons had removed across the Channel. The Continental Congress appointed him as its commissioner of accounts in France.[28] When peace came he returned to London as United States Consul.

[24] JQA to JA, The Hague, June 6, 1796. *Writings,* I, 490.

[25] JQA to Charles Adams, The Hague, June 9, 1796. *Writings,* I, 493.

[26] JQA to JA, No. 22, The Hague, June 24, 1796. *Writings,* I, 497.

[27] JA to JQA, Quincy, August 25, September 19, 1795. Adams MSS.

[28] *Journals of the Continental Congress* (Library of Congress Edition), XV, 1126. Wharton: *Revolutionary Diplomatic Correspondence of the United States,* III, 536. Edward S. Delaplaine: *The Life of Thomas Johnson* (New York, 1927), pp. 104–19; and Allen French: *The First Year of the American Revolution* (Boston, 1934), pp. 286–93. Charles Albro Barker: *The Background of the Revolution in Maryland* (New Haven, 1940), p. 342.

Joshua Johnson and his family returned to the United States after Louisa's marriage. President John Adams made him Director of Stamps. After the removal of the Government to the new capital at Washington the Johnsons established themselves within a mile of the White House. Nancy, the eldest sister, and Adelaide, the young-

The Adamses and the Johnsons had seen much of each other when John Adams had been Minister to Great Britain. John Quincy had visited the Johnson home at Shuter's Hill before he was old enough to shave.[29] He probably never noticed the little Johnson girls much then. Certainly he had never seen nor thought of them since. He did not even call on the family on his passage through London in October 1794.

At twenty-eight, with a career launched, the celibate Minister was in no resolution much longer to forgo the joys and trials of family life. He found himself drifting more and more frequently to the Johnson home and the society of the amiable sisters. At first it was the eldest, Nancy, who seemed to capture his fancy. Louisa Catherine, the second daughter, a girl of twenty, conceived herself to be a young woman of "blasted hopes," already disillusioned about the male sex.[30] But she did not repel John Quincy's attentions when it became clear that they were fixed especially on her. A betrothal took place before he returned to Holland. He came back from The Hague to marry her, in the parish church of All Hallows Barking, July 26, 1797, being then, as will be seen, on his way to another diplomatic post, in Lisbon. The Johnson family, eager to remove to America, had been awaiting his arrival as impatiently as the bride. She was then twenty-two years of age. He had just passed his thirtieth birthday.

In Braintree, Abigail Adams worried about her son's engagement. How about "Maria" — Mary Frazier? Had she no lingering claims? "As you tell me the enthusiasm of youth has subsided," she wrote, "I presume that reason and judgment have taken its place." One thing particularly bothered her. It was not a matter of dowry — Louisa brought none — it was the girl's dubious nationality. "I would hope for the love I bear my country that the Siren is at least *half-blood*." [31]

John Adams looked at it the same way. He felt that his son was making a mistake if only because he wasn't yet sufficiently established in any "regular permanent course" — that is, career — to justify matrimony. "Your son will form some attachment or other in Europe," remarked the sophisticated wife of the Portuguese Minister in Philadelphia. "I sighed, and assented to the probability of it," the Vice President wrote, "but I wished in my heart it might have been in America. But I have not a word to say. You are now of age to judge for yourself; and whether you re-

est, successively married Walter Hellen of Washington. John Quincy Adams and his family boarded with the Hellen family when he was United States Senator, from 1803 to 1808. Carolina Marylanda Virginia married Andrew Buchanan (1) and Nathaniel Frye (2); Harriet married George Boyd; Catherine Maria Frances married William Steuben Smith, nephew of JQA; Eliza married Senator John Pope of Kentucky. There was also a brother, Thomas B. Johnson.

[29] *Letters of William Vans Murray to John Quincy Adams, 1797–1803,* W. C. Ford, ed. AHA, *Annual Report* 1912, pp. 358, 637, 676, 679.

[30] Janet Whitney: *Abigail Adams,* p. 264.

[31] AA to JQA, May 20, 1796. Adams MSS.

JOHN QUINCY ADAMS,

MINISTER TO THE NETHERLANDS

PORTRAIT BY JOHN SINGLETON COPLEY, LONDON, 1795
MUSEUM OF FINE ARTS, BOSTON

turn [to England] and choose her or whether you choose elsewhere, your deliberate choice will be mine." He lived to consider the union with Louisa Johnson to be the most important event in John Quincy Adams's life. So he wrote to John Taylor in 1824.[32]

The son made it clear, this time, that "no power on earth" could interfere with his choice.

To marry an Englishwoman — for so Louisa seemed to these good Bostonians — was indeed a questionable venture, a political risk for a future public career. Immediately a local newspaper seized upon the matrimonial handicap and held it up to John Quincy Adams's countrymen. The *Independent Chronicle* of Boston, organ of the Republicans, gleefully informed its readers that: "Young John Adams's negotiations have terminated in a marriage treaty with an English lady, the daughter of one Mr. Johnson, on Tower-Hill. It is a happy circumstance that he had made no other Treaty." [33]

The *Columbian Centinel* loyally came to his aid. The editor, Benjamin Russell, was an old friend of the Adamses. He had printed John Quincy's letters of "Publicola," "Columbus," "Marcellus," and even "Menander." John and Abigail Adams saw to it that he had proper information about their new daughter-in-law. The *Centinel* responded [34] to the *Chronicle's* statement:

> This is an imposition upon the public, who ought to be informed, without derogating from the merits of the ladies of England, that Mrs. A. is an American lady; that her father is a citizen of Maryland, and brother to His Excellency Thomas Johnson, Esq., Late Governor of that State. All who know Mrs. A. speak of her as a lady of distinguished worth, and if every negotiation Mr. A. makes in Europe, terminates as happily for his country, as this will for him, we shall have additional cause to praise the wisdom of that illustrious character, who selected him from his fellow-citizens as one of the representatives of the United States, in the Eastern hemisphere.[35]

As late as his campaign for re-election to the Presidency in 1828, political opponents tried to injure John Quincy Adams in the western counties of Pennsylvania by passing about stories of the President's "English" wife.[36] Other Jacksonites charged that Mrs. Adams was a "European" and that her husband was therefore addicted "to the English System." [37]

[32] JA to JQA, Quincy, May 19, 1797. JA to John Taylor, Quincy, April 13, 1824. Adams MSS.

[33] September 14, 1797.

[34] September 20, 1797.

[35] W. C. Ford prints the two excerpts in *Writings*, II, 192, n. 1. "This [the *Chronicle's* item] induced some friendly correspondent to place the subject in its true light in the *Centinel*. . . ." AA to JQA, Chester, November 3, 1797. Adams MSS.

[36] *Memoirs*, VII, 536.

[37] Jonas Deyo to JQA, September 18, 1828. Adams MSS.

In letters from The Hague to his betrothed and to her family the prospective bridegroom made it perfectly plain that they were going to spend their lives in the plain and energetic environment of the United States and not in the lap of European luxury. "America is my country," he wrote to Louisa; "there all my hopes and all my intentions center, and I know not of any misfortune that could befall myself personally, which I should consider more severe than that of being condemned to a constant residence in any part of Europe." [38]

As in many a successful marriage, it cannot be said that the nuptials sprang from any deep romantic love on either side. Nor was it a connection of the type sought by ambitious European diplomats. But it made a satisfactory union for a good republican family, and they became a most devoted couple. The principal worry of John and Abigail after the event was that their brilliant son's wife might be spoiled by the glitter and elegance of European courts for the simple and frugal life of an American statesman. Actually Louisa Johnson Adams never displayed any great enthusiasm for court functions at her husband's various posts of duty, and seems rather to have shunned much of the social life of the foreign service.

From time to time John Quincy Adams reviewed and appraised his marriage as objectively as possible. As the years wore on, he found his state of wedlock by no means flawless, but nevertheless "highly favored" above the generality of mankind, more so than he really deserved.[39]

Louisa, although of delicate health, outlived her husband by four years. From a patriotic point of view the success of their union is attested abundantly by the survival of the Adams family and its continuing successes and distinctions in the nation's history.

The individual portraits herewith reproduced show the groom and bride in 1795 and 1797. The Copley, painted during the London interlude, was a present from the artist's wife to Abigail Adams.[40]

[38] JQA to Miss Louisa C. Johnson, The Hague, December 21, 1796, February 7, 1797. *Writings,* II, 70, n. 1, 108, n. 1.

[39] "Our union has not been without its trials, nor invariably without dissensions between us. There are many differences of sentiment, of tastes, and of opinions in regard to domestic economy, and to the education of children, between us. There are natural frailties of temper in both of us; both being quick and irascible, and mine being sometimes harsh. But she always has been a faithful and affectionate wife, and a careful, tender, indulgent, and watchful mother to our children, all of whom she nursed herself. I have found in this connection from decisive experience the superior happiness of the marriage state over that of celibacy, and a full conviction that my lot in marriage has been highly favored." *Memoirs,* II, 282–83, July 26, 1811. See also ibid., VI, 46.

[40] JQA to AA, London, July 29, 1797. *Writings,* II, 195.

LOUISA CATHERINE JOHNSON ADAMS

MINIATURE BY J. T. BARBER, LONDON, 1797
OWNED BY MRS. ROBERT HOMANS

4

Adams's inept diplomacy at London must have ruined any unmentioned chance he might have had to succeed Thomas Pinckney in the highest post abroad when the South Carolinian retired in 1796 from the London Legation. Fortunately his official conversations in England remained inconspicuous at home. The opposition press could not know of them. Not even the historians have had occasion to notice them. When the President and Vice President and Secretary of State thought of their Minister Resident at The Hague, they preferred to remember his admirable letters on warring Europe [41] rather than his discomfiting conferences with Lord Grenville and his rather ridiculous fears of being made a minister "by construction" to the Court of St. James's.

John Adams readily enough imputed his son's unpleasant experience in official London to British jealousy, envy, and hatred. "Don't suffer their little contemptible passion and sordid interests to hurt your feelings," he wrote from Quincy.[42]

As for President Washington, he promptly promoted John Quincy Adams from the grade of Minister Resident to that of Minister Plenipotentiary to Portugal.[43] Perhaps he went benevolently out of his way to accomplish the younger Adams's promotion before his father might be elected President and find it embarrassing to improve the employment of his own son. At least Abigail Adams thought so.[44]

Promotion from the grade of Minister Resident to Minister Plenipotentiary doubled the diplomat's salary to $9,000. The transfer of posts allowed a supplement for "outfit" equal to one year's salary – construed to be his former salary of $4,500 – and Lisbon was a much cheaper place to live in than The Hague. The step up in rank and pay made it possible for him to look forward to supporting a family out of his salary and savings – which were to remain his sole source of income throughout his life. He decided to give the diplomatic career a three years' trial, as his father advised, before returning to America.

John Quincy Adams had learned things that could not be learned out

[41] "Your details, observations, and conjectures concerning the powers at war and the issue of the extensive and destructive conflict are highly interesting." Timothy Pickering to JQA, Department of State, September 3, 1796. DS, *Instructions, U.S. Ministers*, III, 238.

[42] JA to JQA, Quincy, June 10, 1796, and Philadelphia, April 5, 1796. Adams MSS.

[43] The President sent in the nomination to the Senate, May 28, 1796. That body unanimously approved, May 30, 1796. *Memoirs*, I, 195. In the House of Representatives there was objection to the additional expenses incurred by new Ministers Plenipotentiary to Spain (David Humphreys) and Portugal (JQA), and the appropriations passed by a vote of 39–25. See *Annals of Congress*, 4th Cong., 1st Sess., 1795–6, pp. 1487–98.

[44] AA to JQA, Quincy, August 10, 1796. Adams MSS.

of books. His residence at The Hague had taught him, and he helped to teach his own country, how the French Republic had changed from a chariot of liberty to a Juggernaut car of conquest and plunder. As he surveyed the European scene, he trembled at every new turn in the foreign policy of the French Revolution, at every maneuver of the opposition party in the United States in sympathy for France. His fears of French diplomacy, however, had not warmed him to England, and his awkward experience at London had increased his congenital dislike for the British court. England, to be sure, was protecting herself from French conquest. But in Adams's opinion she would exploit her victory, if she won it, to establish her dominion over the seas more arbitrarily than ever, at the expense of small neutrals like the United States. While Britain weakened by war and America strengthened by peace, every true American must feel a double satisfaction. "Between the United States and Great Britain no *cordiality* can exist," he concluded. "I do not think it is on our part to be desired. But peace may, and I hope will, continue, notwithstanding all the conspiracies that may be formed against it in America and in Europe." [45]

He went back to Holland more determinedly neutral, more implacably American than ever. His appreciation of Washington's neutral policy, to which he himself had been able to make a modest contribution, exalted his regard to a real and unqualified veneration.[46] Even though it was obvious that his own father, Vice President John Adams, might become Washington's successor, John Quincy Adams regretted "for the peace and happiness of the United States" the first President's decision to retire at the end of his second term.[47]

Upon Washington's retirement the presidential contest of 1796 had naturally fallen between John Adams and Thomas Jefferson. French diplomacy worked desperately for Jefferson. When the votes were counted, Adams had 71 ballots, Jefferson 68, of a total of 138 electors, each of whom had to vote for two names. To be elected a President must have a majority of the electors. Adams thus had but two votes to spare, and received only three votes more than his rival. By the peculiar provisions of the original Constitution the runner-up in the contest automatically became Vice President. Had President John Adams died in office, Vice

[45] JQA to JA, No. 18, London, March 20, 1796. *Writings*, I, 478.

[46] "At the present moment if our neutrality is still preserved, it will be due to the President alone. Nothing but his weight of character and reputation, combined with his firmness and political intrepidity, could have stood against this torrent that is still tumbling with a fury that resounds even across the Atlantic. He is now pledged, and he is unmoved. If his system of administration now prevails, ten years more will place the United States among the most powerful and opulent nations on earth." JQA to Sylvanus Bourne, London, December 24, 1795. *Writings*, I, 467.

[47] JQA to Joshua Johnson, The Hague, July 11, 1796. JQA to Joseph Pitcairn, The Hague, August 11, 1796. Adams MSS. JQA to Christopher Gore, The Hague, July 26, 1796. *Writings*, II, 13, n. 1.

President Thomas Jefferson, leader of the opposition, would automatically have become President.

It is a measure of Jefferson's character and patriotism that he advised his friends that he would be ready to step aside in favor of Adams, his senior in life and rank,[48] if the election for lack of a majority should be thrown into the House of Representatives. And the dispatches of a disappointed French diplomat in Philadelphia are testimony to Jefferson's patriotism, to the fact that he would put America first. "Jefferson," wrote Adet, as he prepared to withdraw from the country after the election of Adams, "is an American, and, as such, he cannot sincerely be our friend. An American is the born enemy of all the people of Europe."[49]

Adet's judgment corroborated John Quincy Adams's appraisal of the great man of his youth, if not his faith in Jefferson's politics. But it was George Washington who remained John Quincy Adams's hero of history *sans peur et sans reproche*. He was deeply affected when the General died. He named his first child George Washington Adams, born in Berlin, April 13, 1801.[50] Washington's character, he wrote from Prussia, would to all ages be a model of human virtue untarnished by a single vice. "The loss of such a man is a misfortune to mankind. To our country it is a heavy calamity."[51] His was "one of the greatest names that ever appeared upon earth for the pride and consolation of the human race. I feel it as an inestimable happiness to have been the contemporary and countryman of that man."[52]

George Washington's foreign policy now passed unchanged into the hands of President John Adams. To him fell the heavy task of preserving American neutrality during the rupture with France that followed Jay's Treaty with England.

[48] Thomas Jefferson to James Madison, Monticello, December 17, 1796. *Writings of Thomas Jefferson*, Memorial Edition (Washington, 1903), IX, 351.

[49] "Washington's Farewell Address: a Foreign Policy of Independence," loc. cit., p. 267.

[50] "My child was yesterday [May 4, 1801] baptised by the name of George Washington; and may the grace of Almighty God guard his life and enable him, when he is come to manhood, to prove himself worthy of it! I was not induced merely by the public character of that great and good man to show his memory this token of respect. President Washington was, next to my own father, the man upon earth to whom I was indebted for the greatest personal obligations. I knew not whether upon rigorous philosophical principles it be wise to give a great and venerable name to such a lottery-ticket as a new-born infant—but my logical scruples have in this case been overpowered by my instinctive sentiments." JQA to TBA, quoted without date by Dorothie Bobbé in her sprightly (but undocumented) book on *Mr. and Mrs. John Quincy Adams* (New York, 1930), p. 113, who explains that she had read the correspondence and private papers of John Quincy and Louisa Catherine Adams, John and Abigail Adams, Thomas Boylston Adams, and Joshua Johnson, among others.

[51] JQA to Joseph Pitcairn, February 4, 1800. *Writings*, II, 451, n. 1.

[52] JQA to William Vans Murray, February 11, 1800. *Writings*, II, 453.

CHAPTER V
The Mission to Prussia
(1797–1801)

It must always happen, so long as America is an independent Republic or nation, that the balance of power in Europe will continue to be of the utmost importance to her welfare. The moment that France is victorious and Great Britain with her allies depressed, we have cause for alarm ourselves. The same thing is true when the reverse of this happens.

THOMAS BOYLSTON ADAMS
TO JOSEPH PITCAIRN, OCTOBER 23, 1799 [1]

THE THREE trial years that John Quincy Adams had planned to dedicate to diplomacy were drawing to a close. At The Hague in 1796 after returning from the special mission to London he had almost made up his mind to retire from the foreign service. He was losing touch with the center of his ambition, his own country. His father was warning that his contemporaries were getting ahead of him in private business and public attention. The life of a diplomat was pleasant enough, John Adams knew, but too long a period abroad might ostracize [2] a man in American politics, and even soften his industry.

Already Adams's friends in Boston, like Sam Cooper and Harrison Gray Otis, were members of the Massachusetts House of Representatives, where their fame was spreading faster than his. The longer he remained abroad, the more hopeless his chances seemed to be. He had been struggling to put by enough money from his salary to marry Louisa Johnson. If he took her home to the United States a year hence, at least they could live there cheaply during the early drudgery of a law practice. Or it might be necessary for him to go home alone and labor and save for a few

[1] "Letters of Thomas Boylston Adams to Joseph Pitcairn," *Quarterly Publications of Historical and Philosophical Society of Ohio,* XII (No. 1, January–March 1917), 29.
[2] JA to JQA, June 10, 1796. Adams MSS.

years in the American vineyard, perhaps in one of the Southern states, before sending for his betrothed.

The truth is that John Quincy Adams had no real devotion to the law. He preferred history and literature. After his return to The Hague from his London "dissipation" he immersed himself in long hours of "literary idleness" — that is, of systematic devotion to his books. He finished Gibbon. He applied himself to Adam Smith's *Wealth of Nations,* "a book to be reread and studied and meditated on." At last he got through Milton's *Paradise Lost.* He read Hume and Rousseau, and Luzac's tedious *Richesse de la Hollande.* He learned to read Italian and took up Ariosto's *Orlando Furioso.* He sampled English translations of the classics, Pitt's *Æneid,* Pope's *Homer,* Rowe's *Pharsalia* of Lucan. He read Caesar again in the original, and Cicero, Terence, Tasso, and Tacitus.[3] Many an hour he lavished on Tacitus, for him the greatest of historians. He thought of devoting himself to a life of letters and redeeming the sad literary reputation of America in Europe.[4] But all the while it was politics that fired his real ambition. Provided he could support a family on his salary, diplomacy might yet afford a springboard into national politics.

It was a great heartener to receive from President Washington promotion to the grade of Minister Plenipotentiary even though it were to Portugal. It made Adams feel that he could risk a few more years of political ostracism in the not uncomfortable foreign service. His father, too, was greatly pleased, despite his recent warnings to his son to come home before he got stuck for life in the diplomatic service. John Adams changed his mind about John Quincy's future. "I am still delighted with your Facts, your Opinions, your Principles, and your Feelings. I believe them just," he wrote. "I do not approve of your projects of quitting the diplomatic career at present; much less of your thought of settling in the Southern States." [5] "Go to Lisbon," he again wrote after taking over the Presidency, "and send me as good intelligence from all parts of Europe as you have done." [6]

[3] Mr. Henry Adams, 2d, culled these readings for me from JQA's Diary.

[4] JQA to JA, No. 25, The Hague, November 25, 1796. *Writings,* II, 45.

[5] "You need not be anxious," he continued, "about the succession to the Presidency, for whoever shall be chosen I dare answer for it, he will not disgust you, either by promoting others over you, or by any other ill treatment. No man who has been mentioned or thought of, but has a just value of your merits. Even if your father should be the person he will not so far affect a disinterest as to injure you. If Jefferson, if Henry, if Jay, Hamilton, or Pinckney should be elected, your honour and promotion will be in no hazard." JA to JQA, Quincy, October 28, 1796. Adams MSS. "If you become a southern man, who shall I leave my Hill to? I have given it the name of *Peacefield.* Shall Charles or Thomas have Peacefield?" JA to JQA, Quincy, November 11, 1796. Adams MSS.

[6] JA to JQA, Philadelphia, March 31, 1797. Adams MSS.

1

The two Adams brothers were at Maasluys, in July of 1797, waiting for a passage across the Channel, en route via London to the new post in Portugal, when John Quincy got first news from his friend and successor, William Vans Murray,[7] that President Adams had made him Minister Plenipotentiary to Prussia. His astonishment at the abrupt change of destination was complete. As yet he had not the slightest idea of the reason for the shift in missions. Already he had bought his passage and shipped his personal effects to Lisbon, including the precious library that he had begun to accumulate, and had rented a house there. He had committed himself to $2,500, personal expense [8] impossible to recover, certainly most embarrassing to lose on the eve of one's marriage. And, of course, it upset all pretty anticipations of a young couple imagining what their new residence would be in Lisbon. All these fond preparations and pleasing images now had to be adjusted from pleasant Portugal to bleak Berlin.

Hasty rearrangement of his plans, official and personal, did not disconcert the new Minister Plenipotentiary as much as the thought of taking the appointment from the hand of his own father. Already he had expressed his nervousness about such a possibility, in a letter to his mother reciting the following anecdote: "Louis the 14th was one day expressing his astonishment, at the stupidity of a certain ambassador at his Court. 'He must be the relative of some Minister.' I have no desire," added John Quincy, "to be the application for a similar reflection." [9]

At first President John Adams had been bothered about how he should treat his own son: whether, for example, to withhold merited promotion. All misgivings disappeared after he consulted General Washington and showed him one of John Quincy's letters to his mother full of earnest scruples about accepting any office through his father's favor.[10]

"The sentiments do honor to the head and heart of the writer," replied Washington to his successor, "and if my wishes should be of any avail, they should go to you in a *strong hope,* that you will not withhold merited promotion from Mr. Jn°. Adams because he is your son. – For without in-

[7] "I am very glad Mr. Murray arrived before your departure from The Hague. This interview must have been of service to him and to the Public; he earnestly wished for it before he sailed. I hope your Brother and you will maintain a constant correspondence with him and the envoys at Paris, particularly my ancient and never failing friend Mr. Gerry." JA to TBA, East Chester, October 25, 1797. Adams MSS.

[8] JQA to AA, No. 33, Berlin, January 19, 1798. Adams MSS.

[9] JQA to AA, The Hague, August 16, 1796. Adams MSS.

[10] "I had hoped that *my mother* knew me better; that she did me the justice to believe, that I have not been so totally regardless or forgetful of the principles which my education has instilled, nor so totally destitute of a *personal* sense of delicacy, as to be susceptible of a wish tending in that direction [of improvement in his situation at his father's hands]." JQA to AA, The Hague, November 14, 1796. *Works* of JA, VIII, 529 n. 1.

tending to compliment the father or the mother, or to censure any others, I give it as my decided opinion, that Mr. Adams is the most valuable public character we have abroad, and that there remains no doubt in my mind that he will prove himself to be the ablest, of all our diplomatic corps." [11]

Such assurance made it easy for John and Abigail Adams to put aside their hesitations. "Merit in my family deserves as much of its Country as in another," wrote the President to John Quincy. He even promised his son – gratuitously – to move him to a post "nearer home" or another court of his preference in Europe as soon as his work was done at Berlin. That could mean only London or Paris. "Minister's relative!" John Adams exploded, recalling his son's anecdote about the inept Ambassador at Louis XIV's court, "I hope the puppies don't call the President of the United States a 'Minister'!" [12]

The son perforce assented to his latest designation, though not without perfunctory expostulation and expression of a determination to be recalled as soon as his mission to Berlin had accomplished its purpose.[13] He was the last person in the world to gainsay the dictum of the great Washington, notably this particular, pleasing dictum, nor could he very well oppose the will, the very kindly will, of the second President of the United States, his father.

The new post did not involve any elevation of rank or salary for the appointee above the promotion he had already received.[14] It did mean the additional public expense of another legation abroad. The Senate after considerable debate confirmed the nomination, 19–9. The opposition restricted their spoken objections to this unnecessary (so they averred) expansion of the diplomatic service. "Old school-fellow" Benny Bache went further in the columns of his *Aurora*. To the lively vexation of the

[11] George Washington to JA [Philadelphia], February 20, 1797. *Works* of JA, VIII, 529.

[12] JA to JQA, East Chester, November 3, 1797. Adams MSS. I have put the French expression in English, and also written out abbreviations, from the original.

"You would not have been sent to Berlin at this time if Mr. Washington had continued in office, I fully believe," wrote Abigail, "but I can tell you where you would have been employed, as one of the envoys to France. This was the desire and opinion of all the Ministers, and nothing but your near connection with the Chief Magistrate prevents your being nominated." AA to JQA, Chester, November 3, 1797. Adams MSS.

[13] JQA to JA, No. 44, London, July 22, 1797, Nos. 51, 52, Berlin, January 3, 31, 1798, to AA, No. 28, The Hague, June 26, 1797; London, July 29, 1797, *Writings*, II, 192; Nos. 31, London, October 7, 1797, 32, 33, Berlin, December 18, 1797, January 19, 1798. Adams MSS.

[14] President Adams took care to correct his son's credentials to Prussia, drafted by Pickering, so that they referred to him as "late Minister Plenipotentiary to the Court of Portugal," rather than late Minister Resident to the Netherlands. *Documents Relating to New England Federalism*, Henry Adams, editor (2d. ed., Boston, 1906), p. 337. Hereinafter cited as *N.E. Federalism*.

Adamses,[15] he represented the nomination as proof of the aspiring views of the President for his own family and their personal profit.

Debate in the House of Representatives delayed the dispatch of commission, full powers, and instructions, so that Mr. and Mrs. John Quincy Adams had three months of uninterrupted leisure for a honeymoon in England. Finally on the 18th of October 1797, accompanied by brother Thomas,[16] still serving as secretary, they took passage from London. Eight rough and stormy days and nights brought the trio to Hamburg. There they had a week of rest. Then five more days of severe jolting by stage and bad roads, with uncomfortable nights in indifferent German inns, brought them to Berlin on the 7th of November. Ordinary travel for the diplomat of those days, it proved hard on Louisa. First she, and then Thomas, were ill at the new post.[17] It was the beginning of many such trials. During the first three years of their residence in Berlin Mrs. Adams was almost continually unwell and despondent.[18] Her poor health weighed heavily on the Minister's spirits all through the Prussian mission.

2

The purpose of Adams's mission to Prussia was a new treaty with that kingdom. Expiration of the ten-year pacts with Prussia and Sweden had presented an opportunity to revise two of the original five treaties[19] of commerce and amity of the United States with European nations and to bring them in line with the maritime principles of Jay's Treaty with England, the newly accepted standard of American neutrality. There was also the possibility of brand-new treaties of the same reformed type with Russia, Denmark, and the Porte. Secretary of State Pickering specifically directed Adams: (1) to abandon the now embarrassing principle of free ships free goods; (2) to repeal the prohibition of privateering in case of war between the two parties, so unique a feature of the Prussian Treaty of 1785 – the United States Government had come to the conclusion that as a small-navy power, unable to equip a big public fleet, it would be advantageous to retain the right to use privateers; (3) to add ships' timbers, naval stores, and wrought iron to the contraband list; (4) to omit the article of the first Prussian treaty, which had exempted the ships of

[15] AA to Mrs. Mary Cranch, Philadelphia, June 3, 8, 1797. *New Letters of Abigail Adams*, pp. 93–7.

[16] Thomas resigned his position as Secretary of Legation and left Berlin for home on September 30, 1798. Thomas Welsh, son of the Dr. Welsh with whose family John Quincy Adams had lived when a young lawyer in Boston, succeeded him. *Writings*, II, 371.

[17] *Writings*, II, 232; *Memoirs*, I, 200–3.

[18] JQA to Mrs. C. Johnson, Berlin, April 18, 1801, announcing the birth of a son to her daughter. Houghton Library, Harvard University.

[19] With France (1778), the Netherlands (1782), Sweden (1783), Prussia (1785), Spain (1795).

each party from embargoes in the ports of the other, making them henceforth liable to general embargoes.[20] The proposed variations from the former Treaty of 1785 all followed Jay's Treaty or at least were not contrary to it.[21]

In addition to the negotiation of fresh treaties with Prussia and Sweden the younger Adams was also expected to serve as his father's observer of the general European scene.[22] "You have wisely taken all Europe for your theatre, and I hope you will continue to do as you have done," the President wrote. "Send us all the information you can collect. I wish you to continue the practice of writing freely to me, and cautiously to the office of State." [23]

In Adams's first official conversations with Count Haugwitz, one of the three ministers in the Prussian Foreign Office,[24] that functionary suggested the desirability of another concert of Armed Neutrality to be directed this time as much against France as against England.[25] "Would it not be possible," Adams immediately wrote the President, "to send full powers and proper instructions to concert and conclude upon a general system of maritime neutrality similar to that which took place during the American war?" [26]

In the Farewell Address, George Washington, thinking as John Quincy Adams did, had warned his countrymen not to allow their nation to become entangled in the *ordinary* vicissitudes of European politics or the *ordinary* combinations of European wars and enmities. Now his disciple in policy was advising that the United States, which had just ratified Jay's Treaty, should turn about and join a new armed neutrality, a European combination to enforce against Great Britain and other belligerents the very principles that it had just agreed at London to relinquish for the duration of the war.

Such a step would produce just what the French Directory so far had been unable to accomplish: war between the United States and Great Britain. The very catastrophe which Adams had feared most of all for his country, being plunged into the European "vortex" for the advantage of some other nation, would certainly have followed any entrance of the

[20] The United States had laid a general embargo in 1794 in the Anglo-American crisis, which occasioned "disagreeable comparisons and real inconveniences" because of exemptions in the treaty with Sweden, similar to the Prussian treaty.

[21] Instructions of Timothy Pickering to JQA, Department of State, Philadelphia, July 15, 17, 1797. *Writings*, II, 188–91.

[22] Uriah Tracy to Oliver Wolcott, Sr., May 27, 1797. Gibbs, op. cit., I, 538.

[23] JA to JQA, Philadelphia, June 2, 1797. *Works* of JA, VIII, 545.

[24] It was the custom of the Prussian Foreign Office to maintain several ministers of state. In 1797 there were three: the Baron Philip Charles von Alvensleben, senior Minister; Count Finck zu Finckenstein, and Count Christian August Heinrich Kurt von Haugwitz.

[25] JQA to the Secretary of State, No. 116, Berlin, February 19, 1798. *Writings*, II, 257.

[26] Berlin, February 25, 1798. *Writings*, II, 263.

United States into any such combination. The President seized hold of his son's diplomatic coat-tails and brought him down to earth, by means of an instruction from Timothy Pickering, Secretary of State.

John Adams, too, had once looked with favor on the idea of another Armed Neutrality. "The Armed Neutrality ought to be revived," he had written to his son during the Anglo-American crisis of 1794.[27] But times had quickly changed after the ratification of Jay's Treaty. The ensuing rupture with France, and renewed French campaigns for the invasion of England and the domination of the seas, plus French maritime decrees out-Englishing England, had altered John Adams's point of view by 1798. He had come to see that France could be an even more dangerous mistress of the seas than England. If anything further were necessary to convince him it was recent French maritime practice.

A proclamation from Paris of January 18, 1798 announced that the character of a vessel, whether neutral or enemy, would be determined by her cargo; in consequence every vessel loaded in whole *or in part* with English merchandise was declared lawful prize no matter who might be the owner of the latter; and further, every foreign vessel that had entered an English port during the course of her voyage was forbidden to enter a French port except in stress of weather.[28] The arbitrary French decree was a prototype of Napoleon's later Milan and Berlin decrees in the fully developed Continental System. It went much further than the British practice of merely taking enemy goods on neutral ships.[29] All that was now necessary to provoke French seizure was to have something on board that might once have been English, like a keg of nails.

In the face of possible war with France, the Secretary of State informed John Quincy Adams that the United States could not enter into any neutral concert which would *hamper England* in her military operations against the "execrable government" and "monstrous tyranny" of France. If there were to be a combination of the neutral powers to protect their commerce, it must be directed against France rather than England.[30] That is not what the Prussian Minister had proposed: what Haugwitz had suggested was to be directed as much against France as against England. Even that would be likely to hamper England.

John Quincy Adams quickly reasoned himself into his father's point

[27] JA to JQA, Philadelphia, April 23, 1794. Adams MSS.

[28] *ASPFR,* II, 151. *Writings,* II, 240, n. 2.

[29] An order in council of January 25, 1798 — possibly a reply from London to the French decree — indulged neutral commerce by permitting a circumnavigation of the Rule of the War of 1756, through the device of allowing neutralization of enemy goods by breaking the voyage of the neutral ship at a neutral port between belligerent colony and mother country. See British order in council of January 25, 1798. PRO, P.C. 2, Vol. CL, pp. 90–1. This had been allowed to the United States since Jay's Treaty.

[30] Secretary of State (Timothy Pickering) to JQA, May 26, 1798. *Writings,* II, 259, n. 1.

of view, as in his new post of duty he studied the conflicting interests of the prospective armed neutrals.[31] He concluded that the best policy for the United States would be to have nothing to do with another Armed Neutrality.

3

It was Adams's challenging assignment, in the revised system of American neutrality, to persuade a friendly government, Prussia, to abandon old treaty principles hitherto considered favorable to her own interests, principles once applauded by friends of peace in the Old World and the New. That Prussia would modify her position on free ships free goods the way the United States had done in Jay's Treaty seemed to him highly problematical. Therefore he suggested to the Secretary of State that he be authorized to propose to the Prussian Government either that Prussia abandon free ships free goods altogether, or that this principle should govern the treaty parties only in case all the belligerents in a war had subscribed to the same dictum.[32] Pickering,[33] who had already instructed Adams not to include free ships free goods in the new treaty, was willing to accept the second alternative, if necessary. After all, it amounted to about the same thing as the first one.

Despite the historical significance of his suggestion – we may call it the "Adams formula" for free ships free goods – the Minister was not called upon to apply his proposed solution in the Berlin negotiations of 1798–9. As the ally of Great Britain, Prussia had thrown free ships free goods altogether overboard in the recent war against France.[34] For the time being, at least, her Government had no desire to return to that principle of the Freedom of the Seas.

[31] "When this plan of a new armed neutrality was first in agitation I was inclined to think we might take a part in it as far as could be consistent with our engagements, and so wrote home. The principles are more liberal than those of England and if generally adopted would prove a real benefit to humanity. But from the moment when the drift of the two *great* parties to this league [i.e., the drift of Russia toward the occupation of Constantinople in any war over neutral rights, and of Prussia toward the occupation of Hanover] I have been convinced that our policy is to have nothing to do with it, and all my dispatches have been calculated to impress as much as possible that opinion." JQA to William Vans Murray, January 27, 1801. *Writings,* II, 497.

[32] *ASPFR,* II, 252.

[33] Secretary of State to JQA, No. 10, Trenton, September 24, 1798. Adams MSS. See also JA to JQA, Quincy, October 16, 1798. Ibid. A copy of this No. 10 is not preserved in the Department of State Records though referred to in later instructions to Adams. Perhaps it got lost from the archives during the removal of the Government Departments to Trenton during the yellow-fever epidemic of that year.

[34] "The United States of America are not entirely wrong in complaining about the theory we adopted during the war with France." Memorandum of Herr Renfner, of the Prussian Foreign Office, for the Ministers of Foreign Affairs. *Preussiches Geheimes Staatsarchiv,* Berlin-Dahlem, Rep. XI, 21A, p. 36. Conv. 2, *Amerika, Vereinigten Staaten, 1795–1804.*

With both the United States and Prussia in agreement on main points, the new treaty was a matter only of time and patience. The negotiation can be traced in a series of four memorials that Adams submitted to the Prussian ministers and in the four replies that the latter returned to him. The exchanges began in July 1798 and consumed a full year. They were accompanied by oral conversations of which there is no record, and finally by treaty *projets,* annotated back and forth. Memorials and *projets* are preserved in the Prussian archives along with the later treaty drafts in John Quincy Adams's own copperplate handwriting.[35] He wrote and rewrote these documents three times over. They reveal an able, patient, straightforward, and conciliatory American diplomat, and one must say the same for the Prussian officials with whom he dealt. The whole business went slowly forward in perfect good will and courtesy.

The resulting treaty, which John Quincy Adams signed on his thirty-second birthday, July 11, 1799, conformed to the new system of Jay's Treaty with England. It omitted free ships free goods altogether, basic principle of the Freedom of the Seas. It did not in so many words put ships' timbers and naval stores on the contraband list. Nevertheless it as much as included them by resurrecting from the former Treaty of 1785 the supplementary general descriptions: "and in general whatever is comprised under the denomination of arms, and *military stores, of what description soever.*" [36] But the unique provision of the "ancient" Treaty of 1785, providing compensation for intercepted contraband, still stood in the new Prussian-American Treaty of 1799 and was renewed throughout the nineteenth century and inherited by the German Empire in 1871. The United States as a neutral appealed to it in the famous case of the *William P. Frye* in 1915.

All the other points that his instructions suggested Adams easily secured. The Prussian negotiators, with suitable expressions of sadness, agreed readily enough to drop out of the new treaty the former prohibition of privateering by either party against the other in case of war between them. With this omission disappeared also [37] the previous immunity of private property on the seas in case of war between the two parties. The Prussians also accepted Adams's proposal to admit the operation of a *general* embargo, as well as other smaller points that his routine Dutch experiences had impelled him to propose.

The United States and Prussia had made their peace, for the time being, with British sea power, in the presence of the conquering forces of the French Revolution. The Prussian-American Treaty of 1799, with its

[35] *Preussiches Geheimes Staatsarchiv,* Rep. XI, 21A, Conv. 2. *Amerika, Vereinigten Staaten,* No. 7, No. 8. I examined these documents in Berlin-Dahlem in 1929. Photostats of them are now in the Library of Congress, Division of Manuscripts. The memorials and replies are printed in *ASPFR,* II, 244–69.

[36] Italics inserted.

[37] Adams's correspondence makes no comment on this.

revision of maritime principles, bore testimony to that fact. It failed to define the legality of a blockade, without which neutral rights meant little. But the two signatories still nursed the shadows of their liberal principles. "The two Contracting Parties," recited Article II, "propose, after the return of a general Peace, to agree, either separately between themselves, or jointly with other Powers alike interested, to concert with the great maritime Powers of Europe, such arrangements, and such permanent principles as may serve to consolidate the liberty and safety of the neutral Navigation and Commerce in future Wars." A quarter of a century later, long after the return of general peace, Secretary of State John Quincy Adams, recalling the Prussian treaties, would draft a Project for the Regulation of Commercial and Maritime Neutrality, and propose it hopefully to the Mistress of the Seas as a model treaty for a general international code.[38]

Adams's next object, a treaty with Sweden, never materialized. As long as the United States and France were on the verge of open war, Sweden was afraid of offending *la Grande Nation,* as the French Revolutionaries boastfully called their country, by making a treaty with the United States. Also, and quite understandably, the Swedish Government felt slighted that its invitation to the United States to join the abortive Armed Neutrality of 1794 had gone unanswered for several years.[39] At all events it was not interested in negotiating any new treaty designed to undo the precious principle of small-navy carrier nations: free ships free goods. It did propose repeatedly a naval concert for joint protection of the trade of Swedish, Danish, and American ships in the Mediterranean Sea against the Barbary States; but the United States, having recently bought a precarious peace with those piratical potentates, shied away from the Swedish proposal.[40]

After signing the new treaty Adams's remaining duty in Prussia was to watch his chosen theater, the whole great stage of international affairs, and to report on it to the Secretary of State. He continued to do this with the same perspicacity that he had displayed in his former listening-post at The Hague. His dispatches from Berlin and his private letters to his parents are first-rate sources – worthy the use of a Sorel – for the diplo-

[38] See below, Ch. XXI.

[39] Secretary of State Pickering directed Rufus King, Minister to Great Britain, to answer it, in instructions of September 17, 1796[8], a copy of which he enclosed in his No. 11 of November 6, 1798, preserved in JQA's Instructions and Incoming Official Correspondence. Adams MSS.

[40] JQA to the Secretary of State, Nos. 110, 113, 114, 120, 121, 133, 139, 160, 168, 170, and JQA to Secretary of State, Hamburg, June 25, 1801, with enclosures; Secretary of State to JQA, No. 10, Trenton, September 24, 1798. A few of these are printed in *Writings,* Vol. II. The others are to be found in Adams's dispatches from Berlin, as preserved in DS, in JQA's own letterbook, and in his book of Instructions and Incoming Official Correspondence (particularly for No. 10, of September 24, 1798).

matic history of Europe during those convulsive years. As he surveyed the European scene from the Prussian capital, his gaze kept turning to Paris and to President John Adams's efforts to keep the United States out of war with France after the spectacular diplomatic rupture of 1796.

4

Already the French Directory had refused to receive a new American Minister, Charles Pinckney, while it gave a fraternal farewell to James Monroe. From distant Berlin, Adams watched Talleyrand and his diplomatic hatchetmen trying to bully or bribe or split apart the bipartisan peace mission that President John Adams sent to Paris to try to mend the break with France: John Marshall, Charles Cotesworth Pinckney, and Elbridge Gerry. Anxiously John Quincy urged his father to be moderate but firm, to preserve neutrality, to keep the United States out of the "vortex." Above all, he prescribed union and military preparedness for his weak and divided countrymen.

Talleyrand's tactics, so successful in Europe, failed in America. The return of Marshall and Pinckney and the publication of their famous "X Y Z" papers united the country in a wave of indignation. The President's messages reflected the tone of his son's letters from Berlin. "I will never send another Minister to France," he declared to Congress (June 21, 1798), "without assurance that he will be received, respected, and honored, as the representative of a great, free, powerful, and independent nation."

Congress responded to President Adams's requests for the creation of a new navy and army. It went beyond what he asked. It raised a new army, which John Adams placed under the command of General Washington, but with Alexander Hamilton actually at the head, at Washington's insistence, as Inspector General. It set up a war loan. It declared abrogated the Franco-American treaties of 1778, both of amity and commerce and of alliance, as well as the consular convention of 1788. It suspended commercial intercourse with France and French colonies (revolted Santo Domingo was later excluded). It authorized American armed ships, public and private, to protect American commerce against the retaliatory French decrees and to capture French *armed* vessels.

Federalists of all shades were delighted at the increased national unity and the new legislation to put the country on a war footing. They enacted supplementary laws to increase the navy still more. Without the President's express recommendation, but certainly not over his opposition, they passed the Alien and Sedition Laws to stamp out foreign propaganda and political intrigue of the kind France was using to undermine hostile regimes in Holland and the neighboring states of Europe. The Federalists triumphed in the Congressional elections of 1798. Very definitely the United States was not going to be "the Holland of the New World."

The dashing naval duels that followed greatly exhilarated and unified American public opinion. They made it evident to the French Foreign Minister that America would and could strike back in her own defense, that a real offensive war might follow if France kept on with her policy. Vice President Jefferson, France's persistent friend, took pains to warn him that the United States might be driven into England's arms.

The new and independent spirit cheered John Quincy Adams in Berlin and made him hope that France might after all change her bullying tactics. He heartily approved of the Alien and Sedition Acts and was thoroughly disgusted at John Marshall for supporting the Virginia and Kentucky Resolutions against them.[41]

Pickering and the Essex Junto – that is to say, the New England Federalists, always excluding the Adamses – wanted war, and alliance with England. For them Great Britain remained "the only barrier to the dreadful deluge."[42] "At present Britain appears," wrote Pickering to John Quincy Adams, "to be the only bulwark against the universal domination of France by sea, as well as by land."[43] Even the President's most valued counselor, Abigail Adams, began to look on England as "the only barrier between France and universal domination." "God Grant the fate of Pharaoh and his Hoast," she wrote her sister, "to those who attempt to cross the channel."[44]

John Adams knew there was no real danger. The British naval victories of Camperdown (October 11, 1797) and Aboukir (August 11, 1798) had shown that the dike would hold. The Essex Junto was not so much afraid of the invasion of French arms as it was of French ideas. They, and the hysterical orthodox New England clergy[45] behind them, wanted war in order to put the Republican opposition in an intolerable position[46] as the friends of France and irreligion. They wanted to extinguish that party and all it stood for in American politics and life.

Under these circumstances, no Adams could bring himself to favor an alliance with England. Public opinion might welcome dissolution of the

41 JQA to William Vans Murray, Berlin, February 5, March 12, April 13, April 27, 1799. Adams MSS.

42 So Harrison Gray Otis, influential member of Congress, described it. Samuel Eliot Morison's biography of *Harrison Gray Otis* (2 vols., Boston, 1913) affords unequaled insight into the thoughts and feelings of the Essex Junto, as well as an excellent analysis of the international situation. See p. 69 for the quotation.

43 March 17, 1798. *Writings*, II, 241.

44 Abigail Adams to Mary Cranch, Philadelphia, June 4, 1798. *New Letters of Abigail Adams*, p. 186.

45 Vernon Stauffer: "New England and the Bavarian Illuminati," *Columbia University Studies in History, Economics, and Public Law*, Vol. LXXXII, No. 1 (New York, 1918), pp. 229–345.

46 I am indebted to Dr. Manning Julian Dauer, Jr., and to the Library of the University of Illinois, for the opportunity of reading his instructive thesis on "The Basis for the Support for John Adams in the Federalist Party" (1938), a work that unfortunately has never been printed.

old "impolitic" treaties with France, as did John Quincy Adams in Berlin.[47] But the American people would never have substituted for them a new alliance with the old enemy that would have put the United States back under the shadow of the British Empire, making it again a certain partner to Britain's wars in Europe, submitting its citizens to be impressed for service in British ships of war. The reply of the House of Representatives to the President's address had made this clear:

> Disdaining a reliance on foreign protection, wanting no foreign guarantee of our liberties, resolving to maintain our national independence against every attempt to despoil us of this inestimable resource, we confide, under Providence, in the patriotism and energies of the people of these United States for defeating the hostile enterprises of any foreign Power.

President John Adams went out of his way to approve heartily of this expression, in his answer:

> The generous disdain which you so coolly and deliberately express, of a reliance on foreign protection, wanting no foreign guaranty of our liberties, resolving to maintain our national independence against every attempt to despoil us of this inestimable treasure, will meet the full approbation of every sound understanding, and exulting applauses from the heart of every faithful American.[48]

All historians of the French imbroglio seemed to have overlooked the plain and obvious significance of this controlling resolution.

Even Alexander Hamilton opposed an actual alliance with Great Britain. He thought Britain's interest would secure her military co-operation anyway: "On the other hand, a treaty might entangle us. . . ."[49]

5

Talleyrand was pursuing a master plan of foreign and colonial policy into which no American diplomat was able to penetrate: a peace of victory on the Continent of Europe and a colonial empire in the Mississippi Valley. Such spirited American resistance was startling, ominous. A pre-

[47] "There were in these treaties advantages to France, which she has forfeited ten thousand fold, and which perhaps ought never to have been granted to her; there was a certain degree of dependence upon France involved in them, which has always been burthensome, and would have become continually more so, the longer it had lasted. There were guaranties unwise, impolitic, and which might have drawn us very unnecessarily into war of no concern to us." JQA to William Vans Murray, Berlin, July 24, 1798. Adams MSS.

[48] For the address, reply, and answer see *Annals of Congress*, 5th Cong., 3d Sess., 1797–9, III, 24, 39–42.

[49] Alexander Hamilton to Timothy Pickering, May 27, 1798. Pickering Papers, MHS.

JOHN ADAMS AS PRESIDENT

PORTRAIT BY GILBERT STUART, PHILADELPHIA, 1798
OWNED BY MRS. ROBERT HOMANS

mature war with the United States, above all an Anglo-American alliance against France, would spoil his grand design.

As a part of his larger policy the French Foreign Minister moved to preserve peace temporarily with America. He sent Louis Pichon, a French diplomat with American experience, to The Hague as Secretary of Legation for the purpose of opening a contact with Murray there.[50] Led on by Murray, whom John Quincy Adams coached from Berlin,[51] Talleyrand finally sent a letter over his own signature to Pichon, for conveyance to President Adams directly. "You were right," the French Minister affirmed, "in asserting that every plenipotentiary whom the Government of the United States will send to France, to terminate the differences which subsist between the two countries, will undoubtedly be received with the respect due to the representative of a free, independent, and powerful country." [52]

These were the assurances that John Adams had required. They were the very words that he had stipulated. True enough, they were not direct assurances to the United States Government, but more direct avowals could be secured before entering on final negotiations. Talleyrand was eager to treat, Murray thought. "I enjoy great pleasure," he added, conveying the Talleyrand-Pichon letter to the President, "having received from Mr. A. [J. Q. A.] a concurrence of opinions on the points I have stated to him." [53]

Murray kept John Quincy Adams apprised of the whole affair and acted in close collaboration with him. He even sent him a copy of the Talleyrand-Pichon letter so that his colleague in Berlin might express to his father any "free ideas" he might have on the subject. Murray also took care to send duplicates of his dispatches to the President by Thomas B. Adams, returning from Prussia via Hamburg after four years of intimate and confidential service with his brother.[54] Thomas Adams disembarked in New York on Friday evening, January 11, 1799, posted his letters and dispatches to Philadelphia the next day, and himself left for that city—twenty-four hours by stage—as soon as he could take care of his baggage.[55] He reached his father's house on Tuesday, January 15.[56]

[50] E. Wilson Lyon has revealed, from the archives of the French Foreign Office, the diplomacy of "The Directory and the United States," in *AHR*, XLIII (No. 3, April 1938), 514–31.

[51] W. C. Ford edited the "Letters of William Vans Murray to John Quincy Adams, 1797–1803," in *Annual Report* 1912 of AHA, pp. 347–715.

[52] September 28, 1798. *ASPFR*, II, 239.

[53] *Letters of Murray,* 481. For Murray's letters to John Adams, see *Works* of JA, VIII, 677–91.

[54] JQA wrote to AA, Berlin, October 8, 1798, that he withheld no confidence from his brother. Adams MSS. See also *Letters of Murray,* p. 481.

[55] TBA to JQA, New York, January 12, 1799. Adams MSS.

[56] *Berlin and the Prussian Court in 1798, Journal of Thomas B. Adams, Secretary of the United States Legation at Berlin,* edited by Victor Hugo Paltsits (New York Public Library, 1916), p. 40, *et passim.* TBA to J. Pitcairn, Quincy, March 2, 1799.

The President knew how his eldest son felt, if only from Murray's dispatches, but he also had Thomas to talk to.

Should the United States, already twice rebuffed, now send a third mission to the tricky Talleyrand?

John Quincy Adams was convinced that the French Government was willing to negotiate. The reason, he surmised, was simply that the resolute attitude of the United States threatened to throw it into the arms of Great Britain and to deprive France of her remaining colonies in the New World. He did not guess the big reason: Louisiana; nor did any other American diplomat. In an official dispatch, No. 137 of October 6, 1798 to Pickering, which it is reasonable to suppose may have reached Philadelphia even before Thomas Adams's arrival,[57] John Quincy urgently advised that the "spirited and prudent" Murray be empowered to enter into preliminary discussions at The Hague with an authorized French representative. The purpose would be first to make certain that France was ready to offer terms which would ensure the success of a final negotiation,[58] if and when diplomatic relations were formally resumed at Paris.

Presumably John Adams read his son's dispatch No. 137, unless Pickering deliberately withheld it from the President.[59] Knowing as we do the inveterate desire of both Adamses for "an everlasting neutrality in all the wars of Europe,"[60] and how much confidence the father placed in his son's judgment, it is hard to resist the conclusion that John Quincy Adams's counsel tipped the scales in the President's mind and made him decide in favor of still another negotiation with France.[61]

"Letters of Thomas Boylston Adams to Joseph Pitcairn," *Quarterly Publications of the Historical and Philosophical Society of Ohio*, Vol. XII, No. 1 (January–March 1917), p. 24.

[57] "The enclosed letters are to be delivered to my brother, excepting the letter to the Secretary of State, marked 2, which I wish to be forwarded by any other early opportunity, and with directions to be sunk in case of capture." JQA to Joseph Pitcairn at Hamburg, October 6, 1798. Adams MSS.

[58] JQA to the Secretary of State, Timothy Pickering, No. 137, Berlin, October 6, 1798. *Writings*, II, 372.

[59] Pickering did not acknowledge its receipt to JQA, nor even comment on it to him. He acknowledged receipt of all dispatches to No. 147 in a letter to Adams of August 6, 1799. DS, *Instructions, U.S. Ministers*, V, 199. No copy of No. 137 exists in the State Department Records, but this is true of many other of Adams's dispatches, copies of which are in his letterbook.

[60] JA in Boston *Patriot*, No. XVIII. See note below.

[61] In reviewing the controversy in 1807, public letters to the Boston *Patriot* (*Works* of JA, IX, 241–311), ex-President Adams said (ibid., 244) that Talleyrand's letter clinched his decision, after reports from the returned Gerry and Logan, together with the reading of letters from Americans in France like Joel Barlow, Nathaniel Cutting, and Richard Codman among others, to their correspondents in America. "But the testimonies of Mr. Codman, Mr. Cutting, Mr. Barlow, and Mr. Logan, *and all other private communications*, though they might convince my mind, would have had no influence to dispose me to nominate a minister, if I had not received authentic, regu-

It is perhaps not without significance that on January 15, 1799, presumably after receiving the European letters that Thomas had posted from New York, John Adams suddenly requested the Secretary of State to draw up a project of a treaty and consular convention such as, in the Secretary's opinion, might be acceptable if proposed by France.[62]

Fortified by his son's advice, Adams sent his famous message of February 18, 1799 to the Senate, accompanied by a copy of Talleyrand's letter. He proposed a renewal of negotiations without a let-down of determined preparations for war. He nominated William Vans Murray, not for preliminary discussions as John Quincy Adams had suggested, but for a resumption of diplomatic relations and a definitive negotiation.

The Federalist leaders were thunderstruck. The President had not consulted them! Recovering to some degree from the shock of the Chief Magistrate's unexpected decision, they proposed putting the negotiation "in commission," as Pickering expressed it.[63] That is, they wanted to group Murray with two Federalist colleagues. John Adams consented readily enough. He nominated Chief Justice Oliver Ellsworth, a proved Federalist, and Governor William R. Davie of North Carolina, a more neutral figure politically. Meanwhile he had laid down the condition suggested by his son, that no negotiation was to start until Talleyrand's letter to Pichon had been confirmed by a similar one to Murray as one of the new Commissioners to France. Until that was received, neither Ellsworth nor Davie was to set forth.

Some of the Federalist Senators had advised nominating Rufus King, Minister Plenipotentiary in London, and John Quincy Adams, Minister Plenipotentiary in Berlin, to serve with Murray. The President responded

---

lar, official, diplomatic assurances [Talleyrand's letter to Pichon]." Italics inserted. Gibbs (in his *Memoirs,* II), the apologist for the Federalist war policy and for the action of Hamilton's men in Adams's Cabinet, analyzes the President's decisions and policy most severely and unfairly. Compare the temperate and generally adequate reply by Charles Francis Adams in his edition of his grandfather's *Works* of JA, I. One should also consult the works of Hamilton and Pickering (Upham's) for details of Adams's conflict with them.

It was the opinion of Robert Liston, British Minister at Philadelphia, that the elder Adams had been driven to the "hazardous resolution" by accounts received from his son. In his dispatch No. 17, Philadelphia, March 4, 1799, to Lord Grenville, Liston, speculating on the possible reasons for President Adams's decision "to patch up a precarious peace with the rulers of France," concludes that it was either (1) due to a conviction, from reading his son's dispatches, of the hopelessness of the position of the continental sovereigns against France, or, more likely, (2) a diplomatic "counterpart to the insidious professions of friendship and offers of negotiation by the French Government. He has, I believe, no faith in the sincerity of their overtures, and no intention to abate the claims of America." PRO, F.O., 5, Vol. XXV. In either case the influence of JQA was equally evident.

[62] *Works* of JA, VIII, 621.

[63] *Writings,* II, 412, n. 2.

that the nomination of either would probably defeat the whole measure.[64] King was Minister to France's principal enemy. He would have been regarded as a British spy in Paris. To nominate the President's own son would have furnished obvious ammunition to those opposed to the mission. Besides, John Quincy Adams had important work to do in Prussia.

John Adams's independent step exasperated the Essex Junto almost beyond measure, but leading "characters" of the day supported him: Washington, John Jay, Henry Knox, Patrick Henry. Even Hamilton refused to oppose the President. So the Essexmen had to stomach their disgust. They bided their time, and with Hamilton's aid and abetment determined to set Adams aside in the coming presidential election. In vain they turned their faces toward Mount Vernon. But General Washington did not choose to run [65] in 1800 any more than in 1796. The electoral hopes of the High Federalists died with the Father of His Country, December 14, 1799.

John Quincy Adams's own feeling about his father's great decision was one of satisfaction, despite reminders from Rufus King that the "good" men in America disagreed upon the wisdom of the step.[66] To his intimate correspondents the younger Adams explained the President's new move. It had not surprised him. The reasons for it were obvious: (1) both nations had manifested, despite their hostilities, a "clear and unequivocal aversion to a formally declared war" — and the American House of Representatives had made a declaration against an alliance with England; (2) it would be more advantageous to treat in France than in the United States with "that universal firebrand, called a French Minister"; (3) the internal revolutions in the French Government were so numerous that it would be prudent to have ministers there on hand to take advantage promptly of more favorable moments for negotiation as they might come up; (4) "I considered [note the past tense] the measure wise in respect to its effects on our relations towards England, who will certainly think us in her power, and treat us accordingly, in proportion as she sees the door of reconciliation between us and France shut." [67]

To Hamilton's close friend King, himself one of the "good" men — the High Federalists called themselves "the wise and the good" — who disapproved of the mission, John Quincy Adams stressed the "unequivocal madness" of war with France without a British alliance. He disarmingly reminded his colleague of the explicit resolution of the House of Repre-

[64] JA to AA, February 22, 1799. *Works* of JA, I, 545. See also Letter V to the Boston *Patriot*. Ibid., IX, 249.

[65] Washington to Governor Jonathan Trumbull, Mount Vernon, August 30, 1799. *Writings of Washington*, Bicentennial Edition, XXXVII, 348.

[66] Rufus King to JQA, London, January 25, April 2, 12, July 2, 17, November 15, 1799. Adams MSS.

[67] JQA to William Vans Murray, Berlin, May 14, 1799; to Joseph Hall, Berlin, November 19, 1799. *Writings*, II, 420, 438–42.

sentatives against any alliance.[68] This being so, and France having manifested a willingness to negotiate, a negotiation was indicated.

6

As Ellsworth and Davie were preparing to set forth to join Murray in Europe, the war took a new turn unfavorable to France. Great Britain in 1799 raised a Second Coalition (Russia, Austria, Portugal, Sardinia, Naples, and the Ottoman Empire) against the Great Nation.

At first the Allies seemed to be carrying everything before them. An Anglo-Russian expedition landed in the Netherlands. Austrian forces started to drive the French out of Switzerland and the Rhineland. An Austro-Russian army pushed them out of most of nothern Italy. *La Grande Nation* seemed to be tottering.

In America the Federalists rejoiced. Hopefully Pickering delayed issuing final instructions to the Commission. He wrote John Quincy Adams that great events in Europe would probably cause the "proposed" mission to be suspended at least for the present.[69] General Alexander Hamilton hastened from New York to Trenton, temporary seat of government, to canvass the situation with his puppets in President Adams's Cabinet. The High Federalists were all agreed on the desirability of halting the mission. Hamilton told the President at Trenton that he was sure that the Stadtholder would be restored and Louis XVIII put on the throne of France before Christmas.

"I should as soon expect," replied John Adams, who had been reading his son's dispatches, "that the sun, moon and stars will fall from their orbits, as that events of that kind take place in any such period, but suppose such an event possible, can it be any injury to our Country to have envoys there? It will only be necessary for them to wait for new commissions. And if France is disposed to accommodate our differences, will she be less so under a Royall than a Dictatorial Government? Have not the Directory Humbled themselves to us more than to any Nation or Power in contest with her? If she [France] proves faithless, if she will not receive our Envoys, does the disgrace fall upon her, or upon us? We shall not be worse off than at Present. The people of our own Country will be satisfyed that every honorable method has been try'd to accommodate our differences."[70]

Hamilton and the Essex Junto wanted war. Adams preferred peace.

The President ordered Ellsworth and Davie forthwith to join Murray in France for their important business. In so doing, he split the Federalist

[68] JQA to Rufus King, Berlin, May 25, 1799. *Writings*, II, 422.

[69] Secretary of State to JQA, No. 19, Department of State, Trenton, October 4, 1799. DS, *Instructions, U.S. Ministers*, V, 219.

[70] So Abigail Adams related the conversation to her sister Mrs. Mary Cranch, Philadelphia, December 30, 1799. *New Letters of Abigail Adams*, p. 224.

Party hopelessly, but he saved the peace honorably and profitably for his country. The rupture was completed, irreparably, when in the spring of 1800 President Adams summarily rid himself of Hamilton's most obnoxious liegemen in his Cabinet.[71]

John Quincy Adams had nothing directly to do with this vitally important decision of his father on foreign policy, against the wishes of the High Federalists. Nevertheless his remarks on Secretary of State Pickering's intimation that the mission to France might be suspended, in view of encouraging events in Europe, are highly interesting. In his dispatches and letters home he had been conservative in appraising the early Allied victories. It proved well that he had been so cautious. By the time Pickering's letter reached him in the Prussian capital, the military situation had reversed itself, suddenly and completely. General Bonaparte had returned from Egypt. The *coup d'état* of 18th Brumaire had abolished the Directory and put France under the control of the Corsican adventurer, as First Consul, for a term of ten years. Everything, replied the American Minister to Prussia, urged that the Commissioners be sent forthwith to France.[72]

In the new military situation so favorable to France, the American Commissioners opened their negotiations in Paris. Their instructions, like those to Pinckney, Marshall, and Gerry before them, were in effect to replace the old treaties, already abrogated unilaterally, by a new treaty on the lines of Jay's Treaty with England. It would provide for adjudication of American claims for spoliations, "under color" of French maritime decrees, by a mixed commission similar to that set up by the Anglo-American treaty.[73]

This time Talleyrand received the Commissioners deferentially. He presented them to the First Consul. Bonaparte was anxious to encourage them. News of George Washington's death recently had afforded an opportune occasion to touch and to beguile American opinion. The First Consul ordered the pennons of France's victorious armies to be draped with crape for ten days.[74] What a conspicuous contrast to George III's silence when Rufus King appeared in mourning at the royal levee!

The American Commissioners were still engaged in their negotiations

[71] McHenry promptly resigned upon invitation. Pickering said he could not afford to do so because he needed the salary. So the President had to put him out. The equally disloyal Wolcott enjoyed Adams's confidence unsuspected to the end; the President even appointed him a Federal judge when the Secretary of the Treasury resigned a few weeks later.

[72] JQA to Secretary of State, No. 158, Berlin, November 29, 1799, received June 29, 1800. DS, *Letters of J. Q. Adams, Minister U.S. to Berlin, 1799–1801,* in volume of *Duplicate Letters.*

[73] *ASPFR,* II, 301–6.

[74] JQA to the Secretary of State, No. 161, Berlin, March 8, 1800. *Writings,* II, 454. Cf. Rufus King's account of British reaction in *Life and Correspondence of Rufus King,* III, 202.

when Bonaparte crossed the Alps and broke the back of the Second Coalition by his brilliant victory of Marengo (June 14, 1800). Talleyrand, who had gone into eclipse temporarily following Brumaire, climbed back into power under the First Consul. But there were no more scandalous demands for personal graft in tribute from foreign envoys. Bonaparte wanted peace to consolidate France's train of victories and his own personal position and to build up a new colonial empire in the Mississippi Valley. Necessary steps toward this were amity with the United States, the retrocession of Louisiana to France, and finally a victorious end of war with Great Britain. Under his new master Talleyrand took these successive steps as rapidly as possible. Through regularly empowered French Commissioners he pursued the negotiations with the United States in the spirit of his assurances to President Adams.

The American plenipotentiaries were unable to cover the spoliation claims, which Secretary Pickering had "expected" as an "indispensable condition" of a treaty, unless they would admit the continuing (that is, after July 7, 1798) [75] force of the Franco-American treaties and alliance. Since they were under instructions to get rid of the entangling alliance, they could not admit that the old treaties continued in effect after Congress had declared them abrogated by its one-sided resolution of July 7, 1798. Bonaparte was willing enough to cancel the former treaty obligations and with them any American claims against France for violation of them, but he insisted on renewing the ancient maritime principles in any new treaty. The Americans on the other hand were trying to dilute the Freedom of the Seas to the standard of Jay's Treaty in any new arrangement with France.

The negotiations came to a head when the First Consul triumphed over Great Britain's allies on the Continent. Across the Channel his last obstinate enemy still controlled the seas. As a last effort to overpower Britain on her own element Bonaparte was seeking to erect another Armed Neutrality of the North, with the United States a member, and thus to bring a naval combination into the war against England. Signing the United States up again to the principles of Freedom of the Seas in a new French treaty would be a step in that direction. So the French negotiators insisted on putting free ships free goods into the treaty, together with a restricted list of contraband like that of the Armed Neutrality of 1780, not including naval stores or foodstuffs. The proposed new French treaty did not define blockade any more than the old, and this makes one wonder whether Bonaparte was contemplating paper blockades of England as early as 1800.

The Americans could take peace on these conditions, consistent with the former attitude of their country, or leave open the rupture with France as a general peace approached in Europe. Straining their instruc-

[75] Date of unilateral abrogation of the French treaties by act of Congress.

tions, they chose for peace, the Freedom of the Seas, and the abrogation of the old treaties, and accordingly signed the Convention of Morfontaine on September 30, 1800.[76]

Although the new French convention differed from Jay's Treaty in that it stipulated free ships free goods and did not specifically define naval stores as contraband, the British Government — to which Rufus King submitted the document — made no objection.[77] After all, the Franco-American pact did not violate any obligation of the United States to Great Britain, and if France wished to commit herself to novel principles of neutral rights, that was her business; a treaty between the United States and France could not bind Great Britain to observe those principles toward a neutral any more than the former Franco-American Treaty of 1778 had been able to do. The very fact that France had thus resolved the dispute with America was proof that she was no longer insisting that the United States compel Britain to observe free ships free goods and let naval stores and provisions pass free in neutral bottoms to French ports.[78] Incidentally, the British Government was then in the midst of negotiations of its own with France and doubtless hoped that peace would soon dissipate all issues over neutral rights.

John Quincy Adams congratulated his friend Murray upon successfully "steering the diplomatic ship through a furious sea away from a long ridge of rocks under the lee . . . by a narrow passage into a snug little harbor sheltered from every blast." News of the treaty was the happiest tidings he had heard for years. No matter if it signalized the break-up of the Federalist Party. No matter if it meant the loss of the Presidency in the next election. No matter if his father would have to go home for good to Quincy. It would be an honorable retreat. The President had acted "not as the man of a party, but as the man of the whole nation."[79]

7

Historians have long disputed the causes of John Adams's defeat in 1800 and the precise effect of each. Looking back today upon that historic political schism, we can see that it was not his foreign policy that deprived him of re-election. The second President's attitude toward France helped rather than hurt him with the voters. It was the cleavage between agrarianism and mercantilism within the party, which Adams tried so hard to reconcile,[80] that brought about the downfall of the Federalists. In the election of 1800 Adams ran far ahead of his party, Jefferson and

76 For the record of the negotiations see *ASPFR*, II, 295–345.

77 *ASPFR*, II, 343.

78 A. B. Darling: *Our Rising Empire* (New Haven, 1940), p. 385.

79 JQA to Murray, Berlin, October 30, 1800. *Writings*, II, 471–4. JQA to Murray, Berlin, December 16, 1800. Adams MSS.

80 Dauer, op. cit.

Burr away behind theirs.[81] Thanks to his foreign policy, Adams himself was almost re-elected. His defeat, or his near triumph, whichever way one sees it, was, as his son so proudly felt, an honor to himself, to his family, and to his country. It was better to have lost the Presidency than to lead the country into an unnecessary war to keep the Federalist Party in power.[82] No one after his generation has risen up before the bar of history to challenge John Adams's moral victory.

The High Federalists, the "good" men, made a last stand in the "lame-duck" Senate against the convention with France – to the disgust of John Quincy Adams in distant Berlin.[83] They rejected the instrument, January 23, 1801, by a vote of 16 yeas, 14 nays (20 yeas were required for the necessary two-thirds majority). President Adams urged them to reconsider, and on February 3 the Senate consented to and advised ratification by a vote of 22 yeas, 9 nays, subject to the expunging of Article II [84] and a limitation of duration to eight years. First Consul Bonaparte in exchanging ratifications, July 31, 1801, agreed to the eight-year term and accepted "retrenchment" of the second article, provided the parties re-

[81] He got 65 electoral votes to Jefferson's 73 as compared with 71 to 68 in 1796. The Republicans won the Presidency, not by any certain popular majority, but because they manipulated more astutely the method of choosing electors in Virginia and Pennsylvania, and had the advantage of Aaron Burr's skillful ward-heeling in New York City in the election of the New York legislature in May 1800 – a change of 250 votes in New York City would have made Adams President by 71 to 61 (for Jefferson) in the Federal election of November. It was in the House of Representatives, and indirectly in the Senate, that the real magnitude of the Federalist collapse appeared, as contrasted with Adams's loss of the election by only 5 electoral votes. The expiring House of Representatives had 73 Federalists, 33 Republicans. The new House had 68 Republicans, 38 Federalists; the Senate, overwhelmingly Federalist before the election, was Republican by a bare majority after the sweep of 1800. See Dauer, op. cit.; C. A. Beard: *Economic Origins of Jeffersonian Democracy* (New York, 1915); Edward Channing: *History of the United States*, IV, 233–7; Morison: *H. G. Otis*, I, 177–88. For composition of the new Senate, see Henry Adams: *Life of Albert Gallatin* (Philadelphia, 1879), p. 260.

[82] "So long as the power was held by the Federalists, their principles were better calculated to promote the national prosperity than those of their opponents. But if they had adopted for a maxim that a foreign war must be fostered *for the sake* of maintaining an army and increasing the public debt, it was time that they should be removed from the management of affairs." JQA to JA, Berlin, March 24, 1801. JQA Papers, LC.

[83] "Of any good which will result from this refusal of compromise [the French treaty] I have no hope. Of great evils that may arise from it there is strong ground for apprehension." Ibid.

[84] "Article II. The Ministers Plenipotentiary of the two Parties, not being able to agree at present, respecting the Treaty of Alliance of 6th February 1778, the Treaty of Amity and Commerce of the same date, and the Convention of 14th November 1788, nor upon the indemnities mutually due, or claimed, the Parties will negotiate further on these subjects at a convenient time, and untill they may have agreed upon these points, the said Treaties, and Convention shall have no operation, and the relations of the two Countries shall be regulated as follows." Then follow the other articles of the treaty.

nounced their pretensions under it. President Jefferson thought it necessary to resubmit the convention to the Senate, which declared it to be "fully ratified," December 19, 1801, by a vote of 22 yeas, 4 nays.[85] Thus the United States and France canceled the obligations of their respective nations and their nationals against each other. So ended the historic Franco-American pact, that life-saving alliance which had so deeply entangled the United States in the "vortex" of European diplomacy.

The United States, whether under the Administration of President John Adams or his successor, Thomas Jefferson, refused to have any more to do with the Armed Neutrality of 1800 signed (December 16–18) by Russia, Prussia, Sweden, and Denmark-Norway. The famous league collapsed when the British Navy blasted Denmark out of it and young Alexander I, ascending the throne of Russia upon the assassination of his father Paul, deserted the combination.

Collapse of the Armed Neutrality of 1800 ended Bonaparte's fond hope of any immediate victory over England. The colossus of the land realized that on the ocean he was helpless against the leviathan of the seas. He decided to make a compromise peace that would open the oceans again and allow him to build up a colonial empire in the Mississippi Valley while he consolidated and expanded his power on the Continent of Europe. Preliminaries with Great Britain were signed at London, October 1, 1801, one year and a day after the Convention of Morfontaine with the United States and the secret Treaty of San Ildefonso with Spain for the retrocession of Louisiana. The definitive Treaty of Amiens followed, March 27, 1802.

The Corsican's next coup was to make himself sole chief of the French state. This was easy, under a new constitution of his own dictation. A *senatus consultum* of August 1, 1802 declared Napoleon Bonaparte to be First Consul of France for life and decreed the erection of a statue of peace, with the successful general holding in one hand the laurel of victory and in the other hand the senatorial decree. The Government of France had ended up in a single person, as John Quincy Adams had predicted. Napoleon was now but a step from the imperial diadem. On May 18, 1804 an obedient Senate proclaimed him Emperor of the French.

8

During the stirring scenes that brought Napoleon Bonaparte to the top in France and Thomas Jefferson to the Presidency in America, John Quincy Adams had pursued his leisurely duties in Berlin. He and Mrs. Adams played their modest role in the continual rounds of court functions and ceremonies and the social activities of the diplomatic corps. If official life was sometimes wearisome and uninspiring, the Minister seems to have performed his part dutifully. His official and personal correspond-

[85] *Senate Executive Journal,* I, 365–98.

ence from The Hague and from Berlin reveals no personal friction, altercation, or quarrels, such as hasty commentators have been too prone to attribute to him. If Adams was not a gay and lively court figure, he was a pleasant and correct diplomat, socially as well as officially. He certainly had no trouble with anybody, either at The Hague or at Berlin, nothing resembling the mild contretemps in London, when he had fancied that the British Foreign Office was trying to construe him into being a Minister to the Court of St. James's.

Official life in Berlin did not break up his usual discipline of reading or interfere with his severe habit of study. In his home at the corner of Friedrichstrasse and Behrenstrasse[86] he applied himself to German assiduously several hours a day. To perfect himself in that language he made a poetic translation of Wieland's popular romance *Oberon,* a labor that slumbered unpublished until 1940.[87] He also translated into English Gentz's *Origin and Principles of the American Revolution Compared with the Origin and Principles of the French Revolution,* a seventy-three-page pamphlet published anonymously "by an American Gentleman" in Philadelphia in 1800. He thus acquired a reading knowledge of German and an enduring fondness for German literature. After a great struggle he made himself tolerably proficient in the spoken tongue. He was the first American to help overcome the prejudices of the English- and French-speaking world against the German language and literature.[88]

Adams still longed to indulge in more literary expression. It was at this period that he made a contributing connection with the *Portfolio,* one of the early periodical vehicles of American letters. He even aspired to be a poet, but never became more than a habitual rhymster.[89] The most ardent of John Quincy Adams's admirers, after reading his prose and verse, may be well content that he never deserted politics for belles-lettres. He did not have the original mind necessary for a career in creative letters. His mental processes were too extractive, analytical, reflective. He would have made an admirable historian. Exposition and argumentation were his forte. His own artificial verses describe, they do not feel. "I know well enough that the Star at my birth did not make me

[86] The Adamses at first had lodgings at Captain Stanckar's house at the Brandenburg Gate. They moved to the house on the Friedrichstrasse, May 1798. Diary, February 20, March 27, May 1, 1798.

[87] A. B. Faust published it, with a learned introduction, and annotation, together with excerpts, hitherto unprinted, from Adams's Diary, describing the progress of his German studies: *Oberon, a Poetical Romance in Twelve Books. Translated from the German of Wieland (1799–1801),* by John Quincy Adams (New York, 1940).

[88] "The flimsy prejudices of the French and English nations against the German language have long blinded them to its excellencies of literature, and even at this day the English men of letters whom I meet in this country in general dispute the merits of German literature, as the continental connoisseurs even to this day scruple to acknowledge an English school of painting." JQA to William Vans Murray, Berlin, November 22, 1799. Adams MSS.

[89] JQA to William Vans Murray, Berlin, November 12, 1799. Adams MSS.

a poet," he confessed in later life.[90] His real emotions he buried in his Diary, never expecting it to be printed.

As soon as the Prussian treaty was signed, Adams and his wife began to travel about Germany. The welcome vacation from office toil greatly benefited both of them. It included a trip out of Brandenburg into Saxony and Bohemia in 1799, during which they enjoyed together the galleries of Dresden and increased their acquaintances among German officialdom.[91] In 1800 they made a trip through Silesia. He recorded his travels and impressions in a series of letters to his brother Thomas in Boston. His own observations in these letters were rather superficial, the more valuable matter having been taken from German tourists and other writers on the province. But Thomas Adams released them for publication in the *Portfolio* in 1801, without John Quincy's express permission. He nevertheless republished the letters in 1804, and French and German editions followed in 1805 and 1807.

Now that Louisa's health had improved following the birth of their first son, John Quincy Adams grew more and more content with a position that afforded him an agreeable living and gave him leisure for literary activities. The diplomatic service had got him in its easy grip. He shrank from returning to the weary labors of the bar. He no longer asked to be recalled,[92] though he expected to be ordered home if a new administration came into power in 1801.

Perhaps Jefferson would have kept in the service the experienced and competent Minister Plenipotentiary, once a wide-eyed boy during their long walks and talks in Paris. But John Adams never gave his successor a chance to do so. Straightway after Jefferson's election he ordered his son back home.[93]

The vicissitudes of American politics, always fearsome to the Adamses, had brought to an untimely end, so it seemed, the unique and promising career of a man who George Washington had said would soon become America's ablest diplomatist. Reluctantly John Quincy Adams came home to begin all over again the dry and drudging practice of the law.

[90] JQA to William Montgomery, Washington, December 27, 1827. JQA to Robert Walsh, Jr., Washington, February 10, 1829. Adams MSS.

A selection of John Quincy Adams's verses was published posthumously: *Poems of Religion and Society, by John Quincy Adams, with Notices of his Life and Character*, by John Davis and T. H. Benton (New York, 1850; Auburn and Buffalo, N.Y., 1854).

[91] A series of letters to his friend William Vans Murray, United States Minister at The Hague, describes this trip in great detail.

[92] JQA to AA, Berlin, July 11, 1800. Adams MSS. See also JQA to JA, June 19, 1800, ibid., and JQA to AA, Berlin, April 14, 1801. *Writings*, II, 529.

[93] "The objects of your mission to Berlin having been entirely accomplished," wrote Secretary of State John Marshall to JQA on February 3, 1801, "the President is of opinion that you may be permitted to return to the United States." DS, *Credentials*, I, 112. Adams received the recall, May 4, 1801.

CHAPTER VI
The Young Senator and the Louisiana Purchase (1801–1806)

I would fain be the man of my whole country.

DIARY OF JOHN QUINCY ADAMS, JANUARY 28, 1802

IT was to a fortunate homeland that John Quincy Adams returned after the election of President Thomas Jefferson. The appearance of the country had greatly improved since he left it in 1794. Everywhere he found the marks of peace. How greatly it contrasted with the European countries depressed by years of revolutionary upheavals and wars! The standard of living had steadily improved for the average man. Luxurious new mansions, or "palaces," had sprung up for the more wealthy.[1] The general well-being was testimony to the success of the foreign policy of George Washington and John Adams, which Thomas Jefferson took over and continued in all essentials: "peace, commerce, and honest friendship with all nations, entangling alliances with none."

1

In prosperous America, John Quincy Adams started in to repair his own fortune. He had lived within his salary while abroad.[2] He had saved carefully. His "Waste Book and Journal,"[3] begun on January 1, 1802, lists his total property at $43,702.54. It included two houses in Boston valued at $6,000 and $5,000, and $11,100 in eight-per-cent U.S. stock (purchased at 110), and his treasured library, valued at $5,000. Where he had been able personally to manage his investments, he had prospered. Where his sojourn abroad had induced him to entrust his business affairs to friends or relatives at home, he had suffered heavily. There was at least $9,000 in uncollectable debts. Some of his savings he had placed in the hands of his old friend Dr. Thomas Welch to be invested in Boston

[1] October 13, 1801. *Writings,* III, 1.

[2] ". . . I can and will continue fully within my means." JQA to AA, No. 31, London, October 7, 1797. Adams MSS.

[3] Adams MSS.

real estate.[4] This small sum melted away under the good doctor's mismanagement and incompetence. A larger amount, between six and ten thousand dollars, he had sent to his brother Charles to be invested. Charles's poor judgment contributed to the loss of most [5] of the money in speculative enterprises undertaken before his early death on November 30, 1800.

Adams still had funds enough to set up a law office in State Street under the *Centinel* printing shop. He was able to buy and furnish a home at 39 Hanover Street, Boston, and to support himself and family, now including two sons, until his law practice should begin to yield a living. He got a little business at the outset by serving as a commissioner of bankruptcies, a temporary appointment that lay within the authority of the Federal judge of that district, John Davis. But he soon lost that petty office and its fees. The Republican Congress amended the law and provided for permanent appointment of commissioners by the President. Jefferson unwittingly overlooked the boy friend and admirer of his Paris days. This oversight sorely strained the personal regard that Abigail Adams had retained for the Virginian statesman amidst the buffetings of opposing politics. She could never quite believe it had not been an act of personal political reprisal.[6] Her son seems to have taken the matter more philosophically.

The retired diplomat bent his body over the grindstone of the law, but the political urge kept stirring in his breast.

"Walked in the mall just before night," he wrote in his Diary on January 28, 1802. "I feel strong temptation and have great provocation to plunge into political controversy. But I hope to preserve myself from it by the considerations which have led me to the resolution of renouncing. A politician in this country must be the man of a party. I would fain be the man of my whole country."

That is how he had looked on his father, the President, during the French crisis: "not as the man of a party, but as the man of the whole nation."

Already the younger Adams had more of an entrée into politics than he realized. His diplomatic success abroad and his brilliant letters about the Jacobin dangers in France — and in America — had long since made him an ornament to Massachusetts Federalism, an "excellent young man." [7]

[4] AA to Mrs. Mary Cranch, Philadelphia, June 1, 1798. *New Letters of Abigail Adams*, p. 183. JQA to AA, October 8, 1798, March 16, 1799; and AA to JQA, January 29, 1801. Adams MSS.

[5] Two thousand dollars, lent by Charles Adams to Justus B. Smith, brother of Col. William S. Smith, husband of John Quincy Adams's deceased sister Abigail, was recovered, with interest, from the estate of the latter in 1820.

[6] For the exchange of letters in 1804, see *Letters of Mrs. Adams*, pp. 389–99; and *Writings of Jefferson*, Memorial Edition, XI, 28, 42, 49.

[7] Henry Van Schaak to Theodore Sedgwick, Pittsfield, June 9, 1797. Theodore Sedgwick Collection, C. 95. MHS.

It was natural that his fellow townsmen should think of him for public service at home.

Their first trust was to elect him to the State Senate in April 1802 "on the Federal list." It was the novitiate of his legislative labors. He was not able to effect much good or prevent much evil. He attempted some reforms and aspired to check some abuses, but with little success.[8] For example, he tried unsuccessfully to secure proportionate representation for the Republican minority among the members that the Senate elected to the Governor's Council; and he opposed chartering a new bank in Boston because the stock was not open to general subscription but only to "every gentleman of respectable character" according to a list drawn up by his Federalist friends. He lacked experience. He was too eager to challenge and charge single-handed without working up alliances and support beforehand. He soon got to be known as "unmanageable."[9]

Nevertheless the solid men of Massachusetts called on him during the year 1802 for two public addresses, which he considered no inconsiderable incidents in his budding political career. One was to the Massachusetts Charitable Fire Society. It was nothing startling. In elegant periods replete with classical allusions he advised the people of Boston to build their houses of brick and stone instead of wood. The other was a Plymouth Rock oration. It was more thoughtful. He extolled the heroic virtues of the Pilgrim Fathers and argued for their right, and that of all Europeans, to form settlements in the American wilderness and establish sovereignty over the aborigines. Little did he then imagine that later the thesis of his patriotic speech of 1802 would be of service to him in the negotiations for peace at Ghent in 1814. Nor could he then foresee that one day he would turn around and challenge the right of any European power to occupy more territory or to make further colonial establishments on the Continent of North America.

Adams was Federalist candidate for election to the House of Representatives from the Boston district in November 1802. He lost, 1,840 votes to 1,899 for his opponent, Dr. Eustis.[10] His defeat was a fortunate one because of another opportunity that Fate was holding for him just around the corner. The term of United States Senator Jonathan Mason was due to expire on March 4, 1803, and the incumbent declined to be a candidate for re-election. Opposition within the Federalist Party to Timothy Pickering, ex-Secretary of State, whom John Adams had dismissed from that office a year previously, greatly improved John Quincy Adams's prospects. Despite Adams's independent outlook and his opposition to

[8] *Writings*, III, 10.

[9] Fisher Ames to Christopher Gore, February 24, 1803. *Writings*, III, 11, n. 3.

[10] "I had a majority of votes in Boston; but two or three neighboring towns [Charlestown, Medford, Hingham, Malden] annexed to the Congressional district and a rainy day lost me the election by forty or fifty votes." *Writings*, III, 10; *Memoirs*, I, 256.

the bank, the party caucus agreed that if Pickering should not be elected to the long term on two trials, then the members would vote for Adams on the third test. This happened, actually on the fourth ballot. Thus at the age of thirty-five he became United States Senator from Massachusetts.

A second vacancy unexpectedly appeared, because of the resignation of Senator Dwight Foster. Then the General Court elected Pickering, fifty-eight years old, for the shorter term. So it was that the two wings of the Federalist Party in Massachusetts, represented by the Adamses on the one hand and by the Essex Junto on the other, balanced each other uncomfortably in the United States Senate. John Quincy Adams, previously sounded, let it be known that he harbored no feeling against Pickering because of the latter's dissidence from former President John Adams. But almost from the first a chasm opened between the younger, senior Senator, and the older, junior Senator from Massachusetts, men so different in temperament, in judgment, and in national outlook and patriotism.

Another financial reverse now beset the Adamses, father and son. A few weeks after his election John Quincy Adams learned of the failure of the London banking house of Bird, Savage & Bird. They were the bankers of the United States Treasury in the British capital. Through them the Adams family had been accustomed to transfer their personal funds from Europe to America. John Adams had just turned over to his son the business of collecting some matured United States bonds underwritten by Dutch bankers, securities that he had purchased as a patriotic example when personally negotiating the war loans during the American Revolution. Bird, Savage & Bird had the collected funds when John Quincy Adams drew on them for his father's affairs only to have the drafts come back in his own name protested, with charges. At the same time the son also had a smaller amount of money on deposit with the Birds, $1,333.33, and had been drawing on it to furnish his office and new house. His Federalist friends Rufus King, Christopher Gore,[11] and Samuel Williams,[12] then in London, came unrequested to his aid. They got the drafts safely covered for a total of £2,872.

To remit that amount immediately to London, John Quincy Adams borrowed against his own credit from Benjamin Pickman of Salem. To satisfy this new debt he sold his Boston real estate, including the recently purchased Hanover Street house. Thanks to the co-operation of his father, whose funds were those principally involved, John Quincy came out at the end of the year, at least so he felt, with very little net change in the value of his own estate. He was much grieved to have been involved in

[11] One of the American Commissioners on the mixed claims commission then sitting in London under Article VII of Jay's Treaty.

[12] United States Consul and agent for the prosecution of claims and appeals. Jefferson removed him in 1802.

an agency that should have lessened the comfort of his father and mother in their old age. Eventually the London bankers paid off in full. The last payment came shortly after the death of John Adams, twenty-three years later.[13]

This financial upset, and his aversion to the law, made the United States senatorship all the more acceptable. His law practice was still too light to support a family. Waiting for the Senate to convene in the autumn, he had plenty of time to read: Shakespeare, Rousseau, Luzac, Robertson's *History of America* (the only one there was!), Plautus, Juvenal.

Adams entered the Senate as an independent and refractory Federalist — that is to say, an Adams Federalist. As a Federalist, even as an Adams Federalist, he could have no career in national politics and leadership. The Federalist Party as a national organization was a dead carcass. He knew it before he went to Washington.[14] He did not want to be a party man, he did not want to be a Federalist, but he had to have a party to put him into national politics, and the Federalist Party had done that. He tried to be loyal to it. At the very beginning of his senatorial career a vital issue appeared to test his party fealty and his political courage. It was Louisiana, key to the larger mystery of French policy that had so puzzled American diplomatists in Europe.

2

President John Adams had brought about peace with France. For his successor, Thomas Jefferson, it was a peace of hope and promise. For Napoleon Bonaparte it was a peace of beguilement. He had made a treaty to content American public opinion while secretly he acquired Louisiana from Spain and prepared the way for a colonial empire in the Mississippi Valley. On October 1, 1800, the day after the signature of the Convention of Morfontaine with the United States, Napoleon's plenipotentiary in Spain had signed the secret Treaty of San Ildefonso, providing for the retrocession of Louisiana to France.

Promptly following the preliminaries of peace with England the First Consul, with the tacit consent of the British Government, had set in motion his plans for the occupation of Louisiana with an army of veteran troops for whom some military employment must be provided. One ex-

[13] *Writings,* III, 13, n. 1; *Memoirs,* I, 263. Diary, October 1, 7, December 21, 1801. JQA to Benjamin Pickman, April 25, September 5, 1803. Adams MSS.

[14] "Whatever the merits or demerits of the former administrations may have been, there never was a system of measures more completely and irrevocably abandoned and rejected by the popular voice. It never can and never will be revived. The experiment, such as it was, has failed, and to attempt its restoration would be as absurd as to undertake the resurrection of a carcase seven years in its grave." JQA to Rufus King, Boston, October 8, 1802. *Writings,* III, 9.

peditionary force of 20,000, under his brother-in-law, General Leclerc, sailed to Hispaniola in November 1801. After quelling the Negro revolt of Toussaint L'Ouverture in Santo Domingo the troops were destined to go to New Orleans. From the army that had been assembled in Holland for the invasion of England, Bonaparte set aside another force of 2,400 men to embark from Hellevoetsluis in the autumn of 1802 for the mouth of the Mississippi. Meanwhile the King of Spain caused to be suspended at New Orleans (October 6, 1802) the right of deposit [15] that Pinckney's Treaty had guaranteed to citizens of the United States navigating the Mississippi River.

This measure suited perfectly the purposes of Talleyrand and his Corsican master. "The difficulty of maintaining it [suspension of the American right of deposit]," wrote the ex-Bishop of Autun, "will be much less for us than establishing it." Assiduous scholars have not been able to find extant a scrap of documentary evidence to prove [16] collusion between France and Spain. Perhaps no evidence is necessary. As the late Frederick Jackson Turner has pointed out, the whole tenor of French diplomacy from 1792 to 1803 revealed Bonaparte's stratagem to intrigue with the citizens of the American West, to use control of navigation to influence them, to make of the Indians a barrier to American western expansion, and gradually to widen the borders of his province until the Gulf of Mexico should become a French lake, and perhaps the Alleghenies the boundary of the United States.[17] The men of the Western waters needed no documentary proof of these designs.

Up the Mississippi flew like wildfire the news that Spain had suspended the right of deposit. It alarmed the Western citizens on the eve of French entry into Louisiana. It furnished political ammunition for Federalists seeking to undermine the confidence of the agrarian West in President Jefferson. They brought forth resolutions in Congress for the immediate occupation of New Orleans. They did not want Louisiana — on the contrary — but they did want to stir up the West against Jefferson in the next election, that of 1804. Undismayed, Jefferson was quietly waiting for a war in Europe so that he could exploit the distresses of that Continent to the advantage of the United States in the Mississippi Valley. "I did not expect that he [Bonaparte] would yield till a war took place between France and England," he explained later. "My hope was to palliate and endure, if Messrs. Ross, Morris [spokesmen in the Senate of the Federalist opposition], etc. did not force a premature rupture, until the event [i.e. of a new European war]. I believed the event was not very distant, but acknowledge it came on sooner than I had expected." [18] The

[15] See above, p. 48.

[16] Spain restored the right of deposit, after American protest and claim for damages, before turning over the province to France.

[17] *AHR,* X (No. 2, January 1905), 277.

[18] Henry Adams: *History of the United States,* I, 435.

Federalists forced the President's hand. With this issue they threatened to revive as a power again to be reckoned with in American politics.

The step that Jefferson took to save the West, and with it Western voters for the Republican Party, was another special mission to France like those which Washington and Adams had nominated to London, Madrid, and Paris in times of great foreign crises. The President's French friend Pierre S. duPont de Nemours, had just sent word from Paris that Napoleon, faced with war in Europe, might sell New Orleans and the Floridas to the United States. Du Pont even enclosed a treaty project, sale price $6,000,000, for Jefferson to present to the French ruler. Jefferson dispatched James Monroe again to France as Minister Plenipotentiary and Envoy Extraordinary to assist the regular Minister, Robert R Livingston, in renewed efforts to persuade Bonaparte to sell New Orleans, or the Floridas, or both, to the United States.

In his vast and shifting combinations Bonaparte had turned to Louisiana only when Nelson and the British Navy had blocked him in Egypt and Syria. By 1803 his plans had broken down in America too. The army that he had sent to Santo Domingo, and further reinforcements, wasted away from warfare and yellow fever so that it could not go on to Louisiana. Its commander, General Leclerc, perished from the disease. In Europe the coldest winter in decades froze the transports tight in the harbor of Hellevoetsluis, delaying the departure of another expeditionary force for New Orleans. Quickly the First Consul turned his plans of colonial empire back to the Mediterranean. To compensate for the failure of his American project he resolved on war again in Europe as a prelude to a conquest of the East. The new war would place French eagles at the gates of India. Meanwhile an invasion of England would bring that foe to her knees and open the oceans to France. Empire overseas, in North America, everywhere, could come later.

During the Peace of Amiens, Bonaparte's diplomatic interventions in Italy and Switzerland had built up a causeway of conquest from Italy across the Strait of Otranto into the Ottoman Empire. Confronted by this upset of the balance of power, Great Britain refused to evacuate Malta, as required by the peace treaty.

"I must have Malta or war," the First Consul said to the British Ambassador at a court reception in the presence of the diplomatic corps. To provoke Great Britain to war he openly threatened an attack on Egypt.[19]

Bonaparte expected Great Britain to capture Louisiana immediately. Therefore it would be better to let the United States buy the province and keep it until England was finally defeated and prostrate and America helpless before the conqueror of the Old World. So he sold New Orleans and the whole vast unexplored territory of Louisiana, lock, stock, and barrel, to the United States, through its plenipotentiaries Livingston and

[19] E. Wilson Lyon has analyzed Napoleon's plans and motives in regard to *Louisiana in French Diplomacy, 1759–1804* (Norman, Okla., 1934).

Monroe. Monroe reached Paris barely in time to take part in the big deal just before the papers passed. The price was 60,000,000 francs payable on easy terms: in six per-cent United States Government bonds, to be redeemed $3,000,000 a year beginning in 1818. The First Consul sold the bonds — to London bankers — to get cash to prepare his army for the invasion of England! The United States also assumed the payment of claims of its citizens against France, up to 20,000,000 francs. It was the best buy of choice real estate that history can show.

Again Europe's distresses were the advantage, this time the salvation, the great boon in amplitude, of the United States. A diplomatic miracle had suddenly unblocked the West and doubled the territory of the United States overnight.

3

The vast territorial acquisition of the Louisiana Purchase would present to John Quincy Adams the continental fencing-field for his own finest achievements. Therefore everything that he said or thought or did about Louisiana is of interest.

As a diplomat in Europe, Adams had reported dutifully from The Hague and Berlin such rumors as he picked up about the retrocession of Louisiana to France. At first they had not been too alarming, for France could scarcely take delivery of the province as long as her enemy Britain controlled the Atlantic. But the rumors persisted, particularly after signature of the Franco-American Treaty of Morfontaine and during the ensuing Anglo-French peace discussions. They disturbed the satisfaction that the Adamses derived from the peace settlement with France. What if John Adams and his son proved to be the dupes of the clever Corsican? What if, after all, the treaty with France, in which they took such pride, should prove to be only a prelude to a French military occupation of the Mississippi Valley, to cooping up the United States behind the Allegheny Mountains?

The younger Adams's first reaction to the danger, while he was still in Europe, was typically Federalist-minded. The Virginia and Kentucky resolutions of 1798 and 1799, looking toward nullification; the gestures of Virginia for self-defense; the over-representation of the slave-holding states in the House of Representatives due to the notorious three-fifths ratio of the Constitution — all these political developments at home had disheartened him. Then came the not unexpected news of the Republican triumph of 1800, which he regarded as a sectional victory of the South and West. To him as a New Englander it was almost the last blow. What did it matter, after all these calamities, if Bonaparte did cross the Atlantic! "Let them take Louisiana!" he wrote in discouragement from Berlin to his friend William Vans Murray.[20]

Such a lament was almost as close to the Essexmen as Quincy was tc

[20] April 7, 1801. *Writings,* II, 525–6.

Boston. But the difference between Adams and the Essex Junto was that he was determined to support the Constitution and the Union, while the Essexmen under Pickering's leadership looked to separation of New England from the Union as the answer to Jefferson's election and the Louisiana Purchase.

After a first moment of despair Adams took some sober second thoughts. Quickly his national instinct righted his imagination. "We must be upon our guard," he wrote from Hamburg to his father in Quincy. France might want Louisiana *"in order to obtain a powerful influence over the United States."* [21] Henceforth there was no wavering. John Quincy Adams was a nationalist first and foremost. He could not reject Louisiana. He became a continentalist.

A series of unavoidable delays prevented the new Senator's arrival at Washington in time to vote on the Louisiana treaties in the special session of Congress that President Jefferson called for October 17, 1803. As he and his wife were driving into the "City" of Washington in the twilight of October 20, at the end of a trying three weeks' trip from Boston, they met the carriage of their old Massachusetts friend Samuel Otis, Secretary of the Senate, returning from the President's House. That official had just delivered the resolution of advice and consent of the Senate to the ratification of the Louisiana treaties, voted 24 to 7.[22] All the Federalist Senators present had voted against them: Hillhouse and Tracy (Connecticut), Olcutt and Plumer (New Hampshire), Pickering (Massachusetts), and Wells and White (Delaware).

John Quincy Adams believed with John Adams [23] and Thomas Jefferson, as well as with the High Federalists Rufus King and Alexander Hamilton, in the annexation of Louisiana, if only as a means of keeping Napoleon Bonaparte out of that region for the peace and safety of the United States. He was further convinced that the loss of power and influence of his section would be more than compensated by the extension of national power and security. At least so he recalled a quarter of a century later [24] after he had done so much to confirm American sovereignty

[21] *Writings*, II, 531.

[22] Diary. There were three treaties relating to the procurement of Louisiana: the treaty of cession, actually signed on May 2, 1803; the convention assuming the claims of American citizens against France, signed actually on May 8 or 9, 1803; and the convention fixing the manner in which the United States would pay for Louisiana, signed sometime before May 13. All were then antedated to April 30, 1803, presumably in the apprehension that England might already have declared war before the treaties had been signed and might consider Louisiana really enemy property and subject to capture.

[23] "I do not disapprove of your conduct in the business of Louisiana. I think you have been right, though I know it will become a very unpopular subject in the Northern States. . . ." JA to JQA, February 25, 1804. *Writings*, III, 30, n. 1.

[24] Henry Adams: *Documents Relating to New England Federalism, 1800–1815* (Boston, 1905), p. 148 – hereinafter cited as *N.E. Federalism*. This is his memory twenty-five years later. The entry in the *Memoirs* for April 8 and 10, 1804, notes

to the Pacific Coast. He was the only Federalist member from New England in either house of Congress to support the acquisition of Louisiana.[25] He voted for the House bill creating the necessary bonds for the Purchase and providing for the payment of the spoliation claims of American citizens assumed by the United States as part of the Louisiana bargain. But he joined his Federalist colleagues in voting against all the other Louisiana legislation at that session: against the bill enabling the President to take possession and to provide temporary government under officials of his sole appointment; against the bill creating the District of Louisiana and the Territory of Orleans, and extending enumerated laws of the United States over them, including tax laws; and against the famous Mobile Act, enabling the President to take over West Florida as a part of the Louisiana Purchase if and when he should see fit.

These laws, declared Adams, violated the third article of the treaty of cession [26] and breached the Constitution of the United States as well. They were opposed to the principles of American independence: to no taxation without representation, to the right of self-determination. They were also oppressive to the natural rights of the people of Louisiana.[27] As a remedy Adams proposed a constitutional amendment giving to the Congress the power to incorporate within the Union the inhabitants of all territories previously not within the limits of the United States, to make them citizens, and to make laws for their governance.[28] Then the

"long conversations" with King, and Wolcott, on "public affairs," without recording details. His letters of "Publius Valerius" of 1804 defended the acquisition of Louisiana. See below, p. 131.

[25] JQA to CFA, Meridian Hill, Washington, April 30, 1829. See also *Letter of the Hon. John Quincy Adams in Reply to a Letter of the Hon. Alexander Smyth to His Constituents* (Washington, 1823). Adams published this document again during the presidential campaign of 1828, with the addition of his speech in the Senate on November 3, 1803, in support of the payment, and a letter from Jefferson to William Dunbar on the unconstitutionality of the Louisiana Purchase.

[26] "Article III. The inhabitants of the ceded territory shall be incorporated in the Union of the United States and admitted as soon as possible according to the principles of the federal Constitution, to the enjoyment of all the rights, advantages and immunities of citizens of the United States, and in the mean time they shall be maintained and protected in the free enjoyment of their liberty, property and the Religion which they profess."

[27] "Notes on a Speech of Motion." *Writings*, III, 26–8. Everett Somerville Brown printed "The Senate Debate on the Breckinridge Bill for the Government of Louisiana, 1804," from notes taken at the time by Senator William Plumer of New Hampshire. *AHR*, XXII (No. 2, January 1917), 340–64. See also *William Plumer's Memorandum of Proceedings in the United States Senate, 1803–1807,* E. S. Brown, ed. (New York, 1923), pp. 75–6, 103–4, 143–9. Plumer's journal is a valuable source for Adams's senatorial career because it covers almost precisely the years of his senatorship. Hereafter cited as *Plumer's Proceedings U.S. Senate.*

[28] "Congress shall have power, at such times and in such manner as they may deem expedient, to incorporate within the Union, the inhabitants of all such territories, heretofore not within the limits of the United States, as have been or may be ceded by

new land and its peoples could be received into the Union. Only two other Senators voted for it, his colleague Pickering of Massachusetts, and Hillhouse of Connecticut. Both were arch Federalists and obstructionists. They supported the amendment for reasons opposite to Adams's. They knew it would fail.

During the debate on the Louisiana territorial bill Adams brought forward three resolutions of protest based on the principle of no taxation without representation.[29] He got practically no support for them. The bill passed the Senate by a vote of 21 to 3, Adams in the minority, and became law February 24, 1804.

When John Quincy Adams as Secretary of State negotiated his famous Transcontinental Treaty with Spain procuring the territory of Florida for the United States, he must have remembered his constitutional scruples of 1804. He included an article (VI) promising incorporation of the inhabitants of the ceded territory within the Union "as soon as may be consistent with the principles of the Federal Constitution," with admission to all the privileges, rights, and immunities of citizens of the United States.[30]

In February 1806 he did oppose the notorious "Two Million Act," under which Jefferson made ready to traffic with Talleyrand for that West Florida which he so stoutly claimed to the public had been already purchased from France as a part of Louisiana. "West Florida I consider as our own," Adams told the Senate. "We have bought and paid for it." [31]

He was not opposed to southern and western expansion like the High Federalists. He thought that Jefferson's Florida diplomacy was too weak,

treaty, duly ratified, to the United States; and to extend to the said inhabitants all the rights, privileges and immunities which are enjoyed by native citizens of the United States under the Constitution. And Congress shall also have power to make all such laws for the government of such ceded territories, and of their inhabitants as may be necessary to fulfil with good faith the conditions of cession, and as may best conciliate the protection of the liberties, property and religion of the said inhabitants with the rights of the United States, of their citizens, and of the respective States, under the Constitution." *Writings,* III, 20.

[29] "*Resolved,* That the people of the United States have never, in any manner, delegated to this Senate, the power of giving its Legislative concurrence to any act for imposing taxes upon the inhabitants of Louisiana without their consent.

"*Resolved,* That, by concurring in any act of Legislation for imposing taxes upon the inhabitants of Louisiana without their consent, this Senate would assume a power unwarranted by the constitution and dangerous to the liberties of the people of the United States.

"*Resolved,* That the power of originating bills for raising revenue, being exclusively vested in the House of Representatives, these resolutions be carried to them by the Secretary of the Senate: that, whenever they think proper, they may adopt such measures as to their wisdom may appear necessary and expedient for raising and collecting a revenue from Louisiana." *Annals of Congress,* 8th Cong., 1st Sess., 1803–4, pp. 127–8, January 6, 1804.

[30] See below, Ch. XVI, Section 4.

[31] *Plumer's Proceedings U.S. Senate,* p. 413.

too furtive. It would limit further expansion west. "He [the President] is now prepared for a negotiation by which he may renounce all our claims upon the western boundary and pay several millions to get the Floridas." [32] In vain Adams moved that the bill be committed to a select committee with instructions to inquire whether West Florida was or was not included in the Louisiana cession.

Senator Adams also voted against another bill passed at the same time further to appease the French jobber. This was the act excluding American ships from commerce with the revolted French colony of Santo Domingo. He further opposed confirmation of the nomination of General Armstrong for the mission to France as "one of the most disgraceful acts of Mr. Jefferson's Administration." Certainly Adams's stand on the Florida question could not have ingratiated him with the President any more than his vote for the Louisiana appropriation had pleased the Federalists. He was getting more and more independent, more unmanageable.

In voting against the Louisiana territorial bill in 1804, Adams voted against a provision in it that prohibited the importation of slaves from abroad into the Territory of Orleans either directly or by way of a state that permitted such importation. "Slavery in a moral sense is an evil," he declared in the debates, "but as connected with commerce it has its uses. The regulations added to prevent slavery are insufficient. I shall therefore vote against them." [33]

During the progress of the bill he recorded himself against an amendment, carried by a vote of 21 to 7,[34] to prohibit the importation of any slave except by a citizen of the United States going to the territory for actual settlement.[35] "I am opposed to slavery," he explained, "but I have in this bill voted against the provisions introduced to prohibit and lessen it. I have done this upon two principles, 1. That I am opposed to legislating at all for that country. 2. I think we are proceeding with too much haste upon such an important question." [36]

In view of Adams's later opposition to the slave trade and to the expansion of slavery it is interesting to note that at this stage of his political career he took no opportunity to record himself unequivocally against either of these evils and to vote against them. His principal grievance voiced against slavery during his Senate years was the compromise article in the Federal Constitution which allowed five slaves to be counted as three whites in apportioning representation in the lower house of Con-

[32] *Memoirs,* I, 402, 405. *N.E. Federalism,* p. 175.

[33] "The Senate Debate on the Breckinridge Bill," loc. cit., p. 346.

[34] The minority opposition can scarcely be said to have constituted a sectional block: Adams of Massachusetts; Baldwin and Jackson of Georgia; Condit and Dayton of New Jersey; Samuel Smith of Maryland.

[35] *Annals of Congress,* 8th Cong., 2d Sess., 1804–5, pp. 239–46, 255. February 1, 17, 18, 1804.

[36] "The Senate Debate on the Breckinridge Bill," p. 346.

gress.[37] It should be noted, however, for the benefit of his later career, that he advocated the propriety and necessity of the Senate's receiving and at least hearing a Quaker petition for restraining the increase of slavery, as far as the Constitution would permit.[38]

The fact that Adams had approved the purchase of Louisiana, had attended a banquet of the Republican members of Congress to celebrate the acquisition of that territory,[39] had voted for the financial measures necessary to complete the Purchase, and wanted an amendment to let Louisiana and more and more territories into the Union pleased the Republicans and annoyed the Essex Junto. His disgruntled constituents saw in Louisiana a continental covey of future democratic states, the final doom of the Federalist Party, the end of rule by the "well-born," "the wise," and "the good." Senator Pickering complained about his colleague to the Essexmen. The Junto scowled and growled among themselves about the young Senator's "erratic" opinions and "independent" attitude, and his ambitions.

"Like a Kite without a Tail," declared Stephen Higginson, the big Boston banker, "he will be violent and constant in his attempts to rise . . . and will pitch on one side and the other, as the popular Currents may happen to strike, without soaring to his intended point. His views are ambitious, even to the Chair of State . . . he will beside be often misled by his visionary scheme of building up a third and independent party. . . ."[40]

"'Curse on the stripling, how he apes his sire,'" wrote silk-stockinged Theodore Lyman, Jr., he who was to be the first "historian" of American diplomacy,[41] to Timothy Pickering.[42]

Both these bigwig Federalists had opposed John Adams's treaty of amity with France. Both had been against the acquisition of Louisiana, like all Essexmen. At that very moment their leader, Pickering, was urging that the New England States secede from the Union and create a Northern Confederacy, if possible with New York, rather than be swallowed up by the Republican West and South in a greater United States.

"The Hon. John Quincy Adams will certainly be denounced and excommunicated by his party," hopefully declared the Republican Worces-

[37] "Every planter south of the Potomac has three votes in effect for every five slaves he keeps in bondage; while a New England farmer, who contributes ten-fold as much to the support of the Government, has only a single vote." "Publius Valerius" (JQA), in *Repertory,* November 8, 1804.

[38] *Plumer's Proceedings U.S. Senate,* p. 250.

[39] Ibid., p. 122.

[40] *Letters of Stephen Higginson,* J. F. Jameson, ed., *Annual Report* 1896 AHA, I, 839–40.

[41] Author of *The Diplomacy of the United States* (2 vols., Boston, 1828). It is a lazy man's ill-digested compilation of well-known printed state papers of the time.

[42] *Writings,* III, 30.

ter *Aegis* December 4, 1803. "On the leading questions in the Senate he has acted and voted with the friends of the Administration. On the Resolution for carrying into effect the Convention with France for the purchase of Louisiana [by appropriating the necessary moneys] he directed a concise, nervous, manly, energetic, and unequivocal eulogy on the measure." [43]

The Louisiana procurement, the Mobile Act, and Jefferson's attempted jobbery with Talleyrand for Florida produced a spectacular quarrel between the President and the Spanish Minister in Washington, the Marquis de Casa Yrujo. Before it came to the surface, Yrujo made the mistake of accepting Jefferson's fellowship at Monticello after he had just attempted to suborn a Federalist editor in Philadelphia to attack the President. Later realization that Jefferson knew of this underhand business when he was lavishing traditional Virginian hospitality upon the Spanish Minister caused the Marquis infinite mortification. At the climax of the quarrel Secretary Madison told Yrujo that his presence was no longer desired at Washington. Yrujo stood on his diplomatic immunities and refused to leave the capital: "I intend remaining in the city, four miles square, in which the Government resides, as long as it may suit the interests of the King my master or my own personal convenience." [44]

John Quincy Adams had nothing to do with this acrimonious affair. He could well have remained on the sidelines. But as a Senator and former diplomat his patriotic indignation flamed up at Yrujo's impertinence. Unasked, and characteristically without securing any support beforehand, he brought in a bill enabling the President to send out of the country any foreign minister who abused his diplomatic privilege by committing acts indictable for violation of municipal laws, or who entered into conspiracy against the Government of the United States, or who treated the President with disrespect. To prevent such ejectment from being considered as an act of war the bill contained a section requiring the President to make a statement of the reason for expulsion in any given case.

Adams's speech on the bill was an interesting and cogent analysis of its relation to the Constitution of the United States and to the law of nations. His proposal and his remarks were nevertheless a curious and thankless gesture.[45] The Secretary of State told him that he approved the bill in principle, and the President was reported also to be well pleased with it, but the Administration forces did not lift a finger to support it, despite their vexation with Yrujo. Actually the President had the power to expel if he chose to use it. No other senator spoke for Adams's supererogatory measure. His colleagues listened respectfully to his learned dis-

[43] For the speech (not in *Annals*) see T. H. Benton: *Abridgement of the Debates of Congress,* III, 18–19.

[44] Henry Adams: *History,* III, 187.

[45] See *Annals of Congress,* 9th Cong., 1st Sess., 1805–6, pp. 92–4, 146–62, 166, February 12–March 9, 1806. *Memoirs,* I, 408, 412.

course; then they voted down the bill, 24 to 4. Even Adams supposed the President might have the power anyway.

4

Soon John Quincy Adams became one of the busiest members of the Senate. Despite his feeble political power, he served on many special committees: for revising the articles of war; the Library of Congress (his favorite committee duty); appropriation of moneys to lay out roads from the Atlantic Ocean to the Ohio River; memorials of merchants on spoliations; New Orleans territorial legislation (1806); revision of Senate rules; petitions of Georgia land claimants; seamen's funds; impressed seamen; laws of the District of Columbia; suspension of the writ of habeas corpus, at the time of Burr's conspiracy; expulsion of Senator John Smith of Ohio, a participant in Burr's enterprises;[46] the "financeering bill" (1807); and many other committees big and little. Much of this labor was unrewarding, imposed on him because of his capacity and willingness for hard work; but one pleasing recognition of his public service was a Doctor of Laws degree from Princeton (then called New Jersey College) in September 1806.

Had there been a Senate committee of foreign relations at that time, Adams doubtless would have been a member. Immediately upon his first arrival in Washington, he was appointed to an *ad hoc* committee of three to report on an important treaty: the convention that Rufus King signed with Lord Hawkesbury in London, May 12, 1803, just after Livingston and Monroe had put their names to the Louisiana treaties in Paris. It provided for adjusting the northeast and northwest boundary gaps of the United States,[47] left open since the Treaty of Peace and Independence of 1783; the northeast gap to be closed by survey of a mixed commission, the northwest gap by an agreed line straight from the northwesternmost corner of the Lake of the Woods to the source of the Mississippi River (Article V of the convention).

John Quincy Adams, spokesman for the special committee on this treaty, in correspondence with the Secretary of State and in report to the Senate, opposed the boundary change in the Northwest. It would have let British territory come south to the waters of the Mississippi River. It would also have prejudiced the still unsettled northern boundaries of Louisiana. Such a boundary rectification, if ratified, would have set far to the south of the latitude of the Lake of the Woods the point of departure from which the northern boundary of Louisiana, still undetermined, might

[46] As chairman of this committee Adams brought in a report favoring expulsion, but the Senate failed by one vote to muster the necessary two-thirds majority. Smith later resigned under a weight of obloquy.

[47] "Jay's Treaty and the Northwest Boundary Gap," *AHR*, XXVII (No. 1, April 1922), 465–84.

some day be drawn due west. Had the Senate consented to this article of the convention, the United States very likely would have lost, in the subsequent boundary settlements with Great Britain, a strip of territory 152 miles wide all the way across to the Pacific Ocean through the present states of North Dakota, Montana, Idaho, and Washington, including Puget Sound. Perhaps it would not be too far-fetched, looking at the map from our historical vantage-point of today, to call this territory "the Adams Strip." [48]

Despite the disapproval of Secretary of State Madison,[49] the Senate amended the convention by cutting out the fifth article, thus leaving the northwest boundary gap still open. The British Government refused to accept the amendment. That killed the treaty.[50]

It is not too much to say that defeat of the King-Hawkesbury Convention was the most important service that John Quincy Adams rendered to his country as Senator from Massachusetts. It made it easy for him later, as Secretary of State, to fix the boundary along the line of 49° from the Lake of the Woods to the "Stony Mountains" in the Convention of 1818 with Great Britain. Already in 1803 Adams had set up a diplomatic springboard for a later leap of sovereign title over the Rocky Mountains along the proper parallel of latitude.

On domestic issues Senator Adams at first generally opposed the Administration. He voted against conviction of the judges whom the Republican House of Representatives impeached before the Senate in their unsuccessful attack upon the Federal judiciary. He also enthusiastically supported the constitutional amendment that his colleague Pickering introduced, under instructions from the Massachusetts legislature, to do away with the three-fifths ratio for the apportionment of membership in the Federal House of Representatives.

On the other hand, he voted against the much-needed Twelfth Amendment to the Constitution to reform procedure in the electoral college [51] — and for a peculiar technical reason. Adams insisted on retaining an original feature of the amendment as it came from the lower house, which would have provided, in the contingency of no majority for any candidate in the electoral college, for election of the President by the House of Representatives, voting by states, from the *five* highest runners-up for that office in the electoral college. He had some good historical and mathematical reasons for preferring five instead of three candidates. When the

[48] See Map 1.

[49] *Memoirs,* I, 273. The amendment passed, 22–9 (Adams, of course, voting in the affirmative); then the Senate advised and consented unanimously to the amended convention. *Senate Executive Journal,* I, 463.

[50] *ASPFR,* II, 584–91; *Annals of Congress,* 8th Cong., 1st Sess., 1803–4, pp. 76–228, November 15, 1803 to January 9, 1804; *Writings,* III, 19; *Memoirs,* I, 273–94.

[51] Requiring presidential electors to cast their ballots specifically for candidates for the Presidency and Vice-Presidency — so as to make impossible another election of the leader of the opposition as Vice President, as in Jefferson's case in 1796.

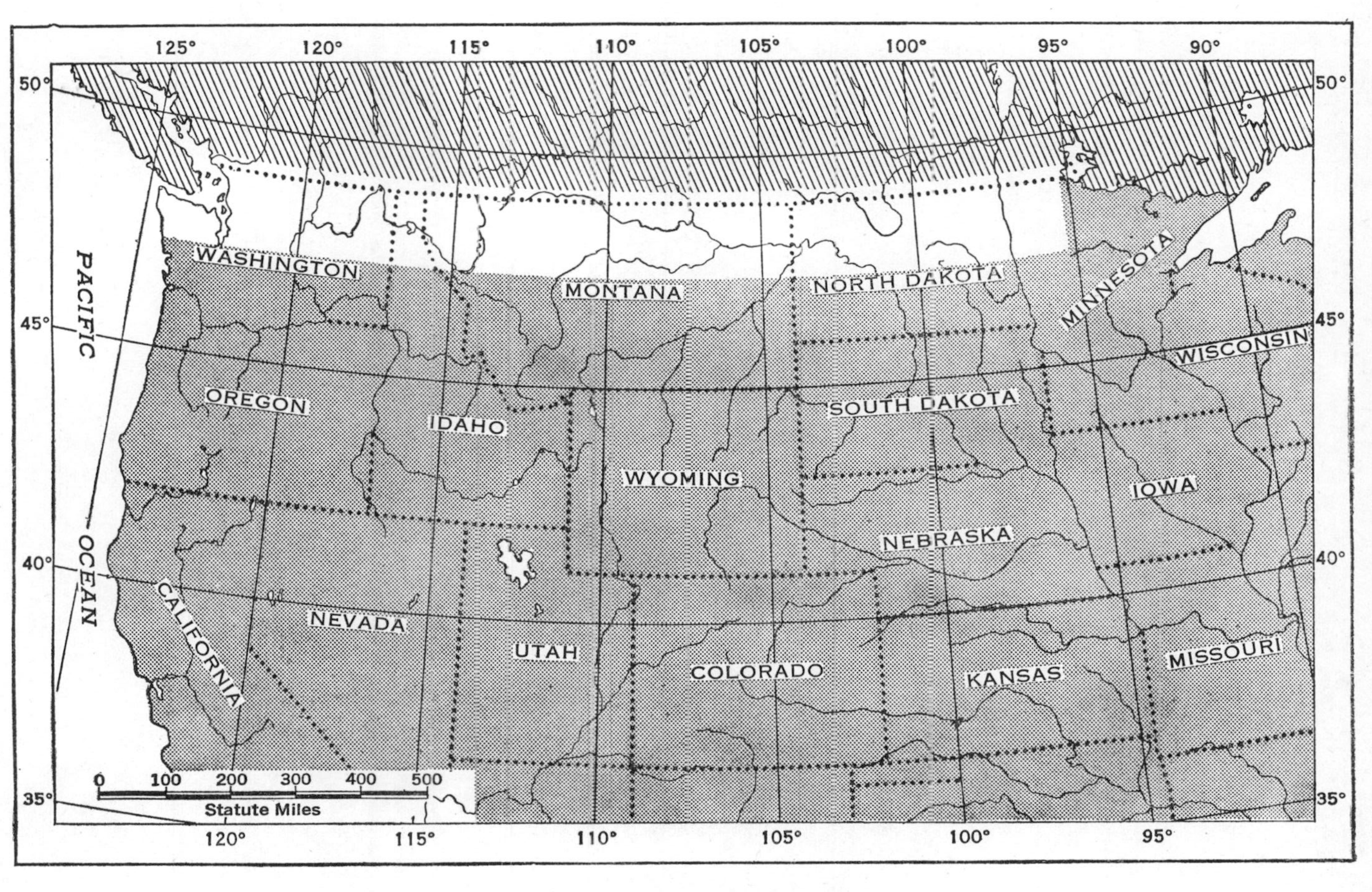

MAP 1 *The "Adams Strip"*

Senate amended the House bill to limit the number to three he would not vote for the amendment at all. If he had had his way in 1803 he might never have become President of the United States in 1825, for his chances in the election of that year would have been greatly diminished if four competitors instead of two had remained to oppose him before the House of Representatives.[52]

Another constitutional proposal he made in the Senate anticipated a feature of the Twentieth Amendment. It would have provided for designation by Congress of a person to act as President until the next election, in case of a deadlock in the House of Representatives.[53] Such a provision would have been comforting in the famous disputed election of 1876.

How important it is in politics, when proposing such a thing as a constitutional amendment, or even a constitutional innovation, or a bill, or a resolution, on anything important, to work up in advance some support for it, above all to give it an attractive name! If one can baptize something with a catching label, like the American System, the Era of Good Feeling, or the Good Neighbor Policy, one does not even have to be originator of the idea. Henry Clay, for example, was not the real father of the American System; neither of the American System in foreign relations – that was John Quincy Adams – nor of the American System in domestic politics – protective tariff, internal improvements, scientific disposal of public lands, all supplementing each other to bind the nation together in stable power, union, and prosperity – that was John Quincy Adams too.

Young Senator Adams, original sponsor of the American System, did not get any farther with his scheme for a Federal plan of internal improvements, proposed in the Senate in February 1807, than he had with his proposals for constitutional amendments.[54] The Senate voted down his resolution without a record vote and without trace of debate. Senator Henry Clay, present, made no move to support it. Yet it is Henry Clay, the eloquent champion in later decades, whose name is indissolubly associated with the American System.

52 Note by CFA in *Memoirs*, I, 275.

53 *Annals of Congress*, 8th Cong., 1st Sess., 1803–4, pp. 126–35, December 1, 1803.

54 "*Resolved*, That the Secretary of the Treasury be directed to prepare, and report to the Senate at their next session, a plan for the application of such means as are constitutionally within the power of Congress, to the purposes of opening roads, for removing obstructions in rivers and making canals; together with a statement of the undertakings of that nature now existing within the United States, which, as objects of public improvement, may require and deserve the aid of Government." *Annals of Congress*, 9th Cong., 2d Sess., 1806–7, p. 77. Worthington C. Ford has described Adams's consistent advocacy of a national system of internal improvements: "A Lost Opportunity – Internal Improvements," in *Indiana Historical Society Publications*, VI (No. 1, 1916), 55–81.

5

Life in the still shapeless and insalubrious "Federal City" on the banks of the Potomac presented a great contrast to the refinements of European capitals. How different it was even from other American communities, busy Boston, studious Cambridge, or quiet Quincy, or bustling New York and prosperous Philadelphia, all of which John Quincy Adams knew so well! The District of Columbia was still a vast area of vacant swamp and scrub land marked out with stakes and unpaved lanes and public circles full of weeds. The dispatches of European diplomats marooned in Washington in these early bucolic decades are full of the discomforts of heat, cold, mud, and insects, and the lack of all the refinements and conveniences of urban society. There was no hospital, there were few doctors, there was no museum, not even a picture gallery. It was a community of small unsightly government buildings, boarding-houses, and stables. The city boasted one crude theater, but the performances were poor. There was not yet a park or a fountain.

Adams's copious Diary and letters say nothing about these obvious shortcomings of the ugly place. He drew no contrasts to the disadvantage of the United States. He was quite content with Washington, capital of his youthful country, city of the future.

Senator and Mrs. John Quincy Adams boarded with the family of one of Louisa's sisters, Mrs. Walter Hellen, in a house about two and a half miles from the Capitol toward Georgetown. Usually he kept busy in the Senate till four o'clock in the afternoon. Then a walk home, or perhaps a ride in some friend's carriage, and dinner with the home folks before turning to public papers or writing letters or reports far into the evening. Occasionally he and Louisa would take a canter on horseback [55] in the empty spaces of the Federal City. He led a quiet home life in the urban wilderness. When work or outside engagements were not too pressing, he would play with the Hellen children in the early evening, read aloud to the ladies — Louisa and her sister — or peruse his beloved classics. Then a last habitual glance at the thermometer, a banking of his chamber fire, and to bed at eleven o'clock.

Whenever he could — in the summer recesses of Congress — he journeyed back to see the old folks in Quincy. He liked to visit the Braintree farmhouse where he was born, to wander, gun in hand, over the adjacent fields and marshes and back into the Blue Hills. In 1803 he bought from his father the original Penn's Hill farm, with the two old houses, and made a summer home there.

Abigail Adams kept a watchful eye upon her Senator son, even when he was in Washington. From Quincy by correspondence she nursed his colds and distempers with advice on diet and exercise. She commended to him

[55] Diary, November 27, 1804.

ABIGAIL ADAMS

PORTRAIT BY GILBERT STUART, BOSTON, 1804
OWNED BY MRS. ROBERT HOMANS

Lord Chatham's advice on social trifles and personal carriage.[56] Unbend in company, she urged. Lighten your brow with agreeable trifles. Don't get careless about your clothes.[57]

Even with his parents he was a stiff and reserved man. When he returned to Washington in the autumn of 1804 after a visit to Quincy, he wrote home to express what satisfaction he had felt in residing again that summer under his father's roof.

"I have only to hope," he said, in the heavy language of those days, "that a certain stiffness of temper, which I have not always had enough under controul, has not borne the appearance at times of a departure from that affection and respect which my duty cannot more forcibly enjoin than my heart is ever willing to pay." [58]

"You must not let the mind wear so much upon the body," replied Abigail. "You eat too little and study too much." [59]

She took care to tell him how to dress for his public duties: "Now I hope you never appear in Senate with a beard two days old, or otherwise make what is called a shabby appearance. Seriously I think a man's usefulness in society depends much upon his personal appearance. I do not wish a Senator to dress like a beau, but I want him to conform so far to the fashion, as not to incur the character of singularity, nor give occasion to the world to ask what kind of mother he had? or to charge upon a wife negligence and inattention when she is guiltless. The neatest man, observed a Lady the other day, wants his wife to pull up his coller, and mind that his coat is brush'd." [60]

Though their own domestic establishment in the capital permitted little entertaining, Senator and Mrs. Adams dined out a good deal. The distinction of his family, the old friends of his father, his own personal qualities, together with his diplomatic experience and travel, made him and his wife frequent dinner guests at the President's home, with the Secretary of State, and at the tables of the British and French Ministers. He enjoyed those social occasions, particularly when the conversation turned to history, literature, or science — as it always did at Jefferson's dinners.

Jefferson's talk continued to fascinate him almost as much as it had as a boy in Paris. "Mr. Jefferson tells large stories," he noted after his first dinner at the White House. "You never can be an hour in this man's com-

[56] AA to JQA, Quincy, November 11, 1804. Adams MSS.

[57] AA to JQA, Quincy, November 18, 1804. Adams MSS.

[58] JQA to JA, Washington, November 19, 1804. Adams MSS.

[59] AA to JQA, Quincy, December 18, 1804. Adams MSS.

[60] AA to JQA, Quincy, March 24, 1806. That the young Senator minded his mother well about his clothes and daily shaving is attested by a letter which she wrote ten years later to "His Excellency, John Quincy Adams, Minister Plenipotentiary from the U.S.A. to the Court of St. James's, London: I had the pleasure to hear from you by Mrs. Sweet, and in letters from Mrs. Tarbell, who writes that she saw you in good health, and in your person very *neat*." AA to JQA, Quincy, May 2, 1816. Adams MSS.

pany without something of the marvellous. . . . His genius is of the old French school. It conceives better than it combines." [61]

As a grown man and United States Senator he could not swallow without a grain of salt all the table tarradiddle of the White House. He just couldn't bring himself to believe Jefferson could have learned Spanish in nineteen days with the help of Cabot's grammar and a copy of *Don Quixote* on a passage to Europe! Nor that it had ever been twenty below zero in Paris by Fahrenheit six weeks steady without a let-up, as Jefferson said it had been during his diplomatic winters in France. "He loves to excite wonder. Fahrenheit's thermometer never since Jefferson existed was at twenty degrees below in Paris. It was never for six weeks together so low as twenty degrees above zero." [62]

Jefferson's risibles must have twitched to know the way his matter-of-fact Federalist friend set down in his Diary the reasoned impossibility of some of these harmless after-dinner whoppers.

Senator Adams tried to believe that his contacts with Jefferson were purely social and coolly formal. But no Jefferson could converse long with an Adams without introducing some political subjects, and no man, certainly not an old friend, could keep coolly formal with Thomas Jefferson throughout many conversations. They soon fell into discussion of international politics.

At the first dinner party, on November 23, 1804, Jefferson commented on how the French Revolution had finally turned out so contrary to all expectation. Everything that had happened in France for the last twelve of fifteen years now seemed like a dream. He wished France could return to the Constitution of 1789 and call back the Old Family. Although by that Constitution the French Government was much too weak, particularly in having a legislature in one branch, yet it was better than what France had under Napoleon. "This is one of the most unexpected phases," noted Adams, "in the waxing and waning opinions of this gentleman concerning the French Revolution."

Jefferson's serious reflection marked the complete disappearance of the French Revolution as an issue in American domestic politics. Disagreement on the principles and effect of that Revolution had been the sharpest political issue between Jefferson and the Adamses. Those early differences were now rapidly melting away.

Adams had increasing reason to suspect that his father's successor might have him in mind for a presidential appointment. Soon after his return from Berlin his brother-in-law, Colonel William Smith, reported that Jefferson had said as much. One evening in November 1804, just after Abigail Adams had taken her old friend to task for dismissing her son from the office of commissioner of bankrupties in Boston, Jefferson, as if to make amends, made an interesting suggestion to the Senator. He mentioned the great difficulty he had in getting fit persons for government

[61] *Memoirs,* I, 317. [62] *Memoirs,* I, 331.

appointments in Louisiana. He would give all creation, he said, for a young lawyer of good abilities, who could speak the French language, to go to New Orleans as one of the judges of the Superior Court. The salary was $2,000. John Quincy Adams could easily have named a "character" fully corresponding to the one the President had in mind. He did not respond to the overture. He no longer thought of settling in one of the Southern states or territories.

At least one other suggestion came indirectly from President Jefferson. As the Senator was passing through Philadelphia on his way to the capital in November 1805, an old friend of the family, Dr. Benjamin Rush, called on him. Rush told Adams that Madison had spoken very favorably of him. The Secretary of State had said that the President's opinion was "equally advantageous." In short, Jefferson wanted to employ him on some mission abroad if he desired it.[63] Adams replied that he was obliged to Mr. Jefferson and Mr. Madison for their good opinions, but that he had never asked any office of any man. He certainly would not solicit Mr. Jefferson for any office whatsoever. However, should Mr. Jefferson nominate him for any post abroad to which he thought him competent, he would not refuse it merely because the nomination came from Mr. Jefferson. In short, Adams was willing.

6

With his own seat in the Senate apparently secure until 1809, John Quincy Adams played only a perfunctory part in state or national politics in the elections of 1804. All he did was to publish some anonymous letters under the pseudonym of "Publius Valerius."[64] These articles were more calculated to justify his own position in the Senate than to support the Federalist candidates of 1804. A senator, declared "Publius Valerius," should not sacrifice the interests of the whole Union to those of a section. And it was the duty of good citizens to acquiesce in Mr. Jefferson's Louisiana Purchase: the resulting shift in the political center of gravity, being founded in nature, could not be resisted, he argued. What he did oppose was the Republican spoils system and the Jeffersonian attack on the Federal courts and their Federalist judges — "a curse upon our prosperity which the blessings of a thousand Louisianas will never compensate." And he argued vehemently against the injustice of the "three-fifths ratio"

[63] Benjamin Rush's son, Richard Rush, later an eminent American diplomat and Cabinet member under Secretary of State and President Adams, actually applied to Adams for appointment as his secretary of legation, presumably in England. Adams assured him that there was no reason to suppose the smallest foundation for the report that prompted the application. "That any such mission is contemplated by the government appears to me not very probable, but if it is, the person selected for it will be different." JQA to Richard Rush, Washington, December 12, 1805. *Writings*, III, 131.

[64] The *Repertory*, October 26, 30, November 2, 6, 1804. *Writings*, III, 46–76.

which gave to the slave-holding states an unfair representation in the House of Representatives, fountainhead of national taxation and expenditure.

How could Adams take off his coat and work for a party whose leaders in New England he knew to be waiting for an opportunity to secede from the Union and establish a Northern Confederacy? Yet he could not come out and denounce the Essex Junto when its plots were so well hidden from him as to be only a matter of notorious hearsay, not provable in a court of law. Like Jefferson he hoped that the defeat of Vice President Aaron Burr in the New York gubernatorial election would break up Pickering's treacherous alliance with that sinister politician. And like Jefferson he waited to see what would happen to Federalism after Hamilton's death at Burr's vengeful hand.

After hearing about Pickering's secessionist plot, Adams no longer made any effort to co-operate politically with his colleague. Independence and Union remained the two keys to his political creed: Union in matters of sectional strain, and Independence in foreign affairs.[65] Henceforth he continued only nominally to be a member of the party that had put him in the Senate. Federalism was a dismal affiliation for a man with national ambitions. "My political prospects have been daily declining," he noted in his journal on the last day of 1804. Again, a year later: "My political prospects continue declining."

It was during this period of dubious political future that Adams accepted the Boylston professorship of rhetoric and oratory at Harvard. A relative of the Adams family, Thomas Boylston, had established the chair in the year 1771, but it was not until 1804 that the fund had accumulated sufficiently to support a professorship and became available. A contemporary kinsman, Ward Boylston, was influential in getting the Harvard Corporation to name John Quincy Adams as the first incumbent. As soon as he heard of the appointment he hurried to the Harvard College Library, got out the three volumes of Leland's *Demosthenes* and the two volumes of Guthrie's *Quintilian,* and planned a program of seven years of scholarly work.[66]

"The term of my public service will soon be at an end," he wrote to Louisa after beginning his lectures in the summer of 1806, "and in the present condition of politics in this state, as well as almost all the rest, there is no danger that when my time expires I shall have the opportunity to continue in public life." [67] With the idea of settling his family again in Boston, permanently, after his senatorial term had finished, he purchased on July 14, 1806 a residence at the corner of Nassau Street (now Tre-

[65] See his autobiographical letter to Skelton Jones, Boston, April 17, 1809. *Writings,* III, 300.

[66] Donald M. Goodfellow has described "The First Boylston Professor of Rhetoric and Oratory" in *New England Quarterly,* XIX (No. 3, September 1946), 372–89.

[67] JQA to Louisa Catherine Adams, Quincy, June 29, 1806. *Writings,* III, 150.

mont) and Frog Lane (now Boylston Street), site of the present Hotel Touraine. There his third and famous son, Charles Francis Adams, was born, August 18, 1807, and named after John Quincy Adams's deceased brother, Charles, and Francis Dana, patron of the boy diplomat on the mission to Russia of 1781–3.[68] The house cost $15,000. Adams went into debt for it.[69] By every indication he was planning to live in Boston for the remainder of his life.

It makes a twentieth-century professor shiver with delight to read how John Quincy Adams laid down to the Harvard Corporation the conditions under which he would accept the appointment, salary $348 a quarter. He declined to take the customary oath of religious test, not because he disagreed with the doctrine but because he could not accept the principle of such a requirement. He refused to have an assistant who could act as his deputy under the control of the university. He insisted upon doubling up his schedule so as to do all his teaching during the summer term, when the Senate was not in session, and having two summers to complete his whole course of lectures.[70] To satisfy him in all particulars, the university had to reform some of its statutes.

Coachloads of his Boston friends drove out to Cambridge to hear his inaugural lecture. His instruction consisted of a course of formal lectures in rhetoric and oratory – one lecture every Friday morning at ten o'clock – and in presiding over students' exercises in declamation beginning at two o'clock the same afternoon. His discourses, prepared with much work and erudition, were published in two volumes in 1810 under the title: *Lectures on Rhetoric and Oratory, Delivered to the Classes of Senior and Junior Sophisters in Harvard University.*[71] He long regarded this work as the greatest literary effort of his life. No author ever pored over his own pages more fondly. He received his printed copy in 1810 in St. Petersburg, and sat up until two o'clock in the morning to read the first volume.[72] Today nobody would read one of the volumes through at one sitting. Its passages are puffy with superfluous luxuriance, full of mixed metaphors, pompous and stilted eloquence. Nevertheless the work receives honorable mention in the *Cambridge History of American Literature.*

The most enthusiastic admirer could not claim John Quincy Adams to be a stylist or a great orator at this period of his life. By his own account

[68] Charles Francis Adams, Jr.: *Charles Francis Adams* (Boston, 1900), p. 3.

[69] Diary.

[70] To Samuel Dexter, chairman of the Committee of the Corporation and Overseers of Harvard University, Quincy, August 6, 1805; to the Corporation of Harvard College, October 11, 1805, June 26, 1806. *Writings,* III, 123, 126, 148. *Memoirs,* I, 373, 443.

[71] See also *An Inaugural Oration Delivered at the Author's Instalment as Boylston Professor of Rhetorick and Oratory, at Harvard University, in Cambridge, Massachusetts, on Thursday, June 12, 1806, and Published at the Request of the Students* (Boston, 1806).

[72] *Memoirs,* II, 148.

he was slow, hesitating, and often confused.[73] Only by infinite pains and care did he finally overcome his own difficulties in public speaking. He himself said to the students of Harvard College: "Rhetoric alone cannot constitute an orator. No human art can be acquired by the mere knowledge of principles. But the artist who understands its principles, will exercise his art at highest perfection." Adams himself became an orator only when he spoke from the heart, as he did during the slavery controversy of his later years.

Some fellow alumni had had him in mind for president of Harvard. After the death of President Willard in 1804, Josiah Quincy, later himself a president (1829–45), urged Adams to be a candidate,[74] but nothing came of it.

For Harvard College he always had a most ardent attachment and deepest reverence.[75] Whether he was at home or abroad, in after years, his alma mater was ever in his mind and heart. All he had ever been in life he owed to Harvard, he declared in his old age. His voluminous private correspondence from abroad contains many references to the college. During his diplomatic missions he was forever presenting books to the library, or executing errands for the president of the college in the purchase of needed volumes in Europe. He headed the list, with a gift of one thousand dollars, of contributors for the establishment of the college's astronomical observatory. After finishing his term as President of the United States, he was elected a member of the Board of Overseers. He served faithfully and ably for eighteen years, from 1830 until his death, in 1848. In 1841 he became the first president of the alumni association. To the end he remained a loyal, conscientious, and grateful son of Harvard, one of her very greatest.

If it had not been for the renewal of war in Europe, John Quincy Adams might never have risen beyond the office of Senator from his native state and professor of rhetoric, perhaps president of Harvard University. It was the reappearance of grave issues of foreign policy and his uncompromising national and patriotic stand on them behind President Jefferson that turned the Essex Junto openly against him, transformed him into an avowed supporter of the Republican Administration, brought about his expulsion from the outraged Federalist Party of Massachusetts, and landed him back in the diplomatic service of the United States.

[73] *Memoirs,* I, 332, 445. [74] *Memoirs,* I, 314. [75] *Writings,* VII, 88.

CHAPTER VII
Politics Stops at the Water's Edge (1806–1809)

I lament the want of *genius* because I want a mighty agent for the service of my country.

DIARY OF JOHN QUINCY ADAMS, JANUARY 31, 1806

As the war in the Old World raged across the Continent of Europe and flamed out over the Atlantic Ocean, each mighty belligerent laid hands on his most deadly weapons of war without regard for treaty obligations or for international law. England proclaimed the offshore blockade and the Rule of the War of 1756. Napoleon, driven from the seas, imposed on Europe the Continental System. The ships and commerce of the United States were caught between the retaliations of the opposing illegal maritime systems. Meanwhile the British Navy continued the hateful and humiliating practice of impressing American seamen.

1

Spectacular announcement to the United States of the growing arbitrariness of the British system was a decision of the Admiralty Judge, Sir William Scott, in the celebrated case of the *Essex*, 1805. Hitherto the British Navy had allowed American neutral ships to circumnavigate, so to speak, the Rule of the War of 1756. They might take noncontraband goods from enemy colonies to unblockaded enemy European ports providing the ship "broke" the voyage by first importing the goods into the United States, thus Americanizing them, and then re-exporting them, perhaps in the same ship, to the originally intended destination. Scott decided that a voyage by a neutral vessel between an enemy colony and the motherland was not really broken by landing the goods and paying duties at a neutral port *if the duties were paid back upon re-exportation;* on the contrary, it constituted a *continuous voyage* between enemy ports in essentially *enemy property,* a trade forbidden in time of peace, hence a violation of the Rule of the War of 1756. Any neutral ship captured while engaging in such a traffic was good prize the same as an enemy ship.

Scott's judicial dictate killed a lucrative neutral wartime American carrying trade from the French and Spanish West Indies to Europe and thereby threw Anglo-American relations into advancing acrimony. British naval commanders promptly brought in to prize courts scores of American vessels engaged in a commerce hitherto unmolested by ten years of custom and sanctioned by British courts (case of the *Polly*, 1802).

Angry protests poured upon Congress from organizations of merchants in the Atlantic seaports: from Boston, New York, Baltimore. The Secretary of State, James Madison, published a long disquisition to prove the illegality of the Rule of the War of 1756 [1] and had it placed on every Senator's desk. He pointed out that British spokesmen had always contended that new principles, like those of the Armed Neutralities and the Freedom of the Seas, did not make international law unless universally accepted. How then could such a purely British innovation as the Rule of the War of 1756 be sanctioned?

Madison and John Quincy Adams saw eye to eye on British maritime practice. To Adams the Rule of the War of 1756 was the taproot of illegal retaliations and counter-retaliations that were building up between the opposing belligerents at neutral expense.[2] The Republican Secretary of State, soon to be President, and the young Senator from Massachusetts developed an increasing respect and friendship for each other.

Adams joined in the protest against British captures and in advocating measures of economic coercion against Great Britain. He helped prepare in committee a series of three resolutions, which the chairman, Senator Samuel Smith of Maryland, presented to the Senate on February 5, 1806. The Massachusetts Senator drafted the first and second resolutions.[3]

The first resolution declared that the captures and condemnations of American vessels and their cargoes under the order of the British Government, on the pretext of their being engaged in a trade with the enemies of Great Britain *not permitted before the war*, were an "unprovoked aggression upon the property of the citizens of these United States, a wanton violation of their neutral rights and a direct encroachment upon their national independence." The second requested the President to "demand and insist upon" restoration and indemnity. The Senate passed the first resolution unanimously — even Timothy Pickering felt it expedient to vote for it. Administration spokesmen induced the Senate to tone down the second resolution by cutting out the words

[1] *An Examination of the British Doctrine, Which Subjects to Capture a Neutral Trade, Not Open in Time of Peace* ([Philadelphia], 1806).

[2] See his letter to Harrison Gray Otis, Washington, March 31, 1808, answering the charges in the Pickering-Sullivan correspondence. *Writings*, III, 212.

[3] *Writings*, III, 133. He also drafted a third resolution, not presented, suspending the power of transfer upon United States bonds or bank stock held by British subjects until the British Government should have given satisfaction for the captures and condemnations.

"and insist upon." Passage of these two resolutions by the Senate was Adams's first triumph as a nonpartisan Senator.

The third resolution recommended nonimportation of British goods as economic coercion by Britain's best foreign customer to bring her to terms. In the debate on it there was talk of a general embargo and even of the sequestration of British property.[4] It was much the same situation and the same debate that had preceded Jay's mission back in George Washington's Administration. This time it resulted in the actual passage of a nonimportation act against England, but not to go into effect until November 1, 1806. In the interval it was expected that a satisfactory treaty could be negotiated with England. Adams was the only Federalist in either house of Congress to vote for nonimportation.[5]

The voice of the Senate impelled the President somewhat unwillingly to send another mission extraordinary, this time to England. He dispatched a Maryland Federalist, William Pinkney, to assist James Monroe, Republican successor to Rufus King at the Court of St. James's. The two plenipotentiaries had instructions to make a new treaty with England on the lines of Jay's old treaty, but to add articles specifically sanctioning the practice of the "broken voyage" and absolutely prohibiting impressment.

The extraordinary diplomatic mission of James Monroe and William Pinkney to London in 1806 failed to settle Anglo-American relations for the duration of the war as Jay had succeeded in doing with his treaty of 1794. After the death of William Pitt, Charles James Fox, traditional friend of the American colonies and of the United States, succeeded Grenville in the Foreign Office. He tried to ease the way for a new treaty by partially and temporarily suspending *operation* of the Rule of the War of 1756 without yielding the principle. This is what Grenville had done when he temporarily lifted the "provision order" during his negotiations with Jay twelve years earlier. But Fox disguised his concession in a paper blockade of France and occupied countries, from Brest to the Elbe, leaving outer zones of this enemy coast open to neutral ships that had circumnavigated the Rule of the War of 1756 by means of a broken voyage.[6] To neutral statesmen the medicine looked worse than the complaint. Unless a treaty were very carefully worded, Fox's prescription might commit the patient to the principle of offshore blockades expanded and contracted at the will of Great Britain. That would be worse than the Rule of the War of 1756.

[4] This would have been a violation of the permanent articles of Jay's Treaty still in force.

[5] *Memoirs*, I, 408, 432.

[6] This blockade, known as Fox's Blockade, declared May 16, 1806, was to be strictly enforced in an inner zone, between Ostend and the Seine. To the remaining outer zones, north and south, neutral ships might bring neutral noncontraband articles (by British definition) provided they were exported from a neutral port.

Nevertheless Monroe and Pinkney put their signatures to a treaty with England on December 31, 1806. Its maritime articles were similar generally to those of Jay's Treaty, condemned by Monroe in 1795. It specifically sanctioned the practice of broken voyage for American carriage of neutral noncontraband articles between a European belligerent country and its West Indian colonies, provided no more than ninety-nine per cent of American import duties were drawn back upon re-exportation of the same goods from the United States, and provided also that the carriage was not to or from a "blockaded" port.

Again, as in 1794, Great Britain seemed to be yielding the substance while not giving up the principle. But the lack of any definition of blockade left a loophole by which at any time she could nullify the concession by the simple act of declaring a coast of her enemy's possessions to be "blockaded." This she freely did in the struggle with Napoleon in the years that followed. Furthermore, at the moment of signing, the British Government made a reservation of complete liberty to retaliate against Napoleon's Berlin Decree (news of which had just arrived in London) *unless it should be effectively resisted by the United States.* Such a reservation completely devitalized the treaty. It reminds one of the way in which the French Revolutionary Governments had insisted, in the previous phase of the war, that the United States should *require* Great Britain to observe toward American neutral ships the principles of the Freedom of the Seas. Now Great Britain was announcing her intention to require the United States to make France do the same thing in regard to blockade. President Jefferson would not go to war to compel France to observe the law of blockade (not defined in the Franco-American Convention of 1800) any more than he would go to war to make Great Britain abandon the Rule of the War of 1756. He refused to submit the negotiated treaty to the Senate if for no other reason than that it did not contain an article forbidding impressment.

Senator Adams thought the President's course on this occasion correct; the treaty if ratified would have entangled the United States in war within twelve months.[7] It may be assumed that he would have opposed the treaty had it reached the Senate.[8] The Federalists certainly would have voted for it. The President's withholding of the document for further improvement put off only a little longer the inevitable break between Adams and the Essex Junto. On issues of foreign policy, the principal issues of the day, he was rapidly becoming an Administration Senator.

[7] JQA so stated in his fragmentary history of *Parties in the United States,* composed in the spring of 1829, after he retired from the Presidency, but not printed until 1941, in New York; see pp. 58–9. See "John Quincy Adams's Accounts of His Break with the Federalists," Appendix 1 of this book.

[8] *N.E. Federalism,* p. 177

2

In the hope that renewed negotiations might yet reach a satisfactory settlement with Great Britain, Congress again postponed enforcement of nonimportation until December 14, 1807. The hope proved illusory. Controversies over the Rule of the War of 1756, the *Essex* decision, and British offshore blockades soon were swallowed up in greater enormities of the opposing belligerents. Napoleon proclaimed his Continental System, a self-blockade of French-controlled Europe against British commerce declared by the Berlin and Milan decrees (November 21, 1806 and December 17, 1807); and Great Britain cut off all commerce with countries from which France caused the British flag to be excluded, unless the trade proceed by way of British ports under British license and toll (orders in council of January 7 and November 11, 1807). These British measures were contrived not only to injure the enemy; they were also particularly designed to take over the profits of neutral wartime carriage. "The only principle on which Government acted," said Spencer Perceval, the Prime Minister responsible for the system, speaking to Parliament on the eve of the War of 1812, "was to secure to the natives of England that trade by means of licenses, the profits of which without them would devolve to the hands of aliens."[9] Thus would neutrals be taxed to protect competing British commerce. Thus would they be forced to contribute revenue to help subsidize Britain's coalitions against Napoleon in Europe.

On paper it looked as if, harried between these two illegal systems, all American neutral commerce to Europe and to European colonies would be cut off by one belligerent or the other. But since Great Britain was Mistress of the Seas, there still remained open to American ships trading under British sufferance and fee a commerce with the British islands and to such ports of Europe as Napoleon could not seal up absolutely against neutrals coming with British license. This trade was due to expand as one European country after another was liberated from Napoleon's power. Then, too, some American ships, equipped with double sets of papers, for England or France, might slip through the imperfect British blockade to French-controlled ports of Europe. In this way a not unprosperous American commerce continued to exist with the Continent.

The Essex Junto preferred to tolerate the irregularities of both belligerents, to accept this still lucrative British-controlled trade, to pay the tribute required by British tariff and licenses, even to submit to the continued pains and humiliations of impressment, rather than risk a rupture with England.

[9] Henry Adams: *History*, VI, 274. So also said James Stephen, leading proponent of the British measures, quite frankly in the House of Commons, March 6, 18. Ibid., V, 61.

A breach in Anglo-American relations would supplement the Continental System by cutting off the United States, the last great neutral, from British trade. That, of course, was just what Napoleon wanted. The Essexmen feared that such a catastrophe would undermine the "last bulwark and barrier" against the tyrant's conquests in Europe; then the United States would be next. They determined to prevent a break at all costs, even that of separating New England from the Union and accepting the protection of Great Britain. As once the Republican Party had lent itself to French sympathy and influence to thwart Federalist foreign policy, so Timothy Pickering and the Essex Junto prostituted themselves to British sympathy and influence to thwart the foreign policy of President Thomas Jefferson, which did not differ essentially from that of his Federalist predecessors, George Washington and John Adams.

In the midst of these European blows at neutral rights British insistence upon impressment brought Anglo-American affairs to a sensational and, so it proved, a prolonged and irreparable crisis. The most humiliating event in a tragic train of blunders, "the last step in a gradation of outrages,"[10] was the *Chesapeake-Leopard* affair. It marked a turning-point in John Quincy Adams's career.

Off the capes of Virginia just outside the three-mile territorial limit, on June 22, 1807 the British warship *Leopard* fired into the U.S.S. *Chesapeake,* at friendly range, after her commander, Commodore Barron, had refused a summons to deliver up alleged deserters from His Majesty's Navy. The American warship, standing out to sea with her deck cluttered with gear, not suspecting aggression, was caught helpless and struck her colors. It would have been more decisive on Anglo-American relations had she gone down with her flag flying. Three men perished in the action and eighteen were wounded, including Commodore Barron. The British impressed four sailors. One of them proved to be a real deserter. Him they speedily court-martialed and hanged from a yardarm. Another was a natural-born American who had been impressed and had "deserted" his kidnappers. A third was also a natural-born American, born in slavery, again escaped from another slavery on the seas. The fourth was a naturalized American citizen also "deserting" from a previous impressment. These sailors the British naval commander forced back into George III's naval service. They must therefore be included in the ledger of history with the approximately 9,000 American citizens, mostly native-born,[11] impressed from American ships before the War of 1812.

Adams was at Harvard busy with his Boylston professorship when news of the *Chesapeake-Leopard* affair stunned the people of Boston

[10] JQA in *N.E. Federalism,* p. 180.

[11] James Fulton Zimmerman: *Impressment of American Seamen* (New York, 1925).

and launched him into a more important period of his life.[12] He immediately proposed that the Federalists express their indignation in a special town meeting. The party leaders hesitated. But the Republicans held a mass meeting of citizens of Boston and neighboring towns. Adams attended, and served on a committee of seven — the other six all Republicans — that drew up resolutions of protest, including the following: "that though we unite with our government in wishing most ardently for peace on just and honorable terms, yet we are ready cheerfully to co-operate in any measures, however serious, which may be judged necessary for the safety and honor of our country, and will support them *with our lives and fortunes.*"[13] The last five words were those of the Declaration of Independence, written by Thomas Jefferson thirty-three years before the *Chesapeake-Leopard* affair.

The Essex Junto were not willing to support with their lives and fortunes the measures that Jefferson's Government might take against Great Britain. One of them, John Lowell, actually justified to indignant John Quincy Adams the action of Vice-Admiral Berkeley, commander of the Halifax station, in directing his captains to search the *Chesapeake* for deserters from certain British ships; that is to say, Lowell justified the impressment of men from the crews of the United States Navy.[14] But the Federalists did not dare remain silent. Two days after the Republican mass meeting the very individuals who had refused to call a meeting at Adams's suggestion caused a town meeting to be held in Faneuil Hall. Essexmen like John Lowell, George Cabot, Judge Theophilus Parsons (John Quincy Adams's old preceptor), and Senator Timothy Pickering stayed away. Adams attended this meeting too. He was chairman of a committee that formulated some resolutions prepared by Jonathan Mason. But the town meeting resolutions were not so strong as those of the Republican mass meeting — the Federalists said nothing about their lives and fortunes.

It was at this time that John Quincy Adams saw a letter from the Governor General of Nova Scotia that was being passed around among the Junto. It stated that the British Government had certain knowledge of a deliberate plan of Napoleon to conquer the British provinces in America and to revolutionize the United States by means of a war between them and Great Britain, and accused the Administration of being party to such a plan.[15] The Essexmen were thinking of supporting

[12] "The really important period of my life began with the British attack upon our *Chesapeake* frigate, in the Summer of 1807." *Memoirs,* V, 136. May 31, 1820.

[13] *N.E. Federalism,* p. 182. Italics inserted.

[14] John Quincy Adams: *Parties in the United States* (New York, 1941), p. 66. See Appendix 1.

[15] *N.E. Federalism,* p. 116. *Parties in the United States,* p. 68. We have only John Quincy Adams's description of the letter. Its text has not yet been discovered and published. For report of the British secret agents in the United States in 1808 and 1809, John Henry, from the Governor General of Canada, and John Howe, from the

the enemy, if Britain should become an enemy of the United States, or at least of not supporting their own Government, but they scorned Adams for his "apostasy" to Jefferson. Adams had every reason long afterward to be proud of his stand. The Essexmen lived to regret theirs. His split from the Federalist Party dates from his presence at the Republican mass meeting.

Such was the state of Anglo-American relations and such were Senator Adams's relations with the Federalist Party and with Jefferson's Administration when Congress met on October 24, 1807, called six weeks earlier than usual because of the critical situation.[16] As a member of a small and decreasing minority party he realized that his opinions and votes had come to be much more often in unison with the Administration of Jefferson than with its opponents. He had met with more opposition from friends in his own party than from their political adversaries.[17] In striving like his father before him to be the man of his whole country he had become like his father a man without a party.

By the time Congress met, national indignation had cooled down somewhat, much to the relief of the peace-loving President. Jefferson was waiting hopefully for Britain's reply to his powerless demands for disavowal of and reparation for the *Chesapeake-Leopard* affair. He had forbidden all British warships the hospitality of American waters; he had concentrated his ridiculous little gunboats in New York, Charleston, and New Orleans; he had warned the states to be ready with their quotas of militia; but Jeffersonian pacifism and national irresponsibility had made the country helpless in the face of grave insult. The only products of the first weeks of Congress were a law definitively excluding British public ships from American ports until due amends were made, and much debate on national defense: gunboats and militia. Neither party was willing to urge resolute and all-out military preparedness. Senator John Quincy Adams as chairman of a committee reported the bill excluding British warships, supported it, and voted for it. Back in Boston the Essexmen accused him of bringing forth an "aggression bill."[18]

The Administration drifted indecisively until December 17, 1807. Then Jefferson received unofficial news of the British order in council of November 11, professedly in retaliation against Napoleon's Berlin Decree. It was evident that no satisfactory arrangement could be negotiated with England or with France. The President had to do something or else submit to the dictates of the belligerents. He consulted

---

Governor of Nova Scotia, and particularly their reports on opposition of New England Federalists to the Administration's foreign policy, see *AHR*, XVII (Nos. 1, 2, 1911–12), 70–103, 332–55, and *Report on Canadian Archives*, 1896, pp. 38–69.

[16] *N.E. Federalism*, p. 185.

[17] *Memoirs*, I, 471.

[18] JQA to JA, December 27, 1807. *Writings*, III, 167.

Republican leaders in both houses of Congress, and recommended, December 18, another characteristic measure of economic coercion: a general embargo, unlimited in time, on all shipping in American ports. It was a Jeffersonian step short of war calculated to coerce the warring European nations into suspending their retaliatory measures so far as the United States was concerned. An embargo would not only deprive the belligerents of American foodstuffs and raw materials. It would also keep American shipping out of their avaricious reach.

At this juncture Adams considered himself in communion with no party in the United States. But he served on a committee with four Republican Senators to consider the President's confidential recommendation. The necessary legislation had to be passed quickly lest shipowners get time to sail their vessels out of port equipped for long voyages, thus defeating the purpose of the proposed law. Reluctantly he gave his consent to it as the only immediate alternative to a war for which the country was not prepared. He further understood the embargo to be a device calculated to help the President in the expected negotiations with the British envoy, Rose. As he was leaving the committee room he observed to a fellow member: "This measure will cost you and me our seats, but private interest must not be put in opposition to public good." [19]

The embargo bill sped through the Senate in one day, 22 to 6. Adams voted in the affirmative with the Republicans against the Federalist Senators. Three days later, December 21, 1807, it passed the House, 82 to 44.

John Quincy Adams, hitherto a hard-working Senator of no political influence, suddenly found himself no longer a nonentity in Washington. In a growing national emergency his colleagues looked to him as a man of experience in diplomacy and foreign policy. They placed him on every committee of national importance. He seized upon his increasing prestige in an endeavor to exercise a leadership hitherto denied him because of his political affiliation, but to no avail. His situation was "singular and critical," he wrote to his father, that of "a leader without followers." After his vote for the embargo he had no Federalist ally in the Senate, and the President's friends in that body still regarded him with distrust and suspicion.[20] "My political prospects are declining," he again recorded, summing up the year 1807 in his Diary, "and as my term of service draws near its close, I am constantly approaching to the certainty of being restored to the situation of a private citizen." [21]

Adams had voted for the embargo reluctantly, preferring to consider it as a temporary expedient, an experiment to see how far the Government might calculate upon the support of the people for the maintenance of their own rights. No sooner was the measure put into effect than he began to hesitate about its expediency, so great was public revulsion,

[19] *Writings*, III, 168–89, n. 2.

[20] JQA to JA, Washington, December 27, 1807. *Writings*, III, 172.

[21] *Memoirs*, I, 498.

particularly in his own section. He introduced (January 11, 1808) a motion for the appointment of a committee to inquire when the embargo could be removed and whether American vessels might then be armed to resist foreign aggression. The motion failed 10 to 17. Of course, it did not satisfy the Federalists at home in Boston; but the Republican Governor James Sullivan applauded his stand.[22]

"My advice to you," wrote John Adams from Quincy, "is steadily to pursue the course you are in, with moderation and caution however, because I think it the path of justice." John Adams, too, had ceased to be a Federalist. Reading the letter over before he sent it, he added: "But you must 'ere long vote for the repeal." [23]

3

The Essex Junto were enraged at the younger Adams for having put country above party, nation above section, as once they had been infuriated at his father for doing the same thing. Alarmed at the prospects of a break with England, they renewed their confabulation and correspondence with British officials. Thanks to the Essexmen the nation was divided when war came in 1812. The end of their road was the defeatist Hartford Convention of 1814.

While the Junto was clamoring against Adams's support of the Administration's foreign policy he attended a caucus of Republican members of Congress (January 23, 1808) for the nomination of candidates for President and Vice President in the election of 1808. His presence at such a conclave signified publicly his change of party allegiance, although he still considered himself an independent in politics. He was not conscious of any change in his political beliefs. Doubtless this feeling of independence helps to explain his curious vote in the caucus.

Senator Bradley of Vermont, who delivered to him the printed circular inviting attendance at the meeting, suggested that Madison was the man for President and expressed the hope that Vice President George Clinton might be unanimously renominated for another term. Clinton represented the irregular Northern wing of the Republicans, malcontents who resented Jefferson's pacifism. He would have been more acceptable to Federalists than Madison. In fact there were some members of the Essex Junto, like George Cabot and Harrison Gray Otis, who wanted to make Clinton the Federalist candidate for President in 1808.[24] Adams voted

[22] *Writings*, III, 187. J. Sullivan to JQA, Boston, November 7, 1807, January 4, 23, April 5, 1808. Adams MSS.

[23] "Parton has denounced you as No Federalist, and I wish he would denounce me in the same manner, for I have long since renounced, abdicated, and disclaimed the Name and Character and Attributes of that Sect, as it now appears. We have no favour to expect from France or England nor from the Partisans of either." JA to JQA, Quincy, January 17, 1808. Adams MSS.

[24] E. Wilder Spaulding: *His Excellency George Clinton, Critic of the Constitution* (New York, 1938), pp. 278–94.

for Clinton as his choice for the first office; then, when Madison was overwhelmingly nominated, he joined the great majority which voiced its preference for Clinton for Vice President.[25]

Undoubtedly the new recruit to the Republican caucus had supported Clinton because he was the Republican least obnoxious to the Federalists. Everybody knew that the Vice President was in his dotage. His judgment was slow and weak. He was hardly competent to preside over the Senate. Inexperienced in parliamentary law, he did not know the most common forms of proceeding and order. "In this respect," Adams had long since noted, "a worse choice than Mr. Clinton could scarcely have been made." [26]

Someone, presumably not a wag, voted for John Quincy Adams for Vice President.[27]

Abigail Adams could hardly believe what she read in the newspapers, that her son had attended a Republican caucus! [28] "Your mother has written you on the subject of caucuses," the ex-President remarked in a letter of his own. "I am not of her opinion." [29]

The rage of the Federalists against Adams was boundless. Pickering had sent a letter to the Governor of Massachusetts for presentation to the legislature condemning the embargo and calling for joint resistance against it by the commercial states. Taking his cue from the Governor of Nova Scotia, he accused the Administration of a secret understanding with the Emperor Napoleon. Pickering's avowed purpose was to stimulate resistance to a law of the Union. It smacked strongly of nullification. "This interposition of the commercial states," wrote John Quincy Adams in historical retrospect, "was the embryo conception of the Hartford Convention." [30]

Quite properly the Republican Governor Sullivan refused to submit such a communication to the legislature. Pickering's Junto friend George Cabot – afterward president of the Hartford Convention – then had it printed in the form of a pamphlet that accused Senator Adams of voting for the embargo on the express recommendation of the President.[31] On the eve of the Massachusetts elections he published it. Obviously it was intended to help bring in a legislature that would not send John Quincy Adams back to the United States Senate when his term expired in the year 1809.

Josiah Quincy, Federalist member of the House of Representatives from John Quincy Adams's own district in Massachusetts, and a personal

[25] *N.E. Federalism*, p. 197.

[26] *Memoirs*, I, 385.

[27] *Memoirs*, I, 506.

[28] AA to JQA, Quincy, February 15, "April," 1808. Adams MSS.

[29] JA to JQA, Quincy, February 19, 1808. Adams MSS.

[30] *Parties in the United States*, p. 85.

[31] *Interesting Correspondence between His Excellency Governor Sullivan and Colonel Pickering* (Boston, 1808).

friend, gently tried to reclaim the fallen Senator from the error of his ways. Adams explained his position:

"In case of war," he said, "opposition [to the Government's foreign policy] must in its nature end, either in a civil war, or in a dissolution of the Union, with the Atlantic States in subserviency to Great Britain. To resist this I am ready to risk, if necessary, every thing I have in life, and even life itself. You, too, ere long," Adams told his friend, "will have to elect which side to take."

"I don't see the prospect in the same light," replied Quincy, kindly, "but if I did, I shall be willing to meet the question when it comes."

Quincy did not say which side he would take. It was evident to Adams that he was already too far pledged to the opposition to retreat.[32] As a matter of fact, Josiah Quincy had never wavered. He remained a consistent Essexman and separatist. But he was one of the few Federalists who did not question Adams's sincerity and disinterestedness.[33]

Adams's patriotic stand against the Federalist Party's truckling to British policy in 1807 echoed his earlier convictions that of all the dangers that encompassed the liberties of a republican state the most alarming was the association of internal faction and external power.[34] It was the lesson he had learned as American Minister to the Netherlands from 1794 to 1797. It recalls his warnings to his father of the fatal designs of the French Directorate to overthrow the Administration of President Washington and to defeat Washington's foreign policy as it was being carried forward by John Adams. It applied to American politics his experience in European affairs.

Senator John Quincy Adams had "aped his sire," to be sure. He was as independent as his father. He was a man of the whole country. He resented the attempt of any European power to take hold of an American political party, whether that power were France or England, whether the party were Republican or Federalist. But he had one misgiving, the Federalist allegation that the Governor of Nova Scotia had planted among the Essex Junto: that Jefferson, the Francophil of yesteryear, had a secret understanding with Napoleon.

The Federalists were ringing this charge through a hundred changes in party newspapers and pamphlets. Might there be any validity in it? Adams himself had received a mysterious warning, apparently from Pichon, Talleyrand's onetime spokesman to President John Adams, that the French Government contemplated a "crusade" in the United States.[35]

[32] *N.E. Federalism,* p. 198; *Memoirs,* I, 510–11.

[33] "His deviation from his friends is perfectly reconcilable with the peculiar texture of his mind, without resorting to any suspicion of his political integrity. I neither join in, nor sanction, any asperities about him." Josiah Quincy to his wife. *Writings* of JQA, III, 172, n. 2.

[34] Above, p. 37.

[35] *Plumer's Proceedings U.S. Senate,* p. 604.

Before replying to Pickering's attack he wanted to be sure of his position. Two of Jefferson's friends in Congress, Senator William Branch Giles of Virginia and Representative William Cary Nicholas of the same state, urged him to go to Jefferson himself and get full assurances that in opposing Great Britain's insults the President had no understanding whatsoever with the Emperor of the French.[36]

A confidential interview followed in the White House, March 15, 1808. Senator Adams told Jefferson about the letter from the Governor of Nova Scotia that he had seen being handed about in Boston. The President assured him that there had never been any negotiation upon the subject with France, and that France had never intimated a wish that we should join her in the war. Jefferson also appeared convinced that the British Government did not intend immediate war with the United States.[37]

It was true, of course, that Great Britain, harassed by her distresses in Europe, did not want war with the United States. At the same time her leaders were determined not to relax their arbitrary naval policy. Timothy Pickering and the Essex Junto had persuaded the British envoy, George Rose, that it would be best to continue the maritime measure unabated, taking care to avoid if possible actual warfare. Then in time Jefferson's system would collapse of its own folly.[38]

Jefferson's personal assurances convinced Adams. He publicly replied to Pickering in a long open letter to his old friend Harrison Gray Otis, now a prominent Boston member of the Junto. The pamphlet was only a plausible defense of the embargo as a means of preserving peace while preparing for war.[39] It failed to convince a majority of the Massachusetts voters.

Some of them sent him stinging anonymous letters. "Lucifer, Son of the Morning, how thou hast fallen!" wrote "A Federalist." "We hope not irrecoverably. Oh Adams, remember who thou art. Return to Massachusetts! Return to thy Country. Assist not in its destruction! Consider the Consequences! Awake – Arouse in time!"

An "Observer of Times, Men and Manners" prepared a catechism for his instruction, which read in part:

Ques: "Is the old maxim discarded *Honesty is the best Policy*?"

Ans: "Yes! By modern Rulers."

Ques: "Who saved America in the late Revolution?"

[36] *Memoirs,* I, 518–20.

[37] *Memoirs,* I, 521.

[38] "Their soundest statesmen," reported Rose after consulting with Pickering, "express to me the utmost anxiety that their fellow-citizens should be allowed to bear the whole burden of their follies, and suffer by evils originating with themselves; and they are convinced that the effects of punishment inflicted by their own hands must ere long bring them in co-operation with Great Britain, whilst if inflicted by hers, it must turn them perhaps irrevocably against her." Henry Adams: *History,* IV, 233. *N.E. Federalism,* p. 366.

[39] JQA to Harrison Gray Otis, March 31, 1808. *Writings,* III, 220–2.

Ans: "Washington, with the assistance of other patriots."
Ques: "Have we seen a Washington in our Administration, or in our Councils since he retired from office?"
Ans: "No: John Adams did not possess self-command; Tho'. Jefferson is Bonaparte's Tool."
Ques: "May not the Commonwealth of Massachusetts and the United States be highly benefited by the Son of John Adams?"
Ans: "The Son of John Adams stands at the present time in a very critical and solemn state of responsibility to his God and to his Country. Let him please his God by the *disinterestedness* adorning the character of the *true Patriot,* and the Historians of America will certainly not fail to appreciate his character and celebrate his name." [40]

Federalist journals attacked and called names: "one of those amphibious politicians, who lives on both land and water, and occasionally resorts to each, but who finally settle down in the mud," a "party scavenger," [41] a "popularity seeker," "courting the prevailing party," unworthy of confidence, one of "Bonaparte's Senators," [42] an apostate "associating with the assassins of his father's character." [43] Even his old friend, Russell's *Columbian Centinel* of Boston, would not admit the correctness of his opinions on the embargo, "the most iniquitous measure ever adopted by a government." [44]

Republican sheets naturally defended him and welcomed him. He was a patriot for whom "the nation's thanks will be a never-failing laurel on his brow"; [45] "an Atlas unshaken by the roaring blasts of Federalism"; [46] a "fair and honorable," an "independent" man, "the *greatest ornament* and the *ablest member of the American Senate,* who if he but persists in his dignified course must one day attain to the highest station in our republic." [47]

Old John Adams was quick to read the handwriting on the wall of his son's new political bedchamber. He did not disapprove of his support of the Administration's foreign policy, or even his attendance at the Republican caucus. With him, too, politics had always stopped at the water's edge. But he thought John Quincy finished politically, and bluntly wrote him so. "Return to your professorship, but above all to your office as a lawyer. Devote yourself to your profession and the education of your children." [48]

[40] Adams MSS.
[41] *Hampshire Gazette,* Northampton, April 20, 1808.
[42] Salem *Gazette,* January 22, April 15, 26, May 10, 1808.
[43] Greenfield *Gazette,* May 16, 1808.
[44] February 20, March 30, 1808.
[45] *National Aegis,* Worcester, May 15, 1808.
[46] *Essex Register,* Salem, February 16, 24, April 30, May 4, 7, 1808.
[47] *Independent Chronicle,* Boston, January 14, 18, May 8, 1808.
[48] January 8, 1808. *Writings,* III, 189, n. 1.

Spurred on by the Essex Junto and suffering from paralysis of commerce caused by the embargo, the Massachusetts Federalists were quick to confirm John Quincy Adams's separation from the party. As soon as the new legislature met at the end of May 1808, they proceeded by a narrow vote, 248 to 213, to elect James Lloyd, Jr., as his successor to the United States Senate. It was six months before the normal time for such a choice. To make the rebuke unmistakable, the General Court accompanied it by positive instructions to its Senators to urge repeal of the embargo. Adams resigned immediately, June 8, 1808. In effect the legislature of Massachusetts had "recalled" him.[49] Lloyd straightway succeeded him in the vacancy.

The Essex Junto took immeasurable satisfaction in the discomfiture of the "scoundrel." So did their confidant George Rose, who referred to the Junto as "that honorable confraternity." "In Professor Adams's downfall, at which I cannot but be amused," he wrote hopefully from London to the conspirator Pickering in Washington, "I see but the forerunner of catastrophes of greater mark." [50]

4

The ousted Senator resisted temptations to re-enter politics as a Republican candidate in the ensuing campaign of 1808. Committees of Republicans repeatedly waited on him at his home in Boston and urged him to run for the lower house of Congress on their ticket. Greatly inclined to do so, he told them that he believed their party's cause to be that of the country. But he could not bring himself to oppose his old friend Josiah Quincy, the Federalist incumbent. He also declined, largely on his father's advice, to lend himself to a movement conceived by Dr. Eustis to make him Governor of Massachusetts.[51]

Reduced to the status of a private citizen in Massachusetts, John Quincy Adams had almost as much influence on foreign policy in the deliberations of Congress as he had enjoyed while Senator. His Republican friends in Congress wrote to him for advice.[52] He warned them that persistence in the embargo might drive New England Federalists into armed insurrection. His opinion, voiced through the New England Republican members of Congress, softened the original determination of Jefferson and his

[49] W. C. Ford discusses "The Recall of John Quincy Adams in 1808," in MHS, XLV, 354–75.

[50] *N.E. Federalism*, pp. 369, 372.

[51] *Memoirs*, I, 536–43. *Writings*, III, 260, n. 1.

[52] Orchard Cook to JQA, November 10, 27, December 17, 29, 1808, and January 1, 1809; William Branch Giles to JQA, November 7, December 9, 25, 1808, January 25, 1809; Ezekiel Bacon to JQA, November 9, December 11, 1808, January 9, 1809; Samuel Mitchell to JQA, December 3, 1808, January 30, 1809; Joseph Anderson to JQA, December 6, 1808, January 3, 13, 1809. Adams MSS. Adams's answers are printed in *Writings*, III, 242–8.

successors in power to persist in the embargo. At Adams's suggestion [53] and under Gallatin's leadership [54] they substituted, for complete embargo, a nonintercourse with Great Britain and France. Thus they relieved American commerce by opening it with other countries, with the promise of opening it also with the belligerent power that would relax its illegal measures. Gallatin thought this would eventually bring conciliation with Great Britain and unite both countries against France – a Hamiltonian concept.

5

Once more the perturbations of American domestic politics seemed to have brought a public career to an end. To support his family the recalled Senator turned again to the pickings of a law practice made meager by many years of absence in public service, and to the pleasanter occupations of his Boylston professorship. In a spirit of political martyrdom [55] he accepted his fate and looked forward to dedicating himself to the fine

[53] JQA to Ezekiel Bacon, November 17, 1808. *Writings,* III, 250. In a letter to CFA of December 2, 1828, JQA recalled that it was his letters to Bacon of November 17 and December 21, 1808, and still another one of 1809, that had "urged the substitution of non-intercourse for the Embargo";

"There are three things on which I wish you to fix your attention . . . to the vindication of your father's good name:

"1. That I gave the first warning to Mr. Jefferson to be upon his guard against the intrigues of the British Government through the Governor of Nova Scotia, with the disaffected party in New England.

"2. That although living as a private citizen in 1808–9 I was the efficient cause of the substitution of the Nonintercourse for the embargo, which I verily believed saved the country from a civil war.

"3. That Mr. Jefferson to the last moment of his life, and under the fiend-like temptations of a tampering miscreant upon his resentments against me, bore witness clear, explicit, and unqualified to the integrity and disinterestedness of my conduct at that trying time." Adams MSS.

See also Appendix 1.

[54] "Yesterday I spent an hour with Mr. Galatin [*sic*] when he unfolded to me his Plan – a Plan which he thinks will finally prevail. It is this. That we immediately pass a non intercourse, to take effect say first of June next – and as the Bill now reads that it become null towards that Power which may relax – send out the Act – forthwith to E. and to France together with an Act raising the E[mbargo] partially say at the same time and arming or granting Letters of Marque etc. – these being made known to G.B. and France – it is expected that the Obstinate Emperor will not alter his course but it is expected that G.B. when she finds the stand we deliberately take, that we have no rebellions, that Madison and a maj'ty of Democrats are chosen – that we shall be fighting a common Enemy (France) with her – and when she finds that we intend living without dishonourable purchases of her Goods etc., then she will study her interests and relax." Orchard Cook to JQA, House of Representatives, Washington, December 29, 1808. Adams MSS. For Gallatin's original enforcement proposals, see H. Adams: *Writings of Gallatin,* I, 428.

[55] JQA to William B. Giles, Boston, December 26, 1808. *Writings,* III, 286.

arts. In the mortification of disappointment the soothing love of letters would whisper serenity and peace.[56]

Governor Sullivan of Massachusetts urged Jefferson to requite Adams,[57] but the Virginian retired to Monticello without doing anything for him. After Adams's vote for the embargo had made him clearly a man without a party, Senator Giles, Republican whip in the Senate, hinted that there might be bright prospects for him in the Madison Administration. The ex-Senator from Massachusetts did not dash such prospects from his contemplation. "In any support I have given or ever should give to this [Jefferson's] or any other administration," he told Giles, "I have been and shall be governed solely by public considerations, and the belief that the administration aims at the welfare of the nation." [58]

His Federalist enemies maliciously interpreted his support of Republican foreign policy as a bid for a diplomatic appointment. Had he counted on any such appointment he would hardly have accepted the Boylston professorship in 1805, gone into debt to buy a house in Boston in 1806, and moved his family into it in 1807.

Adams was in Washington arguing a case in the Supreme Court – the famous case of *Fletcher* v. *Peck* – when President Madison was inaugurated, March 4, 1809. Two days later without any previous sounding Madison offered him the post of Minister Plenipotentiary to Russia. Apologizing for lack of an earlier notice, he said he wanted to send the nomination to the Senate in half an hour in a list of names already prepared.

"How long will the mission probably continue?" asked Adams.

"Indefinitely," responded the President. "It depends upon events. Perhaps three or four years." [59]

Adams accepted on the spot.

At first the economy-minded Senate did not approve. On March 7 that body resolved, 17 to 15, that it was inexpedient "at this time" to appoint a minister from the United States to the court of Russia. It was also too expensive and unnecessary.

The swiftly unrolling scene of Napoleonic Europe soon operated to reverse the Senate's opinion. On June 27, 1809 it confirmed John Quincy Adams by a vote of 19 to 7. Five Federalist Senators, including those from Massachusetts, Pickering and Lloyd, now opposed the nomination vindictively. Two Republicans still thought the mission unnecessary.

Professor Adams received his commission while listening to a Fourth-of-July oration in the Old South Church in Boston.[60] That night he recorded in his Diary his motive for accepting the appointment. As his

[56] *Lectures on Rhetoric and Oratory*, II, 396.
[57] *Writings*, III, 236, n. 1.
[58] *Memoirs*, I, 512–13.
[59] *Memoirs*, I, 545.
[60] "JQA Loquitur." Adams MSS.

final reason he gave his desire to justify the confidence reposed in him by Madison. He promised himself to devote all his powers to the support of the Administration, convinced that it would aim at the welfare of the whole Union.[61] He regarded the new appointment – at least so he said fifteen years afterward – as the judgment of his country on his past conduct in supporting Jefferson's Administration, over the disapproval of his constituents, in the cause of American independence.[62]

John Quincy Adams quickly made ready to depart the scene of domestic politics for honorable exile [63] abroad. It was not very difficult to take leave of the law, but it was with great reluctance that he severed his ties with Harvard.

No coachloads of Federalist admirers drove to Cambridge to listen when he gave his last lecture. Except for his mother, the hall was occupied by students and strangers. The students seemed the only friends he had left – they and the great orators of the past.

> In social converse with the mighty dead of ancient days, you will never smart under the galling sensation of dependence with the world, should a crisis ever occur, when even friendship may deem it prudent to desert you; when even priest and levite shall come and look upon you, and pass you on the other side; seek refuge, my *unfailing friends,* and be assured you will find it, in the friendship of Lælius and Scipio; in the patriotism of Cicero, Demosthenes, and Burke; as well as in the precepts and example of him whose whole law is love, and who taught us to remember injuries only to forgive them.[64]

Nothing better illustrates the newly appointed Minister's complete alignment with the Republican Party under President Madison than his anonymously published letters to the Boston *Patriot* from April to June 1809 reviewing the *Works of Fisher Ames,* the Junto's intellectual giant, who died in 1808. In his last desponding years Ames had loosed his unrivaled powers of style and eloquence to champion the righteousness of British naval policy and power. Hateful of democracy, contemptuous of republican institutions, and convinced that the liberty of the United States depended on British sea power in the struggle with Napoleon, he

[61] JQA to Secretary of State Robert Smith, Boston, July 5, 1809. *Writings,* III, 329. For his reflections similarly twenty years later, see *N.E. Federalism,* p. 26.

[62] "JQA Loquitur." Adams MSS.

[63] "I was proscribed in my native State, for voting the Embargo, and resenting British Impressment and commercial depredation. Mr. Madison sent me for eight years in honorable diplomatic exile in Europe. Mr. Monroe called me back and placed me at the head of the Department of State, for the eight years of his Administration." JQA to Charles W. Upham, Washington, February 2, 1837. "Ten Unpublished Letters of John Quincy Adams, 1796–1837," edited by Edward H. Tatum, Jr., *Huntington Library Quarterly,* IV (No. 3, April 1941), 382–3. For the phrase "honorable exile" used by his friend Ezekiel Bacon, M.C., in 1809, see *Writings,* III, 321, n. 1.

[64] *Lectures on Rhetoric and Oratory,* II, 396–7.

went to his grave defending every act and principle of the British Navy, including the Rule of the War of 1756 and impressment. After his death his intimates published his works, including private correspondence, as a new political bible for Essexmen.

Adams's trenchant review was his best piece of writing thus far in his career. Pitched in patriotic fervor, ardently invoking Union, it vibrated a strong and patriotic tone. Ames's dependence on the British Navy for American protection against Napoleon, declared the reviewer, meant subjection to the Mistress of the Seas, as proved by impressment and by the tribute laid on the American carrying trade in colonial products forced to pass through England and pay toll there. He cited Madison's treatise of 1806 on the Rule of the War of 1756 as an unanswerable vindication of the neutral cause of the United States, and rejoiced that the maintenance of America's national rights had been committed to men of firmer minds than the Essex Junto.

> While we drop a tear of compassion upon the political weakness of Mr. Ames's declining days let us rejoice that the maintenance of our national rights against Great Britain has been committed to men of firmer minds. . . . If the people of this Union were reduced to that deplorable condition of having only to deliberate "whose base herd they would be" – still it would be incumbent upon those who prefer the domination of Britain to that of France, to shew that the British yoke would be the easiest – that the protection of the British navy would be a safe reliance – that by redemption from the Hall of France, we should have a *Paradise regained* in Britain. . . . If our nominal independence of France rested upon no other foundation of power than the navy of England, the consequence would be that we should again be under the domination of England. Her argument would be that in all reason we ought to contribute our share to support the expense of protecting us, and we should soon be called upon for our contribution of men, as well as of money.[65]

The *Review* was anonymous, but its authorship was unmistakable. It stung the Essexmen to a frenzy. They vented their rage on the "apostate" in pamphlets and newspapers long after he had left the country.[66]

6

John Quincy Adams, his wife, and their infant son Charles Francis closed the door of their Nassau Street house on August 5, 1809 and, accompanied by his official family, drove over the Charles River Bridge to

[65] *American Principles: A Review of Works of Fisher Ames, Compiled by a Number of His Friends* (Boston, 1809), pp. 24, 50–1.

[66] *Parties*, op. cit., p. 98. See the reply by John Lowell: *Remarks on the Hon. John Q. Adams's Review of Mr. Ames's Works, With Some Strictures on the View of the Author* (Boston, 1809).

William Gray's wharf at Charlestown, whence they had engaged passage on Gray's ship,[67] the *Horace,* Captain Bickford, for distant St. Petersburg. He took along with him two of his Harvard students who wanted to see Europe under good guidance and to get a little diplomatic experience and knowledge of the world. That was the way he himself had first visited St. Petersburg with Francis Dana in 1782–3.

One of these personal attachés was Francis C. Gray, son of the Lieutenant Governor of Massachusetts, in whose ship the party voyaged. Gray was a big trader to the Baltic ports and wanted his son to get some idea of his business as well as to travel for his health. He was the only conspicuous Federalist merchant and shipper who had supported Jefferson's embargo and turned Republican, like John Quincy Adams.[68] He provided Adams with a letter of credit (never drawn on) and requested a special oversight for his son's education and welfare. Adams rendered the boy this friendly service, counseled the father on commercial houses to handle his business in Russia,[69] and gave useful advice to Gray's business agents and shipmasters.

A second young student friend was Alexander H. Everett, destined as a protégé of Adams to rise high in the diplomatic service of the United States; he was brother of a still more famous later American diplomat, Edward Everett. Young Everett had been reading law in John Quincy Adams's Boston office, and he continued reading international law in Adams's Legation in St. Petersburg until 1811.[70] Senator Samuel Smith of Baltimore, brother of the Secretary of State, also asked Adams to take along his boy, John Spear Smith. All three of these youths served without pay.

At the request of Colonel William S. Smith, with the approval of John Adams,[71] the Minister appointed his nephew William Steuben Smith, son of his sister Abby, as private secretary at public expense. He later received a commission as Secretary of Legation.

[67] The President ordered the *Essex* frigate to Boston to take the Minister to St. Petersburg, but it arrived one day after Adams, eager to embark in time to make his destination before the Gulf of Finland should freeze up in the coming autumn, had taken passage on a private ship. Later he wished he had been on a public vessel, to prevent tiresome visits by British cruisers at the entrance of the Danish sounds, and Danish privateers within them.

[68] James Duncan Phillips points this out in his study of Salem's reaction to "Jefferson's 'Wicked Tyrannical Embargo'" in *N.E. Quarterly,* XVIII (No. 4, December 1945), 466–78, and shows that the embargo injured Gray's business less than most others because his ships traded from one foreign port to another and came home at long intervals.

[69] Correspondence between JQA and William Gray, 1809–14. Adams MSS. JQA to William Gray, St. Petersburg, May 24, 1812. *Writings,* IV, 334–6.

[70] A. H. Everett to Mrs. Lucy Everett, St. Petersburg, October 19, 1810. A. H. Everett, Private Letterbook, 1809–11. MHS. Everett's Commonplace Book in the same collection is full of notes on the classical publicists made while with Adams.

[71] The youth's grandfather.

Adams thus had a small class of future diplomats to coach. Such apprenticeship was the only kind of training that then existed for the foreign service. With the exception of Alexander Everett there were no distinguished graduates of this group, although John Spear Smith became Secretary of Legation in London in 1811.

Mrs. Adams had with her for a companion her younger sister Catherine, who before long was to marry young W. S. Smith, doubly grafting the Johnson family to the Adams stock.

The Adamses' two older sons, George Washington Adams and John Adams, remained in Massachusetts under the care of their relatives.[72]

Out at sea the newly appointed Minister cast his mind back over the turbulent picture of his country's politics and its uncertain future. In a letter to his friend ex-Senator William Plumer, who proposed to write a history of the United States, he said: "I hope that the *moral* of your history will be the indissoluble union of the North American continent."[73]

Union and Independence! Indissoluble union was the watchword of Adams's own politics, as independence and abstention from Europe's wars were the beacon of his foreign policy.

John Quincy Adams was glad to be again in his real profession. Contented, patriotic, and prayerful, he sailed over smooth Atlantic waters to the troubled scenes of Napoleonic Europe.

[72] At first the boys lived in Quincy with Mr. and Mrs. Richard Cranch. Their father entrusted to his brother Thomas B. Adams a general oversight of their education. Mary Cranch was the "Aunt Cranch" of John Quincy's boyhood, Abigail Adams's sister. The boys lived there until the death of Mr. and Mrs. Cranch in October 1811, after which they lived with another sister of Abigail Adams, Elizabeth (Smith) Peabody, widow of the Rev. John Shaw of Haverhill, "Aunt Shaw." She had married Stephen Peabody and lived in Atkinson, New Hampshire (six miles over the Massachusetts boundary), where the Adams brothers stayed and went to school until 1813, when they entered school in Hingham, five miles from their grandparents and Uncle Thomas in Quincy. When JQA became Minister to Great Britain in 1815, they joined their parents in London. Adams MSS. *Writings,* III, 496–8.

[73] *Writings,* III, 340.

CHAPTER VIII

At the Court of the Czar

(1809–1812)

Our attachment to the United States is *obstinate, more obstinate than you are aware of.*

COUNT RUMIANTZOV TO JOHN QUINCY ADAMS, OCTOBER 1810

How Europe had trembled in terror and reeled under the tread of Napoleon's armies since John Quincy Adams left Prussia in the year 1801! From the Danish Sound to Gibraltar, from the Baltic Sea to the Strait of Messina, the aggressive forces of the French Revolution marshaled under the greatest military genius of modern times had spread themselves in conquest over the Continent. The Holy Roman Empire was gone. Ancient monarchies and principalities in Germany, Italy, and Spain had disappeared. In their places stood new puppet states reigned over by members of the Bonaparte family. A united empire seemed about to take shape on the ruins of ancient Europe, an empire that if allowed to assume its final form and power might rule the whole world.

1

Two years after the renewal of war between France and Great Britain in 1803, a Third Coalition (Great Britain, Sweden, Austria, Russia) had risen against the Emperor of the French. To confront his enemies Napoleon turned away from the Channel coast after Lord Nelson and the British Navy had broken up his vast land-and-sea combinations for the invasion of England.[1] From his encampment near Boulogne he wheeled the Army of England – thenceforth the Grand Army – on a rapid march to the Danube. One after another he defeated his foes in a series of brilliant military successes: Austria at Ulm and Austerlitz, in 1805; Prussia (which entered the Coalition after Austria's defeat) at Jena-Auerstädt, in 1806; Russia at Friedland, in 1807. The Battle of Friedland, fought near the Russian frontier in East Prussia, left him victorious over all the mainland of Europe west of the Russian and Ottoman Empires, with the

[1] The naval campaign had already been decided when Admiral Villeneuve's fleet, off Ferrol, was turned back by Cornwallis and Calder in July 1805. Trafalgar, October 21, 1805, was Nelson's *coup de grâce* to the French and Spanish navies.

exception of Portugal, which his troops soon occupied, and Sweden, still insulated from him by the British Navy.

At the Czar's Baltic border Napoleon halted. He wanted a period of peace with Russia in order to perfect his Continental System for the ruin of England and to consolidate his power for the invasion of the Ottoman Empire and the fulfillment of his ambitions in the Near East and India. Alexander I on his part was happy to be able to turn back French armies by a diplomatic give-and-take that left him free to conquer Finland from Sweden and to marshal his resources for an ultimate contest with Napoleon in the Near East. In a dramatic meeting on a raft anchored in the middle of the Niemen River in the summer of 1807 the Imperator of the West and the Cæsar of the East reached an agreement that resulted in the treaties of Tilsit (July 7, between France and Russia; July 9, between France and Prussia). They set their seals on the new map of Europe, entered into a defensive and offensive alliance, and looked to the partition of the European dominions of the Sultan, all except Constantinople. They could not agree who should have that symbol and key of world empire, so they excluded it from their arrangements. The two Emperors pledged themselves to "the equal and perfect independence of all flags at sea" in the final peace with England, an ambiguous phrase that sounded something like the Freedom of the Seas. As for Prussia at Tilsit, she was dismembered, half her domains pieced on to Napoleon's puppet states, her fortresses and ports garrisoned by French troops.

Fifteen years previously, in the Netherlands, John Quincy Adams had first seen rise the "comet or coruscation of the day." Later, from across the Atlantic, he had observed the European sky all alight in its glare from the Tiber to the Niemen. As he watched the brilliant firmament he sensed the ever precarious position of the Corsican constellation. "Bonaparte appears to have at present as much upon his hands as he needs," he wrote as he prepared to sail from Boston, "and what he gains in Germany, he loses, it would seem, in Spain and Portugal, if not in Italy. He has stretched the bowstring till it cracks. He may as well reserve his resentments against us, and I hope he will until he shall see cause to forget them." [2]

This was an accurate trans-Atlantic analysis, as the events of the next five years were to prove, but the bow was bending ever stronger and the string was still stoutly holding when Adams and his family set foot on the quay of the river Neva in St. Petersburg, opposite the magnificent equestrian statue of Peter the Great, October 23, 1809, just before the ice closed in on the Bay of Kronstadt. Only a few days before they disembarked on Russian soil, Napoleon at Vienna had dictated to Austria, defeated for the fourth time, the Peace of Schönbrunn (October 14, 1809), which ceded the Adriatic littoral to him, thus opening up a land corridor of conquest to the Sultan's Balkan frontiers. Meanwhile his ally Alexander

[2] JQA to William Eustis, Boston, July 16, 1809. *Writings*, III, 333.

had brought Sweden to her knees: by the Peace of Fredrikshamn (September 17, 1809) she ceded Finland to Russia and agreed henceforth to exclude English ships from her ports.

In 1810 Napoleon was at the apogee of his power. To achieve the destruction of England he had compelled all the states of Europe to join his Continental System. When they faltered, he successively annexed them to the French Empire. During 1810 he took over the Kingdom of Holland, Oldenburg and northern parts of Berg, Westphalia, and Hanover, Lauenburg, and the Hanse towns of Bremen, Hamburg, and Lübeck. He occupied the whole coast of the North Sea, clear to the frontiers of Denmark, his ally against England since the British bombardment of Copenhagen in 1807 and seizure of the Danish fleet. Finally he took possession of Swedish Pomerania. From these newly occupied Baltic ports French privateers sallied forth to capture neutral ships, mostly American, defying the Continental System in northern Europe.

At the zenith of his career Napoleon divorced the Empress Josephine and made a marriage alliance with Austria, taking to his imperial bed Maria Louisa, an emperor's daughter. Only Great Britain, her storm-tossed fleets forever interfering with his plans on every sea and consequently in every land, notably in Portugal and Spain, seemed now to stand between the Emperor and his final goal. The strong-bent bow was presently to check in the bleak and stormy uplands of Spain, and the tight-stretched bowstring was at last to snap on the frosted steppes of Russia. From the Czar's own capital John Quincy Adams was to watch the great spectacle.

Alexander remained the nominal ally of Napoleon against Great Britain after Tilsit from 1807 to 1812, although most Russian energies were taken up in an effort to conquer the Danubian provinces (Romania) from Turkey, and Finland from Sweden, Britain's last lingering ally of the Third Coalition.

After the renewal of difficulties with Great Britain over neutral rights that followed the *Essex* decision of 1805, President Jefferson, yearning for an early peace in Europe that might relieve the United States of the necessity of "addressing measures to the interest of Great Britain" (that is, nonimportation), had hoped that the two Emperors, Napoleon and Alexander, still enemies in 1806, might find themselves on sufficiently common maritime ground to force Great Britain to accept the Freedom of the Seas in the coming peace settlement. The United States, he promised, would be friendly to the rules of the Armed Neutralities, including free ships free goods, and would even look with favor on the abolition of all contraband, but it could take no part in a European congress and would not even adhere to any guaranty of maritime principles that might be written into the final peace: "It would expose us to all the snares which might be laid for entangling us in the politics of Europe, and in the plans of those who may predominate in the negotiations." So wrote Secretary of State Madison to General John Armstrong, United States Minister Plenipotentiary setting out for France in March 1806. Nevertheless Armstrong was directed to intimate at least to the French Government how much the United States had the Freedom of the Seas "at heart." [3]

If Jefferson saw in the Czar a possible champion of the Freedom of the Seas in the next European peace settlement, Alexander perceived in the United States an offset to British maritime practice. This attraction became more evident in 1807 when Great Britain declared war on Russia following Tilsit, and hostilities seemed likely between the United States and Great Britain after the contemporaneous *Chesapeake-Leopard* affair. That outrage and the crisis with England over neutral rights signalized by the embargo had impelled Jefferson to send William Short on his way as Minister Plenipotentiary to Russia in September 1808. At the same time Great Britain's declaration of war on Russia had induced the Czar independently to commission a chargé d'affaires to the United States. Thus mutual interests served to bring into formal diplomatic relations [4] these distant continental nations of opposite political poles, powers that served to complement each other in world politics despite their ideological divergencies.

Such was the inveterate American interest in the Freedom of the Seas and such was the incipient diplomatic status of Russian-American affairs when President Madison appointed John Quincy Adams as Minister Plenipotentiary to the Czar of Russia, to take the place of Jefferson's appointee, Short, whom the Senate had refused to confirm after he had got as far as Paris and had some preliminary conversations with the Russian diplomatist Rumiantzov at the French capital.

2

The new Secretary of State, Robert Smith, did not prepare any special instructions for the Minister Plenipotentiary to Russia. Instead he gave him copies of the instructions previously issued by Madison to Short in 1808, and also those of 1806 to the Minister to France, General Armstrong.[5] From these documents Adams noted that his principal duties

[3] Secretary of State (James Madison) to John Armstrong, Minister Plenipotentiary to France, March 14, 1806. *Writings,* III, 322–5, n. 1.

[4] The first American Consul to St. Petersburg was John M. Russell, appointed November 24, 1794. Jefferson had sent a Consul, Levett Harris, to St. Petersburg in 1803. This opened the way for the Czar's appointment of André Dashkov in 1808 as Consul General at Philadelphia, with the additional title of chargé d'affaires "near the Congress of the United States." He presented his credentials July 11, 1809. After JQA's arrival in St. Petersburg as Minister Plenipotentiary, the Russian representative to the United States was raised to the same rank. See J. C. Hildt: *Early Diplomatic Relations of the United States and Russia.* Johns Hopkins Studies in Historical and Political Science, Series xxiv, Nos. 5–6 (Baltimore, 1906). Harris's consular correspondence from St. Petersburg, 1803–16, is preserved in DS.

[5] Both printed in *Writings,* III, 321–8.

near the Czar of all the Russias were to create good will, attend carefully to the just rights and interests of the United States, and to secure favorable treatment for American commerce; should the Emperor wish to discuss express stipulations of neutral rights, the Minister might expect further directives on these points. Adams, diplomatic reporter *par excellence,* must have noticed with particular satisfaction the following sentence: "The President will expect from you the most exact and ample communications, for which opportunities may be found."

One might wonder whether the Minister Plenipotentiary of a unique trans-Atlantic republic, so weak in power, so radical in politics, the very antithesis of a czardom, might expect more than perfunctory welcome and treatment in the glittering Russian court whose master had become a pivot in the international politics of Napoleonic Europe. Actually no one could have asked for a more friendly welcome at St. Petersburg, and never did a diplomat step into a situation better conditioned for the success of his mission. Thanks to Russia's necessities, the new American Minister straightway found himself a man of some importance.

The Chancellor, Count Rumiantzov, asked Adams in to see him the same day (October 24) that Consul Levett Harris communicated notice of his arrival, and promised that the Czar would give an audience as soon as he could get up from a slight injury. A few days later Adams and Harris were invited to a splendid diplomatic dinner, magnificent in every particular. The other guests of the Chancellor were bedecked with stars and ribbons beyond anything that our son of the Western World had ever seen even in Paris, London, The Hague, or Berlin; but he felt at home, for he had already dined in that very room as a youth in the year 1781, when the Marquis de Verac, French Minister of that time, had his quarters there. Now he noted that the French Ambassador, Caulaincourt, Duc de Vicence, was the principal personage at the dinner – the same who had carried out the kidnapping from neutral territory of the Bourbon pretender, the Duc d'Enghien, done to death in 1804 on Napoleon's order. Despite the shock of this murder to the Russian court, Caulaincourt had succeeded in convincing the Czar that he was not personally responsible for it. As long as diplomatic relations were suspended between Russia and Great Britain the Duke was the only representative of ambassadorial rank near the Czar's court. His prestige as well as his rank was unequaled. The diplomatic corps always alluded to him, and his successor, as *the* Ambassador. Because of his influence, and of the critical nature of Franco-American relations, Adams cultivated him assiduously.

At the Chancellor's table and afterward the Russian host bestowed many pointed and formal civilities upon the new Minister from the United States.[6] It was the beginning of an increasingly sympathetic relationship which lasted throughout the four tempestuous years of Adams's sojourn at St. Petersburg, never upset by the slightest contretemps. At

[6] *Memoirs,* II, 48–9.

this state dinner, first of many that he attended, Adams met the principal members of the diplomatic corps at once and under the most auspicious circumstances.

The Czar received him a week later at the Imperial Palace. As Adams stepped through the door of the Emperor's cabinet, in which the ruler stood alone, Alexander advanced to greet him.

"I am so glad to see you here," he said, in French.

Luckily for Adams, who conscientiously struggled with Russian during his four years in St. Petersburg, French was then the language of the court. In that tongue he was as fluent as Alexander himself. An extended personal interview followed the exchange of set greetings. Taking Adams invitingly by the arm and walking him over to a window that overlooked the Neva, as if to get out of earshot of the chamber door, the Emperor talked at length. He seemed perfectly apprised of the principal tenets of American foreign policy. Doubtless he had learned of them from Count Rumiantzov's conversations with William Short in Paris.

"With regard to the political relations of Europe, and those unhappy disturbances which agitate its different states," Alexander freely observed, "the system of the United States is wise and just. They may rely on me not to do anything to withdraw them from it. The Continent of Europe is now in a manner pacified. The only obstacle to a general pacification is England's obstinate adherence to a system of maritime pretentions which is neither liberal nor just. The only object of the war now is to bring England to reasonable terms on this subject. She can no longer flatter herself with any support for her system upon the Continent. . . . I am convinced that the good of my Empire, and of Europe, are best promoted by a state of peace and friendship between Russia and France, whose views, I believe from the assurances of that Government, are not all directed to the conquest of England, but merely to make her recognize the only fair and equitable principles of neutral navigation in time of war. The only danger to England from the establishment of these principles would be that France might be enabled, in consequence of them, to form and maintain again a large navy; but that can be no justification for England's maintaining a system oppressive and destructive to the fair and lawful commerce of other nations. The establishment of this just system of maritime rights is the purpose of France.

"As for me," the Czar went on, assuming a firmer tone and more dignified attitude, "I shall adhere invariably to those [principles] which I have declared. I am sensible that it subjects us to inconvenience; that the people suffer privations and some distress under the present state of things. But the English maxims are much more intolerable and, if submitted to, would be permanent."

Nothing that the Czar might say could have conformed more to American hopes for the Freedom of the Seas. Nothing could be better suited to the diplomatic temper of John Quincy Adams, who realized that the

British Navy, acting in purely British interest, must stop Napoleon's power from again crossing the Atlantic, but who smarted under the constant humiliation of British impressments of American seamen and British violation of American neutral rights, and who wanted to stay out of all of Europe's wars and to keep England and France balanced against each other. Amidst the Emperor's animated remarks Adams managed now and then to get in a word emphasizing the policy of his country to steer clear of political ties with Europe.

"The political duty of the United States towards the powers of Europe," he said at the first opportunity, "is to forbear interference in their dissensions. It will be highly grateful to the President to learn that their system in this respect meets the approbation of your Imperial Majesty. They are at once a great commercial and a pacific nation. They are greatly interested in the establishment of a system which would give security to the fair commerce of nations in time of war. The United States, and the world of mankind, expect that this blessing to humanity will be accomplished by your Imperial Majesty himself. The United States, *by all the means in their power, consistent with their peace and their separation from the political system of Europe,* will contribute to the support of the liberal principles to which your Majesty has expressed so strong and so just an attachment." [7]

Having got off to a good start under such high and friendly auspices, Adams's mission in Russia was a success from the first. Despite handicaps of low salary and expense account in the most costly and extravagant court of Europe he and his family remained *personæ gratæ* at the court throughout their long tour of duty there. At levees and balls the Czar always had a pleasant word for the Adamses, with attention to Mrs. Adams and her sister. Frequently – every few days – John Quincy Adams would meet the Emperor walking unattended on the quay or Admiralty Mall, and they would exchange amenities about the weather and even talk business. Adams always admired the young, affable, and elegant Emperor, with his personal disposition, so congenial with everything equitable and humane, and so peculiarly friendly to the United States.[8] He remained convinced that the Czar's personal sentiment was partly responsible for the friendly attitude of the Russian Government,[9] and he exercised all his tact to retain it. The Czar on his part always had a friendly esteem and respect for the republican diplomat who attended all court functions and ceremonies so conscientiously and so agreeably.

The first American Minister's uniform success in Russia was due, of

[7] See *Memoirs,* II, 51–3, and JQA to Secretary of State (Robert Smith), No. 5, St. Petersburg, November 6, 1809. DS, *Despatches, Russia,* I. Italics inserted.

[8] JQA to Secretary of State, No. 23. St. Petersburg, September 5, 1810. *Writings,* III, 489.

[9] JQA to the Secretary of State (James Monroe), St. Petersburg, No. 61, August 2, 1811. *Writings,* IV, 168.

course, to other factors than his own tactful conduct, although a single misstep on the slippery diplomatic ground of St. Petersburg could have spoiled his personal usefulness; it was due also to the obstinate desire of the Russian Government to have in the United States a potential counterweight to British sea power. At one of his first conferences with Count Rumiantzov the Chancellor frankly said that Russia needed some great commercial state to support as a rival to Great Britain and her exclusive maritime pretensions, that the United States of America were such a state, and the highest interest of Russia was to support and to favor them, as by their relative situation the two powers could never be in any manner dangerous to each other.[10]

3

The Adamses arrived at the Russian capital in the midst of the social season, with its long, long nights and scanty hours of daylight. Soon they plunged into a round of court ceremonies and diplomatic dinners, suppers, balls, masquerades, winter sports – sliding on the artificial "ice hills" – parties without end. Aside from almost daily court functions and Count Rumiantzov's numerous diplomatic dinners Adams was most often guest at the French Embassy. He picked up many a useful bit of information at the Duke's magnificent[11] table, where usually he met the diplomatic representatives of Napoleon's various puppet states; then he dined the rounds with them too.

A gay life like this, we know, did not suit his temper perfectly. It interrupted his "systematic occupations." The introspective passages of his Diary characteristically rue the long succession of lost hours, wasted from reading and study, never wasted to his country. "It is a life of such irregularity and dissipation as I cannot and will not lead." Much time passed before he felt free to devote himself to congenial interests in St. Petersburg and environs: the theater and opera, the academies and learned societies, libraries and museums, private picture galleries, gardens and resorts; to pursue his hobby of comparative weights and measures, and to visit such factories as there were – "I wish I could visit a manufacture once a week, and spend three hours at every visit."[12]

John Quincy Adams realized well enough that extravagance and dissipation had become a public duty, and he did not shirk, either in body or in spirit, the inevitable tours of hospitality. He talked brightly through the long dinners; he discreetly sampled the liqueurs of his Russian hosts; he walked the polonaise at the court balls and diplomatic dances; he played chess with the more staid members of the corps; he sat down to

[10] *Memoirs*, II, 65.

[11] JQA described the opulence of one of the French Ambassador's dinners in a long letter to his mother, March 22, 1810. *Writings*, IV, 27–34.

[12] *Memoirs*, II, 322.

cards with the dowagers; he went conscientiously to the *Te Deums* and important funerals. What bothered him most of all, even more than the time lost from his beloved books, was the high cost of official life at the Russian court.

On the banks of the Neva it was almost a part of the law of nations that a minister should reside in splendor and magnificence. The Russian officials all lived above their salaries, many of them conspicuous for never paying their debts, others notorious for making both ends meet by means that in the United States would have been deemed dishonorable but which in Russia were much less disreputable than too severe an economy. Most members of the diplomatic corps had large salaries and expense accounts. The French Ambassador's official expenses were a million rubles ($350,000 U.S. at that time) a year.[13] Napoleon encouraged heavy expenditures on the part of his ambassadors as well as among his officers, not liking to have men too independent about him — such at least was the diplomatic gossip in St. Petersburg. The Dutch Minister spent fifty thousand rubles ($17,500 U.S.) a year. The Swedish Minister was modest: he claimed one could live decently on twenty thousand rubles ($7,000 U.S.) — he had a salary of thirty thousand plus a military pension of three thousand.

The salary of a minister plenipotentiary of the United States, $9,000 a year, plus an equal amount as "outfit" for travel to a post and setting up an establishment there, was next to that of the President ($25,000 a year) the highest pecuniary emolument at the disposal of the Republic. The Vice President and cabinet officers got only $5,000 and justices of the Supreme Court $3,500, the Chief Justice $4,000.[14] To the American people a minister's salary seemed extravagant. But Adams, truly an economical man, felt cramped and greatly embarrassed at the court of Alexander of Russia. It was impossible to rent a furnished house or apartment. The bare walls of a single floor or house big enough to hold his family cost $1,500 to $2,000 a year, and furnishings five times as much more. Not an article of clothing that he brought with him was suitable for attendance at the numerous court functions, and the cost of a lady's dress was far more expensive and her wardrobe must needs be more varied than that of a man. And one had to keep three times as many servants as elsewhere.

Adams finally established his family in their first comfortable home in St. Petersburg. It was a house, rented at 6,000 rubles a year, in the Novy Pereulok (New Place) where it met the Moika Canal. But his household troubles had just begun. "Since we entered this house, my monthly expense books amount to double what they were the first month," he noted in his Diary. "We have a maître d'hôtel, or steward; a cook, who has under him two scullions — mujiks; a Swiss, or porter; two footmen; a mujik

[13] *Memoirs,* II, 72, 132. *Writings,* III, 435.

[14] *An Account of the Receipts and Expenditures of the United States for the Year 1810* (Washington: A. & G. Way, Printers; 1812).

to make the fires; a coachman and postillion; and Thomas, the black man, to be my valet-de-chambre; Martha Godfrey, the maid we brought with us from America; a femme-de-chambre of Mrs. Adams, a house-maid and a laundry-maid. The Swiss, the cook, and one of the footmen are married, and their wives all live in the house. The steward has two children, and the washerwoman a daughter, all of whom are kept in the house. I have baker's, milkman's, butcher's, greengrocerman's, poulterer's, fishmonger's, and grocer's bills to pay monthly, besides purchases of tea, coffee, sugar, wax and tallow candles. The firewood is, luckily, included as a part of my rent. On all these articles of consumption the cook and steward first make their profits on the purchase, and next make free pillage of the articles themselves. The steward takes the same liberty with my wines." [15]

To cut down costs and pilfering, Adams dismissed the cook and engaged a caterer to furnish dinners at twenty rubles a day.

The first United States Minister to Russia simply could not repay all the official hospitality and that of colleagues and still live within his means. "Friends" offered to loan him money. He found himself placed between the alternatives of squandering within two or three years the means of subsistence of his family and education for his children or of incurring a reputation for parsimony, not to call it by a harsher name. To keep rigorously within his Yankee means threatened to expose him personally to social obloquy and might even have an injurious effect on the reputation and interests of his country.

Alarmed by John Quincy's discouraging letters about the high cost of living at the Russian court, Abigail Adams sat down and wrote a letter from Quincy to President Madison asking him to order her son home. The President promptly obliged, furnished the diplomat with a letter of recall to present if he so desired, and sent him a commission – unanimously ratified by the Senate – as Associate Justice of the Supreme Court of the United States. But the Minister declined the new appointment and set himself resolutely and uncompromisingly to make his income cover his outgo. To that principle he held obstinately during the remainder of his sojourn in Russia.

Once he had successfully made the rigorous adjustment, he found himself leading as agreeable and comfortable a life as he could expect anywhere outside his own country. He went to dinners and parties to which he could reciprocate only in the most limited way. The diplomatic corps did not seem to mind. Maybe they comprehended the parsimony of republics, maybe they secretly admired it. As a matter of fact, Mrs. Adams was unwell and withdrawn from society a great deal of the time, and he went alone, or with one of his secretaries, to many of the diplomatic dinners. These circumstances afforded some justification for less entertainment on his part. Notwithstanding their handicaps the Adamses continued to be popular and successful until the end of their stay. There is nothing

[15] *Memoirs,* II, 193.

to show that the United States suffered from its economy in this instance, as it has in so many others since. Only its representative suffered.

The Czar understood Adams's situation. One bright spring morning when the two met on the Fontanka, near the bridge under which the canal joined the river, Alexander asked Adams if he was going to take a house in the country for the summer. Adams answered no, that he had for some time had the intention, but he had given it up.

"Why so?" the monarch asked, and, seeing the American hesitate, relieved him from some of his embarrassment by saying good-naturedly: "Financial considerations, perhaps?"

"Well yes, Sire, in large part," Adams had to admit, putting on as good humor as possible.

"Well enough," the Czar responded. "You are quite right. One must always balance income and outgo."

A maxim worthy of an Emperor, thought Adams to himself, though few emperors practice it.[16]

Actually Adams and his family did get into the country that summer, after all. His landlord sold over his head the house he had rented in the capital city, and the new owner would not renew the lease. By good fortune he rented at a moderate price a delightful summer villa on Apothecaries' Island, in the Nevka River, one of the streams that flow from the mouth of the Neva into the Bay of Kronstadt, not far from the Imperial Summer Palace. In this "Russian arcadia" he passed one of the pleasantest summers of his life.[17]

4

In making known to the Czar and his Government how much the United States had at heart the Freedom of the Seas, without being able or willing to go to war for it, or guarantee it, or be entangled for it, and in getting expressions from Czar and Chancellor of Russia's determined loyalty to those maritime principles, John Quincy Adams at the outset acquitted himself perfectly of one of the principal objects of his mission. The other specific task was protection of American shipping in the ports of Russia. At this point we must recall the provisions of the Non-Intercourse Act of March 2, 1809 and some of its results. The technicalities of this American legislation and its complicated relations to trade and diplomacy in the Baltic gave Adams a vital, though neutral, role in the denouement of the vast European tragedy that led to the final downfall of Napoleon.

[16] *Memoirs*, II, 268.

[17] JQA to JA, St. Petersburg, July 26, 1811; to AA, October 2, 1811. *Writings*, IV, 146,231. At the close of the summer the Adamses took another house, at 5,000 rubles annual rent, on Vosnesensky Prospekt and Ofitserskaia Street, where they dwelt until Adams left for Göteborg in 1814, soon after which Mrs. Adams and son Charles moved to smaller quarters.

This latest American measure of economic coercion had repealed the embargo except so far as it related to Great Britain or France, or their colonies or dependencies, *or places in the actual possession of either.* The new law still denied American harbors to French and British ships, henceforth on pain of confiscation, but provided that if either France or Great Britain should so revoke "or modify" her edicts as that they should cease to apply to the United States, then the President could lift all restrictions in favor of the party so doing, but would continue to enforce the act against the nation persisting in its illegal measures. It was at once an act to relieve American trade from total stoppage and a well-freighted bid for the revocation of their retaliatory systems by the rival belligerents one after the other. Meanwhile it gave relief from the hated embargo by allowing American trade with those European countries which were the unwilling allies of France but not yet actually in French occupation: the small German states, Denmark-Norway, Sweden, Prussia, Russia, Portugal, Spain, also Brazil and the revolted American colonies of Spain.

The new Latin American revolutionary governments were quick to open their ports to the Stars and Stripes, but none of the European states except Russia dared to receive American ships. For Napoleon was ordering his puppets to enforce his Continental System: to confiscate or to sequester (which amounted to the same thing) American vessels which had on board British goods or goods of British origin, or which had touched at a British port, paid British tariffs, bought a British license, or submitted to visit and search by a British naval officer.

Great Britain was first to invoke the contingent provisions of the non-intercourse law in an effort to get the American restrictions lifted as against trade with her dominions and to have them continued against her enemy.

Immediately news of the act reached London, a new order in council of April 26, 1809 modified the obnoxious orders of 1807 so as to permit direct American trade to Baltic countries – that is, without stopping at British ports, paying British duties, and buying British licenses – and to all European ports north of the river Ems not in French possession. In London this was esteemed to be a most important concession to the United States,[18] and indeed it was, but it missed the mark of conciliation because it insisted on substituting for the old orders a "paper blockade" of the remaining coasts of Europe occupied by French forces: from the Ems River southwestward around the Spanish Peninsula (except where

[18] "You will not fail to observe that the Substitution of a simple Blockade of the Countries, an Intercourse with which remains interdicted to Neutrals, for the circuitous Voyage touching and paying Duty in the Ports of England, entirely relieves the Retaliatory System [of England against France] from that Objection which appears to have been most sensibly felt in America, as a Grievance and an Injury." George Canning, British Foreign Minister, to David Erskine, Special Envoy to the United States, May 2, 1809. *Instructions to British Ministers to the United States, 1791–1812*, B. Mayo, editor. *Annual Report* 1936 AHA, III, 270.

French control was interrupted by British occupation or native revolt in Portugal and Spain) and along the Mediterranean and Adriatic shore to include northern Italy. All these coasts were to be treated as before; that is, "as if the same were actually blockaded by His Majesty's Naval forces in the most strict and rigorous manner."[19] It was of course impossible to assert a blockade over that extensive coastline and still conform to the definitions of the United States and of the historic Armed Neutralities.

The new order in council of April 26 was part and parcel of the specious project of George Canning for Anglo-American agreement, whereby Great Britain would repeal her naval measures so far as the United States was concerned, *provided* the United States would let the British Navy enforce the Rule of the War of 1756 and American nonintercourse with the interdicted coasts of France and of French dominions and satellites. In other words, Great Britain would repeal her orders in council forbidding American neutral trade to *all* French belligerent ports if the United States would forbid its citizens and their ships to trade to those same ports and let the British Navy enforce the prohibition!

Already before the conciliatory order of April 26 was issued in London a special British Envoy Extraordinary and Minister Plenipotentiary, David Erskine, had taken an unauthorized step in Washington toward Anglo-American reconciliation. He signed an exchange of notes with Secretary of State Robert Smith on April 18–19, 1809 to carry out the contingent provisions of the Non-Intercourse Act. The United States agreed to lift nonintercourse with British dominions and Great Britain repealed its orders in council so far as the United States was concerned, *unconditionally*. As soon as he learned of this agreement, Canning repudiated it on the ground that Erskine had violated his instructions. News of the British disavowal of the Minister's arrangement had reached Boston two weeks before Adams left that port for Russia.[20] President Madison immediately reimposed the statutory prohibitions against Great Britain, but the interval in which they had been suspended had allowed upwards of six hundred American ships to leave port with cargoes of raw materials for the relief of English consumers. Doubtless some of these vessels after discharging their cargoes in English ports took on English goods for carriage to the ports of Britain's enemy Russia before returning home across the Atlantic.

Amid these diplomatic equivocations the new British blockade order of April 26, 1809 remained in force. As noted, it allowed a direct American neutral trade to enemy states not actually under French dominion or occupation – that is to say, the Baltic countries. The purpose of the new measure was as much to frustrate the Continental System in northern Europe as it was to conciliate the United States. If it did not achieve its

[19] *ASPFR*, III, 241.

[20] JQA to the Secretary of State (Robert Smith), Boston, July 18, 1809. Adams MSS.

American objective it was to be successful in attaining its European goal, for it really encompassed Napoleon's ruin by provoking him to war with Russia in a vain effort to enforce his system. As will appear later, Napoleon on his part tried to offset British diplomatic inroads in the Baltic by luring the United States into a war with Great Britain.

The Baltic states, Denmark-Norway, the Duchy of Mecklenburg, Prussia, Sweden after 1809, and Russia had joined the Continental System to the extent of excluding from their ports British ships and goods and also neutral vessels bringing goods of British origin, including "colonial" goods like sugar, cotton, rice, coffee, indigo, all noncontraband luxury articles of European consumption. But none of them accepted the system willingly. Even Denmark, victim of British bombardments and Napoleon's only sincere ally, resented the French Emperor's commands to enforce his decrees. All of them had been members of the Armed Neutralities. All still favored those principles, which were also American principles. All preferred to admit American neutral goods in American neutral ships. The degree to which they considered American ships and cargoes to be actually British enemy vessels and thus subject to capture depended upon Napoleon's power over them; and his power over Denmark, with his legions on the frontier of Holstein, was much greater than over Russia.

Denmark-Norway asserted sovereignty over the Sound, or passage into the Baltic, and the right to levy toll. If a neutral ship did not stop to pay toll it ran the risk of capture; if it stopped to pay, it put itself in reach of Danish privateers, to be seized as a British enemy ship in disguise. Many American vessels successfully ran the Danish gantlet into the open waters of the Baltic. Sometimes they lent themselves to the shelter of British convoy, directly or indirectly. Frequently British vessels would disguise themselves as American ships, with false papers almost perfectly forged in London. The American Consul at St. Petersburg, Levett Harris, made a fortune, at the cost of his own reputation, by clearing doubtful ships and cargoes through the venal Russian neutrality commission that passed upon their authenticity.[21]

[21] *Memoirs,* IV, 283, V, 329. W. D. Lewis, an American merchant in Russia, came home in 1819 and accused Harris of prostituting his office corruptly for personal gain. Harris promptly sued him for libel, for $50,000 damages. In the ensuing long-drawn-out trial, finally decided in the Supreme Court of Pennsylvania, Harris's counsel acknowledged readily enough that their client had made a fortune, but explained that his intercessions with the Russian board of commissioners had been in his capacity as merchant, not consul! The court awarded $100 nominal damages to Harris, which Lewis considered a moral victory.

JQA's papers contain summaries of arguments on both sides, reported to him, and copies of his own depositions. William D. Lewis to JQA, Philadelphia, February 15, 1827. Adams MSS.

There is no printed report on this famous case of ***Harris* v. *Lewis,*** but there are meager references to it in the old manuscript dockets, 1820–7, of the Supreme Court of Pennsylvania, Eastern District.

Thanks to the ease with which a British ship and crew could be made to look like an American ship and crew, to the temporary suspension of nonintercourse with Great Britain by the short-lived Erskine Agreement, to the difficulty of enforcing the Non-Intercourse Act so as to prevent an American ship stopping at England en route to the Baltic, and thanks also to Russian demand for overseas commodities exchanged against her own products, British colonial products continued to get into Russia under the American flag. At profitable prices they flowed overland from that Empire through the Continental System into central and western Europe, defying Napoleon's prohibitions.

When the *Horace* passed through the Sound in 1809 bearing the first American Minister to St. Petersburg, there were thirty-six American prizes which Danish privateers had taken into the harbors of the Christiansund, and sixteen more in the ports of Jutland proper, worth some five million dollars.[22] There they awaited judgment for having violated the Continental System. Their captains and agents appealed to Adams for protection. Although not commissioned to deal with the Government of Denmark, the American Minister to Russia did go so far as to call at the country residence of the Danish Chancellor, Count Bernstorff, to intercede as well as he could under the circumstances. The Chancellor was not at home, and time was pressing to complete the voyage before late autumn frosts should close up the Gulf of Finland, so Adams left with the American Consul, a Danish subject who seems not to have been wholly disinterested, some remarks to be presented by him on behalf of the captured vessels.[23]

John Quincy Adams was not one of those timid career diplomats whose rule for sure promotion in the course of time is to avoid any mistake by never assuming any initiative. His first diplomatic move upon arriving in St. Petersburg was to importune the Czar's Government to use its influence with Denmark for the release of the captured American ships being held in the ports of Holstein. In so doing he was acting on his own responsibility. He could easily have avoided any such duty. Danish-American affairs lay outside his mission, as did all Danish-Russian affairs. Count Rumiantzov frankly told him that he thought nothing could be done under the circumstances, but the Czar, anxious to cement friendship with the United States as well as to keep up the flow of Russian exports, overruled the Chancellor and did make effective representations to Denmark. Thereupon the Danish Government promptly released the ships detained in Holstein harbors, only a portion of such seizures made under French pressure. For this the Czar received the formal thanks of the United States Government. Adams's services in this instance alone were worth hundreds of thousands of dollars to his countrymen, a few of whom in

[22] JQA to Secretary of State (Robert Smith), No. 2. Elsineur, October 4, 1809. DS, *Despatches, Russia*, I.

[23] *Writings*, III, 343–59. *Memoirs*, II, 22–37.

the Senate and in the press [24] had opposed a legation in Russia as a useless expense.[25]

Adams next addressed himself with the aid of Levett Harris to American ships detained in Russian ports on suspicion of false colors or cargoes of enemy goods. Invoking the Russian-American principles of the Freedom of the Seas, he urged that vessels and cargoes be released for the advantage of both Russian and American commerce. There followed a struggle of influence between the American Minister and the French Ambassador. Some twenty-three American ships, after being detained at Archangel, Kronstadt, Riga, and other Russian ports through the winter of 1810–11, were eventually released in time for spring navigation. "It seems you are great favorites here. You have found powerful protection," the defeated Caulaincourt acknowledged.[26]

Adams won out because the Czar, for the prosperity of his own realm, had determined to free himself of the Continental System. By a ukase of December 19/31, 1810 he declared Russia's independence of Napoleon. While still formally excluding enemy products this decree regulated imports into Russia in such a way as to discriminate prohibitively in favor of goods customarily imported in American ships and against imports from France. The principal French exports to Russia were either excluded altogether or, as in the case of wines, required to come by sea, which amounted to the same thing.[27] From then on, John Quincy Adams had no troubles. American ships, excluded by the Continental System from all the other Baltic nations, flocked to Russian harbors and were received there without restraint. As the year 1811 wore toward its end, first American and then even British flotillas began to arrive in ballast from England to take back Russian naval stores.[28]

Alexander had turned the Continental System against Napoleon himself. He had refused to stultify Russian principles of the Freedom of the Seas and to cripple such Russian commerce as survived the war. Because

[24] See *Columbia Centinel* of Boston, December 23, 1809.

[25] Before the collapse of the Continental System, Danish naval forces captured 160 American ships, of which 42 were actually condemned. For spoliations and delay the United States held Denmark responsible after the war. The total American claims then entered amounted to $2,262,280.36½. In 1830 Denmark settled them for a lump sum of $650,000. George W. Erving, who was sent as a special minister to Denmark in 1811 to negotiate a settlement of these claims, estimated their real value at $1,750,000. If this is correct, the United States compromised at thirty cents on the dollar, not to mention arrears of interest. For the Danish spoliations and American claims see *ASPFR*, III, 327, 344, 523, 529–36, and J. B. Moore: *Digest of International Arbitrations to which the United States has been a Party,* V (Washington, 1898), 4549–73.

[26] *Memoirs,* II, 226. See also H. Adams: *History,* V, 419.

[27] A printed copy in English is enclosed with JQA's No. 37 of January 27, 1811 in DS, *Despatches, Russia,* I. For French text of the ukase see *Le Moniteur,* January 31, 1811.

[28] Heckscher: *Continental System,* pp. 235–6.

of this the United States had no spoliation claims against Russia after peace descended on Europe, as it did against France and the nations which Napoleon forced into his system and obliged to obey his imperial decrees. The Czar's decision was an easy victory for Adams over the most powerful diplomatic representative in Europe, the French Ambassador at St. Petersburg.

The Russian ruler's refusal to carry out the Continental System and his eventual admission of British ships and goods destroyed that system and helped to bring the two allied Emperors into collision.[29] It is testimony to Adams's diplomatic talent that amid these thickening clouds of Franco-Russian distrust, rivalry, and war he kept on ever friendly terms with the French Ambassadors, both the Duc de Vicence and his successor, Count Lauriston.

5

While the Minister of the United States was thus securing from the Russian Government the favor of intercession with Denmark for the release of American prizes and was successfully protecting the neutral rights of his countrymen in Russian ports, he received instructions to take up a special subject that had been presented by the Russian Minister at Washington, André Dashkov. It was a problem big with importance for the disputed sovereignty of the United States on the Pacific Coast.

In the middle of the previous century Vitus Bering, a Danish navigator in the Czar's employ, had carried the Russian flag from Siberia to North America. Later the Czar "by right of possession" had conferred upon the Russian-American Company a hunting and commercial monopoly on the North West Coast. The Company founded an island settlement at Sitka (New Archangel, latitude 57° 30′) in 1799 and pursued a precarious existence based on the fur trade with the not always friendly Indians of those inhospitable shores. No precise boundaries marked off Russian sovereignty over what is now called Alaska, neither north nor south along the coast nor into the interior. The Czar did not then seem to attach much importance to this remote extreme of his empire where his domains entered the New World. The Russian-American Company's monopoly extended by its charter as far south as 55° N.L. It is worth noting for the future that the Company also received the right to make new discoveries north and south of 55° and to claim them as Russian possessions, "according to prescribed rules," in regions not previously occupied by or become dependent upon any other nation.[30]

[29] For the correspondence of Napoleon and Alexander I, in detail beyond the subject of this study, see Serge Tatistcheff: *Alexandre Ier et Napoléon (1801–1812) d'après leur correspondance inédite* (Paris, 1891); and Albert Vandal: *Napoléon et Alexandre Ier, l'Alliance Russe sous le Premier Empire* (3 vols., Paris, 1891–6). Eugene Tarlé has written a scholarly and more recent account of *Napoleon's Invasion of Russia, 1812* (translated from the Russian, New York, 1942).

[30] See Map 6.

To the south of Bering's Sea the Russian advance came into conflict with unmarked Spanish pretensions resting on voyages as far as Mount St. Elias (60° N.L.); with British assertions of sovereignty over the same coast going back at least to the maritime exploring expeditions of Captains Cook (1778) and Vancouver (1792) and the overland journeys of Alexander Mackenzie (1793) and Irwin Fraser (1808); and with American claims based on Robert Gray's discovery of the Columbia River (May 11, 1792) and the expedition of Lewis and Clark (1803–6), not to mention the Louisiana Purchase. Out of such a territorial tangle of disputed sovereignty the United States by skillful diplomacy was peaceably to win its way through to unchallenged title to the golden western shore of the later Continental Republic. John Quincy Adams as Secretary of State would play an important part in this great achievement, in his diplomacy with Spain, Great Britain, and Russia.

The Russian proposal, first made at Washington in January 1810, looked innocent enough, and possibly was. The Czar's Minister, André Dashkov, disclosed that he had instructions to negotiate a convention by which the United States would prohibit its citizens from trading in arms and munitions of war with the natives *in Russian possessions* on the North West Coast of America. Such a treaty, he suggested, would help secure the safety of American citizens as well as the Russian trading establishments; it would also increase the trade of both and generally strengthen friendly relations between the two countries.

Now a prohibition of this kind by the United States, embodied in a convention with Russia, would have amounted to formal recognition of Russian sovereignty over a vast and unbounded area of North America. At one stroke of the pen it might have seriously weakened or possibly destroyed vitally important American territorial pretensions in that region, depending on how far south the Russian territories overlapped American claims. Even Robert Smith, prompted perhaps by President Madison, seems to have been alive to this danger. The Secretary of State asked Dashkov if he was authorized to fix a southern limit to the Russian possessions. Informed that the Russian Minister had no such power, Madison transferred the whole question to John Quincy Adams at St. Petersburg for further discussion, with proper warnings about the necessity of first fixing a boundary "as little advanced southerly as may be." [31]

When Adams brought up the subject with Count Rumiantzov, the latter held forth an additional inducement for such a convention: the Russian Government would turn over to American neutral ships the trans-Pacific carrying trade between the Russian-American Company's settlements and Canton. Adams asked the Chancellor to point out the southern boundary of Russian territory on the North West Coast. He received only the reply that this would require some consideration, since Russian maps included

[31] Secretary of State (Robert Smith) to JQA, May 5, 1810. DS, *Instructions, U.S. Ministers,* VII, 90–3.

the whole of Nootka Sound (on Vancouver's Island) and down to the mouth of the Columbia.[32]

From previous correspondence of Consul Harris with Count Rumiantzov, containing memorials[33] of the Russian-American Company, the American Minister learned that Russia had already claimed as far south as the great River of the West, named by its discoverer, Captain Gray, after his Boston trading ship, the *Columbia,* and definitely claimed for the United States by Lewis and Clark in 1804. Careless diplomacy in accepting the Russian proposal without limiting Russian claims would have frustrated epic American achievements and the claims to sovereignty that flowed from them.

In a later interview Adams repeated the question: "What is the boundary line within which it is the wish of your government to extend the prohibition?" The Chancellor responded merely by promising to make a full report to the Emperor of Adams's observations. Really, he said, the Russian Government had no great solicitude in the matter. As to the fixing of a boundary, it would be most advisable to defer that to some future time. Meanwhile American ships would be free to trade with Russian settlements. "Our attachment to the United States is *obstinate, more obstinate than you are aware of.*"[34]

Adams thought the inveterate friendship of the Russian court for the United States and a desire for American trade made the time propitious for a commercial treaty. He recommended such a step to the Secretary of State.[35] In due time he received instructions to go ahead and negotiate a treaty on a conditional most-favored-nation basis for commerce, complete freedom of the seas for neutrals in time of war except to ports really blockaded, and the abolition of contraband if such could be done by ignoring it altogether. The instructions also proposed an innocuous temporary compromise article for the North West Coast: most-favored-nation trading privileges for American citizens trafficking with Indians "who may be under the control of the Russian Government"; and citizens of the United States not to be molested in trading with the independent tribes of Indians except in firearms and ammunition, and even so only during an actual war between those tribes and Russia. Trade on that coast was to be on a "mutually liberal" footing pending ultimate settlement of precise boundaries.[36] Without recognizing unreservedly Russian sovereignty at

[32] JQA to Secretary of State, No. 27, St. Petersburg, October 12, 1810. DS, *Despatches, Russia,* I. *Memoirs,* II, 152–3, August 28, 1810.

[33] *Writings,* III, 477 n. JQA to Secretary of State (Robert Smith), No. 25, St. Petersburg, September 30, 1810. DS, *Despatches, Russia,* I.

[34] Ibid., No. 27, St. Petersburg, October 12, 1810. See also *Memoirs,* II, 179–80. October 9, 1810.

[35] JQA to Secretary of State (James Monroe), St. Petersburg, April 29, 1811. *Writings,* IV, 63.

[36] Secretary of State (Robert Smith) to JQA, February 1811, enclosing Heads of Treaty. DS, *Instructions, U.S. Ministers,* VII, 149–54.

the expense of American claims, this formula was calculated to take care of professed Russian desires to limit the arms trade with hostile Indians.

The Chancellor's reaction was cordial enough. "It is the interest of Russia," he repeated, "to encourage and strengthen and multiply commercial powers which might be the rivals of England, to form a balance to her overbearing power." [37] But treaty negotiations never actually got started. Increasing uncertainty of peace between France and Russia and between the United States and Great Britain made it impossible to go ahead. "We cannot know from day to day whether there will be any commerce," Rumiantzov acknowledged. "It is impossible to do anything more than provide for the day that is passing over our heads. What will come tomorrow is beyond all human foresight. What, for instance, would be the consequence of a war between the United States and England, which you have told me you think probable, and which I think so myself?" [38]

Both men had to admit that an Anglo-American war would stop all American commerce with Russia. So the two Governments awaited more peaceful times for the conclusion of their first treaties, of boundary in 1824,[39] of commerce in 1832.

6

When John Quincy Adams went out to The Hague as Minister in 1794 he had unexpectedly found himself studying vital American interests at the very epicenter of European diplomacy. So it was to be at distant St. Petersburg sixteen years later. Tremendous issues and bitter rivalry were pushing France and Russia toward war: the Polish Question, the Eastern Question, the Czar's desertion of the Continental System, the rapid advance of French annexation and occupation during the year 1810 from the North Sea to the Baltic, ever closer to the Russian frontier. As the Emperor of the French became more and more embarrassed by the Spanish revolt at one end of the Continent, the Czar of all the Russias became more and more independent of his great ally at the other end. Napoleon came to the fateful decision that success of his Continental System against Britain required him to reduce Russia to his will, even as he had subjected Prussia and Austria and had annexed the Netherlands, before he could bring down England and at last fulfill his vast ambitions for the conquest of Constantinople and the East. He hoped to make a wide sweep of conquest through Russia to India by way of Moscow and Persia, with the Russian Army serving as an "auxiliary force" after Alexander's de-

[37] *Memoirs,* II, 271–2. June 4, 1811.

[38] *Memoirs,* II, 289–90. August 5, 1811.

[39] See below, Ch. XXV, Section 4.

In 1813 the commission of three (Adams, Bayard, Gallatin) appointed to negotiate a peace with Great Britain under Russian mediation also were empowered to negotiate treaties of commerce with Great Britain and with Russia.

feat.[40] In the Czar's capital Adams was best located to watch the diplomatic revolution that followed, and then the tragic invasion that was to end the conquering Corsican's dreams of world domination, serving as a model for Adolf Hitler's military strategy and downfall a century and a quarter later.

As early as the autumn of 1810 Adams reported an increasing opinion throughout Europe that the alliance between Russia and France would not be very long-lived.[41] Although Napoleon was not yet ready to strike in the season of 1811, a sort of public instinct everywhere sensed that war between the two empires must come. At the diplomatic dinners of the Chancellor and of the Ambassador the American Minister felt the atmosphere increasingly charged with a new potential. At court functions he noted how frequent and how animated were the conversations apart between the Czar and Napoleon's representative. At first furtively and then openly the diplomatic corps began to speculate on the imminence of hostilities. Adams talked about it frankly with the Ambassador and with the Emperor himself while the diplomatic atmosphere thickened through that tense winter of 1811–12.

One after another the storm signals broke out indicating a return of the conflict to northern Europe, and Adams reported them to Washington from his station on the Neva. In the autumn of 1811 Russian troops engaged in the Turkish war retired to the north of the Danube and contingents began to move over to Russia's Polish frontier.[42] In January 1812 the Czar made a treaty of alliance with Sweden, his recent enemy. In February Count Rumiantzov told Adams that he expected France to attack as soon as the season allowed.[43] In May Alexander made peace with Turkey on the line of the Prut River and shifted his remaining troops to confront the army that Napoleon was mobilizing in Saxony. More and more the Czar turned toward England, still a nominal enemy, as hostilities approached with France, and also glanced toward Napoleon's nervous Austrian ally.

In Europe the dreaded war came ever closer to the north. Out walking one frosty spring day in March 1812 Adams met the Emperor as was his wont. After exchanging the usual amenities the Czar broke out:

"And so it is that, after all, war is coming which I have done so much to avoid – everything. I have done everything to prevent this struggle (*cette lutte*), but thus it ends. . . . Everything points toward war, however. *He* keeps on advancing. He began by taking Swedish Pomerania –

[40] Tarlé, op. cit., pp. 4–5.

[41] JQA to Secretary of State (Robert Smith), No. 30, St. Petersburg, November 6, 1810. DS, *Despatches, Russia,* I.

[42] JQA to Secretary of State (James Monroe), No. 67, September 12, 1811. DS, *Despatches, Russia,* II.

[43] JQA to Secretary of State (James Monroe), No. 79, St. Petersburg, February 7, 1812. DS, *Despatches, Russia,* II.

now he has just occupied[44] Prussia — he can't advance much farther without attacking us."[45]

In the tragic days ahead, and particularly in the peace settlement that followed in 1815, Czar Alexander was John Quincy Adams's hero, the only truly moderating influence in Europe, "the Titus of the Age, the Delight of Human Kind."[46]

The Czar's manner became steadily more grave and less cheerful as Adams met him on their promenades. Presently he left for the front. On June 25, 1812,[47] the French Army crossed the Russian frontier. The French Ambassador and the diplomatic representatives of France's puppets and allies, except the Ministers of Denmark and Sardinia, cleared out of Russia and turned their archives over to Adams for safe-keeping; a British Ambassador and a Turkish Minister reappeared in the capital city of St. Petersburg.

Napoleon did not get as far as St. Petersburg. Instead he led his Grand Army of over half a million men, Frenchmen and puppet allies, including Italians, South Germans, Saxons, Poles, Prussians, and even Austrians, across the steppes on the fatal march to Moscow, that bleak Scythian city, soon mantled with the freezing cold and snows of a starving Russian winter.

Most of the diplomats, and the generals, expected an easy triumph for Napoleon's hosts, just as in 1941 the diplomatic and military authorities of our day expected Hitler's hordes to cut through Russia like a knife through cheese. But Adams was skeptical of Napoleon's ability to conquer such a country. "The Fabian system of warfare," he wrote to his father as the Grand Army advanced into Russia, "which succeeded in our Revolutionary War, and which has recently been successful against the Generals of Napoleon in Portugal, is now systematically tried against himself. It probably was never brought to a severer test; but the modern Alexander may after all be destined like his predecessor to be arrested in his career of domination by the Scythians."[48]

Adams was quick to realize the implications of Napoleon's Russian disaster for American diplomacy and for world politics. "The great events daily occurring in the country whence I now write you," he observed when French defeat seemed certain, "are strong and continual additional warnings to us, not to involve ourselves in the inextricable labyrinth of

[44] Napoleon, keeping his garrisons in adjacent duchies, had evacuated Prussia in 1808.

[45] *Memoirs*, II, 352. March 19, 1812.

[46] JQA to AA, Ghent, June 30, 1814. Adams MSS. See also JQA to AA, Reval, May 12, 1814, and to Louisa Catherine Adams, Ghent, July 2, 1814. *Writings*, V, 43, 55.

[47] JQA to Secretary of State (James Monroe), No. 90, St. Petersburg, July 1, 1812. DS, *Despatches, Russia*, II.

[48] JQA to JA, St. Petersburg, August 16, 1812. Adams MSS.

European politics and revolutions. . . . The politicians [i.e., the Essex Junto] who have been dreading so long the phantom of universal monarchy may now rest their souls in peace."[49]

On the last day of 1812 he described to his mother the calamity that had overtaken Napoleon on his retreat from Moscow:

"Of the immense host with which six months since he invaded Russia, nine-tenths at least are prisoners or food for worms. They have been surrendering by ten thousands at a time, and at this moment there are at least one hundred and fifty thousand of them in the power of the Emperor Alexander. From Moscow to Prussia, eight hundred miles of road have been strewed with his artillery, baggage wagons, ammunition chests, dead and dying men, whom he has been forced to abandon to their fate — pursued all the time by three large regular armies of a most embittered and exasperated enemy, and by an almost numberless militia of peasants, stung by the destruction of their harvests and cottages which he had carried before him, and spurred to revenge at once themselves, their country, and their religion. To complete his disasters the season itself during the greatest part of his retreat has been unusually rigorous, even for this northern climate; so that it has become a sort of by-word among the common people here that the two Russian generals who have conquered Napoleon and all his Marshals are *General Famine* and *General Frost.* There may be, and probably is, some exaggeration in the accounts which have been received and officially published here of the late events; but where the realities are so certain and so momentous the temptation to exaggerate and misrepresent almost vanishes. In all human probability the career of Napoleon's conquests is at an end. France can no longer give the law to the continent. . . . A new era is dawning upon Europe."[50]

To General Famine and General Frost he might have added General Kutuzov and the generality of the Russian people. Their casualties were greater even than those in Napoleon's army, but they saved their own country.

Adams's reports of French losses proved to be no exaggeration — on the contrary. Of the 600,000 men whom Napoleon led into Russia, only 30,000 staggered back across the Niemen in December 1812. The Corsican returned to Paris without even a personal military guard. France's whole position in northern Europe and Germany collapsed. In the wake of French defeat arose the triumphant Fourth Coalition.[51]

"The general result has been the natural and obvious consequence of the preceding campaign of 1812." So John Quincy Adams summed up for the appraisal of his father at home the transformed European situation at the beginning of 1814. "The fatal blow to the exclusive dominion of

[49] JQA to TBA, St. Petersburg, November 24, 1812. *Writings,* IV, 408.

[50] *Writings,* IV, 421–2.

[51] JQA to Secretary of State (James Monroe), Nos. 102 to 112, St. Petersburg, December 11, 1812 to May 31, 1813. DS, *Despatches, Russia,* II.

France upon this Continent was given by the immediate hand of Heaven."[52]

Simultaneously with the French invasion of Russia the War of 1812 between England and the United States, so unwelcome to Russia, so desired by France, so feared by John Quincy Adams as the undoing of American independence, had broken out in the New World and raised new problems of diplomacy for the American Minister at St. Petersburg, whose mission so far had been a perfect success.

[52] JQA to JA, No. 29, St. Petersburg, January 2, 1814. Adams MSS.

Portions of this chapter originally appeared in the *Virginia Quarterly Review*, XXI (No. 4, Autumn 1945), 553–68.

CHAPTER IX
The War of 1812
(1812–1814)

A nation, coextensive with the North American Continent, destined by God and nature to be the most populous and most powerful people ever combined under one social compact.

JOHN QUINCY ADAMS TO ABIGAIL ADAMS,
ST. PETERSBURG, JUNE 30, 1811

THE SECOND war between the United States and Great Britain was due to a complex of at least three "causes" that came together in the spring of 1812: (1) impressment, an ever hateful thing and justification for war if there ever was one, but never an issue for which alone the United States had been willing to fight; (2) neutral rights, concerning which Napoleon beguiled President Madison into believing that Great Britain was a more heinous offender than France; (3) American agrarian expansion, the popular desire, particularly in the inland West and South, to take advantage of the European war and to requite British frontier Indian outrages by conquering Canada from Great Britain and incidentally Florida from Britain's ally Spain. None of these issues of itself would have resulted in war. Together with the difficulties of communication in those days, they combined to defeat Madison's strategy of auctioning the giant belligerents out of their respective systems of retaliation.

1

The measures initiated by Jefferson and continued by Madison lent themselves to exploitation by French diplomacy. Napoleon wished to bridge the Atlantic with his Continental System by constraining the United States to close its ports like a subject European country to all intercourse with Great Britain. It had been his consistent effort, ever since the Armed Neutrality of 1800, to marshal the remaining neutrals of the world into an unbroken circle of enemies against the Mistress of the Seas.

Against this stratagem Russia and the United States were the last to hold out. To bring Russia back into his system he made war on that country, unsuccessfully. To keep the United States in line he mobilized all the craft of his diplomacy, successfully. He "hoodwinked" President Madison into believing that France's obnoxious decrees were revoked while Britain's orders in council were not, and thus maneuvered the trans-Atlantic Republic back into the Continental System and then into war with England. The Emperor's purpose was to occupy his inveterate enemy across the Channel with an American war while he engaged in his Russian campaign. After he knocked out Russia and conquered the East he would turn finally on England. Then all would be over.

From Peter the Great's Baltic "west window" John Quincy Adams anxiously watched the diplomatic controversy. He saw what Madison the auctioneer was determined not to see: that Napoleon's real purpose was to "rivet upon us the fetters of France" in order to get the United States into the war on his side.[1] By the same token it would be the real interest of America, as it had been ever since 1793, to stay out of the European conflict.

Adams suffered for his country under the tyranny of British naval measures and the ever smarting humiliation of impressment. He considered the kidnapping of American citizens, native-born or naturalized, as abominable as the slave trade itself.[2] He was willing to go to war with England to do away with impressment if it could be done successfully; but he did not think his nation stood a chance to win against the British Navy, and besides his countrymen would not fight over impressment alone. As to a conquest of Canada, he felt that a few more years of peace in America and of war in Europe would so bankrupt and exhaust Britain that all her possessions in the New World would inevitably and peacefully fall to the United States anyway.[3]

It had been a primary article of John Quincy Adams's political creed that all that was necessary to proceed "with giant strides to honor and consideration and national greatness" was the preservation of the Union.[4] Now war threatened the Union and with it the vision of a continental future so nobly begun.

The Louisiana Purchase, for which he had voted in the Senate against the desires of the Essexmen, had been the first giant stride to honor and consideration and national greatness. To protect the unbounded upper reaches of that vast procurement the young Senator had blocked ratifica-

[1] JQA to TBA, St. Petersburg, November 6, 1811. *Writings*, IV, 273.

[2] *Memoirs*, II, 422.

[3] JQA to TBA, St. Petersburg, November 24, 1812. *Writings*, IV, 407.

[4] "There is no one article of my political creed more clearly demonstrated to my mind than this, that we shall proceed with giant strides to honor and consideration, and national greatness, if the union is preserved; but that if it is once broken, we shall soon divide into a parcel of petty tribes at perpetual war with one another, swayed by rival European powers, whose policy will agree perfectly in the system of keeping us at variance with one another, and who will at the same time govern and despise the party they may respectively protect." JQA to Charles Adams, The Hague, June 9, 1796. *Writings*, I, 493.

tion of the King-Hawkesbury Convention of 1803. The next year Lewis and Clark had penetrated beyond the Purchase, across the "Stony Mountains," down the Great River of the West to the Pacific Ocean. In Russia, John Quincy Adams in 1810 conserved American claims to the North West Coast in his discussions with the friendly Count Rumiantzov. Then the Astorians established their post at the mouth of the Columbia in 1811. On the eve of the War of 1812 Adams's continental instincts had quickened to the conviction that, if only the Union could be preserved, by keeping clear of the "vortex," it was the destiny of the United States peaceably to expand by further giant strides over the whole Continent of North America.

Could the Union be preserved while the youthful nation grew up to take the giant strides? It was Adams's continual fear that Junto Federalism would break up the Union, kill the nation, and destroy its continental future.

"If that Party [Federalist] are not effectually put down in Massachusetts," he wrote to his mother from Russia in the summer of 1811, "as completely as they already are in New York, and Pennsylvania, and all the southern and western states, the Union is gone. Instead of a *nation, coextensive with the North American continent, destined by God and nature to be the most populous and most powerful people ever combined under one social compact,* we shall have an endless multitude of little insignificant clans and tribes at eternal war with one another for a rock, or a fish pond, the sport and fable of European masters and oppressors." [5]

"The whole continent of North America appears to be *destined by Divine Providence* to be peopled by one *nation,"* he wrote to John Adams a few weeks later, "speaking one language, professing one general system of religious and political principles, and accustomed to one general tenor of social usages and customs. For the common happiness of them all, for their peace and prosperity, I believe it indispensable that they should be associated in one federal Union." [6]

Union was John Quincy Adams's watchword for national greatness, as the balance of powers, executive, legislative, and judicial, had been John Adams's formula for constitutions.[7] Independence, Union, Neutrality in Europe's war, Manifest Destiny on the American Continent, these were the basis of Adams's foreign policy in 1812 to secure the American way of life. To be sure, the phrase Manifest Destiny was not coined until 1845, but Adams for one had stamped its metal in 1811.

[5] JQA to AA, St. Petersburg, June 30, 1811. *Writings,* IV, 128. Italics inserted.

[6] JQA to JA, St. Petersburg, August 31, 1811. *Writings,* IV, 209. First italics inserted.

[7] "*Union* is to me what the *balance* is to you, and as without this there can be no good government among mankind in any state, so without that there can be no good government among the people of North America in the state in which God has pleased to place them." JQA to JA, St. Petersburg, October 31, 1811. *Writings,* IV, 267.

Adams's hope that his country could keep out of the European war seemed to be realized – at the eleventh hour. Whether as a result merely of the American restrictive measures, as he himself believed, or of a more complicated economic crisis in England, which historians have not yet explained, the British Government found itself in an increasingly desperate position. By the President's imposition of nonimportation in 1811, and a second congressional embargo in 1812, the United States in effect had again stepped back into Napoleon's Continental System. This final embargo was the "wrenching stroke," so Adams believed, "to the stubbornness of the British Ministers." [8]

It were folly for any British Government not to use all efforts to preserve peace with the United States and reopen an alternate reservoir of overseas commerce. Late in 1811 Great Britain had made belated satisfaction for impressment at least from public ships of war: His Majesty's Government restored to the *Chesapeake* the American sailors taken from her deck in 1807. The King paid reparations to the families of American citizens killed or injured in the outrage. Prime Minister Perceval's Government was already tottering under the weight of the orders in council when a demented subject assassinated him (May 11, 1812). A complete new Ministry then came in under Lord Liverpool, Viscount Castlereagh in charge of Foreign Affairs. With the approbation of all parties the new Government hastened to repeal (June 25, 1812) the obnoxious orders in council and the paper blockade of 1806, so far as they concerned the United States.

It looked as though the easy ingenuity of Madison's measures short of war had won a complete diplomatic victory. First Napoleon had been persuaded to repeal his Berlin and Milan Decrees. Then Great Britain in her turn had been forced to yield, however unwillingly. Each side had consequently revoked its illegal measures against the United States. Peace seemed assured.[9]

The British concessions came too late to save the situation. A week before, on June 18, 1812, the United States Congress, under the lead of the Expansionists of 1812, had declared war, by a vote of 79 to 49 in the House of Representatives, and 19 to 12 in the Senate. "Its principal cause and justification," John Quincy Adams felt when he heard the news of war, "was removed precisely at the moment when it occurred." [10]

[8] JQA to AA, St. Petersburg, July 13 [12], 1812. *Writings*, IV, 368.

[9] "I please myself with the hope that these great and real concessions extorted from the stubbornness of the British councils, though at the last extremity, will preserve us from that greatest of scourges, war. Though until the Orders in Council were removed I thought that war inevitable, I cannot think it so now, as the great objects for which we have been struggling have been substantially yielded." JQA to Benjamin Waterhouse, St. Petersburg, July 25, 1812. *Writings*, IV, 381.

[10] JQA to TBA, St. Petersburg, September 29, 1812. "Correspondence of John Quincy Adams, 1811–1814," edited by Charles Francis Adams, Jr., in *Proceedings of the American Antiquarian Society*, n.s., XXIII (April 1913), 120. This publication of

To the American diplomat in the distant Russian capital this war seemed to have come upon this country by a sort of "fatality." "I must lament, deeply lament," he wrote to his father, "that the change of system which at the same time had taken place in England, could not be known to produce its effects upon the deliberations of Congress." [11]

If only there had been an Atlantic cable in 1812! If Congress had known of the fall of the Perceval Government and the impending repeal of the orders in council, the vote for war might not have carried. A shift of only four votes in the Senate would have stopped a declaration.

Adams adjusted himself as best he could to the fact of war. Perhaps, after all, it was necessary to redeem the national spirit. "If it had been possible for us to avoid a War at this time," he reflected amidst the tread of marching Russian patriots, "and even to have enjoyed many more years of Peace, war must after all have come at last, and if we are so disqualified for it now [12] is it not possible that in the progress of enervation and languor which another long period of inaction would have produced, the very spirit of independence itself might have been extinguished, and we should have really [become] what Fisher Ames said we were ten years ago 'of all men on earth the fittest to be slaves.'" [13]

So, with peace in his own heart, John Quincy Adams found comfort in war as a bitter school for patriotism.[14] It would be thus in America as it was in Russia.

The War of 1812 would unexpectedly bring to him new diplomatic labors. Negotiations for peace started as soon as war began.

2

As Napoleon marshaled his legions for the attack on Russia, Count Rumiantzov in his conferences with Adams had shown increasing anxiety about the possibility of war between Great Britain and the United States. If Russia should switch friends and enemies, it was better that her new ally,[15] Great Britain, be relieved from any hostilities with the United States. Incidentally such a war would close off American commerce to Russia. This was the view of the Czar's Government.

The French Ambassador in St. Petersburg was just as anxious for the

---

the more important letters from Russia contains a number not included in Ford's edition of the *Writings* of JQA.

[11] November 5, 1812. Adams MSS.

[12] Hull's surrender of Detroit, August 16, 1812.

[13] Ibid. (note 11).

[14] "The calamities of war are always deplorable, but they seem to be a necessary furnace for the refinement of nations. Thirty years more of peace would have made cowards of us all and destroyed the character of man in America." JA to JQA, Quincy, December 23, 1813. Adams MSS.

[15] Russia and Great Britain promptly made peace and an alliance, in June 1812, as soon as Napoleon began war on Russia.

United States to go to war against England, for the advantage of French policy.[16] Again the trans-Atlantic Republic had become a pawn in the power politics of Europe.

Despite the common belligerency of France and the United States, Madison's Government kept clear of a French alliance. France had despoiled American neutral commerce almost as much as Britain. If French depredations were any less in amount it was only because France lacked the naval power to do as much harm. The American people actually had less love for their cobelligerent Napoleon than for England, their enemy. Nevertheless it was with relief that in October 1812 John Quincy Adams opened a dispatch from Secretary of State James Monroe assuring him that, come what might, the United States would not form any closer connections with France,[17] the enemy of Russia as well as the enemy of Great Britain.

Count Rumiantzov received this news with lively satisfaction. "Do you have any objection to my communicating this to the British Ambassador, Lord Cathcart?" he asked.

Cathcart, one of the bombarders of Copenhagen, had just arrived at St. Petersburg. Despite the American declaration of war, he had left a card at Adams's house, and Adams returned the call. Their countrymen had begun to kill each other on the high seas and on the Continent of North America, but both diplomats expressed the wish that their differences might be yet amicably settled. They did not avoid each other at court functions.

The Chancellor's question was a full-sized diplomatic poser to be answered yes or no on the spot. Adams had no authorization to pass any such assurance on to the enemy. It was clearly safer for him personally to say yes, he did object. Absolute certainty that the United States would not make common cause with France might make the British Government indifferent to peace with America. On the other hand, it might promote a spirit of pacification. It was with this latter hope that Adams promptly risked the answer: no, he did not object.[18]

The Czar's Government already had sounded out Adams on the acceptability of Russian mediation to end the Anglo-American war. At the moment the American Minister had not received any statement from Washington, not even the one that led to the exchanges of amity just mentioned. He could have responded, securely and unexceptionably, that he had no authority to say anything, that he must refer the question at

[16] JQA to Secretary of State (James Monroe), No. 70, St. Petersburg, October 3, 1811. *Writings,* IV, 232–6.

[17] The Secretary of State to JQA, July 1, 1812. *ASPFR,* III, 625.

[18] "In calculating the operation of a generous purpose even upon the mind of an inveterate enemy, I feel an irresistible impulse to the conclusion that it [the enemy's mind] will be generous like itself [the generous purpose of the American Minister to St. Petersburg]." JQA to the Secretary of State, No. 102. St. Petersburg, December 11, 1812. *Writings,* IV, 417.

once to his Government. But that would have required at least six months of war before an answer could be had merely to the question whether the United States would welcome an *offer* of mediation.

Again Adams did his utmost toward restoring peace with England. He assured Rumiantzov that although he was not authorized to say so, he was certain that his Government, however it might reply to the Emperor's offer of mediation, would be sure to consider it as a new evidence of His Majesty's regard and friendship, and that he personally did not know any obstacle or difficulty in the way of accepting the offer.

"I lament the war," he declared to the Russian Chancellor, "particularly as occurring at a period when, from my good wishes for Russia and for the Russian cause, I should rejoice to see friendship and harmony taking place between America and England, rather than discord and hostility. I know the war will affect unfavourably the interest of Russia. I know it must be highly injurious both to the United States and to England. I can see no good results likely to arise from it to anyone." [19]

Thus did John Quincy Adams, six months away from his Government, stretch his powers and responsibility. Instead of reproving him for taking so much discretion, Secretary of State Monroe commended him, in the name of the President, for all his work so far in Russia.[20]

Napoleon's defeat in Russia and the shameful failures of the initial American campaigns against Canada and Florida, plus the opposition of New England to the war, made the United States Government eager, anxious for peace. Madison snapped up the Czar's proffer of mediation without even waiting to see if Great Britain would do so. He quickly appointed two special plenipotentiaries to serve with the independent-minded Adams to negotiate peace under Russian mediation: Albert Gallatin, Secretary of the Treasury, and Senator James A. Bayard of Delaware, a Southern Federalist.

The British Government responded to Adams's hope for peace negotiations, but not through Russian mediation. It was unwilling to submit such issues as impressment and blockade to the mediation of a sovereign who had proclaimed to the world the principles of the Armed Neutralities of 1780 and 1800. Lord Castlereagh insisted that impressment was a problem of internal government, constituting a sort of family quarrel, not susceptible to outside mediation however friendly. But he wrote to Secretary Monroe that England was ready to negotiate directly with the United States. She would be willing to appoint plenipotentiaries to meet American representatives either at the neutral city of Göteborg or in London, for the conciliatory adjustment of the differences between the two states, "upon principles of perfect reciprocity, not inconsistent with the established maxims of public law, and with the maritime rights of the British

[19] JQA to Secretary of State (James Monroe), Nos. 95, 98, St. Petersburg, September 30, October 17, 1812. *Writings,* IV, 389, 401. *Memoirs,* II, 401–3, 412, 415.

[20] Secretary of State (James Monroe) to JQA, April 26, 1813. *Writings,* IV, 477.

Empire." It is important to keep this precise wording in mind. It became the "frame of reference" for the negotiations at Ghent.

The Czar's mediation offer and Adams's response to it had the effect of bringing the two enemies to discuss peace between themselves. That much alone was a great boon in the existing state of the world, with British triumphs girdling the globe and the prospect ahead of having to face the mightiest belligerent in the world disengaged from all other foes.

Gallatin and Bayard joined Adams in St. Petersburg in July 1813. They lingered there fruitlessly for six months before being notified of Britain's formal refusal to mediate.[21] British influence isolated them from any direct contact with the Czar, then on the field of battle in Germany. Eventually they got tired of waiting and started home by way of Amsterdam with the expectation of feeling out the enemy at closer quarters. From Holland they went to London, with the permission of the British Government. There they paved the way for direct negotiations with the enemy, to take place as soon as the President should commission plenipotentiaries for that purpose.

The British Government was not averse to negotiating at Göteborg, even though Sweden had been a member of the Armed Neutralities of 1780, 1794, and 1800. Sweden looked devoutly to London for such a consummation of her territorial ambitions in the coming European peace settlement. The annexation of Norway meant more to that country in 1814 than Freedom of the Seas. But Castlereagh preferred to hold the parleys in London if acceptable; if not, then at some spot closer than Sweden to the center of European affairs. Gallatin was not opposed to London. He thought it desirable to keep as closely as possible in touch with Castlereagh.[22] Bayard, for one, would not consent to negotiate in the enemy's capital.

Gallatin and Bayard finally compromised on the city of Ghent, in Dutch

[21] "Their refusal [of the British Government] was [finally] communicated, not to the Chancellor, and Minister of Foreign Affairs, at St. Petersburg, but directly to the Emperor himself at Töplitz, at the most critical moment of the eventful campaign of 1813. The Emperor, whether absorbed by the immense combination of military movements and of multifarious negotiation in which he was then involved with all Europe, or whether purposely forbearing to make known a document marking the distrust in which he was held by his most important ally, never communicated to his own Chancellor, the rejection by Great Britain of his mediation. The knowledge of the fact came to the American Plenipotentiaries through other channels, and after repeatedly writing to the Chancellor for an official communication, which might warrant them in considering the negotiation as closed, which the Chancellor has repeatedly informed them he was not enabled to make; Messrs. Gallatin and Bayard, at the close of the month of January 1814 left St. Petersburg and proceeded to England, leaving me to receive any official communication which might afterwards be made by the Russian Government on the subject of the Mission." JQA's "Observations submitted with my accounts to be settled." Washington, November 26, 1817. Adams MSS.

[22] *A Great Peacemaker: The Diary of James Gallatin, Secretary to Albert Gallatin, 1813–1827, with an Introduction by Viscount Bryce* (New York, 1914), p. 14.

Flanders (Belgium), a newly liberated country still garrisoned by allied troops and therefore only nominally neutral. Much nearer to England than Göteborg, Ghent was also conveniently on the way from London to Paris and to Vienna, where Europe's statesmen soon would make the big decisions of world politics. The United States was still counting on the continental powers to write the Freedom of the Seas into the coming general peace settlement and to influence Great Britain in favor of those principles in any separate Anglo-American treaty.

Madison was as quick to accept Castlereagh's offer to discuss peace directly as he had been to grasp at Russian mediation. He nominated a new peace commission of five men, including the three who had been named to the Mediation Commission, and two new members: Henry Clay of Kentucky, Speaker of the House of Representatives, and Jonathan Russell, an adopted son of Massachusetts, then rising in the diplomatic service as first Minister to be appointed to the court of Sweden. The Senate confirmed them all. Since it accepted Gallatin only after he had ceased to be Secretary of the Treasury and after earlier acceptance of the other four, it was John Quincy Adams, named first in the President's joint commission, who became chairman of the Peace Commission.

In St. Petersburg, Adams received his new commission, together with advice from the Secretary of State that if peace were made it was the President's intention to make available to the public his further services, next time as Minister to Great Britain. Hurriedly he arranged the affairs of his Legation, appointed Levett Harris [23] chargé d'affaires, and took leave of the Russian court. Already he had said good-by to Count Rumiantzov. The Chancellor, caught between France and Great Britain in 1812, had fallen back on his own great rule of diplomacy: always love your friend as though one day he might be your enemy, and always hate your enemy as though one day he might become your friend.[24] After Napoleon's flight from Russia the rule would work no more. Count Nesselrode, closer to the Czar in the new Anglo-Russian alliance and accompanying the Emperor in the field, was taking over the actual direction of foreign affairs. Rumiantzov's authority flickered out with the failure of his mediation between the United States and Great Britain.

It was with real regret that Adams saw the Chancellor disappear from the Foreign Office. Of all the statesmen with whom he had dealt he had never known one of such irreproachable public integrity and private

[23] Harris, the Consul at St. Petersburg, had held the office of secretary to the Mediation Commission and in that capacity had accompanied Bayard and Gallatin to Amsterdam and London. It was therefore necessary for Adams to summon him back. During the period between Adams's departure and Harris's return to the Russian capital, the Minister's nephew and private secretary, William Steuben Smith, had charge of the Legation. Smith would join him at Ghent, on the way back to the United States, September 17, 1814. Even then Adams did not entrust the confidential record of the negotiation to him until after the peace was signed.

[24] *Memoirs,* II, 481.

honor. Rumiantzov had been a real friend to America. At his last interview he repeated to Adams what he had already said to Gallatin and Bayard, that his heart was American and that if it were not for his age and infirmities he would certainly go to America (presumably as Russian Minister to the United States). He had been a staunch advocate of a general treaty embodying the principles of the Armed Neutralities against the maritime pretensions of England.[25] That was the reason for his downfall in Britain's hour of triumph.

It was now time for Adams to part from his family. Louisa and little Charles Francis accompanied him out from the city as far as the posthouse opposite the Grand Duke Constantine's summer palace. There at half past four in the afternoon of the rapidly lengthening daylight on April 28, 1814, at the close of their fifth Russian winter, he embraced wife and son in farewell. They would have to wait through still another long winter in the Czar's whitened capital.

3

The Peace Commission over which John Quincy Adams was to preside in Ghent was the strongest delegation that the United States could have sent abroad. Four of the five men were as able and competent as any group they might expect to meet from any nation anywhere.

Gallatin, senior member if not the ranking spokesman of the group, was born and educated in Geneva, the son of a capable Swiss family, friends and correspondents of Voltaire. He still spoke English with a strong accent. As an orphan he had come to the United States during the American Revolution and soon found himself a tutor in French at Harvard College. At the close of the war he invested his patrimony in western Pennsylvania lands and grew up with the country there. He entered the United States Senate in 1793. In the following year a Federalist majority expelled him from that body on the uncertain technical ground that he had not been a citizen of the United States for the required ten years. Later, in 1794, he persuaded his radical and misguided countrymen of the Whisky Rebellion to submit peaceably to the laws of the nation. He became a prominent Republican leader in the House of Representatives. As Secretary of the Treasury he was Jefferson's most important subaltern next to Madison. Spokesman for the Madison Administration in 1814, he was easily the most eminent man on the Peace Commission. He was also the most urbane, notably when contrasted with Adams, a typical Yankee in manner, or with Clay, the outspoken Westerner. Adams had not known Gallatin very well in Washington. In St. Petersburg the two men quickly came to appreciate each other's qualities and abilities.

[25] JQA to the Secretary of State (James Monroe), No. 128, St. Petersburg, February 5, 1814. *Writings,* V, 15–18.

James A. Bayard bore an old Huguenot name. A graduate of Princeton College, he became a leading lawyer in Wilmington, Delaware. As a Federalist Senator from the State of Delaware he had helped make the political deal that decided the contested election of 1800 in favor of Jefferson over Aaron Burr. Adams had first met Bayard in London in 1795 when the latter represented American spoliation claims in British courts on appeal from orders in council. In the Senate later he had admired his colleague's superior eloquence, but noted: "His manner is always commanding, rather than conciliatory." [26] The two men had clashed in the Senate on small issues. They grated a little on each other during the idle months at St. Petersburg. Bayard, who was unwell, found Adams harsh in manner, careless of trifles. He was too retired, so the Senator fancied, from the social activities of the diplomatic corps. Adams on his part was somewhat reserved toward Bayard because his fellow Commissioner had discussed the qualities of his colleagues with the Commission's secretarial staff. But at Ghent Adams found Bayard "entirely *another man,* with good health, good spirits, good humour, always reasonable," and "an American to the quick." [27]

Henry Clay, rising leader of the West, had commanded the Warhawks in Congress in 1812. As a youth he had read law in George Wythe's famous office in Richmond, Virginia. He had moved over the mountains to Kentucky to become an early apostle of Jeffersonian democracy. He was now an ardent nationalist, although his expansionism of 1812 had been defeated by the disasters of the war to which it led. Adams had first met his Kentucky colleague during the latter's initial short term in the Senate in 1806–7. "A young man, an orator – and a republican of the first fire," he had noted after listening to Clay's maiden speech.[28] Clay was the ablest politician on the Commission. He was the most prominent political leader in the country, a man with his eye on the Presidency. Quite obviously Madison had put him there to represent Congress and to command the confidence of the West.

Jonathan Russell, youngest member of the delegation, was a graduate of Rhode Island College (later called Brown University). He had been a minor leader of the Jeffersonian party in New England. On the eve of the War of 1812 he had served as chargé d'affaires successively in France and in England, in which posts he had carried on an agreeable correspondence with Adams in St. Petersburg. Russell was thoroughly familiar with all the controversies over neutral rights. In 1814 Madison appointed him as the first Minister to Sweden. His new office might help neutral rights in the peace negotiation, particularly if it should take place at Göteborg. Not without considerable ability, Russell was a smaller man than any of

[26] *Memoirs,* I, 402.

[27] *Memoirs,* II, 573–7. *Writings,* V, 66, 161.

[28] *Memoirs,* I, 444. January 15, 1807. Bernard Mayo has written a superb book on *Henry Clay, Spokesman of the New West* (Boston, 1937).

the other plenipotentiaries in political stature and character. In the negotiations at Ghent he supported Clay's views and hung on the Speaker's future for political preferment.

Adams's own position on the Commission was a tribute to his unequaled experience. He knew more about European affairs than any other American. It looked like a tough and unprofitable assignment, from which he was likely to emerge with his own political future much damaged if not forever ruined.[29] Seriously as all his fellow Commissioners undoubtedly took their duties, none of them labored like Adams. He begrudged every minute lost from work. The hours that he took off from official duty he used for indispensable exercise, solitary walks about the city, or for inspection of museums and historical antiquities, or searchings in bookshops. More time than this he would not steal from his writing-table and candle. He could not help noting that his colleagues in their spare hours, of which there always seemed to be plenty, frequented the coffee-houses and public reading-rooms. They took their exercise mostly at the billiard table.[30] More than one morning as he was getting up at dawn to read his Bible he heard a card party breaking up in Clay's room next door.[31]

Despite their individual tempers and differences the American plenipotentiaries managed to live in good and friendly harmony in bachelor quarters at the Hotel Lovendeghem, in the Rue des Champs. At first it was a little difficult for Adams to share their conviviality. "They sit after dinner and drink bad wine and smoke cigars, which neither suits my habits nor my health, and absorbs time which I cannot spare. I find it impossible, even with the most rigorous economy of time, to do half the writing that I ought." [32] Adams himself had given up smoking in his forty-fifth year (1812) after reading a paper by his old friend Dr. Benjamin Waterhouse of Harvard on the injurious effects of tobacco on the human system.[33] He took a table apart while the others dined together.

Such a silly aloofness annoyed his colleagues. Clay spoke to him about it. Thereafter he sat with them. It was good for him. He relaxed still further. He next made it a point to attend all the receptions, dinners, concerts, plays, and card parties that the good people of Ghent, in their eager hospitality, showered on the American delegation. For two months they all dined together regularly, including the secretaries; then it was Russell who dropped out and took separate lodgings, "for some trifling personal convenience of saving of time," so the reformed John Quincy Adams explained.

All the Commissioners had secretaries except Adams.[34] There was also

[29] H. Adams: *History,* IX, 16.

[30] *Writings,* V, 89.

[31] *Memoirs,* III, 32, 39.

[32] *Memoirs,* II, 656.

[33] Donald M. Goodfellow: "Your Old Friend J. Q. Adams," *N.E. Quarterly,* XXI (No. 2, June 1948), 230.

[34] See note 23 above.

Christopher Hughes, secretary to the whole Commission. Two of the delegates had their sons along with them, George Russell and James Gallatin. The Russell boy was a normal enough American youth who excited no comment beyond Adams's later note that he was a lively and intelligent lad.[35] James Gallatin, on the other hand, was a playboy who ended up by becoming an expatriate in France. He left a sprightly diary not without historical value.[36]

No one has set down the individual personalities and characteristics of the five Commissioners more accurately, or more mercilessly in comparison with himself, than John Quincy Adams in his correspondence with his wife during the progress of the negotiations.

There was Gallatin, copiously informed, vivacious in intellect, fertile in resource, coolly argumentative as compared with Adams's own warmth of disputation and temper: "Mr. Gallatin keeps and increases his influence over us all. It would be an irreparable loss to our country if it had been deprived of the benefits of his talents in the negotiation." Gallatin and Adams saw eye to eye on most matters, but privately the Pennsylvanian thought his Massachusetts colleague "deplorable in judgment!" Gallatin was not without his weakness, too, although Adams leaves no notice of it. He prided himself on his European origin and his higher culture. The only real Americans, he thought, were red Indians. "Father . . . is a foreigner and is proud of it," Gallatin's young son wrote in his diary at Ghent.[37] It was possible to flatter the ex-Secretary of the Treasury on his European background. There was none among the British delegation, Adams was sure, equal to Gallatin, or to Bayard.

"Of the five members of the American mission the Chevalier has the most perfect control of his temper, the most deliberate coolness; and it is more meritorious because it is really self-command. . . . I can scarcely express to you how much both he and Mr. Gallatin have risen in my esteem since we have been here, living together."

Clay, thought the self-mortifying Adams, most resembled himself: "There is the same dogmatical, overbearing manner, the same harshness of look and expression, and the same forgetfulness of the courtesies of society in both. An impartial person judging between them I think would say that one has the strongest, the other the most cultivated understanding; that one has the most ardency, the other the most experience of mankind; that one has a mind most gifted by nature, the other a mind less cankered by prejudice." [38]

Russell, noted the senior delegate from Massachusetts, took the least

[35] *Memoirs,* III, 186.

[36] See note 22 above.

[37] *Diary of James Gallatin,* pp. 34–5.

[38] W. C. Ford, when editing the *Writings,* put together a number of these appreciations at the time of "The Treaty of Ghent and After." *Proceedings of the State Historical Society of Wisconsin,* 1914, pp. 78–106. See also *Writings,* V, 148, 238–9.

active part in the business at hand. He had scarcely anything to say either in the conferences with the British plenipotentiaries or in the discussions within the Commission. He followed the lead of Clay. As the youngest member of the Commission, Russell was "more solitary and less social in his disposition than the rest of us. . . . He nevertheless bears his proportion of all the entertainments that we give. But he has a high sense of his personal dignity, and sometimes takes offense where none is intended to be given. This has never happened upon any circumstance connected with the business of the mission . . . but we have seen the manifestations of his temper in the occurrences of social intercourse, as well in our particular circle, as in our relations with the people of the country."[39]

These five distinguished men of such varying backgrounds and personalities represented all sections of the United States and all complexions of political opinion, except of course the defeatist Junto Federalists. Despite their different characters and points of view they held together and always presented a united front to the enemy. Appointment of such a Commission in itself was a political achievement of the first order. It contained one recent Cabinet officer, one Senator, three ex-Senators, as well as the last Speaker of the House of Representatives. Any peace these men could make would get overwhelming national approval, both in the Senate and from the people. Any compromise they refused would most likely unite the country in a more desperate war of defense.

The British Government did not think it necessary to send its best men to treat with the Americans, leaders like Castlereagh, Canning, Wellesley, Grenville, or Wellington. The Liverpool Ministry reserved the ablest officers it could muster outside of the opposition to hold France down and to settle the general peace of Europe at Vienna. The plenipotentiaries who were to take their places across the table from the five Americans were Lord Gambier, Henry Goulburn, and Dr. William Adams.

Gambier was a testy firecracker always sputtering but never going off,[40] a naval officer of some distinction who had received a peerage for his part in the bombardment of Copenhagen in 1807. Young Goulburn was the ablest Commissioner, closest to the Government, and, to use John Quincy Adams's word, the most "inveterate" of the three. He had been a Member of Parliament and an Undersecretary of State successively for Home Affairs and for War and the Colonies. In the last-mentioned office he had become thoroughly familiar with the interests of the Canadian provincials and their desire to protect themselves against the United States by shifting the international boundary far to the south in order to give Great Britain unchallengeable control over the Great Lakes and their rivers and also a military overland road from Montreal to an ice-free port on the Bay of Fundy. Dr. Adams was an expert whose specialty was international and maritime law. In him John Quincy saw a "blunderbuss

[39] *Writings,* V, 238–9. [40] *Diary of James Gallatin,* p. 72.

of the law" with "pretensions to wit."[41] The Adams from Boston was inclined to take the full measure of his English namesake from the fact that he had not been to the theater for ten years. But Dr. William Adams would describe to his astonishment those tricks he had seen an Indian juggler perform and the amazing skill with which that kind of specialist could balance straws on his nose. Goulburn and Adams were Oxford graduates, of Trinity College. The Harvard Adams thought that both had the English prejudice of disliking everything that was not English.[42]

None of these people could hold a candle to any of the American negotiators other than Russell. But after all it was not necessary for Great Britain to have first-rate men at Ghent. Her envoys were near enough to London to refer everything back home for decision. The British Commissioners were little more than messenger boys to Downing Street. Statesmen like Castlereagh, Wellington, and Bathurst were to make the real decisions. They left the leg-work, note-writing, and diplomatic dinners to the three subordinates at Ghent.

These, then, were the men who met in Flanders to make peace between the United States and Great Britain as the wars of the French Revolution and Empire drew to a close after having impoverished and bled Europe for a quarter of a century. At last the Allies had overthrown Napoleon and packed him off to Elba. They had entered Paris and restored the Bourbon monarchy in the person of Louis XVIII. A Congress of the Powers, France included, was about to assemble in Vienna to restore legitimate sovereigns everywhere to the liberated nations. They were ready to remake the map of Europe. Russia, Austria, Prussia, and Great Britain had signed a Quadruple Alliance to protect the European peace settlement against another eruption of the defeated enemy. Great Britain ruled the oceans and blockaded the United States. The Duke of Wellington's veteran armies of the Peninsular War, now victorious in France, were free for service overseas. In London the press was clamoring for punishment of the traitorous Americans, who, so it was asserted, had stabbed England in the back while she was fighting for life or death against the greatest conqueror of modern times. All Europe, except Russia, was now on England's side. Even Alexander I, the champion of neutral rights, was in the embrace of his victorious maritime ally. He was powerless to help his old republican friends across the Atlantic. Things looked bad for the United States all over the world.

In America, President Madison's armies had been barely able to hold the line of the Great Lakes, and that thanks only to Perry's magnificent naval victory on Lake Erie. The projected conquest of Canada had collapsed under the military disasters of 1812 and 1813. Far from conquering Florida, the most aggressive Warhawks were glad enough now to retain Spain's neutrality.

[41] *Writings,* V, 108.

[42] *Writings,* V, 175.

In Madrid, Ferdinand VII back on his throne again was beseeching England to get back West Florida and Louisiana for him.

At Bordeaux, Wellington's veterans were embarking for North America. They prepared to scourge the seaboard cities. They looked forward to the speedy capture of New Orleans, key to the Mississippi Valley. Above that city lay the vast province of Louisiana as a rich prize of war. It could unite British North America with the Gulf of Mexico. Great Britain would then hold the two great rivers of the Continent.

In Lower Canada another British army was poising itself to strike south via Lake Champlain and sever New England from the Union.

In New England the Junto Federalists, in control of Massachusetts and Connecticut, were planning a convention at Hartford to deliberate on ways and means to separate their common interests from the detested war with Mother England. The United States was on the verge of dissolution. It looked as though one more military disaster might be enough to bring it. Visions of a Continental Republic were vanishing from history.

Such was the discouraging situation on both sides of the Atlantic when the American plenipotentiaries finally met their British opposites at Ghent on August 8, 1814.

CHAPTER X
The Peace of Ghent
(1814)

> The situation in which I am placed often brings to mind that in which you were situated in the year 1782. . . . I am called upon to support the same interests, and in many respects, the same identical points and questions. . . . It is the boundary, the fisheries, and the Indian savages.
>
> JOHN QUINCY ADAMS TO JOHN ADAMS,
> GHENT, OCTOBER 27, 1814

In the historic peace negotiations that ended the war of the American Revolution under brighter skies than those of 1814 the British Cabinet had yielded magnificent boundaries to the United States: the St. Croix River on the east, the present river-and-lake line on the north, Florida on the south, and the Mississippi on the west, with free navigation of that river "from its source to the ocean" for American citizens and British subjects. And in their sovereign independence the citizens of the United States preserved the "liberty" if not the right to fish within the territorial waters of remaining British North America as they had done when British subjects. John Adams was proud of the part that he had played in those negotiations. To commemorate the Treaty of Peace and Independence he gave to his new family seat in Quincy the name of Peacefield, and he had a family seal made to pass on to his son and his son's son. Under an arc of thirteen stars for the thirteen United States it showed a pine tree, a deer, and a fish swimming in the sea, symbolic of a continuing right to hunt on land and fish at sea everywhere as before the Revolution. A generation later at Ghent, John Quincy Adams and his colleagues were to encounter the same vital questions that John Adams and his associates had met and conquered at Paris in 1782. Would they be as fortunate as their predecessors? Would John Quincy Adams deserve to take over the seal from his father's hands?

1

Lord Castlereagh's original proposal for direct peace negotiations with the United States had been based on conciliating "the differences between the two States . . . upon principles of perfect reciprocity, not inconsistent with the established maxims of public law, and with the maritime rights of the British empire." Holding strictly to this proposition, John Quincy Adams and his colleagues at Ghent in 1814, and their Government behind them in Washington, preferred to assume that in settling the peace they had to deal only with those ostensible issues which had led to war, like neutral rights and impressment. Thus the boundary question need not enter into the negotiation.

The Commissioners did not admit that a double-barreled expansionist aim, Canada and Florida, had anything to do with the war. They preferred not to say anything about the instructions that Secretary of State Monroe had given them to get Canada if they could at the peace. That part of their instructions the Government never has printed to this day,[1] because its representatives at Ghent maintained so categorically that the United States never had any idea of taking Canada!

At Ghent it was to be merely a question, so the Commissioners elected to believe, whether the British Government could be persuaded to accept a peace abolishing impressment and defining neutral rights according to the American point of view. If not, then it was for the United States to decide, in the discouraging military and diplomatic situation, whether it would make peace without such settlements and let things stand as they were before the war; in other words, whether it would go back to the *status quo ante bellum.*

First instructions to the American Commission had insisted on the abolition of impressment. "If this encroachment of Great Britain is not provided against," wrote Monroe, "the United States will have appealed to arms in vain. If your efforts to accomplish it should fail, all further negotiations will cease, and you will return home without delay." [2] But before peace negotiations finally got under way the pitiful land campaigns of 1813 in North America and the victories of Great Britain and her allies in Europe forced the United States to come down by successive steps from its first high terms. Henry Clay felt that under the circumstances

[1] At one point in the negotiations, Adams proposed avowing to the British Commissioners that the cession of Canada would be for the interest of Great Britain as well as the United States. "My own concern is, that when our instructions come to be published, as they must and will be, they will be compared with the arguments pointedly urged in all our notes, and will countenance a charge of duplicity against us and our Government." *Memoirs,* III, 52.

His Government avoided the charge of inconsistency only by suppressing this part of the instructions. Historians like Henry Adams, Mahan, and Updyke have long since made them public. For the printed instructions, and the correspondence of the American Commissioners, see *ASPFR,* III, 695–726, 730–48.

[2] April 15, 1813. *ASPFR,* III, 700.

it was impossible to insist upon abolition of impressment. He was ready to take the personal risk of violating his instructions rather than block peace on that point alone.[3] Gallatin as soon as he got to Europe wrote back counseling omission of the subject of impressment and neutral rights altogether. "You may omit any stipulation on the subject of impressment, if found indispensably necessary to terminate it [the war]," Secretary of State Monroe finally replied on June 27, 1814, after receiving Gallatin's letter, just before the burning of Washington.[4]

There remained two indispensable conditions to which the American instructions must hold fast throughout: the United States must be left free to maintain naval forces without restriction on the Great Lakes, and in no case could any territory be yielded, either south of the old boundary of 1782 or on the Pacific Coast in the neighborhood of the Columbia River.[5]

The British Government in the smiling hour of victory had no occasion to yield on the question of neutral rights and the practice of impressment. The men at Whitehall were not content merely to evade any statement on these subjects. Colonial officials in Canada and a fur-traders' lobby in London were urging them to make the best of the favorable turn of the war in Europe to get rid of some of the obnoxious conditions of the old Treaty of Peace and Independence, terms that a former British Government had felt obliged to grant to John Adams, Benjamin Franklin, John Jay, and Henry Laurens.

Ever since the end of the American Revolution, British diplomacy had been trying to move the American frontier away from the Great Lakes and their rivers and to bring British territory down to the banks of the Ohio and the Mississippi. Now the big opportunity seemed to be at hand. If everything should go well in the coming campaigns in America, New Orleans and all Louisiana would be taken from the United States, as well as the old Northwest; in New York the south bank of the St. Lawrence would be appropriated, and in Maine all territory east of the Penobscot. Other boundary "rectifications" could give to the King in Canada an all-British military road from Quebec to the Bay of Fundy.[6] The Ministry also wanted to terminate, once and for all, American "liberty" to the inshore fisheries. With his eyes on these objectives Castlereagh based his diplomatic strategy on the principle of *uti possidetis* – that is, keep what you have according to the war map at the time of negotiation and get as much more as possible. That summarizes the first instructions to the British delegation.[7]

[3] Clay to W. H. Crawford, Ghent, July 2, 1814. "Letters Relating to the Negotiations at Ghent, 1812–1814." *AHR,* XX (No. 1, October 1914), 111.

[4] *ASPFR,* III, 704.

[5] Updyke: *War of 1812,* p. 185.

[6] See Map 2 and Map 5.

[7] Of July 28, 1814. *Correspondence, Despatches, and other Papers, of Viscount Castlereagh* (12 vols., London, 1848–53), X, 67–72.

The British Foreign Minister had not hurried to nominate and instruct his peace Commissioners. After their belated appointment he was by no means impatient to get them to their posts. As if to impress the American Commissioners with the good fortune that was rolling up for Great Britain, the Ministry made studious affectation of delay. Britain had just issued in complete and unqualified triumph from her obstinate twenty-year struggle for existence and power. She had humbled, disgraced, and crippled her ancient enemy. She had established her sea power on foundations so firm that she scarcely listened to the protests of her friends against her naval principles. So unbounded was her ascendancy on the ocean that the very allies who had helped her to conquer France were obliged to agree that maritime questions would not be discussed in the coming peace conference at Vienna. Only the resurgence of French power could worry her, and in the summer of 1814 there seemed to be no such possibility.[8] There was every reason to hope that the war map in North America would look better and better for Britain as the year 1814 marched on. Already on the distant North West Coast a British naval force had captured Astoria, base for future territorial expansion through all that part of the Continent. Meanwhile, as British diplomacy so deliberately pursued its way toward a mutilating American peace, the navy was convoying two massive military expeditions, released from the wars of Europe, across the Atlantic: one for operations against the Eastern seaboard states, New Orleans, and the Mississippi Valley; the other to the St. Lawrence estuary for invasion and conquest of the Champlain and Hudson Valleys.

Gloomily the American Commissioners awaited in Ghent the arrival of their adversaries. Only Henry Clay could see grounds for hope. Britain's ever shifting liabilities on the Continent of Europe might make her wish to liquidate the American war. A general peace had to be made at Vienna. The great problems of Germany were still unsettled. Defeated France would seethe and seek the first opportunity to redeem herself from foreign forces. Even the current American campaign might redound to the advantage of the United States instead of Great Britain.

Soon the capture and burning of Washington would dampen even the Kentuckian's inveterate optimism.[9]

2

John Quincy Adams and his colleagues had already been waiting six weeks[10] at Ghent when on August 8, 1814 they had their first meeting at the Hotel des Pays Bas with Messrs. Goulburn and Gambier, and Dr. William Adams.

[8] JQA to William Plumer, Ghent, July 17, 1814. JQA Papers, LC.

[9] Clay to Crawford, Ghent, July 2, October 17, 1814. *AHR*, XX, 111–12, 119–21.

[10] Gallatin did not arrive from London till July 6, five weeks before the negotiations.

Plainly the Americans were on the defensive in the peace negotiations as in the war. After the introductions had taken place and the plenipotentiaries had exchanged their full powers, the chairman of the British delegation, Lord Gambier, spoke first. He expressed the hope for the return of peace under the blessings of a kind Providence. John Quincy Adams answered. He promised for his delegation to meet every sentiment of candor and conciliation with the most cordial reciprocity. Then the British assumed the initiative. Goulburn, their next spokesman, announced there were three principal subjects to discuss:

1. Impressment.
2. "The Indian allies of Great Britain to be included in the pacification, and a definite boundary to be settled for their territory." This point, he said, was a *sine qua non* of peace.
3. "A revision of the boundary line between the United States and the adjacent British colonies."

Having laid down these three points, Goulburn added a fourth:

4. That his Government would not renew the special fishing privileges within British jurisdiction without requiring an equivalent.

The first British territorial demand, presented in the form of an Indian article as a *"sine qua non,"* spearheaded the negotiation. It was the most dangerous diplomatic thrust that could have possibly been aimed at American defense. The British negotiators expected the Americans to break off further parley rather than yield, or at least to send home for additional instructions. In either case the negotiations would lag along until friendly New England might be split off from the rest of the Union by an invasion of the Champlain and Hudson Valleys, New York City overpowered, Baltimore and Washington destroyed, New Orleans captured, and the Mississippi Valley opened to British occupation. With the campaigns of 1814 completed in North America, Britain would be in an even better position to negotiate. She might then take Louisiana too. Such were the British designs, militarily and diplomatically, according to their widest expectations and possibilities.

John Quincy Adams asked for time to confer with his colleagues. Monroe's new instructions of June 27 had just arrived. Grudgingly the British Commissioners allowed one day. Next morning Adams responded for the American delegation. On the first point, impressment, they had instructions. On the second point, Indians, they had none, but of course a peace would be made with the hostile tribes as soon as one was first made with Great Britain, if not before. On the third point, boundaries, they also had instructions. On the fourth, the fisheries, he asserted, they had none. Then he presented two additional subjects for discussion: definition of blockade and of neutral and belligerent rights, and claims for indemnification on account of maritime spoliations both before and during the war. He expressed surprise that the British representatives had brought up such points as boundaries and Indians. They had no relation to Castlereagh's formula for the negotiations, asserted Adams. Nevertheless he and his colleagues would listen to what the British had to say on these points, even discuss them. The Americans were taking great care to avoid responsibility for breaking off the negotiation.

"If we enter into a discussion," asked Goulburn, having in mind the *sine qua non* of the Indians and their boundary, "couldn't we expect that it would terminate in your agreeing to a provisional article, which you would sign subject to the ratification of your Government?" [11]

Adams said no. By now Clay, Gallatin, and Bayard had spoken out vigorously defending American Indian policy and the complete sovereignty of the United States over the natives and the territory occupied by them. The British Commissioners urged the Americans to consult together by themselves for an hour and see if they could not agree to a provisional article. But they had no desire nor need to deliberate further. They held their ground. The whole westward-rolling future of their country depended on their stand at Ghent.

Here it was that the British frontal assault first faltered. The delegates from London proposed to adjourn the conference until they could consult *their* Government. After one more session and much wrangling on the form of the protocol or minutes of their discussions, in which detail the Americans felt obliged to yield to British desires, and following a ceremonial dinner, they adjourned for a few days. Adams drafted a dispatch to the Secretary of State recounting progress so far. After much correction by the other Commissioners he sent it on in a cartel ship for which the British Admiralty graciously granted a pass.

Weighed down by twenty years of warfare in the Old World, the British Government preferred a triumph on the Continent of Europe to a complete victory in North America. Given the explosive condition of France and the volatile situation of the European peace map, Liverpool and his colleagues were not anxious to prolong the conflict in America by standing fast at Ghent. In new directions to the British delegation Castlereagh told them to try again to get the Americans to agree to sign a *provisional* article on Indians and boundaries, subject to approval by their Government (*sub spe rati*). If the American Commissioners would sign an article on this basis, said Castlereagh, Great Britain would not dispute their free *commercial* navigation of the Great Lakes, provided the United States Government would stipulate not to preserve or construct any fortifications upon the shores of the Lakes, or near them, nor to maintain or construct any armed vessels upon those inland seas or the rivers flowing into them. With the Indian question out of the way, added Castlereagh, there would remain for discussion the rearrangement of the northwestern boundary between Lake Superior and the Mississippi, and on the side of Lower Canada — that is, the St. Lawrence River and Maine.

Thus the British Government proposed at the very least, in addition

[11] *Memoirs,* III, 8.

to separating the Indian tribes and their vast hunting grounds from American sovereignty, to cut off the northwest and northeast corners of the United States in order to bring Canadian territory down to the navigable portion of the Mississippi River and to make possible a secure overland communication between Quebec and warm water. The free navigation of the Mississippi (which, like the American inshore fishery liberties, might be asserted to have ended with the war) would also have to be provided for. Perhaps the conquest of New Orleans and Louisiana would take care of that.

However unsatisfactory these latest instructions might prove to be when presented to the Americans, they represented the first British concession. Instead of insisting that the boundary of Canada be brought down to the Ohio River, they revived as a substitute the old historic project of making the American Northwest into an Indian barrier state. Had the American diplomats only known it, the British Foreign Minister was willing to make even greater concessions. To strengthen Britain's position at the coming European peace congress the Liverpool Government was prepared, if necessary and as a last recourse, to make peace in North America on the basis of the *status quo ante bellum* [12] without any decision on the points in dispute at the commencement of hostilities. But matters had not come to that pass yet.

"With respect to the Indians," Castlereagh directed, "you will repeat that their being expressly included in the peace is considered to be a *sine qua non;* and that, with respect to their limits, the British Government is prepared, as the least objectionable arrangement to the United States, to take the Treaty of Greenville, subject to certain modifications,[13] as a basis for negotiation; and having agreed as to the general boundaries, to stipulate, mutually with the American Government, against any acquisition, by purchase, on the part of either state." [14] A postscript cautioned Goulburn and his associates not to leave any doubt about the islands of Passamaquoddy Bay being considered as within the British boundary line. It now remained to be seen, observed Castlereagh, whether the negotiation could be continued with some prospect of advantage, or whether the peace conference would have to be suspended until the American negotiators could receive further instructions.

Taking the former Indian Treaty of Greenville as a basis of negotiation was a dextrous move. By the terms of that treaty, concluded directly between the United States and the Western tribes back in 1795, the Indians

[12] Memorandum of Cabinet, December 26, 1813, of instructions for Castlereagh to take with him to the Continent. C. K. Webster, ed.: *British Diplomacy, 1813–1815. Select Documents Dealing with the Reconstruction of Europe* (London, 1921), pp. 123–6.

[13] Presumably the elimination of the reservations for military posts and the right of way to them.

[14] Lord Castlereagh to the Commissioners at Ghent, Foreign Office, August 14, 1814. *Correspondence of Castlereagh*, X, 90–1.

retained proprietary possession to a great area of land within the Northwest Territory west of a line running through the present State of Ohio from the mouth of the Cuyahoga River on Lake Erie (Cleveland) to the Ohio River (near Louisville, Kentucky). The United States reserved sixteen strategic places in the Indian area of the Northwest Territory for military posts, including those at Michilimackinac and Detroit, with a right of way to them across Indian lands. If one overlooked the sinister intrusion into American sovereignty of British protection over the Indians, it might be argued plausibly that Great Britain in her proposed Anglo-American treaty urged no more for the Indians than the United States itself had already granted directly to them before the war.

Careful study of the wording and punctuation of the new British instructions suggests that they had watered down the original ultimatum about the Indians so as merely to include the tribes somehow in the peace treaty without necessarily providing a boundary for them at the expense of the United States. At any rate this was a construction to which the Cabinet could further retreat in case of necessity.

Castlereagh himself brought these latest instructions to Ghent, on his way to Paris and Vienna, and explained them orally. He was there when Goulburn, Gambier, and William Adams drafted their next note. He found them still persuaded that the Americans would accept the frontier and Indian arrangements.[15] So he did not choose to interpret their new instructions to allow a further retreat, at least for the moment.

[15] James Gallatin's *Diary*, first printed in 1914, contains the following passages:

"August 23. Lord Castlereagh arrived here today on his way to Vienna.

"August 24. He had a long conference with father. I was present. He said he had written to Lord Liverpool. . . . [*sic*]"

This convinced W. C. Ford that Castlereagh had a secret conference with Gallatin behind the back of the latter's colleagues.

Goulburn wrote Lord Bathurst, who was serving as Secretary for Foreign Affairs in Castlereagh's absence on the Continent, from Ghent, Sunday, August 21: "Lord Castlereagh arrived here at a very late hour on Thursday [August 18] and left us again on Saturday morning [August 20]."

The American Commissioners wrote to Secretary of State Monroe, August 19, 1814: "It is proper to note that Lord Castlereagh had arrived last night in this city, whence it is said, he will depart tomorrow." *ASPFR*, III, 708.

Castlereagh wrote Liverpool from Paris, August 28: "During my stay of the greater part of two days at Ghent I did not see any of the American Commissioners. They did not call upon or desire to see me, and I thought my originating an interview would be considered objectionable and awkward by our own Commissioners."

A search made for me by Mr. Donald H. Sheehan, Curator of Manuscripts of the New York Historical Society, in the Gallatin Papers there, for the month of August 1814, revealed nothing to indicate that Castlereagh was or was not at Ghent on the 23d or 24th of August.

I am inclined to accept the categorical statement of a man of Castlereagh's weight of character, with the precise dates and other evidence in his letters, corroborated by the report of the American Commissioners, against the apparently opposite statement of the irresponsible playboy, James Gallatin, with his mistaken dates and uncertain use of the pronoun "he"; but an examination of Castlereagh's private papers may throw

The peace discussion resumed on August 19.

"Is the proposition respecting the Indian pacification and the boundaries still presented as a *sine qua non*?" asked Bayard.

"Undoubtedly it is," was the reply.

"How about the one relating to the Lakes?" Bayard persisted, recurring to the proposal to exclude American armament from those waters and from the frontiers.

"One *sine qua non* at a time is enough," replied the man of the law, Dr. William Adams, sententiously.

"In requiring us to keep no naval forces on the Lakes, and no forts on their shores," inquired Gallatin, "do you reserve the right of keeping them there yourselves?"

"We certainly do," declared the British envoys.[16]

John Quincy Adams suggested that no further conference would be desirable until his side received a written statement of the British proposition. Both groups agreed to this. Henceforth the negotiation took the form of memoranda and countermemoranda as influenced by the tide of war in North America and the ebb and flow of prospects for a lasting peace in Europe. There were half a dozen of these exchanges written before matters came to a climax. It was a good thing to have it all down in black and white in case the negotiations should break off, as Adams expected, and the war should go on. Then the record might convince American opinion everywhere of the hopelessness of peace and unite all sections in continuing a war for the preservation of the nation's territory and sovereignty.

Clay was not so sure there would really be a rupture. An expert at cards and the Western game of brag, he believed the British might be bluffing. An inconceivable idea, thought Adams, no match for Clay at brag or bluff.

All five of the Commissioners agreed that their opponents were stalling for time. The prospect of further military disaster hung heavy on their minds and hearts. John Quincy Adams thought of the new British armies on the move against America, and the Essexmen's opposition to the war. "We shall be brought again to the trial whether we can maintain the Independence once achieved and the Union founded by our fathers," he wrote to one of those founding fathers back at Quincy. "If our Dissensions should be buried in our Dangers we have ultimately nothing to fear. I will trust in the mercies of a righteous Providence, and pray that the Hand of Heaven in the midst of Chastisement may also be a hand of Deliverance." [17]

Adams drafted a reply to the first British written statement, refuting

---

more light on the puzzle. See *Supplementary Despatches, Correspondence, and Memoranda of Field Marshal Arthur Duke of Wellington, edited by his son, the Duke of Wellington* (15 vols., London, 1858–72), IX, 188–96.

[16] *Memoirs,* III, 18–19.

[17] JQA to JA, No. 33, Ghent, August 20, 1814. Adams MSS.

its position, refusing to accept the *sine qua non* of Indians or any boundaries for them. He was willing to let the negotiation break off on the Indian issue alone, not to mention the boundaries. Again his colleagues went over his handiwork. They left it in "shreds and patches." Then they slept on what was left and went at it again till late the next evening, "sifting, erasing, patching, and amending until we were all wearied, though none of us were yet satiated with amendment."

The most the American Commissioners could finally offer was assent to a treaty based on the *status quo ante bellum,* with a provisional article by which each party agreed to make peace separately with the Indians within its own territory. In this way the Anglo-American treaty would at least promise to the tribes an end of hostilities. The United States further proposed that each nation agree to try henceforth to keep its Indians from committing hostilities against the other, and to prohibit them from trading in the territory of the other. Such stipulations would have confirmed the full sovereignty of each party over the aborigines within its own territory.

When after four days' labor the American delegation finally delivered the note, on August 25, scarcely the fifth part remained of Adams's original composition.[18] It was perfectly evident that his colleagues regarded him only as a nominal chairman. Henceforward it was Gallatin who was the chief draftsman and spokesman. They all looked more and more to him for guidance, and the Genevan's moderating influence presided over the American Commission. Adams yielded to it not ungracefully.

At this juncture the British Commissioners thought the negotiation was all over, but they did not dare to quit without orders from London.

Castlereagh, to whom the decision was referred in Paris, advised against a rupture. He wrote to the Prime Minister that he would have been inclined to state the proposition as to Indian limits "less peremptorily." That is, he now disapproved of making a *sine qua non* out of the Indian boundary, over and above a mere Indian pacification.

"The substance of the question is," said Castlereagh, "are we prepared to continue the war for territorial arrangements? And if not, is this the best time to make our peace, saving all our rights and retaining the fisheries, which they do not appear to question (in which case the territorial questions might be reserved for ulterior discussion), or is it desirable to take our chance of the campaign, and then to be governed by circumstances?"[19]

The Cabinet followed Castlereagh's suggestion to cut down the *sine qua non* still further, but first made another play for time in the hope of favorable military news from North America. When Goulburn presented the second British note (September 4, 1814) with the latest terms, as drafted by the Foreign Office, it turned out to be a repetition of argu-

[18] *Memoirs,* III, 21–3. The American note was dated August 25, 1815.

[19] *Supplementary Despatches of Wellington,* IX, 192–3.

ments marshaled and phrased for the attraction of High Federalist opinion in New England. It accused the United States Government of pursuing "in recent years" – that is, since Jefferson's inaugural – a policy of territorial aggrandizement and conquest: the steady acquisition of Indian lands and of Louisiana, Florida, Canada – in sum, the road to war.

So indignant were the American Commissioners that they did not perceive at first that the enemy had dropped his unconditional insistence upon the Indian boundary.

"Mr. Bayard pronounced it a very stupid production," John Quincy Adams noted in his Diary. "Mr. Clay was for answering it by a note of half a page. But I neither thought it stupid nor proper to be answered in half a page." [20]

Again Adams had his eye on the record to be spread before his countrymen in case of failure of the negotiations.

Adams and Clay at first were in favor of standing out against any inclusion of the Indians in the peace. If the negotiations were going to break off, it were better to break on that issue than on any other. "If that would not unite our people it was a hopeless pursuit."

"It is a bad point to break on," Gallatin kept saying to his fellow Commissioners, looking the while very earnestly in Adams's direction.[21] They all agreed it was.

Gallatin favored a very careful analysis of the British note, with minutes by all, before they decided on an answer. Clay assented to this, with the others, but he professed to be so disgusted that he sent a note to Goulburn requesting a passport from the British Navy to return home. Possibly the Kentuckian was bluffing a bit himself.

The second formal American reply of September 9 was merely a long repetition of arguments in defense of the territory and sovereignty of the United States. It ended with a frank declaration of the inadmissibility of an Indian boundary or of any exclusive military possession of the Lakes by Great Britain. This was better ground to break on, if break they must. Then the enemy would appear to be continuing the war to conquer American territory.

There seemed little hope of peace unless the British would lower their demands. In the interest of diplomatic decorum the two delegations continued not inimically to exchange rather dull dinners. On one such uninspiring occasion, September 15, Gambier asked Adams if he was returning immediately to St. Petersburg. "Yes," was the reply. "That is, if you send us away." [22]

3

Henry Clay's optimism about the European situation was not ill-grounded. The British Government in London, if not in Upper Canada, really wanted peace just as much as the Americans did. It was facing

[20] *Memoirs,* III, 31. [21] *Memoirs,* III, 38. [22] *Memoirs,* III, 36.

intricate questions in the coming peace conference at Vienna. Any failure to adjust the new map of Europe satisfactorily to the continental allies, with their divergent interests, might realign the land powers under the Czar in favor of the principles of the Freedom of the Seas and a personal union of Russia with a restored Kingdom of Poland. In Paris the Duke of Wellington was sitting on a powder keg, even with Napoleon exiled to Elba. Exhausted by a long war, and still in the midst of an unsettled European situation, the Liverpool Ministry did not want to break off the subordinate parleys at Ghent over territorial questions in North America. That would only fire American patriotism to fight on another year against conquest and weaken the force of British diplomacy at Vienna. After all, asked Lord Liverpool of his Ministers under the burden of all these anxieties, could Great Britain be bound in honor to do more than insist that the Indians should be included in the peace only to the extent of having restored to them the rights and privileges they enjoyed before the war? [23]

Consequently the third British note, after more arguments directed to public opinion in case the negotiations should fail, came down by implication to a still much smaller *sine qua non:* merely to include the Indians in the peace treaty somehow, without requiring a boundary for them. Soon afterward news arrived that the United States had made with one group of the hostile tribes a second Treaty [24] of Greenville (July 16, 1814) imposing its own terms on them directly. The fickle savages had switched their allegiance and agreed to declare war on their British ally! Henceforth the Indian question was academic to the British Government, like impressment and the Freedom of the Seas to the United States following the armistice between Great Britain and France. The British also ceased to insist on American disarmament on the Lakes and frontier.

Britain's once formidable ultimatum had been reduced to acceptable, face-saving proportions. The first faint breath of peace had stirred the autumn leaves at Ghent. It had not yet touched the worried cheeks of the five American envoys.

John Quincy Adams made the major contributions to the next countermemorandum,[25] although he was chagrined at the way his colleagues pruned down his verbiage. In answer to the "insolent charges" of the last British note he prepared a statement, fashioned after the argument of his Plymouth Rock oration of 1802,[26] defending the Indian policy of the United States.

[23] Liverpool to Bathurst, September 14, 1814. *The Bathurst Manuscripts* (Report of the Historical MSS. Commission, London, 1923), pp. 286–8. The American Commissioners received the third British note on September 19, 1814.

[24] JQA first noted the news on September 29. *Memoirs,* III, 43. The American Commissioners conveyed it to the British Commissioners at Ghent on September 30. PRO, F.O., 5, Vol. CII. Transcript from Canada Archives. Courtesy of Mr. Gustave Lanctot, Archivist.

[25] September 26, 1814. *ASPFR,* III, 719–21.

[26] Above, p. 113.

It was the moral and religious duty of a civilized nation, he declared, to settle, cultivate, and improve the Indian territory, extinguishing step by step the right of savages tribes by fair and amicable means – a principle, said he, perfectly recognized by the law of nations. Bayard agreed to say it was the duty of a civilized nation. Clay would not deny all this, but he thought the free use of the words God, Providence, and Heaven so much cant. Russell, who was now attaching himself to Clay's political future, laughed outright at Adams's use of those terms. Gallatin admitted the weight of the argument, but gently told Adams that they must be careful to avoid ridicule.

The Commissioners retained Adams's principle after making over its wording to their hearts' content. With less quibbling they accepted his second proposition, for an article of reciprocal amnesty designed to satisfy British concern for their Indian allies and at the same time to preserve American sovereignty over them. As finally phrased, it offered peace and amnesty to the tribes on both sides of the frontier, with all the rights, privileges, and possessions they had at the commencement of the war. On their part the Indians must demean themselves peaceably and conformably to their duties *to their respective Governments.*

The British would not accept Adams's formula outright. They had just got the good news of the capture and burning of Washington, though the Star-Spangled Banner still waved over Baltimore and General Ross had fallen in his attempt to take that port.

The fourth British memorandum, of October 8, 1814, was another long manifesto, ending with their final "ultimatum": the text of an article by which each side, reciprocally, agreed to make peace with the hostile Indian tribes, restoring to them all the possessions, rights, and privileges that they might have enjoyed previous to such hostilities – providing that the tribes in each case should agree to cease hostilities as soon as notified of the peace treaty between Great Britain and the United States.

These words were enough, even if they did not expressly acknowledge American dominion over the Indians within the boundaries of the United States, as Adams's proposed article would have done; but the British did not contest it, and that was enough. Nervous at the shaky state of affairs in France, fearful of the cost of another year's war in America, and anxious for the return of a general peace after a generation of exhausting wars all over the world, Great Britain, still without information as to the outcome of the campaign in North America, had come down a long way from her initial attempt to drop her boundary south to the Ohio River. Her ultimatum was something the Americans could accept with honor. They were quick to do so in face of the menacing military situation in the United States. It was the turning-point. The American negotiators now asked their British opposites to submit the draft or project of a final treaty.

News of the American victory on Lake Champlain at Plattsburg (September 12, 1814) arrived at London while the Cabinet was formulating its fifth statement for the messenger-diplomats to deliver at Ghent. As for a treaty project, declared this document, the British plenipotentiaries had already made plain their principal demands in their very first conference. Now, after Plattsburg, they dropped all mention of naval armaments on the Lakes. But again they came back to the principle of *uti possidetis*, with "mutually convenient modifications," as the basis for a final territorial settlement. They asserted once more that Great Britain considered the fisheries "liberty" of the Treaty of Peace and Independence to have lapsed because of the natural effect of war on treaties.

So far as the northwestern boundary was concerned, declared Gambier, Goulburn, and William Adams, there would be no objection to the line from the Lake of the Woods to the Mississippi, "the intended arrangement of 1803." This was the line of the unratified King-Hawkesbury Convention that John Quincy Adams had blocked in the Senate at the time of the Louisiana Purchase. He was not likely to sell out the West by agreeing to it in 1814. If he, or any of the delegation, had been so inclined, then Clay certainly would have raised a cry against any relinquishment of territory, any such abortion of future American expansion.

What was the war map of October 1814? What were the territories that Britain still hoped, with flagging confidence, to hold in the peace?

British forces occupied Fort Michilimackinac on the little island that stands at the entrance of the three largest Lakes, Huron, Michigan, and Superior. They possessed Fort Niagara on the American shore of Lake Ontario below the Falls. They held all of Maine east of the Penobscot. On the other hand the Americans had possession of Fort Erie on the Canadian side of the Niagara River at the outlet of Lake Erie, thus balancing the British hold on Fort Niagara. They also held Fort Malden (Amherstburg) and Ontario's western peninsula across the river from Detroit. Most important of all, their fresh-water navy dominated the whole system of the inland seas. They were in a position to take Fort Michilimackinac at their convenience.

The Foreign Office instructed its agents at Ghent to put forward the following modifications of the war map, in addition to the proposed rectification of the northwest boundary: (1) restoration to the United States of the province of Maine east of the Penobscot (keeping the disputed Moose Island in Passamaquoddy Bay) in exchange for the return of Fort Erie; (2) British forces to continue in possession of Fort Niagara, which would then remain the key to southern Ontario; (3) rectification of the "uncertain" boundary at the "northwest angle of Nova Scotia" so as to secure the northern part of Maine for a strategic military road on British soil to the mouth of the St. John River.[27] These were the minimum boundary changes that the British Government had intended to get from the

[27] Bathurst to the Commissioners, Foreign Office, October 18, 1814. *Correspondence of Castlereagh*, X, 168–70.

beginning of the negotiation.[28] Would it be possible now to achieve even this minimum?

Britain's repeated insistence on the war map as the basis for peace discouraged the Americans. Macdonough's victory on Lake Champlain and the ensuing break-up at Plattsburg of Prevost's invasion, not to mention the bloody repulse of Drummond's attack on Fort Erie, had not properly raised their spirits. They were more impressed by the enemy's recent occupation of eastern Maine and by the fact that the renewed demands for territorial cessions had followed hard upon his seizure of that province. They also feared greatly for the fate of New Orleans, to which the expedition under Admiral Cochrane had set sail after the burning of Washington and the failure to take Baltimore. But once more and without hesitation they refused [29] to treat upon the basis of *uti possidetis,* "or upon any other principle involving the cession of a part of the territory of the United States." They asked their adversaries at last to lay all their cards on the table, to submit the draft of a proposed treaty. They declared they had no objection to stating all their own demands in a simultaneous exchange of treaty drafts.

There were no hopes for peace, Adams and his colleagues reported to the Secretary of State as they were preparing this note; the British envoys were referring the subject again to their Government only to gain time.[30]

"Our prospects are not more promising than they have been from the beginning," John Quincy Adams wrote gloomily to Abigail. "You can easily judge how all our exertions are affected by the accounts that are daily arriving from America." [31]

Clay alone was hopeful. The events at Baltimore and Lake Champlain, he privately wrote Monroe, would help. Just as the British had abandoned piece by piece their original *sine qua non* of an Indian barrier state and their high demands excluding American armament from the Lakes, so they would give up their present territorial demands. If they were beaten at New Orleans, peace would certainly ensue.[32] Everybody at Ghent, including the British mission, expected that London would await the out-

[28] See "Intended Instructions" to the British Commissioners, marked "not used," and published by W. C. Ford, together with the actual instructions and essential documents of the correspondence of the British Commissioners at Ghent, in MHS *Proceedings,* XLVIII (1914–15), 138–62. These intended instructions had also said: "Some such boundary also must be assigned to Louisiana as may exclude the Citizens of the United States from any interference with the British Settlements on the Columbia River" (p. 140). It is most significant for the history of the Oregon Question that the British did not come back to this in any of the actual instructions. See below, Chs. XXIV, XXV.

[29] The fifth American note, or countermemorandum. *ASPFR,* III, 725.

[30] October 25, 1814. *ASPFR,* III, 711–12. See also Gallatin to Monroe, August 20, 1814. *Writings of Gallatin,* I, 637–40.

[31] JQA to AA, No. 64, Ghent, October 22, 1814. Adams MSS.

[32] Clay to Monroe, October 26, 1814. Monroe Papers, LC.

come of the campaign against Louisiana before settling on final terms of peace in America. Otherwise that expedition was a waste of time and money.

Goulburn and his associates strengthened this impression when they asserted they had no new demands to make. They had already stated their terms clearly enough. If the Americans did not agree to the *uti possidetis,* then let them present a treaty draft of their own, to which they would promptly receive a counter-*projet.*[33] Certainly it looked as if the British were seeking quite deliberately to gain time for Cochrane's convoy to get to the Gulf of Mexico.

Not without emotion John Quincy Adams beheld himself fighting the same old fight his father had fought a generation before in Paris, against the same old foe, for the same great stakes of empire: boundaries, fisheries, and the Indians.

"The situation in which I am placed," he wrote to his father in Quincy, "often brings to mind that in which you were situated in the year 1782, and I will not describe the feelings with which the comparison, or I might rather say, the contrast, affects me. I am called to support the same interests, and in many respects, the same identical points and questions. The causes in which the present war originated, and for which it was on our part waged will scarce form the most insignificant item in the Negotiations for Peace. It is not impressment and unalienable allegiance, blockades and orders in Council, colonial trade and maritime rights, nor belligerent and neutral collisions of any kind that form the subjects of our discussions. It is the boundary, the fisheries, and the Indian savages."[34]

After a long review of the negotiations and the dilatory tactics of the British representatives he begged his father to send him all possible information on the fisheries.

John Adams forwarded his son's letter to the President at Washington. "All I can say," he added to Madison, "is that I would continue this war forever, rather than surrender an acre of our territory, one iota of the fisheries, as established by the third article of the treaty of 1783, or one sailor impressed from any merchant ship. I will not, however, say this to my son, although I shall be very much obliged to you, if you will give him orders to that effect."[35]

The haughty tone of the British adversaries at Ghent, demanding that the American plenipotentiaries be the first to lay all their cards down, exasperated the latter, but they waived the point of procedure. They were determined to leave no stone unturned for peace with territory and sovereignty still intact. They fell to work again with a will. For the next ten days they drafted and redrafted, under Gallatin's leadership, the project

[33] From the British to the American Ministers, Ghent, October 31, 1814. *ASPFR,* III, 726. The sixth British note.

[34] JQA to JA, No. 34, Ghent, October 27, 1814. Adams MSS.

[35] JA to James Madison, Quincy, November 28, 1814. *Works* of JA, X, 105.

of a proposed treaty. It contained the agreed Indian pacification article, now harmless enough. It also included all the other things that the United States Government would like to have but did not really expect to get: abolition of impressment; definition of blockade and neutral rights; indemnity for spoliations; reciprocal prohibition of the use of Indians in warfare; settlement of the northwest boundary gap according to the proposals of 1807 [36] rather than the provisions of the unratified King-Hawkesbury Convention of 1803: that was to say, the line of 49° N.L. from the Lake of the Woods west *as far as the territories of both parties should extend in that direction,* excluding the North West Coast and all territory beyond the Rocky Mountains.

These were the articles they proposed on paper. They did not expect to get much more, really, than the *status quo ante bellum.* Their latest instructions allowed them to fall back on that. The principal difficulty presented itself when these five independent-minded men, representing all sections of the Union, tried to agree among themselves on what to do about the fisheries question.

4

The British had categorically asserted that the war had put an end to the American fishery "liberty," at best a privilege rather than a right. Monroe's instructions had warned the Commissioners not to let that subject come into discussion. Yet not to mention the fisheries now, after their opponents had put a caveat in the record, would let the liberty lapse by a failure to defend it.

The American privilege to participate in the inshore fisheries of British North America and the British right to the free navigation of the Mississippi, and the effect of war on both treaty stipulations of 1783, presented interesting equivalents for British and American diplomats to balance against each other and for different sections of the United States to appraise in terms of local interest. In such a measurement of values the Mississippi navigation was an empty right unless British traders could get into the river from Canada, while the fisheries continued to be a real and profitable enterprise for Yankee mariners.

Great Britain had ceased to attach any real value to the Mississippi Question after it had become evident that traders would never be able to reach the river direct from British territory in the north. Nobody at Ghent seems to have realized how valuable the free navigation of the Mississippi might soon be to British ocean-going steamboats coming into the continental waterway from the Gulf of Mexico. But all the plenipotentiaries knew that the North Atlantic fisheries were New England's most important industry as well as a national nursery for seamen. There was no real comparison between the two benefits. The British were ready to

[36] During the negotiations between Monroe and Pinkney and Lords Auckland and Holland in London. *ASPFR,* III, 160–85, IV, 377.

let the navigation of the Mississippi go unless they could have access to the river from the north. The Americans were determined not to give up their claim to the fisheries.

Such considerations led the British Commissioners to argue that the war had ended the former treaty privileges, at least the fishery liberty. On the other hand the Americans were disposed to contend that the articles of the Treaty of Peace and Independence, anyway the fishery article, lasted as long as American independence itself.

At first blush it might seem that if both articles survived, the American fishery benefit would be a boon to the East, and British navigation of the Mississippi a blow to the West and South. The latter sections would get nothing out of the fisheries, and the Mississippi would remain open to the British flag. Remembering that the British could not enter the Mississippi from the north, what harm could come from a continuation of the theoretical right? John Quincy Adams thought, no harm. The British had enjoyed their right for thirty years without being able to exercise it. On the other hand, the fisheries were a very real benefit to New England, particularly to Massachusetts.

It was Gallatin, a Pennsylvanian, a western Pennsylvanian, but eminently a nationalist, who proposed putting into the American treaty *projet* an article suggesting continuance of the fishing liberties for citizens of the United States and the free navigation of the Mississippi for subjects of Great Britain.

Clay bitterly opposed this concession. The exclusive navigation of the Mississippi, he argued, was far more valuable to the United States than the fisheries. Adams was in favor of proposing Gallatin's article, or of taking the ground that "the whole right to the fisheries was recognized as a part of our independence, that it could not be abrogated by the war, and needed no stipulation for its renewal." [37]

The Commission voted (November 5) three to two, Clay and Russell dissenting, to include such an article, but all five reversed the vote when Clay declared he would not sign any treaty that restored the navigation of the Mississippi to Great Britain. They therefore left all mention of both the Mississippi and the fisheries out of their treaty draft. At the same time they protected their claim to the fisheries by a caveat of their own, phrased by Clay along the lines of Adams's alternate argument, in the covering note that delivered the *projet*.[38]

[37] *Memoirs,* III, 60–4, 71–3.

[38] "In answer to the declaration made by the British plenipotentiaries respecting the fisheries, the undersigned, referring to what passed in the conference of the 9th of August, can only state that they are not authorized to bring into discussion any of the rights or liberties which the United States have heretofore enjoyed in relation thereto. From their nature, and from the peculiar character of the treaty of 1783, by which they were recognized, no further stipulation has been deemed necessary by the Government of the United States to entitle them to the full enjoyment thereof." *ASPFR,* III, 733.

The promised British counter-*projet* proved to be only a list of alterations and additional propositions made in the margin of the American draft. One of these was a clause stipulating the right of British subjects to have access from British territories to the Mississippi River, by land or inland navigation through the territory of the United States, together with a right to the full navigation of the river.[39] The British proposal would have left an unbounded area of the Northwest open to the goings and comings of British traders, old friends and allies of the Indians. And it said nothing about American fishing liberties.

Clay flared up again at any mention of the Mississippi. Over his negative vote and that of Russell, the Commission finally adopted, *and all signed,* Gallatin's proposal to offer an article continuing both the navigation of the Mississippi and the fishery liberty. The American offer was calculated to make the navigation more than an empty right. It offered an access for British subjects to the upper waters of the river across American territory from some one point of their own territory within three hundred miles of the Lake of the Woods, subject to the payment of customs duties.[40] The actual wording of this proposal carefully avoided any admission of the one being an equivalent for the other, although the American Commissioners undoubtedly so considered it in their own intimate discussions.

Fortunately for the United States the British Commissioners flatly rejected this offer. Failure of war and diplomacy to bring British territory down to the banks of the upper Mississippi already had spoiled the usefulness of the old right to navigate that river "from its source to the ocean." Of what value, then, was such a right if British subjects had to travel hundreds of miles across American territory to get to it and then pay customs when they crossed the American boundary on the way? They abandoned the subject altogether.

The fisheries liberty now fell back to its moot position outside the proposed treaty of peace. The British continued to declare that it had lapsed with the war. The Americans had asserted that no war could destroy it any more than independence itself.

5

Leaving the fisheries question to be settled after the peace, the negotiators spent considerable more time arguing about the eastern boundary of the United States. They agreed to the appointment of four joint commissions to survey and adjust uncertainties in the old northern frontier all along the way; but there was a long wrangle as to whether Moose Island in Passamaquoddy Bay, occupied by the British during the war, was to be given up under that article of the treaty calling for the restora-

[39] November 26, 1814. *ASPFR,* III, 732–40.

[40] Protocol of conference of December 1, 1814. *ASPFR,* III, 742.

tion of all territory taken by either party during hostilities or after the signing of the treaty,[41] or whether it should be regarded as a part of the disputed northeastern frontier. On Moose Island was the town of Eastport, District of Maine, which sent a delegate to the General Court of Adams's own State of Massachusetts. At his insistence the Commission held out against any phraseology that would acknowledge this island as British; finally they agreed to regard it as disputed but to leave it in British possession pending the decision of one of several joint boundary commissions.

There had been still another debate on how to set up the joint boundary commissions: for the settlement of the title to Moose Island and of the islands in Passamaquoddy Bay; for regulation of the northeastern boundary line; and for settlement of certain minor questions along the boundary line of 45° N.L., and the river-and-lake boundary in the north. The Americans wanted in each case a commission of three, one representative of each nation and an umpire selected by the two, three so as to be sure to get the line settled permanently one way or the other, as in the case of the St. Croix River controversy of a generation before. The British insisted on a commission of two, one from each party, so as not to fix the boundary unless it was as they wanted it; if the two deadlocked, then they proposed a "friendly sovereign state" as the final arbitrator, under the persuasion that Great Britain would be likely to have more influence than the United States over a European sovereign.[42] The Americans made the mistake of accepting this arrangement. It brought the ultimate loss in the Webster-Ashburton Treaty of 1842 of 3,207,680 acres of territory that John Quincy Adams's father and his colleagues of 1782 had won in the Treaty of Peace and Independence. On the other hand, the Passamaquoddy Commission in 1817 awarded Moose Island, Dudley Island, and Frederick Island to the United States, and the other big islands of the bay, including Grand Manan, to Great Britain. So it was that Adams saved Eastport, eventually, for the United States.[43]

The negotiators had completed their work. The five American plenipotentiaries were ready to sign the final treaty, based almost[44] altogether on the *status quo ante bellum*, a compromise peace leaving none of the original issues settled. But on the most vital point of all there was no compromise at Ghent. Adams, Bayard, Clay, Gallatin, and Russell all successfully resisted the British design to deprive the Republic of any of

[41] See Map 2, insert.

[42] Updyke: *War of 1812*, p. 318.

[43] See Map 2, insert.

[44] The provisions of the "permanent" articles of Jay's Treaty, the first ten articles, which ended with the war, were not renewed. They had stipulated, among other things, free navigation of the Mississippi, free trade and passage for British subjects across the frontier overland from Canada with the Indians in American territory, with the right to own houses and lands without harming American citizens. The lapse of these articles was a great advantage for the United States.

its territory, either by changing frontiers or by setting up an Indian barrier state south of the boundary of 1783, or in the guise of an "Indian boundary" of any kind.[45] The courageous envoys saved the West, and with it the Far West of the future, for the United States and for American expansion through to the other ocean. Here, in this achievement, was a real diplomatic victory.

Adams and his coadjutors at last had brought the enemy's representatives at Ghent, always under the pressure for peace in London, down from the high horse of their first demands to acceptable terms. It remained for the Liverpool Government, beset still by the anxieties of European politics, to tell their plenipotentiaries across the Channel whether to sign the treaty and get the American war out of the way.

6

While the five American delegates were preparing a treaty *projet* according to their taste, the Government in London was anxiously scanning the European situation and the relation of the American war to it. The peace conference had begun at Vienna and the victorious Allies were disputing among themselves about the Polish Question, the Saxon Question, the Italian Question, and many others. Castlereagh was also doing his best to keep neutral rights off the agenda and to hold the Allies together under British principles in the hour of triumph. His hand would be strengthened if Britain could be rid of the remaining war across the ocean and on the ocean. Paris was in a ferment of plotting against the restored Bourbons, and the British Government feared for the personal safety of their Iron Duke, who commanded the occupation of the city. They even thought of withdrawing Wellington from the French capital on the pretext of giving him a command to finish up the American war, or of sending him to Vienna as a negotiator. But really, in case of another outbreak in France, he would be more needed there than across the Atlantic, as he himself pointed out. In the Government's worry over the general situation the Prime Minister submitted to Wellington himself whether he should take the field across the Atlantic and what to do with the American war.

The incisive reply of Britain's great warrior and statesman settled the business. He was not unwilling to go to America if ordered. He believed that there were sufficient land forces there to carry on the costly war another year at least. But he bluntly told the Government that after the defeat on Lake Champlain and the loss of naval power on the Lakes there could be no compelling reason in the current negotiations at Ghent for demanding territorial cessions. He counseled a peace on the basis of the

[45] Charles M. Gates considers this the most significant feature of the Treaty of Ghent in his study of "The West in American Diplomacy, 1812–1815," in *Mississippi Valley Historical Review,* XXVI (No. 4, March 1940), 499–510.

status quo ante bellum — which the Americans had not been unwilling to accept from the beginning.[46]

It was about this time, if we can believe at all the *Diary* of Albert Gallatin's frivolous son, that Wellington wrote a "strictly confidential" friendly note to Gallatin at Ghent, assuring that he had brought all his weight to bear for peace. "As I gather," wrote the Duke, upon what authority we do not know, "Mr. Madison and Mr. Monroe gave you full power to act, without even consulting your colleagues on points you considered of importance. I now feel that peace is shortly in view. Mr. Goulburn has made grave errors and Lord Castlereagh has read him a sharp lesson."[47]

The British Cabinet followed Wellington's advice. They were further impelled to it by the unified resistance of American public opinion, except for Junto extremists, to the original British territorial demands, and by the opposition of Parliament itself. With the American treaty *projet* before him, Lord Liverpool wrote to Castlereagh, November 18, 1814: "I think we have determined, if all other points can be satisfactorily settled, not to continue the war for the purpose of obtaining or *securing* any acquisition of territory. We have been led to this determination by the *consideration of the unsatisfactory state of the negotiations at Vienna, and by that of the alarming situation of the interior of France.* We have also been obliged to pay serious attention to the state of our finances . . . under such circumstances, it has appeared to us desirable to bring the American war if possible to a conclusion."[48]

The British Government gave up hopes for the capture of New Orleans even as Cochrane's fleet was approaching the Mississippi Delta. The Prime Minister sent the order to sign the treaty, without waiting a few weeks more to see the outcome of the campaign.

At last the Hand of Heaven, for which John Quincy Adams had prayed at Ghent in the midst of chastisement, had appeared over Europe as the Hand of Deliverance for America. If it had not been for Britain's worries on that Continent no group of American envoys, however able, could have saved their country. But again, if it had not been for the European situation, the United States would never have become involved in the world conflict, "kicked into the war" by Great Britain, to use one of the Essexmen's choicest phrases of scorn for Madison's Government.

[46] Wellington to Liverpool, Paris, November 9, 18, 1814. *Supplementary Despatches,* IX, 424, 435.

[47] "Father burnt this dispatch and does not even know that I have recorded it. I wanted to copy it, and was doing so when he took it off the table and burned it. . . ." *Diary of James Gallatin,* p. 34.

[48] Italics inserted. *Supplementary Despatches of Wellington,* IX, 438. Dudley Mills has explained the significance of "The Duke of Wellington and the Peace Negotiations at Ghent" in *Canadian Historical Review,* II (No. 1, March 1921), 19–32. See also my *Diplomatic History of the United States* (Henry Holt and Company, 1942), pp. 166–71.

7

The envoys signed the peace at the residence of the British Commissioners on the night before Christmas 1814, ushering in a day of peace and good will on earth. Lord Gambier expressed the hope that the treaty would be a permanent one. Said Adams for his delegation: "I hope it will be the last treaty of peace between Great Britain and the United States." [49]

"I cannot close the record of this day," he wrote that night in his Diary, "without an humble offering to God for the conclusion to which it has pleased him to bring the negotiations for peace at this place, and a fervent prayer that its result may be propitious to the welfare, the best interests, and the union of my country." [50]

Before leaving Ghent the American delegation gave a dinner in honor of the peace to the British envoys and the dignitaries of the city. Gambier rose to give the first toast: "The United States of North America!" Adams requested and received permission to forestall him: "His Majesty the King of England!" It was indeed a gallant gesture for an Adams, for George III still lived. At this moment the orchestra of the Society of St. Cecilia struck up *God Save the King*. Then Gambier gave his toast. The musicians played *Hail Columbia*. Adams gave another toast: "The Sovereign Prince of the Netherlands!"

Within the next few days there were other dinners at which the orchestras played repeatedly *Hail Columbia* and *God Save the King*. The Hanoverian Lieutenant General at Ghent gave one for the Intendant and Mayor and the English, Hanoverian, and Belgian officers. As a grand climax the burghers gave an elaborate banquet, with American and British flags intertwined under olive branches at the head of the hall. There were many more toasts. Adams raised his glass last of all to the hosts of the peace conference: "Ghent, the City of Peace; may the gates of the Temple of Janus, here closed, not be opened again for a century." [51]

It was to be just a century before the gates of Janus would swing open again at Ghent.

The Americans were more popular with the inhabitants of the city than the British, who still garrisoned the place. This was demonstrated when Adams and his colleagues gave their landlords at the Hotel Lovendeghem permission to auction off their furniture. Under the name of effects belonging to the plenipotentiaries the resourceful auctioneers emptied at brisk prices all the upholsterers' shops in town, at least so Adams wrote to Louisa. "Even the furniture from the British hotel was sold at our house, for the sake of putting it in favor. The worst part of the joke was that they put off quantities of bad wine, as if it had been ours. We did not leave a bottle for sale." [52]

[49] *Memoirs,* III, 126.

[50] *Memoirs,* III, 127.

[51] *Memoirs,* III, 131, 137–9.

[52] *Writings,* V, 268.

THE SIGNING OF THE TREATY OF GHENT, 1814

PAINTING BY SIR AMÉDÉE FORESTIER, 1914, ON LOAN, 1949, TO THE DEPARTMENT OF STATE FROM THE NATIONAL COLLECTION OF FINE ARTS, SMITHSONIAN INSTITUTION

As identified at the National Collection of Fine Arts for the Department of State, the persons are:

BRITISH DELEGATES [*left to right*]: 1. Anthony St. John Baker, Secretary 2. Henry Goulburn, Plenipotentiary * 3. William Adams, Plenipotentiary * 4. Admiral Lord Gambier, Chief Plenipotentiary *

AMERICAN DELEGATES [*continuing left to right*]: 5. John Quincy Adams, Chief Plenipotentiary * 6. Albert Gallatin, Plenipotentiary * 7. Christopher Hughes, Secretary 8. James A. Bayard, Plenipotentiary * 9. Henry Clay, Plenipotentiary * 10. Jonathan Russell, Plenipotentiary * 11. Unidentified

* Signer

The negotiators immediately rushed three copies of their treaty by way of London to the United States, accompanied by a protocol of their conferences with the British Commissioners leading to the final signature of the peace. Russell signed the joint report, but in a separate letter to the Secretary of State reserved the occasion to explain later why he had differed from the majority of his colleagues when they had proposed to continue both the fisheries and the navigation of the Mississippi—an offer that the British Commissioners had rejected. This he did at great length in a private letter to the Secretary of State on February 11, 1815. More will be heard of Russell's dissent much later. It was a seed of future action against a brother Commissioner, planted, as John Quincy Adams discovered seven years later, to take rancorous root in the soil of sectional prejudice and party politics.[53]

In London the Prince Regent speedily ratified the treaty. He had already given his plenipotentiaries the power to bind, ratify, and confirm in his name when they signed. The American Commissioners of course could not do this for their Government. The Senate of the United States first had to advise and consent by a two-thirds majority of Senators present before the President could ratify.

The British Government feared that President Madison might try to "trick" them out of ratification. Perhaps it recalled how Jefferson in 1807 had refused even to submit a treaty to the Senate because it did not contain an article prohibiting impressment. At the last moment Lord Liverpool had insisted on a stipulation that hostilities should not cease until both parties had ratified. That meant that if Admiral Cochrane's expedition took New Orleans, Great Britain would not have to give it back if the United States did not ratify. In that contingency the London Government had good reason to believe that the New England States, with their tendency toward separation from the Union, would not be indisposed to listen to a separate peace proposal.[54]

Before the treaty reached Washington, stirring news had arrived, February 11, from New Orleans. General Pakenham's British troops had landed and marched against the city, only to be thrown back and their commander killed in Andrew Jackson's magnificent victory of the 8th of January 1815. This triumph did not abate the desire for peace in Washington when the first copy of the treaty reached the capital, February 14. As soon as the Senators read the document and a summary of the diplomatic record [55] of the negotiation submitted therewith, they unanimously

[53] *The Duplicate Letters and the Navigation of the Mississippi* (Washington, 1822), p. 141. See below, Ch. XXIV, Section 5.

[54] Liverpool to Castlereagh, December 23, 1814: *Supplementary Despatches of Wellington*, IX, 495.

[55] Despite the contentions of Clay, supported by Bayard and Russell, that the original diplomatic documents of the Commission be sent to the Department of State immediately, Adams insisted, as chairman of the Commission, in retaining custody of the archives until otherwise directed by the Government, or by the Commission in a for-

advised and consented (February 17, 1815) to its ratification. They were greatly pleased with the end of the war without loss of territory, climaxed with such a thrilling victory over a veteran British army. At eleven o'clock that night the Secretary of State exchanged final ratifications with the British Minister. Next morning (February 18, 1815) the President promptly proclaimed the treaty.

Everybody, East and West, North and South, was delighted with peace. Even the Essex Junto had to like it, for peace, peace at any price, was what they had been crying for, and here was peace, and peace with national dignity.

John Adams was greatly proud of his son's work at Ghent, particularly his stand for the inshore fisheries. Jubilantly the onetime Peace Commissioner of 1782 sent orders to London to have a new die made for the family escutcheon. Under the thirteen stars, the pine tree, the deer, and the fish swimming in the sea were now engraved the words from Horace: "*Piscemur, venemur, ut olim*": Fish and hunt we will as heretofore.[56] Before he died, the old statesman of Quincy passed the seal thus embellished down to John Quincy, and he in turn in his old age passed it on to his son Charles Francis Adams.

After two years of bitter humiliation the honor of the United States at last had been redeemed in the Cabinet and in the field. The delegates from the Hartford Convention, the Essex Junto defeatists of 1814, slunk home in obscurity, speedily to become forgotten men. The future belonged to Adams, to Jackson, to Clay, to the new nationalists, to the continentalists.

---

mal meeting of the same (which did not come to pass). They would be useful, he declared, in the new assignment that the Commission had received to negotiate a treaty of commerce with Great Britain. For Clay's squabble with Adams on this point, see *Memoirs,* III, 129–44. I have found no record to establish when the Commission's files reached the Department of State. They are now in the National Archives.

[56] The seal is now in the museum of the Massachusetts Historical Society. See Henry Adams, 2d: *A Catalogue of Books of John Quincy Adams with notes on Adams Seals,* p. 140. JA to JQA, Quincy, April 15, 1815, and JQA to JA, London. The English translation above given is by JQA in an anonymous communication sent to the *National Gazette,* June 17, 1822. For line-cut of seal see title page and front binding of the volume now in the reader's hands.

CHAPTER XI

Minister to Great Britain (1815–1817)

The avowed and true policy of Great Britain . . . in the existing state of the world . . . is to appease controversy, and to secure, if possible, for all states a long interval of Repose.

CASTLEREAGH TO CHARLES BAGOT, BRITISH MINISTER AT WASHINGTON, MOST PRIVATE AND SECRET, NOVEMBER 10, 1817[1]

BEFORE the Commissioners could proceed with their next assignment, a general treaty of commerce with Great Britain, they must first know the fate of their treaty of peace. While waiting for word from Washington they all betook themselves to the more agreeable scenes of Paris.

1

Thirty years earlier John Adams had lingered with his son in the French capital, hoping to make a treaty of commerce with Great Britain as soon as the Treaty of Peace and Independence of 1783 should be ratified. Now the son, waiting there under the same circumstances in his generation, eagerly revisited the landmarks of his boyhood. How they had been scarred by the tremendous cycle of history that had intervened since then! But Paris was still there in all its essential aspects, the Tuileries, the Palais Royal, the restored Bourbon court, the Louvre, the Bois, the courts of justice, museums, historical monuments, parks, squares, boulevards, book stalls – above all, the theaters.

The idle diplomat reveled in the old familiar scenes. His long and wide experience at European courts and chancelleries meant plenty of society. He wined and dined with many old friends of his father and himself: with Lafayette; with Count Barbé Marbois, who had been Secretary of the French Legation in Philadelphia thirty years before; with Madame de Staël, whom he had first met in St. Petersburg; with LeRay de Chaumont and de Castries, names famous in the diplomacy of the American Revolution; with Lafayette's brother-in-law, the Count de Tracy, whose

[1] PRO, F.O., 5, Vol. CXX.

son, Victor, Adams had succeeded in getting paroled from Russian captivity when in St. Petersburg. It was at the Tracys' that he met the famous scientist Alexander Humboldt.

Like a famished man Adams indulged his old passion for the theater. Several nights a week found him at one or another of the numerous playhouses. "The tendency to dissipation at Paris seems to be irresistible. There is a moral incapacity for industry and application, a *mollesse* against which I am as ill guarded as I was at the age of twenty." [2] When he had exhausted the repertory of the Opéra, the Théâtre Français, the Odéon, he visited marginal products at the Porte St. Martin, and the Feydeau. He much admired the great Talma, then at the height of his powers.

Paris had its serious interests too. Adams listened to long trials at the courts of justice and studied the court proceedings. He passed many hours in the museums and picture galleries. He nodded with some of the sleepy academicians at the Institute. With his colleagues on the Peace Commission he made his bow at the court of Louis XVIII. In the interview the King asked the tactful question: "Are you in any way related to the celebrated Mr. Adams?"

Meanwhile Louisa and ten-year-old Charles Francis were on their adventurous way across war-torn Europe in a trying winter stage-journey from St. Petersburg.[3] Soon the whole family would be reunited. The two older boys were already at sea to join their parents in England. As Mrs. Adams and young Charles were entering Paris, Louis XVIII, his court, and the diplomatic corps — all excepting the American Minister, William H. Crawford — were hastening away from it. Napoleon Bonaparte had come back from Elba.

For the last several afternoons John Quincy Adams had been walking the boulevards watching for the Emperor's entry. It was hard to believe that the exiled leader, with scarcely a battalion of troops to start with, could walk into possession of all France. Now he was in the Tuileries again. On the streets the bill-posters were busy scraping the official fleurs-de-lis off the walls and pasting up the imperial eagles.

Adams in his day, like historians in our day, looked upon Bonaparte as a unique product of the French Revolution. Throughout the Consulate he had felt that France was better off with Bonaparte than without him.[4] Then the conquests of the Empire led him to regard the great man as a misfortune to Europe. But it made him wince to realize that the restored Louis XVIII was only a "Vice-Roy" under the Duke of Wellington.[5] In

[2] *Memoirs,* III, 154.

[3] Her grandson, Brooks Adams, published "Mrs. John Quincy Adams's Narrative of a Journey from St. Petersburg to Paris in February, 1815" in *Scribner's Magazine,* XXXIV (October 1903), 449–63.

[4] *Writings,* II, 169, 442, 462, 467.

[5] *Writings,* V, 307.

THE SIGNING O

PAINTING BY SIR AMÉDÉE FORESTIE
FROM THE NATIONAL COLL

As identified at the National Colle

BRITISH DELEGATES [*left to right*]: 1. Anthony St. Joh
ipotentiary * 4.

AMERICAN DELEGATES [*continuing left to right*]: 5.
7. Christopher Hughes, Secretary 8. James A. Bayar

* Signer

' THE TREATY OF GHENT, 1814

1914, ON LOAN, 1949, TO THE DEPARTMENT OF STATE
:TION OF FINE ARTS, SMITHSONIAN INSTITUTION

›n of Fine Arts for the Department of State, the persons are:
ıaker, Secretary 2. Henry Goulburn, Plenipotentiary * 3. William Adams, Plen-
niral Lord Gambier, Chief Plenipotentiary *
ın Quincy Adams, Chief Plenipotentiary * 6. Albert Gallatin, Plenipotentiary *
'lenipotentiary * 9. Henry Clay, Plenipotentiary * 10. Jonathan Russell, Pleni-
entiary * 11. Unidentified

The negotiators immediately rushed three copies of their treaty by way of London to the United States, accompanied by a protocol of their conferences with the British Commissioners leading to the final signature of the peace. Russell signed the joint report, but in a separate letter to the Secretary of State reserved the occasion to explain later why he had differed from the majority of his colleagues when they had proposed to continue both the fisheries and the navigation of the Mississippi — an offer that the British Commissioners had rejected. This he did at great length in a private letter to the Secretary of State on February 11, 1815. More will be heard of Russell's dissent much later. It was a seed of future action against a brother Commissioner, planted, as John Quincy Adams discovered seven years later, to take rancorous root in the soil of sectional prejudice and party politics.[53]

In London the Prince Regent speedily ratified the treaty. He had already given his plenipotentiaries the power to bind, ratify, and confirm in his name when they signed. The American Commissioners of course could not do this for their Government. The Senate of the United States first had to advise and consent by a two-thirds majority of Senators present before the President could ratify.

The British Government feared that President Madison might try to "trick" them out of ratification. Perhaps it recalled how Jefferson in 1807 had refused even to submit a treaty to the Senate because it did not contain an article prohibiting impressment. At the last moment Lord Liverpool had insisted on a stipulation that hostilities should not cease until both parties had ratified. That meant that if Admiral Cochrane's expedition took New Orleans, Great Britain would not have to give it back if the United States did not ratify. In that contingency the London Government had good reason to believe that the New England States, with their tendency toward separation from the Union, would not be indisposed to listen to a separate peace proposal.[54]

Before the treaty reached Washington, stirring news had arrived, February 11, from New Orleans. General Pakenham's British troops had landed and marched against the city, only to be thrown back and their commander killed in Andrew Jackson's magnificent victory of the 8th of January 1815. This triumph did not abate the desire for peace in Washington when the first copy of the treaty reached the capital, February 14. As soon as the Senators read the document and a summary of the diplomatic record[55] of the negotiation submitted therewith, they unanimously

53 *The Duplicate Letters and the Navigation of the Mississippi* (Washington, 1822), p. 141. See below, Ch. XXIV, Section 5.

54 Liverpool to Castlereagh, December 23, 1814: *Supplementary Despatches of Wellington*, IX, 495.

55 Despite the contentions of Clay, supported by Bayard and Russell, that the original diplomatic documents of the Commission be sent to the Department of State immediately, Adams insisted, as chairman of the Commission, in retaining custody of the archives until otherwise directed by the Government, or by the Commission in a for-

advised and consented (February 17, 1815) to its ratification. They were greatly pleased with the end of the war without loss of territory, climaxed with such a thrilling victory over a veteran British army. At eleven o'clock that night the Secretary of State exchanged final ratifications with the British Minister. Next morning (February 18, 1815) the President promptly proclaimed the treaty.

Everybody, East and West, North and South, was delighted with peace. Even the Essex Junto had to like it, for peace, peace at any price, was what they had been crying for, and here was peace, and peace with national dignity.

John Adams was greatly proud of his son's work at Ghent, particularly his stand for the inshore fisheries. Jubilantly the onetime Peace Commissioner of 1782 sent orders to London to have a new die made for the family escutcheon. Under the thirteen stars, the pine tree, the deer, and the fish swimming in the sea were now engraved the words from Horace: "*Piscemur, venemur, ut olim*": Fish and hunt we will as heretofore.[56] Before he died, the old statesman of Quincy passed the seal thus embellished down to John Quincy, and he in turn in his old age passed it on to his son Charles Francis Adams.

After two years of bitter humiliation the honor of the United States at last had been redeemed in the Cabinet and in the field. The delegates from the Hartford Convention, the Essex Junto defeatists of 1814, slunk home in obscurity, speedily to become forgotten men. The future belonged to Adams, to Jackson, to Clay, to the new nationalists, to the continentalists.

---

mal meeting of the same (which did not come to pass). They would be useful, he declared, in the new assignment that the Commission had received to negotiate a treaty of commerce with Great Britain. For Clay's squabble with Adams on this point, see *Memoirs*, III, 129–44. I have found no record to establish when the Commission's files reached the Department of State. They are now in the National Archives.

[56] The seal is now in the museum of the Massachusetts Historical Society. See Henry Adams, 2d: *A Catalogue of Books of John Quincy Adams with notes on Adams Seals*, p. 140. JA to JQA, Quincy, April 15, 1815, and JQA to JA, London. The English translation above given is by JQA in an anonymous communication sent to the *National Gazette*, June 17, 1822. For line-cut of seal see title page and front binding of the volume now in the reader's hands.

CHAPTER XI

Minister to Great Britain (1815–1817)

The avowed and true policy of Great Britain . . . in the existing state of the world . . . is to appease controversy, and to secure, if possible, for all states a long interval of Repose.

CASTLEREAGH TO CHARLES BAGOT, BRITISH MINISTER AT WASHINGTON, MOST PRIVATE AND SECRET, NOVEMBER 10, 1817[1]

BEFORE the Commissioners could proceed with their next assignment, a general treaty of commerce with Great Britain, they must first know the fate of their treaty of peace. While waiting for word from Washington they all betook themselves to the more agreeable scenes of Paris.

1

Thirty years earlier John Adams had lingered with his son in the French capital, hoping to make a treaty of commerce with Great Britain as soon as the Treaty of Peace and Independence of 1783 should be ratified. Now the son, waiting there under the same circumstances in his generation, eagerly revisited the landmarks of his boyhood. How they had been scarred by the tremendous cycle of history that had intervened since then! But Paris was still there in all its essential aspects, the Tuileries, the Palais Royal, the restored Bourbon court, the Louvre, the Bois, the courts of justice, museums, historical monuments, parks, squares, boulevards, book stalls – above all, the theaters.

The idle diplomat reveled in the old familiar scenes. His long and wide experience at European courts and chancelleries meant plenty of society. He wined and dined with many old friends of his father and himself: with Lafayette; with Count Barbé Marbois, who had been Secretary of the French Legation in Philadelphia thirty years before; with Madame de Staël, whom he had first met in St. Petersburg; with LeRay de Chaumont and de Castries, names famous in the diplomacy of the American Revolution; with Lafayette's brother-in-law, the Count de Tracy, whose

[1] PRO, F.O., 5, Vol. CXX.

son, Victor, Adams had succeeded in getting paroled from Russian captivity when in St. Petersburg. It was at the Tracys' that he met the famous scientist Alexander Humboldt.

Like a famished man Adams indulged his old passion for the theater. Several nights a week found him at one or another of the numerous playhouses. "The tendency to dissipation at Paris seems to be irresistible. There is a moral incapacity for industry and application, a *mollesse* against which I am as ill guarded as I was at the age of twenty." [2] When he had exhausted the repertory of the Opéra, the Théâtre Français, the Odéon, he visited marginal products at the Porte St. Martin, and the Feydeau. He much admired the great Talma, then at the height of his powers.

Paris had its serious interests too. Adams listened to long trials at the courts of justice and studied the court proceedings. He passed many hours in the museums and picture galleries. He nodded with some of the sleepy academicians at the Institute. With his colleagues on the Peace Commission he made his bow at the court of Louis XVIII. In the interview the King asked the tactful question: "Are you in any way related to the celebrated Mr. Adams?"

Meanwhile Louisa and ten-year-old Charles Francis were on their adventurous way across war-torn Europe in a trying winter stage-journey from St. Petersburg.[3] Soon the whole family would be reunited. The two older boys were already at sea to join their parents in England. As Mrs. Adams and young Charles were entering Paris, Louis XVIII, his court, and the diplomatic corps – all excepting the American Minister, William H. Crawford – were hastening away from it. Napoleon Bonaparte had come back from Elba.

For the last several afternoons John Quincy Adams had been walking the boulevards watching for the Emperor's entry. It was hard to believe that the exiled leader, with scarcely a battalion of troops to start with, could walk into possession of all France. Now he was in the Tuileries again. On the streets the bill-posters were busy scraping the official fleurs-de-lis off the walls and pasting up the imperial eagles.

Adams in his day, like historians in our day, looked upon Bonaparte as a unique product of the French Revolution. Throughout the Consulate he had felt that France was better off with Bonaparte than without him.[4] Then the conquests of the Empire led him to regard the great man as a misfortune to Europe. But it made him wince to realize that the restored Louis XVIII was only a "Vice-Roy" under the Duke of Wellington.[5] In

[2] *Memoirs,* III, 154.

[3] Her grandson, Brooks Adams, published "Mrs. John Quincy Adams's Narrative of a Journey from St. Petersburg to Paris in February, 1815" in *Scribner's Magazine,* XXXIV (October 1903), 449–63.

[4] *Writings,* II, 169, 442, 462, 467.

[5] *Writings,* V, 307.

also allowed American ships to trade directly between the United States and the British East Indies ports of Calcutta, Madras, Bombay, and Prince of Wales' Island (Penang) on most-favored-nation terms.

At that time the arrangement was considered to be a stopgap for four years. Except for the prohibition of discriminatory duties it provided for little more than agreement on existing practice.[14] This latter provision was a great step ahead. Nondiscrimination became one of the abiding principles of American foreign policy, and the Convention of 1815 a model for similar pacts between the United States and other countries.[15] Repeatedly renewed in 1818 and thereafter, it is still in effect.[16]

During the discussions the British Commissioners tried without success to secure for their subjects in Canada a freedom to the fur trade with Indians south of the American boundary line as before the war. The American Commissioners countered by demanding an equivalent: permission to float products down the St. Lawrence River for exportation in British ships from Montreal. The British Government would not allow this privilege, and was equally unprepared to let American ships into the British West India Islands or British North America. The whole question of trade with the British colonies was to occupy Adams again as Secretary of State.

An interesting feature of this negotiation of 1815 was the question of the *alternat*, which arose when the texts were being prepared for formal signature. In making a treaty or convention, which sovereign should stand first in the title, preamble, and body of the document, wherever it is necessary to mention both together? Whose plenipotentiaries should put their names above or before the other's when signing the instrument? European custom had dictated an alternation of precedence, called the *alternat*. For a diplomat to overlook the right of his sovereign to the *alternat* accepted for that sovereign an inferior position.

Sometimes the representatives of a little country did not dare to ask for an equality of position in this respect. That had been the case of the new-born United States in its first treaties. The European powers had looked upon the trans-Atlantic Republic as a parvenu among sovereign states, which ought to bow before divine-right kings and high mightinesses and was not entitled to have diplomatic representatives above the rank of minister plenipotentiary and envoy extraordinary.

In our very first treaties, of commerce and of alliance with France in

---

Nation, the two Contracting Parties reserve to themselves respectively the Right of regulating or diminishing, in such case, the amount of said drawback." For the negotiations see *ASPFR*, IV, 7–18.

[14] JQA to Richard Rush, instructing him to secure a renewal of the treaty, No. 5, May 22, 1818. DS, *Instructions, U.S. Ministers*, VIII, 193–6. *ASPFR*, IV, 371.

[15] Richard Rush: *Memoranda of a Residence at the Court of London* (2d ed., Philadelphia, 1833), p. 412. See below, Ch. XXII.

[16] So I am informed by Dr. Hunter Miller, onetime treaty editor of the Department of State.

1778, the name of the Most Christian King led that of the United States all the way through. Among all the treaties so far concluded by the United States (including John Quincy Adams's Treaty of 1799 with Prussia) there had been only two exceptions to this subordinate position: in the Treaty with Spain of 1795 Thomas Pinckney signed his name above that of the Prince of the Peace, although His Catholic Majesty held precedence throughout the text of the instrument. In the three treaties between the United States and France in 1803 the *alternat* prevailed perfectly for the first time. In the Treaty of Ghent, His Britannic Majesty ranked before the United States, as he had in the Treaty of Peace and Independence and in Jay's Treaty, and Gambier, Goulburn, and William Adams had signed their names over those of John Quincy Adams, Bayard, Clay, Russell, and Gallatin. It had galled Adams at the time,[17] and it disturbed Secretary of State Monroe, who wrote a remonstrance to him, with admonition for the future.[18]

After the negotiators in London had agreed on the articles of the Convention of 1815, Adams called the attention of the British plenipotentiaries to the *alternat*. With regard to the order of signatures they offered no positive objection, although Dr. Adams, the legal expert, declared he did not know of any such usage. Mr. Goulburn said the same. Adams told Goulburn that if he would take the trouble to inquire at the Foreign Office he would find it to be universal practice. The British representatives objected that to put in the *alternat* would require changes all through the document, and that the copies could not be absolute duplicates with this alternating precedence!

The two delegations then separated, each to prepare its own copy for signature the following Monday. Before the British delivered to the Americans their draft, His Britannic Majesty ranking first, they suggested that a fair American copy could be made from that text. Discussing the matter with Gallatin, Adams determined to introduce the *alternat* into the American counterpart of the British draft. He showed to his colleague the Secretary of State's instructions to him on that point.

Gallatin thought the matter of no importance. So did Clay.

When Adams showed Gallatin the draft he had made, with the *alternat* in it, the latter said in a peremptory and somewhat petulant manner:

"Oh, that is entirely wrong; it will throw the business into confusion."

Gallatin insisted on a new copy without the *alternat*.

"Mr. Gallatin, you and Mr. Clay may do as you please," Adams retorted in a heated and angry manner, "but I will not sign the treaty without the alternative observed throughout."

"Now don't fly off in this manner," admonished Gallatin.

"Indeed, sir," replied Adams. "I will not sign the treaty in any other form. I am so far from thinking with Mr. Clay that it is of no importance, that I think it by much the most important thing that we shall obtain by

[17] *Memoirs*, III, 242.

[18] Miller: *Treaties*, II, 583.

this treaty. The treaty itself I very much dislike, and it is only out of deference to you and Mr. Clay that I consent to sign it at all. I should infinitely prefer to sign no treaty at all, being perfectly convinced that we obtain nothing by it but what we should obtain by the regulations of this Government without it." [19]

Adams was everlastingly right on the point under discussion. Moreover, he had the Secretary of State behind him. His colleagues yielded good-humoredly. When the Americans presented their copy for signature along with the British copy, the British plenipotentiaries made no objection to any of the transpositions that had brought in the *alternat.* American and British delegates signed the alternating copies placing their names in parallel columns, the American column at the left on the American copy, and the British column at the left on the British copy.[20] The American signatures were alphabetical in their own column.

Thus did John Quincy Adams place the protocol of the American Republic on full equality with that of Great Britain. When he became Secretary of State in 1817 one of his first acts was to send out a standing instruction to the United States Minister to Great Britain, and later to all heads of missions, to maintain the *alternat.*[21] Thenceforth, except for inadvertent lapses, the practice has prevailed in all the bilateral treaties of the United States. Multilateral treaties, however, are signed in alphabetical precedence. In 1945 when the United Nations signed the peace charter at San Francisco the Big Five, except the United States, signed alphabetically, next the small powers alphabetically in their subordinate rank; the United States of America, in an unprecedented gesture of hospitality, signed last of all.

As the two delegations took leave of each other after signing the Convention of 1815, Goulburn said to John Quincy Adams: "Well, this is the second good job we have done together."

"Yes," replied Adams, "and I only hope we may do a third, going on from better to better." [22]

3

The hope of an improving relation with Great Britain sustained John Quincy Adams in his mission at the Court of St. James's during the two years following the War of 1812. His was the task of vigilantly guarding the rights and honor of his country as established in the Treaty of Ghent and in the Commercial Convention of 1815 and seeking to reach further agreement on some of the vexing issues of neutral rights and commerce which those treaties left unsettled. Above all, he worked to bring about

[19] *Memoirs,* III, 240–6.

[20] JQA to Secretary of State, No. 3. London, July 14, 1815. DS, *Despatches, Great Britain,* XIX.

[21] *Writings,* VI, 246.

[22] *Memoirs,* III, 248.

for the first time between the two nations a spirit of real reconciliation and mutual respect.

Castlereagh, greatest diplomatist of British history, was now at the height of his powers and prestige. He was just returned from his success at the Conference of Vienna, where England got everything she wanted and no other power got anything that England really did not want it to have. Rich, aristocratic, brilliant, with the world at his beck in 1815, the Secretary of State for Foreign Affairs could easily have assumed an arrogant, supercilious, or condescending tone. "His deportment is sufficiently graceful," noted Adams after his first conference, "and his person is handsome. His manner was cold, but not absolutely repulsive." [23]

The Foreign Minister proved always ready to receive Adams and to keep his appointment or to make proper excuses when prevented. He was polite and frank, and the many and sometimes lengthy interviews always went off in an unruffled manner. The two men soon learned to respect each other. Through them the two Governments came to place good faith in each other, even when they could not agree on principle. Of all British statesmen of Adams's time Castlereagh was the most steady and successful advocate of Anglo-American reconciliation.

The complete peace of the world and the prevailing will of all the powers in the unexcitable years immediately after Waterloo made easier Adams's task of ameliorating relations with the mother country. "The world of Europe is in a glassy calm," he wrote to his father. "Not a breath of wind or a ripple of water is moving." [24] The principal problems which he had to handle during these tranquil times were: the execution of the Treaty of Ghent and the Commercial Convention of 1815; rival naval armaments on the Great Lakes; a more comprehensive treaty of commerce, to include an agreement also on neutral and belligerent rights and impressment; and the fisheries. In addition to these special questions were the ever increasing routine tasks of the Legation: for instance, the relief of indigent American seamen released from the British Navy, which took up more of the Minister's time than any other single duty.

Thanks to Castlereagh's loyal policy of conciliation, John Quincy Adams's efforts to ensure the territorial integrity of the United States according to the terms of the Treaty of Ghent were far more successful than the similar representations that his father had made in London after the Treaty of Peace of 1783. It must be acknowledged that in 1815–17 the United States had a certain military leverage which it lacked in 1784–96. For example, it refused to evacuate Fort Malden in Ontario until the British garrison withdrew from Michilimackinac.[25]

Despite the opposition of fur-trading interests and local officials in

[23] *Memoirs*, III, 205.

[24] No. 46, February 24, 1816. Adams MSS.

[25] A. L. Burt, op. cit., p. 374. This work presents the frontier situation with scholarly detail.

Canada the restoration of the frontier posts presented no insurmountable difficulty. Nevertheless, Adams had to call the attention of the British Government repeatedly and very forcibly to some disagreeable frontier incidents in which officers and colonial officials regrettably had departed from the fairness and liberality of their Government's instructions to them, making the execution of them "so different from them in Spirit, so opposite to them in effect." [26] He was referring to British Colonel Nicholls's incendiary intrigue in Spanish Florida and his alliance with the Creek Indians of the Southwest.[27] On the extreme northwestern frontier the intrusive conduct of Colonel James furnished another occasion for protest.[28]

The American Minister's vigorous but perfectly temperate remonstrances won Castlereagh's respect for his power of dialectics. He immediately repudiated Colonel Nicholls, and he assured Adams that very strong instructions would be sent out to observe American jurisdiction on the northern frontier.[29] The diplomatic exchanges proved good practice for Adams. He would have to deal with these same questions again as Secretary of State.

The Great Lakes were a zone of danger at the outset of these mutual strivings for Anglo-American amity. Colonial officials had been disappointed at the failure of their statesmen to exclude the Americans altogether from those waters, or at least to limit their naval armament there. After Ghent an increase in British fresh-water warships gave the signal for a race in armaments on the inland seas of the Continent. It threatened to provide a continual stimulus to suspicion and ill will along the border. Small but provocative incidents occurred on each side, including the firing of shots at an American ship on Lake Erie in 1815 and the boarding of American vessels.[30] Incidents like these could bring on larger collisions. Adams, under instructions [31] from his Government, proposed, January 25, 1816, a reciprocal reduction of armaments upon the Lakes.

As early as the peace negotiations of 1782 John Adams had favored the elimination of any garrisoned or fortified frontier. The idea of abolishing naval armaments on the Lakes went back to the definitive peace negotiations of 1783. It had been in the mind of Alexander Hamilton as early as 1782. At Hamilton's suggestion John Jay had proposed it during

[26] JQA to Lord Bathurst, 25 Charles St., Westminster, September 25, 1815, enclosed in JQA to Secretary of State, No. 15, September 26, 1815. DS, *Despatches, Great Britain*, XIX.

[27] For Nicholls, see below, Ch. XV, and *ASPFR*, IV, 546–62.

[28] JQA to Secretary of State, No. 40, London, April 15, 1816. *Writings*, VI, 18.

[29] JQA to Bathurst, September 25, 1815, note 26 above. *Memoirs*, III, 330.

[30] JQA to Secretary of State, No. 53, London, August 24, 1816. JQA to Castlereagh, London, August 29, 1816, enclosed in JQA to Secretary of State, No. 55, September 18, 1816. DS, *Despatches, Great Britain*, XXI. *Memoirs*, III, 425.

[31] Secretary of State to JQA, November 16, 1815. *Instructions, U.S. Ministers*, VII, 8.

his negotiation of 1794. It then had proved unacceptable to Lord Grenville.[32] After Ghent it struck Lord Castlereagh as perfectly reasonable. It would be ridiculous and absurd, he said, to keep a number of armed ships parading the Lakes in time of peace; everything beyond what was necessary to guard against smuggling would be calculated only to produce mischief.[33] "But you know we are the weaker party there," he observed. "Therefore it was that we proposed at Ghent that the whole Lakes should belong to one party – all the shores; for then armaments would not be necessary."

"The proposition at Ghent to which we objected," Adams reminded him, "was that the disarming should be all on one side." He continued with a most diplomatic allusion, which may have been designed to make the American proposal seem like a British idea originally: "There was indeed afterward intimated to us by the British plenipotentiaries an intention to make us a proposal so fair and reasonable that it was thought no objection could be made against it. We did suppose that it was this identical proposition which I am now authorized to make. It was not, however, brought forward, nor was any explanation given by the British plenipotentiary of what they had intended by their offer."

"Well," Castlereagh said, after some further conversation, "I will propose it to the Government for consideration." [34]

Still not sure how far Castlereagh would go, Adams repeated the offer in a formal note of March 21, 1816.[35]

There was nothing else for Great Britain to do but to welcome the proposal. In any naval race on the Great Lakes the United States was in a position to surpass all British efforts. But Castlereagh transferred the negotiations across the Atlantic because of Adams's lack of powers to conclude any definite arrangement. Meanwhile the two diplomatists entered into a gentleman's agreement that pending the negotiation in Washington neither Government would begin any new armaments on those frontier waters.[36] The ultimate result was the celebrated Rush-Bagot Agreement [37] of April 28–9, 1817 limiting naval armament by both

[32] See Helen Dwight Reid: *International Servitudes in Law and Practice* (Chicago, 1932), p. 200, and my article: "Alexander Hamilton and the Limitation of Armaments," *Pacific Review,* II (No. 4, March 1922), pp. 587–602. Note also JA to Benjamin Franklin, April 16, 1782. Wharton: *Revolutionary Diplomatic Correspondence,* V, 544.

[33] JQA to the Secretary of State, No. 30, London, February 8, 1816. *Writings,* V, 497–500. *Memoirs,* III, 288–9.

[34] *Memoirs,* III, 286–8.

[35] JQA to Lord Castlereagh, London, March 21, 1816, enclosed in JQA to Secretary of State, No. 36, March 22, 1816. DS, *Despatches, Great Britain,* XX.

[36] A. L. Burt, op. cit., p. 390.

[37] Approved and consented to, in treaty form, by the United States Senate, April 16, 1818. For relevant correspondence between the British Minister, Charles Bagot, and the Acting Secretary of State, Richard Rush, see Miller: *Treaties,* II, 644–54, and *ASPFR,* IV, 202–7. The standard work on the subject is James Morton Callahan: *The*

parties on the Great Lakes to a specified number and size of ships barely adequate for customs regulations.[38] It was the first instance of reciprocal naval disarmament in the history of international relations, the most successful and the most lasting precedent, and certainly an advantageous arrangement for the larger interests of the United States.

Nothing could have offered a greater earnest of the permanently peaceful intentions of the British Government in this new epoch of Anglo-American reconciliation. As John Quincy Adams realized, disarmament on the Lakes gave to the United States a powerful compensation against overwhelming British sea power on the oceans. As the United States rapidly grew in resources, population, and military potential, a defenseless Canada inevitably became more and more a hostage, if indeed such were at all needed, for the friendly conduct of the British Navy toward the populous and undefended cities of the Atlantic and later the Pacific Coast of the Continental Republic. After 1842 the land defenses on both sides of the Canadian land frontier began to fall into decay.

4

A vexing dispute between the United States and Great Britain arising out of the Treaty of Ghent related to the evacuation by the British Army of escaped slaves who had sought refuge with the enemy. Article I of the treaty had stipulated:

> All territory, places, and possessions whatsoever taken by either party from the other during the war, or which may be taken after the signing of this Treaty, excepting only the Islands hereafter mentioned,[39] shall be restored without delay and without causing any destruction or carrying away any of the Artillery or other public property originally captured in the said forts or places, and which shall remain therein upon the Exchange of the Ratifications of this Treaty, or any Slaves or other private property. . . .

Neutrality of the American Lakes and Anglo-American Relations, Johns Hopkins University Studies in Historical and Political Science, XVI (Baltimore, 1898), 1–199. Rush had nothing to do with the negotiation of the agreement which bears his name. That was the work of James Monroe as Secretary of State. After Monroe succeeded to the Presidency, Rush signed the notes as Acting Secretary of State.

[38] The existing naval ships on both sides were not destroyed nor disarmed, but only *decommissioned.* Not until 1831 did the United States reduce the number of its ships to the level agreed upon in 1817, and the British Government did not do so until 1834. Albert B. Corey has analyzed "Canadian Border Defense Problems after 1814 to their Culmination in the 'Forties," in *Report* of the Annual Meeting of the Canadian Historical Association held at Ottawa, May 23–4, 1938 (Toronto, 1938), pp. 111–20. See also same author's examination of *The Crisis of 1830–1842 in Canadian American Relations,* in the Carnegie Endowment Series, The Relations of Canada and the United States (New Haven and Toronto, 1941), Ch. X.

[39] These were the islands in Passamaquoddy Bay. See above, p. 215.

To the consternation of the United States, the British Government interpreted this phraseology to apply only to slaves who were actually in British garrisoned places after the signature of the treaty, not to the hundreds who found themselves on British ships in American territorial waters. In obedience to his instructions,[40] Adams protested the carrying away of these slaves and the refusal of the British Government to deliver them up or to make compensation for them. It was even suspected that some unscrupulous naval captains had sold the liberated Negroes to West Indian planters.

Thanks to his recently having insisted so obstinately, as titular head of the Peace Commission, on personally retaining custody of the documents relating to the negotiation of the Treaty of Ghent, Adams was able to show Castlereagh how the British negotiators had allowed to be transposed to the end of the clause, above quoted, the words: "or slaves or other private property." At the time they had been well aware of the reason for this change in position: namely, to exclude the slaves and other private property from assimilation to public property within the evacuated places. But Castlereagh would not admit either the plain sense of the article or the inference to be drawn from the way the negotiators had drafted it. The British Government had allowed no indemnity for slaves carried off after the former War of American Independence, despite a provision in the Treaty of Peace of 1783 against "carrying away any negroes." It seemed determined not to allow it this time either.

Lord Liverpool, the Prime Minister, a man of remarkable mildness and amenity of manners, was equally adamant. "I do not think," he said to Adams, "they can be considered precisely under the general denomination of private property. A table or a chair, for instance, might be taken and restored without changing its condition; but a living and a human being is entitled to other considerations."

"The treaty has made no such distinction," Adams found himself obliged to say. "The words implicitly recognized slaves as private property. They are in the article alluded to: 'slaves or *other* private property.' I do, however, readily admit the distinction suggested by you. Most certainly a living, sentient being, and still more a human being, is to be regarded in a different light from the inanimate matter of which other private property might consist, and if on the ground of that difference the British Plenipotentiaries had objected to restore the one, while they agreed to restore the other, we should have readily discussed the subject. . . ."[41]

The Prime Minister's well-aimed moral thrust did not deflect Adams from his diplomatic duty. So pertinaciously did he carry out his instructions in long conversations and voluminous notes on this issue that the British Government finally adopted his suggestion that the question be

[40] Secretary of State to JQA, November 16, 20, 1815. DS, *Instructions, U.S. Ministers,* VIII, 3, 9.

[41] *Memoirs,* III, 257–9.

submitted to arbitration,[42] thus following the precedent of the Treaty of Ghent for the settlement of other anticipated disputes like the northeastern boundary.

Castlereagh and Adams also had some conversations about the African slave trade. In Article X of the Treaty of Ghent the two parties had agreed to use their best endeavors to promote its entire abolition.[43] The Foreign Minister, explaining British intentions in Lord Exmouth's famous punitive expedition against the Dey of Algiers in 1816,[44] declared that Great Britain after imposing a peace upon that potentate would willingly co-operate with the other nations interested in making the Barbary powers observe the principles of civilized nations in the future, by supplying her proportion of the requisite naval force.

"But," he added, "it is her intention to combine this purpose with that of completing the abolition of the African slave-trade, and to obtain the assent of the nations which will contribute to the joint armament to put down forever the Barbary piracies, to allow the same joint application of power to arrest every ship pursuing the traffic in black slaves."

"This seems perfectly fair to me," responded Adams.[45]

Apparently in these early discussions John Quincy Adams did not at the very first see the objections that might arise to foreign visit and search of American vessels suspected of that nefarious African commerce, as long as Great Britain refused on her part to give up the right of visit and search for the impressment of seamen, including American citizens, deserted from her navy. But he soon became suspicious when the English emancipator, James Wilberforce, sounded him out as to whether the United States, together with all other maritime powers, would consent that ships under its flag might be searched and captured by British cruisers patrolling against the slave trade.

Wilberforce, leader of the "Saints" in the House of Commons, was one of the most influential members of Parliament; moreover, he was brother-in-law to James Stephen, whose famous pamphlet, *War in Disguise, or the Frauds of Neutral Flags,* had defended the Rule of the War of 1756 and

[42] Below, Ch. XIV.

[43] "Whereas the Traffic in Slaves is irreconcilable with the principles of humanity and Justice, and whereas both His Majesty and the United States are desirous of continuing their efforts to promote its entire abolition, it is hereby agreed that both the contracting parties shall use their best endeavors to accomplish so desirable an object."

[44] Adams had much discussion with the British Foreign Office over Britain's policy toward the Barbary States, particularly concerning Article XVIII of the Treaty of 1815 between the United States and Algiers, by which the Dey of Algiers agreed to refuse entrance to prizes made by the enemies of the United States, and to admit American warships with their prizes. Great Britain served notice on Algiers that this article was incompatible with British-Algerian treaties since 1698. Nevertheless the article was repeated in the Treaty of 1816 between the United States and Algiers. *Memoirs,* III, 355–60, *et passim.* JQA to Secretary of State, Nos. 45, 47, London, May 18, June 22, 1816. DS, *Despatches, Great Britain,* XX.

[45] *Memoirs,* III, 428.

is supposed to have inspired the Orders in Council of 1807, of baleful memory.[46] Adams feared that Wilberforce's proposal might sanctify a "bare-faced and impudent" attempt to obtain in time of peace a right of visit and search – and impressment – which had been so abused in time of war.[47]

Kidnapping American citizens and forcing them to fight in British warships against Britain's enemies, including their own country, was as odious to Adams as enslaving African Negroes and selling them to sweat out the rest of their lives on American plantations. Nevertheless, international agreement for the suppression of the slave trade became a very real and pressing humanitarian problem. It was another Anglo-American question to which he would soon have to devote himself as Secretary of State.

5

Of all the issues left unsettled by the Treaty of Ghent that of the fisheries was nearest to John Quincy Adams's heart and home. It soon became evident that Great Britain was prepared to deny at least the inshore fisheries to citizens of the United States. In July 1815 there were detentions in Nova Scotian territorial waters. A British sloop-of-war, the *Jaseur*, warned American fishing vessels not to come within sixty miles of the coast. To Adams fell the congenial task of defending his countrymen's fishery rights and liberties. The London Government speedily revoked the *Jaseur* order and sent out instructions to naval officers on that station not even to interrupt the American fishermen who might have proceeded to British coasts within the existing year, but to allow them to complete their fares, then to give notice that the "privilege" could no longer be allowed and they must not come back the following year.[48]

"I think I have sent you proofs enough of the importance of the fisheries to your Country," wrote old John Adams, "and my advice is to demand your recall and refuse your signature to any compact which shall directly or by implication surrender one tittle or iota of the Treaty of 1783 relative to the fisheries." [49]

Fortified by long and impassioned letters from his father in Quincy, original defender of the fisheries, the American Minister threshed over the old arguments in numerous memoranda and conversations at the Foreign Office. Again and again John Quincy Adams insisted, as he had asserted at Ghent, and as his father before him had contended at Paris, that the inshore fisheries were a part of the original division of the British Empire in 1783, that they were part and parcel of American independence itself. Soon the British Government dropped all pretense to exclusion

[46] See above, p. 140. H. Adams: *History of the U.S.*, III, 50–3; IV, 57, 100, 102.

[47] *Memoirs*, III, 556–8.

[48] *ASPFR*, IV, 348–60. *Writings*, V, 377–91, 409, 445, 472–87. *Memoirs*, III, *passim.*

[49] Quincy, June 7, 1815. Adams MSS.

of American fishermen from their rights on the high seas, and finally Lord Bathurst (who took charge of Foreign Affairs during Castlereagh's absences from Whitehall) stated the Government's willingness for the "modified renewal" of the liberties in question. Adams received powers to negotiate a convention for that purpose. Before they arrived, Castlereagh had transferred that negotiation to Washington too, doubtless with the hope of getting it out of the hands of an Adams.[50] Meanwhile the British Government extended from year to year the suspension of trespass proceedings. It was one of Adams's tasks during the remainder of his mission in London to keep these prohibitions and seizures in a state of suspense.[51]

6

After over a year of discussing the various problems of Anglo-American relations Adams, under authority of his Government,[52] proposed a far-sighted treaty intended to take care of all outstanding issues between the two countries, to guard against all future misunderstandings, and to promote and perpetuate good will and peace in the future. It contained proposals under four heads: (1) Reciprocal liberty of commerce between the United States and the British West India Islands, and between the United States and British North America, without discrimination by either party against the other. (2) An adjustment of the impressment issue [53] by a stipulation that neither the United States nor Great Britain should employ in their naval or merchant service the seamen of the other, with the exception of those *already* naturalized. (3) The Freedom of the Seas, by an agreement on neutral and belligerent rights. (4) Arbitration by a friendly sovereign of the dispute concerning slaves carried away from the United States by British forces after the ratification of the Peace of Ghent.[54]

The proposed treaty seemed so much more advantageous to the United States, in the immediate picture of international relations, than for Great Britain that Castlereagh, with the greatest politeness, declined the opportunity.

50 "I flatter myself, however, that you have been fortunate in the translation of this controversy to Washington." JA to JQA, Quincy, August 26, 1816. Adams MSS.

51 In 1817 when negotiations halted at Washington, Castlereagh renewed the no-trespass warnings, and some more seizures occurred, but the Halifax Admiralty courts released the ships and the British Government extended the informal arrangements another year, after negotiations had resumed. Burt, op. cit., pp. 398–410.

52 Secretary of State to JQA, May 21, 1816. DS, *Instructions, U.S. Ministers,* VIII, 61, 66.

53 Adams was not sympathetic to this proposal which he presented, under instructions, on impressment. He felt that the British Government would not understand such an agreement as implying or intending an engagement to renounce the practice of taking men from American vessels in the event of a future maritime war. JQA to Secretary of State, No. 56, London, September 27, 1816. *Writings,* VI, 95.

54 *ASPFR,* IV, 106–22. *Writings,* VI, 80–6, 98–101.

"This Government still adheres to . . . their ancient colonial policy," he told Adams. If the United States desired to retaliate by refusing clearance to British vessels for the West Indies, as a recent act of Congress had threatened, that was only fair on their part, he declared, given the existing situation. He did offer some very minor concessions,[55] and was willing to agree on reciprocal liberty of trade across the common frontier waterways of North America subject to the tariff charges of either party without discrimination – because this was more advantageous to Great Britain than to the United States. On impressment he was courteous but adamant. "Who are we to understand by the seamen of the other?" he had already asked the American Minister, and finally had begged him not to propose any formal article on that subject, but rather to let the controversy sleep in peace.[56]

Adams's London mission was by no means unsuccessful. He had made no mistake. He had quarreled with nobody. He had put at least three issues in the way of settlement: naval armaments on the Great Lakes, the abducted slaves, and the inshore fisheries. By firmness, dignity, tact, patience, and good will in his diplomatic conversations with Castlereagh he had done much to open the road to permanent amity after nearly half a century of dispute, rancor, wars, and mutual suspicion between wars. He had brought to bear the qualities that were most needed in the fatigued aftermath of the War of 1812. On its part the British Government, if it had not gone out of its way to make particular advances, had responded at least not unsympathetically to American overtures. Its conspicuous statesmen began to drop their old tone of distrust and condescension, certainly toward Adams. As Castlereagh said, England wanted appeasement of controversy and repose all over the world. She wanted it in North America as well as in Europe. And a concern at rising American naval power had replaced the old contempt that the British nation once felt for America and for Americans.[57]

In the new atmosphere the Liverpool Government, under the guidance of England's great diplomatist, was willing to let bygones be bygones, to live and let live. A new day was faintly dawning in Anglo-American relations, at least in the eyes of leaders like Castlereagh. John Quincy Adams was first to greet it and to encourage it.

7

Gradually Adams made himself felt in English public life. He received numerous invitations to speak at ceremonial functions. He rose frequently to conventional toasts, always in a friendly and open manner. His *Mem-*

[55] Most-favored-nation privileges at free ports there, which were negligible, and right to go to Turk's Island with exports, for salt.

[56] *Memoirs,* III, 283–8, 395–8, 423.

[57] *Writings,* VI, 141–3.

oirs record a number of these specimens of "tablecloth oratory," of which the following is a good sample. Responding on Easter Monday 1816, at a Mansion House dinner, to the Lord Mayor's toast: "To the President of the United States," the American Minister said:

> My Lord, I pray your Lordship to accept my hearty thanks for the honor which you have done my country in drinking the health of its Chief Magistrate. I receive it as an earnest of peace, harmony, and friendship between the two countries. To promote peace, harmony, and friendship between Great Britain and the United States is the first duty of my station. It is the first wish of my heart. It is my first prayer to God. I hope it will not be deemed unsuitable on this occasion to recur to considerations of a religious nature.
>
> In ordinary cases, and at ordinary times, it may be proper and sufficient for Britons and for Americans to say to themselves, It is our interest on both sides to live in peace, harmony, and friendship together. But, my Lord, the event which was yesterday commemorated by religious solemnities, and which is this day commemorated at this table in the convivial and loving cups of your Lord and Ladyship, is the most important event that ever occurred upon this globe. It is an event in which we are all interested – a pledge to us all of immortality. It is the warrant to us all of another state of existence, where all is peace, harmony, and friendship. May it ever have the proper influence on the minds of your Lordship's countrymen and mine! May it ever remind them of a higher motive than any possible temporal interest to peace, harmony, and friendship!
>
> In return for your Lordship's obliging toast, I beg leave to drink, All religious blessings and all temporal prosperity to the Metropolis of the British Empire and its Chief Magistrate.[58]

Adams made real reconciliation between the two Governments and peoples the devout purpose of his mission – "sweet reconciliation," as Benjamin Franklin would have put it.

"My special duty at present is to preach peace," he wrote his father. "And from the bottom of my soul I do preach it, as well to those to whom, as to those from whom I am sent. I am deeply convinced that peace is the state best adapted to the interest and the happiness of both nations." [59]

As Minister to the Court of St. James's, John Quincy Adams began to experience some of the trials since common to every American representative abroad. Before the War of 1812 Americans visiting Europe for amusement or education were not sufficiently numerous to constitute much of

[58] *Memoirs,* III, 333.

[59] JQA to JA, Ealing, May 29, 1816. *Writings,* VI, 38. "You preach peace, and you are right. God and man will approve your doctrine, your exhortation, your instruction, your admonition. If all is overruled, it will not be your fault." JA to JQA, August 26, 1816. Adams MSS.

a problem for any legation. After the Peace of Ghent, however, crowds of young men, particularly from Boston, set forth to learn of the charms and culture of Europe before settling down to life. Most of them passed through London, eager to make the acquaintance of their illustrious countryman, the Minister. Many of them had sought letters of introduction from ex-President John Adams and his wife, for whom it was hard to refuse friends. The tourists often expected a family welcome at their fellow American's house and table. Some of the more distinguished would be delighted to be presented at court. Others even wanted to be his private secretary in order to see Europe with dignity and, as they expected, with ease.

In addition to fellow Bostonians with an itch for travel and education, there were always young relatives who wanted to be legation secretaries. One nephew, William Steuben Smith,[60] he had accepted at St. Petersburg in order to please the boy's grandparents, John and Abigail Adams. The young man, well intentioned enough in that extravagant Russian society, got imprudent and careless with money, so much so that he became an anxiety to the Minister, who did not regret leaving him behind in Russia for a time even though it meant being without a private secretary during most of the laborious days at Ghent. Next Adams soon found himself with William's brother, John Adams Smith, on his hands in London. Grandmother Abigail, saying nothing to her son, had sent a letter to Mrs. Madison, and other friends in Washington, recommending the boy, and the President obligingly had appointed him. The Minister had to swallow his vexation and set aside any uneasiness about nepotism. To his surprise the last secretary, like his first, his own brother Thomas Boylston Adams, turned out to be an industrious, attentive, and faithful assistant.[61]

Besides the public business with the British Government, and all the official dispatches to the Secretary of State in Washington, the Legation was in correspondence with ministers, agents, or consuls of the United States in Russia, Great Britain, Ireland, Gibraltar, Malta, Denmark, Holland, France, Spain, Italy, the German States, the Barbary Coast, and Brazil, and with the commanders and supply agents of American naval squadrons operating in the Mediterranean. And every American private citizen who had a claim of some kind on his Government called for the interposition of the Minister. Every projector of absurd ventures, every inventor of impossible contrivances, whose wonder-working genius had not been duly retained and encouraged by the British Government, sought out the patronage of the United States. The multitudes of people who ap-

[60] Son of John Quincy's beloved sister, Abby, and Colonel William S. Smith. Abigail Adams, daughter of John and Abigail Adams, died August 15, 1813. Her husband, Colonel Smith, died June 10, 1816.

[61] AA to JQA, Quincy, August 15, September 30, October 23, 1816; JQA to AA, Nos. 77, 80, October 1, 1815, February 27, 1816. Adams MSS. JQA to JA, Ealing, August 1, 1816. *Writings*, VI, 60. *Memoirs*, III, 275.

plied by person or in writing for what was either improper or impossible to grant were so importunate, so unreasonable, and sometimes so insolent as almost to plague the life out of the Minister, who could not or at least would not close his doors to them.

"One would imagine," wrote the harassed public servant to Abigail, "that the American legation at London was the moon of Ariosto, or Milton's Paradise of Fools — the place where things lost upon the Earth were to be found." [62]

Frequently in those days of economic depression and social malaise, when England seemed on the verge of revolution, John Quincy Adams went into his own pocket to pay the way home of some distressed compatriot or to relieve a needy family, American or British; and more than once such people took advantage of him, particularly his own countrymen. Because Thomas B. Adams in Boston managed his brother's accounts and business affairs during the second European sojourn, some of these cases reached the ears of Abigail. She had to warn her son to be careful or he would go the way of his father! "Your father suffered from swindlers, and if I had not been a little more wary, and looked into characters with rather more facility, Colonel Norton would have got his hundred guineas instead of 50 which never have been or will be paid. I name this as only one instance out of many." [63]

8

The two years spent in England were among the pleasantest of Adams's long life. His contentment did not come from diplomatic functions and state ceremonies. He mistrusted and despised the ruling classes of England. He associated with them as little as was decently possible. Rather he sought the society of thinkers and scholars, like Jeremy Bentham, and took his pleasure in the theaters, concerts, museums, and bookstalls of London town.

Soon after arriving in London, Louisa solved the urgent problem of their domestic establishment by finding a little country house at Ealing, eight miles from Hyde Park Corner — that is, within two hours' coaching distance of town. There the Minister spent most of his time. He did not travel outside the environs of the metropolis. The Legation maintained a chancery first at 25 Charles Street, Westminster, then at 13 Craven Street, and later at 28 Craven Street, where Adams's Secretary of Legation and nephew dwelt. There the Minister and his lady always had available a couple of chambers when they came to town.[64] It was convenient for over-

[62] JQA to AA, No. 84, Ealing, March 25, 1816. Adams MSS.

[63] AA to JQA, Quincy, March 22, 1816. Adams MSS.

[64] JQA to Samuel Thornton, August 9, 1815. Diary, August 15, December 26, 1815. From May 22 to August 5, 1815 the Adamses lived at No. 67 Harley St., Cavendish Square, in lodgings kept by one W. Mills.

night sojourns after attending official functions during the bustling London session with its levees, drawing-rooms, routs, and balls.[65]

Mrs. Adams went to London very little, except for dutiful attendance at court functions, and occasionally to visit a particular friend, like Mrs. Charles King,[66] or to attend concerts or the theater with her husband and sons. To the diplomatic dinners of his colleagues and London officialdom Adams more often betook himself alone, or in the company of John Adams Smith. One of the strongest reasons the Minister had for dwelling outside of London was to escape from the frequency of invitations at late hours, which consumed so much precious time and entailed the perpetually mortifying consciousness of inability to return civilities in the same manner.[67]

His determination to maintain his family on his official salary met an even more severe test in London than in St. Petersburg. "No Minister of the United States at this Court has ever found it profitable," he wrote to the Secretary of State, "to limit his expense within the public allowance of salary and outfit. . . . The permanent missions abroad must be exclusively given to men of large fortune, willing to expend it liberally, or there must be a considerable increase of the salaries." [68]

To old John Adams this was nothing new. "The corps diplomatique will say 'Adams lives *dans la plus infame oeconomy,*'" wrote the first American Minister ever to walk up the stairs of St. James's. "Their coachmen and footmen will look down on yours with the utmost scorn and contempt. Their secretaries, and gentlemen *attachees* [*sic*] *à l'ambassade* will smile and leer and sneer and shrug their shoulders. *Quid inde?* Your father has seen and felt all this before you." [69]

Despite the financial handicaps, and the entire simplicity of Adams's own habits and character, nobody seems to have complained. Neither the British Government nor, remarkably enough, his own compatriots took notice of his economy. On the contrary, people respected his republican simplicity. In the long line of eminent men who have distinguished their country at the Court of St. James's, none ever brought a broader mind, a warmer heart behind a serious mien, wider culture and learning, or as regular, punctual, and comprehensive hard work and application to business.[70] In the language of that day, John Quincy Adams helped to elevate

[65] JQA to AA, No. 75, Boston Terrace, Ealing, August 24, 1815. Adams MSS.

[66] Daughter-in-law of Rufus King.

[67] *Memoirs,* III, 323.

[68] No. 12, London, July 12, 1816. *Writings,* VI, 51.

[69] JA to JQA, Quincy, October 13, 1815. Adams MSS.

[70] See Charles King's *Eulogy on John Quincy Adams* (printed by E. Sanderson, Elizabethtown, N.J., 1848) for a characterization of him as Minister to Great Britain. On the other hand a recent eminent British scholar, C. K. Webster, avers: "The great John Quincy Adams, who left [England] in 1817 to become Secretary of State to Monroe, was as bitter and hostile to Britain as Richard Rush, his successor, was friendly and conciliatory." Professor Webster concedes that: "Nevertheless Adams was a man

the American character in the estimation of Britain and of the European nations.

The comfortable little country house with its laurel-bordered garden at Ealing, rented from a Miss Clitherow for 260 guineas a year, already had the name of Little Boston House – after one Lord Boston, a kinsman of the owner. The ready-made name suited this Yankee family to perfection. The English countryside was a paradise compared with the rigors of life in the climate of St. Petersburg. For the first time in his life John Quincy Adams began to take on weight and soon arrived at those plump and well-nourished proportions which characterized his person in later decades.

In his rural retreat the Minister found satisfaction in the education of his sons. He walked and talked with the boys in many a country ramble. George was already a nervous, overgrown boy of unsteady health, who thought he wanted to be an army officer. John, a small, active lad, apple of his grandfather's eye, aspired to a career in the navy. Eager young Charles, his father's little companion on the quays of the Neva, was not yet decided on what to make of life, but he also inclined to the navy.

The father did not discourage the boys in their martial ardor. A fencing master took his place in their schooling. It was at this time that the Minister injured his right hand by the kickback of a pistol while teaching the boys target practice. The most painful result was that for several weeks he could not write, a calamity for any Adams. He nearly blinded himself reading while he had to be idle with his pen.

The two older brothers, fresh from the United States, attended a boys' school close by. George Washington Adams for a while also got personal tutoring from his father in preparation for Harvard College. At night with his sons and other young friends John Quincy Adams studied the heavens, teaching the names and positions of the major constellations.[71] One of the

of such great capacity, honest character and lofty moral principles that in the long run he served well the interests of the two peoples. . . . He remained, however, always and above all, an intensely patriotic American." See C. K. Webster: *The Foreign Policy of Castlereagh, 1815–1822* (London, 1934), pp. 45, 440–1. Hereinafter referred to as Webster: *Castlereagh*. These are attributes which British scholars so justly admire in their own great statesmen, Winston Churchill for example.

Professor Webster doubtless overlooked Charles Bagot's dispatch of September 20, 1817 from Washington (*Writings* of JQA, VII, 189 n. 2), telling how he had conveyed to the President "the satisfaction which His Royal Highness had derived from the conciliatory conduct of Mr. Adams during the period of his mission in England, and of the constant desire of His Royal Highness the Prince Regent to preserve and strengthen those friendly relations between the two countries which had been so auspiciously commenced."

However galled he may have been at the British ruling classes, John Quincy Adams was a sincere friend and admirer of English liberalism and a patient worker for Anglo-American peace and equality.

[71] JQA to AA, Nos. 75, 76, Boston House, Ealing, August 24, September 11, 1815. JQA to Miss Clitherow, Little Boston House, January 2, 1817. Diary of JQA, Adams MSS. JQA to AA, Ealing, June 6, 1816; to JA, Ealing, October 29, 1816. *Writings*, VI, 40–4, 111–18.

youthful star-gazers was the gentle Ellen Nichols, the schoolmaster's daughter, his "little favourite." She it was who wrote letters to "sweet Mr. Adams" after he became Secretary of State, and received back verses from him in "the Land of Columbus, the World of the West," until her sad death in 1818.

At Ealing, John Quincy Adams was also able to devote himself more to correspondence with his aged parents. He scoured the book market for his father. He exchanged long letters with the sage of Quincy on all sorts of subjects: international politics, the state of England, including the inveterate English character; Junto Federalism and its dangers for the Union; the two great New England hurricanes of September 1815, sunspots and frosts – 1816 was "the year without a summer"; political science, constitutions and governments; Unitarianism, theology, public morals, preachers of perpetual peace, philosophical discussion and badinage, and books, books – books of all epochs and their authors. These subjects overflowed affectionately into long letters to Abigail too, crowded further with intimate details of family news.

In the eyes of the elder statesman his son's epistles long since had become historical documents, as in truth they were. "Why are all your letters for thirty years, public and private, hidden from the world? I conjecture, and I weep." [72] Meanwhile the younger Adams was thinking already of editing his father's papers, a task that the continuing pressure of public affairs ever obliged him to postpone. It was his son Charles Francis Adams to whom finally fell the task of preparing for publication the *Works of John Adams,* his grandfather, as well as the monumental *Memoirs of John Quincy Adams,* his father.

As the peaceful years followed each other at Ealing, the grandparents in Quincy yearned increasingly to embrace their distinguished son and his family once more before they died. The old gentleman sorely missed the boys John and George and their endearing frolics about the Big House. Charles he had not seen since he was a baby. "Oh, how I want John to divert me and George to assist me!" he wrote wistfully to their father. "I can scarcely get a book from my Office without him. Charles is a little Jewell too! How delighted I should be to have them all about me. Yet they would devour all my Strawberries, Raspberries, Cherries, Currents, Plumbs, Peaches, Pears and Apples. And what is worse, they would get into my Bedchamber and disarrange all the Papers on my Writing Table." [73]

Old John Adams felt, too, that John Quincy Adams's political career could not afford further delay in Europe. "A man should be in his own country." [74] The ex-President warmed with anticipation as he read in the newspapers that the newly elected James Monroe planned to make John

[72] JA to JQA, Quincy, September 23, 1816. Adams MSS.
[73] JA to JQA, Quincy, August 27, 1815. Adams MSS.
[74] JA to JQA, Quincy, November 26, 1816. Adams MSS.

Quincy Adams his Secretary of State.[75] "My advice," he wrote to his son, "is to accept it without hesitation and share the fortunes of your country whatever they may be. You are now approaching fifty years of age. In my opinion you must return to it, or renounce it forever. I am well aware of the critical situation you will be in. I know you have not the command of your feelings, nor the immutable taciturnity of Franklin and Washington. But you must risque all." [76]

John Quincy Adams welcomed the call home. England was the home of freedom and liberal thought, and yet it retained into the nineteenth century a vast amount of cruelty and oppression. His sojourn in London had made a stronger American of him.

Already, wrote Abigail, people were beginning to mention him as "worthy to preside over the Counsels of a Great Nation." [77] John Adams, on his part, made the most of that mention and saw that it got into the newspapers so that still more mention could be made of their son.[78] Ever since Thomas Jefferson's time the office of Secretary of State had been a stepping-stone to the Presidency.

[75] JA to JQA, November 26, 1816. Adams MSS.

[76] JA to JQA, Quincy, March 13, 1817. Adams MSS.

[77] AA to JQA, Quincy, March 12, 1817. Adams MSS.

[78] Upon the death of Thomas McKean, last surviving member of the "first American Congress" (Stamp Act Congress of 1765), and fellow member with Adams of the Continental Congress of 1774, John Adams published in *Niles' Weekly Register* for July 12, 1817 a series of eight letters written by McKean to him through the years 1812 to 1817. The penultimate letter, of November 20, 1815, referring to possible candidates for the next Presidency, concluded: "Mr. John Q. Adams has been named, but it [is] not known whether this may not create jealousy or injure him with the present administration, which his friends would by all means avoid." The last letter, June 17, 1817, contained this paragraph: "It seems that the office of secretary of state, the talents of the candidates being equal, is the stepladder to the presidential chair, at least it has been so in the case of the last three presidents. Now as your son, the Honorable John Quincy Adams, is appointed to that station, if he makes the best advantage of his situation, it is more than probable that he may be the next president of the United States."

CHAPTER XII
The Department of State
(1817–1825)

Extend, all-seeing God, thy hand,
In mercy still decree,
And make to bless my native land
An instrument of me.

JOHN QUINCY ADAMS, UPON TAKING OVER
THE DEPARTMENT OF STATE,
SEPTEMBER 21, 1817[1]

THERE were three Americans with outstanding qualifications for the office of Secretary of State in 1817: Albert Gallatin, John Quincy Adams, and Henry Clay.

Gallatin was undoubtedly the ablest. His actual diplomatic labors had been less than those of Adams, but his experience with men and measures was far broader and more distinguished. He knew how to handle people better perhaps than any other political figure of the day in the United States. If he was more urbane, more European in manner than native politicians, there was no doubt about his Americanism. And he knew American politics from A to Z. He had been a constant worker for and mentor of the Republican Party ever since its inception. He had presided over the Treasury with consummate success for twelve years. He had played the major role at Ghent, harmonizing and uniting his colleagues; the American Commissioners, including Adams, acknowledged this ascendancy, and their British opposites sensed it. If he did not know European courts as intimately as Adams, he could divine them easily. But Gallatin was not so bold and aggressive as Adams at a time when a vigorous and upstanding independent position vis-à-vis European nations was needed.

The eminent Swiss-American did not fit the picture. For one thing he was a foreign-born citizen at a time when the Secretary of State was coming generally to be regarded as the customary successor to the chief magistracy. And on his visit home in 1815–16 he had favored Daniel D. Tompkins of New York instead of James Monroe for the presidential

[1] See *Memoirs,* IV, 8, for the complete poem of six stanzas.

nomination. Monroe does not seem even to have considered Gallatin for a place in his Cabinet. Nor had Gallatin any desire to be a principal figure in the new Administration. He had outgrown the old Jeffersonian dogmas in the Republican Party, now the National Republican Party, and had become weary of politics. Already in 1816 he had declined President Madison's invitation to come back to the Treasury.[2] He had no further ambitions. He was willing to rest on his laurels, to keep a post of greater ease and emolument, to stay on in Paris as American Minister. Gallatin was a frugal, a wise, a very wise man, and consequently he had a happy, a useful, and a tranquil old age.

Henry Clay had the greatest natural talents of the trio. He was a born leader, a man of flashing action, impatient of details, shrinking from close application or studious labor, the opposite of Adams. A Virginian by birth, he regarded himself as the heir apparent of the old Jeffersonian Republicans, wrapped in a fresh national mantle after the War of 1812. President Monroe, in his efforts to include all geographical sections of the Union and all shades of Republican leadership in his Cabinet, offered Clay the post of Secretary of War, but the dashing young leader of the West would have nothing but the Department of State, traditional stepping-stone to the Presidency, and he opposed Adams for that office on the ground that he was not a real Republican.[3] Clay, too, would have made a good Secretary of State; he did make a good Secretary of State later under Adams himself; but Monroe hesitated for political reasons to appoint him: if he should do so, the President feared that all the states north of the Potomac would oppose his Administration from the start on the ground that he was trying to appoint essentially another Southern man as his successor in the White House.[4]

With Gallatin and Clay canceled out of the political equation, John Quincy Adams remained Monroe's logical choice. Now in his fiftieth year, he was certainly the most practiced of all American diplomatists. In his long career he had committed no mistake and made no enemies, and he had raised respect for his country at every post of duty. His judgment was sound. He had become what we would call today the leading American "expert" in international relations. Beyond the ken of any of his countrymen he knew and sensed the European diplomatic world, its politics and its personalities, in one of the most involved periods of modern history.

What appealed to President Monroe more than Adams's experience and competence in the field of foreign affairs was his political suitability. Absent in distant St. Petersburg or in London during the last two presidential contests, he had kept clear of all domestic politics and personal rival-

[2] H. Adams: *Gallatin*, pp. 559–60.

[3] *Memoirs*, IV, 73, 131.

[4] James Monroe to Thomas Jefferson, February 23, 1817. *Writings of Monroe*, S. M. Hamilton, ed. (New York, 1898–1903), VI, 2–4. Monroe expressed himself in a similar way to General Andrew Jackson. Ibid., 4–6.

ries. He had never sought any office. President Monroe turned to him because he was the one perfectly qualified Northern and Eastern man, a safe appointment. The Senate confirmed the nomination promptly and all but unanimously.[5] Everywhere the public applauded.

Once, back in the days of Jay's Treaty, young John Quincy Adams had thought James Monroe an egregious and dangerous bungler in diplomacy. Certainly since then the Virginian had done little in his missions in France,[6] Spain, and England to enhance his reputation. But disappearance of the French issue, and politics, and time, had softened this earlier judgment. As Gallatin later remarked, "seventeen years of French yoke" had united the old political parties as far as union was practicable in a free country.[7] The Federalists had all but vanished after supporting England in the War of 1812. Writing in his later years eulogistic popular biographies of Madison and Monroe,[8] Adams would pass by most gently the violent issues over foreign policy that had divided the two parties in the administrations of Washington and John Adams. In 1817 it was easy for him to take first place under President Monroe, the "Jacobin" of 1794, and to give him full loyalty, politically and personally, as a faithful subordinate.[9]

1

As soon as possible after receiving President Monroe's notification Adams and his family packed up their belongings and engaged passage for New York. They left their pleasant home at Little Boston with many a lingering and regretful look behind. In London, Lord Castlereagh gave a most cordial and friendly farewell dinner to Mr. and Mrs. Adams. Finally the retiring Minister went through the ceremony of taking leave of the obtuse, frivolous, and dissolute Prince Regent, "a Falstaff without the wit, and a Prince Henry without the compunctions." On June 15, 1817

[5] There was one vote against confirmation.

[6] Monroe, of course, had little to do with the Louisiana Purchase, except to sign the treaties connected with it.

[7] H. Adams: *Gallatin*, p. 600.

[8] See his *Eulogy of the Life and Character of James Monroe*, delivered at the request of the Corporation of the City of Boston, August 25, 1831 (Boston: J. H. Eastburn; 1831), republished and expanded in his *Lives of James Madison and James Monroe* (Buffalo: Geo. H. Derby and Co.; 1850), dedicated to the Friends of Republicanism.

[9] "His [the President's] motives were altogether of a public nature," Adams wrote to his mother from London, "and I trust I shall be duly sensible of the personal, as well as the political duties which this unsolicited and spontaneous confidence imposes upon me. . . . I shall enter upon the functions of my office with a deep sense of the necessity of union with my colleagues, and with a suitable impression that my place is *subordinate.* That my duty will be to *support,* and not to counteract or oppose, the President's administration, and that if from any cause I should find my effort to that end ineffectual, it will be my duty seasonably to withdraw from the public service. . . ." *Writings,* VI, 178–82.

all embarked at Cowes on the ship *Washington,* Captain Jacob Forman. On the uneventful passage of fifty days the returning diplomat whiled away the time at chess. At last they anchored off Sandy Hook Lighthouse on a fine clear morn, August 6, 1817.

John Quincy could hardly wait for a decent leave-taking from the round of hospitality tendered by the citizens of New York. One hundred eminent persons gave him a dinner at Tammany Hall, among them John Jacob Astor, the fur magnate; General Morris, Marshal of the District; and Governor DeWitt Clinton. Next day the Mayor and Corporation of the City offered another banquet in his honor at the Hotel Bellevue. But first he made formal visits to the City Hall, the Academy of Arts, the Historical Society, the Cabinet of Natural History, the Museum. Last of all he had to sit for another portrait.

Meanwhile word sped to Quincy that they had reached the United States safely. Old John Adams and Abigail were in raptures of anticipation.

"Yesterday was one of the most uniformly happy days of my whole long life," wrote the ex-President to his son in New York. "A thousand occasions exalted the delight . . . a succession of warm showers all day: my threshers, my gardners, and my farmers all behaved better than usual, and altogether kept me in a kind of trance of delight the whole day. Kiss all the dear creatures for me, Wife, George, John and Charles. I hope to embrace them all here in a few days. God Almighty bless you all. So prays John Adams." [10]

"God be thanked," wrote Abigail. "We now wait in pleasing expectation of welcoming you, one and all, to the old habitation, altered only by the depredations of time, like its ancient inhabitants. Come then all of you; we will make you as comfortable as a cup of cold water, tempered with love and affection, can render you. Tell the children I am sorry that they were not here a week earlier, to have been present at the wedding of their cousin Susan. . . ." [11]

The family planned to take one of the new steamboats to New Haven, changing there to another for New London, and thence by stage to Providence and Boston. That morning the confirmed diarist wrote so late in his journal – until seven o'clock – that they missed the boat at the wharf. The smoking, lumbering monsters of Long Island Sound would not wait for tide nor wind, nor even five minutes for a Secretary of State. Not till afternoon did the frustrated passengers manage to get away on a sailing packet.

At Providence the returning native hired a special stage to drive directly into Quincy. About ten o'clock of a hot summer morning one of Abigail Adams's nieces who lived with her at the time, Louisa Smith, came running into the house shouting that a carriage and four horses were

[10] JA to JQA, Quincy, August 10, 1817. Adams MSS.
[11] AA to JQA, Quincy, Sunday evening, August 10, 1817. Adams MSS.

coming down over Penn's Hill on the turnpike from Milton (the present Adams Street).

Abigail bustled to the door. In a few minutes the stagecoach swung up to the gate. Young John was the first to jump out, then George, half-crazy with joy, crying: "Grandmother! Grandmother!" Charles, the youngest boy, descended half-frightened. Not feeling the keen remembrance of persons and things or the same close affection that had bound the other two brothers to the old folks, the little fellow approached his grandparents with more deference and respect. By this time the father and mother were out of the stage embracing their parents and rejoicing. Louisa Adams was looking better than ever Abigail had seen her, and younger too. All the travelers were sunburned, brown, and well. "I had the inexpressible happiness," John Quincy wrote in his Diary, "of finding my venerable father and mother in perfect health." [12]

Uncle Peter Boylston Adams, John Adams's brother, hurried in from the neighborhood. That evening brother Thomas and his increased family came in from their abode in the old birthplace for dinner: five nephews and nieces, Elizabeth, Abigail, Thomas Boylston Adams, Jr., Isaac Hull Adams, and John Quincy Adams, 2d. We may be sure they all had more than a "cup of cold water." Then the neighbors began to flock in. It was Charles's tenth birthday. They measured him then and there with his brothers and, it is to be hoped, marked up their heights on the door-jamb: Charles four feet four; John four feet nine and a half; George five feet seven and a half,[13] already half an inch taller than his father.

John Quincy Adams drank in the delights and affections of the old familiar home. He went swimming again from Black's Wharf. He visited his former haunts in Boston. He walked about and saw with astonishment how the city had grown and improved during the last eight years. There was the Central Wharf, and masses of new houses and shops on New Cornhill and Common Streets. Half the town was transformed, elegantly and comfortably too. He noted with regret how Beacon Hill had been cut down; it had almost disappeared. Friends in Quincy, Cambridge, and Boston engaged him through the pleasant weeks in a continual round of hospitality and "dissipation."

Before he set forth for Washington the citizens arranged a public dinner in his honor, with his father especially invited. Two hundred persons attended, most of them old friends and acquaintances. William Gray, from whose dock the ship *Horace* had sailed with the Adamses to St. Petersburg, presided. Governor Brooks and ex-Governor Phillips, Chief Justice Parker, Judge Story, Generals Dearborn father and son, David Humphreys the diplomat and friend of Washington, President Kirkland of

[12] *Memoirs,* IV, 5.

[13] *Memoirs,* IV, 5. Diary. AA to Harriet Welsh, Quincy, August 18, 1817. Adams MSS.

Harvard, Dr. Nathaniel Freeman, and Adams's favorite naval hero, Captain Isaac Hull, were all there.[14]

The month in Quincy sped by all too fast for everybody. During a round of visits and personal business the Adamses managed to attend the Harvard commencement. On September 9 John Quincy and Louisa bade their aged parents farewell again in front of the Old House.

The boys remained for the time being in Quincy. They were all three of them destined for Harvard College. Awkward, fast-growing, nervous George was constantly at his books. He showed signs of genius, erratic genius, at least so his grandparents had thought.[15] George worked for the best part of a year with Mr. Gilman, the mathematical tutor in Cambridge, in whose family he lived; then he entered Harvard in 1818, after the winter term. He graduated in 1821. The two younger boys immediately entered Mr. Gould's Boston Latin School. They boarded at the home of the old family friend, Dr. Welch. Uncle Thomas Boylston Adams kept a general oversight of their studies. John was more devoted to sports, shooting and fishing, than his older brother, though reasonably studious in term-time. He was a member of the notoriously rowdy class of 1823 at Harvard. Charles, in his grandmother's judgment, was "a thinking boy . . . much surer in the end." He went to college in 1821 when scarcely fourteen years old and was graduated with the class of 1825.

For the next several years the boys could see their parents in Washington only rarely, but all three visited their grandparents every chance they got, week-ends and vacation. They were a continual delight to the old people, who always kept a loving eye on their progress.[16]

The absent father was not so gentle with his children as their warm-hearted grandfather and grandmother. John Quincy Adams's love for his sons knew no bounds. Let one of them fall seriously ill and it affected him beyond power of expression.[17] But his ambition for them as future scholars and statesmen, the next generation of Adamses in the service of the Union, also knew no bounds. Affection must never yield to duty. He wrote them preachy admonitions about their shortcomings, with injunctions to early rising, keeping a diary, industry, perseverance, punctuality, temperance, and churchgoing, regulating and disciplining the schedule of their lives from morning to night. He seemed to forget the irregular hours and joys of his own youth as a law student in Newburyport or as a member of the Crackbrain Club in Boston.

[14] *Memoirs,* IV, 6–7.

[15] "George is a treasure of diamonds. He has a genius equal to anything; but like all other genius requires the most delicate management to keep it from running into eccentricities." JA to JQA, Quincy, March 4, 1811. Adams MSS.

[16] JA to JQA, Quincy, December 7, 1818, February 3, May 3, May 21, 1819, September 8, 1820, October 7, 1822. AA to JQA, Quincy, October 15, December 14, 1817. Diary for August 25–September 9, 1818. Adams MSS.

[17] Diary, March 26, 1820.

When lively young John grumbled about his studies and Uncle Thomas's overseeing and reminded his father that when in England the more he was indulged, the harder he had studied, the unbending parent wrote back from Washington that the more the son had been indulged, the more he had encroached upon indulgence. "You boast of your studying hard, and pray for whose benefit do you study? Is it for mine, or for your uncle's? Or are you so much of a baby that you must be taxed to spell your letters by sugar plums? Or are you such an independent gentleman that you can brook no control and must have everything you ask for? If so, I desire you not to write for anything to me." [18]

During John's course at Harvard his father learned from President Kirkland that the boy stood only 45th in a class of 85 students. For that reason he refused to grant his son's request to visit his parents in Washington for the Christmas holidays of his junior year: "I could take no satisfaction in seeing you. I could feel nothing but sorrow and shame in your presence until you should not only have commenced but made large progress in redeeming yourself from that disgraceful standing." [19]

After this letter John's [20] standing rose rapidly to 24th. Then his father wrote him he would not attend his commencement unless he finished at least 5th in his class. Alas, he never graduated. He was expelled for participation in the student riot or "Great Rebellion" of 1823. All the protests and expostulations of Secretary of State John Quincy Adams to President Kirkland to get his son reinstated were unavailing. Not until 1873 did the Harvard Corporation bestow posthumous degrees on John Adams 2d and his companions, "as of the Class of 1823." [21]

To George his father wrote from Washington an unbelievably severe letter ordering him to stop reading the Greek Testament – too easy for him – and quit skulking from real study, and not to presume to compete for any of the Boylston prizes during his first year at college.[22]

It is a wonder that such a message did not take the heart out of the boy. George Washington Adams did win one of the two first Boylston prizes in his junior year, 1820. Of the two second prizes then awarded, Ralph Waldo Emerson received one, and Josiah Quincy the other.[23]

Such unheard-of parental injunctions may have held the boys' noses

[18] JQA to John Adams, Jr., Washington, November 17, 1817. *Writings,* VI, 258–9.

[19] JQA to John Adams, Jr., Washington, December 15, 1821. Adams MSS.

[20] "That active, enterprising, and ardent creature, John, only wants the curb and rein." At the same time she warned her diplomatist son: "You must not look for old heads on young shoulders." AA to JQA, Quincy, August 15, 1815. Adams MSS.

[21] S. E. Morison: *Three Centuries of Harvard* (Cambridge, 1936), p. 231.

[22] JQA to GWA, May 21, 1818. *Writings,* VI, 278–80.

[23] The other first prize went to Thomas Farr Capers. Records of Harvard College. Courtesy of Mr. Clifford K. Shipton, Archivist of Harvard University. "Our George has gained the first prize, and bears his honour meekly. He is a dutiful son." JA to JQA, Montezillo, September 8, 1820. Adams MSS. John Adams sometimes called his Quincy home Montezillo, apparently in imitation of Jefferson's Monticello.

down to the academic grindstone but could not have warmed their hearts. On at least one occasion Louisa persuaded her husband not to send a shockingly harsh letter to George upbraiding him for allowing himself to be drawn into a student riot at the beginning of his college career. Neither John Adams nor Abigail had ever written in such a way to their sons. Their letters had always breathed affection first and any duty next.

With Charles Francis, who had entered college too young to get along well at first, the father got to be more patient and understanding. And in turn the boy grew to understand his father better than he did his brothers. Eventually, after the death of John Adams, John Quincy Adams was able to carry on with Charles Francis the same kind of learned correspondence that the grandfather had exchanged with John Quincy in a previous generation.

2

An alternating succession of six stages and six steamboats brought the Secretary of State and Mrs. Adams from Quincy to the nation's village capital on the afternoon of September 20, 1817, the day he had promised to be there.

Adams reported to the President at the Executive Mansion the evening of his arrival. Monroe had just come back from his four months' tour of the Eastern and Western states. The White House, recently rebuilt after the War of 1812, was still so redolent of fresh paint and plaster that the Chief Executive was getting away again as quickly as he could to his farm in Loudon County, Virginia, leaving the Government again with the chief clerks and the heads of departments so far as the latter had been appointed.

Adams realized that one of his duties would be to work in close and sometimes trying counsel with Cabinet colleagues during the next few years. His experience in the Senate, in the Mediation Commission at St. Petersburg, and in the Peace Commission at Ghent had long since made him aware of the dangers as well as the advantages of teamwork in government. The new post called for loyal collaboration among strong and politically ambitious men. He had resolved from the first moment of his appointment to do his utmost to pull together with his colleagues under Monroe's chieftainship.[24]

President Monroe completed his appointments of heads of departments only after Adams's arrival in Washington.

William H. Crawford of Georgia, Secretary of the Treasury, was the most impressive personally. A native Virginian of gigantic stature and

[24] "I know something of the difficulty of moving smoothly along with associates, equal in trust, justly confident of their abilities, disdainful of influence, yet eager to exercise it, impatient of control, and opposing real, stubborn resistance to surmises and phantoms of encroachment, and I see that in the nature of the thing an American President's Cabinet must be composed of such materials." JQA to AA, London, May 16, 1817. *Writings*, VI, 180.

handsome face, descendant of a Scotch frontier family, he was a lawyer and plantation-owner, a former Senator, more recently Minister of the United States to France. He had killed a man, Peter L. van Allen, in a duel in 1802, but another opponent, James Clark, had crippled his left wrist with a pistol ball at ten paces in 1806. He was a man of native sagacity, studious disposition, clear if not always sound judgment, and engaging affability, vastly entertaining as a raconteur. Already he was the most popular politician in the Cabinet and a presidential aspirant. At the Republican Party caucus in Congress preliminary to the election of 1816 he had been a candidate, and had come near to succeeding President Madison. He had the support of the more radical, states'-rights wing of the party, and was an inveterate political enemy of General Andrew Jackson. Adams soon came to regard him as a man of mediocre talents and a political intriguer, a person whose main interest was to advance himself politically by embarrassing the Administration, particularly in its foreign policy, on which, in the opinion of the Secretary of State, rested the most important and critical interests of the country. "Crawford is not a worse man than the usual herd of ambitious intriguers – perhaps not so bad as many of them. I do not think him entirely unprincipled, but his ambition swallows up his principle." [25]

John C. Calhoun of South Carolina, Secretary of War, was Adams's strongest colleague. Tall and erect, with gray-blue eyes flashing out from beneath a commanding brow, he was of Scotch-Irish frontier stock, a graduate of Yale College, bred to the law in Connecticut, settled in the lowlands of his home state, already a successful planter with a rich wife. At this early period of his career Calhoun was, like Adams, an eager nationalist, an advocate of internal improvements, tariff, and national bank. Elegant, graceful, easy, above all cogent, he was marked for leadership. Adams admired the distinguished Southerner. He found him candid, self-possessed, honorable, independent in his thinking, keen, quick-minded, discriminating, sound, lucid, judicious, and comprehensive, and forceful in expressing his ideas, but very sensitive to public opinion. At this period of their careers the two men were very like-minded in their national outlook.[26]

Benjamin Crowninshield, Secretary of the Navy, of ancient Dutch lineage, came to Washington from the world-famous counting-house of Crowninshield & Company of Salem. He was an irresolute and vacillating person. In deference to his wife he remained in the capital only when Congress was in session. Barely competent to handle the navy during those doldrum years, he was never a figure in national politics. In his passive way Crowninshield was a friend and supporter of John Quincy Adams. He quit office in 1818, to be followed by Smith Thompson, of

[25] *Memoirs*, IV, 242.

[26] Charles M. Wiltse has written the most recent and the best book on *John C. Calhoun, Nationalist, 1782–1828* (Indianapolis, 1944).

New York — a would-be presidential candidate. Thompson left the Cabinet in 1823, as soon as he realized he had not the slightest chance for the Presidency, and was succeeded by Samuel Southard of New Jersey — "dear Samuel" to President Monroe.

The Attorney General, William Wirt of Maryland, was a respectable lawyer who looked like the poet Goethe. He was a man of vivid imagination, a music-lover, of ingenuous, playful disposition, with little taste for politics, although he had already written an indifferent life of Henry Clay. "He has two faults," Adams immediately noted, "which may have an influence in the affairs of this nation — an excessive leaning toward State supremacy, and to popular humours." [27] In Cabinet discussions Wirt, like Adams, strayed as little as possible from the affairs of his own Department. He remained Attorney General for twelve years, until General Andrew Jackson became President.

Last of all was John Quincy Adams, the Secretary of State, "premier" of the Cabinet in the public fancy of the day. He appeared to contemporary portrait-painters and observers as a short, stocky man of vigorous health, plump in figure, with a well-shaped bald head, a composed countenance, a manner circumspect and cautious, reserved but not always distant, grave but not always forbidding, plain in dress, with a not unkindly face and a quick, black, penetrating eye.[28] One of the most entertaining dinner companions of his day in a select group,[29] he had before the world at large few of the social graces of his colleagues and rivals in the Cabinet. In the pitiless pages of his intimate Diary the subject painted himself less charitably and perhaps more truly: "I am a man of reserved, cold, austere, and forbidding manners; my political adversaries say, a gloomy misanthropist, and my personal enemies, an unsocial savage. With a knowledge of the actual defect in my character, I have not the pliability to reform it." [30]

A man who felt that way about himself was likely to be that way sometimes, particularly toward importunate and impertinent office-seekers. But a man who knew his defects was more likely to control them, and John Quincy Adams generally appeared as men and women of good will have described him. He was the distinguished diplomatist, the scholar in politics, without a personal following, but a real son of the American Revolution, a man to be reckoned with; everybody realized that.

27 *Memoirs,* IV, 83.

28 *Letters from Washington, on the Constitution and Laws; with Sketches of Some of the Public Characters of the United States. Written during the Winter of 1817–18. By "A Foreigner"* (Washington, 1818), pp. 43–8. Worthington C. Ford identified the author as George Watterson. He was Librarian of Congress and in that office saw much of the Secretary of State. Anne Royall also draws a pen-portrait of Adams in *Sketches of History, Life, and Manners, in the United States. By a Traveller from Kentucky, Who Started on Her Tour, July 1, 1823* (New Haven, 1826).

29 "Autobiography of Martin Van Buren," in *Annual Report,* 1918, of AHA, p. 272.

30 *Memoirs,* IV, 388.

The Cabinet discussions were a matching of men and stature, of judgment, of character. Three of the members – not to count Smith Thompson, who in 1823 accepted an appointment to the Supreme Court – were plausible presidential aspirants. Of the three, Crawford had the greatest strength. Calhoun had the most promise for the future. Adams enjoyed the most personal eminence. Outside the Cabinet, General Andrew Jackson really had a larger popular following than any of the politicians. Speaker Henry Clay reflected more political luster. In New York two more presidential aspirants pitted themselves against each other and canceled each other out of the national picture: Vice President Tompkins and Governor DeWitt Clinton.

The word "Cabinet" was then only just coming into occasional usage. Monroe himself always referred to it as a meeting of the "Administration." The President was slow and deliberate in procedure and relied greatly on advice, assuming for himself the final decision. He frequently consulted the Republican ex-Presidents, Thomas Jefferson and James Madison, and kept them apprised of all greater affairs. Like George Washington he customarily laid before the Cabinet all matters of any great importance, particularly questions of foreign policy,[31] which were the most significant questions of the day. Monroe's practice gave to meetings a greater importance than they might have had under a more willful or dynamic chief executive.

Throughout the eight years of his Presidency the Cabinet was a jockeying ground for presidential candidates. The meetings there opened up a new scene for John Quincy Adams and gave him a closer view of the inside workings of the political world of Washington.

"My office of Secretary of State," he soon realized, "makes it the interest of all the partisans of the candidates for the next Presidency (to say no more) to decry me as much as possible in the public opinion." [32]

All his life he had been ambitious for a high political career, even as his parents had thirsted for it in his behalf. He wanted the Presidency as much as any one of the colleagues with whom he debated in Monroe's Cabinet. He wanted it to come to him in good time, unsolicited, a reward for distinguished and patriotic public service. It would be the fulfillment of his parents' long desire that one day he should become guardian of his country's laws and liberties. Now that he was so obviously on the way to the White House, he was more determined than ever not to seem to lift a hand for it.[33] He had no political following, no machine, hardly a party.

[31] At first President Monroe tried to maintain a confidential liaison on foreign policy, via the Secretary of State, with the chairman of the Committee on Foreign Affairs of the House of Representatives, John Forsyth of Georgia; but this fell to the ground when Forsyth proved unable to stand up to Henry Clay's opposition. *Memoirs*, IV, 31, 65, 66.

[32] *Memoirs*, IV, 62.

[33] *Memoirs*, IV, 64.

All he could do was to stand on his record as a diplomatist. That record he embellished at every opportunity. He defended it most jealously and laboriously against all attacks and imputations. It was his stepladder to the Presidency. Political opponents would do their best to knock it out from under him.

All this interesting inside politics, as well as the outside politics of Speaker Henry Clay and General Andrew Jackson, may be put off to another volume, as Adams now put them off in order to give attention to the organization of the Department of State and the United States foreign service, to the foreign diplomatic corps at Washington, and to the official and private life of a Secretary of State on the banks of the Potomac during the Era of Good Feeling. For the next seven years John Quincy Adams's biography is little more than a succession of important chapters in the diplomatic history of the United States.

3

The Department of State was then located in a large brick building on Seventeenth Street, opposite G Street N.W., on the site of the later State War and Navy Building. In January 1820, it moved to the corner of Fifteenth Street and Pennsylvania Avenue, where the north wing of the Treasury Building now stands.[34] It was in the old brick building that John Quincy Adams took up his duties. Robert Brent, a justice of the peace of the District of Columbia, administered the oath of office on Monday, September 22, 1817, in the presence of Richard Rush, Acting Secretary of State until that moment.

At the time the entire staff of the Department consisted of a chief clerk and translator, Daniel Brent,[35] and seven assistant clerks. The total expenditures of the whole Department at home ($19,410) and abroad ($103,652.04) in 1817 were $123,062.04,[36] which was less than the British

[34] The Department remained there until October 1866, when it moved out on Fourteenth Street, near S Street, where it leased the premises now occupied by the Washington Orphan Asylum. In 1875 it moved into the State War and Navy Building, immediately west of the White House where it remained until 1947. For scattered details of the history of the Department, see Gaillard Hunt: *The Department of State of the United States, Its History and Functions* (Washington, 1893).

[35] John Graham had been Chief Clerk from 1807 to 1817; in 1817 Graham was appointed one of the commission of investigation to Buenos Aires and other South American revolutionary communities. Daniel Brent served as Chief Clerk from 1817 to 1833, when he resigned to become consul at Paris.

[36] *Appropriations and Expenditures, Civil and Miscellaneous, of the Department of State, from March 4, 1789 to June 30, 1876.* 44th Cong., 2d Sess., Sen. Ex. Doc. 38 (Washington, G.P.O., 1877), pp. 45, 63. The British Government spent a total of $1,200,000 on its representatives abroad in the year 1822, not including expenses of the Foreign Office in Downing Street.

Foreign Office was spending on secret service alone, not to mention separate expenses of this nature in America, paid from the home account. Of the State Department budget, $3,500 represented the salary of the Secretary of State, increased by Congress in 1819 to $6,000. Lord Castlereagh, Marquis of Londonderry, received £160,000 for ten years of diplomatic service, £16,000 or about $72,000 a year at the rate of exchange then prevailing. John Quincy Adams, citizen of Quincy, Massachusetts, received approximately $40,000 for his seven and a half years of labor as Secretary of State, and no perquisites.[37]

Obviously Adams could not live on his salary, put his sons through college, and entertain with the decency and dignity required by his office. His family expenses for the first full year in Washington as Secretary of State were approximately $11,000. Every year his own expenses exceeded his salary by four to five thousand dollars.[38] Only the fact that he had kept rigorously within his official income while Minister abroad now enabled him to afford the new office. Under the management of his brother Thomas his personal estate had prospered. He was worth one hundred thousand dollars when he got home and settled accounts. This was invested mostly in bank stock and would yield him about six per cent. Reaching into his private income for the first time, he was able to support the burden of office.

The new Secretary found public business painfully in arrears and accounts unsystematically kept. The able but unmethodical Monroe had paid little attention to details when he had held the office. Rush had kept things going since he had been in charge, but, being only temporarily in authority, he had done little to catch up on back correspondence or to organize the ever present routine into a smoothly running system. A multitude of dispatches and letters had been lying for some time on the Secretary's desk. Every day's mail brought many others. Important letters were missing or misplaced. Even the translation of the recent Swedish Treaty of 1816 could not be found, nor could the most important paper of all relating to claims against Sweden be located.

Adams settled down immediately to digest all this matter and to bring some order into the mass of papers. One of the first things that he did was to have prepared an index of diplomatic correspondence. Each dispatch from every American Minister abroad found entry in it, as soon as received, with a calendar of its contents and enclosures. He inaugurated a similar register for the consular correspondence and another one for the notes received from foreign ministers. This enabled him to take up more

[37] For Castlereagh's emoluments see Webster: *Castlereagh*, p. 38, and H. W. V. Temperley: *Foreign Policy of Canning* (London, 1925), pp. 279–81, 284, hereinafter referred to as Temperley: *Canning*. Canning cut down the expenses of the Foreign Office considerably. His biographer notes that he received a total of only £60,000 for his thirty-four years of public service, seven of which were as Foreign Minister (1807–9, 1822–7).

[38] *Memoirs*, V, 239.

pressing matters first, and finally to bring the whole correspondence to date in an orderly manner.[39] In 1822 he established a register of departmental correspondence.[40] He also formulated a general standing instruction applicable to all newly appointed Ministers to foreign countries, to accompany particular and personal instructions in each instance.[41] He reorganized the financial accounts. He established the State Department library. He supervised with incessant vigilance the minutest details and general routine of his office. But he never did find time to write his projected manual upon the Department of State, its history, organization, and functions.

Compared with the present enormous and multitudinous business of the Department of State and the foreign service, in which the work of any one embassy would equal that of the whole Department in 1817, one would think that Adams's duties as Secretary would not have been too laborious. Actually he was busier than ever before in his life. Despite the expansion of American foreign contacts since Jefferson's first incumbency of the Department, the Secretary of State still personally read the dispatches of all ministers and consuls abroad. He gave his close attention to the notes from foreign representatives in Washington. He drafted and redrafted the replies to them in his own hand, a labor long since delegated to numerous assistants, who are now subordinate to an Undersecretary in order that the Secretary may devote himself exclusively to matters of the highest policy.

In addition to this diplomatic work, and the supervision and administration of the Department itself, Adams labored at the ancillary duties of this office: affixing the great seal to all commissions signed by the President by and with the advice and consent of the Senate, countersigning and recording the same, acting as one of the commissioners of the sinking fund, superintending the census, keeping a register of Federal officers, collecting the laws of the several states, transmitting presidential warrants for the pardoning of criminals, and for extradition; managing the

[39] *Memoirs,* IV, 9, 98, 100.

[40] The following order is extant in Adams's handwriting:

Department of State, Washington, July, 1822

The following regulations are to be observed with regard to the correspondence of this Department.

1. A register is to be kept of all the letters and despatches received at the Department in which all the letters are to be entered as they are received from day to day.

2. The Chief Clerk will take care to have these entries made every day, and in case of his absence Mr. Bailey will attend to that duty.

3. After making the entries they will put on file all the letters requiring no answer. But they will return to the Secretary every letter which requires an answer from him and take his directions concerning any other answer to be given.

Adams MSS.

[41] *Memoirs,* V, 143–4.

custody, printing, and distribution of acts and resolutions of the Congress, and of the territorial legislatures; and administering the consular service.[42] He was also called upon by a resolution of Congress to print the Records of the Federal Constitutional Convention of 1787, and the Secret Journals of the Continental Congress.[43]

Whenever he could find any spare hours, he worked on one of the greatest and most continuous interests of this the earlier period of his life. While in Russia he had taken up the study of weights and measures. The hobby grew into a scholarly but none the less agreeable duty when he returned home to take up his new office in the Department. Under the Constitution, Congress had received the power to establish a uniform system of weights and measures throughout the Union, but nothing had ever been done about it. Responding to a reminder from President Madison, Congress on the next to the last day of his Administration, March 3, 1817, had passed a resolution calling upon the Secretary of State to prepare and submit a statement on the weights and measures existing in the several states and foreign countries, and to make propositions for a uniform system such as might be adopted by the United States. It was the sort of thing a cabinet officer usually passes on to a literary or scientific hack, only signing the prepared work. Not so John Quincy Adams. He fell upon the task with gusto and devoted all his spare time to it for the next three years. By spare time is meant getting up at three or four o'clock of a summer's morning and cutting vacations short. The resulting *Report on Weights and Measures*[44] is a classic, a sadly neglected American classic, in the historiography of modern science.

Adams approached his assignment from a philosophical, sociological and psychological (these two words were not then known, but he sensed their domain), and historical, as well as from a scientific point of view, embellishing his narrative with the balanced periods of a stately professional rhetoric. He took the greatest pride in the finished essay, which he submitted to the Senate on February 22, 1821. It was the same day as the

[42] "List of Duties Assigned by Law to the Secretary of State." In JQA's handwriting. Adams MSS.

[43] *Journals, Acts and Proceedings of the Convention, assembled at Philadelphia, Monday, May 14, and dissolved Monday, September 17, 1787, which formed the Constitution of the United States* (Boston: Thomas B. Wait; 1819).

Secret Journals of the Acts and Proceedings of Congress, from the First Meeting thereof to the Dissolution of the Confederation, by the Adoption of the Constitution of the United States. Published under the direction of the President of the United States, conformably to the resolutions of Congress of March 27, 1818, and April 21, 1820 (4 vols. Boston: Thomas B. Wait; 1820–1).

[44] *Report on Weights and Measures,* by John Quincy Adams (Washington: Gales & Seaton; 1821). Donald M. Goodfellow has described this "Neglected American Classic" in *Carnegie Technical,* IX (No. 4, April 1945), 18–19 ff. See also H. G. Good: "To the Future Biographers of John Quincy Adams," *Scientific Monthly,* XXXIX (September 1934), 247–51.

definitive ratification of his famous Transcontinental Treaty with Spain, and the natal anniversary of his illustrious patron.[45] He regarded the report as almost as important as the treaty itself, one of the great achievements of his life. It was the most authoritative treatment of the subject up to that time. Indeed it remains so now. In it he urged that the United States fix a standard of weights and measures in conformance with its own system of units; then consult with other nations, particularly Great Britain and France, for the ultimate establishment of a world-wide uniformity based essentally on the metric system.

For the average man, even for John Quincy Adams's learned father, the report was too erudite, what the lowbrows today would call too highbrow. John Adams acknowledged it with kindly thanks and proper praise — as did most of John Quincy Adams's distinguished correspondents at home and abroad — but he did not read it through. Only a glance showed him that it was a "mass of historical, philosophical, chemical, metaphysical and political knowledge." So the great document remained to Adams's countrymen then and since. It illustrates a belief in one of John Quincy Adams's political predispositions and fundamental tenets: the possibility of improving associated man through scientific planning enacted into law. As President he would stake the success of his Administration on that belief, in the shape of internal improvements for transportation among the states of the Union under national planning, sponsorship, and control — and would lose.

Despite the burden of his many official occupations as Secretary of State, Adams took a broad interest in the activities of philanthropical and learned societies all over the land. Among the organizations to which he was proud to belong were: the Massachusetts Historical Society, for forty-six years; the American Society for Amelioration of the Condition of the Jews (vice president), the Franklin Society of Brown University (honorary member), the American Bible Society (president), the Boston Athenæum, the American Academy of Language and Belles Lettres, the American Philosophical Society, the Columbian Institute (president), and, much later (1833), the American Antiquarian Society.

The weight of responsibility and onerous detail, made all the more oppressive by a succession of visitors in his office, left him no time for reading, hitherto the passion of his life, except for the daily chapters of the Bible before breakfast. He could only look fondly at his Cicero and his Tacitus and occasionally read a line or two: but to live without a Cicero or a Tacitus, that was like losing a leg to stand on.[46]

The pleasantest assignment of seven years and a half in the Department of State was that of officially conveying to his aged father, and other surviving signers, two copies of an engraved facsimile of the original

[45] Below, Ch. XVI. [46] *Memoirs,* IV, 361.

Declaration of Independence, struck off by order of Congress.[47] Another agreeable duty was that of receiving, as Secretary of State and as President, General Lafayette as guest of the Republic on his farewell visit of 1824–5.

It was well that Adams had accepted his high office resolved in advance to be a cheerful and loyal subordinate. In those days it was customary for a Secretary of State in his official notes to refer to the President in the same stereotyped manner that a European foreign minister would refer to the king or emperor whom he served. "It is the desire of the President," "the President believes," "it will be satisfactory to the President" – such was the accepted phraseology. With James Monroe these were not empty words. When Adams used language like this in a note, one may be sure that he had consulted the President. It was the Chief Magistrate's exact opinion personally rendered.

John Quincy Adams as Secretary of State did not "dominate" the President. On the contrary, Monroe maintained the closest oversight of foreign affairs. He read the most important dispatches from the ministers abroad. He went over Adams's drafts for instructions to them. Often he enlarged upon, modified, or cut down what the Secretary proposed to say. Occasionally, as in the case of the reply to the protest of the Spanish Minister at General Andrew Jackson's invasion of Florida in 1818, he would actually draft a diplomatic note, almost word for word. On at least one important occasion, that of the impressment issue with Great Britain,[48] he seems to have given oral instructions to a minister abroad which his Secretary of State did not approve.

A mass of letters and memoranda in the President's own hand testifies to this minute and laborious superintendence.[49] Often he would tell the Secretary of State exactly what he wanted him to say in a diplomatic dis-

[47] Department of State
Washington, 24 June, 1824

Sir, In pursuance of a Joint Resolution of the two Houses of Congress . . . and by direction of the President of the United States, I have the honour of transmitting two facsimile copies of the Declaration of Independence. . . .

Of this Document, unparalleled in the Annals of Mankind, the original deposited in this Department exhibits your name as one of the subscribers. . . . While performing the duties thus assigned to me, permit me to felicitate you and the Country which is reaping the rewards of your labours, as well that your hand was affixed to this record of glory, as that after the lapse of near half a century, you survive to receive this tribute of reverence and gratitude from your children, the present fathers of the Land.

With every Sentiment of Veneration, I have the honour of subscribing myself, your Fellow-Citizen.

John Quincy Adams.

Adams MSS.

[48] See below, p. 287, n. 29.

[49] Letters of James Monroe to JQA, 1798–1831. Adams MSS. Most of the letters are printed in *Writings of Monroe.* Copies may be found in Monroe Papers, LC.

cussion. "I submit to your consideration," or "I am inclined to think you had better," or "it does not appear to me to be necessary," or "I should be glad to," run these directives, or, more informally, "you had better." Rarely do they lapse into a categorical imperative: "Mr. Adams will." Numerous conferences between President and Secretary of State perfected this intimate supervision.

Monroe was not "his own Secretary of State" in the sense that he kept anything away from the Secretary's cognizance, or took it out of his hands,[50] or refused to listen to his advice, but there is no question that he kept his finger on everything. James Monroe made an ideal President. He had in John Quincy Adams a perfect Secretary of State, the most able and experienced adviser available. Jefferson applauded the President's good sense in appointing Adams. "They were made for each other," he is said to have remarked. "Adams has a pointed pen; Monroe has judgment enough for both and firmness enough to have *his* judgment control." [51] So it proved in fact. The two statesmen got along in close confidence, in the most friendly fashion, and in mutual respect, esteem, and loyalty.[52]

Official hours of the Department were from nine o'clock in the morning until three in the afternoon, but this meant for clerks only. They were hardly ever long enough for the Secretary. The mere handling of official papers absorbed most of that time. A succession of interviews and diplomatic conferences often kept him until late in the afternoon. At least once the janitor unwittingly locked him in the building when all others had gone home for the night. After office duties there were the receptions and dinners that the Secretary had to attend or to give. Many mornings he would have to get to his desk hours before the office opened in order to keep abreast of the coming day's work.

"I would not care a farthing about Spain," wrote old John Adams to his son when the Spanish treaty and other duties threatened to prevent the Secretary's annual vacation visit home. "I would leave the census to my clerks, and throw the weights and measures into the mire, and my office, too, rather than be the greatest slave of the blackest in Virginia." [53]

John Adams in his day in harness had always managed to spend long summers in Braintree. John Quincy Adams with his genius for taking infinite pains – if that be genius – remained, as always, a slave to his desk.

[50] For a small but irritating exception, see below, Ch. XIV.

[51] E. F. Ellet: *Court Circles of the Republic from Washington to Grant* (Hartford, Conn., 1869), p. 123.

[52] A number of letters written by ex-President Monroe to JQA attest this. "It would afford me great satisfaction," wrote Monroe to Adams from Oak Hill, Virginia, June 30, 1829, "if we resided near each other, and could frequently meet, and indulge in that free and confidential communication, which it was, during our residence in Washington, our practice to do. It will always afford me pleasure to hear from you, and of your family. . . ." Adams MSS.

[53] JA to JQA, July 26, 1820. Adams MSS.

CHAPTER XIII
The Foreign Service Abroad and the Diplomatic Corps at Washington (1817–1825)

Truth, virtue, honour, the dignity of human nature

. . . are the touchstones by which the conduct of

nations as well as individuals is to be tested.

JOHN QUINCY ADAMS TO WILLIAM PETERKIN,
WASHINGTON, JULY 20, 1821 [1]

THE NEW Secretary of State had relatively little to do with appointments in the foreign service,[2] despite the numerous applications from old friends, acquaintances, and relatives. He had even less to do with Federal appointments outside his own Department. President Monroe, who had been Secretary of State under President Madison, who in his time had served President Jefferson in the same capacity, already had filled up most of the legations abroad by the time Adams reached Washington. He continued personally to attend to the vacancies that occurred until Adams's own election to the Presidency. In order to picture the American diplomatic service during John Quincy Adams's long term as Secretary of State let us notice the principal officers.

1

To fill the post in London, Monroe sent forth the able and equable Richard Rush of Pennsylvania. He had been President Madison's Attorney General, was an old friend of the Adams family, and had served as Secretary of State ad interim pending John Quincy's arrival in Washington. The eminent Gallatin stayed on at Paris. Clay's political equerry, Jonathan Russell of Massachusetts, continued for the time being at Stockholm. Monroe recalled him in 1818, much to Adams's satisfaction. George W. Erving, another Massachusetts man, an old appointment of Monroe, remained as Minister in Madrid. He seems never to have had Adams's full confidence, particularly during the important negotiations of 1817–19. John Forsyth, newly appointed Senator from Georgia, suc-

[1] Adams MSS.

[2] *Memoirs*, IV, 307.

ceeded him in 1819, notwithstanding the Secretary of State's strong "disinclination."

Adams attributed the appointment of Forsyth, "a man of some talents, but very indolent," to Crawford and the extensive political patronage exercised by Forsyth's relatives.[3] The indiscretions and indecorum of this Minister at Madrid soon alienated even his patrons, but he kept his post till 1823. His successor, Hugh Nelson of Virginia, was Monroe's appointment.[4] William Pinkney of Maryland went out to St. Petersburg, by way of a special mission to Naples to collect claims. Dr. William Eustis of Massachusetts, another friend of the Adamses, was nominally Minister in the Netherlands; actually he dallied in London two years and so exasperated the President that he recalled him in 1818. That rid the service of another Massachusetts man. Thomas Sumter, Jr., had been Minister Plenipotentiary to Portugal, at the court of Rio de Janeiro, since 1809; in 1819 Monroe appointed the prudent and industrious John Graham of Maryland, formerly chief clerk of the Department of State, to that post (at Rio), and later General Henry Dearborn of New Hampshire (at Lisbon, 1822–4), whom Adams would not himself have recommended for the position.[5]

All these officers were of strong Jeffersonian background. Monroe also was responsible for naming the new ministers to Latin America in 1822–4, following perfunctory consultation with his Secretary of State: Richard C. Anderson, of Kentucky, to Colombia; Caesar A. Rodney, of Delaware, to the United Provinces of the Rio de la Plata; Heman Allen, of Vermont, to Chile. The President's principal concern in dictating the diplomatic appointments, like those of his Cabinet, seems to have been to obtain a viable sectional balance within the National Republican Party, by then virtually the only party in the United States.[6] As an avowed and loyal subordinate Adams accepted with at least outward equanimity the presidential nominations in his Department, although sometimes he fretted inwardly at the shadows of backstairs influence.[7]

Monroe did accept the Secretary's suggestion of Henry Middleton of South Carolina to succeed G. W. Campbell – a Monroe man – at St. Petersburg, but it was Calhoun who originally mentioned the fellow South Carolinian to his colleague. Adams thought it a good idea to appoint a Southern man because he would be especially vigilant regarding the slave-owner's interests during the coming arbitration by the Czar of the controversy between the United States and Great Britain over slaves taken away by the British Army at the close of the War of 1812.[8] And the

[3] *Memoirs,* IV, 263, 521–2.
[4] *Memoirs,* VI, 128.
[5] *Memoirs,* V, 515–16.
[6] *Memoirs,* VI, 123, 128.
[7] *Memoirs,* IV, 187.
[8] *Memoirs,* IV, 474. JQA to Henry Middleton, Charleston, S.C., Washington, January 17, 1820. Adams MSS.

Secretary of State succeeded in placing his old protégé since Russian days, Alexander H. Everett, as chargé d'affaires in the Netherlands (1820–4) after Monroe removed Eustis from The Hague. He was also responsible for the appointment of his Harvard classmate and fellow law student with Judge Parsons at Newburyport, James Murray Forbes, since 1801 an officer in the consular service, as special agent to Buenos Aires in 1820; later, upon the death of the first United States Minister, chargé d'affaires, 1824–31. Other minor appointments of Adams may have been J. J. Appleton [9] of Massachusetts, and Christopher Hughes, the Baltimore wit, who had served as secretary to the Peace Commission at Ghent and had once solicited from its chairman a list of readings in international law. Appleton served as chargé d'affaires in Portugal 1819–21, Spain 1822–4, and Sweden 1826–30. Hughes got an appointment as secretary of legation (1816–18), later chargé d'affaires at Stockholm (1819–21) and The Hague (1825–30), but Adams even as President never was able to get him confirmed as minister. All of these friends and protégés supplemented their official dispatches with a copious private correspondence, keeping the Secretary posted on personalities, motives, and political gossip in their several quarters of the world. As Secretary of State and later as President, Adams continued to write them personal advice on perfecting their profession. An insistent admonition, confirmed by his own experience,[10] was that every American who had been in Europe for five or six years ought to go home for a while to be "new tempered."

One of the Secretary's first acts was to draw up an outline of standing instructions to be furnished to each head of a diplomatic mission departing for his post. It enumerated the papers he was to take with him: his credentials, powers, ciphers, letters of credit, a list of printed state papers, passport, paper for dispatches, an engraved design of the proper uniform for an American Minister at a European court (knee breeches, cutaway coat, with lots of gold braid and frogs), standard directions as to diplomatic practice, and the general duties of an American Minister abroad. The standing instructions also included two important admonitions: always preserve the *alternat,* never accept presents from foreign sovereigns.[11]

To present a foreign diplomat with valuable tokens of esteem was the long-established custom in European chancelleries, particularly after the signature of a treaty, or upon the leave-taking of a minister *persona grata:* jewels, bediamonded snuffboxes, often large gifts of outright cash. Lord Castlereagh in the course of his renowned negotiations at Paris and Vienna had received twenty-four snuffboxes, each worth a thousand

[9] Chargé d'affaires ad interim in the Netherlands, 1817–19. Transferring him to Lisbon opened up a place at The Hague for Everett.

[10] JQA to A. H. Everett, London, July 17, 1815. JQA Papers, LC.

[11] "Form of Personal Instructions to the Ministers of the United States — to be variously modified in particular cases." Adams MSS.

pounds sterling, besides other articles equally expensive. Royal tips like these ran into big money. Diplomats came to count them as a part of their professional take. In England it was confirmed usage to give a present of one thousand pounds to an ambassador upon the termination of his mission, to a minister five hundred pounds. Ten per cent was customarily deducted as a douceur to the master of ceremonies.[12] Needless to say, it was an insidious practice capable of exercising a softening and even unpatriotic influence over a diplomat who did not want to lose his final gratuities. It was for this and other reasons that the Constitution of the United States had prohibited any public official from accepting gifts from a foreign government without the consent of Congress.

The custom had often bothered John Quincy Adams in his diplomatic missions. Sometimes it had been difficult to decline the present without offending the court functionary who shared in it or giving umbrage to the sovereign in whose name it was offered. When he left The Hague in 1797 the Dutch Government wished to bestow upon him the usual present of a gold chain and medal. He got around a categorical refusal by promising to ask his Government for permission to receive it.[13] At the court of Berlin it was customary for the King to present a thousand ducats to each person engaged in drawing a treaty. When Adams exchanged ratifications of the Prussian-American Treaty of 1799, Count Haugwitz, in deference to American principles, gallantly said that in this case the present could be forgone on both sides. He then offered a snuffbox with the King's picture. Adams avoided any disrespect by leaving the box with the court while he wrote a perfunctory request to his Government to be allowed to receive it.[14] In the case of his Russian mission there was no embarrassment because he sent in his letter of recall from London through the Russian Ambassador. At the end of his assignment in England in 1817 he politely but firmly declined the customary five hundred pounds offered to retiring ministers. The assistant master of ceremonies acquiesced "with apparent cheerfulness though probably not without reluctance"[15] — the Constitution of the United States had deprived that official of a sub-tip of fifty pounds.

In reporting each of these instances Adams had expressed himself strongly in favor of the constitutional prohibition against acceptance of such presents. As Secretary of State his first instruction to Richard Rush, outgoing Minister to Great Britain, contained a prohibitory order, which he later made standard to all heads of missions embarking for their foreign posts. Adams described the obnoxious practice at some length. "It

[12] *Memoirs*, III, 527–9.

[13] JQA to the Secretary of State, No. 102, The Hague, June 20, 1797. DS, *Despatches, Netherlands*, II.

[14] JQA to the Secretary of State, No. 165, Berlin, June 24, 1800. DS, *Letters of J. Q. Adams, Minister to Berlin, 1799–1801.*

[15] *Memoirs*, III, 528.

is expected by the President," he declared, "that every offer of such present which may in future be made to any public minister or other officer of the government abroad, will be respectfully but decisively declined." [16]

Would it not be well if all American public officers, as well as their wives and families, had followed the letter and spirit of these instructions since that time? "An officer or employee of the Service," reads the Foreign Service Act of 1946, "shall not ask or, without the consent of Congress, receive, for himself or any other person, any present, emolument, pecuniary favor, office, or title from any foreign government."

2

When John Quincy Adams took office the foreign diplomatic corps in Washington consisted of representatives from nine European countries. Later, after the recognition of the independence of the new states of Latin America, the number increased to fifteen. Four of these officers had the rank of Minister Plenipotentiary and Envoy Extraordinary in 1817, the highest rank in Washington. They were the Ministers of France, Great Britain, Russia, and Spain.

The most distinguished person in the corps and the oldest and most eminent of all was an envoy of slightly lower rank. He was the Minister Plenipotentiary of Portugal, the Abbé José Francisco Corrêa da Serra, scientist, historian, economist, doctor of canon law, Knight of the Orders of Nossa Senhora da Conceição, and of Christ, and onetime priest. A member of most of the learned societies of the day, this philosopher and wit, old friend of Presidents Jefferson, Madison, and Monroe, was one of Europe's real luminaries. He had known the United States since his first visit in 1797 as a liberal in exile. As a man of erudition he outshone everyone in Washington, even in all America. Jefferson wanted him for a professor or, better, president of the University of Virginia.

Adams took an immediate liking to this learned and amiable diplomat, friend of liberal principles.[17] The always friendly relations between the

[16] *Writings*, VI, 246–7. This was reinforced by a circular instruction of Secretary of State Louis McLane, January 6, 1834, to the ministers, consuls, and diplomatic and commercial agents of the United States, directing them that, "in future, they will not, unless the consent of Congress shall have been previously obtained, accept under any circumstance, presents of any kind whatever, from any King, Prince, or foreign state." Circular Instructions, DS.

When the United States Consul in Madeira sent Adams a shipment of wine as a gift, the Secretary insisted on a bill at regular prices. "This request is founded upon a principle which I have always considered as resulting from the spirit if not the letter of the Constitution of the United States.

"While holding an employment in the public service I have always felt myself interdicted from the acceptance of any present of value, not only from foreign sovereigns, but from any other person." *Writings*, VII, 32.

[17] *Memoirs*, IV, 326–7.

United States and Portugal suffered a greater strain over privateering spoliation claims of each against the other during these years than at any other time in the history of the two nations. Thanks to the friendly intimacy of two scholars in politics, there was no break. Sad to relate, after the Abbé returned home in 1820 he became ill, and rancorous at the failure of the United States to do justice to Portugal's claims. Then he completely forgot his American friends and distinguished himself by his bitter opposition to the United States.[18]

The French Minister, Baron Guillaume-Jean Hyde de Neuville, born in the year of American independence, was a confirmed and devout royalist. Throughout the French Revolution he was a faithful follower of Louis XVI and his heirs, a devout adherent of their cause, and an adventurous worker for it in dangerous employments. He and his family refused to accept the Napoleonic regime and spent seven not unpleasant years of exile in the United States, where he was at first a generous critic, then an ardent admirer of our republican institutions. A follower of Chateaubriand, he found immediate employment in the French Foreign Office after the Restoration, and returned to America as Minister (1816–18). Physically impressive, with large and open-faced countenance and stately carriage, he was usually tranquil in temper, consistent in politics, loyal in personal and conjugal relationships, restrained in judgment, and full of good will for the United States, once the host of his former exile.[19] The Baroness shared equally with her husband the same high esteem and regard.

With France, Adams had bothersome but no really vital issues to settle. The principal difficulty was the regulation of commercial relations upon a basis of complete reciprocity, something he was never able to achieve fully in the stopgap treaty of 1822.[20] The Secretary was to find the friendly Baron a useful informal conciliator in the protracted negotiations with Spain.[21]

Adams's appraisal of Hyde de Neuville should not be passed by without noticing the French Minister's opinion of the Secretary of State, written to the Quai d'Orsay three months after the latter had taken office,

[18] Joseph Eugene Agan printed an excellent biographical sketch and characterization of "Corrêa da Serra" in *Pennsylvania Magazine of History and Biography,* XLIX (January 1925), 1–43, and an account of his diplomacy in *The Diplomatic Relations of the United States and Brazil,* Vol. I (Paris, 1926), left incomplete at the author's early death.

[19] *Memoirs,* IV, 303, V, 137.

[20] See Ch. XXII, below.

[21] See Ch. XVI, below. The Vicomtesse de Bardonnet, his daughter, edited three volumes of *Mémoires et souvenirs du Baron Hyde de Neuville* (Paris, 1888–92), which fail to do justice to the adventures of his royalism during the Revolution or the secrets of his diplomatic career. For Hyde's characterization of John Quincy Adams, see Vol. II, p. 328. For a characterization of Hyde see the preface by Marie Jeanne Drury to the letters published by her in *Chateaubriand et Hyde de Neuville, ou trente ans d'amitié, correspondance inédite* (Paris, 1929).

in respect to the developing Latin-American policy of the new Administration: "Mr. Adams, a calm and very well educated man, and the American who knows Europe best at the present time, favors good measures [*penche pour les mesures sages*]. I happen to know that he has dared to take a stand quite strongly, on several occasions, against indiscreet and purely fanciful ideas."

Don Luis de Onís y Gonzales, fifty-five years of age, was quite the opposite of Hyde de Neuville, in character and in temperament. He had over a third of a century of experience in the field or in the Foreign Office at Madrid. He had come to the United States in 1809 as unrecognized representative of the nationalist republican Junta only to remain as the Minister of absolutist King Ferdinand VII. A gentleman most respectable and amiable in private life, he was not a person of wide culture or reading. He was a man of the world, experienced, vigilant, laborious, ever attentive to his duties.

If there is too glib a readiness in English-speaking countries to dub a Spanish diplomat a "wily Don," as Adams did, Onís nevertheless lent some reason to the custom. Easily variable in his political complexion, he was a man of mental reservations, hackneyed in the traditional ways of Spanish diplomacy, full of ingenious contrivances and devices, of workings and windings. Here is Adams's further description, noted down after eighteen months of contact with him: "Cold, calculating, wily, always commanding his own temper, proud because he is a Spaniard, but supple and cunning, accommodating the tone of his pretensions precisely to the degree of endurance of his opponent, bold and overbearing to the utmost extent at which it is tolerated, careless of what he asserts or how grossly it is proved to be unfounded, his morality appears to be that of the Jesuits as exposed by Pascal." [22]

It was with Spain that Adams was to conduct the most important negotiations of his career. On Onís fell the duty of watching over the complicated and dangerous relationships of the Republic of the North with Spain's revolted provinces in the New World, and of fighting with the Secretary of State a rear-guard diplomatic campaign for defense in North America of the dissolving Spanish Empire, responsibilities to task the ablest head and bow the broadest shoulders.

The British Minister, the Right Honorable Charles Bagot, was a well-bred, genial, and cheerful Englishman of thirty-five years and limited intellectual powers. In Adams's estimate the mediocrity of Bagot's talent had made for his success in diplomacy — as a conciliator.[23] George Canning had made him Undersecretary of Foreign Affairs for a few weeks during the Portland Ministry in 1809, when affairs were going least well with the United States. Now, after the War of 1812, Castlereagh sent him to the United States "to lay aside all unpleasant recollections, to smooth

[22] *Memoirs*, IV, 305–6.

[23] *Memoirs*, IV, 339.

all asperities between the two nations, and to unite them in sentiments of goodwill as of substantial interest."

Privately Bagot looked down his nose on American life and personalities. His personal correspondence was full of sneers and gibes at them.[24] Publicly he managed to "accommodate" himself successfully to customs and people, if not to the trials of the "swamp" and "desert" of Washington and its terrific summers.[25] Indeed, he became a very popular Minister. He was the plenipotentiary who had signed with Richard Rush the agreement for the limitation of naval armaments on the Great Lakes. Fortunately Adams — "Squinty"[26] to Bagot amidst his own choice coterie — could not read the British Minister's private letters and he retained a high opinion of his services in Washington. Their official discussions did not go badly. During Bagot's sojourn in Washington the more important negotiations, ending in the Treaty of 1818, took place in London. He went back to England in 1819 and had a good career, the high light of which was as Governor General of Canada, 1841–3. We shall meet him again as British Minister in St. Petersburg in 1823–5.

The truth is that no representative of His Britannic Majesty in those days enjoyed a tour of duty in the United States. "I doubt," acknowledged John Quincy Adams when Bagot and his family left Washington, "if any British Minister who ever was here felt any wish after getting home to come back in the *same capacity*. It is the real *purgatory*, and so is the condition of an American Minister in London."[27]

Stratford Canning, cousin to the illustrious George Canning, succeeded Bagot in Washington, 1820–3. He too despised American manners and customs and made fun of them to his sophisticated cronies in England. Of all the foreign diplomats this Englishman most resembled Adams himself, although twenty years younger. "I shall always receive any observations that you make to me with a just deference to your advance of years — over mine," was one of Stratford Canning's early assurances to John Quincy Adams. This equivocal compliment the Secretary accepted with no more than a Frenchman's bow.[28]

Like Adams, Stratford Canning owed much of his success to the remarkable qualities of his mother.[29] While still an undergraduate at Cambridge, he had engaged in his first secretarial mission, to Copenhagen.

[24] Webster: *Castlereagh, 1815–1822,* p. 442.

[25] "Sir, it is dreadful — it is deleterious — it leads to madness. Ice houses take fire and scream because they cannot bear it. There is no enjoyment here — all I can hope to do is to prevent being unhappy." Bagot to Sneyd, June 12, 1816. Quoted by G. P. de T. Glasebrook: *Sir Charles Bagot in Canada* (London, 1929), p. 3.

[26] Perhaps because of a long-standing affliction, caused by too much reading, that inflamed his eyes.

[27] JQA to John Adams Smith, Washington, May 17, 1819. Adams MSS.

[28] *Memoirs,* V, 195.

[29] His father died when Stratford was an infant

At the age of twenty-four he was Minister Plenipotentiary to the Sublime Porte. On the eve of Napoleon's invasion of Russia, it was Stratford Canning, abandoned at Constantinople for two years without instructions from his Government, who personally mediated between Russia and Turkey while England was still technically at war with Russia. The resulting Peace of Bucharest (1812) was a spectacular triumph for the young Minister Plenipotentiary. It disentangled Russian armies from a costly Balkan campaign and made the Czar that much more useful to England in the speedy reversal of alliances that followed. Later, as Lord Stratford de Redcliffe, "the great Elchi," he was to enjoy one of the notable British diplomatic careers of the nineteenth century. Stratford Canning was as proud an Englishman on his part as Adams was a patriotic American.

Outside of the circle of his intimates Canning was cool, stiff, often contentious, sometimes even rude. One evening, at a ball given by the French Minister in honor of the Duchesse d'Angoulême's birthday, Canning conspicuously left before supper. Afterward Hyde de Neuville, when sitting beside his English colleague at President Monroe's table, expressed his regret at the circumstance. Canning answered that there were some places at which he took pleasure in staying and others where attendance was mere compliance with forms! Hyde's personal representatives speedily arranged a duel before Canning went to bed that night. Only by the narrowest of margins did the Englishman's friends manage to get him out of it.[30]

Castlereagh's tight rein somewhat curbed Stratford Canning's bluntness when dealing with the Secretary of State. Even so, Adams found the British Minister not always easy to get along with. The two men were so much like each other that they struck sparks continually.

When the British Minister finally took leave, Adams summed him up in his Diary as follows: "a proud, high-tempered Englishman, of good but not extraordinary parts; stubborn and punctilious, with a disposition to be overbearing, which I have often been compelled to check in its own way. He is, of all the foreign Ministers with whom I have had occasion to treat, the man who has most severely tried my temper. Yet he has been long in the diplomatic career, and treated with Governments of the most opposite characters. He has, however, a great respect for his word, and there is nothing false about him. This is an excellent quality for a negotiator. Mr. Canning is a man of forms, studious of courtesy, and tenacious of private morals. As a diplomatic man, his great want is suppleness, and his great virtue is sincerity."[31]

[30] "I now perceive on looking back," recalled Canning in his memoirs, "that I should have acted with more true courage if I had declined the challenge as resting on no warrantable grounds." *Memoirs,* V, 460. Stanley Lane-Poole: *Life of the Right Honourable Stratford Canning* (London, 1888), I, 313.

[31] *Memoirs,* VI, 157.

The Secretary of State sent his official blessing on Stratford's[32] diplomatic conduct at Washington to the latter's superiors in Downing Street: "His conduct during his residence here has been, in all the social relations, exemplary. His official conduct has also been satisfactory, in every particular concerning which, notice need be taken to his Government. He has a very high sense of honour, and connected with it, a quality inestimable in statesmen, a conscious sense of moral obligation. With such dispositions the occasional asperities of deportment, keenness of sensibility, and inflexibility of temper which he manifests may be, and have been overlooked."[33]

On his part Stratford Canning looked back on Adams as "more commanding than attractive in personal appearance, much above par in general ability, but having the air of a scholar rather than a statesman, a very uneven temper, a disposition at times well-meaning, a manner somewhat too often domineering, and an ambition causing unsteadiness in his political career. My private intercourse with him was not wanting in kindness on either side. The rougher road was that of discussion on matters of business. The irritation of a sensitive temper had much to excuse it in the climate."[34]

This characterization of the Secretary of State reflects certain English qualities which the experienced Adams very deliberately cultivated in dealing with Stratford Canning's own torvity. Happily the bluff sincerity of both men, their complete honesty, and the underlying will of both Governments to peace served to temper the sharpness of their discussions. They respected each other and got along.

The Russian representative in 1817 was still André Dashkov, who had

[32] Throughout these chapters Stratford Canning, later Lord Stratford de Redcliffe, will be mentioned frequently as Stratford, to distinguish him from his famous kinsman George Canning, British Foreign Minister and finally Prime Minister.

[33] JQA to Richard Rush, No. 72, Washington, July 29, 1823. DS, *Instructions, U.S. Ministers*, IX, 163.

[34] "He had a trick [Stratford Canning continued in his recollections] when I was with him on some point of difference between the two Governments of leaving open the door into the room occupied by his secretaries and giving them a high opinion of his national spirit by some expression which I could not allow to pass without a corresponding comment. Every year on the recurrence of 4 July, a public speech is made by someone appointed for the purpose, and Mr. Adams on its first anniversary after my arrival in America was selected for that annual display of patriotic oratory. He took advantage of the opportunity to ingratiate himself with his new political allies by language offensive to England and altogether adverse to that friendly understanding which his Government as well as ours professed a desire to maintain, and of which he was the official organ to one of the parties. The diplomatic body formed a portion of the audience and I avoided my share, *the lion's*, of the annoyance, only by making a short holiday excursion to Harper's Ferry. . . . I had fortunately seen enough of the orator to anticipate the turn which his unbridled eloquence was likely to take. Under much waywardness on the surface there lay a fund of kindly and beneficent intentions which ought to go down the stream of time with the record of his life and characteristic qualities." Lane-Poole: *Stratford Canning*, I, 309.

been in the United States ever since 1809 as chargé d'affaires and Consul General, Minister since 1811. He was *persona non grata* when Adams took office, owing to the violent and obnoxious manner in which he had protested the arrest of the Russian Consul Kosloff,[35] at Philadelphia. The new Secretary of State had little to do with him, except to receive him as compassionately as possible upon his formal leave-taking.[36] The Chevalier Pierre de Poletica, his successor in office and rank, who had already been Secretary of Legation, presented his credentials in August 1819. He was a Ukrainian whose name suggests a remote Greek ancestry, but his mother was a captive Turkish woman. Underneath an unprepossessing appearance he had a warm heart and kindly nature. A competent diplomat of long experience, he was greatly interested in art and literature, and became the intimate of such men as Pushkin, Karamzin, and Zhukovsky. In Washington he seemed a busy, bustling person. Adams found him too inquisitive, likely to be "troublesome," and on the whole prejudiced against the United States.[37] Major Baron de Tuyll van Serooskerken, Poletica's successor (1823–6), was a Russian diplomat of ancient and noble Dutch ancestry, a man of much more conciliatory disposition. The Secretary of State had to handle Poletica and Tuyll in such a way as to preserve the traditional cordial relations with Russia in dealing with such questions as the North West Coast and the Holy Alliance. No one could perform this difficult task better than John Quincy Adams, with his long and successful experience in St. Petersburg and his happy personal acquaintance with Alexander I.

Among the minor figures were: Peder Pederson, Minister Resident of Denmark, 1815–30, and before that chargé d'affaires since 1803; Frederick Greuhm, a young bridegroom, Minister Resident of Prussia from 1817 until his decease in 1823 – the first foreign minister to die in the United States, whose obsequies brought up melancholy problems of diplomatic etiquette; the improvident J. W. Ten Cate, and the elegant and courteous Viscount Goupy de Quabeck, successively chargés d'affaires of the Nether-

[35] Kosloff, accused of rape of a twelve-year-old employee in his house, was arrested and brought before the Pennsylvania state courts. Upon the application of the United States District Attorney the court released him on the ground that only Federal courts had jurisdiction over foreign consuls. Since there was no Federal law to cover that crime, no further action was taken. Upon being duly informed, the Emperor of Russia, at first offended by the arrest of his Consul, recalled both Kosloff and Dashkov. For the case, see John C. Hildt: *Early Diplomatic Negotiations of the United States with Russia* (Baltimore, 1906).

[36] *Memoirs,* IV, 231–2.

[37] *Memoirs,* IV, 401. Lane-Poole: *Stratford Canning,* I, 313. B. Modzalevsky's scholarly article on Poletica in *Russky Biografichesky Slovar* (*Russian Biographical Dictionary*), XIV (St. Petersburg, 1905), 327–9 (translated to me by Professor George Vernadsky). Poletica published in French in 1821 an anonymous sketch of the United States: *Aperçu de la situation intérieure des États-Unis d'Amérique et de leurs rapports politiques avec l'Europe,* printed in English translation (Baltimore: E. J. Coale; 1826).

lands, succeeded in 1825–32 by a minister plenipotentiary and envoy extraordinary, the Chevalier C. P. E. J. Bangeman Huygens; and Baron Berndt Robert Gustav Stakelberg, chargé d'affaires of Sweden and Norway, 1819–32, an unimportant-looking man who seemed frightened out of his wits that his place might not be secure. Of the important additions to the corps made by the arrival of the Latin-American representatives in 1822 and afterward there will be something to note later on.

Nothing is more evident to one who reads the record of the State Department during the Monrovian years than that Secretary of State John Quincy Adams stood head and shoulders above the European diplomats at Washington, in learning, in ability, in experience, in professional competence, in character.

3

Since Thomas Jefferson's Administration there had been little or no ceremony in the reception and entertainment of the diplomatic corps. He had regarded precedence and protocol as so much monarchical falderal, ill befitting the chief magistrate of a real republic. At the Executive Mansion Jefferson introduced for his receptions and diplomatic dinners the rule of *pêle-mêle* – that is, no rule at all, first come first greeted, take anybody in, no place-cards, sit anywhere you can find a place. Under such a dispensation nobody had precedence. There was the famous incident where the author of the Declaration of Independence appeared in carpet slippers to receive the first call of the British Minister, Anthony Merry. Merry and his successors always regarded this, and the lack of precedence in Jefferson's hospitality, as a studied affront to George III. Formality can be overdone in high places and become ridiculous, but the same is true of informality. It is doubtful whether Jefferson's *pêle-mêle* placed the corps at its ease.

President Monroe, with John Quincy Adams's full sympathy, desired to return to the formality and dignity of George Washington and John Adams, to place ministers from abroad on the same footing that the American Ministers enjoyed in European courts, to make intercourse between them and the Chief Magistrate more reserved. As soon as he was inaugurated, the President gave notice of his intention and began the practice of keeping foreign representatives at a cool and cautious distance.[38] No longer could diplomats drop in at the White House for a cup of tea or a chat as they did in the days of Jefferson and Madison. James Monroe opened his drawing-room on alternate Wednesday evenings for invited visitors, including foreign diplomats, but henceforth for business of state a foreign minister would have to make an appointment through the Secretary of State. American diplomatic etiquette took on more of the conventions of European practice.

[38] *Memoirs,* V, 62.

John Quincy Adams as Secretary of State managed to be less formal than the President, at least in his own home. He let it be known to inquiring friends, like the Abbé Corrêa da Serra, that he was at home every evening and would be glad to have anyone drop in. Actually, of course, much of the Secretary's time was taken up in the social functions of the capital, and few would have dared, without some good reason or previous understanding, to intrude upon the rare free evenings he had with his family. Louisa set apart Tuesday evenings to receive during the season. These evenings — usually attended by fifty to a hundred persons — were cheerful and informal. The Adamses also gave the usual diplomatic dinners and an occasional ball near the Christmas holidays, at which the attendance of their sons, when available on vacation from college, came to be more and more an enlivening feature.

The Secretary's wife devoted herself unstintedly to her social duties, well aware that the public eye was on her husband as a presidential possibility. She carefully planned out the Tuesday evenings, the dinners, and the dances. A visiting Massachusetts Congressman records that Mrs. Adams was "on the whole, a very pleasant and agreeable woman, but the Secretary [had] no talent to entertain a mixed company, either by conversation or manners." [39]

No one was more painfully conscious of this limitation than John Quincy Adams himself. "I was not formed to shine in company nor to be delighted with it," he had long since acknowledged in his Diary. His mother had often chided him about this shortcoming, but he could never get over it. "I am a silent animal," he said of himself. He was grateful to his wife for balancing the meagerness of his own chit-chat. But on one occasion, when he had worried overmuch at the lateness of the ladies, and whether they would come at all, he was so pleased with the ensuing fullness and gaiety of the party that after the last guest had left — so remembrance has it — he actually danced a reel with his wife and sons, much to the merriment of the onlooking servants.

Louisa took satisfaction in the success of her own entertainments, but social calling was a real torment to her. For the sake of her husband's career she made the necessary visits to wives of public officials, as well as to those of newly arrived foreign diplomats, scattered as they were through the open distances of Washington City. Sometimes she would spend a whole afternoon making the rounds of the boarding-houses looking for the wives of Congressmen who had left their cards. Often it was a vain quest. One evening, according to well-authenticated family recollections, she came back worn and weary from rumbling over the rutty roads of the District of Columbia, but triumphant. She had made eleven successful calls within a compass of six miles.

At first the Secretary rented a house from his chief clerk, Daniel Brent. It stood at the northeast corner of 4½ Street, and F Street, N.E., later John

[39] John T. Morse, Jr.: *John Quincy Adams* (Cambridge, 1886), p. 104.

Marshall Place, where the Municipal Center Building now stands. It was about a mile from the Capitol Building and a mile and a quarter from the Department. He made the walk daily to his office in precisely twenty-two minutes. Present-day Washingtonians would smile at the rent paid, $650 per annum. In April 1820 he bought a house on F Street, lots 8 and 16, square 253, 1333–5 F Street, N.W.,[40] and built on a coachhouse and stable. He could not then have realized that there he was to make his habitation for the greater part of the remaining years of his life. The new residence gave him greater comfort with his books and papers. Louisa liked it because it boasted a ballroom for entertaining.[41]

It was there that the famous ball was given in 1824 in honor of General Andrew Jackson on the anniversary of the Battle of New Orleans. A thousand persons jammed the house. A poem by John T. Agg described the festivities and some of the guests:

> Belles and matrons, maids and madams,
> All are gone to Mrs. Adams'.[42]

During these years as Secretary of State the family consisted at first of Mr. and Mrs. Adams and their youngest son, Charles, who came down from the Boston Latin School and had a none too satisfactory experience preparing for college in Mr. Ironside's school before he entered Harvard in 1821. There was also Mary Catherine Hellen, an orphaned niece, daughter of one of Louisa's sisters. On vacations the two older boys came down from Cambridge.

After Harvard all three sons successively studied law with their father in Washington in preparation for the Suffolk County bar. John Quincy Adams tried to give the young men an education like his own — so far as it could be done in America — as preparation for the call of public service.[43] John served as private secretary to his father during the latter's Presidency. He married his cousin Mary Hellen in the White House in 1828 and settled down to a none too successful law practice in the capital, where he died in 1834. George, and several years later Charles, went back to Boston to study law with Daniel Webster, who had an office on the corner of Court and Tremont Streets, where John Quincy Adams had practiced in 1792 to 1794. They became members of the Massachusetts

[40] The site of the present Adams Building, now (1949) occupied by a clothing store. The original house remained in the possession of the Adams family until 1884. *A History of the City of Washington, Its Men and Institutions,* by Allen B. Slauson, editor (Washington, D.C.: Washington *Post;* 1903), p. 403. I am indebted to Miss Mercedes Jordan of the Public Library of the District of Columbia for details regarding Secretary Adams's residence in the city.

[41] William M. Meigs: *The Life of Charles Jared Ingersoll* (Philadelphia, 1897), p. 129.

[42] Marian Gouverneur: *As I Remember, Recollections of American Society during the Nineteenth Century* (New York, 1911), pp. 279–80. *Memoirs,* VI, 229.

[43] JQA to CFA, Washington, March 26, 1828. Adams MSS.

bar. Each in his time entered politics. Unstable health cut short George's promising career. In a moment of mental derangement he fell or jumped – nobody really knows which – from a Long Island steamboat while on the way to visit his parents in Washington, in April 1829. Charles Francis was the only son to become a statesman. He followed along in the footsteps of his father and grandfather in Boston: law and politics. As John Quincy Adams became the companion and counselor of old John Adams, so Charles Francis Adams grew up to carry on the same role with John Quincy Adams. Charles Francis's notable diplomatic career did not begin until after his father's death. At the beginning of the Civil War, President Abraham Lincoln appointed him Minister to the Court of St. James's, the third Adams to hold the post.

The Secretary preserved his health against the climate of the capital and the piling labors of his office by faithful exercise, walking and swimming. He had always been fond of bathing in sea and stream. Stories are legion, many of them authentic, of his swimming in the Potomac River on hot summer days, even late on into his Presidency. It was his favorite diversion. Stratford Canning recalled how the Secretary of State was reported at an early hour of the morning to be floating down the Potomac with a black cap on his head and a pair of green goggles on his eyes. Often that was all he did wear. On his fifty-seventh birthday he swam for an hour and five minutes without touching ground, in company with his son John and his valet, Antoine Giusta. It was not unusual for him to spend one or two hours of any early morning in the water, sometimes unaccompanied, despite the remonstrances of his friends.

"Swam the Potomac with John," he recorded for August 25, 1824, "Antoine crossing at the same time in a boat close at hand . . . I was exactly an hour and a half from shore to shore. John was ten minutes less." The river was a mile wide at the place.

On an occasion during the first year of his Presidency, John Quincy Adams, aged sixty-two, nearly drowned when a squall capsized the boat in which he and Antoine were crossing the river with the intention of swimming back.[44] After that he restricted himself to ten-minute baths, diving from a rowboat and swimming back to the favorite rock where he always left his clothes.

Whenever he could, Adams got home to Quincy for a month's vacation in midsummer. It was there on the shore of the old Bay State, amidst the stone-cropped fields and low hills of his childhood, that the firmest affections of his life were fixed. Return to the old home and its surroundings never failed to stir his deepest emotions. Only one such visit could be made as Secretary of State during the lifetime of his mother. When he started back to Washington in September 1818, he left her in apparently better health than she had enjoyed for years.[45] A few weeks after his re-

[44] *Memoirs,* VII, 27.

[45] JQA to J. A. Smith, Washington, November 7, 1818. Adams MSS.

turn to Washington he received a letter from George that chilled his heart. Abigail Adams had died on October 28, 1818 in the seventy-fourth year of her notable life.

"Had she lived to the age of the Patriarchs," wrote her grief-swept son in his Diary, "every day of her life would have been filled with clouds of goodness and love. There is not a virtue that can abide in the female heart but it was the ornament of hers. . . . Never have I known another human being the perpetual object of whose life was so unremittingly to do good. . . . Her price indeed was above rubies. . . . Life is no longer to me what it was; my home is no longer the abode of my mother. While she lived, whenever I returned to the paternal roof I felt as if the joys and charms of childhood returned to make me happy. All was kindness and affection, at once silent and active as the movement of the orbs of heaven. One of the links that connected me with the former ages is no more." [46]

A sense of inconsolable bereavement lingered heavily in his breast as he turned to the tasks of his office: dissipation of the old issues with England; settlement of the Florida Question with Spain; the relations of the United States to new states of Latin America, and to the Old World in general; above all, advancing the continental future of his native land in North America.

[46] *Memoirs,* IV, 157–8, 202.

CHAPTER XIV

Issues with England: The Treaty of 1818 (1817–1818)

Piscemur, venemur, ut olim.

MOTTO ON THE ADAMS FAMILY SEAL

AFTER the War of 1812 it became the task of John Quincy Adams, first in London and then in Washington, to co-operate with the British Government to effect a lasting reconciliation. He strove to achieve this while jealously guarding the vital interests of his native land and the basic principles of American foreign policy. His negotiations with England were complementary to his contemporaneous negotiations with Spain. An object of both was to push the recognized boundaries of the United States through to the Pacific Ocean.

Thanks to Castlereagh's policy of appeasement and repose, and to the intrinsic strength of the American position, Adams already had made a good beginning while Minister in England. He had elicited the readiness of the British Government to adjust, through further negotiations in Washington, the vexing questions of naval armament on the Great Lakes and the North Atlantic coastal fisheries, and to arbitrate the mutually unpleasant issue of the abducted slaves. As Secretary of State it was now his hope to build upon these beginnings a satisfactory settlement at least of all the outstanding territorial and commercial questions if not also to secure the Freedom of the Seas and the abolition of the hateful practice of impressment.

1

The most immediate issue and, of course, the one that touched Adams closest personally was the fisheries. It has been noted that Castlereagh had transferred that question to Washington in 1816. The Foreign Minister hoped to settle the disputed fishing liberty by some sort of compromise. Impressed by Adams's arguments,[1] he proposed to "renew" the *liberty* of inshore fishery on certain stipulated coasts of British possessions in North

[1] ". . . many of the considerations which had been urged by Mr. Adams, on behalf of the American citizens formerly engaged in this occupation [the fisheries], had operated so forcibly in favor of granting to them such a concession as might be consistent with the just rights and interests of Great Britain, that I have been furnished with full powers . . . to conclude an arrangement upon the subject. . . ." Bagot to Monroe, Washington, November 27, 1816. *ASPFR*, IV, 365.

America,[2] provided the United States would give it up on all the other coasts; thus the British would conserve their principle while yielding some of the substance.

In Washington, Charles Bagot had made three successive offers to the American Government to confine the fishing liberties: (1) to the southern coast of Labrador only, (2) to the southern coast of Newfoundland only from Cape Ray to the Rameau Islands, (3) to both these stipulated coasts and nowhere else. One after another Secretary Monroe had declined them all. Then the British Minister asked the United States to indicate the coasts of its preference for the exercise of the liberty. To have indicated anything less than all of the coasts would have conceded the British point that the liberty did not survive the War of 1812.[3] President Monroe waited for Adams's arrival to put the fishery question back into his hands as the best advocate possible.

There was only one man in the United States who was a more uncompromising champion of the American fishery liberty than John Quincy Adams. That was his father, John Adams. It was he who had accepted the flaw in the fishery article of 1782, the word *liberty* for inshore fisheries instead of the word *right*, used when referring to the Grand Banks and the high seas. Both Adamses had long since convinced themselves that in this case liberty and right meant one and the same thing: a natural right inseparable from independence. Old John Adams of Peacefield even favored war, as a last resort, rather than yield an "iota" of that liberty which he had caused to be engraved and re-engraved on his family seal, to be passed down to his son and his son's son.

John Quincy Adams clove to the same conviction. "I am afraid we shall have to fight for this matter, in the end," he frankly told Bagot in one of their first interviews, "and I am so confident of our right that I am for it." [4] But nothing was more distant from the President's mind than a desire to fight over the fisheries. Adams had to tone down his stand. "For my part," he was obliged to explain to the British Minister, "I have always been averse to any proposal of accommodation. I think our whole right, as stipulated by the [definitive] Treaty of 1783, so clear that I am for maintaining the whole, and if force were applied to prevent our fishermen from frequenting the coast, I would protest against it, and reserve the right of recovering the whole by force whenever we shall be able. However, it has been determined otherwise, and a proposal has been promised. Perhaps we shall ultimately offer to give up the right of drying and curing on the shore, and reserve the whole right of fishing." [5]

But President Monroe decided to compromise the fisheries issue. Adams, who had just taken up his office pledged in his own heart to be a loyal subordinate, had to accept the sensible orders to do so. The candid biographer must conclude that the New England patriot found in Mon-

[2] See Map 3.
[3] *ASPFR*, IV, 364–6.
[4] *Memoirs*, IV, 61.
[5] *Memoirs*, IV, 96.

roe's authority a not uncomfortable way of loosing himself from the intractable consequences of a most inconvenient and not invulnerable conviction.

2

While the fisheries dispute befogged Anglo-American relations in the North Atlantic and only the forbearance of the British Government prevented hostile collisions on the coasts of Newfoundland, another territorial question was taking shape on the shores of the distant North Pacific to test the conciliatory dispositions of both nations. For a long time Adams had been familiar with this protean subject. Like so many of the disputes with Great Britain that he was called upon to handle, it went back to his father's diplomacy. The Treaty of Peace and Independence had left a serious boundary gap at the northwest corner of the United States, because of the geographical ignorance of the negotiators on both sides. A few years after independence the Canadian pathfinder and fur-trader David Thompson, of the North West Company, had discovered that a line *due west* from the northwesternmost point of the Lake of the Woods to the Mississippi River – the description of the Treaty of 1783 – was geographically impossible because the Mississippi had its source 152 miles south of the latitude of that particular point. It is recalled that British diplomacy repeatedly tried to close the gap by bringing His Majesty's territory south to the Falls of St. Anthony (St. Paul, Minnesota) in order to get into the river at its navigable portion.[6]

To the historian of today there was much more involved in this early phase of the northwest boundary issue than Britain's entering the Mississippi from the north for the benefit of the North West Company and its fur-traders. For one thing, which nobody knew about then, the fabulous Mesabi iron range of northern Michigan and Minnesota, lodestone of a future industrial continent, lay within the territory that Great Britain would have acquired. More important still, if British territory had been brought south to such a point on the Mississippi, it would have prejudiced the future northern boundary all the way westward to the Columbia River basin.

The United States had always resisted any extension of British territory southward to touch the Mississippi, once it was discovered that geography had happily left the river altogether in American territory. John Jay in his celebrated negotiations of 1794 in London instinctively had withstood the British proposal. He agreed to let a joint commission close the boundary gap. The commission never met. It has been noted how Senator John Quincy Adams had opposed a somewhat similar proposition in the unratified King-Hawkesbury Convention of 1803, for fear it would prejudice

[6] "Jay's Treaty and the Northwest Boundary Gap," *AHR,* XXVII (No. 1, April 1922), 465–84.

the northern boundary of Louisiana, and thereby saved the future "Adams Strip." [7]

Lewis and Clark's expedition to the Pacific Coast and their establishment of a post at Point Adams at the mouth of the Columbia River on the south bank, in the winter of 1805–6, expanded the significance of the Louisiana Purchase and of the northwest boundary. The next year, 1807, Monroe and Pinkney, in their continuing negotiations at London for another general treaty to replace Jay's Treaty, agreed with Lords Holland and Auckland to accept the line of 49° N.L. westward from the longitude of the Lake of the Woods "as far as the respective territories of the two parties extend in that quarter." No convention was concluded because the negotiation broke down over other, maritime, questions.[8] They excluded from the scope of the article the North West Coast and all territories west of the "Stony" Mountains. John Quincy Adams in Russia sensed the significance of the Pacific North West for the future Continental Republic. He eluded Count Rumiantzov's efforts to make a commercial and territorial treaty, which might have shut out the United States from regions as far south as Nootka Sound,[9] or even the Columbia River.

As diplomats argued over the boundaries, the rival fur-traders of the United States and Canada made their plans for the occupation and exploitation of the Columbia River basin. In the year 1811 John Jacob Astor's Pacific Fur Trading Company succeeded in forestalling by a narrow margin the North West Company of Canada and planting a post at Astoria near the mouth of the river. The Astorians, pushing up the Columbia after building their post, met David Thompson and a fleet of Nor'westers coming downstream with the object of planting a trading factory at its mouth. Outdistanced in reaching their objective, the Canadian *voyageurs* retreated to the Spokane country to bide their time.

During the War of 1812 Astor's Canadian partners, fearing British conquest from the sea, sold Astoria to the North West Company. They renamed it Fort George. Sale of this private property to British subjects did not affect the question of national sovereignty over it. In December 1813 the British sloop-of-war *Racoon,* Captain Black, arrived at Astoria with orders to take the fort and destroy the American settlement. Finding new British owners already in possession, under the American flag, Captain Black merely hauled down the Stars and Stripes, ran up the Union Jack, and sailed away to other theaters of war. He had effected a bloodless capture, a temporary conquest, nothing more. The same settlement lived on under British colors. Final sovereignty depended on the terms of the treaty of peace.

At the behest of Astor, Secretary of State James Monroe instructed

[7] Above, Ch. VI. See Map 1.

[8] *ASPFR,* IV, 377.

[9] Above, Ch. VIII. Nootka Sound is on the west coast of Vancouver Island at about 49° N.L. See Map 6.

John Quincy Adams and his fellow Commissioners at Ghent not to sign any treaty that ceded territory to the enemy. Specifically they were not to agree to anything that would disturb the title of the United States to the Columbia River. The American plenipotentiaries faithfully observed the injunction.

The Ghent negotiations ended without any agreement on the northwest boundary. They did not even close the gap between the Lake of the Woods and the Mississippi River.[10] The peace treaty did stipulate in unequivocal language that all territories, places, and possessions taken by either party from the other during the war[11] were to be restored after the peace "without delay." Plainly Great Britain was thus bound to replace the American flag above Fort George even though the property was still owned by British subjects. After that the whole larger question of sovereignty remained to be settled over the North West Coast, that remote and legendary shore,[12] so inconsequential to the destiny of the British Empire, so vital to the future of the United States.

Upon the re-establishment of diplomatic relations Secretary of State Monroe, again prodded by John Jacob Astor, advised the British chargé d'affaires in Washington, Anthony Baker, of the intention of the United States to reoccupy without further delay the post on the Columbia River according to the terms of the Treaty of Ghent. He asked for a letter to the British commander there to facilitate the restoration. Baker replied that he had no instructions on the subject. He added that he doubted if anyone was there, because the forces which had captured the post had broken up the settlement and left the site deserted.[13]

The only effect that this exchange had was to warn the North West Company of American intentions. It caused them to importune the British Government not to abandon sovereignty over the territory, to which they had just sent out £150,000 of goods for the Indian trade. They were expecting to develop a considerable settlement in Oregon. The Canadian traders feared that the United States in occupying the place again might exclude them from trading with the Indians, as had happened since the peace in the mid-continent south of the acknowledged boundary. The North West Company appealed to the British Government for protection of their post on the Columbia.[14]

[10] Article VII provided for a joint commission of two members to fix the boundary between Lake Superior and the northwesternmost point of the Lake of the Woods, according to the true intent of the Treaty of 1783, and to particularize the northwesternmost point of the Lake of the Woods.

[11] Excepting the islands in Passamaquoddy Bay, which were left in British occupation pending adjudication of title to them by a joint commission.

[12] See Map 6.

[13] *ASPFR,* IV, 852.

[14] Katherine B. Judson has set forth the "British Side of the Restoration of Fort Astoria," in *Oregon Historical Quarterly,* XX (1919), 243–60, 305–30, from the relevant British archives. See also A. L. Burt: *U.S. and British North America,* pp. 413–14.

Two years later President Monroe took the matter into his own hands. Without consulting the British Government further, he decided on a course of action. He ordered the U.S.S. *Ontario,* Captain James Biddle, with an American Commissioner, J. B. Prevost, to the mouth of the Columbia peaceably to take possession of the region by some appropriate act, without using force on any British establishment they might find there. Adams took over the Department of State just soon enough to write the instructions.[15] He joined Captain Biddle with Prevost in the commission. The duty performed, Captain Biddle on the return voyage was to leave Prevost in Peru as a special agent of the President there.

Rumors that the *Ontario* had set forth for the North West Coast brought Bagot on the run to the State Department.

"I have been informed, and the North West Company has been informed," said the British Minister, assuming a very grave air and tone, "that the corvette *Ontario* has been dispatched from New York on a voyage around Cape Horn, for the purpose of disturbing the British settlement at the northwest coast of America, and therefore I have come to enquire if this is so."

"Neither the *Ontario* nor any other vessel of the United States," Adams quickly answered, "has any order to disturb any British settlement whatever. But you know that we had, before the war, a settlement at the mouth of the Columbia, which may be renewed, and that we had discovered the river. Our settlement, you know, was broken up by force during the war. After the peace the restoration of it was demanded by the Secretary of State in a note to Mr. Baker, which he had answered by stating that no possession of the place had been taken by the British, but that they had immediately withdrawn after destroying the American settlement."

"Captain Cook discovered the river," Bagot roundly asserted. "In 1787 [*sic*] [16] Great Britain spent upwards of three million sterling upon a contest for that territory with Spain – for then we had only Spain to dispute with for it – and I think Great Britain has some claim to the country from the time of Drake's discovery."

"You have a better claim from Sebastian Cabot, or Sir Walter Raleigh," said Adams sarcastically.

"No," Bagot solemnly affirmed, "that question is settled." [17]

"In my opinion," vouchsafed Adams, "it would hardly be worth the while of Great Britain to have any differences with the United States on account of the occupation of any part of so remote a territory."

[15] *Memoirs,* IV, 11.

[16] Presumably he referred to the Nootka Sound Controversy of 1790. Needless to say, Captain Cook never knew of the Columbia River, nor even of Puget's Sound, though he discovered Fuca Straits. He did put in at Nootka Sound on Vancouver's Island in 1778.

[17] *Memoirs,* IV, 24–5. November 24, 1817.

Bagot shook his head. "It is a serious matter," he said.[18]

The British Minister went back to the Legation and looked into the archives. Then he submitted a note presuming that the purpose of the *Ontario's* voyage was *to establish a settlement* in the neighborhood of the Columbia River. He explained that the post in question had not been "captured" during the late war. The Americans had retired from it under an agreement with the North West Company, so there was not anything to restore.[19] Under these circumstances he demanded an "explanation" of the voyage of the *Ontario*. The note was in effect a caveat filed on general principles. Adams did not reply to it.

Had a less forthright and conciliatory statesman than Lord Castlereagh, for instance his rival George Canning, been in charge at this time, an ugly situation easily could have developed. Delay in submitting a counterproposal for limited coastal fishery liberties, together with the freshening westerly squalls along the undefined boundaries of British North America, disturbed Castlereagh in his desire for Anglo-American cordiality. Meanwhile larger diplomatic problems were reappearing on the Continent of Europe. The British Foreign Minister needed the friendship of the United States.

The Holy Alliance was attempting to mobilize the power of the old Quadruple Allies to straitjacket Europe under the government of divine-right monarchs. Some of the old Allies were even thinking of helping Ferdinand VII of Spain to regain control of his revolted American provinces. Henceforth British policy might have to work with the United States in the New World rather than against it. Hostilities with America had already become if not "unthinkable" at least unwise, if only because the United States was one of Britain's most valuable foreign customers at a time when she was making every effort to recover from the Napoleonic wars. Already, since the War of 1812 and the Rush-Bagot Agreement of 1817, Canada had become a hostage for Anglo-American peace. In any third war with the United States, Great Britain could no longer find a fifth column in America. The Essex Junto was dead. Maritime New England would be a determined spearhead of national union in defense of its fisheries.[20]

Castlereagh immediately sent out orders to the British naval commander on the Pacific Station, at Valparaiso, "to obviate a very unpleasant collision" by anticipating the purpose of the *Ontario* and co-operating with it. There could be no doubt of the right of the United States to occupy Fort George, he wrote Bagot, instructing him at the same time to protest against the brusque way in which it was being done and to register Britain's denial of American sovereignty over the North West Coast.[21] He offered to submit the question of dominion over the Columbia River, and also the whole boundary west of the Lake of the Woods, to

[18] Judson, op. cit., p. 312.
[19] November 26, 1817. *ASPFR*, IV, 852.
[20] Burt, op. cit., p. 403.
[21] Ibid., pp. 412–15.

a mixed commission, like that set up under the Treaty of Ghent to settle the disputed northeast boundary.[22]

Meanwhile the British sloop-of-war *Blossom*, Captain Frederick Hickey, proceeded to the Pacific Ocean. It found one of the American Commissioners, Prevost, at Callao, Peru. As a result of some misunderstanding, which John Quincy Adams decided was only too characteristic of joint commissions, Prevost had allowed Captain Biddle to go on alone in the U.S.S. *Ontario* to take possession of Fort George.

Biddle reached the Columbia River in summer, 1818. He anchored outside the bar on the morning of August 19 and went with a boat's crew into the estuary. They first set foot on the north bank behind Cape Disappointment. There they ran up the American flag and saluted, with three cheers. They turned up a sod of earth and nailed a leaden plate to a tree trunk – symbols of possession. In the distance the ship's guns roared a salute. Then they crossed the river, four miles wide at that point, and made their way up the south bank to Fort George. There Captain Biddle paid a polite call on the Chief Factor, James Keith. He explained his mission. He did not pull down the British flag. Instead he went a half mile away and nailed up a board in a rather secluded and unfrequented spot on Point George. On it he had painted in large letters:

Taken possession of in the name and on
the behalf of the
United States
by Captain James Biddle, commanding the
United States sloop of war, *Ontario*
Columbia River, August 1818.

Biddle's party camped overnight at Chinook Point. Next morning they rowed back to the *Ontario* and sailed away.[23]

In Valparaiso, meanwhile, Captain Hickey explained to Prevost his instructions from the British Government to co-operate in the restoration of Fort George to the United States according to the terms of the Treaty of Ghent. Prevost decided to go on to the Columbia with the British officer in the *Blossom*. They entered the river on October 1. A few days later, on October 6, Captain Hickey and Factor Keith, acting under orders of the British Government, formally and handsomely handed over the post to Prevost. He received it in the name of the United States. At last the Union Jack came down. The Stars and Stripes broke out in the autumn sun. Then the *Blossom* and its official passengers sailed back to South America.

Prevost sent in a long report to the Secretary of State describing the country, the fur trade, and the advance of Russian activities from the

[22] Richard Rush to JQA, London, February 14, 1818. JQA to Richard Rush, May 20, 1818. *ASPFR*, IV, 853.

[23] T. C. Elliott described this interesting "Event of One Hundred Years Ago," *Ore. Hist. Quar.*, XIX (No. 3, September 1918), 181–7. Judson, op. cit.

north.[24] Under the American flag the North West Company remained in possession of its property notwithstanding the fact that the purchase from Astor had taken place during time of war.[25] Its trade continued unmolested while the two Governments opposed each other's sovereignty over all the territory stretching between Russian America and Spanish California west of the Rocky Mountains.

Having restored the American flag, John Quincy Adams was not eager to begin a quarrel over the Columbia River country. There were more important questions to be dealt with first. There was the northern boundary of Louisiana east of the Rocky Mountains to be settled with Great Britain. There was the western and southern boundary of Jefferson's great procurement to be fixed with Spain. There were numerous other issues with Great Britain: fisheries, colonial commerce, abducted slaves, neutral rights, impressment. Above all there was the great problem of the newly revolted states of Spanish America, involving the relation of the United States with both Britain and Spain. It would be better if the Columbia River could wait awhile.

Adams instructed Rush casually to remark to Lord Castlereagh that there had been no idea that the Government of Great Britain wanted to start questions of title with the United States on the shores of the South Sea. The interests involved, he declared, were too small a concern for either party: but if the United States left Great Britain in undisturbed enjoyment of all her holds upon Europe, Asia, and Africa, she ought not to be jealous of extension of "*our natural dominion of North America.*" Such an intimation, Adams went on to say, would afford a suitable occasion for opening a frank, candid, and unreserved mutual communication of views of policy on the affairs of South America. His purpose was to encourage a more perfect concert of measures for the total independence of the Spanish-American provinces, in the face of allied Europe.[26]

It will be more appropriate in later chapters to dwell on this bold inspiration for an Anglo-American rapprochement for the independence of the New World, and also on the separation of European (not to mention Asian and African) and American polity.

Having taken the forthright step of restoring the American flag on the Columbia River, Castlereagh directed Bagot to invite the United States Government to furnish its new Minister to London, Richard Rush, with powers to sign a treaty for settlement of the boundary in the West and also the dispute over slaves carried away by British forces after the peace. Preferably each controversy would be referred to a joint commission.[27]

[24] *ASPFR*, IV, 854–6.

[25] T. C. Elliott has explained "The Surrender at Fort Astoria in 1818," in *Ore. Hist. Quar.*, XIX (No. 4, December 1918), 272–82. See also Judson, op. cit.

[26] JQA to Richard Rush, Department of State, Washington, May 20, 1818. *Writings*, VI, 319–32. Italics inserted.

[27] Ibid.

3

Already President Monroe's Administration had been seeking, through the instrumentality of Richard Rush, to build up an even broader-based settlement than that suggested by Castlereagh. The United States wanted a treaty that would do more than resolve these disputes which were, after all, only a minor matter for the British Government. Monroe and Adams wanted to put at rest the great and difficult problems of colonial commerce and the Freedom of the Seas. And Rush's original instructions, at Monroe's own impulse rather than with Adams's approval,[28] had authorized him to put forward successive compromises for a settlement of the impressment issue. The final offer was to exclude by statute all "native born British subjects" from American ships of war and merchant marine if Great Britain would formally give up the practice of impressment.[29] Such was what the American Peace Commissioners had been originally instructed to propose in 1813.[30] Such was what Adams himself had proposed in London in 1816 under instructions, but against his own better judgment.[31]

The first British reaction was discouraging. When Rush presented his final proposal, in July 1818, the Conference of Aix-la-Chapelle was still some months in the future. Castlereagh admitted that such a law would be a "step forward," but declared that his Government was unwilling to meet it by giving up in any treaty, whatever its terms, the right of entering foreign vessels to look for British subjects. He did not, however, dismiss any further discussion of the subject.[32] We shall see presently that he later came back to Rush's proposals. The Foreign Minister was even less encouraging on the American offer of complete reciprocity of commerce and navigation between the United States and British dominions in North America, including the West Indies; the British Government, he repeated, was not ready to abandon its colonial system. It would do no more than renew the limited Commercial Convention of July 3, 1815.

Adams had not heard fully the result of Rush's conversations with Castlereagh when, in response to the British proposals already made for a settlement of the issues of slaves, boundaries, and fisheries, he drew up, at the President's direction, instructions to a new diplomatic commission to make a general treaty of amity and commerce to settle all the issues be-

[28] *Memoirs,* IV, 147.

[29] Such specific instructions do not appear in the letters of JQA to Richard Rush, serially numbered, nor in any private letter. It seems likely that Rush's written instructions on this point were expanded orally by the President, with Adams's knowledge. Adams never personally approved of them. *Memoirs,* IV, 147.

[30] *ASPFR,* III, 696, 739.

[31] Above, p. 235, n. 53.

[32] *ASPFR,* IV, 373–5. Richard Rush: *Memoranda,* pp. 227, 307. Richard Rush to Secretary of State, November 10, 1817 to June 20, 1818. DS, *Despatches, Great Britain,* XXII. Private letters of Richard Rush to Monroe, in Monroe Papers, LC.

tween the two countries. The experienced Gallatin was ordered across the Channel to assist Rush in the negotiation.

From his own long experience in London, dating back to his first conversations with Lord Grenville in 1795, the Secretary had little expectation that Great Britain would concede anything on impressment or on the Freedom of the Seas. That being the case, he had no desire to embarrass the proposed commercial negotiation with questions of maritime regulations adapted to a state of warfare. He did not want to draw into further discussion such subjects as blockade, contraband trade with enemies or their colonies, or even impressment, unless such a wish should be manifested on the British side. In the latter case the Commissioners were to be governed by the instructions already issued to Rush.[33]

Nor was there much hope, from the account of Rush's first conversation with Castlereagh, that Great Britain would accept complete reciprocity of trade in American and British vessels, on equal terms, between the United States and British dominions in North America, including the British West Indies. The independence of the United States had at least one advantage to British navigation: it had wiped out the competition of Yankee shipping in the carrying trade between England and the remaining colonies, and between the colonies themselves. In case of the expected refusal, the Secretary of State indicated that the United States would accept a renewal for a term of years of the very meager Convention of July 3, 1815. This was the treaty that Adams, Gallatin, and Clay had signed in London prohibiting reciprocally any discriminations against the citizens or subjects of either party in the direct trade between the United States and the United Kingdom. If necessary, said Adams, Monroe's Administration would accept this limited trade with the "old country" and abide as cheerfully as possible the result of a dubious and undesirable "experiment" of closing the doors against each other's flag in North America – a threat that the United States might exclude British ships coming from British colonies.

The only objection that Lord Castlereagh had been able to make to the proposed complete reciprocity of commerce between the dominions of each party in North America had been that the British colonial system had been "long established." Such a statement, felt Adams, was nothing more than the age-old argument of existing abuse against proposed reform.[34] He might have added that it was most inconsistent. At the very moment that Great Britain was excluding the flag of the United States from the Atlantic ports of British North America and the West Indies she was insisting upon the entrance of British vessels into the ports of Spanish America, despite the existence for centuries of Spain's colonial monopoly.

Turning to other issues – slaves, the boundary west of the Lake of the

[33] *ASPFR*, IV, 372, 378. The initial instructions to Rush of November 6, 1817 are printed from the original manuscript in JQA's *Writings*, VI, 233–50.

[34] *ASPFR*, IV, 376.

Woods, and the settlement at the mouth of the Columbia River — the Secretary of State noted the willingness of the British Government to submit each of these questions to two-men joint commissions like the boundary commissions set up by the Treaty of Ghent. Castlereagh had suggested such a reference as a first step; then if two commissioners disagreed he would submit the controversy to the arbitration of a friendly sovereign, presumably the Emperor of Russia.

Adams was not willing to place in the uncertain channel of arbitration such immense territorial questions, so important to the continental future of the United States, so relatively insignificant for Great Britain. He quickly discovered serious objections to such procedure. The Czar also had pretensions to territory on the North West Coast. The territorial dispute, furthermore, was not analogous to the controversy over deported slaves that had arisen from opposing interpretations of the language of the first article of the Treaty of Ghent, on which the two Governments were still disagreed. The conflicting claims to the North West Coast did not involve the interpretation of a treaty. It was a matter of give and take. If compromise were the object, said Adams, it would be much better to reach it directly than to entrust the concessions to commissions supposed to be judicial in nature.

Thus by implication the Secretary of State left these three issues to be settled somehow by Gallatin and Rush but with admonitions that the utmost that the American Commissioners could offer on the boundary was the agreement that had been initialed back in 1807. That was the line of 49° westward from the Lake of the Woods as far as the respective territories *of the two parties* extended in that quarter, with exclusion from this formula of all the region west of the Rocky Mountains. Great Britain, insisted Adams, had no valid claim upon this Continent south of 49° N.L. But as a last stand he was willing to accept — what Monroe had always been willing to take — the line of 49° all the way through to the Pacific Ocean.

Next in hand came the fisheries. John Quincy Adams, in obedience to the President rather than by his own option, at last indicated the choice of shores for a perpetual liberty. He was careful to use language that did not disclaim the contention of John Adams and the Government of the United States throughout the controversy, that the War of 1812 had not terminated the fishery liberty. He was willing to desist from the liberty generally in return for a permanent right, good even against war, on stipulated coasts.[35] It was another proposed compromise.

[35] "The President authorizes you to agree to an article whereby the United States *will desist from* the liberty of fishing and of curing and drying fish, within the British jurisdiction *generally,* upon condition that it shall be secured as a permanent right, not liable to be impaired by any future war, 'from Cape Ray to the Rameau Islands, and from Mount Joli, on the Labrador Coast, through the strait of Belleisle, indefinitely north, along the coast; the right to extend to curing and drying the fish' as well

To secure the substance more or less without abandoning altogether the principle of contest, as circumstances may require, has always been the essence of Anglo-American appeasement: in Jay's Treaty of 1794, in the Treaty of 1818, in the Treaty of Washington of 1871, placing the *Alabama* claims in the way of settlement; in the War Claims Agreement of 1927. Now it has been one side, now the other, to which the principle was more important than the substance. In 1818 the substance was more important to the United States than the principle. But Adams strove for the honor of his family as well as the consistency of his country to save the principle too, or at least the shadow of it.[36]

4

The British Government readily accepted the expanded negotiation. On the eve of his departure for Aix-la-Chapelle, Castlereagh did everything personally and officially to expedite matters. He left the actual labor to two of his subordinates who had signed the Convention of July 3, 1815: Henry Goulburn, also remembered for his part at Ghent, and Frederick John Robinson, president of the Board of Trade and now a member of the Cabinet. Both sides quickly agreed to renew indefinitely the convention they had signed three years before. Then they took up the issues of fisheries, northwest boundary, and deported slaves before they tackled the more difficult problems of colonial commerce, the Freedom of the Seas, impressment, and the slave trade. Each of these settlements or near settlements deserves some particular notice.

Gallatin and Rush succeeded in getting an even more extensive inshore fishing liberty than John Quincy Adams's instructions had prescribed. The Secretary had demanded permanent rights on the southern shore of Newfoundland and on the Labrador Coast. The treaty secured them on the shores of the Magdalen Islands too. It stipulated for the inhabitants of the United States the liberty "for ever" in common with British subjects to take fish of every kind on the following coasts, bays, harbors, and creeks of His Britannic Majesty's Dominions in America: southern Newfoundland from Cape Ray to Rameau Island, on the western and northern coast of Newfoundland, from Cape Ray to the Quirpon Islands, on the

as to fishing." JQA to Albert Gallatin and Richard Rush, Washington, July 28, 1818. *ASPFR*, IV, 375–8.

In the quotation above I have italicized the words *will desist from*. Italics of the word *generally* are original with JQA. The words in single quotation marks – i.e., the designated stretch of coastline on which the inshore fisheries were to be retained – are taken from a slip of paper in President Monroe's handwriting found among JQA's private papers. Adams MSS.

[36] For the official documents see *ASPFR*, IV, 378–406. See also Richard Rush's "Notes of the Joint Negociation at London in 1818 – from the Unofficial Journal of one of the Plenipotentiaries," about ten pages of MS. written on both sides. Monroe Papers, LC.

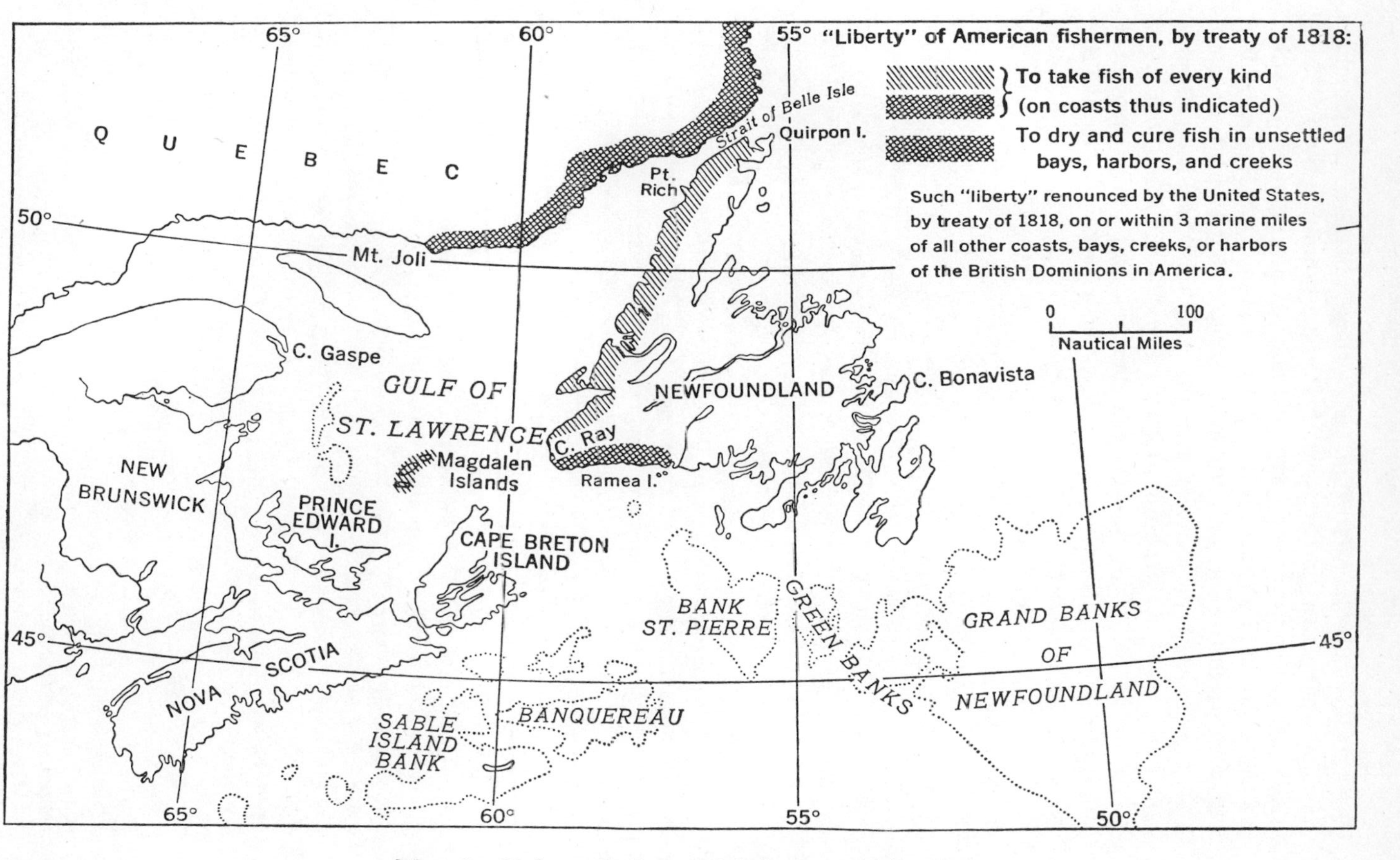
"Liberty" of American fishermen, by treaty of 1818:
To take fish of every kind (on coasts thus indicated)
To dry and cure fish in unsettled bays, harbors, and creeks
Such "liberty" renounced by the United States, by treaty of 1818, on or within 3 marine miles of all other coasts, bays, creeks, or harbors of the British Dominions in America.
0
100
Nautical Miles
65°
60°
55°
50°
45°
QUEBEC
Strait of Belle Isle
Quirpon I.
Pt. Rich
Mt. Joli
C. Gaspe
GULF OF ST. LAWRENCE
NEWFOUNDLAND
C. Bonavista
C. Ray
Magdalen Islands
Ramea I.
NEW BRUNSWICK
PRINCE EDWARD I.
CAPE BRETON ISLAND
BANK ST. PIERRE
GREEN BANKS
GRAND BANKS OF NEWFOUNDLAND
NOVA SCOTIA
SABLE ISLAND BANK
BANQUEREAU

Map 3 *Fishery Rights and Liberties*, 1776–1818

shores of the Magdalen Islands, and on the coasts of Labrador indefinitely northward from Mount Joli, without prejudice to any exclusive rights of the Hudson's Bay Company; also the liberty "for ever" to dry and cure fish in any of the unsettled coasts of Labrador as long as they remained unsettled. In return the United States renounced any liberty to exploit the remaining inshore fisheries of British North America.[37]

What the British objected to during the negotiation was not at all the stretches of coast demanded by the Americans, but rather any language [38] which would imply that the old liberty had not been abrogated by the recent war, or that the newly granted liberty (as Goulburn and Robinson preferred to construe it) would be safe against a future war. The Americans on the other hand stuck to John Quincy Adams's desire for phraseology expressing a survival of the old liberty. For the future they accepted a liberty "for ever" instead of an express provision, which they would have preferred, that the article could never be abrogated by war. The British strenuously resisted even these two words, but finally accepted them.

Whether such language will survive the effect of war on treaties doubtless will never be tested [39] because of the good nature of Anglo-American relations since then. The fact remains that the American Commissioners in 1818 accepted a weaker phraseology on this point, even as John Adams in 1782 had tolerated the weaker word *liberty* instead of the absolute word *right* for the inshore fisheries. The language of the treaty saved to some degree the contentions and the honor of both and yielded the principal substance to the United States. It was another compromise.

In the discussions about the boundary the British Commissioners made a final effort to close the northwest gap by dropping the line from the Lake of the Woods down to the Mississippi and providing for (but not restoring – that would have been inconsistent with their fishery contention) the future navigation of the river from its source to the ocean. Finding that the American plenipotentiaries were forbidden by their instructions to accept any lowering of British territory to the latitude of the Mississippi, not to mention its free navigation,[40] they readily agreed to

[37] "And the United States hereby renounce forever," stated Article I of the Convention of 1818, "any liberty heretofore enjoyed or claimed" to the other coastal fisheries within the three-mile limit of British jurisdiction; admission was granted, however, to enter bays and harbors on those other coasts for the purposes of shelter, repairs to damages, the purchase of wood, and obtaining water, and for no other purpose whatever.

See Map 3.

[38] Such as: "shall continue to enjoy unmolested the liberty," – proposed by the Americans.

[39] See the judicious commentary of Albert Gallatin to JQA, No. 86, Paris, November 6, 1818. *Writings of Gallatin*, II, 75–82.

[40] Adams's instructions made no mention of the navigation of the Mississippi, for the logic of his arguments for the survival of the fishing liberty after the War of 1812 would have required him to acknowledge the continued right of the British to the

extend the line of 49° N.L. westward to the Rocky Mountains.[41] There they stopped.

Gallatin and Rush proposed to carry the line right straight through to the Pacific Ocean. Robinson and Goulburn declined this but intimated that they might take it a little farther along over the mountains, as far as the Columbia River, then down the great River of the West to salt water. Warned by their chief that Great Britain could have no valid claims on the Continent south of 49° – if indeed they needed such a warning – the American plenipotentiaries refused to yield. Then their British friends proposed to leave the region west of the mountains, and lying between 49° and 45°, free and open to the subjects and citizens of both states for the purpose of trade and commerce. Let it be agreed, they suggested, that neither would exercise against the other any sovereign or territorial authority, all without prejudice to any claim of either party or to the pretensions there of any other power. This would have cut the United States out of any worth-while claim to territory west of the mountains and north of 49°. It would have given to Great Britain at least as good a claim as the United States to what soon came to be known as the Oregon Country – that is, the Columbia River basin, Puget Sound, and the Olympic Peninsula. Gallatin and Rush refused to fall into this territorial trap. They contested Britain's claim to the region north as well as south of the line. They had been willing to accept the line of 49° only as a compromise.

Article III of the Treaty of 1818 finally agreed to leave the whole North West Coast of America, without mention of its boundaries north or south, "free and open, for the term of ten years . . . to the Vessels, Citizens, and Subjects of the Two Powers" without prejudice to the claims of either party, or to those of any other power or state, "the only object of the High Contracting Parties in that respect, being to prevent disputes and differences amongst Themselves." It was still another compromise prolonging the status quo, meanwhile agreeing quite peaceably to disagree. It left either party completely free to exercise acts of sovereignty within the disputed area.

Actually this article of the convention was a temporary waiver of discussion of sovereignty. Nobody expected it to set the question at rest, least of all Adams. "It will certainly come upon us again," he noted, "for which I ought to be prepared. Let me remember it."[42]

There was no danger that he would forget it.

---

free navigation of the Mississippi. By keeping the British away from the Mississippi he made any such navigation undesirable to them.

[41] Since it was still uncertain whether the "northwesternmost point of the Lake of the Woods," hitherto the western terminus of the boundary, was in fact north or south of the latitude of 49°, the treaty provided that a boundary line would be drawn north or south from that point, as geography might require, to the latitude of 49° N.L., thence along that line westward to the "Stony Mountains."

[42] *Memoirs*, V, 260.

Lord Castlereagh's previous willingness to arbitrate the controversy over deported slaves led to a quick agreement. The two parties concurred in Article V of the Convention of 1818 to refer to some friendly sovereign or state — it proved to be the Czar of Russia — the question whether the true intent and meaning of the Treaty of Ghent entitled the United States to the restitution of, or full compensation for, all of the slaves carried away. Subsequently they selected the Czar of Russia as the arbitrator and further conferred upon him the office of mediator in the negotiations that must ensue between them in consequence of the award they had requested. On April 22, 1822 Count Nesselrode handed down the Czar's opinion that the United States was entitled to indemnity. Under his mediation the United States and Great Britain signed a convention (June 30/July 12, 1823) providing for two mixed commissions with umpires to sit at Washington (1) to fix the average value of each slave for which indemnity was due, and (2) to determine the number of slaves and other private property for which compensation must be paid.

The first mixed commission succeeded in performing its duty acceptably to both parties, but the second commission disputed and wrangled ineffectually. In 1826 the two Governments concluded a convention by which Great Britain agreed to pay to the United States the sum of $1,204,960 in full satisfaction of all obligations. Congress then had to set up an American commission to distribute the money to the claimants, finally completed in 1828.

This whole affair of securing "justice" for the slave-owners injured by loss of their human property took four years of patience and labor of John Quincy Adams as Secretary of State and President.[43]

5

These important Anglo-American negotiations in London on the eve of the Conference of Aix-la-Chapelle came close to settling at least two of the unsolved issues that then stood in the way of a complete Anglo-American rapprochement: the question of reciprocal trade between the United States and the remaining British colonies of the New World, and the issue of impressment.

Goulburn and Robinson expressed a willingness to allow to American and to British vessels equally a direct commerce between the United States and the British West Indies in several important commodities of that trade, not however including sugar and coffee and specifically excluding salt provisions of all kinds. Not very preposterously they reserved for their Government a right to levy lower, preferential, duties on the allowed products when imported into the British West Indies from British North America in British ships, the only vessels that could legally engage in the intercolonial trade. They also planned that sugar and coffee would

[43] J. B. Moore: *Digest of International Arbitrations*, I, 350–90.

reach the United States only in British ships by way of Nova Scotia or New Brunswick. Despite these significant reservations the concession offered in the direct trade was a very considerable one. It would have opened an irreparable hole in the dike of mercantilism. As for trade between British North America and the United States, Goulburn and Robinson advanced no proposition for overland commerce or by inland waterways. All they offered was a limited reciprocity of maritime carriage of enumerated home products between the United States and the Maritime Provinces.

The American Commissioners did not consider the complicated British propositions to be real reciprocity within the meaning of their instructions. They saw at once how the articles were contrived to favor British intercolonial commerce carriage at the expense of American goods and ships. Nevertheless the two plenipotentiaries agreed to send the drafted articles along to their Government *ad referendum.* In his dispatches to John Quincy Adams on this point Gallatin dwelt on Robinson's persuasion that Great Britain was bound to recede further with the passage of time, that an unlimited intercourse (except perhaps in salt provisions) would be certain to follow these limited beginnings.[44]

President Monroe referred the proposed British articles to the Senate. After careful consideration the newly established Committee on Foreign Relations [45] made a confidential report which evidenced a willingness to go a long way toward meeting them — farther, indeed, than the Administration itself was willing to travel. Adams canvassed the complicated subject with at least two opposition Senators, Rufus King of New York, and Harrison Gray Otis of Massachusetts. King opposed it. Otis seemed to favor it. At the President's request he went over the matter with Crawford, Calhoun, and Attorney General Wirt. They finally agreed to instruct Rush to accept a reciprocity limited, as the British proposed, to the direct trade in enumerated articles; but only upon condition that the duties upon imported articles should not be higher when carried into the British West Indies from the United States than when similar articles were imported from other foreign countries *or from British colonies or dominions themselves.*

The Secretary of State embodied these requirements in two new articles to be added to those which the British Government had offered. The purpose was to give effect to reciprocity in fact as well as in words in such direct trade as might be opened up between the United States and the British West Indies.[46] Adams and his colleagues hardly expected the

[44] H. Adams: *Gallatin,* p. 571, and *Writings of Gallatin,* II, 86.

[45] Established December 10, 1816. Eleanor E. Dennison has written a careful study of *The Senate Foreign Relations Committee* (California: Stanford University; 1942).

[46] "It is far better for the harmony of the two nations [he said] to avoid any bargain, in which either party, after agreeing to it, should have, by the experience of its effect, the sentiment of having been *overreached* brought home to its councils. . . .

British Government to abandon its sovereign right to intercolonial preferential duties. Nor did they think Britain would give up the right to exclude all foreign ships from the intercolonial trade. Without such concessions, not unreasonable legally, real and effective reciprocity in the permitted articles of direct trade would be largely nominal. Favored by lower preferential duties, the acceptable commodities would flow back and forth between the United States and the West Indies in British ships through convenient colonial vestibules in Quebec, New Brunswick, Nova Scotia, and Bermuda.

When Rush took up the subject again with Lord Castlereagh, he met the expected objections. Without hesitation Castlereagh declared that the American proposals were not of a nature to form the basis of any agreement between the two countries.

"They would effect," said the Foreign Minister, "an entire subversion of the British colonial system." He went on to describe that system in language which echoed the eighteenth century.[47] All this did not slacken his efforts to subvert the whole Spanish colonial system by insisting on freedom of trade for British subjects and ships in all the ports and regions of South America.

Neither the American Revolution nor the revolution of the Spanish colonies had yet taught their full lesson to the British Tory Government. The United States on its part was not willing to take half a cake of British West Indian trade. Both nations fell back on their respective navigation laws. Most obstinately and unprofitably they continued to exclude each other's ships from any commerce between their possessions in the New World. The issue remained for John Quincy Adams to struggle with in Anglo-American relations throughout the remainder of his administrative career.

On impressment, touchiest question of all, the British Government showed a surprising readiness to treat. At this particular juncture of world politics Lord Castlereagh on his own initiative had brought up the subject in preliminary and informal conversations with Rush before the arrival of Gallatin from Paris. He actually offered, with two changes, to accept the proposals that Rush had made at the beginning of his mission: to abolish impressment, subject to an agreement by each party not to allow *henceforth* the natural-born subjects or citizens of the other party to serve in its navy or merchant marine. These were Castlereagh's two proposed modifications: (1) the treaty or convention to be limited to a term of years, eight, ten, or twelve, with liberty to each party to denounce it

---

But, to whatever arrangement we subscribe, we are convinced it can answer no useful purpose, unless it should prove to be founded on the reciprocity of real effects, instead of hinging upon that of words." The Secretary of State to Richard Rush, Washington, May 7, 1819. *ASPFR*, IV, 402–3. *Memoirs*, IV, 316, 322, 323.

[47] *ASPFR*, IV, 405.

upon a notice of, say, three or six months; [48] (2) "that the British boarding officer, entering American ships at sea for a purpose justified under the laws of nations, should have the liberty of calling for the list of the crew, and, if he saw a seaman known to him, or on good grounds suspected of being an Englishman, that he should have the further privilege of making a record or *procès verbal* of the fact, in such a way as to have the case distinctly brought under the attention of our [i.e., the American] Government, though by no means withdrawing the man from the ship."

The first proposed modification, the Foreign Minister observed to Rush, would be a regulation to guard against any irrevocable relinquishment of the right of impressment, which British opinion "or even prejudice" might not, after a trial, be willing to tolerate. The second would operate as a further incentive to the faithful execution by the United States of its domestic legislation for prohibiting the service of native-born British seamen.

Rush thought the first point unobjectionable, but objected strenuously to the second. "It comes as a first objection," he wrote to Secretary Adams, "and we may therefore hope to get rid of it altogether." With much elation he declared to his chief that at last the British Government seemed ready to abandon the ancient practice to which it had clung so long and so tenaciously. Anxiously he waited for Gallatin to join him to bring the work to a decision.[49]

Once more the European situation came to the help of the United States. It should have made it possible to clear up the impressment issue altogether. At Aix-la-Chapelle, Castlereagh's chief anxiety would be to stem the efforts of Alexander I to transform the Quadruple Alliance from the specific purpose (as interpreted by Great Britain) of protecting the peace settlement of 1815 against another eruption of France, into the vague interventionist motives of the Holy Alliance. He also intended to appeal to the Christian professions of the legitimist monarchs of Europe to acknowledge a reciprocal right of visit and search of each other's merchant ships in time of peace for the suppression of the African slave trade. In reality this would have been tantamount to a mandate to the British Navy, which had so abused that right in time of war, particularly in the impressment of American seamen. Castlereagh did not want the powers of the Holy Alliance to find a possible supporter in the United States, too sorely rebuffed at his hands on the issue of impressment.

Just before his departure for the port of embarkation Castlereagh called Rush to his office. The American Minister found the Secretary's coach waiting to take him to a Channel port. Hastily the Foreign Minister announced the decision of his Government finally to accept the American proposal for

[48] The provision for denunciation and termination upon prescribed notice, Castlereagh pointed out, would be similar to the provision in the Rush-Bagot Agreement for the limitation of naval armament on the Great Lakes.

[49] *ASPFR*, IV, 379.

the abolition of impressment and to waive the second suggested British modification. Proposals to that end, he promised, would be put into shape as soon as Rush and Gallatin were ready with theirs on the fisheries and the West Indies. "The great principle at last being settled," said Castlereagh warmly, "that on your engaging not to employ British seamen, we will cease to impress them from your vessels, I hope all details will be easily arranged."[50] Castlereagh left for the European Congress hopeful that he need expect no embarrassments from the other side of the water.[51]

The British Commissioners had submitted definite articles for a special treaty abolishing impressment during at least a term of years. In doing so they had formally expressed their conviction that, with all the difficulties that surrounded the issue it should be sufficient to satisfy their American friends of the earnest disposition of Great Britain to go to every practicable length to connect the two countries in the firmest ties of harmony.[52] The British draft treaty abolished impressment reciprocally on the "high seas" for a period of ten years. There were, however, some conditions attached. The treaty was terminable at any time after six months' notice; and it introduced a new proviso: nothing in the treaty should protect the vessels of either party which might find themselves in the ports or "maritime jurisdiction" of the other.

Gallatin and Rush made no objection to the time limits, or to the principle allowing impressment of subjects or citizens within the proper territorial waters of either party. They succeeded in adding the "narrow seas" to the "high seas" where impressment was to be prohibited. They further introduced the qualification "as acknowledged by the law of nations" after the words "maritime jurisdiction" to define the area where impressment was to be legal.

The British delegates promptly accepted these important amendments as well as minor verbal changes. But on the very threshold of success the negotiation stumbled fatally over small technical obstacles.

The second article of the proposed treaty provided that each party should draw up and deliver to the other within eighteen months following "signature" a list of all the naturalized seamen known to be in its maritime service at that date. Thenceforth no person whose name was not included in that list could claim the privileges of American citizenship under the treaty. The American negotiators explained in great detail that it would be impractical and impossible to get up a definitive list because of the previous deficiencies of their Federal and state registration laws. Therefore they reserved the right of any individual to show good proof

[50] Rush: *Memoranda,* pp. 383–4.

[51] "I could not help thinking that he [Castlereagh] may have deemed it best to go off, in his semi-sovereign capacity, freed from all prospective embarrassments upon the ocean from a quarter so formidable as the United States, in the possible contingency of England intending to take any high tone at the Congress." Richard Rush to James Monroe, Private, London, September 6, 1818. Monroe Papers, XX, LC.

[52] Rush: *Memoranda,* p. 436.

of his former naturalization after the ratification of the treaty. Constitutional doubts over *ex post facto* legislation, doubts that seem today quite absurd, impelled them to insist that the list itself go into effect only at ratification of the treaty rather than from its signature. These objections quite absurdly convinced the British negotiators in their turn that there would be a big loophole for hordes of British seamen to naturalize themselves before the treaty went into effect. They refused to entertain the American reservations. So no special anti-impressment treaty was signed.

It seems a pity that the two Governments got so near to a settlement of the historic dispute only to fail so miserably. Had Gallatin and Rush signed the treaty, there is good reason to think that Monroe would have accepted it notwithstanding Adams's advice against agreeing to any treaty that would permit impressment in the future under any circumstances anywhere.[53] Monroe had decided to accept the arrangement, subject to abrogation at four years' notice.[54] Whether he would have agreed to Castlereagh's term of six months' notice remains a question. Six months' notice would have enabled Great Britain to throw off the prohibition of impressment soon after the beginning of the next war. If Monroe had accepted such a short term for the giving of notice to abrogate – a condition that went far to nullify the value of the American concession henceforth not to employ any native-born British subjects in the United States merchant marine – such a treaty would still have had to get the approval of two thirds of the Senate.

6

The four-point Treaty of 1818 (fisheries, slaves, boundaries, trans-Atlantic commerce) arrived in Washington without any settlement of the other major issues. With all its limitations it was a sturdy advancement of Anglo-American amity. No less an authority than Professor A. L. Burt has pronounced it the most important treaty in the history of Canadian-American relations.

The Senate promptly and unanimously ratified President Monroe's first treaty, negotiated under the direction of Secretary of State John Quincy Adams. For one thing it secured the fisheries, and that was due to the unremitting efforts and arguments of the Adamses, father and son. The father's success in preserving the inshore fisheries in 1782, albeit in equivocal language, the son's determination not to yield them at Ghent, and his later obstinate and resourceful insistence that the liberty lived on after the War of 1812 saved this valuable resource for their countrymen. The compromise of 1818 secured for New England fishermen a continued enjoyment to this day of the best inshore fisheries of British North America almost as if they were a part of the United States itself, and that without extending to British subjects reciprocally any liberty to fish within Amer-

[53] *Memoirs*, IV, 147–51.

[54] *Memoirs*, IV, 150.

ican territorial waters. *Piscemur, venemur, ut olim.* Thanks to John Adams and to John Quincy Adams, their fellow countrymen would fish and hunt as of yore.

The boundary articles were of even greater importance to the United States. Article III by taking the boundary westward to the Rocky Mountains secured beyond any cavil of future doubt or challenge for the United States the northwestern part of Minnesota and most of North Dakota and Montana. It was a rich territory with room for homesteads for millions of American citizens and natural resources still uncalculated. The boundary settlement of 1818 further gave diplomatic momentum for carrying the line across to the Pacific Ocean. As the Republic grew westward in strength it was easily able, in 1827, to renew the article on the North West Coast (Article III) for another period of twenty years.

The Convention of 1818 was of great advantage to each party in the existing diplomatic situation. It enabled Great Britain to turn her attention to the European situation undistracted by the prospect of any trouble with the United States. It left Monroe's Government free to drive home its contemporaneous negotiation with Spain without fear of any difficulties with Great Britain.[55] Even as he handed the British treaty to the President, John Quincy Adams was deep in diplomatic discussions with the Spanish Minister in Washington for a treaty that would carry the acknowledged southern boundary of the United States all the way across the Continent.

[55] "To stave off all danger of immediate collision with Britain on this point [the fisheries] by a compromise, involving, as we would hope under all the circumstances no essential sacrifices, besides being a course having reasons to recommend it in the abstract, seemed to be peculiarly advisable at a moment when we desire to be left as free as possible to pursue whatever line of policy we may think fit in regard to Spain." Richard Rush to James Monroe, Private, London, October 22, 1818. Monroe Papers, XXVII, LC.

CHAPTER XV
The Florida Question (1817–1818)

On s'agrandit toujours un peu dans ce monde.

CZAR ALEXANDER I TO JOHN QUINCY ADAMS
ON THE OCCUPATION OF WEST FLORIDA,
MAY 6, 1811

A CAPTIVATING school of historical scholarship during the last half-century, rising from the inspiration of Frederick Jackson Turner, has evoked the phenomenon of a westward-marching frontier as a fundamental explanation of American nationhood and character particularly during the eighteenth and nineteenth centuries. He who finds in the frontier the great historical secret of the nation, if there it really is to be found, must think back and wonder how the country happened to have a frontier moving westward across the Continent all within the United States of America. The historian of the frontier, or of immigration, or of the rise of urban life, or of the Industrial Revolution, or of changing society in North America, all these and other specialists ought not to overlook the biggest wonder of all: how this Republic came to possess the favored expanse of territory that makes possible its varied history, its wealth, its power in the world for human freedom.

Surely the creation of the Continental Republic from Atlantic to Pacific represents the greatest single achievement of American nationality, the basis of all subsequent accomplishments. Diplomatic history cannot explain it all, of course, but the handling of American foreign affairs during John Quincy Adams's life-span ought to have major meaning for the general historian. In helping to lay the foundations of American foreign policy during those decisive years, and in making good our sovereignty over much of the Far West, as well as Florida, Adams played an increasingly important and successful role.

1

John Quincy Adams's Treaty of 1819 with Spain was the outcome of that Florida Question which President Thomas Jefferson and his Republican diplomats had conjured out of the Louisiana Purchase. As a young Senator in Washington, Adams had been opposed to Jefferson's Florida policy as too weak. He was disturbed and disgusted at the President's attempt to purchase from France what he said he had already bought from Spain. Consequently Senator Adams had voted against the Mobile Act of 1804 and the Two Million Act of 1806.[1] There is no contemporaneous record of his opinion on another major expression of policy toward Florida and all the adjacent Spanish borderlands: the No-Transfer Resolution of January 15, 1811.

This important statement of Congress, standing as it does half-way between Washington's Farewell Address and the Monroe Doctrine, was to govern Adams's action as a diplomatist. Passed while Spain's provinces in South America were declaring their independence one by one, and the Floridas, bereft of defense, had become an international No Man's Land, the No-Transfer Resolution declared:

> Taking into view the peculiar position of Spain and her American provinces; and considering the influence which the destiny of the territory adjoining the southern boundary of the United States may have upon their security, tranquillity, and commerce: Therefore,
>
> *Resolved, by the Senate and House of Representatives of the United States of America in Congress assembled,* that the United States, under the peculiar circumstances of the existing crisis, cannot without serious inquietude see any part of the said territory pass into the hands of any foreign Power; and that a due regard to their own safety compels them to provide under certain contingencies, for the temporary occupation of the said territory; they, at the same time, declare that the said territory shall, in their hands, remain subject to a future negotiation.

Under authority of this resolution and a sequent enabling act the armed forces of the United States occupied West Florida (as far east as the Pearl River) on the eve of the War of 1812 and during the early months of that conflict, and also attempted ineffectually to occupy East Florida.

Adams was United States Minister to Russia at the time. He found himself asserting in St. Petersburg what he had declared in the Senate five years previously: that West Florida was part of the Louisiana Purchase, and that it was Spain that had started a controversy with the United States.

Czar Alexander spoke to him about the subject one day when they met promenading on the banks of the Neva.

"I hear you have lately made an acquisition."

"I suppose you mean in Florida," Adams assumed.

"That is what I mean," replied the Emperor. "But," he continued complacently, "it appears to have been a spontaneous movement of the people themselves, who were desirous of joining themselves to the United States."

[1] See above, Ch. VI.

"So it appears from the accounts I have seen," the American Minister agreed, "but I have no communication from my Government on the subject. This was a part of the territory ceded by France to the United States in the Louisiana Treaty. Spain, however, has entered into a controversy with us about it, upon which negotiations were pending at the time when the great changes in the Government of Spain itself took place. Since then the people of that country have been left in a sort of abandonment by Spain, and must naturally be very desirous of being annexed to the United States."

The Emperor smiled and bowed. "One keeps on growing bit by bit in this world" (*"On s'agrandit toujours un peu dans ce monde"*), he acknowledged.[2]

To Alexander, Florida was like Finland.

The two men took polite leave of each other and continued their separate walks. Their two countries, the expanding Czardom of the East and the growing Republic of the West, also continued their respective national promenades east and west from opposite sides of the globe, finally to confront each other amidst the chill fogs of Bering Sea.

The Emperor Alexander, or for that matter anyone else who took the trouble to look at the map of North America, would have seen at once the vital significance of the Floridas to the security of the United States. In the hands of any foreign power they were a pistol pointed at the heart of the future Continental Republic. East Florida was the butt of the pistol, Pensacola the trigger-guard, and the "panhandle" of West Florida was the horizontal barrel with its muzzle pressed against the nation's life-artery, the Mississippi River, just above New Orleans. Spain had been too feeble to load the pistol and pull the trigger, but not her ally England, nor her enemy Napoleon if he could lay hands on the weapon.

Since Jefferson's Administration too many spectacular events had attested to the strategical danger of these collapsing Spanish provinces: the Corsican's invasion of Spain itself; British invasion of West Florida during the War of 1812, and alliance with the Indians there; the dreadful massacre by the savages of some five hundred American settlers, including the scalping of two hundred and fifty men, women, and children at Fort Mims, north of the boundary line, not to mention designs to stir up a slave rebellion in the Southern states; and finally the military campaign against the Mississippi Valley that ended in the Battle of New Orleans. Both Great Britain and France must be kept out of Florida. It did not need an Adams to see that. We may be sure that he approved of the No-Transfer Resolution. The War of 1812 had demonstrated the vital danger of foreign intervention in that Spanish borderland.

[2] *Memoirs,* II, 261.

2

After the War of 1812 Great Britain under Castlereagh's policy of appeasement and repose abandoned all responsible activity in Florida, but her former agents there did not cease their plottings or mitigate their hostility to the United States. A British officer, one Colonel Nicholls, had organized the hostile Indians during the war. Thus they found themselves well supplied with arms and ammunition. They and fugitive slaves who joined them manned the redoubtable Negro Fort on the Apalachicola a few miles south of the boundary of the United States. Following the Peace of Ghent this same Nicholls tried to get the Creek Indians north of the line to repudiate the pacification that General Jackson had imposed on them in 1814. At his base of operations among the Seminoles in Florida, Nicholls signed a treaty of alliance offensive and defensive between Great Britain and the Creek Indians dwelling within the United States.

Both Bathurst and Castlereagh had assured Adams, when he was American Minister in London in 1816, that the British Government would not ratify or countenance any such pact. They disavowed Nicholls and his treaty, albeit not in any public manner. At the same time they bestowed distinctions on him and the Indian chiefs who visited London in his retinue, and sent the native leaders back to Florida loaded with presents. One of them, the famous Prophet Francis, returned clad in the bright red uniform of a British officer. Associated with Colonel Nicholls in Florida were another English military adventurer, the "notorious Woodbine," and an elderly Scotch trader, Alexander Arbuthnot.[3] Later a British officer named Robert C. Ambrister also appeared to seek his fortune among the hostile Indians of Florida.

As if to explain these dubious activities, a rumor had got around that Great Britain was going to receive the Floridas as a reward for mediating between Spain and her revolted colonies.[4] On instructions from Secretary of State Monroe, Adams had brought up the subject with Castlereagh in London in 1816.

"This [Nicholls] affair has given the more concern to the Government of the United States," he declared to the British Foreign Minister, "because they have received strong and confident intimations from various

[3] In December 1818 Adams forwarded some sheets of a journal in Arbuthnot's handwriting taken from his papers at the time of his capture, which definitely established his connection with Nicholls and Woodbine in these hostile proceedings. JQA to Richard Rush, No. 14, Washington, December 3, 1818. DS, *Instructions, U.S. Ministers,* VIII, 279–85.

[4] In 1815 the Spanish Minister at Washington, Luis de Onís, urged his Government to offer Florida to England if the latter power would cause Louisiana to be restored to Spain. Arthur Preston Whitaker: *United States and the Independence of Latin America* (Baltimore, 1941), p. 203.

quarters that there had been a cession of Florida by Spain to Great Britain."

"As to that," Castlereagh immediately assured him, "I can set you at ease at once. There is not and never has been the slightest foundation for it whatsoever. It never has been even mentioned."

"I am sure the American Government will receive with much pleasure the assurance given me by your Lordship that no such cession has been made."

"None whatever," the Foreign Minister repeated. "It has never been mentioned, and, if it had, it would have been decisively declined by us. Military positions may have been taken by us during the war, of places which you had taken from Spain, but we never intended to keep them. *Do you also observe the same moderation,*" he warned. "If we should find you hereafter pursuing a system of encroachment upon your neighbors, what we might do defensively is another consideration."

"I do not precisely understand what your Lordship intends by this advice of moderation," Adams professed. "The United States have no design of encroachment upon their neighbors, or of exercising any injustice toward Spain." [5]

Mutual disavowals of any aggressive diplomacy followed, and mutual asseverations that the policy of each country toward the revolution of Spain's colonies was one of strict neutrality. But clearly the Floridas were the key to the attitude of the United States toward the revolutions of Mexico and South America. And clearly the United States had a much more vital interest than England in the fate of those provinces.

One thing was certain when the wars had ended in Europe and North America: the United States, having extricated itself safely from the world conflict, did not wish forthwith to fight another war with Spain – and perhaps with allies of Spain in Europe – for the independence of Spanish America. Rather, it preferred to take advantage of that Empire's exhaustion in Europe and continuing distresses in America to secure the peaceful possession of the strategic borderlands, notably the Floridas, so necessary for the preservation of its own security and independence.

To achieve this purpose there was good diplomatic ammunition at hand. Spain had not lived up to her treaty obligation of 1795 [6] to keep the Indians within her territory at peace with the United States. Confronted by widespread revolutions, she could not live up to it even if she wanted to. Consequently the United States held Spain heavily responsible in damages for the devastation wrought by Spanish Indians north of the Florida boundary. There were numerous other useful claims, already presented, which American diplomacy since Jefferson's time had hoped to cancel in return for the Floridas: claims for damages due to arbitrary suspension of the right of deposit at the mouth of the Mississippi, guaranteed by

[5] *Memoirs,* III, 289–91, January 25, 1816. Italics inserted.

[6] Above, p. 48.

Pinckney's Treaty; and old unsettled claims for spoliations during the European war in violation of the Freedom of the Seas (Articles XV and XVI of Pinckney's Treaty). The Spanish Government had recognized the force of these when it signed a convention in 1802 to adjudicate them, but it had indignantly refused to ratify it after learning of the Louisiana Purchase.

Following the re-establishment of peace in 1815 Secretary of State James Monroe had tried to settle Spanish-American relations, including the Florida Question, by offering to accept as the southwestern boundary of the Louisiana Purchase the line of the Colorado River of Texas, which runs southeast through the middle of the present state. He was even willing to retreat if necessary to the Sabine (western boundary of the State of Louisiana),[7] abandoning all claims to Texas if Spain would yield both Floridas.[8] All spoliations and other claims would be mutually canceled. To the north of Texas, Monroe would have left the western boundary of Louisiana to be settled by a joint commission. But the Spanish Government, though not unwilling to let the Floridas go if the United States would first make the *amende honorable* of handing back what it had already taken of them, still insisted that the Mississippi River must be the boundary; in other words, that the whole Louisiana Purchase, one half the then United States, was invalid. Such was the posture of the controversy when John Quincy Adams, already well schooled in the Florida Question, took over the Department of State.

3

Spain's hold on the Floridas weakened as the war in South America began to shift in favor of the insurgent governments. The success of the movement for independence was due principally to the patriots' own heroic efforts, but at least something may be ascribed to the neutrality of the United States. It made it possible for revolutionary agents to procure and export contraband of war from North American ports. The active sympathy of the American people permitted the outfitting of privateers under the belligerent flags of their countries, manned with American crews and captains, all contrary to the laws of neutrality whether domestic or international. Faced by the rising power of the insurgents and the swelling tide of opinion in the Republic of the North, the Spanish Foreign Minister, Pizarro, feared a recognition by Washington of the

[7] Secretary of State James Monroe had instructed George W. Erving, United States Minister in Spain, to go as far as offering the line of the Sabine River in exchange for the Floridas, but Erving never presented this extreme concession. It was the same offer that Secretary Madison had authorized Monroe himself to make when the latter had been Minister to Spain in 1806. Philip C. Brooks made a careful study in American, British, French, and Spanish archives of *Diplomacy and the Borderlands, the Adams-Onís Treaty of 1819* (Berkeley, 1939). It will be seen that I am much indebted to him in this and the following chapter.

[8] See Map 4.

independence of the rebel states. And he grew increasingly alarmed at the precarious condition of the indefensible borderlands.

So many things betokened more trouble for Spain, in North as well as in South America. There were, for example, the continuous threats of hostile expeditions into Texas and Mexico. Behind the unmarked Florida frontier, plots against New Spain had been shaping and reshaping ever since the time of Aaron Burr's conspiracy. On the Tombigbee River in Alabama Territory a group of Napoleonic exiles and ex-generals were planning to set forth from New Orleans a great filibustering expedition across Texas to place Joseph Bonaparte on the throne of Montezuma. Adams, well informed of this enterprise, let it be understood that he would not interfere with it as long as it was directed toward the independence of Mexico.[9] In their most roseate dreams some of these adventurers looked toward rescuing Napoleon from St. Helena.[10]

Both the Spanish Minister, Luis de Onís, and the French Minister,[11] Hyde de Neuville, protested against such threatening movements: Onís because of the danger to Ferdinand's sovereignty over Mexico; Hyde de Neuville because of Louis XVIII's fear of revival of Bonapartism anywhere in the world.[12] Monroe's Government kept an eye on the conspirators, but took no active step to frustrate them. After all, their immediate field was Texas, and the United States claimed that to be American territory. The President let the plots and preparations ferment for the effect they would have on Spanish-American negotiations. He told his newly established Secretary of State that he wanted to make the Spanish Government understand that it must settle the American claims before the United States attended to the complaints of Spain. Only the opposition of the European powers, particularly Great Britain and Russia, he told Adams, could cause him to relax such a pressure.[13]

[9] P. P. F. De Grand to JQA, with enclosures, Boston, December 14, 1817, January 15, 28, March 21, April 27, 1818. W. Lee to JQA, January 20, 1818. Adams MSS. JQA to P. P. F. De Grand, Washington, January 21, April 20, 1818. *Writings*, VI, 289–91, 310.

[10] Harris G. Warren shows how, in the case of all these filibusters, *The Sword Was Their Passport* (Baton Rouge, 1943). They had no established, or even *de facto*, government back of them.

[11] De Neuville to Rush, September 7, 12, 1817. DS, *Notes from the French Legation*, IV. For exchanges between Onís and Adams, see *ASPFR*, IV, 427, 466.

[12] *Writings*, VI, 213.

[13] James Monroe to JQA, Albemarle, September 1817. Adams MSS.

When the filibusters, under the command of General Charles L'Allemand, actually planted themselves on the Trinity River, near Galveston, Texas, with the possible intention of setting up an independent state there, the President sent a confidential informer, George Graham, to warn them that they were undertaking an unauthorized settlement within the territorial limits of the United States. Walter Prichard has edited documents, including JQA's instructions and Graham's report, relating to this secret, in *Louisiana Historical Quarterly*, XX (No. 3, July 1937), 619–50.

A feeble demonstration of Spanish troops had easily frightened the Frenchmen away before Graham reached the Trinity.

Observing the thickening atmosphere of Washington, Onís and his chief, Pizarro, feared that some sudden move of the United States might bring on a war that would ruin Spain in America once and forever. It could come with the seizure of Florida, for which General Andrew Jackson was so notoriously eager; or with recognition of the independence of the new states of South America, for which Henry Clay was pushing the Administration.

Just such a move seemed to be portended by the posture of affairs at Amelia Island, in the St. Mary's River, between Georgia and East Florida. Some of the revolutionary agents,[14] then in North America seeking political recognition and material succor for their *de facto* governments, had given unauthorized commissions to foreign adventurers like the Scotsman Gregor McGregor and the Venezuelan naval patriot Louis Aury to take over territory on the coast of Florida or Texas to serve as bases for privateers against Spanish shipping. McGregor successfully organized a filibustering expedition out of Charleston and Savannah, which seized Amelia Island. Aury ensconced himself first at Galveston and later superseded McGregor at Amelia. Corsairs and buccaneers sallying forth from that base under revolutionary flags failed to draw the line between privateering against Spanish commerce and freebooting against the commerce of neutral nations, including that of the United States.[15]

The President and his Cabinet agreed with Adams that these "marauding parties" should be broken up immediately. Monroe announced[16] orders for subjection of both buccaneering strongholds on the ground that they menaced the peace and tranquillity of the United States and the lawful commerce of its inhabitants. That is, he based his action on the authority of the No-Transfer Resolution of January 15, 1811: the "tranquillity" and "commerce" of the United States were endangered. Naval and military forces took over Amelia Island, December 23, 1817. McGregor, whom Aury had already pushed out of that pirates' nest, retired to England and made plans for a descent on Tampa from the Bahamas.

4

When Pizarro heard of these events, and of American plans also to occupy Galveston[17] on the Texan coast, he trembled for the security of the

[14] One of these agents was Don Vicente Pazos, of Venezuela, who professed to speak and act in the name of the independent republics of South America *generally*, "as the representative," commented Adams, "of 88 degrees of latitude, and 18 millions of People." JQA: "Pazos – Observations on his Memorial. A Fragment, 1818." Adams MSS.

[15] Maury D. Baker, Jr.: *The United States and Piracy: the Latin American Wars of Independence* (Duke University thesis, 1946, in preparation for publication).

[16] First Annual Message to Congress, December 2, 1817, and Special Message of January 13, 1818.

[17] Orders to occupy Galveston were suspended repeatedly, apparently because Monroe decided (in February 1818) to yield that part of Texas to Spain, in the nego-

King's borderlands in North America. "The difficult negotiation based on the cession of the Floridas will be useless," he declared to the Spanish Minister of War, "as we shall not have them to cede." [18] This is just what John Quincy Adams kept telling Onís in Washington: "If we don't come to an early conclusion of the Florida negotiations, Spain won't have the possession of Florida to give us." [19]

Under all this pressure from the United States, and with Spanish fortunes deteriorating constantly in South America, Pizarro decided to let the Floridas go and draw a boundary line somewhere west of the Mississippi, as near to the great river as possible. In return for this he hoped to pledge the United States not to recognize any of the revolted provinces of Spanish America.

Monroe's announcement of intention to occupy Amelia Island and Galveston spurred Onís to open a general negotiation with Secretary Adams. In a series of notes he developed at great length the historical background of the boundaries of Louisiana and Florida. The purpose was to show that the United States had no right to any territory east or west of the Mississippi Delta.[20]

Without indulging in further historical argument,[21] Adams repeated the offer which Monroe had first made in 1816 as Secretary of State. That was the line of the Colorado River (of Texas) from the Gulf of Mexico to its source "and from thence to the northern limits of Louisiana." [22]

The "northern limits of Louisiana" had never been fixed. Jefferson had assumed that they were the watershed of the Mississippi-Missouri system west of the Lake of the Woods. Diplomatists of the day, and most historical students of the subject since then, accepted the historical fiction that an Anglo-French boundary commission set up by the Treaty of Utrecht (1713) had fixed the boundary between French Louisiana and British North America west of the Mississippi at the line of 49° N.L. That was the line which the United States thus far had been insisting on in all its negotiations with Great Britain. It was that which Monroe and Adams presently would put forward as the minimum requirement of the United States, in the instructions (July 28, 1818) to Richard Rush and Albert

tiations with Onís. In May 1820 an American naval officer, Lieutenant Commander Lawrence Kearney, razed the pirate defenses of Galveston and burned their houses there after their leader, Jean Laffite, had decamped toward the Mexican shore. Baker: *United States and Piracy*, p. 132.

[18] Brooks: *Borderlands*, p. 92, quoting Pizarro to the *Secretario de Guerra*, February 26, 1818.

[19] *Memoirs*, IV, 42. January 14, 1818.

[20] Onís to the Secretary of State, December 6, 10, 29, 1817, January 5, 8, 1818. *ASPFR*, IV, 450–63.

[21] The American position, including the claim to the Rio Grande as the western boundary of Louisiana, had been presented in the negotiations at Washington and Madrid in 1816–17. See *ASPFR*, IV, 423–50.

[22] See Map 4.

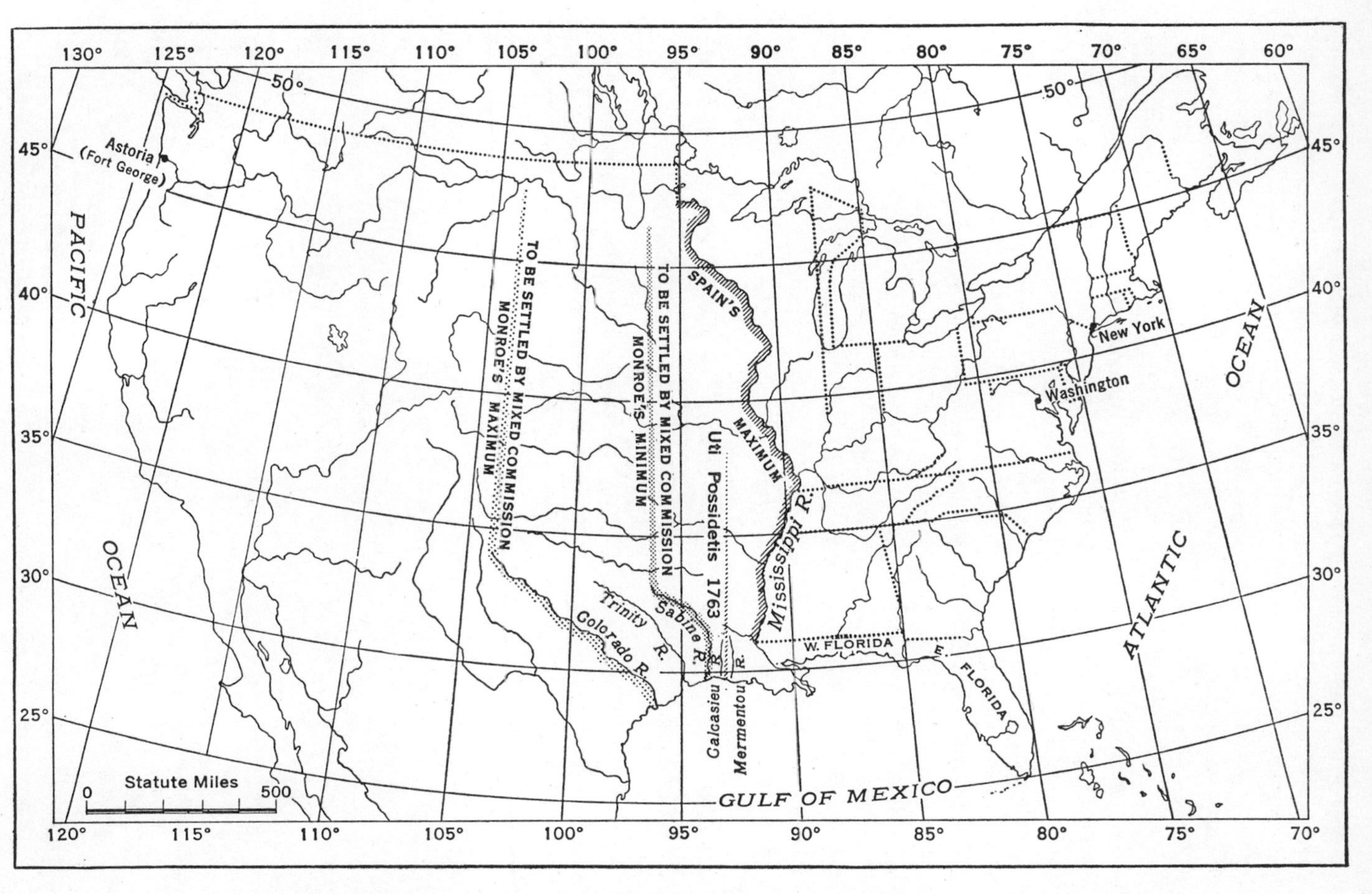

Map 4 *Maximum and Minimum Boundary Claims of the United States and Spain, 1816*

Gallatin, which resulted in the Anglo-American Convention of October 20, 1818.

Adams's first proposal (January 16, 1818) to Onís shows that he had not yet fully perceived the relationship between the Anglo-American boundary question in the Northwest and the Spanish-American boundary question in the Southwest. He was really taking his stand on Monroe's old position vis-à-vis Spain only. A line north from the source of the Colorado River of Texas to the "northern limits of Louisiana" would run up across the prairies just in front of the Rocky Mountains. It would save the Louisiana Purchase, but it would absolutely cut the United States off from the Columbia River country. Nothing could have been farther from Adams's real desire, or from Monroe's, for that matter. They did not realize the full implications for American continental expansion of the Spanish negotiations until, in the summer of 1818, they came to draw up the instructions for the British boundary negotiations.

Here, then, was a golden opportunity for the Spanish Minister. Once, during the American Revolution, Spain had tried to coop the United States up between the Alleghenies and the Atlantic seaboard. Thanks to Europe's distress since then the Republic had doubled its territory, had expanded across the Mississippi to Texas and to the Rocky Mountains, and had laid claims to the Oregon country and the North West Coast, claims at least as strong as any other nation's. Onís realized that the Americans thought it their destiny to expand their homeland all the way across the Continent.[23] Now he had a chance, by taking advantage of Adams's rather careless offer, to halt their westward march, to lock them up, if not east of the Alleghenies, then at least east of the Rocky Mountains. But he did not see his opportunity. Even if he had sensed it, his instructions had tied his hands. He had as yet no powers to accept the Colorado, much less a line run northward from its source to the "northern limits of Louisiana."

What Onís did propose (January 24, 1818) as an alternative was the ancient customary boundary between Spanish Texas and French Louisiana, the *uti possidetis* of 1763. According to Onís's proposal,[24] that customary or historical boundary began at a point half-way between the Mermentau and Calcasieu Rivers, two small parallel streams flowing into the Gulf of Mexico entirely within the State of Louisiana. The easternmost stream, the Mermentau, is about fifty miles from the Sabine, then as now the western boundary of the state. About half-way between the Mermentau and the Sabine is the Calcasieu. Ascending the divide between these little rivers, the putative ancient boundary then proceeded to the north through a barren basin called the Arroyo Hondo, which stretches between Los Adaes, historically the easternmost post of Spain, on the one side, and Natchitoches, westernmost settlement of old Louisiana in the French days, on the other side. From there the historical frontier might be sup-

[23] Brooks: *Borderlands*, pp. 76, 90.

[24] *ASPFR*, IV, 464–7. See Map 4.

posed to run generally north and northwest as far as the eastward-flowing Red River.[25]

The Arroyo Hondo already had served as a neutral barrier zone between Spanish and American forces back in 1806–7. The Spanish Minister now proposed to make these old *de facto* limits the *de jure* boundary between Spain and the United States from the Gulf of Mexico to the Red River. North of that – that is, north of the Red River – he was willing, as a last recourse, to allow the boundary to be marked out by a joint commission.[26]

President Monroe would not accept any line that cut into the State of Louisiana. But he was prepared to meet the Spanish offer in a conciliatory way. He directed the Secretary of State to retreat from the Colorado to the Trinity – half-way between the Colorado and the Mermentau – and to take the Arkansas River as the northern boundary of Spanish dominions as far west as the mountains.

"We may agree to fix the boundary," the President noted for Adams's guidance, "by the Trinity, from its mouth to its source, then to the Arkansas at its nearest point, and along the Arkansas to its source, thence due West to the Pacific, *or to leave the limit in the latter instance to be settled by commissioners.* If this is done, and Florida, west, to the Perdido, is ceded, and the Convention of 1802 ratified, the U States will undertake to pay, in satisfaction of claims, on account of the French spoliations, and condemnations in Spanish ports, a sum not exceeding ——, and will likewise pay to Spain ——."[27]

Here is the first recorded suggestion, not yet conveyed to Spain, of carrying the boundary through to the Pacific Ocean. Was the brilliant inspiration Monroe's or Adams's? The day he signed the Transcontinental Treaty, and five years later when appealing to the voters on his record, Adams claimed that it was his original idea and his alone. In view of these solemn and categorical statements and of his stand throughout the nego-

[25] As far north as Los Adaes this line is slightly to the west of a line advanced by the French geographer d'Anville as the proper boundary between French Louisiana and Spanish Texas, and accepted as such by the learned Mexican antiquarian Padre José Antonio Pichardo in his million-word MS. *Treatise on the Boundaries of Louisiana and Texas,* translated and edited by Professor Charles W. Hackett, and published by the University of Texas (4 vols., Austin, 1931–47; see map in pocket of Vol. II). This MS. was the historical repository for Spanish treaty-makers in 1818–19. The d'Anville-Pichardo line begins at Bahía de la Ascención (present Atchafalaya Bay, westernmost entry into the Mississippi Delta) and follows roughly the western watershed of the Red River, but crosses that stream near present Wichita Falls, Texas, and continues indefinitely in a general northerly direction.

[26] See Map 4.

[27] This is a memorandum in Monroe's handwriting bound between two documents dated February 5 and 23, 1818, in a volume of letters from James Monroe to JQA, 1798–1831. Adams MSS. Italics inserted. Internal and external evidence proves that Monroe was writing this memorandum in response to Onís's note to Adams of January 24, 1818. For the interchange of notes see *ASPFR,* IV, 450–78.

tiations for a boundary to the Pacific, and for other reasons to be advanced in the following chapter, it is not difficult to believe that the President was recording and sanctioning what the two men had agreed to in previous discussions, in which the Secretary of State had come out for a boundary line all the way through to the other ocean.

The other alternative, that of a mixed commission to determine the northern part of the western boundary, is what Onís was now pressing back upon Monroe, through the intermediary of Nicholas Biddle of Philadelphia, who enjoyed a confidential and officious intimacy with the President.[28]

Onís's instructions would not yet permit him to meet the American Government, even at the Trinity. Before making any further concessions west of the traditional boundary of the Arroyo Hondo the Spanish Government had resolved, characteristically, to exhaust every possibility of foreign assistance, particularly that of the ally, England.

5

In vain Spain had importuned England during negotiations at Ghent and had appealed to the powers at the Congress of Vienna to restore Louisiana to its rightful sovereign. All her efforts since then to get their active assistance to save Florida had come to naught. Now her last recourse was British mediation as a means of getting a better treaty with the United States than by direct negotiations. Despite all British efforts to discourage the step, the Spanish Government obstinately persisted in requesting the mediation of the ally. Great Britain had to pay some deference to the importunity in order not fatally to injure at Madrid the progress of a much desired treaty for the suppression of the African slave trade. Just before Adams left London in 1817, Castlereagh intimated that his Government might be willing to mediate between the United States and Spain.

"If the Floridas were ceded to the United States," he asked, "what objection would they have to the Mississippi as a boundary?"

Adams had already explained that West Florida was a part of the Louisiana Purchase. He pointed to a map in the Foreign Office on which a whole range of territory west of the Mississippi was marked Louisiana. "That would be the objection," he said, "but if Spain would but for one moment be rational with us, we could easily come to an accommodation with her."

Castlereagh smiled. "I must admit that Spain is not the easiest of parties to concede," he declared, "and I may say the same of the United States."

"There can be no better judge of stubbornness and compliance," Adams

[28] *Memoirs,* IV, 307. Nicholas Biddle to Monroe, Baltimore, January 28, 1818. Copy in Adams MSS.

answered amiably, "than a party so very easy and accommodating as Great Britain." [29]

Without committing himself officially or personally, the retiring American Minister gave Castlereagh to understand that the United States Government might not be disinclined to accept a British mediation if there were reason to believe that it was tendered in a spirit of peace and impartiality, and not with a desire to support the pretensions of Spain.[30]

After Adams got established in the State Department at Washington, the British Government did suggest, half-heartedly, through Charles Bagot (January 1818) that Spain wanted a mediation, but that Great Britain would offer it only if the United States would join in the request. Nobody in England expected that a request would be forthcoming from the United States.[31] Nobody intended to do anything further if the suggestion was declined. Castlereagh assumed that Spain must and would purchase peace by sacrificing the Floridas; in exchange she should get the best boundary possible on the side of Mexico.[32] It was a correct assumption.

President Monroe weighed the British inquiry in a full Cabinet meeting. Adams was less earnest against it than all the others. He still had doubts whether the United States could escape European interference in this affair, and even larger doubts that it could be finally avoided in the greater, hemispheric conflict between Spain and her revolted colonies. Until the attitude of Europe should be better revealed, he thought it would be more diplomatic to evade but not absolutely to decline the British suggestion.[33] Nevertheless Monroe and his advisers decided, unanimously, to decline it. It was agreed that the Secretary of State should explain to Bagot that they feared acceptance would cause ill will and irritation against Great Britain in the mind of the public. To Onís, Adams explained that the United States had no desire to be drawn into the "labyrinth of European politics." The Spanish Minister did not fail to remind him that Secretary of State Monroe had accepted the Russian mediation offer in 1813. Adams only shrugged his shoulders.[34]

Pizarro would not make another move until he learned the result of the mediation proposal. Meanwhile the negotiations sank into a redundancy of historical argument, at which both Adams and Onís were singularly gifted. What finally constrained Spain to give up the Floridas and

[29] *Memoirs,* III, 549–50, 560.

[30] Castlereagh to Charles Bagot, Private and Confidential, November 10, 1817. C. K. Webster: *Britain and the Independence of Latin America, 1812–1830* (2 vols., London, 1938), II, 489.

[31] Brooks: *Borderlands,* pp. 114–15.

[32] Castlereagh to Bagot, No. 24, most secret and confidential, November 10, 1817. See note 30.

[33] *Memoirs,* IV, 48–51, January 27, 28, 31, 1818. *Writings,* VI, 294–8.

[34] Brooks: *Borderlands,* p. 114. Adams to Onís, March 12, 1818. *ASPFR,* IV, 468. *Memoirs,* IV, 53, 57, 60.

meet the United States half-way across the Continent of North America was General Andrew Jackson's spectacular invasion of those provinces. Although Adams had nothing to do with the inspiration of this additional pressure, nothing could have been more convenient to his negotiations with the Spanish Minister.

6

With revolution and civil war flaming throughout Mexico and South America, Spain was no longer able to control the hostile Indians and fugitive slaves in Florida. The chaotic situation offered to General Jackson's mind an ideal occasion, and justification by treaty, to occupy the remainder of the territory. He was itching for a chance to take possession of East Florida, and of West Florida between the Pearl and Perdido Rivers including the city of Pensacola. The opportunity was at hand.

British officers like Woodbine and Ambrister lingered among the Seminoles and incited them to hostilities. The Scotch trader Alexander Arbuthnot had now taken the place of the discredited Colonel Nicholls as spokesman for the natives along the Apalachicola south of the boundary. From this district they made forays against white settlers north of the line. The Secretary of War ordered Major General Gaines, at Amelia Island, to march against the murderous Seminoles, passing through East Florida if advisable to get at them. He had permission to pursue them into Spanish territory if necessary, but to respect the Spanish authority "wherever it is maintained." [35] Calhoun sent a copy of these instructions to Major General Jackson, ordered to Fort Scott [36] to take charge of the whole campaign. The border captain from the Tennessee frontier had sweeping powers "to adopt the necessary measures to terminate a conflict which it has ever been the desire of the President, from motives of humanity, to avoid."

Before proceeding promptly to his new and wholly congenial task, General Jackson wrote a famous confidential letter to the President, January 6, 1818, suggesting the occupation of all of East Florida.

"The Executive Government had ordered (and, as I conceive, very properly) Amelia Island to be taken possession of; this order ought to be carried into execution at all hazards, and, simultaneously the whole of East Florida seized, and held as indemnity for the outrages of Spain upon the property of our Citizens; This done, it puts all opposition down, secures our Citizens a compleat indemnity, and saves us from a war with Great Britain, or some of the Continental Powers combined with Spain." [37]

Just how the occupation of Florida would save us from a war with

[35] Message of March 25, 1818. *ASPFR*, IV, 183.

[36] On the Apalachicola just north of the Florida boundary.

[37] *Correspondence of Andrew Jackson*, J. S. Bassett, ed. (Washington, 1927), II, 345.

Spain, and perhaps with Spain's allies in the Old World, notably Great Britain, Jackson did not further explain. Probably he meant that the Mississippi Valley, heartland of the nation, would be so safe from invasion if the United States took the Florida pistol into its own hands, that no enemy would attempt it. What he urged, said the General, "can be done without implicating the Government. *Let it be signified to me through any channel, (say Mr. J. Rhea) that the possession of the Floridas would be desirable to the United States, and in sixty days it will be accomplished.*"[38]

Monroe had done this sort of thing more than once before. As Secretary of State with President Madison's sanction he had given just such a sign to General Mathews in 1811 for the occupation of East Florida, only to disavow him when the action became embarrassing. As Secretary of War he had also quite approved General Jackson's initiative in marching into Pensacola and West Florida to meet British invasion during the War of 1812. As President in 1818 he was glad enough to have the fiery Tennesseean at hand to hold over Spain's head during the lagging negotiations between Adams and Onís. He took no step to check Jackson's eager proposal.[39]

The General advanced into Florida with a force of 3,000 men, quickly broke up all Indian resistance, and pursued the fleeing savages eastward as far as the Spanish town of St. Marks, some seventy-five miles east of the Apalachicola and ten miles from the seacoast. That town he occupied over the protest of the local Spanish authorities. Then he turned back and took the post at Pensacola, West Florida, after a show of resistance

[38] Ibid., II, 345–6. Italics inserted.

[39] Years later (1831) when Jackson himself was President a political controversy over the affair developed. The General then asserted that he actually had received a letter from John Rhea, a member of Congress in 1818 from Tennessee, assuring him that Monroe said it was all right to go ahead, and that he discreetly burned the document. The aged Monroe thereupon denied that he had ever given Rhea any such assurance. Rhea, by then a shaky old man, backed up the ex-President equivocally. Historians have never been able to reconcile the opposite statements of the two men, Monroe and Jackson. The late Professor Bassett, scholarly biographer of Jackson and editor of his correspondence, thought that the General must have got his impression from vague and general expressions of approval by President Monroe on another separate matter, which Rhea conveyed to Jackson in a letter, still preserved, of January 12, 1818, not in answer to the celebrated secret epistle of January 6.

Even if Jackson did not get indirect word from the President, was it not a case where silence gave consent? It is certain that the Secretary of War, if not the President himself, well knew the contents of Jackson's letter of January 6 as soon as it was received in Washington. Bassett: *Correspondence of Andrew Jackson,* II, xi, 348. Marquis James reviews the evidence in a similar way in *Andrew Jackson, the Border Captain* (Indianapolis, 1933), p. 408. Richard R. Stenberg presents more searching examination of "Jackson's 'Rhea Letter' Hoax" in *Journal of Southern History,* II (1936), 480–96, and leaves little credence in Jackson's side of the controversy, but does not examine into Monroe's statement that he did not read Jackson's letter of January 6, when Calhoun handed it to him.

by the garrison there. He sent orders to General Gaines to take possession of St. Augustine too.

At the settlement of Suwanee, Jackson captured the trader Arbuthnot and his papers. At St. Marks he took Captain Ambrister, arms in hand, in avowed leadership of the savages. Arbuthnot denied any complicity in the Indian war, but his papers belied him. Ambrister admitted it. A court martial condemned both men, Arbuthnot to be hanged, Ambrister to be shot. Jackson speedily had the sentences carried out on these two British subjects who had done so much to keep alive the Indians' hostility and to give expectation of British countenance and backing. The evidence produced before the military court, and other evidence, conveyed by Adams to Richard Rush for exhibition to Lord Castlereagh, was so complete that there was no protest. The whole affair did not deter the British Government one whit from signing with Rush and Gallatin the Convention of October 20, 1818 for regulation of the northern frontier.

The invasion of Florida brought on a serious debate in Monroe's Cabinet. Calhoun immediately countermanded Jackson's order for the occupation of St. Augustine. The Secretary of War seemed piqued that his own authority had been challenged, or circumvented. He wanted the Government to disavow the General. Crawford, eager to see a presidential candidate ruined, took his stand against Jackson.

Outside the Government, Clay and his cohorts gleefully saw a chance to attack both Jackson and the Administration. They denounced the invasion of Florida without the sanction of Congress, ignoring the No-Transfer Resolution of January 15, 1811. They asserted it was an act of war by the executive in violation of the Constitution. They held it up as a military menace to free men everywhere. They excoriated Jackson. In the Cabinet, Calhoun and Crawford, everybody except Adams, were for the disavowal of Jackson and the immediate restoration of Florida. Calhoun thought the General's conduct should be "the subject of investigation by a military tribunal" – in other words, court martial.[40]

The President was nervous about the political opposition, but he feared more clamor if he disavowed the popular General. He wanted to use the situation to press Spain in the current negotiations without driving that country into war. If he punished or even reprimanded Jackson, it would be a diplomatic advantage for Spain and confirm her in her disposition not to cede the Floridas.[41]

Adams argued at length that there was no real violation of instructions. Jackson's proceedings, he said, had been justified by the necessities of the case and by the misconduct of the Spanish commanding officers in Florida. "If the question is dubious, it is better to err on the side of vigor

[40] Calhoun to JQA, Washington, February 3, 1831. "Letters of John C. Calhoun," in *Annual Report* 1899 of AHA, 285–7.

[41] Monroe to Jefferson, Washington, July 22, 1818. *Writings of Monroe,* VI, 63, 87–92.

than of weakness — on the side of our own officer, who has rendered the most eminent services to the nation, than on the side of our bitterest enemies, and against him." At first he contended that the United States should keep Pensacola, upon the principles on which Jackson had taken it, till Spain should give an adequate guaranty that she would fulfill her engagements by restraining the Indians from hostilities. Finally he conceded that there would be difficulties in holding Pensacola without an act of Congress. He therefore urged that the taking be justified, yet the place restored, on the express condition that thereafter Spain should fulfill her treaty.[42]

It was so decided. The President drafted a note for the Secretary of State to present to Onís. It admitted that Jackson's seizures of Pensacola and St. Marks were the General's own acts. It boldly justified them by the conduct of the Spanish officials who had been concerned with the Indian war, as Adams had contended. It declared that the President was ready to deliver up Pensacola to anyone authorized to receive it. He would give up St. Marks, too, as soon as a Spanish force adequate to hold it against an attack of hostile Indians was ready to take it over.[43] This did not take place until February 1819 as Spain was ceding the Floridas to the United States.

To Jackson, Monroe cordially explained that he had patriotically transcended his authority in attacking the Spanish posts. Florida would therefore be evacuated.[44] Jackson refused to admit that he had gone beyond his orders. There the matter rested, so far as the President and his General were concerned, until many years later.

Monroe was satisfied. General Jackson's action had put just the right pressure on Spain at just the right time. It had turned the situation to the best account for the country.[45]

John Quincy Adams was content too. Andrew Jackson's invasion enabled him to close the Florida Question with the spacious Transcontinental Treaty of February 22, 1819.

[42] *Memoirs,* IV, 107–14.

[43] JQA to Onís, July 23, 1818. *ASPFR,* IV, 498. Monroe to JQA, July 20, 1818. Adams MSS.

[44] "The events which have occurred in both the Floridas show the incompetency of Spain to maintain her authority; and the progress of the revolutions in South America will require all her forces there. . . . If we hold the posts, her [Spain's] government cannot treat with honor, which, by withdrawing the troops, we afford her an opportunity to do." Monroe to Jackson, July 19, 1818. *Writings of Monroe,* VI, 58.

[45] Eight months later, and two weeks before signature of the treaty with Spain, Monroe explained to ex-President Madison: "On the receipt of Genl. Jackson's report of his proceedings there we had three great objects in view, first to secure the constitution from any breach, second to deprive Spain and the allies of any just cause of war, and third *to turn it to the best account of the country.*" Monroe to Madison, February 7, 1819. To Richard Rush he wrote, March 7, 1819, in a similar vein, and added: "*By the pressure on Spain* we have obtained a territory equally necessary to her peace and our own, and have also given some support to the Colonies." *Writings of Monroe,* VI, 87–92. Italics inserted.

CHAPTER XVI
The Transcontinental Treaty with Spain (1818–1819)

The right of the United States can as little compound with impotence as with perfidy.

JOHN QUINCY ADAMS TO GEORGE W. ERVING, AMERICAN MINISTER TO SPAIN, NOVEMBER 28, 1818

THE INDIANS were crushed. The fact that an American General had caught and hanged or shot their British friends and leaders, whom they had regarded as all-powerful, thoroughly discouraged the tribes.[1] On the more cultivated Spanish mind, both in Washington and in Madrid, Jackson's campaign made an even stronger impression.

1

In Washington, Onís announced that he would sign no treaty until the United States first restored Florida to Spanish authority. He demanded a suitable indemnity for the "outrage," and "lawful punishment" of General Jackson for his "flagrant" disobedience of orders.[2] Nevertheless, he continued to discuss things with Adams – on the assumption, he professed, that Florida would be promptly restored. In Madrid, Pizarro protested against the invasion and broke off all discussion with Erving, but he kept on instructing Onís to make further boundary concessions in the west.

In the midst of his protests to the United States and while the Cabinet was debating the action of General Jackson the Spanish Minister had three long conversations with the Secretary of State. Still exploring the terms of peace under the shadow of war, neither diplomat revealed in these tentative discussions just how far he could go to meet the other. Adams did not disclose that the United States was ready to fall back east to the Trinity. Onís did not say that he would retreat west to the Sabine. Onís stressed the ardent desire of Spain for peace. Assuming that of course Jackson would be disavowed, the Spanish Minister tried to sound out Adams about the terms of a treaty settlement to follow. The Secretary of State declared that if Spain would cede the Floridas, and all claims

[1] Bassett: *Jackson*, p. 259.
[2] Onís to JQA, June 9, 17, July 8, 1818. *ASPFR*, IV, 494–7.

could be renounced by each side, he thought the President might be willing to make an agreement to let the western boundary wait.

Spain did not care to let the western boundary wait. What she wanted in these negotiations was to save Texas and the immense territories back of it by yielding the indefensible Floridas. What she also desired was to pledge the United States not to recognize the independence of the revolted provinces in South America.[3]

Onís had instructions not to make any settlement that failed to fix a final boundary in the west. "That is the sole object of the sacrifices which His Majesty is disposed to make of the Floridas," he told Adams, "and I will not advise His Majesty to make any settlement unless it fixes safe and permanent limits west of the Mississippi."

Adams smiled. "If that's the way it is, we can take the Rio Bravo [Rio Grande] del Norte for a frontier."

"Better still the Mississippi," replied Onís in the same tone.

More seriously, he asked the Secretary to take out a map and see if they could not get together on some suggestion. Adams got out a copy of the most recent (January 1, 1818) edition of Melish's *Map of the United States and the Contiguous British and Spanish Possessions,* the latest cartographical authority, on which the opposing diplomatists had been charting their respective claims.[4] Onís pointed out what Spain claimed to be the old boundary of French Louisiana – the Mermentau, or at least the Calcasieu, and the Arroyo Hondo to the north. From the Arroyo Hondo one might continue straight north to the Missouri and up that river to its source. Or a mixed commission could fix the boundary in those parts. Adams insisted that San Bernardo Bay (Matagorda) and the river flowing into it (the Colorado), from the ocean to its source, was as far as the United States could yield.

"And pray what are your plans from there on?" inquired Onís.

"From there on," continued the Secretary, "a line might be drawn to the source of the Missouri, *thence straight to the Pacific Ocean.*"

"So you are trying to dispossess us also of the whole Pacific Coast which belongs to us, and which Juan de Fuca took possession of in the King's name up to 56°!"

"Nonsense," said Adams. "The English pretend the Columbia River is theirs. The Russians have possessions north of it which you have never disputed, and we have more right than anybody else to the River Columbia. We have establishments on its banks, and we need it to keep open our communications with the interior."

"Here are their views, clear enough," wrote Onís to Pizarro, recount-

[3] Pizarro to Onís, April 25, 1818. Brooks: *Borderlands,* pp. 134–5.

[4] The series of maps in the volume in the reader's hands, tracing the Adams-Onís negotiations (see Map 7 at end of book), is based on Melish's cartography, with red cover-tracings of present-day geography.

For notes on Melish, and a facsimile, see Brooks: *Borderlands,* pp. 214–19.

ing the conversations, "and the truth is they are less exaggerated than their real ones. . . . If His Majesty can't get the support of any Power, and hasn't sufficient forces to make war on this country, then I think it would be best not to delay making the best settlement possible, seeing that things certainly won't be better for a long time." He further warned his chief that there was no hope of pledging the United States not to recognize the independence of any of the insurgents; in fact, it seemed that they might soon recognize the Government of Buenos Aires before the year was over.[5]

Such was Onís's official account of the interview in which the Secretary of State broached for the first time *to Spain* the idea of a line through to the Pacific. Adams's Diary[6] agrees with his interlocutor, except that he does not mention having suggested any line north from the source of the Colorado to the Missouri, much less from the latter point due west to the Pacific. We must, I think, accept the accuracy of these details from Onís's dispatch.

What Adams so tentatively suggested – it was not an offer – did not correspond to the boundary proposals that he and Monroe had worked out the previous February. Then they had fixed on the Trinity, from its mouth to its source, thence north to the Arkansas River and up that river to its source (in about 41° N.L. according to Melish). From that point they had thought of a line due west to the Pacific, Adams's idea, *or* a boundary to be fixed by a joint commission, Monroe's solution, or perhaps Onís's suggestion planted in the President's mind through John Jacob Astor.[7] Now, after Jackson's invasion of Florida, Adams was still talking about the Colorado instead of the Trinity. But he was suggesting – to be sure, in a noncommittal way – the source of the Missouri (45° 20′ N.L. on Melish)[8] instead of the source of the Arkansas as the starting-point west to the other ocean. When he spoke of the source of the Missouri he meant what people then and since then have taken it to be – the Three Forks of the Missouri.

In these exploratory conversations Adams had thrown out a suggestion which smacks more of Monroe's previous boundary diplomacy than it does of the Secretary's own developing concepts of a continental boundary. To Onís he had said, in effect: all right, we might conceivably be willing to take the source of the Missouri for a boundary point, but never its watercourse; and we propose to get to the source of the Missouri by drawing a line north from the source of the Colorado River of Texas.

The line that Adams had intimated as a possible western boundary of the United States, from the source of the Colorado River of Texas to the

[5] Onís to Pizarro, No. 134, Bristol, July 18, 1818. *Archivo Histórico Nacional* [Madrid], *Estado, legajo* 5643. Photocopy by courtesy of Dr. Philip C. Brooks.

[6] *Memoirs,* IV, 106–7, July 11, 1818.

[7] Above, Ch. XV, n. 28.

[8] That is, if we assume it to be the source of that tributary, above the Three Forks, called the Jefferson or Beaverhead.

source of the Missouri, corresponded very roughly to the Front Range of the Rockies. He could not think of accepting the upper course of the Missouri River (or any part of the stream) for a boundary, as Onís proposed. That would have abandoned a large area of the original Louisiana Purchase, the part least in contest with anybody. In even conceiving the source of the Missouri for a starting-point of his line west to the Pacific he was going against his better continental instincts, and he soon withdrew the suggestion. It would place the Spanish-American frontier too high up on the map. The object of his diplomacy with Great Britain [9] and with Spain, as he felt his way through the trackless West during the year 1818, was to get possession of Spain's title to the entire Columbia River basin, which he supposed to lie between 41° and 51° N.L.

Onís now retired to his summer residence in Bristol, Pennsylvania, to await the restoration of Pensacola and St. Marks. Following the Cabinet discussions noted in the last chapter, the President drafted the reply that was to be delivered to the Spanish Minister's protest against Jackson's proceedings. Some further deliberation took place between Monroe and Adams about the western boundary. Following this the Secretary quickly took pains to remove any impression that he might have left in Onís's mind that the United States would run any line through to the Pacific from a point as far north as the source of the Missouri River. An occasion for doing so presented itself through the medium of the French Minister, Hyde de Neuville, who from now on assumes a conspicuous place in the negotiations.

At the height of the crisis caused by Jackson's move into Florida, Hyde had offered his good offices to prevent a break. The motive of the French Government is not clearly established. On the surface it was a harmless response to Spain's cries for help against the United States.[10] In his sketchy *Mémoires,* Hyde de Neuville reveals a deep-seated fear of British intrusion in the Caribbean area. Undoubtedly he wanted to strengthen Spain's position there by composing all her differences with the United States on the Continent of North America. It is also quite possible that he felt that the establishment and enforcement of an agreed boundary between the two countries in North America would discourage the filibustering plots of the Napoleonic exiles. Certain it is that the French Government feared the United States might recognize the independence of the new states of Latin America; perhaps here was a way of staving off such a calamity.[11] At any rate, the President and the Secretary of State found

[9] It was on May 19 that Adams first began to discuss with the President the instructions for Gallatin and Rush, insisting on the line of 49° N.L. as the northern boundary of the United States. *Memoirs,* IV, 97. The actual instructions are dated July 28, 1818. *Writings,* VI, 394.

[10] Brooks: *Borderlands,* pp. 124–7.

[11] Dexter Perkins: "John Quincy Adams," in *American Secretaries of State and Their Diplomacy,* IV (New York, 1928), 29–30.

it convenient to avail themselves of Hyde's conciliatory services, as did the Spanish Government.[12]

Whatever the motive of Hyde de Neuville's good offices, they gave Adams a means of drawing back from the dangerous suggestion he had just made regarding a line to the Pacific Ocean as high up as the source of the Missouri. On July 16, 1818, within a week after exploring the map with Onís in Washington, Adams marked on Melish's Map his first definite offer for Hyde to convey to the Spanish Minister: "the boundary which it had been agreed on at the President's that I should be authorized to offer; the Trinity, from its mouth to its source, then a line due north to the Red River, following the course of that to its source, then crossing to the Rio del Norte, and following the course of it, or the summit of a chain of mountains northward and parallel to it; there stop, or take a line west to the Pacific."[13]

On Melish's Map the Rio Grande appears to rise in about 41° 30′. For the United States it was a much better point from which to start due west for the Pacific. Crossing over the Sangre de Cristo Mountains, the proposed boundary would come into the Rio Grande Valley just above the ancient towns of Taos and Santa Fe. Santa Fe, capital of the province of New Mexico, was the King of Spain's first jewel in that part of the world.

One would like to know more definitely the respective contributions of President and Secretary of State to this new boundary offer, which yielded much of Texas and demanded more of Oregon. Later, after the treaty had been signed, when Clay was raising a cry against the abandonment of Texas, Adams, sensitive to Western opposition to himself, declared he had been the last man in the Administration to agree to the Sabine for the western boundary.[14] Ever since Monroe had had anything to do with the Spanish negotiations – ever since 1806 – he had been willing to retreat still farther east, to the Sabine, to give up all of Texas for the Floridas. Therefore it seems most likely that it was the President who commanded the step of retreat eastward from the Colorado. Adams followed his chief with no great if any protest.

But who suggested the new, more southern point of departure *westward* that had been "agreed on at the President's"? According to Adams's later statements the whole idea of a line west was originally his and his alone. That this was true is borne out by Monroe's consistent willingness to leave the northern part of the boundary to commissioners as Onís

[12] After the treaty was signed, Adams instructed Gallatin to express to the French Government the thanks of the President for the "friendly interposition of the French Government with that of Spain," and for the zeal and ability of de Neuville in promoting the amicable settlement between Spain and the United States. JQA to Albert Gallatin, No. 13, Washington, February 27, 1819. DS, *Instructions, U.S. Ministers*, VIII, 301, 302.

[13] *Memoirs,* IV, 110. See Map 7B at end of book.

[14] *Memoirs,* V, 54, 69. March 31, April 13, 1820.

desired, and by Adams's consistent fight for an agreed line to the South Sea. A letter from the President to Adams of July 17, 1818, at the time of the deliberations, reflects a revealing light on the question. "That the alternative, suggested by your conversation with the Minister of France, and examined in conference yesterday, may be again more fully considered, it will be advisable to have before us a project, founded on it. And although I have intimated a preference for the first mentioned mode [i.e., a commission], I am far from being decided, that some other ought not to be preferred."[15] This makes it clear that it was Adams who persuaded Monroe and the "Administration" to go west to the Pacific.

Hyde de Neuville reported that Onís still would not budge from the Mermentau and Arroyo Hondo as the barrier to which the United States must agree. But it would be easy to fix the "termination of that barrier" – so the French Minister reported his Spanish colleague to have said.

The Secretary of State referred the matter to the President. Naturally Monroe would not give up any part of the State of Louisiana, though he was ready to meet Onís at the Sabine, western boundary of the state and of the old neutral barrier zone between the United States and Spain in the years before the War of 1812. Obviously the Sabine was the termination of the barrier that Hyde de Neuville had meant. Again the President proposed to leave the continental boundary, north from the source of the Red River, to be fixed by a joint commission. He directed Adams to intimate to Hyde, for the benefit of Onís, that if Spain would not come to terms on this basis, Congress at its next session was sure to give the Government powers to take the Floridas. He would then reserve American claims to all of Texas as far as the Rio Grande.

The President well knew the advantage he had over Spain. He was determined not to lose it.[16] There was no danger that he would, with Adams in charge of the negotiation.

[15] James Monroe to JQA, July 17, 1818. Adams MSS.

[16] "Mr. Onís ought to know that we make a good concession in giving up all the country between the Rio Bravo [Grande] and the Sabine. I should talk of nothing more then. The course of the Red River must be maintained, commissioners to settle the boundary from its source. After proposing these ideas in a letter, kindly expressed to Mr. De Neuville, I would accept his proposal of suggesting to Mr. Onís the propriety of formulating his propositions, that the affair may be brought to a conclusion as soon as possible. Mr. Onís ought to seek to get rid of the question of sending a person to take possession of Pensacola, which can be done, only, by a prompt arrangement and cession. He may be satisfied that we shall lose, no part, of the ground we have now gained, and that if a cession is not made, the public mind will easily make itself up, especially if nothing unfavorable, occurs, in Europe, to take the Floridas, at the next session, by an act of Congress, and as an indemnity, retaining our full claim to the Rio Bravo. This Government will likewise be forced to submit to that measure, unless, it engages us, in a war, to prevent it, in which case we shall expell Spain from this hemisphere.

"I wish you would propose to our Ministers at London, Paris, and St. Petersburgh, the question, what part, do they respectively think, those governments will take in

Having planted these propositions in Onís's mind and conveyed these threats, through Hyde de Neuville, Adams went on his annual September vacation to Quincy. Upon his return, and following the restoration of Pensacola, Onís renewed direct conversations. He offered a line half-way between the Mermentau and Calcasieu, then following the Arroyo Hondo north to a point between Los Adaes and Natchitoches, thence north again across the Red River (at 32° N.L. and 93° W.L., "according to Melish's Map") to the Missouri and up that river to its source.

That line would have deprived the United States of half the Louisiana Purchase. It would have left the Republic in contact with the Oregon country only by a narrow corridor north of the Missouri, thence across the lofty and most impassable ranges of the Rockies, the present Glacier National Park. Onís further demanded that the navigation of the Mermentau, the Missouri, *and the Mississippi* should be free and open to the subjects of both parties.[17]

Repetition of this offer almost exhausted President Monroe's patience. "It is time to bring Onís to the point," he told Adams. "If he won't agree to reasonable terms, break off the negotiation."[18]

Under these firm orders the Secretary of State conveyed to the Spanish Minister a "final offer." "As the session of Congress is at hand," he warned that procrastinating diplomat, "I am directed to request your immediate and frank reply to this communication."[19]

The "ultimatum" of the United States, as Adams described it to Onís, was the Sabine River from the Gulf of Mexico to 32° N.L., then due north to the Red River, thence up the Red River to its source, "touching the chain of the Snow [Sangre de Cristo] Mountains" in 37° 25′ N.L., 106° 15′ W.L., or thereabouts, as marked on Melish's Map, and following the chain of mountains northward to 41°; *thence along that parallel of*

regard to the dispute between Spain and her Colonies, and in what light they will view an acknowledgment of the independence of the Colonies by the U States? Whether they will view it, as an act of hostility to Spain, and in case Spain declares war on us, in consequence, take part with her in it? Whatever be the course which we pursue, it will be useful and proper for us to have it in our power to lay such a document before Congress, at the next Session, should either House request it." James Monroe to JQA, Albemarle, August 10, 1818. Adams MSS. A copy of the same letter is in the Monroe Papers, LC. For Adams's instructions to the Ministers in London, Paris, and St. Petersburg, see W. R. Manning: *Diplomatic Correspondence Concerning the Independence of the Latin American Nations* (Washington: Carnegie Endowment for International Peace; 1925), I, 74–5.

[17] Onís to JQA, October 24, 1818. *ASPFR,* IV, 526–30. See Map 7 B at end of book.

[18] *Memoirs,* IV, 144. October 26, 1818.

[19] "The President is deeply penetrated with the conviction that further protracted discussion of the points at issue between our Governments cannot terminate in a manner satisfactory to them. From your answer to this letter, he must conclude whether a final adjustment of all our differences is now to be accomplished, or whether all hope of such a desirable result is, on the part of the United States, to be abandoned." *ASPFR,* IV, 531.

latitude to the South Sea. This line, declared the Secretary of State, would not need any commissioners to fix it.[20]

For Spain, Adams's proposed boundary presented the advantage of skirting around the headwaters of the Rio Grande River to the east and north. For the United States it retained the entire Columbia River and all its southern tributaries — at least so it appeared on Melish's Map.[21]

By now Onís had received new instructions, dispatched after arrival in Madrid of the first news of Jackson's invasion of Florida. They enabled him to retreat westward to the Sabine as the eastern boundary of Texas, even to withdraw west of the Sabine if necessary to meet the United States. But as yet he had no authority to accept the Red River as a northern boundary for Texas. Much less was he authorized to draw any line clear through to the South Sea.

It was not necessary for Spain to retreat beyond the Sabine. Onís had already saved Texas for Spain, easily. Henceforward he strove to hold back half of the Louisiana Purchase and to keep Spain's claims to the North West Coast and Oregon country. He accepted Adams's proposed boundary only as far north as the Red River. From there Onís proposed to draw a line due north to the Missouri and up the middle of that river to its source. From that point he left the boundary "unsettled," but said he had no doubt of His Majesty's disposition to agree to the appointment of a joint commission to determine and establish the future boundaries from the source of the Missouri to the *north and west* "in a manner conformable to the titles and documents and possession respectively exhibited."[22] This last, of course, meant nothing, except future uncertainty and trouble.

Repetition of the line of the Missouri, without even the certainty of a commission to mark out anything to the "north and west" of that river, again threw the whole negotiation out of gear. Monroe would have no more of such foolishness. The next day he sent in a message to Congress reviewing the whole question.

Relations with Spain, the President declared, remained nearly the same as they had been at the close of the last session. In the meantime events clearly had proved the ill effect that Spain's policy had had on the friendly

[20] "Unless it be for the purpose of ascertaining the spot where the river falls upon latitude thirty-two degrees north, and the line thence north to the Red River, and the point of latitude forty-one degrees north on the ridge of the Snow Mountains: to which appointment of commissioners this Government will readily agree." JQA to Onís, October 31, 1818. *ASPFR,* IV, 530–1. See Map 7 C at end of book.

[21] On Melish the heads of the small tributaries of the fictitious San Clementini (San Clemente, as Onís called it) are barely north of 41°.

[22] Onís to JQA, November 16, 1818. See Map 7 C at end of book. *ASPFR,* IV, 531–3. Italics inserted. This publication misprints the word *Missouri* as *Mississippi.* Subsequent cartographical studies that accepted the misprint, like Thomas M. Marshall: *History of the Western Boundary of the Louisiana Purchase* (Berkeley, 1914), Map 20, and Paullin and Wright's *Atlas,* Plate 95 A, project a mistaken line. Brooks: *Borderlands,* p. 167, n. 41, first called attention to the mistake.

relations between the two countries, "which it is presumed is at least of as much importance to Spain as to the United States to maintain." He promised to lay the diplomatic documents before Congress.

At the President's direction Adams now withdrew all previous boundary offers. He formally reserved all claims to the Rio Grande River, from the Gulf of Mexico to its source, as the southwestern boundary of the Louisiana Purchase. But the Secretary still left the door of peace ajar for Spain – uncomfortably ajar, but not closed. He stated that he would be willing to talk over things with the Spanish Minister if the latter's instructions would allow him to make a treaty without fixing a western boundary.[23]

The partly open door let in a chill draft from the Texas prairies. More than anything else in these negotiations the Government in Madrid, and its representative in Washington, and the French Minister with his good offices, feared to leave the southwestern frontier wide open into Mexico.[24] The first object of Spain was to fix an honorable and inviolate boundary in the southwest as far east of the Rio Grande as possible.

2

The Secretary of State now turned his attention and energies to public opinion at home and abroad, and particularly to Congress, for the Administration needed a majority for any resolution enabling the Executive to take possession of the Floridas in case of an absolute failure of the negotiation. Supporters of Clay and of Crawford were planning to attack the Government for the invasion of Florida and the execution of Arbuthnot and Ambrister. Pizarro's note of protest against Jackson's action had recently arrived in Washington. It gave to the Secretary of State just the occasion he needed. He answered it in a voluminous instruction to Erving, November 28, 1818, for communication to the Spanish Government. Long before it could be delivered in Madrid he gave a copy of the in-

[23] JQA to Onís, November 30, 1818. *ASPFR,* IV, 545–6.

[24] *Minuta de un informe presentado por el Sr. José Imáz sobre el tratado entre España y los Estados Unidos acerca de límites en la Luisiana y las Floridas.* Archivo Nacional, República de Cuba, Floridas, Legajo 11, Signatura 66. After signature of the treaty of February 22, 1819, Don José Imáz, Minister ad interim of the Exchequer (*Hacienda*) was called upon to study the dossier (*expediente*) of documents made up in the Spanish Department of State relating to the negotiations of the treaty and to render a confidential, unprejudiced report to the King directly on the expediency of ratifying the document. The resulting report affords considerable insight into motives of Spanish diplomacy. In 1851 the Count of Villanueva, Governor General of Cuba, ordered a copy of the Imáz report to be filed in the archives of the *Superintendencia General de la real hacienda de la Isla de Cuba,* in Habana, hereinafter referred to as *Informe de Imáz.* I am indebted to Captain Joaquín Llavarías, Director of the National Archives of Cuba, for particular courtesies extended during my researches in Habana.

struction, with supplementary and supporting papers, to the press in Washington.

The greatest state paper of John Quincy Adams's diplomatic career, this document served as a reply to the propaganda pamphlets with which Onís had been flooding the country,[25] but it had still larger purposes. He wanted particularly to exhibit the American position to the British public. Above all, he wanted to spread it out in the American press. "There is a Key which will explain this," wrote Bagot to his Government in London, "and always will explain every measure of this Government, viz: — Elections." [26]

In justifying Jackson, both for his violation of Spanish territory and for the execution of Arbuthnot and Ambrister, Adams drove home the real lesson of the Florida invasion: Spain must either exercise responsible authority in the derelict province or cede it to the United States. He reviewed at great length the whole background of the "Indian and Negro War" and the "dark and complicated depravity" of British adventurers in Florida ever since the War of 1812. He took particular pains to defend the execution of Arbuthnot and Ambrister. This was not so difficult. But to uphold the seizure of Pensacola, which had sheltered no hostile Indian forces, involved a bit of special pleading.

Jackson, explained the Secretary of State, had learned that the Governor of Pensacola had assisted the hostile Indians in various ways. Therefore he had marched into that part of West Florida. Then the Spanish Governor had warned him that he would be expelled by force if he did not leave immediately. Accordingly the General had seized the town of Pensacola and its fortifications in order to prevent his own ejection from the province. He continued to hold that post and St. Marks because he feared that otherwise they would be used by Spanish authority to protect the savages. "The President will neither inflict punishment, nor pass a censure on General Jackson, for that conduct, the motives

[25] "Verus" was the pseudonym for the following pamphlets issued by Onís:

1. A pamphlet without title in 1810 relating to the occupation of West Florida.
2. *Observations on the Conduct of Our Executive towards Spain* (Georgetown, November 12, 1813).
3. *Observations on the Existing Differences between the Government of Spain and the United States* (Philadelphia, 1817).

In 1820 Onís reprinted the three "Verus" pamphlets in his own account of the negotiations with the United States: *Memoria sobre las negociaciones entre España y Estados Unidos de América, que dieron motivo al tratado de 1819* (Madrid, 1820; Mexico, 1826). An English edition was published in the United States in 1821: *Memoir upon the Negotiations between Spain and the United States, which led to the Treaty of 1819,* with a statistical notice of that country. Accompanied with an appendix containing important documents for the better illustration of the subject. By D. Luis de Onís, Madrid, 1820. From the press of E. Burgos. Translated from the Spanish, with notes by Tobias Watkins (Baltimore: F. Lucas, Jr.; 1821. Washington: E. de Krafft; 1821).

[26] Brooks: *Borderlands,* p. 150.

of which were founded in the purest patriotism; of the necessity for which he had the most immediate and effectual means of forming a judgment; and the vindication of which is written on every page of the law of nations, as well as in the first law of nature — self-defense."

Now came the thrust home. It would be more proper for Spain to investigate the conduct of her Governors of Pensacola and St. Marks. "This inquiry," said the Secretary, "is due to the character of those officers themselves, and to the honor of the Spanish Government."

Seldom with impunity does the foreign minister of one government venture to tell another government publicly what is due to its own honor. In stern and scorching language Adams continued:

> If, as the commanders both at Pensacola and St. Marks have alleged, this has been the result of their weakness rather than of their will; if they have assisted the Indians against the United States to avert their hostilities from the province which they had not sufficient force to defend against them, it may serve in some measure to exculpate, individually, those officers; but it must carry demonstration irresistible to the Spanish Government, that *the right of the United States can as little compound with impotence as with perfidy,* and that Spain must immediately make her election, either to place a force in Florida adequate at once to the protection of her territory and to the fulfilment of her engagements, or cede to the United States a province, of which she retains nothing but the nominal possession, but which is, in fact, a derelict, open to the occupancy of every enemy, civilized or savage, of the United States, and serving no other earthly purpose than as a post of annoyance to them.[27]

The force of this dispatch, and of the papers accompanying it, was prodigious.[28] It undermined the opposition in Congress in the noisy debates that followed. Notwithstanding the eloquence of Henry Clay and of Howell Cobb of Georgia, the House of Representatives voted down by heavy majorities resolutions disapproving the Administration's proceedings. In the Senate they never got beyond a committee report. Adams's paper mollified a hostile reaction of the European governments to which Spain had protested the enormity of Jackson's invasion. In England it had an especially healthy result. Castlereagh told Richard Rush, and Rush wrote it down in capital letters, that public opinion was so heated

[27] JQA to George W. Erving, November 28, 1818. To Luis de Onís, November 30, December 2, 1818. *ASPFR,* IV, 539–612. Italics inserted. See also JQA to Richard Rush, No. 11, December 1, No. 14, December 3, 1818, and No. 16, February 1, 1819. DS, *Instructions, U.S. Ministers,* VIII, 279–85, 289–92, 299–301.

[28] "The paper on our right to the Rio-bravo, and the letter to Erving of Nov. 28. are the most important and are among the ablest compositions I have ever seen, both as to logic and style. . . ." Jefferson to Monroe, January 18, 1819. *Writings of Jefferson* (P. L. Ford, ed.), XII, 113–14.

at the executions of Arbuthnot and Ambrister that war would have occurred if the Ministry had but "held up a finger." [29]

Amidst the public excitement in London,[30] Adams's defense of Jackson stayed the hand of the British Government. With a copy of Adams's defense of Jackson on his desk, Castlereagh acknowledged most equably to Rush that Arbuthnot and Ambrister had met their just deserts.[31] To have lifted a finger, not to mention the mighty naval arm of the British Empire for war, would have wrecked Castlereagh's peace policy with the United States at the very moment when it was beginning to bear fruit. It would have embarrassed him seriously in his collaborations with the European powers, so difficult to hold in balance for Britain's larger interests on the Continent.

In Europe the effect of Adams's paper was electrical. That any foreign nation should presume to touch a hair of a British subject under any circumstances and that His Majesty's Government should decline to insist on prompt and signal atonement were a lesson to the world in the independence and power of the United States on its own Continent. The quietude of the British Government under the lash of an outraged London press was astounding.[32]

"There has been scarcely a pistol flashed since the great gun from Washington to Madrid," wrote John Adams Smith from the London Legation to the Secretary of State,[33] describing the effect of his uncle's spectacular state paper.

John Quincy Adams's great gun cleared the air everywhere. It made an even profounder impression on sophisticated Spanish statesmen than

[29] Rush: *Memoranda,* p. 140. Rush printed the quoted words in capitals.

[30] Alexander Everett reported the uniform opposition of the London press to the Treaty of 1819, as well as to the execution of Arbuthnot and Ambrister, and its "malignant and base attacks on the American character, national and individual." Alexander H. Everett to JQA, London, April 19, 1819. Adams MSS.

[31] They "had identified themselves, in part at least, with the Indians, by going amongst them with other purposes than those of innocent trade; by sharing in their sympathies, too actively, when they were upon the eve of hostilities with the United States; by feeding their complaints; by imparting to them counsel; by heightening their resentments, and thus at all events increasing the predisposition which they found existing to the war, if they did not originally provoke it." Rush to JQA, London, No. 54, January 25, 1819. DS, *Despatches, Great Britain,* XXIII.

To the British Minister at Washington, Castlereagh repeated: "I have stated to Mr. Rush that . . . as it is impossible not to admit, that the unfortunate sufferers, whatever their intentions, had been engaged in unauthorized practices of such a description as to have deprived them of any claim on their own Government for interference in their behalf, it has not been deemed fit, under all the circumstances of this case, to instruct you to take any further step in the business." Brooks: *Borderlands,* p. 117, quoting Castlereagh to Bagot, January 2, 1819, from PRO, F.O., 115/34.

[32] A. H. Everett to JQA, Private No. 2, Brussels, April 11, 1819. Adams MSS.

[33] John Adams Smith to JQA, Private No. 38, London, January 24, 1819. Adams MSS.

it did on the less cultivated Indians along the Apalachicola. It settled the Florida Question.

3

Already the Spanish Government had seen the handwriting on the wall when Jackson's riflemen poured into Florida. It had sensed the fact that no help could be expected from Europe. On October 10, 1818 the Marquis de Yrujo, Pizarro's successor in the Foreign Office, dispatched an instruction based on a draft that the retiring *Secretario* had left on his desk. On the side of Texas, Onís was to obtain the Sabine as a boundary if possible. But if absolutely necessary to avoid a break with the United States, recognition of the revolted provinces of Spanish America, or an invasion of Mexico, he was directed to settle the whole territorial question as best he could, preferably by running the boundary along the Missouri to its source and thence to the ocean *as far north as possible.* These instructions arrived in Washington on January 4, 1819.[34]

At last Spain was ready to accept a transcontinental line. On January 11, 1819 Onís informed Adams that new instructions made it possible to renew the negotiation with a view to compromise. A treaty was now in sight. The two diplomatists got down to exchanging drafts and counter-drafts,[35] assisted by the good offices of Hyde de Neuville. They had little difficulty in agreeing in principle on everything but the boundary west from the Sabine to the Pacific Ocean.

For the next five weeks the Secretary of State and the Spanish Minister wrestled back and forth across the Continent.

Onís first offered to carry the boundary due north from the Sabine to the Missouri and there to accept the line of the Missouri and Columbia Rivers.[36] Presumably this meant westward from the headwaters of the Jefferson River, a tributary source, across the Continental Divide to the headwaters of the Snake (Lewis), the route of Lewis and Clark in 1804.[37] On Melish's Map it was very plausible to link the tributaries of the Columbia system with those of the Missouri system in this way and get a natural boundary easy to follow. Accepting this presumption, Onís proposed the Missouri-Columbia line. It would have taken from the United States the great prairie lands of the Louisiana Purchase: most of the present State of Missouri, a third of North Dakota, half of South Dakota, the eastern watersheds of Wyoming and Colorado, all of Nebraska, Kansas, and Oklahoma.

[34] Brooks: *Borderlands,* p. 155.

[35] The President scrutinized all these drafts with great care, and the Cabinet deliberated on them. For the drafts, or *projets,* see *ASPFR,* IV, 616–23.

[36] January 16, 1819. *ASPFR,* IV, 616. See Map 7 D at end of book.

[37] The source of the Columbia (Lake Windermere) does not appear on Melish. A line "westward" from the source of the Jefferson would not strike the Snake.

Such would have been the mutilation of the Louisiana Purchase by the Missouri-Columbia boundary if one locates the source of the Missouri at the headwaters of the Jefferson; but it would have required very little ingenuity to insist that the source of the Missouri was one of the more northern tributaries, like Dearborn's,[38] the Medicine,[38] or the Marias,[38] so that a line westward would have hit Clark's Fork which flows into the Columbia north of 49° N.L. Indeed it could have met the Columbia itself north of the present international boundary. Such an interpretation would have shut the United States out of the Oregon territory altogether. Needless to say, John Quincy Adams had no intention of inviting it.

The United States was about to exchange ratifications [39] of the Anglo-American Convention of October 20, 1818. Adams had not accepted the line of 49° N.L. of that treaty as the northern boundary with Great Britain westward to the Rocky Mountains merely for the purpose of meeting a western boundary with Spain at the Columbia River. On the contrary, he – that is to say, the American plenipotentiaries acting under his responsibility – had fixed the boundary in the British treaty in order to keep the westering way wide open into Oregon. In the Spanish treaty he was not going to throw away all of what he had just staked out against Great Britain beyond the mountains, or even a part of it. He therefore repeated his "ultimatum" of October 31, 1818, which was: the Sabine, from that river at 32° N.L. north to the Red, up the Red to its supposed source at 37° 25′ N.L., 106° 15′ W.L., "or thereabouts" in the "Snow" Mountains, from there northward along the crest of the mountain range to 41° N.L., thence straight west to the Pacific Ocean.[40] The Secretary of State wanted to confirm American sovereignty in the entire Columbia River basin.

By now Onís had received *carte blanche* to settle the western boundary without further instructions.[41] Having saved Texas, he was fighting a valiant rear-guard action to keep for the dissolving Spanish Empire as much as possible of the North West Coast. Adams's proposed line, from the Red River to 41° N.L. and due west, was too close to the upper waters of the Rio Grande and the settlements of Santa Fe and Taos to suit Spain. It also came out on the Pacific Coast too near San Francisco. The obstinate Minister made another effort against the American "ultimatum." He offered the Sabine River, thence by the 94th parallel of west longtitude to the Red River of Natchitoches, up that stream to longitude 95°, thence north again to the Arkansas, and westward up that watercourse to its source; from the source of the Arkansas the line would run "due west" to the source of the "San Clemente or Multnomah, in latitude 41°," and down that putative river to the Pacific Ocean.[42]

38 As of Melish.
39 January 30, 1819.
40 JQA to Onís, January 29, 1819. *ASPFR,* IV, 616. See Map 7 D at end of book.
41 Brooks: *Borderlands,* pp. 157–8.
42 February 1, 1819. *ASPFR,* IV, 616–17. See Map 7 E at end of book.

There is in fact no San Clemente River, or anything like it. Melish depicts a mysterious "San Clementini" as rising just west of the Continental Divide from the headwaters of the Arkansas, slightly north of 41°. It is the upper part of a long southern tributary of the Columbia like the real Snake, only far to the south and west of the latter. Part of its lower course, where Melish called it the Multnomah, corresponds roughly with the small but famous Oregon river Willamette, flowing into the Columbia near the present city of Portland. Adams referred to the Multnomah (an old Indian name for the Willamette) as "the southern branch of the Columbia River." [43]

Thus on the latest map available to John Quincy Adams and Don Luis de Onís it seemed a simple matter to draw a line across the height of land that separated the headwaters of the Arkansas and Columbia just north of 41° N.L. To Onís, at least, the two rivers made a natural boundary, if one must have a boundary all the way through to the Pacific. The new line was far to the south of the Missouri-Columbia line which Onís had proposed in earlier stages, but it would still maintain Spain's title to the North West Coast as far north as the Columbia.

Anxious for a peace that would leave Spain free to turn her entire attention and energies to the revolted colonies of the south, Onís had offered an immense concession in the northwest. He had left all the Louisiana Purchase north of Texas to the United States. If pressed hard enough he would have yielded Texas too in order to get a fixed frontier.[44] This the Secretary of State, operating without the aid of any secret service, unfortunately never knew.

Onís had at last accepted Adams's principle of a boundary all the way across the Continent. But he had not yet abandoned the whole Columbia basin.

The President was inclined to close with Onís's latest proposal, particularly after Hyde de Neuville had indicated that the Spaniard would retreat to 100° W.L. for a north-south line between the Red and the Arkansas Rivers. But the Secretary of State thought it would not suit the nation. A better boundary could be had, he told Monroe, if Onís intended to make any treaty at all.[45] The First Magistrate swayed a little. At his direction Adams made a further concession. He still stuck to 41° N.L. from the Rocky Mountains to the Pacific Ocean, but he offered a buffer of territory for Spain, north of Texas, that would give more protection to the Spanish towns on the upper Rio Grande: instead of demanding the Red River to its source, he was willing to accept a line from the "great bend" of that river, "between 101° and 102° W.L.," due north to the Arkansas, continuing up the Arkansas River to its source, in latitude 41°, thence westward to the source of the San Clemente or Multnomah," also

[43] *Memoirs,* IV, 237.

[44] *Informe de Imáz.*

[45] *Memoirs,* IV, 244. February 4, 1819.

"in latitude 41°," and along that parallel toward the setting sun as far as the Pacific. But the Secretary insisted that the United States should own the boundary rivers completely and all the islands in them; Spain could come up only to the south and west banks.[46]

Onís countered again. He offered the line of 100° W.L. from the Red River to the Arkansas, thence along the middle of the Arkansas to 42° N.L., and along that line west to the Multnomah.[47] Then he proposed to descend the Multnomah (northwest) to 43° N.L., from there to take the parallel of 43° westward to the South Sea.[48] This would have left the mouth of the Columbia River entirely within the American zone. It would have yielded most of the coastline of Oregon – all except one degree. But it still left Spain a hold on the Columbia basin, on the south and east bank of the Multnomah or Willamette, at least in its upper waters.

James Monroe called his "Administration" together to consider Onís's latest offer. Agreement seemed so near that the President and his Cabinet, except the Secretary of State, were willing to accept it rather than jeopardize a treaty in the last days of its negotiation.[49] The Floridas had been secured, protecting New Orleans on the east. The line of the Sabine would secure Louisiana on the west. General Jackson, whom the President directed Adams to consult, thought Onís's proposed terms would do. He said that the possession of the Floridas was of such great importance to the southern frontier of the United States, so essential even to their safety, that the vast majority of people in the nation would be satisfied with the western boundary, as proposed, *if the Floridas were obtained.* He showed the Secretary on a map the operations of the British forces during the War of 1812. As long as the mouths of the Florida rivers were made accessible to a foreign naval force, Jackson explained, there would be no security for the southern part of the United States.[50] Nobody realized better than the hero of New Orleans the significance of the Florida pistol-barrel if held against the Mississippi River by a foreign enemy.

With Florida secured, what did it matter whether the southern bound-

[46] *Memoirs,* IV, 246. JQA to Onís, February 6, 1819. *ASPFR,* IV, 617. See Map 7 E at end of book.

[47] February 9, 1819. *ASPFR,* IV, 617. Onís said, along that 42d parallel of latitude to the source of the Multnomah, the San Clementini, which is not possible even on Melish's Map.

[48] Onís to JQA, February 9, 1819. *ASPFR,* IV, 617–18. See Map 7 F at end of book.

[49] *Memoirs,* IV, 250.

[50] *Memoirs,* IV, 239. Jackson to Monroe, June 20, 1820. *Correspondence of Jackson,* III, 28.

In view of the fact that American diplomacy had been conditioned in Washington ever since 1805 to try first for the line of the Colorado River of Texas and then to fall back to the Sabine as a boundary in the west if necessary to obtain the Floridas in the east, one must somewhat qualify President Monroe's statements during the Missouri discussions of 1819–20 and afterward that he did not choose to take Texas if only for fear that it would stimulate a harmful sectional controversy over slavery.

ary of the United States beyond the Rocky Mountains be placed at 41° or 43°? But Adams still stood his ground for the Pacific Northwest. Finally, as if to humor the obstinate patriot, the "Administration" authorized the Secretary of State to take from Onís the line of west longitude 100° between the Red River and the Arkansas, and the line of 43° north latitude from the Rocky Mountains to the South Sea, *if* he could get no better boundary terms.[51] Adams accordingly made another try for 102° W.L. and 41° N.L. in those sectors.[52] That is to say, he repeated his last offer of February 6, except that he stipulated more precisely the line of 102° W.L. from the Red River north to the Arkansas rather than "between 101° and 102°."

The long diplomatic contest was now narrowed down to two degrees of latitude in remote reaches of the Continent. Onís was in no position to resist much more. Thanks to Adams's defense of General Jackson's invasion of Florida, Monroe had Congress behind him. If Spain did not come to terms, that body would authorize the President to take possession of the Floridas by force and claim Texas as indemnity for the expenses of so doing. With the odds all against him, the tenacious Spanish Minister finally offered to split the difference between 43° and 41°. On the 15th of February, Hyde de Neuville came into Adams's office to say that Onís would yield the line of 42°. But, he declared, Spain could not accept the humiliation of being restricted to the south bank of the rivers. It was a point of honor.[53]

In a spirit of compromise Adams accepted the line of 42° N.L. from the Rocky Mountains to the Pacific Ocean (the present northern boundary of California, Nevada, and western Utah), and the line of 100° W.L. from the Red River to the Arkansas.[54] He would not yield the river watercourses themselves, even though it was the custom of diplomacy to take the mid-channel, or *thalweg,* of rivers for boundary.

Hyde de Neuville protested that this would be humiliating to Spain. "I can see no humiliation in it," the Secretary briskly told the French Minister. "We are to agree upon a boundary, for which purpose the bank of the river is more simple and less liable to occasion future controversy than the middle of the river. . . . It is of no importance to Spain, who will never have any settlements on those rivers. But the United States will have very extensive settlements upon them within a very few years."[55]

Only half the width of the boundary rivers separated the two contestants for a continent. Adams stood doggedly at the water's farthest edge.

[51] *Memoirs,* IV, 248–56.

According to Melish, the parallel of 43° N.L. crossed the upper waters of the Snake River (in the southern part of the present State of Idaho), and also, farther west, the Multnomah.

[52] February 13, 1819. *ASPFR,* IV, 619. See Map 7 F at end of book.

[53] *Memoirs,* IV, 255. *ASPFR,* IV, 621.

[54] See Map 7 G at end of book.

[55] *Memoirs,* IV, 255.

The Cabinet was excited, trembling for the success of the negotiation. The President was nervous, alarmed, eager to meet Spain in midstream. At a White House reception the evening of February 18 he shook hands most cordially with Onís.

"I will do anything you want," he said. "I have had a personal esteem for you ever since the first day I dealt with you. Have a glass of wine with me."

Onís hastened to write home that all was agreed, not without the resentment of Secretary Adams, who could not forget the shame of having his ultimatum destroyed in all its points.[56]

Monroe's intervention at the eleventh hour made the south bank of the river a point of honor with Adams too. He told Hyde de Neuville that Onís had misunderstood the President's meaning.

"The Secretary of State is the officer through whom the negotiation is to be conducted," he reminded the French Minister. "All immediate applications to the President concerning it are improper. I have taken and shall take no notice of it in this instance; but the President himself will be much and justly displeased if he has reason to think that a complimentary expression of politeness used by him in answer to a remark made to him by a Foreign Minister at the drawing-room were to be construed into an abandonment of an important principle in a pending negotiation."

"That is perfectly just," acknowledged Hyde de Neuville.

When the point came up in the last Cabinet meeting before the treaty, Monroe did not press it.

Onís gave in. He agreed to accept the south and west banks of the Sabine, the Red, and the Arkansas Rivers, where they marked the boundary.

"You are harder to deal with than the President," he said when they met to edit the final text.[57]

4

At last the famous treaty was completely drafted, punctiliously, according to the *alternat*. At Adams's suggestion they agreed to wait two days until Washington's Birthday for formal signature. It is proper now to notice its terms.

Article I proclaimed a firm and inviolable peace and friendship between the United States and His Catholic Majesty.

By Article II the King of Spain ceded to the United States "all the territories *which belong to him,*[58] situated to the Eastward of the Mississippi, known by the name of East and West Florida."

Was West Florida one of the territories that belonged to him at the

[56] Onís to Yrujo, February 19, 1819. Quoted by Brooks: *Borderlands*, p. 162.
[57] *Memoirs*, IV, 269–70.
[58] Italics inserted.

time of the cession? Jefferson and his successors had claimed that since the Louisiana Purchase it was a part of the United States. Onís tried to word this article so as to constitute an unqualified cession of both provinces. By accepting such a wording the United States would have admitted that it had annexed West Florida without any title. Adams resisted any description of the provinces that would convey such an imputation. A comma placed between the word "territories" and the word "which" would have made it absolutely clear that West Florida as well as East Florida was territory that belonged to the King of Spain and was being ceded by him. Neither the English nor the Spanish texts of the original treaty, now in the Department of State Records in the National Archives, contains a comma.

With the territory went, of course, all public property and records.

Article III fixed a transcontinental boundary line between the two countries west of the Mississippi. It began at the mouth of the Sabine River in the sea and continued north along the western bank of that river to the 32d parallel of latitude, thence by a line due north to the Red River, thence westward up the south bank of the Red River to 100° west longitude, thence across the said Red River and due north to the south bank of the Arkansas and westward along that bank to the source in latitude 42° north, and thence westward by that parallel to the South Sea, the whole as laid down in Melish's Map.[59]

The Spanish King ceded to the United States all rights, claims, and pretensions to any territories east and north of the agreed boundary, and, reciprocally, the United States renounced all titles to the west and south of it.

Spanish subjects were to have the right of navigating the Sabine River to the sea, and the Red and Arkansas Rivers only in those portions where they formed the boundary.

Article IV provided for commissioners of each Government to survey the boundary thus established. Before they could meet, Mexico had succeeded to the sovereignty of Spain. Before a commission of the United States and Mexico could mark out the inherited boundary, the latter nation had ceded California and New Mexico to the United States in the Treaty of Guadalupe Hidalgo, signed February 2, 1848, twenty-one days before the death of John Quincy Adams. It is not recorded whether he ever heard the news.

Article V provided for religious freedom for all within the ceded territory, and permission for anybody to remove with the proceeds of his property to Spanish territory if he so desired.

Article VI promised incorporation of the ceded territory within the Union of the United States as soon as might be consistent with the prin-

[59] See Map 7 F at end of book. In case the source of the Arkansas did not lie in 42° N.L. (which proved to be the case), then the boundary was to run north or south (it proved north) from that source until it hit 42° N.L.

ciples of the Federal Constitution, with enjoyment of all the privileges, rights, and immunities of citizens of the United States.

Article VII provided for evacuation of all officers and troops of His Catholic Majesty within six months after the exchange of ratifications.

Article VIII stated that all royal land grants in the ceded region made before January 24, 1818 should be "ratified and confirmed to the persons in possession of the lands, to the same extent that the same grants would be valid if the territories had remained under the dominions of His Catholic Majesty." All grants made after January 24, 1818, date of the first proposal of His Catholic Majesty for the cession of the Floridas, were to be null and void.

When the Spanish Government concluded that it would have to cede Florida to the United States, a court camarilla had prevailed upon Ferdinand to grant private title to most of the land in the lost province to three court favorites in Madrid: the Count of Puñonrostro, under date of December 17, 1817; the Duke of Alagón, under the same date; and Don Pedro de Vargas, under date of January 25, 1818. Thus the first two grants – which comprised all of East Florida except the east coast [60] – had not been outlawed by the treaty date of January 24, 1818. Adams had first proposed invalidating, in the treaty, all land grants made by the Spanish crown after August 11, 1802 (date of signature of the Spanish-American claims convention). Onís would have been quite willing to accept the limitation if it had proved necessary in order to secure a frontier between Spain and the United States in the west, but it did not prove necessary. As it was, he was able to advance the date to January 24, 1818; all grants made after that date were specified to be invalid.

When Adams and Onís read this article to each other before signing, Onís glanced up in a peculiar way, his countenance showing some muscular play.

"What," the Spaniard asked, "do you understand by words 'shall *complete* them'?" referring to the completion of Spanish land grants in the Floridas.

"It is to confirm the benefit of the exception," the Secretary replied, "to grantees in possession, and having commenced settlements."

Onís assented to this explanation. His visage beamed with a ray as if to say: "I have him in my toils."

The look gave Adams a moment of uneasiness. Perhaps there was a snare. But he himself had drafted the article, except for the inserted date.[61] So he continued reading the treaty, article by article, with the Spanish Minister, and they signed it.

Adams had allowed himself to be careless about the royal land grants. As a result he badly stubbed his diplomatic toe. It was Henry Clay, of all persons, who was to awaken him to the facts. Within three weeks after the

[60] For map see Miller: *Treaties*, III, 41.

[61] JQA to C. J. Ingersoll, Washington, August 7, 1821. Adams MSS.

treaty had been signed, the Speaker called on President Monroe to inform him that the grants had been made on January 23, 1818, the day *before* the date stipulated in the treaty! If this were true, the President notified Adams, "a most shameful fraud has been practised on this government." [62] Clay was wrong in some details, but correct in substance. To his chagrin the Secretary found, from his own archives, in the dispatches from Erving, Minister to Spain, that the Puñonrostro and Alagón grants had been made before the outlawing date. This discovery dampened all the vanity and self-conceit that he had derived in bringing the negotiations to a successful conclusion. It confirmed his uneasy inner feeling that the treaty was too good to be true.[63]

To repair the carelessness the Secretary of State, with the President's hesitant backing,[64] instructed the Minister in Madrid to insist, when exchanging ratifications of the treaty, upon an express renunciation by the King of the three grants.[65] This eventually was done, but not without much delay and difficulty.[66]

Article IX mutually renounced all claims of either party against the other. The United States promised to make satisfaction for any injuries sustained by Spanish officers and inhabitants by the late operations of the American Army in Florida.

Article X canceled the Claims Convention of 1802,[67] which Spain had belatedly ratified as a gesture of conciliation on the eve of the treaty. Because of the renunciation of all claims it was no longer necessary.

Article XI provided that the United States would assume payment of the claims of its citizens, renounced as against Spain, up to a total of $5,000,000, and provided for a commission to fix the amount of these claims.

Article XII renewed Pinckney's Treaty of 1795, excepting those articles that had been transcended by the Transcontinental Treaty (II, III, IV, XXI). One of these articles (IV) was the one in which His Most Catholic

[62] James Monroe to JQA, March 8, 1819. Adams MSS.

[63] *Memoirs,* IV, 288. March 1819.

[64] *Memoirs,* IV, 290. March 9, 1819.

[65] Brooks: *Borderlands, passim* (see index), relates the part that the land grants played in the negotiations, referring to Miller: *Treaties,* III, 20–3, 42–9, for the complex details, with dates, and a map of the grants. See also JQA: *Memoirs,* IV, 265, 287, 289–91, V, 271, *et passim,* and *Writings,* VI, 537. In Spain these grants reeked with corruption. As soon as it became apparent that the treaty would annul them, interested parties tried to assign parts of them to American citizens and to influence members of Congress. Joseph Bloomfield to JQA, with enclosures, Burlington, April 12, 1819. Adams MSS. Fortunately there was an honest Administration in Washington at that time, which insisted on cancellation of the grants. The possibilities of corruption of this kind are illustrated by the history of the notorious Perkins Claim and the corruption in Congress at the time of the Alaska Purchase.

[66] For the sequence of events connected with ratification, see below, Ch. XVII.

[67] Providing for the arbitration of American spoliation claims arising since the previous disposal of claims under the Treaty of 1795 (Pinckney's Treaty).

Majesty had guaranteed that the whole length of the Mississippi River, from its source to the ocean, should be free only to his subjects and to the citizens of the United States. Spain's recognition of American sovereignty to Louisiana and West Florida had made that article at last obsolete; no longer could she claim that any portion of her territory touched the river. Thenceforth the Father of Waters poured his murky flood from Lake Itasca to the Gulf of Mexico untinctured by the slightest color of any foreign servitude.

In one respect the Transcontinental Treaty made an important change in a continued article of Pinckney's Treaty. Article XV of the latter, now renewed, had stipulated free ships free goods. Adams now added to it the proviso which he had formulated for the Prussian Treaty of 1799, but had not found it necessary to use at that time: "If either of the contracting parties shall be at war with a third party, and the other neutral, the flag of the neutral shall cover the property of enemies whose Government acknowledge this principle, and not of others." This "Adams formula" was to become a standard feature of American maritime treaties.

Article XIII provided for the return reciprocally of deserters from merchant ships.

Article XIV stated for the record that the United States never had received from France any compensation for spoliations on American ships in Spanish territorial waters, "for the satisfaction of which provision is made by this treaty" (in Article XI), thus leaving grounds for Spain to collect from France if she could.

Article XV admitted Spanish ships and products for twelve years to the ports of Pensacola and St. Augustine without paying any higher duties than imposed on American ships and goods of the same kind.

Article XVI provided for the exchange of ratifications within six months.

5

At eleven o'clock in the morning of February 22, 1819, natal anniversary of Adams's illustrious patron, John Quincy Adams and Onís affixed their signatures to the treaty in the office of the Secretary of State. Late that night, in a mood of religious exaltation, Adams made this characteristic record in his Diary of his contribution to the Manifest Destiny of his country:

> It was near one in the morning when I closed the day with ejaculations of fervent gratitude to the Giver of all good. It was, perhaps, the most important day of my life. What the consequences may be of the compact this day signed with Spain is known only to the all-wise and all-beneficent Disposer of events, who has brought it about in a manner utterly unexpected and by means the most extraordinary and unforeseen. Its prospects are propitious and flattering in an eminent degree. May they be realized by the same superintending

bounty that produced them! May no disappointment embitter the hope which this event warrants us in cherishing, and may its future influence on the destinies of my country be as extensive and as favorable as our warmest anticipations can paint! Let no idle and unfounded exultation take possession of my mind, as if I could ascribe to my own foresight or exertions any portion of the event. It is the work of an intelligent and all-embracing Cause. May it speed as it has begun! for, without a continuation of the blessings already showered down upon it, all that has been done will be worse than useless, and vain.

The acquisition of the Floridas has long been an object of earnest desire to this country. The acknowledgment of a definite line of boundary to the South Sea forms a great epocha in our history. The first proposal of it in this negotiation was my own, and I trust it is now secured beyond the reach of revocation. It was not even among our claims by the Treaty of Independence with Great Britain. It was not even among our pretensions under the purchase of Louisiana — for that gave us only the range of the Mississippi and its waters. I first introduced it in the written proposal of 31st October last, after having discussed it verbally both with Onís and De Neuville. It is the only peculiar and appropriate right acquired by this treaty in the event of its ratification. I record the first assertion of this claim for the United States as my own, because it is known to be mine perhaps only to the members of the present Administration, and may perhaps never be known to the public — and if ever known, will soon and easily be forgotten.[68]

Two days later, February 24, 1819, the Senate unanimously advised and consented to ratification of the treaty. The President immediately signed it, and the Secretary of State and the Spanish Minister sent authentic copies to Madrid for exchange of ratifications within the six months' period prescribed in the instrument. The very day that the Senate thus accepted John Quincy Adams's Transcontinental Treaty without an opposing vote a committee of five of that same body brought in a report severely censuring General Jackson for his activities in Florida, military operations that, in Adams's words, "had been among the most immediate and prominent causes that produced the treaty"! [69] As we have seen, the report came to nothing. Even its authors voted for the treaty.

Could John Quincy Adams have got Texas too, if he had held out for it sufficiently in the negotiations? Presumably yes, at least to the Colorado, perhaps to the Rio Grande, for we know that Onís had received instructions to yield whatever was necessary in that direction. But the fact is that under Monroe's direction no determined effort was made to get Texas. As the President had stated, in his annual message of December 2,

[68] *Memoirs,* IV, 274. [69] *Memoirs,* IV, 278.

1817, the United States stood ready to exchange for Spanish East Florida "something of equal value, west of the Mississippi." It was, he added in parentheses, "a fact well known to the world." That something was the imperfect American claim to Texas. As Adams himself recalled in his old age on the floor of the House of Representatives: "That negotiation was for the purpose of Florida; and as to the boundaries of Louisiana, they had been considered as settled long before."[70] President Monroe in 1819 was abundantly satisfied with Florida. He would have been satisfied with much less than what Adams secured in the final treaty. He himself would never have thought of drawing a boundary line north of Texas from the Rocky Mountains to the Pacific Ocean.

It has sometimes been assumed that Adams relinquished Texas in exchange for Oregon. Onís so averred in his famous *Memoria*.[71] There is no substantiation for this statement. President Monroe had no idea of getting a title from Spain to Oregon as compensation for giving up Texas. Texas was yielded in return for Florida. It was Adams, and Adams alone, who saw the opening for a break through to the Pacific. It was a brilliant plunge. Oregon was his most massive contribution to Manifest Destiny.

Time has confirmed Adams's pardonable pride in his superb if not perfect achievement. Even without Texas the Transcontinental Treaty with Spain was the greatest diplomatic victory won by any single individual in the history of the United States.

[70] *Congressional Globe*, 29th Cong., 1st Sess., I, 663.

[71] See above, n. 25. John Forsyth to JQA, Private, Madrid, September 1, 1820. Adams MSS.

CHAPTER XVII
The Independence of Latin America (1815–1822)

And now, as at the early stage of the French Revolution, we have ardent spirits for rushing into the conflict, without looking to the consequences.

JOHN QUINCY ADAMS TO JOHN ADAMS, WASHINGTON, DECEMBER 21, 1817

LIKE North American independence the revolution of the Spanish provinces in South America prospered on the distresses of Europe. The popular rising in the Peninsula against Napoleon's usurpation paralyzed the authority of the Spanish Empire and provided the opportunity for successful revolt of the overseas colonies against centuries of oppression. It remained for the New World to preserve its emancipation against the legitimist reaction of the Old World after Waterloo. The questions of Latin-American independence,[1] and of America versus Europe, presented themselves to Adams, under President Monroe's guiding responsibility, at the climax of his diplomatic career. Together they constituted nothing less than the problem of how to secure for the New World the full fruitage of the Age of Emancipation: self-determination, independence, and human liberty under popular sovereignty.

1

John Quincy Adams, like most of his fellow citizens, even the most distinguished, had shown little interest in Spanish America and less sympathy for its culture and institutions. His diplomatic career had been concerned altogether with the relations between Europe and the United States during the French Revolution and the Napoleonic wars. His wide reading had not taken him into Spanish literature or history, and he did not really know the Castilian language. He did not regard the Latin-American revolutions as sympathetically as President Monroe, who had

[1] The persistent reader will detect in this and the following two chapters occasional passages taken from my *Early Diplomatic Missions from Buenos Aires to the United States, 1811–1824* (American Antiquarian Society, Worcester, 1940), and *Latin American Policy of the United States* (Harcourt, Brace & Co., New York, 1943).

had a long experience with Spanish affairs as Minister to Madrid and as Secretary of State. He did not consider the cause of the revolted colonies to be identical with that of the North American Revolution of his own boyhood.[2] Nor was he a man to be influenced by the current patriot propaganda, against American neutrality, set on foot by agents of the new states seeking military succors and recognition of their independence. Adams's mental image of the peoples to the south reflected an ignorant miscegenated populace benighted by centuries of political and ecclesiastical tyranny, doubtfully capable of self-government, hardly profitable for the communion of free men. Events were to correct this distorted vision, but only at the convenience of North American foreign policy.

Twenty years before, the French Revolution, to the dismay of President George Washington, had been a powerful agent in the crystallization of American political parties: Federalists and Republicans, the party of the British interest, and the party of the French interest, so foreign observers dubbed them. Each party in its time had been a medium for foreign intrigue against the policy of the Government in power: the Republicans against the foreign policy of Washington and John Adams, the Federalists against that of Jefferson and Madison. It was like the Patriots and the Dutch Orangemen whom young John Quincy Adams had seen disputing away the liberties of the Netherlands. Only the broad Atlantic and the continuing distresses of European strife and war, and George Washington's wise foreign policy, had saved the United States from a similar fate during the great European conflict. Now, as Secretary of State, Adams beheld the old lesson writ large on the horizon of South America. The Spanish-American revolutions, like the French Revolution in Washington's time, would soon awaken in the United States another painful political division for the advantage of foreign powers.[3]

John Quincy Adams's whole diplomatic career, like that of his father, had confirmed the lessons of Washington's Farewell Address: history and experience proved foreign influence to be one of the most baleful foes of republican government. Both Adamses[4] believed in neutrality for Amer-

[2] JQA to A. H. Everett, Washington, December 29, 1817, suggesting a series of newspaper articles along these lines. *Writings,* VI, 280–3.

[3] JQA to Governor W. Plumer of New Hampshire, Washington, December 15, 1817. Adams MSS. JQA to JA, December 21, 1817. *Writings,* VI, 276.

[4] "Our national sympathy with the patriots of S. America is natural and inevitable, though I hope not uncontroulable.

"How will humanity be affected? How shall we be affected? They will be independent, no doubt, but will they be free? General Ignorance can never be free, and the Roman Religion is incompatible with a free government. South America, then, independent of Spain, will be governed by a dozen Royalists independent of each other, and each of them seeking alliances in Europe, and in the United States. Suppose a Confederation of these little sovereigns, will it not be a perpetual struggle which shall be first?

"The relapse of Europe into the principles of monkery and despotism is indeed an awful and direful and rueful subject of consideration. It is portentous of calamities

ica in the wars of the Old World, and in the wars
even wars for liberty itself, fought in the Land o
absolute monarchy of Europe: neutrality in thoug
deed, irrespective of the merits of the contest.[5]

Secretary Adams concluded that Great Britain would
and develop the emancipated trade of the dissolving Span
would be backward about recognizing the independence of th
The Tory Government would be inclined to support its ally,
dinand VII, in efforts to salvage imperial sovereignty over some
reformed colonial system open to British trade. On general prin
London would be likely to oppose Washington. The big question w
would the British Government join in any policy of the Holy Alliance fo
the forceful restoration of Spanish authority in the New World? If Castlereagh were to do so, it would be foolish for the United States to brook the sanction of a united Europe by any premature and crusading recognition of the uncertain republics to the south.

Actually it was Castlereagh's strategy to keep Adams guessing as long as possible, in order to prevent the United States from recognizing a group of new republican nations, so incompatible with the world of restored legitimist monarchies. If and when recognition eventually did become necessary, Britain's eminent Foreign Minister preferred a constellation of Latin-American monarchies under British tutelage.[6]

2

The Latin-American Question, provoked by the movements of the Buenos Aires revolutionary agent in the United States, Manuel Hermenejildo de Aguirre, came up for discussion a few weeks after Adams had taken up his office in the Department of State. In a Cabinet meeting of October 30, 1817 President Monroe presented the following questions:

"Has the executive power to acknowledge the independence of the new states whose independence is not recognized by the parent country and between which parties war exists?

"Is sending a minister equal to recognition?

---

beyond the reach of all human calculation. It is enough to make the best Christians pray for another Voltaire.

"I hope our Government will stand fast in its impregnable fortress neutrality as long as possible," JA to JQA, Quincy, January 5, 1818. Adams MSS.

[5] "By the usual principles of international law, the state of *neutrality* recognizes the cause of both parties to the contest to be *just* – that is, avoids all consideration of the *merits* of the contest." JQA to Gallatin, Department of State, May 19, 1818. *Writings*, VI, 317.

[6] Charles K. Webster: "Castlereagh and the Spanish Colonies," *English Historical Review,* XXVII (No. cv, January 1912), 78–95, XXX (No. cxx, October 1915), 631–45.

it expedient for the United States to recognize Buenos Aires or oth
lted provinces?
What ought to be the future conduct of the U. States towards Sp
nsidering the evasion practised by her government and amounti
refusal to make reparation for injuries?
"Is it expedient to break up the Amelia Island establishment w
of a piratical and highly mischievous nature?
"Is it expedient to act as was accorded in the previous May
pended, i.e. to send a commission to South America to repo
progress of the revolution and the probability of its success?"

Nothing could illustrate better than these queries the inter
of the Florida Question, then in negotiation with Spain, and
of recognition of the new Latin-American countries ce
Buenos Aires. The Cabinet decided affirmatively the last t
Adams argued successfully against the expediency of ack
independence of Buenos Aires and urged that the next di
United States Legation in Madrid be awaited before as
attitude toward Spain; this was also agreed to.[8]

Before Adams had left London, President Monro
rising tide of public sympathy for the revolutionary st
send a fact-finding commission to South America to r
of events. Various delays had prevented the departu
– John Graham, Chief Clerk of the Department of
ney of Delaware, formerly a member of Congres
of the United States; and Theodoric Bland of Ba
Latin-American enthusiast[9] – till after Adams re
while popular sentiment everywhere was risin
triots of the south. Ambitious political person
private individuals would be sure to capitaliz
sympathy for the independence of the new g
appeal of an American System free of the p

Henry Clay, expansionist of 1812, alre
sensed political advantages in it for him
terest in the "Southern Brethren" reflect

[7] From a memorandum of "October, 181
the discussion in a summary way in his Mem
clarity I have quoted the paraphrase of t
Griffin: *The United States and the Disr*
(New York, 1937), pp. 40–1.

[8] *Memoirs*, IV, 13–15. July 28, 1818.

[9] See Laura A. Bornholdt: "Baltimo
Independence." Ph.D. thesis, Yale Uni
ting himself attached to the mission
one year with 100 per cent interest
master of Baltimore, had made to
arrera, in 1816.

ica in the wars of the Old World, and in the wars of the New World too, even wars for liberty itself, fought in the Land of Columbus against an absolute monarchy of Europe: neutrality in thought and neutrality in deed, irrespective of the merits of the contest.[5]

Secretary Adams concluded that Great Britain would seek to hold open and develop the emancipated trade of the dissolving Spanish Empire but would be backward about recognizing the independence of the new states. The Tory Government would be inclined to support its ally, King Ferdinand VII, in efforts to salvage imperial sovereignty over some sort of reformed colonial system open to British trade. On general principles London would be likely to oppose Washington. The big question was: would the British Government join in any policy of the Holy Alliance for the forceful restoration of Spanish authority in the New World? If Castlereagh were to do so, it would be foolish for the United States to brook the sanction of a united Europe by any premature and crusading recognition of the uncertain republics to the south.

Actually it was Castlereagh's strategy to keep Adams guessing as long as possible, in order to prevent the United States from recognizing a group of new republican nations, so incompatible with the world of restored legitimist monarchies. If and when recognition eventually did become necessary, Britain's eminent Foreign Minister preferred a constellation of Latin-American monarchies under British tutelage.[6]

2

The Latin-American Question, provoked by the movements of the Buenos Aires revolutionary agent in the United States, Manuel Hermenejildo de Aguirre, came up for discussion a few weeks after Adams had taken up his office in the Department of State. In a Cabinet meeting of October 30, 1817 President Monroe presented the following questions:

"Has the executive power to acknowledge the independence of the new states whose independence is not recognized by the parent country and between which parties war exists?

"Is sending a minister equal to recognition?

---

beyond the reach of all human calculation. It is enough to make the best Christians pray for another Voltaire.

"I hope our Government will stand fast in its impregnable fortress neutrality as long as possible." JA to JQA, Quincy, January 5, 1818. Adams MSS.

[5] "By the usual principles of international law, the state of *neutrality* recognizes the cause of both parties to the contest to be *just* — that is, avoids all consideration of the *merits* of the contest." JQA to Gallatin, Department of State, May 19, 1818. *Writings*, VI, 317.

[6] Charles K. Webster: "Castlereagh and the Spanish Colonies," *English Historical Review*, XXVII (No. cv, January 1912), 78–95, XXX (No. cxx, October 1915), 631–45.

"Is it expedient for the United States to recognize Buenos Aires or other revolted provinces?

"What ought to be the future conduct of the U. States towards Spain, considering the evasion practised by her government and amounting to a refusal to make reparation for injuries?

"Is it expedient to break up the Amelia Island establishment which is of a piratical and highly mischievous nature?

"Is it expedient to act as was accorded in the previous May and suspended, i.e. to send a commission to South America to report on the progress of the revolution and the probability of its success?"[7]

Nothing could illustrate better than these queries the interrelationship of the Florida Question, then in negotiation with Spain, and the question of recognition of the new Latin-American countries centered upon Buenos Aires. The Cabinet decided affirmatively the last two questions. Adams argued successfully against the expediency of acknowledging the independence of Buenos Aires and urged that the next dispatch from the United States Legation in Madrid be awaited before assuming any new attitude toward Spain; this was also agreed to.[8]

Before Adams had left London, President Monroe, impelled by the rising tide of public sympathy for the revolutionary states, had decided to send a fact-finding commission to South America to report on the progress of events. Various delays had prevented the departure of the Commission – John Graham, Chief Clerk of the Department of State; Caesar A. Rodney of Delaware, formerly a member of Congress and Attorney General of the United States; and Theodoric Bland of Baltimore, a self-interested Latin-American enthusiast[9] – till after Adams reached Washington. Meanwhile popular sentiment everywhere was rising to the cause of the patriots of the south. Ambitious political personalities as well as interested private individuals would be sure to capitalize upon the prevailing public sympathy for the independence of the new governments and the universal appeal of an American System free of the power politics of the Old World.

Henry Clay, expansionist of 1812, already felt the new current and sensed political advantages in it for himself. The increasing popular interest in the "Southern Brethren" reflected the essential anti-Spanish feel-

[7] From a memorandum of "October, 1817" in the Monroe Papers, LC. JQA notes the discussion in a summary way in his *Memoirs,* IV, 15, for that date. For the sake of clarity I have quoted the paraphrase of these questions offered by Charles Carroll Griffin: *The United States and the Disruption of the Spanish Empire, 1810–1822* (New York, 1937), pp. 40–1.

[8] *Memoirs,* IV, 13–15. July 28, 1818.

[9] See Laura A. Bornholdt: "Baltimore as a Port of Propaganda for Latin American Independence." Ph.D. thesis, Yale University, 1945. Bland's principal purpose in getting himself attached to the mission was to collect in Chile a loan of $4,000, due in one year with 100 per cent interest, which his son-in-law Joseph H. Skinner, Postmaster of Baltimore, had made to the self-constituted Chilean agent José Miguel Carrera, in 1816.

ica in the wars of the Old World, and in the wars of the New World too, even wars for liberty itself, fought in the Land of Columbus against an absolute monarchy of Europe: neutrality in thought and neutrality in deed, irrespective of the merits of the contest.[5]

Secretary Adams concluded that Great Britain would seek to hold open and develop the emancipated trade of the dissolving Spanish Empire but would be backward about recognizing the independence of the new states. The Tory Government would be inclined to support its ally, King Ferdinand VII, in efforts to salvage imperial sovereignty over some sort of reformed colonial system open to British trade. On general principles London would be likely to oppose Washington. The big question was: would the British Government join in any policy of the Holy Alliance for the forceful restoration of Spanish authority in the New World? If Castlereagh were to do so, it would be foolish for the United States to brook the sanction of a united Europe by any premature and crusading recognition of the uncertain republics to the south.

Actually it was Castlereagh's strategy to keep Adams guessing as long as possible, in order to prevent the United States from recognizing a group of new republican nations, so incompatible with the world of restored legitimist monarchies. If and when recognition eventually did become necessary, Britain's eminent Foreign Minister preferred a constellation of Latin-American monarchies under British tutelage.[6]

2

The Latin-American Question, provoked by the movements of the Buenos Aires revolutionary agent in the United States, Manuel Hermenejildo de Aguirre, came up for discussion a few weeks after Adams had taken up his office in the Department of State. In a Cabinet meeting of October 30, 1817 President Monroe presented the following questions:

"Has the executive power to acknowledge the independence of the new states whose independence is not recognized by the parent country and between which parties war exists?

"Is sending a minister equal to recognition?

---

beyond the reach of all human calculation. It is enough to make the best Christians pray for another Voltaire.

"I hope our Government will stand fast in its impregnable fortress neutrality as long as possible." JA to JQA, Quincy, January 5, 1818. Adams MSS.

[5] "By the usual principles of international law, the state of *neutrality* recognizes the cause of both parties to the contest to be *just* — that is, avoids all consideration of the *merits* of the contest." JQA to Gallatin, Department of State, May 19, 1818. *Writings*, VI, 317.

[6] Charles K. Webster: "Castlereagh and the Spanish Colonies," *English Historical Review*, XXVII (No. cv, January 1912), 78–95, XXX (No. cxx, October 1915), 631–45.

"Is it expedient for the United States to recognize Buenos Aires or other revolted provinces?

"What ought to be the future conduct of the U. States towards Spain, considering the evasion practised by her government and amounting to a refusal to make reparation for injuries?

"Is it expedient to break up the Amelia Island establishment which is of a piratical and highly mischievous nature?

"Is it expedient to act as was accorded in the previous May and suspended, i.e. to send a commission to South America to report on the progress of the revolution and the probability of its success?" [7]

Nothing could illustrate better than these queries the interrelationship of the Florida Question, then in negotiation with Spain, and the question of recognition of the new Latin-American countries centered upon Buenos Aires. The Cabinet decided affirmatively the last two questions. Adams argued successfully against the expediency of acknowledging the independence of Buenos Aires and urged that the next dispatch from the United States Legation in Madrid be awaited before assuming any new attitude toward Spain; this was also agreed to.[8]

Before Adams had left London, President Monroe, impelled by the rising tide of public sympathy for the revolutionary states, had decided to send a fact-finding commission to South America to report on the progress of events. Various delays had prevented the departure of the Commission – John Graham, Chief Clerk of the Department of State; Caesar A. Rodney of Delaware, formerly a member of Congress and Attorney General of the United States; and Theodoric Bland of Baltimore, a self-interested Latin-American enthusiast [9] – till after Adams reached Washington. Meanwhile popular sentiment everywhere was rising to the cause of the patriots of the south. Ambitious political personalities as well as interested private individuals would be sure to capitalize upon the prevailing public sympathy for the independence of the new governments and the universal appeal of an American System free of the power politics of the Old World.

Henry Clay, expansionist of 1812, already felt the new current and sensed political advantages in it for himself. The increasing popular interest in the "Southern Brethren" reflected the essential anti-Spanish feel-

[7] From a memorandum of "October, 1817" in the Monroe Papers, LC. JQA notes the discussion in a summary way in his *Memoirs,* IV, 15, for that date. For the sake of clarity I have quoted the paraphrase of these questions offered by Charles Carroll Griffin: *The United States and the Disruption of the Spanish Empire, 1810–1822* (New York, 1937), pp. 40–1.

[8] *Memoirs,* IV, 13–15. July 28, 1818.

[9] See Laura A. Bornholdt: "Baltimore as a Port of Propaganda for Latin American Independence." Ph.D. thesis, Yale University, 1945. Bland's principal purpose in getting himself attached to the mission was to collect in Chile a loan of $4,000, due in one year with 100 per cent interest, which his son-in-law Joseph H. Skinner, Postmaster of Baltimore, had made to the self-constituted Chilean agent José Miguel Carrera, in 1816.

ing of his section, the Mississippi Valley, and also the Jeffersonian tincture of his political apprenticeship, but his campaign for recognition of independence of the new states revealed even more his personal ambition. The Kentucky leader discerned a new issue of national and international dimensions to take the place of his militant expansionism, which had died away in the military fiascoes of the War of 1812.

Clay and the Buenos Aires envoy, Aguirre, concerted an attack on the Government's neutral policy. As soon as Congress opened, the Speaker and his cohorts commenced to nag the Administration, protesting against the occupation of Amelia Island as unfair to the revolutionists (it deprived them of a shelter for privateers illegally fitted out in the United States); and urging the immediate recognition of the United Provinces of the Rio de la Plata, the one province where independence had been achieved most substantially. If the Administration resisted, Clay hoped to carry resolutions against it and thus discredit it, and everybody in it, including Adams, Calhoun, and Crawford, before the electorate. It would be the first victory in his political maneuvers for the Presidency.

Nothing could have been more undiplomatic than Clay's and Aguirre's strategy, nor more calculated to prejudice the Latin-American agent and his principals. In protesting about Florida the envoy touched a nerve center of North American foreign policy. Moreover, Monroe was nervous about a possible war with Spain, particularly after the occupation of Amelia Island, and Adams still feared that Spain might find European support. Aguirre was untactful enough to tell Adams that the possibility of the United States becoming involved in war was no just motive why he should not solicit the recognition of his nation. It is no wonder that the President and his advisers, particularly Adams, decided against any recognition at this time.

Clay's group continued to press the subject on the floor of the House of Representatives. They successfully called for papers connected with the Amelia Island affair. They also obtained all correspondence relating to the revolted Spanish provinces.

Adams provided a statement to accompany the documents, stressing the fact that Aguirre had no regular diplomatic title, no powers to treat, and that all his demands for recognition had arisen since the assembly of Congress. But the notes and credentials of Aguirre were published, as he and Clay doubtless had intended, and circulated before a sympathetic public. When the President requested the necessary appropriation for defraying the expenses of the commission of inquiry that he had sent to South America, Clay attached an amendment appropriating $18,000 for a minister and legation in Buenos Aires.

To support the amendment the Speaker, descending from the chair, summoned all the resources of his oratory. The new nations, whatever form of government they might adopt, would be animated by an American feeling and guided by an American policy. "They would obey the laws of the system of the New World, of which they would compose a part, in contradistinction to that of Europe." They looked upon the people of the United States as their brothers in freedom, their great example.[10] "At the present moment," he told his listeners, "the patriots of the South are fighting for liberty and independence — for precisely what we fought for. . . . I ask him [pointing to a member who was a veteran of the Revolutionary War], the patriot of '76, how the heart rebounded with joy, on the information that France had recognized us! The moral influence of such a recognition, on the patriots of the South, will be irresistible." [11]

The Speaker's rhetoric thrilled but did not convince a majority of the House. Many of his friends and colleagues obeyed the head rather than the heart and voted down the amendment, 115 against, 45 for it (March 28, 1818), and Congress adjourned.

As Adams anxiously scanned the European skies for American omens he worked, under Monroe's direction, to detach England from any possible co-operation with the Holy Alliance to suppress the revolutions in Spanish America. To do this he proposed repeatedly to the British Government a concert of measures for the speedy recognition of the new republics.[12] By the summer of 1818 he had become persuaded that the five great European allied powers could not agree on any coercive measures to restore Spanish sovereignty in America, because the real policy of Great Britain was to promote rather than to defeat the cause of independence, although to delay acknowledging it for fear of offending Spain. "They will take special care that the European Alliance shall take no active measures against the independents. . . . There can be no doubt but this appeal of Spain to the thunder bolts of the Allies will terminate in utter disappointment." [13]

The Conference of Aix-la-Chapelle seemed to justify Adams's analysis. The proposed mediation of the European allies between Spain and her revolted colonies failed because England, who had brought it up at the request of Spain, refused to countenance the use of force to carry it into effect. After this Adams kept pressing Britain for joint action in recognizing the independence of the new republics; it would frustrate completely any legitimist plans of the Holy Alliance for the New World. But were the revolutionary states stable enough to stand by themselves?

In July 1818 President Monroe's fact-finding Commission returned from Buenos Aires. A majority were of the opinion that resubjugation of the United Provinces to Spain was impossible. On everything else they were hopelessly divided, so much so that they made separate reports. Rodney's report was so favorable to Buenos Aires that Graham refused to

[10] *Annals of Congress*, 15th Cong., 1st Sess., 1817–18, II, 1482.
[11] Ibid., pp. 1614–15.
[12] JQA to Richard Rush, May 20, 1818. *Writings*, VI, 319–27.
[13] JQA to Thomas Sumter, Jr., Washington, August 27, 1818. *Memoirs*, VI, 452.

sign it. He was very skeptical about the stability and the republican principles of the Buenos Aires government. The not disinterested Bland excoriated the O'Higgins dictatorship of Chile as a viceroyalty of a despotic government in Buenos Aires. So did independent observations from Joel Poinsett of South Carolina, the most experienced *Hispanista* in the United States. The diverse reports [14] may have dulled the edge of public enthusiasm for the patriot cause, but they did not dismay Monroe too much, although they confirmed John Quincy Adams's opinions. The President strained toward recognition, and Adams had to follow with as good grace as possible.

Monroe was able to announce to Congress when it reassembled in November 1818 that no forceful intervention by Europe was likely, and that there was good cause to be satisfied with the course heretofore pursued by the United States. Under the President's impulse the Secretary of State began to sound out the way for recognition. He instructed Richard Rush to state to the British Government that it was the intention to recognize Buenos Aires at an early date, "should no event occur which will justify a further postponement of that intention," and invited Great Britain to do the same in concert with the United States.[15] It was a thankless overture. The significant fact for the evolution of American foreign policy is that Lord Castlereagh, striving to keep the European powers balanced in a perfect concert, and opposed to the creation of more republics over here, persistently refused the overtures for an Anglo-American concert for recognition of Latin-American independence in the face of Spain and the Holy Alliance.

A successor to the departed Manuel Hermenejildo de Aguirre appeared in Washington in the late spring of 1818, the Connecticut Yankee adventurer David Curtis DeForest.[16] This romantic character, who had made a fortune as an outfitter of privateers in Buenos Aires, was now a citizen of two republics, the United States of his youth and the revolu-

[14] The reports are printed in *ASPFR,* IV, 217–348, and in William R. Manning: *Diplomatic Correspondence of the United States Concerning Independence of the Latin-American Nations* (3 vols., New York: Carnegie Endowment for International Peace; 1925), I, 382–514, together with Poinsett's letters from Columbia, S.C. The latter publication is hereinafter cited as Manning.

H. M. Brackenridge, secretary to the Commission, later published his valuable observations in a notable book: *Voyage to South America, Performed by order of the American Government in the Years 1817 and 1818* (2 vols., Baltimore, 1819). A condensed version was published in London in 1820. A German translation appeared in Leipzig in 1821, and a Spanish edition in Buenos Aires as late as 1927. An attempt to counteract the impressions made by the Carrera group (see above, note 9) in both North and South America, it was a far more reliable appraisal than the reports of the Commissioners. Bornholdt, op. cit.

[15] January 1, 1819. Manning, I, 87.

[16] Benjamin Keen has utilized the adventurer's unprinted journals, letterbooks, and account books, for his definitive study of *David Curtis DeForest and the Revolution of Buenos Aires* (New Haven, 1947).

tionary state of the United Provinces of the Rio de la Plata. He returned to his homeland and built himself an elegant mansion facing the New Haven Green. He bore with him a commission as consul general from the government of his second allegiance. The Buenos Aires authorities had given him instructions to secure the recognition of independence by the United States, pending the dispatch of an "ambassador" to Washington, to get promises for material aid from the United States, to distribute letters of marque in North America for Buenos Aires privateers, and to establish a base somewhere for their operations.[17] Florida was enough of an island for DeForest's purposes.

With DeForest and Clay, Adams had to fight all over again the same contest that he had waged the previous year with Aguirre and the Speaker of the House of Representatives. Like Aguirre, DeForest seemed at first content with an informal status — until the meeting of Congress in December 1818. Then he talked with Clay and decided to push the Administration to acknowledge him formally as consul general, and to get his representations into writing so that the opposition in Congress could call for the record and spread it before the public. After a written solicitation to the Secretary of State he appeared at the Department for a long conference, December 14, 1818. Again Adams explained that the President thought that the time had not yet come for formal recognition, as would be signalized by an *exequatur* to him as consul general. At the proper time, however, acknowledgment "would not be withheld," although any recognition by the United States would not decide the extent of territory claimed by Buenos Aires, such as the *Banda Oriental,* Santa Fé, and Paraguay, where separatist movements had gained headway.

It was agreed that the substance of their conversation should be recorded in notes passed between the two men.[18] This was done, and the Secretary added another note protesting against the excesses and irregularities of Buenos Aires privateers and their violation of the neutrality laws.[19] Adams suspected that DeForest himself was commissioning privateers but could not prove it.[20] If the Secretary of State could lay his hands on satisfactory evidence, the soldier of fortune would be at his mercy; for it was against the neutrality laws for an American citizen to fit out or commission privateers for a foreign prince, state, colony, or people to wage war against another power friendly to the United States.

[17] "In case our corsairs should take some island suitable as a base and to which none of the recognized nations should have any right, the said Consul is empowered to set up a municipal government there, taking possession of the island in the name of this government." *Archivo General de la Nación* (Buenos Aires), S1-A2-A4, No. 8.

[18] The interview is recorded by both men, without any substantial discrepancies: in Adams's *Memoirs,* IV, 190–3, December 14, 1818, and in DeForest to Tagle, Georgetown, December 18, 1818. *Archivo General de la Nación* (Buenos Aires), S1-A2-A4, No. 8.

[19] Adams to DeForest, January 1, 1819. Manning, I, 88.

[20] *Memoirs,* IV, 225.

DeForest did not have to wait long for Clay's opposition to rise up to support him in Congress. On January 14, 1819 the House of Representatives passed a resolution requesting information whether any independent government in South America had asked for the recognition of a minister or consul general, and what reply had been made. Adams sent in his correspondence with DeForest and also with Lino de Clemente, agent of Venezuela. He explained that the Government had refused to have any communication with Clemente because he had been one of those who had signed the commission to McGregor to take possession of Amelia Island; as to DeForest, recognition of him as consul general from the United Provinces of South America could not be granted without recognizing thereby the authority from which it emanated as a sovereign and independent power. The Secretary made clear his suspicion that DeForest was working with Clay's opposition by pointing out that in the previous May the envoy had declared himself entirely satisfied with his informal reception, but that shortly after the commencement of the existing session of Congress he had renewed his solicitations.[21]

Prudently Adams held DeForest at arm's length. "In this affair everything is insidious and factious," he had noted while preparing his statement for Congress to accompany the correspondence. "The call is made for the purpose of baiting the Administration, and especially of fastening upon the Secretary of State the odium of refusing to receive the South American Ministers and Consuls-General. DeForest's notes are cunning and deceptive."[22]

A happy inspiration enabled the Secretary of State to put DeForest out of the way and break up his collusion with Clay. When the putative consul general of the United Provinces of the Rio de la Plata next appeared at the Department, Adams deftly reminded him that as an American citizen he was liable to prosecution for violation of the neutrality laws.[23]

The hint was enough. No evidence was necessary. DeForest's attitude changed immediately. He did not care to face a host of lawsuits, the loss of his curiously gotten fortune, perhaps jail itself. He quickly declared himself entirely satisfied with the friendly disposition of the executive and became straightway convinced, as he told Adams, that the proceedings of Clay, with whom he admitted having talked, and of his supporters, had injured rather than aided the cause of South America. He went back to New Haven and his luxurious home on the Green and never seriously bothered John Quincy Adams any more. Soon afterward Adams's magnificent diplomatic victory, the Transcontinental Treaty, temporarily silenced the opposition in Congress. Spain had yielded Florida and acknowledged a new frontier from the Gulf of Mexico to the Pacific Ocean.

21 Adams to President Monroe, for transmission to the House of Representatives, Washington, January 28, 1819. Manning, I, 89.

22 *Memoirs,* IV, 223. January 20, 1819.

23 *Memoirs,* IV, 225. January 22, 1819.

3

The Transcontinental Treaty immediately would have taken the wind out of Speaker Clay's opposition to the Latin-American policy of the Administration had the Spanish King ratified it promptly, as he pledged himself to do. The full powers under which Onís had signed the treaty contained a solemn promise by His Most Catholic Majesty "on the faith and word of a king, to approve, ratify, and fulfill whatsoever might be stipulated and signed" by the plenipotentiary. Now, a Spaniard, particularly a Spanish King, is always proud about his faith and word – that is, his *pundonor.* When the treaty reached Madrid the King's Secretary of State read his handiwork and found it good, but the Council of State objected: too much territory had been ceded, there was no guaranty against recognition of the independence of Buenos Aires, no promise on the part of the United States to enforce its neutrality laws better. So the Council advised that pretexts [24] be sought to delay ratification until more propitious times. Before these considerations the King's *pundonor* fainted forthwith. He sent another Minister, General Francisco Dionisio Vives, on a leisurely trip to Washington, by way of Paris and London, to see if he could get better terms.

Spain's refusal to ratify disgusted Adams and pleased Clay. The Secretary of State by now had despaired for the success of his treaty. He felt that the President's too sympathetic Latin-American policy,[25] so resented by Spain, had ruined a fine negotiation. With the Speaker declaring that Spain by her own default had relieved the United States from a bad bargain, and clamoring in Congress for the immediate occupation of Florida and Texas, Adams counseled the President to recommend to Congress the forcible occupation of the Floridas.[26]

[24] See Miller: *Treaties,* III, 42–53 and map.

[25] *Memoirs,* V, 109. May 10, 1820.

[26] In instructions to Rush (Great Britain), Gallatin (France), G. W. Campbell (Russia), and A. H. Everett (Netherlands), August 23, 1819, Adams declared that if Spain did not ratify, it would remain for the United States to assert its rights "in another form." "Should the opinion of Congress concur with that of the President, possession will be taken of Florida, without any views of hostility to Spain, but holding her responsible for the expenses which may be occasioned by the measure. You will explicitly make it known to the French (Russian) Government that it is not the intention of the United States to disturb the peace of Europe, and that if possession be quietly given of Pensacola and St. Augustine, when required as it probably will be, the further claims of indemnity from Spain, arising from the refusal to ratify the Treaty, will be reserved subject to further amicable negotiation." Letterbook copy of a Circular to Messrs. Gallatin, Rush, and Campbell (*mutatis mutandis*) in DS, *Instructions, U.S. Ministers,* VIII, 358–60. The draft in Adams MSS. is dated August 23, 1819. There is also in Adams MSS. an undated draft of an "act for carrying into execution the Treaty between the United States and Spain, concluded at Washington, February 22, 1819," in JQA's handwriting. It calls for the occupation of East and West Florida and the taking possession thereof, and the removal and transportation of Spanish forces, agreeably to the stipulations of the treaty.

Virgil's colt turned loose at the close of a long winter into a rich meadow, said Attorney General William Wirt, would not enjoy the luxuriant frolic more than General Jackson would be pleased to be turned into the Spanish Provinces, "Cuba included." [27]

President Monroe in his annual message (December 7, 1819) on the state of the Union asked Congress for discretionary authority to take over Florida. In response the Committee on Foreign Affairs of the House reported a bill for the mandatory occupation of the Floridas. Then Speaker Clay opened his attack. Always anxious to win a victory over the Administration, and particularly to discredit the diplomatic achievements of his rival Adams, Clay brought forth two resolutions in the Committee of the Whole of the House of Representatives: (1) Congress alone has the power to cede territory belonging to the United States (Texas, in this instance), and no treaty purporting to alienate any portion thereof is valid without its concurrence; (2) the equivalent rendered by the treaty for that part of Louisiana lying west of the Sabine was inadequate, and it would be inexpedient to transfer that region to any foreign power, or to renew the treaty.[28]

These threatened resolutions, which never got out of committee, helped the treaty more than they injured it. On sober second thought the President, at Adams's suggestion,[29] sent in a special message (March 27, 1820) suggesting delay until the next session of Congress, to give time for the new Spanish Minister to arrive. At the same time the Secretary instructed John Forsyth, the new American Minister to Madrid, that if ratifications were withheld, the United States would insist upon further indemnity, and would reassert "and never again relinquish" its right to a western boundary at the Rio Grande del Norte.[30]

Spain was helpless. Nothing in the international situation could have stopped the United States from occupying the remainder of Florida and marching into Texas. But President Monroe did not want Texas. He feared that the acquisition of that great territory would only serve to reawaken sectional controversy over slavery in the territories, just put to sleep by the Missouri Compromise.[31]

The new Spanish Minister, General Vives, immediately revealed (April 1820) the new terms that Spain demanded as her price of ratification: (1) strengthening of the neutrality laws, (2) a formal guaranty of the integrity of Spain's American possessions, (3) a promise not to recognize Buenos Aires or any of the revolted provinces. In return he offered to annul the Florida land grants. The French Minister, Hyde de Neuville,

[27] William Wirt to John Coalter, Washington, October 25, 1819. *AHR*, XXV (No. 4, July 1920), 692–5.

[28] *Annals of Congress*, 16th Cong., 1st Sess., 1819–20, p. 1719. April 3, 1820.

[29] *Writings*, VII, 3.

[30] *Writings*, VII, 31. May 25, 1820.

[31] Monroe to Jefferson, Washington, May 1820. *Writings of Monroe*, VI, 119.

continued his friendly good offices between the United States and Spain. But Adams refused all of Vives's conditions. The neutrality laws were being enforced, he declared. The policy of the United States toward the revolution was neutrality, and he repeated that it would be a violation of neutrality to agree never to recognize the independence of any of the communities at war with Spain, no matter what should happen. Nevertheless the Secretary of State carefully intimated that his Government "probably would not precipitately recognize the independence of the South Americans." [32]

The words "probably" and "not precipitately" were latitudinarian enough. They gave Spain a last chance to comply. News had reached the United States of an uprising in Spain. At Adams's suggestion the President recommended to Congress still further delay before forcible occupation. As the session of Congress ended, Henry Clay succeeded in carrying (May 10, 1820) a mild resolution: "that it is expedient to provide by law a suitable outfit and salary for such Minister or Ministers *as the President, by and with the advice and consent of the Senate,* may send to any of the Governments of South America, which have established, and are maintaining, their independence on Spain."

Passage of this resolution by a vote of 80 to 75 was a tempered tribute to Clay's long advocacy. Its qualified language, in the words here italicized, strengthened rather than embarrassed the Secretary of State in dealing with Spain. And it left the Speaker's oratory rolling over the prairies and pampas of North and South America, reverberating from crag to crag among the cordilleras of two Continents: "Let us become real and true Americans, and place ourselves at the head of the American System." [33]

Again European events conspired with the distant American scene to relieve the diplomacy of the United States. A liberal revolution in Madrid, which took place just after Vives had departed, together with the likelihood that the United States would occupy the Floridas and also immediately recognize the independence of the revolted colonies, perhaps take Texas too — should Clay's opposition have its way — revived the King's *pundonor* and saved the treaty. Obviously a radical Spanish Government could get no support from European legitimist powers. The Council of State now favored ratification; the new constitutional Cortes secretly gave its approval (September 30, 1820) and formally annulled the Florida land grants. The King finally signed the instrument (October 24, 1820) and sent it to Washington. Because the original term of six months stipulated for exchange of ratifications had long since expired, the President once more submitted the document to the Senate. Again that body advised and consented to ratification (February 19, 1821). This

[32] *Memoirs,* V, 86, 94–5, 104. May 1, 4, 1820.

[33] *Annals of Congress,* 16th Cong., 1st Sess., 1819–20, p. 2228. May 10, 1820.

time there were four opposing votes.[34] Exactly two years had elapsed between signature and the final exchange of ratifications of the treaty, February 22, 1822. Spain had gained at least that much time by her procrastination, but to little avail.

General Vives departed from Washington one of John Quincy Adams's best diplomatic friends. President Monroe appointed General Jackson Governor of Florida with a commission formally to take over the province from Spain. Soon the General got involved in vigorous altercations with the Spanish Commissioner Callava, in Florida, and with the new American judge there, Fromentin. John Quincy Adams continued to defend him in the Cabinet discussions as uncompromisingly as ever, until Jackson, fed up with Florida now that it was a part of the United States, resigned as Governor and went back home to Tennessee for a rest at the Hermitage. "General Jackson has rendered such services to this Nation," Adams told the President, "that it is impossible for me to contemplate his character or conduct without veneration." [35]

With the Transcontinental Treaty duly ratified and the Floridas safely annexed, there was no longer any great reason of international politics to prevent the United States from recognizing the independence of any of the revolted provinces. Since the Conference of Aix-la-Chapelle (September-November 1818) it had been perfectly evident to Adams that England, if she would not join in such a recognition, at least would not oppose it. It was also clear that all danger had disappeared – at least for the time being – of any formidable European reaction to such a step. The United States was free to do as it pleased. In Congress, Clay, on the eve of a temporary retirement from public life, still kept up the fight for recognition. Just before Spain's ratification of the treaty reached Washington he had secured the passage of another resolution.

The first clause, carried 134 to 12, stated: "That the House of Representatives participates with the people of the United States in the deep interest which they feel for the success of the Spanish provinces of South America which are struggling to establish their liberty and independence." The second, voted 87 to 68, declared: "that it will give its Constitutional *support* to the President of the United States, *whenever he may deem it expedient* to recognize the sovereignty and independence of any of the said provinces." [36]

Passage of these unexceptionable resolutions and the ratification of

[34] "Brown of Louisiana, who married a sister of Clay's wife; Richard M. Johnson, of Kentucky, against his own better judgment, from mere political subserviency to Clay; Williams of Tennessee, from party impulses, connected with hatred of General Jackson; and [William A.] Trimble, of Ohio, from some maggot in the brain, the cause of which I do not yet perfectly know." *Memoirs*, V, 285–6.

[35] *Memoirs*, V, 473. January 2, 1822. See also ibid., 440–72. Bassett: *Jackson*, I, 296–321.

[36] *Annals of Congress*, 16th Cong., 2d Sess., 1820–1, pp. 1081–92. Italics inserted.

the treaty marked the complete evaporation of the issue between the Administration and the Speaker on the Latin-American policy of the United States. Shortly thereafter Clay and Adams, conscious rivals for the Presidency, had a long talk about Latin America. Each regretted the difference of views in the past and rejoiced that they were at an end. It is worth while to record Adams's words as expressed in this remarkable interview:

> I have never doubted [he said to Henry Clay] that the final issue of their [the revolted provinces] present struggle will be their entire independence of Spain. It is equally clear that it is our true policy and duty to take no part in the contest. The principle of neutrality to *all* foreign wars is, in my opinion, fundamental to the continuance of our liberties and of our Union. So far as they are contending for independence, I wish well to their cause; but I have not yet seen and do not now see any prospect that they will establish free or liberal institutions of government. They are not likely to promote the spirit either of freedom or order by their example. They have not the first elements of good or free government. Arbitrary power, military and ecclesiastical, is stamped upon their education, upon their habits, and upon all their institutions. Civil dissension is infused into all their seminal principles. War and mutual destruction are in every member of their organization, moral, political, and physical. I have little expectation of any beneficial result to this country from any future connection with them, political or commercial. We shall derive no improvement to our own institutions by any communion with theirs. Nor is there any appearance of a disposition in them to take any political lesson from us. As to the commercial connection, I agree with you that little weight should be allowed to arguments of mere pecuniary interest; but there is no basis for much traffic between us. They want none of our productions, and we can afford to purchase very few of theirs. *Time* must be the test of your opinion and of mine; but, I candidly acknowledge that nothing has occurred hitherto to weaken in my mind the view which I have taken of this subject from the first.[37]

The issue over policy now evaporated, the Secretary of State was in a position to pursue unembarrassed his policy of "unequivocal neutrality" and to carry out his personal assurances to General Vives that the United States would not act "precipitately" in recognizing the South Americans.

Convenient justifications were at hand for leisurely deliberations. In the first place the military situation at the beginning of 1821 was much blacker than at the close of that memorable year. In Mexico, Venezuela,

[37] This is taken from Adams's own account of the conversation of March 9, 1821 (changed into direct discourse), *Memoirs,* V, 324–5. Clay seems not to have recorded his version of the interview.

Colombia, and Peru it was not yet clear whether the revolutions would be successful. In the far south the present Argentina and most of Chile were clear of Spanish troops, but at Buenos Aires all was confusion and anarchy. Disclosure of an intrigue by one of the transitory governments of Buenos Aires to set up a Bourbon monarchy in the United Provinces of the Rio de la Plata [38] disgusted liberals in the United States and in England. Montevideo was in the hands of the Portuguese, and in the interior of the river provinces it was impossible to say who was in authority. The essential requisites for carrying out the responsibilities and duties of a state under international law — the standard that Adams found it convenient to demand — did not yet exist in Latin America. This fact was particularly evident in the depredations of the rebel privateers, in many instances turned pirates.

By sweeping the Spanish merchant marine from the seas the scores of privateers fitted out in the United States had been an important factor in keeping the revolts alive. So had the occasional frigates clandestinely built in the United States or converted from American armed merchantmen in rebel ports. As long as the privateers confined their operations to enemy prizes they were a vexatious but not impossible problem for the Secretary of State in answering the protests of the Spanish Minister. Public opinion tolerated if it did not applaud their deeds, and indulgent juries generally acquitted them when brought to court for violation of law; but when their irresponsible captains began piratically to plunder neutral vessels, and even the shipping of the United States, their popularity declined. Despite prevailing sympathies for the privateers and the difficulties of securing condemnations because of local profits and interests involved, ten men were hanged as pirates in 1820.[39]

The United States had repeatedly protested to the *de facto* governments against these abominations, and Adams was unwilling to recognize the Buenos Aires government until it could demonstrate its power to stop them. To satisfy the complaints the Buenos Aires authorities revoked all commissions to privateers on October 6, 1821. When this became known in Washington it removed the last impediment to recognition.

4

It was characteristic of John Quincy Adams that when circumstances forced him to shift a political position he was able to rationalize his action. With the way now prepared, and indicated by the President, for a

[38] William Spence Robertson: *France and Latin American Independence* (Baltimore, 1939), pp. 157–76; Arthur Preston Whitaker: *The United States and Latin American Independence*, p. 323.

[39] Forty-five men were convicted of piracy, "all cases of privateers under the South American colors." The Cabinet, after discussion, decided ten must be executed and the others reprieved. *Memoirs,* V, 19–21, 55–6, 63–6.

recognition of Latin-American independence without the proffered concert with Great Britain, he proceeded to find a justification for the step that would not conflict with his previous position. An occasion soon presented itself for a pronouncement.

Henry Clay had gone back to Kentucky for a brief period of private life. Responding at Lexington to an ovation of his friends and admirers from far and wide, he had again criticized the Administration for delay in conforming to general sentiment for the recognition of Latin-American independence. He reiterated his own recommendations that the United States should countenance the patriots' cause "by all means short of actual war"; "it would give additional tone, and hope and confidence, to the friends of liberty throughout the world." Finally, he advocated that "a sort of counterpoise to the Holy Alliance should be formed in the two Americas, in favor of national independence and liberty, to operate by the force of example, and moral influence. . . ."[40]

This doctrine invited Adams's powers of animadversion. Meanwhile his dander had risen at the meekness with which newspapers in the United States were allowing to go unanswered certain supercilious British publications on the theme: "What has America done for mankind?" He was especially annoyed by the suggestion of the *Edinburgh Review* in May 1820 that the United States should unite with liberals in Great Britain in supporting the principles of reform and liberty in Spain, France, and Italy in an impending final struggle against established abuse, legitimacy, or tyranny. Adams determined to sound a blast against such doctrine in the Fourth-of-July address that the citizens of Washington invited him to deliver in 1821. At the same time he would formulate a principle to justify colonial revolutions for independence, whether in North America or South America, without rushing in arms to their support. In short, he had discovered for his own serenity and consistency at least an ideological bond which united the cause of Latin-American independence with that of Anglo-American independence.[41]

Delivering the carefully prepared oration from the rostrum of the House of Representatives, the speaker stood before his audience clad in a professor's gown as if to veil his person from the high office of Secretary of State. He began by characterizing the last seven hundred years of English history as a continual conflict between "oppression of power and claims of right." The American Revolution had separated the claims of right from the oppressions of power, at least in the United States, and had built upon the resulting independence a stable and orderly nation based on popular sovereignty and the social compact. Amidst flights of elo-

[40] Such is Whitaker's admirable summary of the Clay speech, in his chapter on John Quincy Adams's 4th-of-July oration of 1821. *U.S. and Latin American Independence*, Ch. XII, "The Reply to Lexington and Edinburgh."

[41] Whitaker, op. cit., p. 361.

quence extolling the cause of 1776, professedly without rancor in 1821, John Quincy Adams blew a "trumpet upon Zion" for two great principles of policy governing "America's" relations with all other nations and peoples: (1) the anticolonial principle; and (2) the anti-entanglement principle; or what we would call today anti-imperialism and absolute nonintervention.[42]

Adams was reflecting in his extravagant rhetoric what he had seen happen to republican France in a previous generation when she began intervening to establish liberty in other lands. He was echoing the Farewell Address of the venerated Washington.

The Russian Minister, Pierre de Poletica, congratulated himself that he (like Stratford Canning) had stayed away from the ceremony, if only because among the toasts offered at the banquet that followed was a "miserable calumny on the Holy Alliance." "From one end to another," reported the diplomat, "Mr. Adams's speech was a virulent diatribe against England." He sent home a printed copy with markings of his own penciled on the margin.[43]

Opposite the sentences laying down fundamental maxims, italicized in the text above quoted, Poletica wrote: "This passage is worth noting because it is the epitome of American policy." Throughout the speech here and there he made his comments. "How about your two million black slaves," the Russian marked against Adams's boast that American independence had presented to mankind the inextinguishable rights of human nature and the only lawful foundation of government. "How about your two million black slaves who cultivate a great expanse of your territory for your particular and exclusive advantage? You forget the poor Indians whom you have not ceased to spoil. You forget your conduct toward Spain."

The patriotic orator, extolling in his peroration the spirit of the Declaration of Independence, had made a final appeal to Britannia, ruler of the waves, "and to every individual among the sceptered lords of mankind: '*Go thou and do likewise!*'" Such an injunction from such a personality, so thinly veiled by professor's gown, shocked the proper susceptibilities of the Russian Minister. "It is an appeal to the nations of Europe to rise against their Governments," he reported, "and it is a Secretary of State, that is Minister of the Interior and of Foreign Affairs, who permits himself language like this on such a solemn occasion."

These moral mentations of a faithful servant of divine-right Czardom

[42] *An Address Delivered at the Request of a Commission of the Citizens of Washington; on the Occasion of Reading the Declaration of Independence, on the Fourth of July, 1821.* By John Quincy Adams (printed by Davis and Force, Washington, 1821).

[43] Poletica to Nesselrode, Philadelphia, July 30, 1821. *AHR,* XVIII (No. 2, January 1913), 327.

remained buried to this day in the archival tombs of St. Petersburg and Moscow.[44]

Stratford Canning also sent home a printed copy of the address. Despite the reflections on George III, and other exceptions, the representative in North America of the Defender of the Faith thought Adams's oration a "masterpiece of eloquence." [45]

Adams was disappointed that the general public had been more captivated by his Fourth-of-July twisting of the lion's tail and by his defense of America's contributions of liberty and self-government to the world than by his essential points: anti-imperialism and nonintervention. Particularly did he deplore the popularity of the "Edinburgh doctrine" of the supposed duty of the United States to take an active part in the impending European conflicts between Power and Right. Henry Clay in his speech at Lexington also had squinted uncertainly in that direction.

"This doctrine has already twice in the history of our country brought the peace and the permanent welfare of the Union into jeopardy," Adams wrote to Edward Everett. "Under Washington's administration at the early stage of the French Revolution; and under the present administration in the efforts to entangle us in the South American conflict. The address has presented a principle of *duty* directly the reverse of that which ought to govern the councils of the Union, and has assigned as a reason for it the inevitable tendency of a direct interference in foreign wars, even wars for freedom, to change the very foundations of our own government from *liberty* to *power*." [46]

He intended his speech to be a reply both to Edinburgh and to Lexington, to be heard and pondered also by the legitimist governments of Europe.[47] The Holy Allies, if they listened to the blast at all, must have noted also its isolationist echo. But there was nothing in it to make them tremble at intervening in South America to restore Spanish legitimacy.

In the Farewell Address, George Washington had counseled his fellow Americans not to entangle themselves by artificial ties in the *ordinary* vicissitudes of European politics, or the *ordinary* combinations and collisions of European friendships or enmities. The question of entanglement with the vicissitudes and combinations, ordinary or extraordinary, of sister nations of the New World had not come up in 1796 for the simple reason that then there had been no other nations in the New World. Now in 1821, as if to make American foreign policy perfectly clear on that

[44] I am indebted to Dr. E. Wilder Spaulding, Chief of the Division of Publications of the Department of State, for procuring through official channels, and with the cooperation of the Soviet Government, a photographic copy of the marked pages of this address.

[45] S. Canning to Londonderry, Separate, Washington, July 30, 1821. PRO, F.O., 5, Vol. CLVIII.

[46] JQA to Edward Everett, Washington, January 31, 1822. *Writings*, VII, 197–207.

[47] JQA to Robert Walsh, Jr., Washington, July 10, 27, 1817. *Writings*, VII, 113–18, 127–37.

point, "Professor" John Quincy Adams, acting independently and on his own responsibility, applied the same doctrine implacably to the New World as well as to the Old World.

5

By the end of the year 1821 the striking victories of the patriots over the royalist forces had weakened Spain's hold on most of the Continent of South America. Mexico and Central America also had established their independence by comparatively bloodless revolutions. President Monroe decided that the time had come to recognize the new states if their good will were to be preserved against the wiles of European diplomacy. Responding to a welcome call from the House of Representatives for documents bearing on the state of the war between the Spanish-American governments and Spain, he sent in a special message (March 8, 1822) declaring that Chile, the United Provinces of the Plata, Peru, Colombia, and Mexico were all in full enjoyment of their independence, and that there was not the remotest prospect of their being deprived of it. Recognition of established independence, he asserted, could not be considered by Spain as a hostile act, and the neutrality of the United States would continue unaltered.

Congress immediately complied (May 4, 1822) by appropriating $100,000 to meet the expenses of "such missions to the independent nations on the American continent as the President might deem proper." The act passed almost unanimously: 167 to 1 in the House, 39 to 3 in the Senate. President Monroe signalized the first act of recognition by formally receiving, in a moment of great and sincere emotion, June 19, 1822, Manuel Torres, as chargé d'affaires of Gran Colombia (which then included New Granada and Venezuela). An invalid with only a few weeks to live, the highly respected Torres [48] was the only accredited diplomatic agent of a Latin-American government then in the United States. The Colombian jurist Dr. José María Salazar [49] succeeded the deceased Torres and represented Gran Colombia on the banks of the Potomac until 1828.

A parade of Latin-American representatives increased the roster and added to the color of the diplomatic corps in Washington as one by one the new states received recognition.

Formal recognition of independence of the new states involved no departure from North American neutrality. Though Spain protested indignantly, she did not break off relations with the Republic of the North.

President Monroe delayed the actual appointment of diplomatic repre-

[48] Nicolas García Samudio has described the *Misión de Don Manual Torres en Washington, 1819–1822, in Capítulos de Historia Diplomática* (Bogotá, 1925).

[49] Envoy Extraordinary and Minister Plenipotentiary, June 10, 1823 to June 27, 1828. See Raimundo Rivas: *Relaciones internacionales entre Colombia y los Estados Unidos, 1810–1850* (Bogotá, 1915).

sentatives of the United States near the governments of the new states until after he should see how the initial step of recognition and the formal reception of their diplomats in Washington would strike the other European powers.[50] Only after hearing that his message to Congress on recognition and the welcome to the patriot envoys were well received in the chancelleries of the Old World did he call upon John Quincy Adams to draw up general instructions for the first North American Ministers to set forth to South America: to Buenos Aires and Colombia.

The President directed his Secretary of State, April 30, 1823, to review the friendly policy of the United States toward the revolution of the Spanish colonies, "pushing their cause everywhere," from its early neutrality to the inevitable recognition of their independence. "Our Ministers will of course not boast of this, but the fact being well impressed upon their minds, will enable them to take proper advantage of it."[51] Monroe carefully perused and amended the instructions that Adams drew up to Caesar A. Rodney, Minister to the United Provinces of the Rio de la Plata, and to Richard C. Anderson, Minister to Colombia, before he gave them his final approval and heartening applause.

The lengthy instructions constituted one of Adams's more important state papers.[52] They may be noted together. Extolling the success of the Spanish-American revolutions, stemming as they did from the principles and examples of the North American Revolution, the Secretary pronounced the final independence of the new nations as among the most important events in human history. The United States, within the proper duties of neutrality, had exercised all its *moral* influence to countenance and promote the cause of independence until the time was actually ripe for recognition. As early as August 1818 it had proposed to Great Britain a joint recognition of the new states. Alas, Britain had held aloof, but at least the proposed Anglo-American concert had served to "disconcert" the projects of the Holy Alliance at the Conference of Aix-la-Chapelle to intervene to restore Spanish sovereignty.

After this long historical review Adams laid down the principles of North American policy toward the new republics to the south: (1) Upholding of the republican principle against Latin-American "hankering after monarchy." (2) Support of the American System of separation from the monarchical and tyrannical system of European polity. (3) As to any inter-American Congress (being considered by Colombia) for articulating

[50] Monroe to JQA, June 10, 1822. Adams MSS.

[51] Monroe to JQA, April 30, 1823. Adams MSS.

[52] Like all of the important instructions drafted by Adams, the President read them carefully. He approved the instructions to Rodney as they stood: "I think it meets the object of making an epoch in our relations with the new independent govts south of the U States, in a manner worthy of our own." In the instruction to Anderson he advised cutting out passages that bore too hard on the conduct of other governments and nations, since the document was likely to be published to the world. Adams MSS. Ford indicates the deleted passages in *Writings,* VII, 441–86.

that system toward republican institutions and political and commercial independence from Europe, the United States would yield its approbation and cordial good wishes: "If more should be asked of them, the proposition will be received and considered in a friendly spirit, and with a due sense of its importance." (4) Treaties of commerce and amity would be welcome on the basis of the most-favored-nation – "the great foundation of our foreign policy" – or, if possible, a reciprocal equality of nations in each other's ports; and the Freedom of the Seas, United States model. The United States stood for republicanism, anti-imperialism, commercial equality with nondiscrimination between nations – in short, for "*civil, political, commercial,* and *religious* liberty." [53]

The phraseology, the technical details, the careful instructions, they were the work of the Secretary of State; the kindling word of welcome to the new Latin-American nations and peoples, it was the voice of President Monroe echoing throughout the documents. Since the Fourth-of-July address of 1821 Adams had warmed himself more and more into the spirit of Monroe. The last paragraph of his instructions to Minister Anderson sounded like a peroration. It was a hopeful accolade to the patriotic cause, quite out of keeping with Adams's own pessimistic analysis of Latin-American politics privately conveyed to Henry Clay only two years before. The words of John Quincy Adams might well have been the words of Henry Clay himself:

> The emancipation of the South American continent opens to the whole race of man prospects of futurity, in which this union will be called in the discharge of its duties to itself and to unnumbered ages of posterity to take a conspicuous and leading part. It invokes all that is precious in hope and all that is desirable in existence to the countless millions of our fellow creatures, which in the progressive revolutions of time this hemisphere is destined to rear and to maintain. That the fabric of our social connections with our southern neighbors may rise in the lapse of years with a grandeur and harmony of proportions corresponding with the magnificence of the means, placed by providence in our power and in that of our descendants, its foundations must be laid in principles of politics and of morals new and distasteful to the thrones and dominations of the elder world, but coextensive with the surface of the globe and lasting as the changes of time.[54]

The friendly Republic of the North was thus the first nation outside the sisterhood of the new states of Latin America to recognize the independence of those nations. This recognition was the greatest assistance

[53] JQA to Caesar Augustus Rodney, and to Richard C. Anderson, Department of State, May 17, and May 27, 1823. *Writings,* VII, 424–86, and Manning, I, 186–209. For enlightening commentary on these instructions, see Whitaker, op. cit., 410–19.

[54] *Writings,* VII, 486.

rendered by any foreign power to the independence of Latin America. The example was to prevail soon on hesitant England and reluctant Europe.

The opposing Latin-American policies of Adams and Clay had approached each other by 1823 so that all difference had melted away on this issue. Warm-hearted Clay, in espousing the ideal of emancipation of the whole New World and its political separation from the European System of divine-right monarchy and power politics, was willing finally to leave Adams to secure the continental interests of the United States first. Cool-headed Adams, after reaching the goal of his diplomatic ambition, a transcontinental republic, the vital territorial basis for the nation, was later careful to take care of Clay's broader American concepts.

The events to be narrated in the next chapters will show John Quincy Adams emerging further from his hitherto confirmed isolationism. Within another twelve months he would formulate principles of American foreign policy — proclaimed by President Monroe in his historic message to Congress on December 2, 1823 — that would include the American Continents within the area of our vital interests. Three years more and John Quincy Adams as President of the United States, with Henry Clay as Secretary of State, would actually accept Clay's Lexington doctrine by sending plenipotentiaries to the Congress of Panama. He would no longer be a "tranquil spectator" of the struggles for liberty in the Land of Columbus, the World of the West. Assisted by Clay he would attempt to drive the foundations of American foreign policy deep into the whole continental ground of the Western Hemisphere.

CHAPTER XVIII
John Quincy Adams and the Background of the Monroe Doctrine (1792–1823)

We shall assume distinctly the principle that the American continents are no longer subjects for *any* new European colonial establishments.

JOHN QUINCY ADAMS TO BARON VON TUYLL,
RUSSIAN MINISTER, JULY 17, 1823

THE MONROE DOCTRINE, as the celebrated message of President Monroe to the Congress on December 2, 1823 came to be called in later years,[1] and as we shall call it by prolepsis, consisted of three principal dicta. They were:

(1) The Non-Colonization Principle applied to South America as well as North America, in "the rights and interests of the United States." On this point the message said: "the American Continents, by the free and independent condition which they have assumed and maintain, are henceforth not to be considered as subjects for future colonization by any European power."

(2) The principle of Abstention from the wars of the European powers in matters relating to themselves, as being in another political system than that of this Hemisphere: "It is only when our rights are invaded, or seriously menaced, that we resent injuries, or make preparations for our defense."

(3) Consequently, the dictum of Hands Off the independent states of the New World: "We could not view any interposition for the purpose of oppressing them, or controuling in any other manner, their destiny, by any European power, in any other light, than as the manifestation of an unfriendly disposition towards the United States."

Before describing the circumstances under which President Monroe pronounced the message, it is worth while to recall the part which John Quincy Adams already had played in articulating these principles.[2]

[1] The phrase "Monroe Doctrine" was not coined until 1852. Dexter Perkins: *The Monroe Doctrine, 1826–1867* (Baltimore, 1933), p. 223.

[2] No later student can touch the subject of this and the following chapter without a word of gratitude to Worthington Chauncey Ford for his pioneer documentary stud-

Rather than consider the three postulates in the sequence in which they lie in the message, it will be better to take them in their historical order: (1) Abstention, (2) Non-Colonization, (3) Hands Off the New World. Adams had long since been intimately associated with the maxim of Abstention. It will soon be evident that he was the sole author of the Non-Colonization Principle. His connection with the precept Hands Off may be postponed to a later and more lengthy portion of this chapter and to the following one. We may now bring together some of his contributions to the Monroe Doctrine before the famous presidential pronouncement of 1823.

1

The dictum of Abstention was common to all the Fathers of American independence, including John Adams. In its classic exposition it was Washingtonian, although Alexander Hamilton was responsible for its phraseology. From the beginning John Quincy Adams had thought like Washington on foreign affairs. His advocacy of Abstention had originally commended him to the serious attention of the first President. In the letters of "Marcellus" in 1794 he had said: "It is our duty to remain, the peaceful and silent, though sorrowful spectators of the European scene." The famous warning of the Farewell Address against entanglement in the ordinary vicissitudes and the ordinary combinations of European wars and politics bears traces of the ideas and phraseology of John Quincy Adams's early diplomatic dispatches from the Netherlands. As early as 1796 he had discerned and labeled "the American System" [3] of polity, as opposed to the European System – two separate systems, two spheres. Years later, as Secretary of State, he had sensed in the South American revolutions the same temptation that had beset his fellow countrymen in the time of the French Revolution: to rush into a foreign conflict to save somebody else's liberty – and perhaps to lose their own. In explaining to Onís why the United States declined the mediation offer of Great Britain in 1818 he said: "It has hitherto been the policy both of Europe and of the United States, to keep aloof from the general federative system of each other." [4] "America," he declared on the Fourth of July 1821,

ies. The first was "Some Original Documents on the Genesis of the Monroe Doctrine," MHS *Proc.*, 2d Series, XV (1902), 373–436, separately published under the title of *John Quincy Adams, His Connection with the Monroe Doctrine (1823)* (Cambridge, 1902). It is to this separate print, a copy of which the late author presented to me in 1925, that I make my page references. A subsequent article, based on the documents printed in the first contribution, appeared in the *AHR*, VII (No. 4, July 1902), 676–96, and VIII (No. 1, October 1902), 28–52.

[3] Above, Ch. III, last page.

[4] "The European states are combined together, and connected with one another by a multitude of important interests and relations with which the United States have no concern, with which they have always manifested the determination not to interfere, and of which, no communication being made to them by the Governments of Europe, they have not information competent to enable them to estimate their extent

"is the well-wisher to the freedom and independence of all. She is the champion and vindicator only of her own." In his instructions to Richard Anderson, first American Minister to Colombia, he repeated the words of "Marcellus." The United States would continue to be "tranquil but deeply attentive spectators" of the war between the new republics of Latin America and Spain. In the Monroe Doctrine the words would be "anxious and interested spectators," in favor of the liberty and happiness of fellow men on the other side of the Atlantic.

If the United States, according to John Quincy Adams, were not going to take the side of republican liberty in another people's struggle, whether in Europe or in America, it certainly would not take the side of absolutism and tyranny anywhere on the globe. Ever since 1818 Alexander I of Russia had been urging the Republic of the West to join the Holy Alliance and thus associate it with the collective mediation of legitimist Europe between Spain and her revolted colonies.[5] In his well-known instructions of 1820 to Henry Middleton, Minister to Russia, the Secretary of State explained for the benefit of Czar Alexander I why the President must decline a Russian invitation to membership in the "League of Peace." On this occasion he repeated the "great rule of conduct" of Washington's Farewell Address: "The political system of the United States is also[6] extra-European. To stand in firm and cautious independence of all entanglement in the European system, has been a cardinal point of their policy under every administration of their government from the peace of 1783 to this day. . . . It may be observed that for the repose of Europe, as well as of America, the European and American political systems should be kept as separate and distinct from each other as possible."[7] This is little more than he already had personally explained to the Czar in St. Petersburg back in 1809.

---

and bearings. The United States, in justice to themselves, in justice to that harmony which they earnestly desire to cultivate with all the powers of Europe, in justice to that fundamental system of policy which forbids them from entering the labyrinth of European politics, must decline soliciting or acceding to the interference of any other Government of Europe for the settlement of their differences with Spain." JQA to Luis de Onís, March 12, 1818. *ASPFR*, IV, 478. This is the state paper that Jefferson praised so highly.

[5] "Correspondence of the Russian Ministers in Washington, 1818–1825," *AHR*, XVIII (Nos. 2 and 3, January, April 1913), 309–45, 537–62. Dexter Perkins has described the relationship of "Russia and the Spanish Colonies, 1817–1818," in ibid., XXVIII (No. 4, July 1923), 656–73. See also William Spence Robertson: "Russia and the Emancipation of Spanish America, 1816–1826," *HAHR*, XXI (No. 2, May 1941), 196–221.

[6] I.e., like that of Persia and Turkey, whom Adams mentioned as having the most to dread from "the overshadowing and encroaching powers" of the Holy Alliance.

[7] JQA to Henry Middleton, Department of State, July 5, 1820. *Writings*, VII, 49–50. "I have read with much satisfaction your project of instructions to Mr. Middleton, for the discharge of his duties, in his mission to Russia. The objects to which you call his attention, are judiciously pointed out, and discussed. . . ." James Monroe to JQA, Highland, July 28, 1820. Adams MSS.

It was not Adams's idea alone. By 1820 the "doctrine of the two spheres," as publicists of the twentieth century call Adams's expressions of 1796, was widely current in American thought. It distilled and crystallized the diplomatic experience of American independence. It was orthodox to all the Fathers, particularly to Thomas Jefferson and John Adams.

John Quincy Adams's American System did not yet embrace the whole Hemisphere. "As to an American System," he exclaimed to President Monroe in 1820 regarding the use of that phrase by the Abbé Correa, "we have it; we constitute the whole of it; there is no community of interests or of principles between North and South America. Mr. Torres and Bolivar and O'Higgins talk about an American system as much as the Abbé Correa, but there is no basis for any such system."[8]

2

The dictum of Non-Colonization was Adamsonian. John Quincy Adams had long since believed that the United States was destined by God and nature peaceably to become a nation coextensive with the North American Continent.[9] Through the first half-century of American independence his continental instincts had nourished an opposition to all colonial dominion first in North America, then in South America. "Our natural dominion of North America" was the phrase he had used when explaining the departure of the *Ontario* to receive the surrender of Fort George at Astoria. In the treaties of 1818 with England and of 1819 with Spain he had successfully asserted that natural dominion.

Adams smarted under the invectives of the British press and English spokesmen against American expansion through the empty Continent. When the Cabinet was discussing the propriety of occupying Texas as well as Florida should Spain refuse to ratify the Transcontinental Treaty, Crawford had quoted William Lowndes, South Carolina's highly respected Congressman, just returned from a European trip, to the effect that in both England and France people seemed profoundly impressed with the idea that Americans were an ambitious and encroaching people. Similar remarks that Alexander H. Everett picked up when passing through London on his way to his post at The Hague had stirred John

[8] Monroe had been telling Adams that the Abbé Correa had been upon a visit to Jefferson, "to whom he talked so much about an American system, in which his Government [Portugal] and ours should be united, and, by concert with the European powers, should agree to keep the coasts of this hemisphere clear of pirates, on condition that they should sweep the seas of the Eastern Hemisphere clear of Barbary pirates. . . ." *Memoirs*, V, 176. September 19, 1820. "The idea [Correa's] has something imposing in it," Monroe had written to Adams on August 11, 1820, "but I am inclined to think, that the effect, would be, to connect us with Portugal, in some degree, against the revolutionary colonies." Adams MSS.

[9] Above, Ch. IX.

Quincy Adams's ire.[10] The way to stop such talk, he felt, was to convince the world that it was inevitable that the United States should peaceably take over all of North America: "any effort on our part to reason the world out of a belief that we are ambitious will have no other effect than to convince them that we add to our ambition hypocrisy." [11]

So far this expression was for the privity only of Monroe's official closet. The pretensions of Britain and Russia to the North West Coast of America (to be considered more particularly in later chapters) gave the Secretary of State occasions for presenting the Non-Colonization Principle first to the British Minister in Washington, and next to the Russian Minister.

"We certainly did suppose that the British Government had come to the conclusion," he said to Stratford Canning, in an oft-quoted conversation, January 26, 1821, concerning the Columbia River, "that there would be neither policy nor profit in caviling with us about territory on this North American Continent."

"And in this," Canning asked, "you include our northern provinces on this Continent."

"No," Adams admitted grudgingly. "There the boundary is marked, and we have no disposition to encroach upon it. Keep what is yours, but leave the rest of the Continent to us." [12]

That John Quincy Adams did not expect Great Britain to keep the rest of the Continent very long is evident from his significant Fourth-of-July

[10] "The Ministerial papers attack the unprincipled ambition of the United States, which they say will never be satisfied until it has invaded one whole American Continent." A. H. Everett to JQA, private, London, April 19, 1819. Received June 17. Adams MSS.

[11] "Nothing that we can say or do would remove this impression [Adams told his colleagues in the Cabinet] until the world shall be familiarized with the idea of considering our proper dominion to be the continent of North America. . . . Spain has possessions upon our southern and Great Britain upon our northern border. It is impossible that centuries shall elapse without finding them annexed to the United States; not that any spirit of encroachment or ambition on our part renders it necessary, but because it is a physical, moral, and political absurdity that such fragments of territory, with sovereigns at fifteen hundred [*sic*] miles beyond the sea, worthless and burdensome to their owners, should exist permanently contiguous to a great powerful and rapidly-growing nation. Most of the Spanish territory which had been in our neighborhood has already become our own by the most unexceptionable of all acquisitions — fair purchase for a valuable consideration. This renders it still more unavoidable that the remainder of the continent should ultimately be ours. But it is very lately that we have distinctly seen this ourselves; very lately that we have avowed the pretension of extending to the South Sea; and until Europe shall find it a settled geographical element that the United States and North America are identical, any effort on our part to reason the world out of a belief that we are ambitious will have no other effect than to convince them that we add to our ambition hypocrisy." *Memoirs,* IV, 438–9. November 16, 1819. Dexter Perkins's classic dissertation: *The Monroe Doctrine, 1823–1826* (Cambridge, 1927) has brought together in a notable chapter Adams's evolving expressions of the Non-Colonization Principle.

[12] *Memoirs,* V, 252. January 26, 1821.

address of 1821, when he affirmed the theory of noncolonization as a principle of anti-imperialism. In a remarkable exegesis of that discourse to his friend Edward Everett he explained that he had meant to point out that, from the moral and physical nature of man, "*colonial establishments cannot fulfil the great objects of governments in the just purposes of civil society.*" The address anticipated a vital question in the national policy of the United States: "whether we too shall annex to our federative government a great system of colonial establishments." It pointed to another principle: "that such establishments are incompatible with the essential character of our institutions." It led to a startling conclusion: "that great colonial establishments are engines of wrong, and that in the progress of social improvement it will be the duty of the human family to abolish them, as they are now endeavoring to abolish the slave trade." [13]

Adams came back to the Non-Colonization Principle again in November 1822 in another conversation with the British Minister, this time on restriction of trade with the British West Indies. "The whole system of modern colonization," he declared to Stratford Canning, "is an abuse of government and it is time that it should come to an end." [14]

The Secretary embodied the principle in a draft of instructions (June 1823) for the guidance of Middleton in St. Petersburg: the United States would contest the right of Russia to any territorial establishments on the Continent of North America. This categorical statement worried the President. After discussing the matter in Cabinet, Monroe decided to recognize the Russian claims north of 55° N.L.[15] But in an interview with von Tuyll on July 17, 1823 Adams managed to say what the President would not let him put into the instructions to Middleton: "I told him specially that we should contest the right of Russia to *any* territorial establishment on this continent, and that we should assume distinctly the principle that the American continents are no longer subjects for any new European colonial establishments."[16]

Adams had summoned forth the Non-Colonization Principle out of his own intuition. He expressed it gratuitously to both the British and the Russian Ministers. Once more before Monroe's famous message of December 2, 1823 he reiterated the idea for the benefit of the British Government. That was when he was drawing up instructions for the guidance of Richard Rush in parallel negotiations by the United States and Great Britain protesting Russian pretensions on the North West Coast. The independence of the South American states and of Mexico, he then stated, had extinguished the exclusive rights of Spain to any part of the Coast, such as she might have claimed at the time of the Nootka Sound Convention of 1790. "A necessary consequence of this state of things

[13] *Writings*, VII, 197–207. January 31, 1822.

[14] *Memoirs*, VI, 104. November 26, 1822.

[15] *Memoirs*, VI, 157–8. July 27, 1823.

[16] *Memoirs*, VI, 163. July 17, 1823.

will be that the American Continents henceforth will no longer be subjects of *colonization*."[17]

Thus all his life John Quincy Adams had been a spokesman of Abstention. And all students of the question have agreed that he was sole author of Non-Colonization. But what of the third dictum – Hands Off the New World, America for the Americans? To understand the provenance of this dogma and Adams's relation to it, we must return again to Europe, to the predicaments of British and of American diplomacy in the face of the Holy Alliance.

3

British policy after the overthrow of Napoleon embraced supremacy on the seas behind a balance of power concerted in the Quadruple Alliance (Austria, Great Britain, Prussia, Russia) to maintain the peace of Europe against another irruption of revolutionary France. Britain's continental allies under the leadership of Alexander I would fain have used the Quadruple Alliance for another purpose: to repress revolution wherever it might raise its head against a legitimist divine-right ruler. To that end the Czar had proclaimed in 1815, under lofty Christian principles, the Holy Alliance. It was signed originally by himself, the King of Prussia, the Emperor of Austria, and all the legitimist monarchs of Europe except the Sultan of Turkey, the Pope, and the Prince Regent of Great Britain. The British Regent could not condemn revolution too directly because his dynasty owed its throne to the Revolution of 1688. Therefore the Regent had to content himself with a personal letter to the Czar applauding the principles of the Holy Alliance without binding his own Government, which was responsible only to Parliament.

For the first few years following the peace settlement of 1815 – that is, until after the Conference of Aix-la-Chapelle – Lord Castlereagh had been able to hold the Quadruple Alliance to its strict purpose as interpreted by his Government; but in 1820 the continental allies got out of British control. At the Conference of Troppau-Laibach (1820–1) the Holy Allies, despite the dissent of Great Britain, gave a mandate to Austria to put down republican revolution in Naples and in Piedmont lest it spread to their own realms. At Verona in 1822 they again overrode British opposition and approved French military intervention in Spain to tear up the new constitution there and restore the absolute authority of Ferdinand VII. They even announced that if Great Britain, ally of Spain since the first Peninsular War, should interfere to assist the Spanish constitutionalists, they would come to the aid of France.

Castlereagh had failed in his task of holding the Quadruple Alliance to the compass of British policy. Overburdened by the immense responsi-

[17] JQA to Richard Rush, Department of State, July 22, 1823. *Writings of Monroe*, VI, 356–7.

bilities and labors of his office, his reason faltered and he made away with his own life on the eve of the Conference of Verona.

Castlereagh's tragic death opened the office of Foreign Affairs to his rival George Canning. Canning was son of an impoverished London barrister of ancient English lineage and Mary Anne Costello, reigning London beauty and in her later years a popular actress. He was the pride of Eton, Oxford, and the Inner Temple. In his youth he had been a liberal Whig, the friend of Burke, Fox, and Sheridan, but the excesses of the French Revolution drove him, like Burke, into the paths of Toryism, and he became Pitt's Undersecretary of Foreign Affairs, 1796–1801 (succeeding George Hammond), and Treasurer of the Navy, 1801–6. When Pitt died he momentarily went out of office. Then he married a rich bride, sister of the Duke of Portland, and came into the Government of his brother-in-law as Secretary for Foreign Affairs, 1807–9. It was Canning who planned the seizure of the Danish fleet after the Treaty of Tilsit, the coup that broke up Napoleon's formidable plans for a northern confederation against England. During his first tenure of the Foreign Office appeared the belligerent orders in council of November 1807, calculated to destroy competing American commerce.

When Castlereagh as Secretary for War diverted English forces originally planned for the Peninsula to stem the French at Flushing, Canning resented the move and intrigued secretly to unseat his colleague, the while preserving outwardly friendly relations with him in the Cabinet. As soon as Castlereagh awoke to the invidious situation, he challenged Canning to a duel. The Ministers fired two rounds at close pistol range. It is a wonder they did not shoot each other dead. Their first shots went nervously wild. Happily Canning's second glanced harmless off a metal button of his opponent's coat, and Castlereagh's next try gave Canning a slight flesh wound in the thigh. The famous encounter ended Canning's first ministerial career; he could scarcely serve in the Cabinet as long as his rival held any office therein.

The two Tory diplomatists, the greatest England ever had, pursued, each in his own way, Britain's interests in holding the balance of power in Europe. Castlereagh, a strong and serene statesman, adroit and tactful in personal diplomacy, strove to keep the balance by grouping the powers lest any one, notably Russia, get out of hand and become preponderant. Canning, a witty littérateur — too much wit, thought John Quincy Adams,[18] for a Secretary of State — and brilliant parliamentarian, did not believe much in the efficacy of the European concert. He sought to maintain the balance in Britain's favor by building up wherever possible irresistible situations with which to oppose and to outweigh his adversaries. One such situation he found ready to hand in Latin America.

When Canning reappeared in the Foreign Office, 1822–7, it was difficult to oppose the Holy Alliance on the Continent of Europe. Welling-

[18] *Memoirs,* III, 337.

ton's army of the Napoleonic wars no longer existed. The fleet was powerless to stop a continental force from crossing the Pyrenees. Moreover, the King, the Duke of Wellington, and influential Tory leaders sympathized with the French intervention as long as it limited itself to the suppression of revolution and did not extend its force to collide with British interests beyond the boundaries of Spain.

With the Quadruple Alliance in ruins in Europe and the political front divided at home, Canning went as far as he could when he stated in the House of Commons that he hoped the Spanish constitutionalists would win out: "Indifference we can never feel towards the affairs of Spain: and I earnestly hope and trust that she may come triumphantly out of the struggle." [19]

As hostilities broke out south of the Pyrenees, the new Foreign Minister communicated to the French Government, through a dispatch (March 31, 1823) to Sir Charles Stuart, the Ambassador at Paris, a formal warning implying that war would follow if France should establish a permanent military occupation of Spain, or should appropriate any portion of the Spanish colonies, or should violate the territorial integrity of Portugal.

Canning concluded his dispatch to Stuart, published in England within five days after its signature, with these words:

> With respect to the Provinces in America which have thrown off their allegiance to the Crown of Spain. . . . Spain has long been apprized of His Majesty's opinions upon this subject. Disclaiming in the most solemn manner any intention of appropriating to himself the smallest portion of the late Spanish possessions in America, His Majesty is satisfied that no attempt will be made by France to bring under her dominion any of those possessions, either by conquest or by cession from Spain.[20]

France had invaded Spain with the mandate of the Holy Alliance. The Quadruple Alliance was dead. How could the unbalance of Europe now be compensated? [21] Where else could Canning rally an opposition to French intervention in the affairs of Latin America, first step perhaps in a revival of a French colonial empire and of French sea power?

There was left only one direction in which to turn. That was across the Atlantic. In the House of Commons on April 16, 1823 Canning made a speech defending British neutrality and specifically opposing repeal of the Foreign Enlistments Act. He went out of his way to extol as a model the American principles of neutrality in the War of the French Revolu-

[19] Temperley: *Canning*, p. 85.

[20] Webster: *Britain and the Independence of Latin America*, II, 111–12.

[21] "Canning had to win diplomatic prestige over Spanish America as a set-off to his diplomatic defeat in Europe." Temperley: *Canning*, p. 103.

tion.[22] A week later he gave a dinner to the diplomatic corps to celebrate the King's birthday. When it came the turn of the American Minister to raise his glass, Richard Rush gave the toast: "To the success of neutrals!" Canning applauded conspicuously and made further flattering references to Jefferson and American neutrality.[23]

Responding to Lord Castlereagh's general policy of appeasement and repose, Anglo-American relations had been ameliorating steadily, notably in regard to the territorial questions on the Continent of North America. The focus of rivalry had now shifted from the Great Lakes and the Northwest to the Caribbean and Cuba. That island had become as essential to the protection of Florida as previously Florida had been to the safety of Louisiana. The integrity of both Florida and Louisiana – that is to say, the security of the westward-advancing Continental Republic – now depended on who possessed Cuba. While the Holy Alliance sponsored the French occupation of Spain and British diplomacy deployed to resist any further intervention of France to restore Spanish sovereignty in the New World, John Quincy Adams had his eyes fixed on England as well as on France. Like his father in his time, he knew that France could not break through British sea power to reach the Western Hemisphere. What worried him was that the Spanish constitutionalists might cede Cuba and perhaps Porto Rico to England as the price of a new Anglo-Spanish alliance in another Peninsular War.

Cuba was of vital interest to the United States, and it was clearly desirable that it should continue for the time being in Spanish hands. Presidents Jefferson, Madison, and Monroe had never been so sympathetic to revolutionary strivings in that island as they had been toward insurrection in the Spanish provinces of the mainland. When an agent, Don Barnabé Sanchez, tried to get the authorities in Washington to encourage a revolution in Havana for the independence of Cuba and its admission into the American Union as a new state, Monroe's Government would not see him or have anything to do with him.[24] The members of the Administration feared that a premature uprising in the Pearl of the Antilles – before the slavery question was settled in the United States [25] – might disturb what Madison had once referred to as the "manifest course of events," and what John Quincy Adams now called "the law of political gravitation" [26] – that is, ultimate annexation to the United States. "The Cuban question," Adams noted after a Cabinet meeting of Septem-

[22] *Speeches of George Canning*, R. Thierry, editor, V (London, 1886), 24–52.

[23] Richard Rush to James Monroe, April 24, 1823. Cited by Whitaker: *U.S. and Independence of Latin America*, pp. 435–7.

[24] Copies of correspondence between Peter S. Duponceau and General John Mason. September 1822. Adams MSS.

[25] "Were the population of the island of one blood and color, there could be no doubt or hesitation with regard to the course they [the United States] would pursue, as dictated by their interests and their rights." *Writings*, VII, 375.

[26] *Writings*, VII, 373.

ber 30, 1822, was of "deeper importance and greater magnitude than had occurred since the establishment of our Independence."[27]

There were at least two contingencies in which Europe's new war might become America's war, Adams believed: a maritime war resulting in the impressment of American seamen, or a war threatening the transfer of neighboring Spanish territory, like Cuba or Porto Rico, in such a way as to endanger the security of the Union. It was such a possibility that led him to apply the No-Transfer Principle of 1811 to the island of Cuba in the summer of 1823 as French armies occupied Spain.[28]

Cuba was also of vital interest to Britain. "It may be questioned," noted George Canning in a Cabinet Memorandum, "whether any blow, that could be struck by any power in any part of the world, would have a more sensible effect on the interests of this country or the reputation of its government." The British Government did not want to see the island transferred to France or the United States any more than the United States cared to have it transferred to Great Britain or France. American possession of Cuba would jeopardize the Jamaica trade and ruin Britain's position and interests in the whole Caribbean.[29] Canning directed his cousin Stratford, Minister in Washington, to inquire into the "designs" of the United States upon that Spanish colony, without putting any categorical questions to Mr. Adams.[30]

During the diplomatic crisis that preceded the French invasion of Spain, Canning proclaimed the intention to land naval forces in Cuba if necessary in order to pursue pirates preying on British shipping. For the benefit of Monroe's Government he directed Stratford to read (but not to give a copy) to John Quincy Adams the instructions of December 1 to Sir Charles Stuart, British Ambassador in Paris, disavowing any thought of taking advantage of such a "trespass" on Cuban soil for the purpose of appropriating any part of Spanish America, and "giving full credit" to the King of France for being actuated by similar principles.[31] Such assurance was not a full pledge to the United States, but it was helpful.

It was at this juncture that President Monroe suggested to his Cabinet the proposing to Great Britain of a mutual self-denial not to take Cuba.

[27] *Memoirs,* VI, 72–3.

[28] Instructions from JQA to Hugh Nelson, the new Minister going out to Spain. Department of State, April 28, 1823. *Writings,* VII, 369–422. See particularly pp. 379–81 of the *Writings.* Whitaker, op. cit., p. 400, has pointed out from JQA's *Memoirs,* VI, 138, that Adams did not believe it was within the competency of the United States to "prevent by war the British from obtaining possession of Cuba, if they attempted to take it."

[29] Webster: *Britain and the Independence of Latin America,* II, 393–4.

[30] George Canning to Stratford Canning, No. 7, Secret, Foreign Office, October 11, 1822 (draft). PRO, F.O., 5, Vol. CLXV.

[31] George Canning to Sir Charles Stuart, No. 15, December 3, 1822. Webster, op. cit., II, 110.

The Secretary of War as well as the Secretary of State immediately objected. Nothing could be gained by it, thought Calhoun. It would involve a proposal to Spain also, said Adams, and would plunge the United States into the "whirlpool" of European politics.[32]

Reassurance soon came in from London after Stratford Canning had reported the absence of any American intention to occupy Cuba.[33] The Prime Minister, Lord Liverpool, assured Richard Rush that the British Government, although it would tolerate no change in the island's sovereignty, had no intention to take over Cuba itself.[34] In this way a sort of gentleman's agreement sprang up between Monroe and Canning in 1823 that it would be best to let Cuba rest in the quiet possession of Spain. Monroe relied on Great Britain to bring France into the informal understanding.[35]

Thus another great issue in Anglo-American relations seemed quieted, the issue of intervention in the New World, notably in Cuba.[36]

4

Now that the two powers had come to see eye to eye on the Holy Alliance and the danger of European intervention in the Western Hemisphere, the opposing attitudes of the United States and Great Britain as to the *independence* of the new states of Latin America remained the only difference of policy in this part of the world. And it was reasonable to expect that the question of independence must soon settle itself.

There were, however, several other long-standing Anglo-American issues of more than regional significance. The Monroe Administration had been striving in vain ever since its inauguration to settle them with Lord Castlereagh: impressment, suppression of the African slave trade, the Freedom of the Seas, and colonial trade, not to mention still unsettled boundary controversies in the northeast and the northwest. It had long been the thought of Monroe and Adams that if these differences could first be settled the way would be open for a concert of policy in regard to Latin America. Now it looked as though the process might be reversed, that a concert of policy toward Latin America might open the way for settlement of the historic controversies between the United States and Great

[32] *Memoirs,* VI, 138. March 17, 1823.

[33] Stratford Canning to George Canning, No. 3, Washington, January 1, 1823 (received February 6, 1823), No. 10 (Secret), January 11, 1823 (received February 14, 1823), and No. 17, February 4, 1823 (received March 10, 1823). PRO, F.O. 5, Vol. CLXXV.

[34] Richard Rush to JQA, No. 298, London, March 10, 1823. Received April 6. DS, *Despatches from U.S. Ministers to Great Britain,* XVIII.

[35] JQA to W. E. Channing, Quincy, July 31, August 11, 1837. *N.E. Quarterly,* V (No. 3, July 1932), 594–600.

[36] Stratford Canning to George Canning, No. 56, Confidential, Washington, June 6, 1823. Webster, op. cit., II, 495–6.

Britain. The disappearance of issues in regard to the former Spanish Empire — above all, the confirmed neutrality of Great Britain in the Spanish-American conflict as well as in the Franco-Spanish hostilities in the Peninsula — promised to make neutral rights and interests as significant to Great Britain as her old belligerent pretensions had been during the last cycle of wars. At least so Adams professed to believe. If this were true, might it not be possible to resolve the vexatious issues that had separated the two Governments since the Napoleonic conflict? With the President's approbation, he began to draw up instructions to Richard Rush in London for another general negotiation with Great Britain to resolve for all time the old disputes that had caused the War of 1812.[37] Parallel to this would be a negotiation with Russia, by Henry Middleton in St. Petersburg, on the question of neutral rights, freedom of commerce on the North West Coast, and boundaries. These two negotiations will be the subject of later chapters. Here we must observe the more immediate significance of Anglo-American affairs for Latin America.

Stratford Canning noted the new and happier spirit in official Washington. "The course which you have taken in the great politics of Europe," he wrote privately to his cousin George, "has had the effect of making the English almost popular in the United States. The improved tone of public feeling is very perceptible, and even Adams has caught a something of the soft infection. The communication of your correspondence with France has also had its effect. On the whole, I question whether for a long time there has been so favorable an opportunity — as far as general disposition and good will are concerned — to bring the two countries nearer together. France for the moment is quite out of fashion. It may possibly be worth your while to give this a turn in your thoughts." [38]

John Quincy Adams broached his plans to the British Minister. "Britain has separated herself from the councils and measures of the alliance," he observed to Stratford. "She avows the principles which are emphatically those of the United States, and she disapproves the principles of the alliance, which this country abhors. This coincidence of principles, connected with the great changes in affairs of the world, passing before us, seems to me a suitable occasion for the United States and Great Britain to compare their ideas and purposes together, with a view to the accommodation of great interests upon which they have hitherto differed."

Stratford Canning preferred to think that this might be a proposal for an alliance, but Adams insisted that it had been always the policy of the United States to hold aloof from the European System of politics. What

[37] JQA to R. Rush, Department of State, July 22, July 28 (No. 71), 1823. *Writings of Monroe,* VI, 356–61.

[38] May 8, 1823. Perkins, op. cit., p. 60, citing PRO, F.O., 352, Vol. VIII, and Stratford Canning Papers. See also Stratford Canning to George Canning, No. 56, Washington, June 6, 1823. Webster, op. cit., II, 495.

he was talking about, he said, was an agreement on neutral rights, impressment, the slave trade, and commerce with the British colonies [39] — the settlement of the already historic Anglo-American issues.

With affairs in this satisfying position, Adams, in tranquil spirit, set forth in mid-August 1823 for his annual vacation with his aged father in Quincy.

5

In London, George Canning chose to interpret the soft American infection as a disposition not so much to define and strengthen neutral rights as to oppose European intervention in Latin America, particularly any threatened French occupation of the island of Cuba. An opportunity to exploit the new feeling presented itself when Rush casually asked about affairs on the Continent. "Should France ultimately effect her purpose of overthrowing the constitutional government in Spain," he remarked, "there is, at least, the consolation left that Great Britain would not allow her to go farther and stop the progress of emancipation in the colonies."

In this transient remark George Canning, prompted by Stratford's suggestions from Washington, was quick to see an opening.

"What do you think your Government would say to going hand in hand with England in such a policy?" he asked Rush. "Not that any concert of *action* under it would become necessary, because I fully believe that the simple fact of our two countries being known to hold the same opinions would, by its moral effect, put down the intention on the part of France, if she entertains it. I base this belief upon the large share of the maritime power of the world which Great Britain and the United States share between them, and the consequent influence which the knowledge of their common policy, on a question involving such important maritime interests, present and future, could not fail to produce everywhere."

"I am unable to say in what manner my Government would look upon such a suggestion . . ." Rush replied, "but I will communicate it in the same informal manner in which you have thrown it before me." Then he added, acutely: "I can hardly do this to full advantage unless you will at the same time enlighten me as to the precise situation in which England stands in relation to those new communities, and especially on the material point of acknowledging their independence."

Canning answered that Great Britain would not object to an accommodation between Spain and the colonies which might even secure to Spain commercial advantages not extended to other nations. Great Britain would not offer her mediation again but would not interfere to prevent a compromise.

"Is Great Britain at this moment taking any steps," Rush asked more

[39] *Memoirs,* VI, 151–5. June 20, 1823.

specifically, "or contemplating any, which have reference to the recognition of these new communities, that being the point on which the United States would naturally feel most interest?"

"None whatever, as yet," admitted Canning, "but she is on the eve of taking one of a preparatory nature, which will leave her at large to recognize or not, according to the position of events at a future period." [40]

This was the first of several conversations between the two diplomatists in August and September 1823 during which Canning proposed in writing that the United States and Great Britain issue a joint declaration of policy in regard to the Spanish-American question as follows:

1. We conceive the recovery of the colonies by Spain to be hopeless.
2. We conceive the question of the recognition of them, as independent states, to be one of time and circumstances.
3. We are, however, by no means disposed to throw any impediment in the way of an arrangement between them and the mother country by amicable negotiations.
4. We aim not at the possession of any portion of them ourselves.
5. We could not see any portion of them transferred to any other power with indifference.[41]

That is to say, Canning sought to implement by an Anglo-American concert the policy of Britain laid down publicly in the instructions to Stuart of the previous March 31.

The British Foreign Minister asked Rush if he had powers to sign a convention, or at least an exchange of notes, on this subject. In repeated conversations until September 26 he urged the desirability of such a joint pronouncement. He stated that he had just received "notice" that as soon as the French occupation of Spain was completed a conference of the Allies would be proposed to discuss the affairs of South America.

Richard Rush had no explicit powers to join in such a statement. But he was willing to risk his career for the independence of the New World.[42] If the step would benefit his own Government, well and good,

[40] Richard Rush: *Memoranda of a Residence at the Court of London* (Philadelphia, 1845), II, 10–13. W. C. Ford printed Rush's correspondence on Canning's overture, together with documents from the Adams papers, hitherto unprinted, in his articles, op. cit. See also the documentary history of the origin of the Monroe Doctrine in S. M. Hamilton's edition of *Writings of Monroe,* VI, 319–444. Manning, III, Nos. 790, 791, 797, printed some important dispatches from Rush, and letters from him to Canning, not previously published. I have put the conversation into direct discourse observing its literal content if not its entire phraseology, which varies slightly but not materially in Rush's different versions.

[41] Canning to Rush, Private and Confidential, Foreign Office, August 20, 1823. Moore: *Digest of International Law,* VI, 389.

[42] J. H. Powell: *Richard Rush, Republican Diplomat, 1780–1859* (Philadelphia, 1942), p. 160. This biography adds a few new interesting details to previous accounts

he would sign; if he proved to be wrong, his Government could disavow him.[43] But first Canning must recognize the independence of the new republics.

The British Foreign Minister was now courting the United States more and more ardently.[44] Through Rush he had sent to President Monroe and to John Quincy Adams prints, corrected in his own hand, of his speech of April 16, 1823 against repeal of the Foreign Enlistment Act: "If I wished for a guide in a system of neutrality, I should take that laid down by America in the presidency of Washington and the secretaryship of Jefferson." [45]

Canning's flatteries did not stop with this compliment. In Liverpool an obscure American diplomat, happening to be in that port at the time of a visit of the Foreign Minister there, was surprised to find himself the object of unusual attentions. Christopher Hughes, John Quincy Adams's old friend from Ghent days, now chargé d'affaires at Stockholm and voluminous private correspondent on European politics, arrived in Liverpool in mid-August 1823 en route to London and St. Petersburg with instructions to Rush and Middleton. The Mayor of the city invited him to a special dinner for the British statesman, and the Steam Boat Company sent tickets for an "aquatic excursion" for the visiting notables. The captain even stopped the boat to take on Hughes after the excursion had been under way for two hours. On board, Canning overwhelmed him with special courtesies and kindness. When they went on shore he took the astonished diplomat's arm and made a great object of showing him the town, as if to demonstrate how warm his feelings were for Britain's great friends and customers. It was, Hughes thought, as if to make up for all Britain's former offenses to the Yankees.

In seductive confidence Canning informed Hughes that the court of St. Petersburg had retracted all the extravagant old claims and pretensions to the control and command of the North Pacific Ocean.[46] "The only question," he said, "to *settle*, is how moderately *we* shall let them

---

of the Rush-Canning conversations, but informs us that the great mass of Rush's papers, now owned by descendants, is still not available to historical scholars. Whitaker, op. cit., however, used the material relating to the immediate background of the Monroe Doctrine.

[43] Rush to JQA, London, August 28, 1823. Manning, III, 1483.

[44] "We were not prepared to acknowledge [Latin-American independence] immediately; and of course we would not stipulate against Spain. Our flirtation therefore went off; but it left a tenderness behind it. It was in the midst of this flirtation that I made the speech at Liverpool. . . ." George Canning to Bagot, Private and Confidential, January 22, 1824. Josceline Bagot: *George Canning and His Friends* (London, 1909), II, 215–18.

[45] *Speeches of George Canning*, V, 50. Rush to JQA, London, July 13, 1823, transmitting copies of the speech, with Canning's personal covering note. Adams MSS.

[46] See below, Ch. XXV.

down, or let them off; or what shall be the nature of the atonement we shall consent to receive for their folly. . . . I conceive your interests are in common with ours in these questions with Russia."[47]

The climax came at the banquet when Canning proposed the health of the overwhelmed chargé. Great Britain and the United States, he said, had already forgotten their former dissensions: "The force of blood again prevails, and the daughter and the mother stand together against the world."[48]

Turning Christopher Hughes over to the hospitality of the Duke of Buckingham,[49] George Canning hastened back to London and conferred with his cousin Stratford, just returned from Washington.[50] Then he renewed his American suit. He pleaded long and passionately with Rush to take the plunge into the vortex of European politics without Britain's first recognizing Latin-American independence.

"If you continue to be unable to assent to my past proposals," said the British Minister, "my duties and station as the organ of this Government may oblige me to call upon you in another way. If a Congress be assembled upon the affairs of Spanish America, I shall ask that you, as the representative of the United States at this court, be invited to attend. If you are not invited, I shall reserve to myself the option of determining whether or not Great Britain shall send a representative to it. Hence you see the complication of the whole subject; hence you see how essential it is, in the opinion of Great Britain, that the United States should not be left out of view, if Europe is determined to take cognizance of the subject."

Rush was impressed, but not convinced. "You can cure the complication at once," he responded. "Let Great Britain immediately and unequivocally acknowledge the independence of the new states. This will put an end to all difficulty. The moment is auspicious, everything invites to the measure, justice, expediency, humanity; the repose of the world, the cause of national independence, the prosperity and happiness of both hemispheres.

47 Christopher Hughes to JQA, private, Liverpool, August 27, 1823. Italics inserted. Adams MSS.

48 *Speeches of George Canning*, VI, 414. "He did not know then," says a most distinguished historian of British diplomacy, "that the daughter and the mother, though they were both to stand against the world, were to stand against it in separation." Temperley: *Canning*, p. 2.

49 Christopher Hughes to JQA, private, Brussels, October 28, 1826, describes how "somehow or other" the Duke of Buckingham "took me into great favor, in the year 1823, as I passed through England." Adams MSS. Canning gave Hughes a letter to Charles Bagot, now British Ambassador to Russia: "I hope he will be as acceptable an accident to you in your Metropolis as he has been to me in mine." "He is not yet recovered from his delight and astonishment of all that befell him at Liverpool," Bagot wrote to Canning on October 29, 1823. J. Bagot: *Canning and His Friends*, II, 199, 200.

50 J. Bagot: *Canning and His Friends*, II, 200.

Let Britain but adopt this measure — so just in itself, so recommended by the point of time before us — the cause of all Spanish American triumphs. The European Congress may meet afterward, if it sees fit!"[51]

A parallel or even joint recognition of independence is what Monroe's Administration had been suggesting to London ever since 1818 in order to detach Britain from the designs of her continental allies. Castlereagh had consistently avoided the proposal. To accept it was almost equivalent to underwriting the Latin-American policy of the United States. Now Canning, his successor, was almost proposing to do that very thing. But he was unwilling to substitute immediate recognition for point 2 of his proposed joint pronouncement. Even if he wished to do so, it was doubtful whether he could have brought around his Tory colleagues, Lord Liverpool and the Duke of Wellington, to immediate recognition of independence of the new republics. He still insisted on leaving this vital question to "time and circumstances," the most noncommittal formula a diplomat could devise. Rush therefore said that he must wait for instructions.

Suddenly Canning cooled off. He ceased to press his startling proposal upon Rush, except to ask that it be kept absolutely confidential. The American Minister became suspicious. He began to doubt the wisdom of signing the joint pronouncement even after prior British recognition of Latin-American independence. Great Britain, he concluded, was more interested in balancing and holding down European power than in protecting the liberties of Latin America. "It is France that must not be aggrandized, not South America that must be made free."[52] He wondered whether the final complete occupation of Spain had led Canning to secure some fresh explanation from France, which would explain the sudden and full pause of his conversations. "I do not know, and most likely never shall know if events so fall out that Great Britain no longer finds it necessary to seek the aid of the United States in furtherance of her schemes of counteraction as against France and Russia."[53]

Rush had guessed the riddle of Canning's sudden silence. The Foreign Minister, uncertain whether Rush could secure the consent of his Government to the British proposal as it stood, did not wait for the correspondence to cross and recross the ocean. Hastily he turned to the French Ambassador in London, the Prince de Polignac. He notified him in effect that Great Britain would not allow France to take advantage of the situation in Spain in order to appropriate any part of Spanish possessions in America, or to act against the "Colonies" by force of arms. Specifically, he required the French Ambassador to pledge formally, in the Polignac Memorandum of October 9, 1823:

[51] Richard Rush to JQA, London, September 19, 1823. Manning, III, 1490.

[52] Rush to JQA, No. 336, October 10, 1823, received November 19. Ford, op. cit., 59–60.

[53] Ibid.

That his Government believed it to be utterly hopeless to reduce Spanish-America to the state of its former relation to Spain.

That France disclaimed, on her part, any intention or desire to avail herself of the present state of the Colonies, or of the present situation of France toward Spain, to appropriate to herself any part of the Spanish Possessions in America. . . .

That she abjured, in any case, any design of acting against the colonies by force of arms." [54]

It was this lone British showdown,[55] the Polignac Memorandum, imposed by the controlling force of the royal navy, that cut short any ambitious adventure that France alone might have developed amid the ruins of Spanish America.

Canning did not inform Rush of the Polignac Memorandum until November 24, eight days before the delivery of President Monroe's famous message to Congress, and did not read to Rush the above-quoted part of the document until December 13, eleven days after President Monroe had had his say in Washington.

In the Polignac Memorandum France had by no means renounced the idea of a European conference to settle the status of the former Spanish colonies. In November 1823 Ferdinand VII requested such a gathering. Canning worked ingeniously to frustrate it. The continental Allies themselves were divided as to the wisdom of a meeting. Had there been a conference it is not likely that it would have sanctioned any reconquest of Latin America. But the conflicting interests of the European powers were not fully understood in Washington in the autumn of 1823 any more than people on this side of the Atlantic knew about the Polignac Memorandum. People feared something ominous out of Europe. John Quincy Adams with his rich background of European politics came closest to divining the real situation. And, of course, he had before him Canning's instruction of March 31 to Sir Charles Stuart, which told the world that Britain would not allow France to intervene in Spanish America.

It is time to turn to the deliberations that took place in Monroe's Cabinet when news arrived of Canning's extraordinary proposals to Rush. Out of them came Adams's formulation of the third dictum of the Monroe Doctrine.

[54] Perkins: *Monroe Doctrine, 1823–1826*, p. 118, citing *British and Foreign State Papers*, 1823–4, XI (London, 1843), 49–54. The officially published version (March 1824) was only a summary of the conversations. Temperley published the whole record for the first time in *The Cambridge History of British Foreign Policy* (London, 1922–3), II, 633–7, and gives an analytic summary of the full conversations in his *Canning*, pp. 115–17.

[55] Technically it was not an ultimatum.

CHAPTER XIX
President Monroe's Message of December 2, 1823 (November–December, 1823)

A combined system of policy.

JOHN QUINCY ADAMS'S RECOMMENDATION TO THE CABINET, NOVEMBER 7, 1823

THE PRESIDENT had Rush's dispatches [1] on his desk when John Quincy Adams called at the White House the afternoon of his return from Massachusetts, October 11, 1823. Calhoun was there at the moment. Presently the Attorney General, William Wirt, came in. Some preliminary discussion took place.[2] Monroe thought the subject demanded the highest consideration. But he did not deem it necessary to postpone a visit to his home in Loudon County, Virginia, which he had planned to take as soon as the Secretary of State got back to Washington. He requested Adams to have copies of the documents sent to him in the country.[3]

1

Amid the cooler breezes of Oak Hill, President Monroe pondered Canning's unprecedented propositions and their significance for American

[1] These were Rush's No. 323 of August 19, and No. 326 of August 28, 1823, enclosing Canning's written proposals for the joint pronouncement. They were received October 9, 1823. *Writings of Monroe,* VI, 361–72.

[2] "Some discussion concerning despatches received from R. Rush with a confidential correspondence between G. Canning and him relating to S. America." Diary, October 11, 1823. The private *Memoirs* contain no entry from September 11 to November 7, 1823. JQA's Journal or Diary is blank from October 11 to November 7. But he kept a line-a-day minute book, for reference in writing up his main Diary. From January 25, 1823 to October 31, 1826 he kept a Short Diary of four or five lines a day, in which he made summary entries when pressure of occupations prevented him from writing up the arrears of his Journal. JQA's Minute Book and Short Diary reveal that the President left on October 12 for a visit to his home in Loudon County, Virginia, and returned on November 5; that on the morning of November 5 he discussed Rush's dispatches with Adams; that Monroe held a Cabinet meeting on November 7 to consider Canning's proposals, and the answer to be made to Tuyll's note; but contain no further details concerning these matters.

[3] Monroe to JQA, Washington, October 11, 1823. Adams MSS

foreign policy at the close of the Age of Emancipation. He was inclined to meet the proposals of the British Government. A successful intervention by the Holy Alliance in South America now might mean an attack soon afterward on the United States. Would it not be best to make sure that Great Britain would be on our side in such a danger? But second thought raised disturbing questions. After all, was this an occasion for departing from the sound and long-established maxim, laid down by George Washington and pursued by Thomas Jefferson, of absention from the ordinary vicissitudes of European politics and the ordinary combinations and collisions of European friendships or enmities? Or was this an ordinary vicissitude? Was it a purely European question? Was it not an American question too?

In this moment for grave consideration President Monroe turned to his two fellow Republican ex-Presidents, Thomas Jefferson and James Madison. For nearly half a century he had contended at their side harmoniously and faithfully for the nation's interests as they had seen them.[4] Perhaps it was only natural that he should seek counsel from them rather than from another surviving ex-President and father of American independence, John Adams, the one-time Federalist. Anyway, the diplomatist son of the sage of Quincy would be on hand in Washington.

The two Virginia ex-Presidents strengthened the disposition of their fellow statesman at Oak Hill to go along with Canning. Neither Jefferson nor Madison insisted on a prior recognition by Great Britain of the independence of the new republics of Latin America. Jefferson considered the question the most momentous since the independence of the United States. He thought that the proposed concert with Great Britain would introduce and establish the American System, "of keeping out of our land all *foreign powers*, of never permitting those of Europe to interfere with the affairs of our nations." If a war resulted it would be our war as well as Europe's war, with Great Britain on our side.

Jefferson had long coveted Cuba. He did not lose that island from sight as he pondered Canning's fourth proposition: "That we aim not at the possession of any portion of them [the Spanish colonies] for ourselves." Under the circumstances of 1823 he concluded that such a self-denial would be worth the price of making it, particularly because it would bind England against taking the island from Spain; it would not necessarily prevent the annexation of a free and independent Cuba some day to the United States.[5]

Madison, too, was entirely in favor of accepting Canning's proposal of

[4] James Monroe to Thomas Jefferson, Oak Hill, October 17, 1823. *Writings of Monroe*, VI, 323–4. The President did not reveal to the Secretary of State his correspondence with Jefferson and Madison until November 15, after he had returned to the White House. Ford, *AHR*, VIII (No. 1, 1902), 29.

[5] Jefferson to Monroe, Monticello, October 24, 1823. *Writings of Jefferson*, Memorial Edition, XV, 477–80.

an Anglo-American manifesto. He suggested a step further: that the two powers join in condemning French intervention in Spain, and in a declaration on behalf of the revolted Greeks in southeastern Europe. "There ought not to be any backwardness therefore, I think, in meeting her [Great Britain] in the way she has proposed. . . . Our co-operation is due to ourselves and to the world: and whilst it must ensure success in the event of an appeal to force, it doubles the chance of success without that appeal. . . . With the British power and navy combined with our own we have nothing to fear from the rest of the nations and in *the great struggle of the Epoch between liberty and despotism,* we owe it to ourselves to sustain the former in this hemisphere at least." [6]

2

With the opinions of Jefferson and Madison in his portfolio, corroborating his own reaction to Canning's propositions, James Monroe returned to Washington on November 4, 1823. Meanwhile surprising new developments had arisen from what was esteemed to be a significant communication from the Russian Minister at Washington.

A "crisis" was heading up in American foreign policy. A formal note from Baron von Tuyll, delivered to Adams October 16, had announced that the Czar, in conformance with the principles of his allies, would not receive any agents whatsoever from any of the rebel governments in America. It suggestively expressed satisfaction that the United States, in recognizing the independence of those Governments, at least had proclaimed its intention *to continue neutral.*[7] Was this not at least an intimation that, if the United States should swerve from neutrality and espouse the cause of the new states, the Czar of Russia, spokesman of the Holy Alliance, would support the authority of old Spain, and of France behind Spain?

In the first Cabinet meeting after his return to Washington the President brought up both Canning's overtures to Rush and Tuyll's note to the Secretary of State. Perhaps the one might be used to offset the other.

Calhoun promptly proposed giving discretionary powers to Rush to join "if necessary" in a declaration with Canning against the interference of the Holy Allies even if it should pledge the United States never to take Cuba or the province of Texas.

"The power of Great Britain being greater than ours to *seize* upon them," declared the Secretary of War, "we should get the advantage of obtaining from her the same declaration we should make ourselves."

John Quincy Adams did not want to bind the United States categorically against its Manifest Destiny. "I do not think the two cases parallel,"

[6] James Madison to James Monroe, Montpelier, October 30, November 1, 1823. *Writings of Monroe,* VI, 394–5. Italics inserted.

[7] Von Tuyll to JQA, Washington, October 4/16, 1823. Ford, op. cit., 32.

he said. "We have no intention of seizing either Texas or Cuba. But the inhabitants of either or both of them may exercise their primitive rights, and solicit a union with us. They will certainly do no such thing to Great Britain. . . . Without entering now into the enquiry of the expediency of our annexing Texas or Cuba to our Union, we should at least keep ourselves free to act as emergencies arise and not tie ourselves down to any principle which might immediately afterwards be brought to bear against ourselves."

"I incline to the same opinion," said Samuel L. Southard, the new Secretary of the Navy. That was about all he did say during the long discussions that followed. He continued to incline toward Adams's views.

"I am averse to any course which would have the appearance of taking a position subordinate to that of Great Britain," affirmed the President. "I suggest sending a special Minister to *protest* against the interposition of the Holy Alliance."

That idea fell rather flat on everybody present.

"Whether we ought in any event to attend a Congress of the Allies on this subject, if invited," observed Adams, "is a question for separate consideration."

"We ought in no case to attend," said Calhoun.

They all assented to Adams's suggestion that since the United States had recognized the independence of the Latin-American states, there could be no object in attending any European congress to consider their fate.

Adams then launched out on the subject of the recent Russian communication.

"It affords," he stated, "a very suitable and convenient opportunity for us to take our stand against the Holy Alliance and at the same time to decline the overture of Great Britain. It would be more candid, as well as more dignified, to avow our principles explicitly to Russia and France, than to come in as a cock-boat in the wake of the British man-of-war."

All acquiesced readily enough in these sentiments. The Secretary of State then read them the draft of a reply to Tuyll, which they approved, together with what he would be prepared to say to the Russian Minister in oral conference.

John Quincy Adams felt that the occasion required a systematic exposition of policy.

"The answer to be given to Baron Tuyll," he observed to the President after the meeting broke up, "the instructions to Mr. Rush relative to the proposals of Mr. Canning, those to Mr. Middleton at St. Petersburg, and those to the Minister who must be sent to France, *must all be parts of a combined system of policy and adapted to each other.*"

Monroe agreed.[8]

[8] *Memoirs,* VI, 177–80. November 7, 1823. Italics inserted.

A week later Adams delivered the American note to the Russian Minister, after the President had revised and simplified it in wording rather than content. It was a most moderate and amicable missive. In carefully courteous language it explained why the United States, acting in its sovereign capacity upon principles different from Russia's, had recognized the independence of the Latin-American republics and received their agents. And what of neutrality? In conferences meanwhile the Secretary had expressed to Tuyll the President's hope that Russia on her part would also continue to observe the same neutrality.[9] If not, then the United States might have to change its own neutral policy.

The President was still unsettled in his mind what to say to Great Britain. As French troops speedily overran Spain he became more and more alarmed. Calhoun seemed to have convinced him that after the fall of Cádiz the Holy Alliance with no more than ten thousand men would restore all Mexico and all South America to Spanish dominion.

"Perfectly moonstruck," was Adams's opinion of the Secretary of War. "I won't deny," he said in Cabinet on the 15th of November, "that they may make a temporary impression for three, four, or five years, but I no more believe that the Holly Allies will restore the Spanish dominion upon the American continent than that the Chimborazo will sink beneath the ocean." Otherwise it had been a mistake for the United States to have recognized the independence of the new republics, much more so now to involve itself in their fate.[10]

More news from Rush,[11] that Canning had unexplainably ceased to refer to his earlier proposals, temporarily lightened the President's anxiety. "Canning has changed his purpose," Monroe told Adams. "Probably some inducement has been presented him, after the French triumph in Spain, to quiet his apprehensions." [12]

Such indeed was the case, although Monroe could not have guessed that the "inducement" was the Polignac Memorandum.

The relief was only momentary. That very afternoon (November 17, 1823) the mild-mannered and kindly Baron von Tuyll dropped another bombshell into the now thoroughly agitated village capital on the Potomac. Faithful to instructions from his Government, he handed in a second note. It was in the form of extracts from recent circular instructions of Count Nesselrode to be read to the Secretary of State and copies furnished if desired. The most significant feature of these documents was a long description, for the edification of the various governments, of Russia's policy — an "*Io Triumphe,*" said Adams, "over the fallen cause of revolution." In exultant tones it reviewed the success of the interventions

[9] For the drafts of JQA's note of November 15, 1823 to Tuyll, and Adams's account for the President of his conferences with the Russian Minister, see Ford, op. cit.

[10] *Memoirs,* VI, 185–6. November 15, 1823.

[11] Rush's dispatches No. 334 of October 2 and No. 336 of October 10.

[12] *Memoirs,* VI, 188. November 17, 1823.

already sponsored by the Holy Alliance for the "liberation" of Naples, Piedmont, and Spain. Nesselrode ended by affirming the Emperor's policy in general to be that of guaranteeing the tranquillity *of all the states of which the civilized world is composed.*[13]

"Does this mean the supremacy of Spain over the revolted colonies?" Adams asked the Minister, at the request of the President, as soon as they had read the documents.

"Yes," answered Tuyll.

At the next Cabinet meeting the President appeared extraordinarily dejected. The Secretary of War added to the gloom.

"This confirms me in the view I have taken of the designs of the Holy Allies upon South America," said Calhoun.

"I am quite confirmed in mine," Adams opposed cheerfully enough.[14] The Secretary of State had definite ideas about dealing with the latest Russian piece.

"My purpose," he told the Cabinet three days later, "would be in a moderate and conciliatory manner, but with a firm and determined spirit, to declare our dissent from the principles avowed in those communications; to assert those upon which our own Government is founded, and, while disclaiming all intention of attempting to propagate them by force, and *all interference with the political affairs of Europe, to declare our expectation and hope that the European powers will equally abstain from the attempt to spread their principles in the American hemisphere, or to subjugate by force any part of these continents to their will.*"[15]

The President approved of this idea. He had always been sympathetic to the freedom of the whole New World. The third dictum of the Monroe Doctrine was crystallizing.

John Quincy Adams had already said Hands Off to Europe, including Great Britain, so far as further colonization was concerned. Now he was proposing to say Hands Off as to conquest of any part of the New World, or intervention in its political affairs. He was advancing from Non-Colonization to Non-Intervention. But he had no idea of evoking a public pronouncement, of proclaiming a national "doctrine" beyond his own Non-Colonization Principle. He had already drafted a statement on that for the President's annual message to Congress. It was the basic principle. It would be enough to tell the world at this time.

It had been Adams's expectation that the systematic exposition of American foreign policy called forth by Canning's proposal and Tuyll's notes would be expressed only in diplomatic correspondence. The replies could be written with an eye to spreading them before the public to justify the American position. If the crisis were weathered successfully it would not be necessary to publish anything. If trouble with Europe followed, Con-

[13] For the Russian note, see Ford, op. cit., pp. 34–7.

[14] *Memoirs,* VI, 190. November 18, 1823.

[15] *Memoirs,* VI, 194. November 21, 1823. Italics inserted.

gress could call for the documents. Monroe agreed, he told the Cabinet, with the *purpose* of the Secretary of State. He then took up some notes that he had made for his annual message to Congress on the State of the Union. As he read them, it became apparent that he had decided to set forth the combined system of American foreign policy, not in a series of diplomatic notes but in a significant statement to Congress and to the world.

The proposed message opened with a tone of deep solemnity and high alarm. Imminent and formidable dangers menaced the country. They called for most vigorous energies and closest union. After this introduction Monroe followed with occasional variations the draft that Adams had sketched out for him a week previously on subjects relating to the Department of State. He stressed the Non-Colonization Principle as applied to Russia and Great Britain earlier in the year. He touched on boundary controversies with Great Britain, on the North West Coast, on the slave trade, on the proposed abolition of private warfare on the seas, on the new Ministers being sent to Buenos Aires and Chile. Then the President passed beyond the content of Adams's draft.[16] He began to mention the recent events in Spain and Portugal. Pointedly he reproved France for her invasion of Spain and for the principles avowed by the King of France to justify it. The proposed message also contained a broad acknowledgment of the revolted Greeks as an independent nation, and a recommendation to Congress of an appropriation for sending a Minister to them.

Calhoun approved it all.

John Quincy Adams objected.

"I wish you would reconsider the whole subject," he told the President, "before you take this course. The tone of the introduction will take the nation by surprise and greatly alarm them . . . like a clap of thunder." [17]

What Adams objected to most was the summons to arms against all Europe, and over objects exclusively European – Greece and Spain – the sudden departure from the policy of George Washington. To champion the cause of conquered Spanish republicans, whom even Britain had been unable to support, would be to charge a windmill whirling in the gales and cross-currents of the Old World. To uphold the cause of the revolted Greeks, so dear to Adams's classical friends in Cambridge,[18] would have

[16] The draft and Monroe's summary notes on "Mr. Adams's sketch" are in the Monroe Papers in the New York Public Library.

[17] *Memoirs,* VI, 195.

[18] Professor Edward Everett of Harvard suggested the sending out of a commission, like the fact-finding commission to South America in 1817–18, to inquire into the progress of the Greek revolution. "If such a course should be adopted, I wish you would persuade the President to make me Secretary of the Commission." Edward Everett to JQA, Cambridge, October 30, 1823. Adams MSS.

"It is supposed to be the purpose of some gentlemen to get Professor Everett appointed U.S. Commissioner to Greece. If he is a Republican he is totally unknown as such. . . . An appointment of Mr. E. in *your Dept.* wd. naturally be attributed *to*

been to take sides with the monarchs of Europe against the Turks of Asia to settle the insoluble Eastern Question. Already Count Nesselrode had been trying to get an American fleet into the Mediterranean as a naval demonstration against the Turks while the Czar made ready to declare war on them from the north. Already Monroe had decided not to make even a commercial treaty with Russia lest it lead to political involvements in the Balkan region.[19] Was there any more reason to get mixed up in the Near East on account of Greece?

Adams unswervingly opposed any European entanglement whether with friend or foe. "Europe has been in convulsions for more than thirty years," he reminded his colleagues. "Every nation almost of which it is composed [has been] alternately invading and invaded. Empires, kingdoms, and principalities, have been overthrown, revolutionized, and counter-revolutionized, and we had looked on safe in our distance beyond an intervening ocean, and avowing a total forbearance to interfere in any of the combinations of European politics. This message . . . would have an air of open defiance to all Europe, and I should not be surprised if the first answer to it from Spain and France, and even Russia, should be to break off diplomatic intercourse with us. I don't expect the quiet which we have enjoyed for six or seven years to last much longer. The aspect of things is portentous; but if we must come to an issue with Europe, let us keep it off as long as possible. Let us use all possible means to carry the opinion of the nation with us, and the opinion of the world."

"There is not the tranquility that you spoke of," Calhoun objected. "There is great anxiety in the thinking part of the nation. There is a general expectation that the Holy Alliance will employ force against South America. It would be proper for the President to sound the alarm to the nation." [20]

The President took the matter under further consideration.

The next day Adams worked on Monroe alone. Anxiously he urged him to abstain from anything in the message that the Allies could make a pretext for construing as an aggression against them.

"The ground I wish to take," he maintained, "is that of earnest remonstrance against the interference of European powers by force in South America, but to disclaim all interference on our part in Europe; to make an American cause, and adhere inflexibly to that." [21]

In the end Adams had his way. Monroe revised his position to conform with the policy that the Secretary of State had recommended for the emergency. But it was the President himself who decided to give forth that policy to the world in a message to Congress. Behind the public message

---

you, and would have a tendency to make the Republicans of N.E. rise up in arms against you." P. P. F. DeGrand to JQA, Boston, January 10, 1824. Adams MSS.

[19] *Memoirs*, V, 429–31.

[20] *Memoirs*, VI, 195–6. November 21, 1823.

[21] *Memoirs*, VI, 198. November 22, 1823.

would be the unprinted diplomatic correspondence of John Quincy Adams with Great Britain and Russia,[22] to be published only when necessary.

Adams now drafted and presented to the Cabinet some observations on the communications received from the Baron von Tuyll. It corresponded to the relevant parts of the President's message as now redrafted to meet the Secretary of State's ideas. Adams added the No-Transfer Principle. He intended the document to be a firm and spirited but withal conciliatory answer to the communications recently received from the Russian Minister. At the same time it would reflect the unequivocal answer to be made separately to Canning's proposals.

"It is meant also," Adams told the Cabinet, "to be eventually an exposition of the principles of this Government, and a brief development of its political system as henceforth to be maintained: essentially republican – maintaining its own independence, and respecting that of others; essentially pacific – studiously avoiding all involvement in the combinations of European politics, cultivating peace and friendship with the most absolute monarchies, highly appreciating and anxiously desiring to retain that of the Emperor Alexander, but declaring that, having recognized that of the South American States, we could not see with indifference any attempt by European powers by forcible interposition either to restore the Spanish dominion on the American Continents or to introduce monarchical principles into those countries, or to transfer any portion of the ancient or present American possessions of Spain to any other European power." [23]

Now the whole matter was determined. The "Gentlemen of the Administration" had agreed on what to say to Canning, through Rush. They had decided how to reply to Tuyll. They had fixed the principles to be stated in the President's message. John Quincy Adams's views by the force of their reason had prevailed over everybody: over President Monroe, over ex-Presidents Jefferson and Madison, over all his colleagues in the Cabinet, Calhoun, Wirt, and Southard.[24] At this moment, when Monroe was making ready to draft his final message, a last most realistic question came up.

After all, asked Wirt, would the United States go to war if the Holy Alliance should act in direct hostility against South America? [25] He did not favor taking any such position without a supporting resolution of Congress.

This most pertinent question gave pause to them all. Adams, too, would have preferred to have Congress surely behind the President. But the

[22] *Memoirs,* VI, 199. November 25, 1823.

[23] *Memoirs,* VI, 199. November 24, 1823.

[24] Crawford, Secretary of War, was not present for the deliberations, because of illness.

[25] *Memoirs,* VI, 202–205. November 25, 1823.

Eighteenth Congress had not assembled. The message was to greet the two houses upon their convening. In a time of profound peace no resolution could be expected unless all the confidential papers could be put before Congress to show the danger. To send them in would be premature. Both Canning and Tuyll had insisted on the wholly confidential nature of their exchanges with the United States. Wirt had won a point. The message as finally worded avoided any unequivocal threat of war.

Here is what President James Monroe said to the Congress of the United States, December 2, 1823, on the relations between the Old World and the New. It is copied from the Senate files, *verbatim et literatim:*

> At the proposal of the Russian Imperial Government, made through the Minister of the Emperor, residing here, a full power and instructions have been transmitted to the Minister of the United States at St. Petersburg, to arrange by amicable negotiation, the respective rights and interests of the two Nations on the North West Coast of this Continent. A similar proposal has been made by His Imperial Majesty, to the Government of Great Britain, which has likewise been acceded to. The Government of the United States has been desirous by this friendly proceeding, of manifesting the great value which they have invariably attached to the friendship of the Emperor, and their solicitude to cultivate the best understanding with his Government. In the discussions to which this interest has given rise, and in the arrangements by which they may terminate, the occasion has been judged proper, for asserting as a principle in which the rights and interests of the United States are involved, that the American Continents, by the free and independent condition which they have assumed and maintain, are henceforth not to be considered as subjects for future colonization by any European Power. . . .

So far the President was using what John Quincy Adams had drafted for the message. There followed about three thousand words dealing mostly with domestic affairs. Then Monroe resumed the subject of foreign relations, turning to the policy recently formulated in the Cabinet as a result of Canning's proposals. It is worth while to note how widely the Non-Colonization Principle was separated, in the body of the message, from the other dicta on foreign policy.

> It was stated at the commencement of the last session [continued the message] that a great effort was then making in Spain and Portugal, to improve the condition of the people of those countries; and that it appeared to be conducted with extraordinary moderation. It need scarcely be remarked, that the result has been, so far, very different from what was then anticipated. Of events in that quarter

of the Globe, with which we have so much intercourse, and from which we derive our origin, we have always been anxious and interested spectators. The Citizens of the United States cherish sentiments the most friendly, in favor of the liberty and happiness of their fellowmen on that side of the Atlantic. In the wars of the European powers, in matters relating to themselves, we have never taken any part, nor does it comport with our policy, so to do. It is only when our rights are invaded, or seriously menaced, that we resent injuries, or make preparation for our defense. With the movements in this Hemisphere we are of necessity more immediately connected, and by causes which must be obvious to all enlightened and impartial observers. The political system of the allied powers, is essentially different in this respect from that of America. This difference proceeds from that, which exists in their respective Governments, and to the defence of our own, which has been atchieved [*sic*] by the loss of so much blood and treasure, and matured by the wisdom of their most enlightened citizens, and under which we have enjoyed unexampled felicity, this whole nation is devoted. We owe it therefore to candor, and to the amicable relations existing between the United States and those powers, to declare that we should consider any attempt on their part to extend their system to any portions of this Hemisphere, as dangerous to our peace and safety. With the existing Colonies or dependencies of any European power, we have not interfered, and shall not interfere. But with the Governments who have declared their Independence, and maintained it, and whose Independence we have, on great consideration, and on just principles, acknowledged, we could not view any interposition for the purpose of oppressing them, or controuling in any other manner, their destiny, by any European power, in any other light, than as the manifestation of an unfriendly disposition towards the United States. In the war between those new governments and Spain, we declared our neutrality, at the time of their recognition, and to this we have adhered, and shall continue to adhere, provided no change shall occur, which in the judgment of the competent authorities of this Government, shall make a corresponding change, on the part of the United States, indispensable to their security.

The late events in Spain and Portugal, show that Europe is still unsettled. Of this important fact, no stronger proof can be adduced, than that the allied powers should have thought it proper, on any principle satisfactory to themselves, to have interposed by force, in the internal concerns of Spain. To what extent, such interposition may be carried, on the same principle, is a question, in which all Independent powers, whose Governments differ from theirs, are interested; even those most remote, and surely none more so than the United States. Our policy in regard to Europe, which was adopted at an early stage of the wars which have so long agitated that quarter of the Globe, nevertheless remains the same, which is, not to interfere in the internal concerns of any of its powers; to consider the Government *de facto;* as the legitimate [*sic*] for us; to cultivate friendly relations with it, and to preserve those relations by a frank, firm and manly policy, meeting in all instances, the just claims of every power; submitting to injuries from none. But, in regard to those continents, circumstances are eminently and conspicuously different. It is impossible that the allied powers, should extend their political systems, to any portion of either continent, without endangering our peace and happiness, nor can anyone believe, that our Southern Brethren, if left to themselves, would adopt it of their own accord. It is equally impossible therefore, that we should behold such interposition in any form with indifference. If we look to the comparative strength and resources of Spain and those new Governments, and their distance from each other, it must be obvious that she can never subdue them. It is still the true policy of the United States, to leave the parties to themselves, in the hope, that other powers will pursue the same course.

3

Looking ahead to John Quincy Adams's Presidency and to his choice of Secretary of State it is proper at this place to notice Henry Clay's comment on the message the day of its delivery, and to say something of Adams's own appraisal of the manifesto and its principles.

Adams called on Clay that evening to make arrangement for the presence of a delegation of the House of Representatives at the obsequies of the Prussian chargé, Frederick Greuhm. Clay mentioned the message. "It seems to be the work of several hands," he twitted good-naturedly. "The War and Navy Departments make a magnificent figure in it, as well as the Post Office."

"There is an account of a full Treasury," Adams reminded his Kentucky rival, "and much concerning foreign affairs, which is the business of the Department of State."

"Yes," acknowledged Clay. "I think the part relating to foreign affairs is the best part of the Message. The Government had weakened itself and the tone of the country by withholding so long the acknowledgment of South American Independence. Even a war for it against all Europe, including even England, would have been advantageous to us."

"A war for South American independence may be inevitable," conceded Adams, "and under certain circumstances might be expedient, but I view war in a different light from you – as necessarily placing high interests of different portions of the Union in conflict with each other, and thereby endangering the Union itself."

"Not a successful war," said Clay, "but a successful war, to be sure, creates a military influence and power, which I consider the greatest danger of war." [26]

Both men were conscious rivals for the succession to the Presidency. Time and circumstances – and James Monroe – had settled the Latin-American policy of the United States. Both Adams and Clay now had other things to think about. With Andrew Jackson in the offing, they might some day be able to agree on a fancied danger of military power and influence to the Republic.

As John Quincy Adams's mind turned toward the next presidential election, as it did more and more frequently, he never thought of taking political credit for the Monroe Doctrine. In "John Quincy Adams Loquitur," the memorandum in his handwriting in which he summed up the diplomatic achievements which might commend him to the suffrage of his fellow countrymen, he said nothing of the part that he had played in the formulation of the message of December 2, 1823. He did not fail to note the Treaty of 1818 with Great Britain, made under his instructions. He took credit for the Spanish treaty and the transcontinental boundary. He included among his accomplishments the Commercial Treaty of 1822 with France, the Russian arbitration of the slave question with Great Britain, the unratified treaty of 1824 with Great Britain for the abolition of the slave trade, the Russian Boundary Treaty of 1824. But not a word about the Monroe Doctrine. Not until 1846, when the principles of President Monroe were beginning to enjoy a classic renown, and were being applied to Texas, California, and Oregon,[27] did he acknowledge, with pride, his responsibility for any of them, and then only for the Non-Colonization Principle. Clearly in his mind that was the most noteworthy feature of President Monroe's message. Abstention dated back to George Washington's Farewell Address. Hands Off, the really most important principle of the Monroe Doctrine, was a principle that he had sponsored in the Cabinet deliberations, but it did not stand out in his mind as much as the Non-Colonization Principle. Hands Off was really a corollary of Non-Colonization.

4

The text of the message and its general popularity in the United States then and since then have tended to overshadow the correspondence that was an important part of the diplomatic picture framed by Monroe and his advisers. Not published until many years later by historians, these documents complete the policy that was molded in the historic deliberations of November 1823.

On November 27 the Secretary of State read to Tuyll his "Observations on the Communications recently received from the Minister of Russia." At the moment Adams considered it the most important state paper he

[26] *Memoirs,* VI, 224. December 2, 1823. [27] *Memoirs,* XII, 218.

had ever written, and it was with some reluctance that he accepted the revisions that Monroe finally had made in it, mostly for amenity's sake. The Government of the United States, stated the document, recognized the right of nations to establish and modify their own governments according to their own judgments. While espousing the republican principle, it had not sought by the propagation of its own principles to disturb the peace or to intermeddle with the policy of any part of Europe. It had recognized the established independence of the former Spanish colonies and entered into political and commercial relations with them: "relations the more important to the interests of the United States, as the whole of those emancipated Regions are situated in their own Hemisphere, and as the most extensive, populous and powerful of the new Nations are in their immediate vicinity; and one of them bordering upon the Territories of this Union." In the existing contest between these states and their mother country the United States would remain neutral as long as the European powers, apart from Spain, did so. "In the general declarations [of the Russian Minister] that the allied Monarchs will never compound, and never will even treat with the *Revolution* and that their policy has only for its object by *forcible* interposition to guaranty the tranquillity *of all the States of which the civilized world is composed,* the President wishes to perceive sentiments, the application of which is limited, and intended in their results to be limited to the affairs of Europe. That the sphere of their operations was not intended to embrace the United States of America, nor any portion of the American Hemisphere."

The "Observations" ended with a reiteration of policy not embodied in the text of the contemporary presidential message, but long since resolved by Congress, on January 15, 1811, namely the No-Transfer Principle. "The United States of America, and their Government, could not see with indifference, the forcible interposition of any European Power, other than Spain, either to restore the dominion of Spain over her emancipated Colonies in America, or to establish Monarchical Governments in those Countries, or to transfer any of the possessions heretofore or yet subject to Spain in the American Hemisphere, to any other European power." [28]

The No-Transfer Policy, stated in the diplomatic documents ancillary to Monroe's message but not in the message itself, was to become just as important a part of the Monroe Doctrine as the three dicta proclaimed in that celebrated state paper. Older than the Doctrine itself, it lay from the beginning in the same bed with the principles of the message. In 1870 President Grant's Secretary of State, Hamilton Fish, definitely wedded the No-Transfer Principle to the Monroe Doctrine.[29]

During the deliberations in the Cabinet, Secretary Adams had been drafting, under the President's eye, the American reply to Canning's proposal. It was in the form of instructions by the Secretary of State to Rush

[28] W. C. Ford, op. cit., pp. 39–40. Not printed in Manning.

[29] Dexter Perkins: *The Monroe Doctrine, 1867–1907* (Baltimore, 1937), p. 25.

in London, dated November 29, 1823, to be read to the British Foreign Minister. In earlier conversations with the British chargé, Addington, Adams had stated, as they discussed Canning's proposals (first revealed to Addington by Adams), that Britain's recognition of Latin-American independence must be *sine qua non* of any joint manifesto. The Secretary certainly gave Addington the cordial impression that if his Government would meet this indispensable condition the United States would join in the proposed manifesto.[30] But the actual instructions to Rush, indited after full Cabinet deliberation, and revised by the President himself, avoided any commitment to a *joint* manifesto even if Great Britain should recognize Latin-American independence. Adams directed Rush to declare that the United States was in agreement with the points proposed by Canning *except his refusal to acknowledge immediately the independence of the new states*, the restoration of which to the crown of Spain he had avowed to be so "hopeless." Only on the basis of such a recognition would the United States be willing to move "in concert" with Great Britain for the purposes specified, and *even then only in separate and parallel, rather than joint action.*

But what if a great emergency, say an attack on the new states of Latin America, should suddenly present itself? "Should an emergency occur," read Adams's instructions to Rush, "in which a *joint* manifestation of opinion by the two Governments may tend to influence the councils of the European allies, either in the aspect of persuasion or of admonition, you will make it known to us without delay, and we shall according to the principles of our Government, and in the forms prescribed by our Constitution, cheerfully join in any act by which we may contribute to support the cause of human freedom, and the independence of the South American nations." [31]

This left to Congress responsibility for any possible joint action with Britain under the circumstances that might exist in the unknown future. And Congress, as will be noted presently, passed no resolution to support the President's announced policy.

On the No-Transfer Policy the United States would concur, but it would not concert with Great Britain. The Secretary made that evident in a separate letter to Rush of November 30 which the Minister might use at his discretion to interpret the stipulations of the open instructions of

[30] Addington to George Canning, Secret and Confidential, No. 20, Washington, November 20; Secret and Confidential (unnumbered), November 20; and No. 21, December 1, 1823. PRO, F.O., 5, Vol. CLXXVII.

Canning considered a dispatch of November 3, originally numbered 18, to be too confidential to be retained in the official archives, and ordered Addington to turn it into a private letter (Conyngham [Undersecretary] to Addington, Private, December 8, 1823). Dr. William Weed Kaufmann has explained the mystery of the missing dispatch No. 18 from Washington, November 3, 1823, in his study of *British Policy and the Independence of Latin America* (MS., Yale University Library, 1948).

[31] Manning, I, 210–12.

November 29. He stressed his country's policy of recognizing the independence of the new states and of opposing the transfer of sovereignty over American territory. "So long as Great Britain withholds the recognition of that [independence]," he stated, addressing himself to the idea of concert of policy with Great Britain, "we may, as we certainly do, concur with her in the aversion to the transfer to any other power of any of the Colonies in this Hemisphere, heretofore or yet, belonging to Spain; but the principles of that aversion, so far as they are common to both parties, resting only upon a casual coincidence of interests, in a national point of view *selfish* on both sides, would be liable to dissolution by every change of phase in the aspect of European politics."

As to the point of Latin-American independence, Adams directed, the President felt that, in reading to Canning the instructions of November 29, Rush might pass lightly over that indispensable condition: it might "best conduce to the ultimate, *entire* coincidence of purposes between the two Governments, to leave the choice of *time* for the recognition which Mr. Canning has reserved, to the exclusive consideration of the British Ministers themselves." That is to say, Monroe and Adams expected that an independent pronouncement by the United States, agreeing with all of Canning's five points except Point 2 – recognition of independence was a matter of time and circumstances – would soon lead Great Britain also formally to acknowledge the independence of Latin America.

Finally, Adams reiterated to Rush, the United States would not attend any European congress that did not recognize the independence of the new states.[32] Well knowing this already, Canning had been insisting to the continental Allies that no general congress on American affairs could be held without the participation of the United States. It was one of the devices he used to frustrate the meeting of such a congress.

5

Within twenty-four hours after pronouncing his immortal message President James Monroe had a dreadful moment. Hardly had the document issued from the printing presses when the possible "emergency" contemplated in Rush's instructions of November 29 seemed actually at hand. Rumors had come in European newspapers [33] that an army of 12,000 Spaniards was embarking to subdue South America, with the backing of the Holy Alliance. Monroe feared that the United States would be called upon immediately to make good the bold words he had just given to the world. If the danger of European intervention were real and imminent, how then would the new Doctrine be implemented instanter?

In the moment of peril, none the less real because fancied, Monroe again showed himself willing to unite with the mother country in measures to prevent the interference of the Holy Alliance in Latin America,

[32] Manning, I, 215. [33] *Memoirs,* VI, 226. December 4, 1823.

even to the extent of sending troops there. Rush must receive instructions to that effect, he informed the Secretary of State. "We should state also, that the attitude taken in the message, in regard to that object [prevention of intervention in South America], was essentially founded, on the proposition made by Mr. Canning to him [Rush]." [34] In his excitement the President seems to have forgotten, at least momentarily, that Canning had already "cooled off," that he might not be holding forth such a "proposition" any more.

Straightway Monroe summoned the Cabinet once more to consider what measures should be taken with England against the Holy Alliance.[35]

Adams thought his chief was unduly alarmed. Apparently – there is no record of what was said at this meeting – he succeeded in calming Monroe, because the ensuing supplemental instructions to Rush still left the United States uncommitted. But they did not close the door to Anglo-American co-operation, if the worst should happen. They made it swing no longer on a prior recognition by Great Britain of the independence of the Latin-American states but rather on an expected declaration by the British Government similar to President Monroe's. The sentiments of the President's message, the Secretary of State explained, were really similar to Canning's propositions. If only England could now make the same kind of pronouncement, "the moral effects upon the councils of the Allies, to deter them from any interposition by force between Spain and America will be complete. It is hoped that nothing further will be necessary. . . . The object proposed in the confidential letters of Mr. Canning thus having been accomplished, the consideration of what remains further to be done will depend upon the definitive movements of the Allies."

Suppose the Allies did move definitively upon Latin America, then what? The flurry after December 2 is interesting because it shows what Monroe was ready to do if the doctrine that he had just uttered had been really and seriously challenged at the moment. He was prepared in his own mind for a very close understanding, even joint military operations with England in case of any actual invasion of the New World. That was the magnetic pole toward which the needle of his compass always kept quivering.

John Quincy Adams, like his father in 1798, kept his nerve as he

[34] "The accounts which, I hear, are just rec'd from England, make it important, that the instructions to Mr. Rush, should be forwarded immediately, and that he be instructed to state, that he will unite with the British Govt, in measures, to prevent the interference of the allied powers, in the affairs of S°. Am., and particularly in sending troops there. We should state also, that the attitude taken in the message, in regard to that object, was essentially founded, on the proposition made by Mr. Canning to him. The instructions should also be hastened to Mr. Middleton, and we must watch the movements of any Congress, should one be assembled. On these points we shall confer when we meet." James Monroe to JQA, December 3, 1823. Adams MSS.

[35] James Monroe to JQA, December 5, 1823. Adams MSS.

watched the needle flutter. Before he committed himself to England for the defense of the Western Hemisphere, he wanted to see what England would do about all the historic issues still left unsettled between the mother and the daughter. He wanted to be sure that the United States and the other republics would be safe from Great Britain herself.

"The President[36] is anxiously desirous," concluded Adams at the end of the notable secret instructions to Richard Rush of December 8, 1823,[37] "that the opening to a cordial harmony in the policy of the United States and Great Britain offered on this occasion, may be extended to the general relations between the two countries."

Here the Secretary of State was referring to the old problems of impressment, neutral rights, the African slave trade, and Britain's colonial trade monopoly. They will all receive due attention in the following chapters of this book. Had Monroe and Adams succeeded in settling those issues with Great Britain, as they had been so earnestly striving to do ever since the War of 1812, had Great Britain been willing to accept the longstanding American invitation to recognize jointly with the United States the independence of Latin America, as these same two statesmen had been working to bring about ever since 1818, then the Age of Emancipation might have closed in a satisfying Anglo-American entente worthy of the rights of man. But because of the British Foreign Minister's blindness, nothing came out of all Monroe's "opening to harmony of policy."

Doubtless Adams so expected. Rush dutifully read to Canning the Secretary of State's instructions of November 29. He had no opportunity to go farther than that. The only comment that Canning would make was that intervening events (signalized by the Polignac Memorandum) had put an end to the state of affairs that had impelled him to make the confidential proposals of the previous year.[38] He had already told Rush (when revealing the Polignac Memorandum) that Great Britain had deemed it indispensable to come to an explanation with France "without any concert with the United States."[39]

The last of the documents relating to the emergency of 1823 is in the nature of an anticlimax. To this date it has not been fully published. It was the instructions of December 23, 1823 to the new Minister, ex-Senator James Brown of Louisiana, going out to Paris temporarily to replace Albert Gallatin at that capital. His departure had been delayed until he could read all the recent diplomatic correspondence. "The relations between Spain and her emancipated American Colonies," Adams instructed him, "will be discussed in the combined councils of the European alliance.

36 Monroe went over this instruction with his usual care before it was sent. JQA's Short Diary, December 8, 10, 1823.

37 For text of the instructions of December 8, 1823, never before printed, see Appendix 2.

38 Richard Rush to JQA, London, February 9, 1824. Manning, III, 1519.

39 Rush to JQA, No. 346, London, November 26, 1823. Manning, III, 1503.

Upon their determination concerning them will depend that of Great Britain, and both will deeply affect the interest of the United States. If the Allies should conclude to interfere in that contest, it will be probably by means of the intervention of France and all the indications thereto are that Great Britain will not accede to it, but oppose it. Those indications, however, are far from being of an unequivocal character."[40]

The Government of the United States, Adams reminded Minister Brown, was not desirous of being admitted as a party of the councils to interfere in the affairs of Europe. As to America, on the other hand, all Europe must know the vital interest of the United States in the affairs of the independent nations of the New World. The President's recent message to Congress would guide Brown in handling this subject. "It is hoped that the European Continental Alliance will ultimately perceive the inexpediency of their interference in the contest between Spain and South America; but, while manifesting on proper occasions the dispositions of this country concerning it *you will avoid any measure by which the Government might be prematurely implicated in it,* and observing with vigilant attention the progress of the Allies with regard to their general policy, and all its applications, will report as frequently as may be convenient the results of your observations."[41]

Thanks to Canning, there was no treaty, no agreement, no unwritten understanding, not even a concert of policy between the United States and Great Britain to uphold the Monroe Doctrine. Both American and British historians know this very well. But it is necessary to reaffirm the fact because over a century later, during the critical autumn of 1940, a historical legend took root that the United States proclaimed the Monroe

[40] "From the latest dispatches received from Mr. Sheldon [chargé at Paris], it appears the British Ambassador at Paris has expressed to the French Minister the expectation of Great Britain that no definitive arrangement concerning South America should be made without consulting the United States; a proposal which was received with assurances that France would determine upon nothing without consultation. Yet Mr. Sheldon supposes that she will object to extending the consultation to the United States."

Sheldon's private letter, of October 30, 1823, received by Adams the same day that he penned the instructions to Brown, is printed by Ford, p. 61, and Manning, II, 1139.

[41] JQA to James Brown, No. 1, Instructions — General, Department of State, Washington, December 23, 1823. DS, *Instructions, U.S. Ministers,* X, 140–52. Italics inserted. Only the last-quoted portions of these instructions have been printed in Manning, I, 221.

A special agent, Alexander MacRae, left separately for Europe by way of England at about this same time. He had instructions from Adams to place himself at the direction of Rush and Brown and to proceed to any place on the Continent where his services might be useful, particularly to act as a secret observer at any European congress that might be assembled. When it was evident that no congress would take place, the President called him home. His return signalized the end of the great "crisis" in American foreign relations. See Henry P. Wriston: *Executive Agents in American Foreign Relations* (Baltimore, 1929), pp. 572–5, 696–7. Adams's Short Diary for December 15, 17, and 21.

Doctrine only after an agreement with Great Britain that the English Navy would protect it if it were challenged. Mr. Walter Lippmann, the eminent journalist who gave birth to this legend, asserted that there was an actual agreement between the United States and Great Britain of August 23, 1823.[42] President Franklin Delano Roosevelt found it necessary to correct this fiction in his historic speech on national security of December 29, 1940: "One hundred and seventeen years ago the Monroe Doctrine was conceived by our Government as a measure of defense in the face of a threat against this hemisphere by an alliance in continental Europe. Thereafter, we stood on guard in the Atlantic, with the British as neighbors. There was no treaty. There was no 'unwritten agreement.'"

But the legend grew and grew,[43] as if it were necessary to support the cause of 1940 by a perverted historical dialectic. It is despite their former differences that the British people and the American people have grown to look with common concern upon the tyrants of the world. That, rather than any pleasing historical fiction, is the most powerful testimony to their solidarity.

6

How did the outside world take the Monroe Doctrine of 1823?

In England the press at first welcomed President Monroe's message in a way that promised well for Anglo-American brotherhood, but quickly changed its tone when the Foreign Minister shook his head.[44] The Monroe Doctrine irked and piqued Canning. For one thing, the British Government would not subscribe to Adams's axiom, emblazoned in the message, that the American Continents henceforth were not to be regarded as open fields for European colonization. More than that, Monroe's manifesto threatened to rob Great Britain of the prestige which her great Foreign Minister was endeavoring to establish over Latin America as a result of having single-handed prevented any possibility of European intervention. Canning hastened to have the relevant part of the Polignac Memorandum lithographed[45] and passed around among the diplomatic corps. He did this not in order to stand shoulder to shoulder with the Monroe Doctrine and strengthen it, but rather to counteract it and to weaken it. Now that the crisis was over, he wanted above all things to undo the diplomatic defeat[46] that he had just suffered at the hands of John Quincy Adams. From then on, the Monroe Doctrine and the Polignac Memorandum were

[42] See New York *Herald Tribune,* August 22, 1940.

[43] Walter Lippmann: *U.S. Foreign Policy: Shield of the Republic* (Boston, 1943).

[44] Alexander MacRae to JQA, private, London, February 7, 1824. Adams MSS. Perkins: *Monroe Doctrine, 1823–1826,* Ch. V, analyzes public opinion, and the reception of the message at home and abroad.

[45] It was one of the first state papers to be reproduced by the new process. Webster, op. cit., I, 23.

[46] "There can be no doubt but that in this exchange of views Canning suffered a severe diplomatic defeat." Webster, op. cit., I, 49.

rival placards over Latin America competing for the diplomatic allegiance of the new states — and for their commerce. Henceforward Canning did everything in his power to break down the influence of the United States in that part of the world and to enhance that of Great Britain.[47]

The British Foreign Minister feared that Adams might publish his overtures of the previous summer. If it became generally known that the United States had insisted on Britain's previous recognition of the independence of the Latin-American Republics as the price of any joint *démarche,* it would have been more difficult to persuade those Governments that they owed their liberties — Canning himself could not allude to their *independence* until 1825 — to the Mistress of the Seas. Canning repeatedly and anxiously urged Rush to keep his "tentative" and "informal" proposals [48] in "sacred confidence." He even caused to be withdrawn from the official Foreign Office files the one document referring to the matter.[49]

Canning was successful in keeping the matter relatively quiet. Monroe had not alluded to the proposals in his message, nor would he turn the documents over to Congress when they were called for.[50] So nothing was published. But the matter was too good to withhold altogether from the "Southern Brethren." Rush had kept the Colombian envoy in London fully apprised of everything that went on between him and Canning. The first proposal that President Monroe made about Canning's overtures was to inform the Colombian Minister, Salazar. Adams did so on November 29.[51] In Santiago, the new American Minister, Heman Allen (whose departure from Washington had been delayed in order to give him full information),[52] told the Foreign Minister of Chile.[53]

Canning earnestly expostulated against the validity of the Non-Colonization Principle, but he soon learned to make the best of the Non-Intervention dictum. He even took some credit for it with his own diplomatic

[47] H. W. V. Temperley: "The Later Latin-American Policy of George Canning," *AHR*, XI (No. 4, July 1906), 779–97.

[48] "It is impossible to accept the point-of-view that these repeated solicitations were merely sounding. There can be no question but that Canning made a direct offer and earnestly pressed it." Webster, op. cit., I, 46.

[49] See above, note 40.

[50] See note 64.

[51] "At P[resident]. U[nited] S[tates]. He appointed a [Cabinet] meeting for tomorrow. Proposal to communicate Canning's overtures to Salazar. . . ." JQA's Short Diary, November 6, 1823. Adams MSS. On November 29 Adams notes that he spoke to Salazar "of the negotiation between Mr. Rush and Mr. Canning, recently commenced, and of the manifestations of the disposition of the Emperor of Russia regarding South America." *Memoirs,* VI, 220.

[52] "It will, I think, be advisable to detain Mr. Allen, for a few days, to allow him to peruse the late dispatches relating to England, etc. as to So. Am. If you concur in this, you had better send and stop him immediately." James Monroe to JQA, November 26, 1823. Adams MSS. See also *Memoirs,* VI, 204.

[53] Manning, I, 214, II, 1092, III, 1503, 1512.

service. Unblushingly he allowed that the President had "assisted" him in safeguarding Latin America. "The effect of the ultra-liberalism of our Yankee co-operators," he wrote to the British Minister in St. Petersburg, "on the ultra-despotism of Aix-la-Chapelle allies, gives me just the balance that I wanted." [54] Without the slightest diffidence he later personally assumed credit for the independence of the new states which American diplomacy had by then impelled Great Britain to recognize for her best interests. "I called the New World into existence," he boasted to Parliament in 1826, "to redress the balance of the Old." [55]

However unjustified the assertion itself, it revealed the *motive* of Canning's diplomacy: to use the United States to keep the balance of power in Europe. The aim of American diplomacy was exactly the opposite: to keep power and politics of monarchical Europe, *including Great Britain,* out of the New World.

The warm republican sentiments of the message, as well as the diplomatic doctrine in regard to the Old World and the New, delighted European liberals. Lafayette thought it was "the best little bit of paper that God ever permitted any man to give to the world." [56] It bothered the chancelleries of the continental powers.[57] The best thing they could do about it, amidst their own cross-purposes of policy, was to keep quiet.

In Latin America also the liberal elements received the presidential pronouncement most cordially.[58] Two Governments, Brazil and Colombia,

[54] Temperley: *Canning,* p. 130.

[55] Ibid., p. 156.

[56] Lafayette congratulated Monroe on the message and said it would delight every liberal mind in Europe. Perkins: *Monroe Doctrine, 1823–1826,* pp. 164–5. To John Quincy Adams the original French paladin of American independence extended himself further: "While the promoters of European emancipation are still endeavouring to make a stand against the successful flood of despotism and aristocracy, which your old friend Alexander is the most violent in pouring upon us, the manly message of the President of the U. S. and the spirited feeling of the people at large and their representatives have produced an admirable and timely impression. I will not undertake to assign to each power of the Hellish Alliance its particular share of the evils to the rising republics of America, nor will I decide whether, between political hatred, and mercantile interest, the British Government will this time behave more honestly than they have done in the affairs of Naples and the peninsula. For my part I would not trust any of them, and feel particularly secure and proud, when the United States, disentangled from binding connections with heterogeneous courts, stands boldly, as the protecting genius of America, to shield both Columbian Continents, against the covetousness of colonization, the intrigues of counter-revolutionary corruption, and attempts of a more violent nature which, disclaimed as they are now, ought to be carefully watched; the more so as there is no knowing how far, in case of success, these rancorous enemies to the rights of mankind might carry their wicked and extravagant hopes." Lafayette to JQA, LaGrange, January 24, 1824. Adams MSS.

[57] Daniel Sheldon to JQA, private, Paris, January 12, 1824. Received March 1, 1824. Adams MSS.

[58] W. S. Robertson: "South America and the Monroe Doctrine, 1824–1828," *Political Science Quarterly,* XXX (No. 1, March 1915), 82–105. Perkins, op. cit., pp. 149–61.

officially endorsed it.[59] But the men at the head of the governing elements realized that it was the British Navy that counted more than the republican ideals of President Monroe. The conservative leaders, those distrustful of republicanism and leaning toward monarchy – in short, the pro-British following – disliked the Doctrine. If there had been any original doubt in their minds about what governed the situation, it was removed when the United States declined the overtures of five of the new states for either actual alliance [60] or assurance of contingent assistance [61] for the enforcement of President Monroe's principles.

If the replies of the United States to these several solicitations were evasive, it must be noted that except in the case of Mexico the importunities were only nominally against the Holy Alliance; really it was the hope of each state to involve the United States in the existing war against the mother country, or in the instance of the United Provinces of the Rio de la Plata in their war against Brazil for the *Banda Oriental.*

Colombia was the first to inquire just how the United States intended to enforce the Doctrine and to ascertain whether it could not be turned to some immediate advantage. Acting on instructions from his Government, the Colombian Minister at Washington asked:

> In what manner the Government of the United States intends to resist on its part any interference of the Holy Alliance for the purpose of subjugating the new Republics or interfering in their political forms; if it will enter into a Treaty of Alliance with the Republic of Colombia to save America in general from the calamities of a despotic system; and finally if the Government of Washington understands by foreign interference the employment of Spanish forces against America at the time when Spain is occupied by a French Army, and its Government under the influence of France and her Allies.[62]

By this time the Polignac Memorandum was known in Washington. Everybody realized Spain could get no help in Europe.

Adams informed the Colombian Minister that the fact that Spain was occupied by France would not change the neutrality of the United States in regard to the employment of Spanish forces in America. The action that the United States might take in any future emergency would depend on Congress. As to the invitation for an actual alliance, the Secretary of State responded:

> As however the occasion for this resort [the President laying the matter before Congress] could arise only by a deliberate and con-

[59] Whitaker, op. cit., p. 538.

[60] As in the case of Chile (1824), Colombia (1824), and Brazil (1825).

[61] As requested by Mexico (1825) and the United Provinces of the Rio de la Plata (1826).

[62] José Maria Salazar, Colombian Minister to the United States, to JQA, Washington, July 2, 1824. Manning, II, 1281–2.

certed system of the allied Powers to exercise force against the freedom and Independence of your Republic; so it is obvious that the United States could not undertake resistance to them by force of Arms, without a previous understanding with those European Powers, whose Interests and whose principles would secure from them an active and efficient co-operation in the cause — This there is no reason to doubt, could be obtained, but it could only be effected by a negotiation preliminary to that of any alliance between the United States and the Colombian Republic, or in any event coeval with it.[63]

That is to say, in John Quincy Adams's own words, the effectiveness of the Monroe Doctrine depended not only on the support of Congress, which the Administration certainly did nothing to foster in the premises,[64]

[63] JQA to José Maria Salazar, Colombian Minister to the United States, Washington, August 6, 1824. Manning, I, 224–6.

[64] On December 24, 1823 the House of Representatives unanimously passed a resolution, introduced by Rollin C. Mallary of Vermont, requesting the President to lay before it such information as he possessed, and which could be disclosed without injury to the public good, "relative to the determination of any sovereign, or combination of sovereigns, to assist Spain in the subjugation of her late colonies on the American continent; and whether any Government of Europe is disposed or determined to oppose any aid or assistance which such sovereign, or combination of sovereigns, may afford to Spain for the subjugation of her late Colonies above-mentioned." *Annals of Congress,* 18th Cong., 1st Sess., 1823–4, I, 867, 869. "We should be very guarded in our answer to it," the President wrote to Adams, December 25. Adams MSS. On January 12, 1824 he replied to the House: "I have to state that I possess no information on the subject, not known to Congress, which can be disclosed without injury to the public good." *Annals,* ibid., p. 986. Henry Clay offered on January 20, 1824 a joint resolution: "That the people of these States would not see, without serious inquietude, any forcible interposition by the Allied Powers of Europe in behalf of Spain, to reduce to their former subjection those parts of the continent of America which have proclaimed and established for themselves, respectively, independent Governments, and which have been solemnly recognized by the United States." Ibid., p. 1104. In the ensuing debates this resolution became tangled up with a previous resolution, supported by Daniel Webster, in favor of the Greek cause. The sentiment of the House was such that neither resolution could be passed without the other, and therefore both were eventually abandoned. Doubtless this was to the relief of the Administration, which had decided, on Adams's advice, not to join or brook the Holy Alliance on European affairs, and did not want to resolve Congress for war on behalf of South America now that the danger of European intervention was passing. For the lengthy debates, see *Annals,* ibid., pp. 1103–23, 1125, 1127–1214. Whitaker, op. cit., p. 545, shrewdly suggests that the Administration passed around a report from Daniel Sheldon, United States chargé d'affaires in France, revealing that the danger of European intervention was over, thanks to the stand taken by England and the anticipated attitude of the United States. It is certain that Monroe directed Adams to have Sheldon's earlier dispatch of October 30, 1823 (Manning, II, 1399), received December 25, to be passed around among the Cabinet, and had a special copy made for himself, perhaps to show to people. James Monroe to JQA, December 25, 1823. Adams MSS. But Whitaker seems to be referring to a later letter of Sheldon, of November 29, 1823, not received until January. Adams and the other Cabinet members were in frequent contact with leading members of Congress.

but also on Great Britain, whose policy since the rebuff of Canning's overtures had to be regarded as by no means certain. After such a statement it was not unnatural that the Latin-American states leaned more and more heavily on British patronage in the rivalry for prestige, trade, and influence between Great Britain and the United States that ensued. British predominance as a low-cost manufacturing nation and as a source of loans to the new governments also proved irresistible attractions.

Nothing is clearer from these diplomatic exchanges and from later debates in Congress, particularly on the Panama Congress, than the unilateral and non-binding character of the Doctrine. Nor was Great Britain after the Polignac Memorandum any more willing than the United States to pledge herself to help the new states of Latin America resist any future attack.[65] She was unwilling to lay down such a pledge either to the United States or to any of the Latin-American states.

Monroe's message, following the recognition by the United States of the republics of Latin America, had the effect of hastening Great Britain's recognition of the independence of the new states *de jure* in 1825 despite their distasteful form of republican government. Her immediate consolation was the continuation of monarchy in Brazil after the separation from Portugal in 1822.[66] British good offices in 1825 brought about a peaceful recognition by the King of Portugal of his son as Emperor of Brazil. "It was a blow," declares Professor Webster, the British authority, "to the United States, which had sought by the inculcation of republican institutions and separation from Europe to enforce its own leadership of the New World." [67]

7

Historical scholars have agreed that there was little danger in 1823 of actual Allied intervention by force to restore Spanish America to Spain. Great Britain stopped any conceivable menace that there might have been from France with the Polignac Memorandum. Because of this fact there has been a tendency to dismiss the Monroe Doctrine as a mere trumpet-blast safely and somewhat impudently blown behind the pro-

[65] George Canning to H. G. Ward, British Minister to Mexico, No. 11, September 9, 1825. Webster: *Great Britain and Latin America,* I, 478.

[66] The United States had recognized the Portuguese monarchy in Rio de Janeiro ever since its transfer there from Lisbon in 1808. It had a Minister at that court since 1809. It involved no wrench of policy to recognize the new Brazilian monarchy in 1824 after its separation from Portugal. Monroe hoped that monarchy in Brazil would soon be succeeded by a republic, as had been the case with Iturbide's short-lived monarchy in Mexico. In any case the United States was pursuing a fundamental of its foreign policy, the recognition of new governments, regardless of political character, which were able to fulfill their responsibilities under international law. The founders of American foreign policy, notably John Quincy Adams, did not make use of recognition as a diplomatic weapon. They could still remember the days when their own nation had appealed for recognition.

[67] Op. cit., I, 63.

tection of the British Navy, and from that to conclude that it did no real good to Latin America.

This is an exaggerated and distorted view. We have observed that Monroe and his advisers did not know of the Polignac Memorandum. Canning's representation to Rush had much alarmed them. Except for John Quincy Adams they really feared that some sort of European mischief was immediately afoot in the New World at the cost of republican independence. Under the circumstances Monroe's message was a courageous and independent declaration calculated to suit the policy of the United States rather than that of Great Britain.

It is true that the Doctrine had no real force behind it. It was only a pronouncement, but it contained powerful words nevertheless, words that both served the immediate interests of the United States and exalted for the whole Hemisphere the ideals of independence and the sovereignty of the people. The service to the New World of the Monroe Doctrine *at the time of its origin* was not in preventing European intervention against the independence of an American state but rather in galvanizing the preponderant *republican character* of the new states at the outset.

The United States was loyal to the ideology of the Anglo-American Revolution and the French Revolution, which had inspired the ideology of the Spanish-American Revolution. Those ideas were anathema to the Holy Alliance and to Tory England. It would be a long time before the United States would be in a position alone to make good the principles of Non-Colonization and Non-Intervention in the face of any conceivable challenge. Nevertheless they did honor in 1823 to the American statesman who formulated them, to the President who pronounced them, to the Republic that sponsored them, and to the New World that listened to them.

8

What is the answer to the much discussed question of the "authorship" of the Monroe Doctrine? One thing is certain. It was a native national product. No one person was its author. It grew out of a half-century of American independence and republican success stemming from the distresses of monarchical Europe during the Age of Emancipation. It embodied the experience of American diplomacy from the time of George Washington, Alexander Hamilton, John Adams, and Thomas Jefferson to that of James Madison, James Monroe, Andrew Jackson, Henry Clay, and John Quincy Adams. It crystallized the instinctive aversion of American popular sovereignty to European monarchy, colonization, and imperialism. It was inseparable from the continental [68] expansion of the United States. It was a voice of Manifest Destiny.

If we mean divining, sensing, seizing, adapting, and combining, at just the right moment in history, all this national and continental feeling and

[68] I.e., the Continent of North America.

experience into a "combined system of policy" for the United States,[69] then John Quincy Adams more than any other single person helped to formulate the principles of the Monroe Doctrine. But President James Monroe was responsible for the message itself, for the pronouncement to the world, and for the actual phraseology – and punctuation – of that manifesto, except for the lines on the Non-Colonization Principle, which were Adams's words. The Secretary of State deferred loyally to his leadership. The "most significant of all American state papers" [70] appropriately bears the name Monroe Doctrine.

[69] *Memoirs*, VI, 200. [70] So termed by Dexter Perkins.

CHAPTER XX
The Slave Trade and Slavery (1823–1825)

Stratford Canning: Can you conceive of a greater and more atrocious evil than this slave trade?

John Quincy Adams: Yes. Admitting the right of search by foreign officers of our vessels upon the seas in time of peace; for that would be making slaves of ourselves.

THE UNEXPECTED diplomatic discussions that preceded the famous presidential message of December 2, 1823 served only to interrupt the persistent and pacific efforts of the Monroe Administration to reconcile all issues outstanding with Great Britain.

Already John Quincy Adams had made no inconsiderable progress toward Anglo-American concord. Under Lord Castlereagh's guidance the British Government, despite inveterate hostility of public opinion toward America,[1] had been willing to compromise the fisheries controversy. It had abandoned the navigation of the Mississippi River. It had agreed to arbitrate American claims for Negro slaves evacuated to freedom by British forces withdrawing from the United States during the War of 1812. It had given up the old alliances with the savage Indians north and south. It had accepted the facts of an American Louisiana and an American Florida. It had urged Spain to do the same. Great Britain had become generally reconciled to the northern frontier of river-and-lake and 49° west at least to the Rocky Mountains. To be sure, strategists and diplomatists at Downing Street still hoped somehow to clip off the top of the new State of Maine so as to make possible an all-British military road from Montreal to an ice-free harbor on the Bay of Fundy, but the Treaty of Ghent had left that dispute in the last analysis to be settled by the arbitration of a friendly sovereign. And if Great Britain still nursed claims to the Columbia River and the North West Coast she no longer expected to block off expansion of the United States across the Continent to the Pacific Ocean.

[1] *Memoirs,* IV, 310.

1

In the diplomatic situation after Waterloo when Great Britain was turning more and more toward America to balance the power of the Holy Alliance in Europe, it had been easy enough to clear away the small obstacles to trans-Atlantic harmony, small at least to England. After all, they involved only North America. They did not threaten the supremacy of British sea power. They did not menace the established monopoly of trade and navigation with the remaining British colonies in the New World. Therefore they yielded readily to Castlereagh's policy of appeasement and repose.

With George Canning back in the Foreign Office could the Liverpool Government be expected to yield further in more vital questions, issues that according to traditional imperial thought touched the heart of sea power and commercial prosperity? Could it bring itself to open the commerce of the West Indies and British North America to the American flag on terms of entire equality with the Union Jack? Would it accept the Freedom of the Seas? Would it agree to abolish warfare against private property on sea as it was abolished on land? Would it acknowledge the right of expatriation? Was it ready to give up altogether the practice of impressment? And would the United States on its part accept the controlling lead of British sea power for the abolition of that curse of civilized life, the African slave trade?

Britain's new need for Anglo-American solidarity had given Adams fresh hope for the settlement of these larger controversies. That is what he had in mind when he told Stratford Canning that the "great changes in the affairs of the world" offered a suitable occasion for the United States and Great Britain to compare their ideas and purposes together with a view to the accommodation of important interests upon which they had heretofore differed.[2] The great changes then taking place in the world were, of course, the successful revolution of the Spanish colonies and its effect on obsolete systems of colonial monopoly; France's invasion of Spain; and the dissolution, so far as England was concerned, of the European alliance. Britain's new role of neutrality in the face of these events, Adams had suggested, ought to make her conscious that her interests were the same as those of the United States: the interests of a *neutral* rather than a belligerent power.[3]

It was to these corrosive issues remaining to afflict Anglo-American relations that John Quincy Adams had addressed himself in the summer of 1823 in a series of fresh instructions to Richard Rush in London. In these directions he reviewed, one by one, and then all together, the outstanding issues with general reflections on the significance of each and all to American foreign policy. Their preparation constituted one of the

[2] *Memoirs*, VI, 152–3. June 20, 1823.

[3] JQA to Richard Rush, No. 71, July 28, 1823. *ASPFR*, V, 530.

major labors, though certainly not the greatest achievement, of his diplomatic career. There were nine separate instructions, plus treaty drafts, totaling some twenty-five thousand words, exclusive of supporting documents.[4] He wrote them out in his own hand in the months of June and July 1823 after much deliberation in the Cabinet and intimate consultation with the President. As usual Monroe went carefully over all the drafts and made frequent changes in tone and content but not in principle.

The group of instructions presented a grand analysis of unresolved Anglo-American controversy. They provided for Rush's precise and detailed guidance a full statement of the American position on the right of search and the slave trade; impressment; the Freedom of the Seas; colonial commerce and consular intercourse; the navigation of the St. Lawrence River; the Northeast Boundary Question; the North West Coast, and the Columbia River. They also included a directive on a new and minor difficulty concerning the fisheries, a subject ever dear to any Adams.

These remarkable documents help to expose historically the foundations of American foreign policy. For the sake of clarity it is best to devote a separate chapter to each of the major problems they touch upon, as we follow Adams's further strivings for Anglo-American concord. In doing so it will be necessary to bring up something of the background of each and occasionally to carry the narrative through the period of Adams's Presidency. These diplomatic controversies and the acerbities of domestic politics that accompanied them are just as much chapters of Adams's personal biography as they are of the history of American diplomacy. Except for his annual summer vacations in Quincy they constituted almost the whole of his life during the period of his Secretaryship of State.

First comes the question of visit and search in time of peace, precipitated by Lord Castlereagh's persistent demand for co-operation among the maritime powers for suppression of the African slave trade. Unless the

[4] The nine instructions of JQA to Richard Rush are: No. 64, June 23, 1823, concerning commercial intercourse between the United States and British colonies, *ASPFR*, V, 511–20. No. 65, June 24, 1823, concerning the right of search and the suppression of the slave trade, *ASPFR*, V, 333–7. No. 66, June 25, 1823, concerning the arbitration of the northeast boundary according to the fifth article of the Treaty of Ghent, *ASPFR*, V, 523–7. No. 67, June 26, 1823, concerning consuls in British colonial courts, *ASPFR*, V, 527–8. No. 68, June 27, 1823, concerning French interference with American fishery liberties on the west coast of Newfoundland, *ASPFR*, V, 528–9. No. 69, June 27, 1823, enumerating the five foregoing instructions, and apprising him that he is to receive later instructions on the subject of the North West Coast, and on maritime law. No. 70, July 22, 1823, concerning the North West Coast, *ASPFR*, V, 446–8. Parallel to the latter are JQA's instructions of the same date, July 22, 1823, to Henry Middleton at St. Petersburg, dealing with the same subject, *ASPFR*, V, 436–7. No. 71, July 28, 1823, concerning maritime questions, *ASPFR*, V, 529–33. No. 72, July 29, 1823, containing general reflections on the purpose and object of the instructions. Nos. 69 and 72 are not printed. The originals of the nine instructions are in DS, *U.S. Ministers*, IX, *Instructions*, 324–400, X, 61–80, 165–8. Drafts in various stages and Monroe's suggested revisions are in the Adams MSS.

United States was prepared to meet Great Britain half-way in the solution of this pressing humanitarian problem, there would be little chance for success in settling the other issues. The question involves the whole tremendous subject of African slavery and John Quincy Adams's slowly crystallizing ideas and feelings toward that institution.

2

Since the discovery of the New World, Christian slave-traders from Europe had taken a total of 24,000,000 persons out of Africa to the New World. Half of these died on the way – 12,000,000 souls. Back of these agonies to body and spirit was the tragic loss of life in the savage warfare of the African tribes that supplied the civilized traders with their human cargoes. Reckoning in the native wars and man-stealing, the eminent Negro historian W. E. B. Du Bois estimates that the slave trade cost Africa 100,000,000 lives.[5] It was one of the greatest atrocities in modern history even when measured against the monstrous genocide of our own times.

It is to England's unfading honor and glory that the successful movement for the abolition of the African slave trade began in that same island kingdom whose merchants and navigators, whose monarchs and whose governments once had lent themselves so avidly to the planting of Negro slavery in America. British humanitarianism brought about the abolition of slavery itself by judicial decree in 1772 in the United Kingdom, and the prohibition of the slave trade by act of Parliament in 1807. So effective was the agitation of John Wesley, Clarkson, Wilberforce, Brougham, and a host of other Christian leaders that whilst the famous *Asiento* article of the Treaty of Utrecht, giving to the Royal African Company a monopoly of importing slaves into the Spanish possessions of America, was regarded in its day as one of the greatest triumphs of the pacification of 1713, that feature of the Final Act of Vienna which appealed most to public opinion in 1815 was the article morally condemning the African slave trade.[6]

The return of peace brought an actual increase in the malignant commerce. According to an estimate of the African Society, slave-traders carried 60,000 victims across the Atlantic in the year 1816 alone.

Statesmen like Castlereagh and Liverpool at first had been skeptics. They had opposed as sentimental and impractical the movement for abolition of the traffic. But the swelling voice of public opinion forced the Tory Government to do something about it. Castlereagh finally became an enthusiastic and unremitting advocate. The Final Act of Vienna

[5] *Encyclopedia Americana*, article on "The Negro in America," cited by Klingberg. Note 6, below.

[6] Frank K. Klingberg: *The Anti-Slavery Movement in England, a Study in English Humanitarianism* (New Haven, 1926), quoting Baines, out of Gomer Williams: *History of the Liverpool Privateers and Slave Trade.*

paid at least a compliment to his insistence; so did the Treaty of Ghent.[7] Under British urging, supported if not stimulated by Czar Alexander I, all of the European powers except Spain and Portugal abolished one by one the shameful commerce in human beings. In 1817 Great Britain paid subsidies to the two Iberian monarchies to outlaw the trade and to conclude treaties allowing a mutual right of visit and search for its suppression. Somewhat similarly the Netherlands agreed by treaty with Great Britain in 1818 on a limited right. Despite the imperfect success of his diplomatic program, Castlereagh more than any other man excepting Wilberforce prepared the way for eventual extinction of the trade. The labor that the Foreign Minister devoted to this business so increased the heavy load of his responsibilities that in the opinion of his latest biographer it contributed to his untimely breakdown and tragic end.[8]

Allowance of the right to visit and search Spanish, Portuguese, and Dutch ships suspected of carrying on the slave trade was not sufficient to suppress the evil. The traders shifted their false cover to other flags, notably to French and American colors. Obviously it was necessary to set up some sort of international machinery that would give, under the mantle of reciprocity, a sanction to the British Navy in time of peace to visit and search the ships of all nations for the sole purpose of doing away with the thriving abomination. Castlereagh conceived of a league of the maritime powers, including the United States, to suppress the Barbary pirates in the Mediterranean. This would have involved only a belligerent right of visit and search. The next step would be to use such a league against slave-traders as well as pirates. John Quincy Adams when Minister in London had thought well of Castlereagh's idea until he realized that it was leading up to a right in time of peace which the navy had abused so outrageously in time of war.

Adams was not the only diplomatist to distrust British motives. At a special conference called in London early in 1818 to consider ways and means of suppressing the inhuman slave trade Castlereagh was unable to make any progress because of the resistance of France, whose territory was still occupied by allied troops, and of Russia, traditional champion of the Freedom of the Seas. Nor was he any more successful later in the same year at the Conference of Aix-la-Chapelle, where he strove for universal abolition of the traffic and a multilateral convention granting a mutual right of visit and search for its suppression.

While the great powers of Europe were considering the British proposals, Castlereagh turned to the United States. Here as in England an abolitionist sentiment was making itself felt among the politicians.

[7] "Whereas the Traffic in Slaves is irreconcilable with the principles of humanity and Justice, and whereas both His Majesty and the United States are desirous of continuing their efforts to promote its entire abolition, it is hereby agreed that both the contracting parties shall use their best endeavours to accomplish so desirable an object." Article X, Treaty of Ghent.

[8] Webster: *Castlereagh,* pp. 454–66.

From the dawn of independence the people of the United States had been generally adverse to slavery and the slave trade. Between 1770 and 1798 every one of the colonies or succeeding states prohibited the importation of slaves and forbade its citizens to engage in the commerce. The Continental Congress abolished slavery in the Northwest Territory in 1787, and the new Congress re-enacted the law.[9] In the Constitution it seemed easy to leave the ultimate fate of slavery itself to the authority of the individual states, at least within their own boundaries. To satisfy South Carolina and Georgia, however, a compromise article (Article I, Section 9) stipulated in euphemistic but unequivocal language that Congress could not prohibit the importation of slaves into any state before the year 1808. It seemed certain that before that year all of the states would themselves have put a stop to such importation, which indeed they did.

While it was still unconstitutional to prohibit the importation of slaves into such states as desired to allow it, the Federal Government did everything within its power to cripple the evil commerce. An act of Congress of March 22, 1794 forbade American citizens or foreigners residing within the United States to engage in the maritime slave trade, and another law of May 10, 1800 prohibited citizens from owning interests in foreign slave-traders. Federal legislation of April 7, 1798 and March 26, 1804 estopped the importation of slaves directly from abroad into the *territories* of Mississippi and Louisiana.

When in 1803 South Carolina alone reopened her ports to the importation of African slaves a wave of indignation swept through the states to the north. On March 2, 1807 (twenty-three days before the abolition of the slave trade by Great Britain) President Jefferson signed an act prohibiting the trans-Atlantic slave trade as soon as constitutionally possible; that was immediately after December 31, 1807. Penalties were too light — fines ranging from $800 to $10,000 —, and the law was never adequately enforced. A supplementary act of 1818 providing new sanctions, including imprisonment, had little effect. It was too easy for illegal privateers and foreign slave-traders to smuggle in their forbidden cargoes from the buccaneering ports of the Spanish borderlands. Finally the act of May 15, 1820 branded direct participation in the slave trade as piracy punishable by death. Still the business flourished. The Industrial Revolution in England and the new prosperity of cotton culture which rested on it were reconciling Southern politicians to slavery and even ingratiating them to the slave trade itself.

The increasing sentiment behind national legislation prohibiting American citizens from engaging in the slave trade included a body of opinion friendly to international co-operation for its suppression. In 1817 a special committee of the House of Representatives reported in favor of a limited

[9] Act of August 7, 1790.

mutual right of visit and search. A motion to the same effect passed the Senate by a vote of 17 to 16.[10]

Lord Castlereagh promptly took advantage of the movement in Congress. He handed to Richard Rush copies of the treaties that Great Britain had concluded with Spain, Portugal, and the Netherlands, and invited the negotiation of a similar one with the United States. Taken together these treaties contained the following provisions: (1) a reciprocal right of visit and search to a limited number of armed vessels of each signatory for the carefully restricted purpose of capturing vessels flying the flag of either party *and found to have slaves on board,* (2) sending the captured ships in for trial before mixed tribunals of the treaty powers, (3) in the case of the Dutch treaty alone, allowance of the right of visit and search even when the suspected vessel was sailing in the convoy of a public ship of the other treaty party. They were the articles that Castlereagh was endeavoring to put into similar treaties, bilateral or multilateral, with the other powers of Europe, and now with the United States.

The nominal reciprocity of such treaties could not disguise the necessity of British sea power for their effectiveness. To make Castlereagh's plan successful the maritime nations would have to put their commerce and peace trustfully under the authority of the British fleet. It would be the same navy that had kidnapped free white men from ships legally sailing under the American flag. It would be the same government that after the return of peace had still been unable to agree with the United States on the abolition of impressment. Memories of recent wars were still too warm both in Europe and in America for rival powers to give any worldwide acceptance to Castlereagh's worthy purpose.

The able and high-minded Rush was not unsympathetic. Transcendent evils of the trade, he told Castlereagh, had roused throughout all ranks in the United States a zeal corresponding to that of Great Britain for its extirpation. But he was also obliged to say that he had no instructions; he could only refer the subject to Washington.[11]

To John Quincy Adams fell the duty of answering the British proposal, following deliberations of President Monroe's Cabinet. It is now time to take notice of the development of Adams's own personal feelings toward slavery and the slave trade.

3

John Quincy Adams had not been conspicuous in the United States as an antislavery man any more than Castlereagh in England. His early letters published and unpublished had very little reference to slavery or the slave trade. It is recalled that he once thought of quitting the diplo-

[10] Klingberg: *Anti-Slavery Movement,* p. 166, citing *Annals of Congress,* 15th Cong., 1st Sess., 1818–19, I, 71, 73–8, 94–109.

[11] *ASPFR,* V, 69–72.

matic service to settle in one of the Southern states. Certainly it was not with the intention of being a reformer. As a young Senator from Massachusetts he made no great fuss in Washington about these evils. For one reason or another he opposed the bill prohibiting the importation of slaves from abroad into Louisiana.[12] He argued against prohibiting importation of slaves into the United States by any act passed before 1808.[13]

Since 1808 Adams's diplomatic career had kept him out of domestic politics. His duties as American Minister abroad and as Secretary of State at home had brought him into public contact only with the international problems arising from the existence of slavery in the United States. In this capacity he never allowed a foreign government to exploit any personal squeamishness he had about the domestic institution of his country. He loyally presented the claims of Southern owners for indemnification for their slaves abducted by British forces after the peace of Ghent. He pressed forward conscientiously with the arbitration and final settlement of that issue. He lent the assistance of the Department of State to Southern citizens attempting to extradite escaped slaves from Canada.[14] He showed no sympathy for the American Colonization Society, organized for the purpose of establishing liberated slaves in a free state in Africa. It meant imperialism, he told the President in 1819, the grafting of an overseas colonial establishment upon the Constitution of the United States.[15] Adams would never change his mind about the Society. Even in his later crusading antislavery years he continued to regard it as wild and visionary, "an abortion," an uncomely moral project for relieving the slave states of free Negroes.[16]

Adams's inner convictions on slavery and politics first began to crystallize during the debates in Congress over the admission of Missouri into the Union. "I take it for granted," he wrote in his Diary, "that the present question is a mere preamble – a title page to a great tragic volume." [17]

Adams believed that Congress, which had the constitutional right to dispose of and make all needful rules and regulations respecting the ter-

[12] See above, Ch. VI.

[13] *Plumer's Proceedings U.S. Senate,* pp. 353–4. The *Annals of Congress* for January 27, 1807, when this bill passed, do not reveal a roll-call.

[14] Stratford Canning to Castlereagh, Confidential, No. 25, Washington, April 27, 1821. PRO, F.O., 5, Vol. CLVIII.

[15] "There are men of all sorts and descriptions concerned in this Colonization Society: some exceedingly humane, weak-minded men, who have really no other than the professed objects in view, and who honestly believe them both useful and attainable; some, speculators in official profits and honors, which a colonial establishment would of course produce; some, speculators in political popularity, who think to please the abolitionists by their zeal for emancipation, and the slave-holders by the flattering hope of ridding them of the free colored people at the public expense; lastly, some cunning slave-holders, who see that the plan may be carried far enough to produce the effect of raising the market price of their slaves." *Memoirs,* IV, 292.

[16] *Memoirs,* VI, 363, VIII, 309, IX, 437.

[17] *Memoirs,* IV, 502. January 10, 1820.

ritories or other property of the United States, possessed therewith the power to regulate slavery in the territories. But he did not think that Congress had any right to abolish slavery within a state where it already existed.[18] And he did not consider it compatible with the Constitution to require a restriction upon slavery as a condition for admission of a new state into the Union *out of territory where slavery already existed.* Specifically he did not believe that Congress had a right to impose such a restriction on Missouri. He privately urged Massachusetts members of Congress, particularly Daniel Webster and Harrison Gray Otis, to compromise this "first" Missouri question.[19] "If a provision could be obtained excluding the introduction of slaves into future territories," he told two antislavery friends and political supporters, William Plumer, Jr., and Arthur Livermore, Representatives in Congress from New Hampshire, "it will be a great and important object secured." [20]

The more he thought about compromise the more doubts assailed him. One winter afternoon in February 1820 while the debates were running on in Congress, he had a long conversation in the Department of State with his then respected friend and colleague John C. Calhoun.

"I do not think it [slavery] will produce a dissolution of the Union," Calhoun told him, "but, if it should, the South would be from necessity compelled to form an alliance, offensive and defensive, with Great Britain."

"That would be returning to the colonial state," replied Adams.

"Yes, pretty much," admitted Calhoun, "but it would be forced upon us."

"If by the effect of this alliance, offensive and defensive, the population of the North should be cut off from its natural outlet upon the ocean," asked the Massachusetts man, "do you think it would fall back upon its rocks bound hand and foot, to starve, or would it not retain its powers of locomotion to move southward by land?"

"Then," said Calhoun, "we shall find it necessary to make our communities all military."

The two men talked on and on about the perilous subject. They did not notice the hours slip by until long past Calhoun's customary dinner hour. Evening shadows were already shrouding the State Department when the Southerner walked down the steps to Pennsylvania Avenue.

After his colleague left the office, Adams's mind raced on in a momentous train of thought. "Slavery," he told himself, "is the great and foul

[18] JQA to Jonathan Jennings, July 17, 1820. *Writings*, VII, 53.

[19] Edward Everett to JQA, March 28, 1827, and JQA to Edward Everett, Washington, April 11, 1827. Adams MSS.

[20] *Memoirs*, IV, 530. February 23, 1820. See also *The Missouri Compromise and Presidential Politics, 1820–1825, from the Letters of William Plumer Jr., Representative from New Hampshire.* Everett Somerville Brown, ed. (Mo. Hist. Soc., St. Louis, 1926), pp. 15–17, 117–19.

stain upon the North American Union, and it is a contemplation worthy of the most exalted soul whether its total abolition is or is not practicable: if practicable, by what means it may be effected, and if a choice of means be within the scope of the object, what means would accomplish it at the smallest cost of human sufferance. A dissolution, at least temporary, of the Union, as now constituted, would be certainly necessary, and the dissolution must be upon a point involving the question of slavery, and no other. The Union then might be reorganized upon the fundamental principle of emancipation. This object is vast in its compass, awful in its prospects, sublime and beautiful in its issue. A life devoted to it would be nobly spent or sacrificed."[21]

Prophetic musings! But they quieted down under considerations of practical politics and presidential aspirations. Already the Missouri excitement was threatening to obscure the luster of Adams's diplomatic triumph over Spain in 1819. Henry Clay was still trying to stir up the West against final acceptance of the Transcontinental Treaty because it did not secure Texas as well as Florida. Eastern opposition to the expansion of slavery had become so pronounced that it was now doubtful whether the Senate would have accepted the treaty had it taken in Texas too.[22] Adams did not want to antagonize any group if he could help it. Nor had the time yet come to take an uncompromising stand against slavery in American politics.

"As a servant of the whole Union," he told Senator Ninian Edwards of Illinois, "the interests of every part of the Union are equally dear to me. There is neither East, West, North, or South to my duty or my feelings. But as an Eastern man I should be disinclined to have either Texas or Florida without a restriction excluding slavery from them, and if I were now a member of either House of Congress I would offer resolutions that the treaty ought not now to be accepted without an article prohibiting and excluding slavery from the territory to be acquired."[23]

Fortunately for him he was not a member of Congress. He was Secretary of State. He did not need to offer any resolutions. Nor did he try to get anybody else to offer them. It was not his part to make trouble for his treaty. Nor did he do anything about the Missouri question. He kept quiet. He had solid reasons for not wanting to obtrude his views on anybody.[24]

In the Cabinet, Adams agreed with Calhoun and the other colleagues

[21] *Memoirs,* IV, 531. February 24, 1820.

[22] Monroe to Jefferson, Washington, May 1820. *Writings of Monroe,* VI, 119.

[23] *Memoirs,* V, 54.

[24] "When the first Missouri question was before Congress, my opinion was that the restriction proposed upon that State was not compatible either with the Constitution or with the Louisiana Convention. I had many solid reasons for not *obtruding* this opinion at the time upon any one. But I did not disguise or dissemble it to any one who desired to know what my opinion was." JQA to Edward Everett, April 11, 1827. Adams MSS.

that Congress had a right to prohibit slavery in the territories. He marveled that strict constructionists like Crawford, Calhoun, and Wirt would admit this. These gentlemen, in the simplicity of their hearts, he said to himself, have come to a conclusion in direct opposition to their premises, without being aware or conscious of inconsistency.[25] He held with Crawford, that such a prohibition would be binding upon states afterward created out of such territories.

Walking home together in friendly discourse from the Cabinet meeting, Adams and Calhoun again discussed the question long and earnestly.

"The principles which you have avowed," Calhoun admitted, "are just and noble; but in the Southern country, whenever they are mentioned they are understood as applying only to white men."

He pointed out that slavery was a social necessity for manual labor in the South, and the best guarantee for equality among the whites.

"I cannot see things in the same light," answered Adams.

The subject kept stirring in Adams's mind after the two men took leave of each other.

"It is among the evils of slavery," he reflected, astonished that a man of Calhoun's mental and moral powers could identify liberty with the color of a man's skin, "that it taints the very sources of moral principle. . . . The impression produced upon my mind by the progress of this discussion is, that the bargain between freedom and slavery contained in the Constitution of the United States is morally and politically vicious, inconsistent with the principles upon which alone our Revolution can be justified; cruel and oppressive, by riveting the chains of slavery, by pledging the faith of freedom to maintain and perpetuate the tyranny of the master; and grossly unequal and impolitic, by admitting that slaves are at once enemies to be kept in subjection, property to be secured or restored to their owners, and persons not to be represented themselves, but for whom their masters are privileged with nearly a double share of representation. The consequence has been that this slave representation has governed the Union. . . . I have favored this Missouri Compromise, believing it to be all that could be effected under the present Constitution, and from extreme unwillingness to put the Union at hazard. But perhaps it would have been a wiser as well as a bolder course to have persisted in the restriction upon Missouri, till it should have terminated in a convention of the States to revise and amend the Constitution. This would have produced a new Union of thirteen or fourteen states unpolluted with slavery, with a great and glorious object to effect, namely, that of rallying to their standard the other States by the universal emancipation of their slaves. If the Union must be dissolved slavery is precisely the question upon which it ought to break."[26]

The Missouri Compromise Act provided that Missouri might be ad-

[25] *Memoirs,* V, 5. March 3, 1820.

[26] *Memoirs,* V, 11–12. March 2, 1820.

mitted into the Union without any restriction on slavery, and enabled a territorial convention to draw up a constitution for the proposed state; it also prohibited slavery in the territories of the United States north of 36° 30′ north latitude. The state constitution adopted under this enabling act required the legislature to frame laws to restrict the immigration of free persons of color into the state — an outright infringement upon the constitutional rights of colored citizens of the other states. The latter provision caused great opposition among many representatives from the Northern states when the joint resolution for the formal admission of Missouri came up in Congress in November 1820, just before the re-election of President Monroe. It produced the "second" Missouri question.

John Quincy Adams could not look complacently on this new Missouri issue.

Dr. William Eustis, member of the House from Adams's district in Massachusetts and a long-standing friend, consulted him on the problem.

"The clause in their Constitution," said Eustis, "is directly repugnant to the article in the Constitution of the United States. I have no doubt of that, nor do you. But what is to be done?"

"The course appears to me very obvious," Adams declared. "Pass a resolution declaring that State to be admitted from and after the time when they shall have expunged from their Constitution the article repugnant to the Constitution of the United States."

"I intend to do so," assented Eustis, "but I distrust many of those who are on the free side of the question."

Eustis brought up the resolution, only to have it defeated by a large majority. In a memorable conversation with Judge Henry Baldwin, a member of the House from Pennsylvania, Adams let himself out on the subject.

"Those who now object to the admission of Missouri," remarked Baldwin, "wish to reopen the whole controversy."

"That would be quite unjustifiable," Adams declared, "but the article in the Missouri Constitution is directly repugnant to the rights reserved to every citizen of the Union in the Constitution of the United States. Its purport goes to disenfranchise all the people of color who are citizens of the free states.

"If I were a member of the Legislature of one of those States," he continued, "I would move for a declaratory act, that so long as the article in the Constitution of Missouri depriving the colored citizens of the State, say of Massachusetts, of their rights as citizens of the United States within the State of Missouri, shall subsist, so long the white citizens of the State of Missouri shall be held as aliens within the Commonwealth of Massachusetts, not entitled to claim or enjoy within the same any right or privilege of a citizen of the United States."

He would go farther, he asserted, warming up to the subject that had so bothered his conscience. If Missouri were admitted with such an article in her constitution it would be a violation of the Constitution of the United States. Until the citizens of Massachusetts should be restored their full constitutional rights in Missouri, no clause or article of the Constitution of the United States should be so construed as to authorize any person whomsoever to claim the property or possession of a human being as a slave. "I would prohibit by law the delivery of any fugitive slave upon the claim of his master," he affirmed. "I would do this not to violate, but to redeem the Constitution of the United States."

This was dangerously close to nullification. It foreshadowed the later unconstitutional resistance of the North to enforcement of the Fugitive Slave Act. It actually anticipated even a dissolution *de facto* of the Union.

"That dissolution would have commenced by the article in the Missouri Constitution," Adams went rapidly on. "If acquiesced in, it will change the terms of the federal compact [using a phrase of the Virginia and Kentucky Resolutions and the Hartford Convention], change its terms by robbing thousands of citizens of their rights. And what citizens? The poor, the unfortunate, the helpless. Already cursed by the mere color of their skin, already doomed by their complexion to drudge in the lowest offices of society, excluded by their color from all the refined enjoyments of life accessible to others, excluded from the benefits of a liberal education, from the bed, from the table, and from all the social comforts of domestic life, this barbarous article deprives them of the little remnant of right yet left them — their rights as citizens and as men."

A new and impassioned eloquence had seized for the first time upon the former professor of rhetoric who had lamented that his speech was so slow, so hesitant, so halting, so confused.

"If the dissolution of the Union must come," he exclaimed to Baldwin, "let it come from no other cause but this. If slavery be the destined sword in the hand of the destroying angel which is to sever the ties of this Union, the same sword will cut in sunder the bonds of slavery itself. A dissolution of the Union for the cause of slavery would be followed by a servile war in the slave-holding states, combined with a war between the two severed portions of the Union. It seems to me that its result must be the extirpation of slavery from this whole continent; and, calamitous and desolating as this course of events in its progress must be, so glorious would be its final issue, that, as God shall judge me, I dare not say that it is not to be desired."

Baldwin did not interrupt him until the end of this prophetic outburst.

"I entertain different opinions from yours of this class of the population," the Judge then responded quietly. "I think they are far more mischievous than useful. Of all the petty crimes committed in the part of the country where I reside, nine-tenths are by free people of color. I believe it is the same throughout the country, though there may be an exception in the Eastern States. All the States make laws for the exclusion of paupers and vagabonds, and persons whose residence within the State would become a nuisance. For my part, I am willing to admit Missouri in any form in which it has been proposed, with the condition or without it." [27]

It was a weak rejoinder, by a man whom nobody now remembers, to a noble discourse by a statesman of whom the world was to hear much more on this score, but only in a second, crusading career of his life.

Congress proved unwilling to disturb the Missouri Compromise. After much debate it finally passed a resolution admitting Missouri into the Union on the condition that the obnoxious clause in her constitution be not construed, and no law be ever passed, in derogation of the rights of a citizen of another state. Henry Clay got the compromise through, and it was a sensible one for the time. The antislavery impulse had not become sufficiently confirmed in the Northern states for any leader to challenge the South, and the Union, in 1820, on the issue of slavery.[28] Had the controversy been precipitated then, the United States would have broken up irrecoverably. For the North in 1820 did not have the will to go to war to save the Union over any issue of slavery. It could not have suppressed a war for Southern independence at that time. Nor did the South itself want independence then: there were too many Southern as well as Western and Northern statesmen who had their eye on the Presidency of the United States. The majority North and South was anxious to compromise.

John Quincy Adams also was unwilling to disturb the Missouri Compromise. He thought it morally bad but temporarily expedient. It was necessary because of the inherent defects of the Constitution of the United States, the original compromise of 1787 in regard to slavery. "There must be a conflict at some time upon this very question between free and slave representation," he noted in his Diary at a dispassionate moment, "but this is not the time, nor was this the proper occasion, for contesting it." [29]

For the present, he had already concluded, the contest is laid asleep.[30]

Put to sleep by the Missouri Compromise, the issue remained uneasily dormant in Adams's conscience as long as he remained Secretary of State and President. Later these questionings would consume his mind and heart. Amidst the throbbing antislavery crusade of the thirties they would transform his whole political outlook and lead him into another career of his life: the Old Man Eloquent against slavery expansion. In the year 1820 he sensed this career only in the most exalted moods.

[27] *Memoirs,* V, 205–11.

[28] "I have abstained, sometimes perhaps too pertinaciously abstained, from all participation in measures *leading* to that conflict for life and death between *Freedom* and *Slavery,* through which I have not yet been able to see how this Union could ultimately be preserved from passing." JQA to Charles Hammond, Ohio Anti-Slavery Whig, Washington, March 31, 1837. Printed in William Henry Smith's biographical sketch of *Charles Hammond* (Chicago Hist. Soc., 1885), pp. 67–70.

[29] *Memoirs,* V, 308.

[30] *Memoirs,* V, 10–12. March 2, 1820.

For the time being Adams had all he could do to defend his diplomatic record against the attacks of equally ambitious and more unscrupulous rivals without getting involved in the sectional controversy. Spain had not yet ratified the Transcontinental Treaty. Clay's admirers were snickering at Adams's expense. They were saying that Onís had bamboozled him in the matter of the Spanish land grants. The partisans of Crawford, and Crawford himself, were exultant as they contemplated a slur upon the sagacity of the experienced Secretary of State. They delighted in the apparent failure of the negotiation because that would bring disgrace on him.[31] It was not the time to go out of his way to charge windmills.

Not until 1823, when rival politicians were searching out his record, did Adams explain why he had opposed the early laws against the slave trade. It would have done no good, he professed fifteen years after the event, to prohibit the importation of slaves from abroad into Louisiana when the same persons could be landed at Charleston and sent from South Carolina into the territory. This explanation ignores the fact, doubtless forgotten, that during the progress of the Louisiana territorial bill through the Senate he had voted on January 26, 1804 specifically against the amendment which prohibited that very possibility.[32] As to prohibition of the trade, he said in 1823, it was unconstitutional to prohibit it before 1808, therefore it was unconstitutional to pass an act for that purpose before 1808 even though the prohibition was not to go into effect until that year.

At best these were *ex post facto* rationalizations put forward at a time when he was anxious not to alienate any section of the country in the impending presidential campaign of 1824. He repeated them during the campaign of 1828.[33]

4

President Monroe put to the Gentlemen of the Administration Castlereagh's first proposal of 1818 for a reciprocal right of visit and search for the suppression of the slave trade. Unanimously they agreed that it ought not to be acceded to. The Secretary of State faithfully embodied their objections in instructions to Richard Rush and Albert Gallatin in London.[34] At Monroe's earnest suggestion Adams forbore entering into the

[31] *Memoirs*, V, 290.

[32] *Annals of Congress*, 8th Cong., 1st Sess., 1803–5, p. 240. See above, p. 122. This volume of the Debates and Proceedings of Congress was not printed until 1852. JQA's *Memoirs* for that date do not record the details of the debate and amendment to the bill.

[33] *Letter of the Hon. John Quincy Adams, in a Reply to a Letter of the Hon. Alexander Smyth, to His* [*Va.*] *Constituents* (Washington, January 1823). Reprinted in 1828 with Adams's speech in the Senate of November 3, 1803, on the Louisiana legislation and treaty, and a letter from Thomas Jefferson to William Dunbar, distrusting the constitutionality of the legislation.

[34] This was his argument: (1) The participation of the United States in mixed tribunals would be unconstitutional because they would constitute a court consisting

congenial task of exposing the unpleasant historical background of visit and search. Instead he expressed a wish for the success of the European treaties in extirpating "the root of numberless evils, the traffic in human blood." He stressed the determination of the United States Government to co-operate to the utmost extent of its constitutional powers "in this great vindication of the sacred rights of humanity."[35]

The utmost extent of American co-operation proved to be no more than naval instructions to a feeble anti-slave-trade patrol intermittently stationed off the coast of Africa to cruise in company with corresponding British units against slave-traders without recognizing the right of visit and search or sending in captured traders to any but American courts. When American cruisers visited, searched, captured, and sent to the United States some suspected ships flying the French flag, Adams repudiated the action as well as any right or intention to search French ships in time of peace.[36] This attitude and the excessive delicacy with which the Government instructed its naval commanders in exercising visit and search even against vessels suspected of piracy almost completely frustrated efforts to protect American commerce from these enemies of all mankind.[37]

Castlereagh persisted. He seemed to think the attitude of the United States traditional rather than reasonable, that its constitutional scruples would yield to the humanitarian drift. The appearance during the Missouri debates of an opposition to the expansion of slavery within the United States must have heartened the British Foreign Minister. He instructed Stratford Canning to take every opportunity in his conferences

---

partly of foreign judges not amenable to impeachment for corruption and deciding upon the statutes of the United States without appeal. "The constitutional objection may be the more readily understood by the British Cabinet if they are reminded that it was an obstacle proceeding from the same principle which prevented Great Britain from becoming, formally, a party to the Holy Alliance." (2) The condition of blacks in the United States made it impossible for the Federal Government to guarantee the freedom of slaves, liberated from the traders, in the states where they could be received only as slaves, or to control them in the states where they would be recognized as free. (3) Most important of all there was a universal repugnance of public opinion in the United States to admitting any right of visit and search in time of peace "under any circumstances whatever." So obnoxious to "feelings and recollections" was such a proposal that there would be no prospect of securing the advice and consent of the Senate to ratification of a treaty.

[35] JQA to Richard Rush and Albert Gallatin, Department of State, November 2, 1818. *ASPFR*, V, 72–3.

[36] Hugh G. Soulsby: *The Right of Search and the Slave Trade in Anglo-American Relations, 1814–1862* (Baltimore, 1933), pp. 13–38.

[37] "Whatever well-grounded suspicions you may entertain [that a vessel had been fitted out and intended for piracy] you will not molest her, unless you have satisfactory evidence that she has either *attempted* or *actually committed* some piratical aggression on some merchant vessel of the United States." Navy Department Records (National Archives), Private Letters, Perry, May 29, 1819. Cited by Baker: *United States and Piracy.*

with Adams to keep the American Government in the uncomfortable position of continually having to explain why it refused to co-operate in such a good cause. So unremittingly did Stratford keep at the Secretary of State that the latter had to tell him, "in a tone which it was impossible not to understand," that the Government already had been too much pressed upon the subject.[38]

Still the British Minister kept coming back to the charge.

Adams finally made a suggestion, albeit in a negative sort of way. "Unless Britain will bind herself," said the Secretary, "by an article, as strong and explicit as language can make it, never again in time of war to take a man from an American vessel, we never for a moment can listen to a proposal for allowing such a search in time of peace."[39]

The British Government never came forward with such an offer. Nor did Adams ultimately insist upon it as a condition.

"The main purpose for which we wish to obtain your assent to the principle of search," Stratford Canning observed one day, still pursuing the disagreeable subject, "is that it might be urged as an example to France."

"We would rather wish France to adhere to our principles in this respect," replied Adams, "than to give them up."

"Can you conceive of a greater and more atrocious evil than this slave trade?" Stratford challenged.

"Yes," Adams promptly responded. "Admitting the right of search by foreign officers of our vessels upon the seas in time of peace; for that would be making slaves of ourselves."[40]

John Quincy Adams and he alone, so Stratford believed, was responsible for the continuing resistance of the American Government. At least two members of the Cabinet,[41] he reported, were in favor of a mutual right of visit and search, but the Secretary of State's "ascendancy" over the President was complete.[42] In vain the British Minister visited New England and searched about to identify Adams indirectly with some group surreptitiously interested in the heinous business. The only explanation of the Secretary's uncompromising stand, he concluded, was his presidential ambitions: visit and search was too popular an issue to abandon so near to the national elections of 1824.[43] That this explanation was not altogether wrong will be seen presently in Adams's shift in posi-

[38] S. Canning to Castlereagh, private and confidential, March 8, 1821, PRO, F.O., 5, Vol. CLVII. *Memoirs,* V, 321.

[39] *Memoirs,* V, 448. December 4, 1821.

[40] *Memoirs,* VI, 37. June 29, 1822.

[41] Presumably Wirt and Thompson.

[42] Presumably it was Crawford, Adams's rival for Monroe's succession, who tipped Canning off to these inner secrets of Cabinet discussions. JQA to Joseph Blunt, Washington, June 6, 1824. Adams MSS.

[43] Stratford Canning to George Canning, No. 56, Confidential, Washington, June 6, 1823. PRO, F.O., 5, Vol. CLXXVI.

tion as public sentiment in the United States seemed to crystallize in favor of the British proposals.

A campaign began in the House of Representatives in December 1821 in favor of granting the right of visit and search. The House called upon the President for information relating to any negotiations with foreign powers for the suppression of the slave trade. Adams promptly supplied the relevant documents. Next a special committee presented a history of the movement for abolishing the traffic in human beings. Its report took care to include the published minutes of the international conference of January 1818 in London and the discussions at Aix-la-Chapelle. It presented Lord Castlereagh's own voluminous evidence and arguments to support a recommendation for endowing an international police force with adequate power and authority to put an end to the evil.[44] In April 1822 another committee, after reviewing ineffectual efforts to suppress the trade, advocated treaties with one or more of the maritime powers of Europe agreeing to a restricted and reciprocal right of visit and search for the sole purpose of suppressing the trade. This is just what Castlereagh had been urging.

"Your committee cannot doubt," concluded the report of 1822, "that the people of America have the intelligence to distinguish between the right of searching a neutral on the high seas, in time of war, claimed by some belligerents, and that mutual, restricted, and peaceful concession by treaty, suggested by your committee, and which is demanded in the name of suffering humanity."[45]

Even though the House of Representatives took no action on these reports, they revealed an increasing divergence of opinion between the executive and legislative branches of the Government. They encouraged Stratford to press the Secretary of State all the harder. But his chief, the British Foreign Minister, died before he could take advantage of the humanitarian movement that he had so correctly sensed.

George Canning, Castlereagh's flashing successor, promptly took up the campaign where his rival had laid it down. As a disciple of William Pitt, Canning had always been a crusader against the trade. He directed his cousin Stratford in Washington to urge the United States to concede a reciprocal right of visit and search if only for a short time: two or three years might be enough to sweep the atrocious commerce from the African and American seas. Incidentally, Canning observed, this would be the best and perhaps the only remedy against the great and growing evil of piracy in the American seas.[46]

Stratford despaired of success unless there should crystallize some popular movement in support of the British desire. The Secretary of

[44] *ASPFR,* V, 69–126.

[45] *ASPFR,* V, 140–1.

[46] George Canning to Stratford Canning, October 11, 1822. PRO, F.O., 5, Vol. CLXV.

State had made the British envoy "sick at heart" with his inveterate resistance to anything which under any stretch of the American imagination sometime might lend cover somewhere to the hateful practice of impressment. The British Minister in Washington defied Adams either to accept the British proposal already offered or to suggest before God and man an alternate plan of equal efficacy.[47]

John Quincy Adams had to look for an alternative. For the movement against the slave trade was coming to a head much faster than the British plenipotentiary realized. On February 28, 1823 the House of Representatives by an overwhelming vote of 131 to 9 passed a resolution calling upon the President to negotiate with the maritime powers "for the effectual abolition of the African slave trade, and its ultimate denunciation, as piracy, under the law of nations, by the consent of the civilized world." [48] The resolution focused the sun-glass of humanitarian opinion upon the Executive. It made it morally and politically impossible for the Monroe Administration to hold unswervingly to its old position. But how could John Quincy Adams, who had told the British Government that the United States could not concede the right of visit and search in time of peace *under any circumstances whatever,* now accept Castlereagh's proposal without abandoning a traditional stand with which he had identified himself for years before the patriots of his country?

Adams was always writing letters of advice to his sons on religion, life, and politics. They throw much light on his own mental processes, character, and biography. Three years after this particular agitation over the slave trade his eldest son, George Washington Adams, took his seat in the Massachusetts legislature. From the White House the father wrote a letter that might have reflected his own searchings of mind and heart with regard to the suppression of the slave trade. "Your intention to act and vote according to your own sense of right," Adams advised his son, "even at the hazard of losing your popularity, is right; but you must also be careful to avoid taking the side which is both unpopular and wrong; and if the popular sentiment be strong and urgent you should reconsider your own impressions, whether they may not be erroneous." [49]

Under strong and urgent popular sentiment John Quincy Adams in March 1823 reconsidered whether his impressions of the slave trade might not be erroneous. He had been popular and right, there was no doubt about that, in denouncing the historic British abuses of the right of visit and search. He was becoming unpopular in resisting Lord Castlereagh's program for the suppression of the trade; the resolution of the House of Representatives had made that clear. He had also been wrong; his own conscience told him that. The people had been right.

[47] Stratford Canning to JQA, January 29, 1823. *ASPFR,* V, 327.

[48] *Annals of Congress,* 17th Cong., 2d Sess., 1822–3, pp. 1147–55. Soulsby, op. cit., pp. 25–9.

[49] JQA to GWA, Washington, July 5, 1826. Adams MSS.

Reconsideration of his own impressions led to a legal revelation. The United States by municipal legislation had abolished the slave trade and branded it as piracy punishable by death. Let the United States now join with other nations, one or more, in declaring the slave trade piracy under the law of nations – as the House of Representatives had just called upon the Executive to do – and the odious commerce would become piracy in international law. Pirates are the enemies of all mankind. All nations are perpetually at war with them. Therefore there would be a *belligerent* right of visit and search for the purpose of detecting enemies and capturing slave-trade pirates masked under false colors.

Adams had found a way to meet the British position without deserting any of his old defenses against the practice of impressment and without enabling his political adversaries to turn on him for deserting a traditional American principle of the Freedom of the Seas. His discovery of such a bridge of reason is an interesting event in a chapter of American diplomatic history. It is of far greater significance in his own biography and in the general history of the United States, for it brought him to the road that was to lead finally, through winding political vistas, into the antislavery crusade of his second career.

The express and almost unanimous sense of the House of Representatives, so the Secretary of State formally advised the British Minister, at last made it possible to offer an effective substitute for the mutual right of visit and mixed tribunals for the trial of offenders, to which the United States could never be reconciled. As an alternative to the British proposal Adams now proposed denunciation of the slave trade as piracy punishable as such when participated in by the citizens or subjects of the respective nations. If Great Britain approved the idea, then it might be *separately* urged on France and the other maritime powers of Europe.

Stratford transmitted the proposition to his Government, not without expressing ponderously to Adams the thought that, however well it might be received in London, it could not but excite fresh sentiments of regret that the "American Administration" had seen fit to regard so unfavorably the principal measure proposed on the part of His Majesty. He took care to justify at length the principle of mixed tribunals and carefully restricted *reciprocal* right of visit and search. Perhaps the whole arrangement need be no more than temporarily necessary. Under no stretch of the imagination would it lead to "vexatious exercise of authority."

In this formal exchange of views each diplomat was playing to public opinion.[50] The slightly invidious phrase "American *Administration,*" as distinct from the people, is worth noting.

In glorifying the British campaign against the slave trade His Majesty's Minister in Washington had made no reference to the old grievance of impressment. His failure to do so gave Adams the opening he was look-

[50] President Monroe submitted the correspondence to the Senate, with the Convention of March 13, 1824. *ASPFR,* V, 326–30.

ing for to justify his own traditional opposition, and to pour into a final statement for all the world to read the impassioned voice of his country crying out against the evil of impressment while not refusing to enter into an engagement to pursue and punish slave-trading pirates as the common enemies of the human race. In this way would he keep himself before his countrymen as the unyielding champion of their most sacred cause as well as the friend of all humanity black and white. And he would have to leave the public mind in no doubt about his own consistently implacable opposition to any right of visit and search *in time of peace.*

The tireless Secretary sweated out two long papers on the right of search. Between sessions at his sticky desk he went for long swims in the Potomac. One document was an instruction to Richard Rush recapitulating the whole subject of the slave trade and enclosing the draft of a convention that the United States was willing to sign. Rush was to present the project to the British Government only after "adequate assurance" that Parliament would make the slave trade piracy as Congress had done on this side of the water. The other paper was a reply to Stratford Canning's last note.

The President presented Adams's drafts to his Cabinet for consideration.[51]

The proposed convention, of eleven articles, allowed a reciprocal right of visit and search for the sole purpose of suppressing the slave trade, but only on condition that both countries should declare their citizens and subjects engaging in it guilty of the crime of piracy. Captured vessels and people were to be sent in for adjudication by the tribunals of the country to which such slave ship should belong. Careful restrictions guarded against "vexatious or abusive exercise of the right," including indemnities for such abuse. No merchant ship of either party under convoy of a public vessel should be subject to visit and search. "No person shall be taken out of the said visited or captured merchant vessel of either nation by the commanding officer of the visiting vessel, or under his order." Adams intended this last stipulation to be a binder against impressment.

Adams's project [52] was a victory for Stratford Canning and for British and American humanitarianism back of British diplomacy. Except for the provision requiring captured ships to be sent in to the courts of their own country it was just what George Canning had been proposing all along. The exception itself proves the case for Canning. He was just as unwilling as John Quincy Adams (in the case of American citizens) to have one of His Majesty's subjects, an alleged slave-trader, tried in any but British Courts.[53]

[51] James Monroe to JQA, June 20, 22, 1823. Adams MSS.

[52] *ASPFR*, V, 335–7.

[53] "Notwithstanding the flagrant character of the crime, His Majesty's Government, though prepared to consent, eventually and conditionally, to attach a Capital Punishment to the Commission of it, would feel, on that very account, reluctant to

Crawford, spokesman and heir to the Southern democracy, leading candidate to succeed Monroe in 1825, objected to the argument against the right of search as Adams had stated it in the note to Stratford Canning. "It is completely given up in the project of a Convention," he told the Cabinet, "and therefore the argument might be represented by the British as a mere declaration against a practice which the project essentially conceded."

Crawford was correct. The Secretary of State had been fully aware of this point when preparing the documents. "There are two objects to be aimed at in them," he explained: "one, fully to justify the repugnance which we have hitherto manifested against the right of search as practised by Great Britain in war; the other, to carry into effect the resolution of the House of Representatives. . . . To piracy, by the law of nations, search is incident of course, since wherever there is a right *to capture* there must be a right to search. . . . All that is left to us is to keep it still flexibly within the class of belligerent rights, as exercised only against pirates, the enemies of all mankind."

Calhoun objected to the admission in any form of the right of search by foreign officers. "We should say at once," he declared, "that we will never concede the right of search for slaves unless Britain will renounce search for her seamen in our vessels in war."

Already Adams had suggested that to Canning in almost those very words.

"I am willing to make the one the condition of the other," he now assured the Gentlemen of the Administration. But he never actually went that far. All that he did was to make sure that no British naval officer searching an American ship suspected of engaging in the slave trade could take out any member of the crew. He was even then drafting an elaborate convention on the Freedom of the Seas and the abolition of impressment, but it was not to be a condition precedent for American agreement to the right of visit and search for the suppression of the slave trade. Rather he proposed to offer the latter in the hope that Great Britain thus pleased would then agree to the former.

The Cabinet agreed that the project for a convention should go out to England, but that Adams's letter to Stratford should be modified.[54]

Monroe and Adams again went over the draft of the reply to the British Minister. The President cut out a large section and substituted a milder abridgment. The deleted paragraphs were the heart of Adams's paper, pulsing with a patriotic indictment of impressment as a "deadly source of unextinguishable war."

---

make an unqualified transfer of their authority over the offenders, when British Subjects, to any foreign power." George Canning to William Huskisson and Stratford Canning. Foreign Office, January 22, 1824. Huskisson "Papers Relating to the Affairs of America." WRC.

[54] *Memoirs,* VI, 148–9. June 19, 1823.

"My motives," he protested to the President, "are to exhibit to the people of this country and to the world, the real grounds of objection to the right of search. I am satisfied that views unfriendly to your Administration, *and to me personally*, are mingling themselves with this subject. . . ."

Monroe's view prevailed. He staunchly maintained the American principle but toned down his Secretary's bitter strictures. After all it was past history. "I wish to avoid everything," the President explained, "which by irritating them, might give the British Ministers the opportunity of imputing insincerity or ill will to us. I wish to gain over to our views Mr. Wilberforce and his party, and to discard for that purpose, all that [which], by touching their national pride would turn against us." [55]

Thus it was that the most eloquent passages Adams ever penned in a state paper went unused. They came from a long and painful history. They were full of feeling. Some of the paragraphs are the kind which schoolboy orators might have declaimed during generations to follow. Perhaps it is better that they were left unrecited. Today they can do no harm. The reader will find them printed in Adams's *Writings*.[56]

Adams gave Stratford Canning very clearly to understand that the various subjects of the general negotiation were not inseparably connected: "A convention, if practicable, on the slave trade," he remarked to the British Minister, "would probably be best in a separate shape, as admitting more conveniently the accession of other powers, to which, in common with Great Britain, the proposal of constituting that traffic piracy will be offered." [57]

In the ensuing negotiations in London, George Canning would not fail to take advantage of this opening to separate the slave trade from the other less desirable subjects of negotiation, the old historical controversies.

As Stratford took leave of the United States, Adams further explained the purpose of his own government in the coming negotiations at London: "a more permanent and a more harmonious course of public policy between our two governments than has ever existed since the period of our independence." [58] By this he did not mean an alliance, as both Cannings wanted to believe. He was striving for a concert of peace before thinking of a concert of power. The basis of his proposed Anglo-American concert would be the principles and interests of American foreign policy as they had crystallized during his lifetime: abstention from the ordinary vicissitudes, combinations, and collisions of European diplomacy; the Freedom of the Seas and the abolition of impressment; the end of the Brit-

[55] *Memoirs*, VI, 150. June 20, 1823. Italics inserted.

[56] Vol. VII, 498–516.

[57] Stratford Canning to G. Canning, Confidential, No. 56. Washington, June 6, 1823. PRO, F.O., 5, Vol. CLXXVI.

[58] JQA to Richard Rush, No. 72, July 29, 1823. DS, *Instructions, U.S. Ministers*, X, 165–8. *Memoirs*, VI, 150–4.

ish colonial monopoly under a strict and real reciprocity between the United States and remaining British possessions in the New World; freedom to navigate the St. Lawrence through British territory out to the open ocean; and, as will be seen in the following chapters, freedom for the United States to expand its territory through to the Pacific Ocean, to become a Continental Republic. In order to put Britain in a mood for all this, Adams would be willing to allow a belligerent right of visit and search for suppression of the piratical slave trade, and he would if necessary consider some sort of compromise on the northeast and northwest boundaries.

5

No sooner had Rush announced to the British Foreign Office the receipt of his new instructions and powers than the rapidly moving events on the Continent of Europe, already described in previous chapters, interrupted the negotiation and led George Canning to propose a concert of power between Great Britain and the United States without first recognizing the independence of the Latin-American Republics, not to mention any of the basic American principles which Adams had formulated for a concert of peace. Instead of an Anglo-American *entente* on his terms Canning got the Monroe Doctrine. That soured any disposition he might have had to assist further American diplomatic triumphs.

In the revised situation of 1824 Britain's brilliant Foreign Minister made the first move. Astutely he proposed that the suppression of the slave trade be discussed separately from the general negotiation. Rush assented, acting under the authority of Adams's instructions. Thus Canning easily satisfied himself that the United States would not really make the abolition of impressment a condition of agreeing to a mutual right of visit and search for the suppression of the African slave trade. He had easily cut out Britain's chief interest from the herd of American principles. And Rush lost control of the general negotiation at the very outset.

Straightway Canning appointed special commissioners to deal with the American Minister: William Huskisson, president of the Board of Trade, who had participated in the negotiations of 1818 with Rush and Gallatin and was completely conversant with all the complications and interest of British commercial policy, and Stratford Canning, just back from the United States and thoroughly familiar with American questions. The British plenipotentiaries assured Rush that Parliament would pass a law making the slave trade piracy for British subjects, *provided* they could agree on all other articles of Adams's draft convention. In this way they made the desired treaty a condition of the legislation, rather than the legislation a condition for the treaty as Adams had first planned.

Following this assurance it did not take the negotiators long to conclude an agreement on the slave trade. The resulting Convention of

March 13, 1824 included all the principal features of Adams's draft project mostly in his own language: (1) that the citizens and subjects of both parties participating in the African slave trade should be punishable as pirates; (2) that the two navies join with each other in suppressing the trade reciprocally allowing a right of visit and search of each other's merchant ships except when in the presence of a public ship-of-war of their own nation; (3) that the captured ship be sent in to its own country to be tried before its own tribunals; (4) that no individual belonging to the crew[59] was ever to be taken out of an accused vessel; (5) that the officer of the capturing vessel be held to strict responsibility to prevent any vexatious or abusive exercise of the stipulated right of visit and search.

Rush accepted certain minor modifications of the American plan. One was that the citizens or subjects of either party taken might be sent home for trial. He also agreed that although the crew of a pirate slave-trading ship could not be removed from the vessel, they could be laid under necessary restraint while being brought in; otherwise it might be impossible to handle such desperate characters. Finally he consented to an arrangement by which the slaves could be taken from the captured ship when necessary to assure them humane treatment. None of these changes essentially altered the principal object of Adams's original project.[60]

As soon as the convention was signed, and only after it was signed, the British Government brought up in Parliament a bill making the slave trade piracy. It became law March 31, 1824, before President Monroe could send in the treaty to the United States Senate.[61] It served as the "adequate assurance" that the American Government had required.

6

The almost unanimous expression of opinion in the House of Representatives had convinced the Administration that the country wanted to acknowledge a reciprocal right of visit and search, carefully qualified, for the suppression of the African slave trade, piracy or no piracy.[62] Adams had gone ahead and drafted a convention for that purpose. The British Government had accepted it, practically as he had written it out, and the President had recommended its ratification to the Senate.

[59] Adams had originally used the word "person." This would have prohibited slaves from being removed for better treatment.

[60] The original draft and signed convention are printed in *ASPFR,* V, 319–24.

[61] Huskisson and Stratford Canning to George Canning, March 13, 1824, communicating the signed convention, suggested the immediate passage by Parliament of the act making the slave trade piracy under capital punishment, for British subjects, in order that that law might serve as necessary assurances to the Senate when that body deliberated on advising and consenting to the ratification of the treaty. Huskisson "Papers Relating to the Affairs of America." WRC.

[62] JQA to Joseph Blunt of New York. Washington, June 6, 1824. Adams MSS.

Hitherto the Senate had ratified, practically unanimously, all of Adams's treaties, whether signed by him as a plenipotentiary (like the Prussian Treaty of 1799, and the Treaty of Ghent, 1814) or negotiated under his responsibility as Secretary of State (treaties with Great Britain, 1818; Spain, 1819; [63] France, 1822; [64] and three other treaties were to follow with similar unanimity: Tunis, 1824; Russia, 1824; [65] Colombia, October 3, 1825. Already by the end of 1823 his treaty record was getting too impressive to please his rivals.[66]

Adams had to learn the lesson that every American Secretary of State has to learn if he does not know it already from having served in the Senate: namely, that the upper house rarely rejects a treaty on its merits alone but rather because someone wants to make political capital by embarrassing the Administration. In this case the friends of Crawford wanted to eliminate Adams as a rival contender for the Presidency in the November election, but there was another reason for the opposition, portentous for the future fate of the Union. "Crawfordism has taken the alarm," Adams noted in his Diary, "lest this concert between the United States and Great Britain for suppressing the slave trade should turn to a concert for the abolition of slavery." [67]

Quickly the Senate opposition seized hold of Adams's original convictions and brought them to bear against him: they accused him of abandoning to Great Britain America's traditional opposition to visit and search in time of peace. It was not enough for him to argue, as he did in an unsigned editorial in the *National Intelligencer,* that the convention only acknowledged a reciprocal *belligerent* right of visit and search in the eternal war of all civilized nations against pirates.[68] The convention itself said nothing about *belligerent* rights.

The Southern Senators and Crawford's Northern allies could not muster enough votes to defeat the treaty outright.[69] Therefore they attached

[63] Four votes were cast against the Spanish treaty when submitted for advice and consent the second time, in 1821.

[64] On this treaty the Senate voted for the treaty on two separate votes: unanimously for the treaty plus the first separate article; 41 to 3 for the second separate article. *Senate Executive Journal,* III, 329–30, January 31, 1823.

[65] One vote opposed.

[66] Six treaties were concluded during Adams's Presidency: Central America, 1825, unanimous. Denmark, 1826, unanimous. Mexico, 1826, three votes opposed, but first article unanimously *rejected;* 1828 (boundary treaty), three votes opposed; 1828 (amity and commerce), unanimous. Prussia, 1828, unanimous. Sweden and Norway, 1828, unanimous. Hanseatic Republics, 1827, unanimous.

[67] *Memoirs,* VI, 328.

[68] *National Intelligencer,* May 12, 1824. There is a draft of this editorial in JQA's handwriting in the Adams MSS., dated May 2, 1824.

[69] In a letter of June 6, 1824 to Joseph Blunt of New York, Adams explained in detail political reasons behind the unexpected opposition in the Senate and pointed out that it consisted altogether of Crawford partisans. Adams MSS. Blunt made use of this in two unsigned editorials in "The Right of Search." See New York *American,*

qualifying amendments. One amendment changed the treaty from a *perpetual* obligation to one that could be terminated by six months' notice by either party. This amendment was carried almost unanimously, 34 to 2; but it was nothing that would have prevented Great Britain from ratifying the treaty on her part. Then the opposition opened fire on Article I of the convention, which allowed the right of search for slave-trading pirates on the coast of America as well as Africa. There was where British cruisers used to lie in wait before the War of 1812 to impress sailors from American ships. The article would have subjected the exclusive American coastwise trade to visit and search. In advising and consenting to the ratification of the convention by a vote of 29 to 13, the Senate voted against this article (yeas 23, nays 20, under the two-thirds rule, of course). Of the eight Northern Senators who voted against the article, six, at least, were conspicuously Crawford men.[70]

Canning would have been willing to accept minor modifications, but he could not swallow this capital, crippling amendment, omitting the coast of America. So the convention died. It is worth noting that on March 9, 1825 a new Senate unanimously rejected another treaty for the suppression of the slave trade, negotiated by President Adams with the Republic of Gran Colombia, even though it had carefully omitted the coast of America from the right of visit and search.[71] The slavery question had again entered American politics through the narrow treaty door of the Senate and was making rude headway.

Not until 1862 after the Southern states had seceded, could the United States make a treaty for the suppression of the slave trade. Then the Senate accepted without demur Lord Castlereagh's old plan, with reciprocal right of search, mixed courts and all. The Treaty of 1862 even provided for a joint search by American and British naval officers of suspected ships *under convoy.* No harm resulted. Nothing but good, the complete eradication of the African slave trade, followed that treaty.

June 28, 29, 1824. See also Washington *National Journal,* July 8, 16, 1824 and *National Intelligencer,* July 12, 17, 27 ("Veritas"), 1824.

[70] Knight of Rhode Island; Chandler and Holmes of Maine; Lowrie of Pennsylvania; Thomas of Illinois; Van Buren of New York. See *Senate Executive Journal,* III, 384–5, May 22, 1824.

[71] Ibid., III, 448, March 9, 1825.

CHAPTER XXI

The Freedom of the Seas and the Abolition of Private Warfare on the Ocean

(1823–1825)

> Neither of the contracting parties shall authorize their public vessels to capture or destroy them [merchant ships] or grant or issue any commission to any private armed vessels, empowering them to take or destroy such trading vessels, or interrupt such commerce.
>
> FROM ARTICLE IV OF JOHN QUINCY ADAMS'S PROPOSED CONVENTION FOR REGULATING THE PRINCIPLES OF COMMERCIAL AND MARITIME NEUTRALITY

WITH the question of the slave trade temporarily out of the way, by signature of the treaty of March 13, 1824 – never to be ratified – the negotiators in London had turned to the more difficult subjects of Anglo-American controversy still unresolved: the Freedom of the Seas, impressment, colonial commerce, navigation of the St. Lawrence River, the ever recurring fisheries question, the Northeast Boundary Question, the North West Coast and Oregon. John Quincy Adams as Secretary of State and later as President continued his anxious concern in all these problems. Most exalted of all of them was the Freedom of the Seas and abolition of private warfare on the ocean.

1

In the unpublished reply to Stratford Canning on the right of visit and search and in the instructions to Richard Rush of June 23, 1823, reviewed in the last chapter, Adams was building toward something even more far-reaching than putting an end to the kidnapping of white men by press crews and the enslavement of black men by international traffickers in human flesh. He envisaged nothing less than a profound revolution in the laws of warfare at sea. He aspired to write one of America's birthrights into international law: the Freedom of the Seas, American principles of neutral rights laid down in the "Plan of 1776." He hoped also to abolish privateering and "private warfare" upon the oceans – that is, the capture of enemy private property. He wanted to codify propositions to that effect recommended by Dr. Franklin in 1783 and adopted by the Continental Congress in a new supplementary "Plan of 1784." [1]

So far only one treaty had been concluded embodying the concepts both of 1776 and of 1784. That was the ten-year treaty with Prussia, already defunct, which John Adams, Benjamin Franklin, and Thomas Jefferson had signed at Paris in 1785. John Quincy Adams now revived all those advanced principles and drafted them into a "Project for Regulating the Principles of Commercial and Maritime Neutrality." This he sent to Richard Rush as the basis of a proposed Anglo-American convention which, if concluded, would become the model for a multilateral pact among all the maritime powers of the world. Perhaps that would be the harbinger of a millennium that would see the final abolition of those twin curses of humanity, slavery and war.

Adams was a devout convert to this brave new world on the oceans only since the War of 1812. In the past, before the European belligerents had built up their opposing maritime systems, he had been a believer in privateers as a "militia moving upon the water." But the piratical enormities of South American privateers had shaken his approval of that means of warfare. In the past, too, he had all but renounced the principle of free ships free goods, following Jay's Treaty with England. The "Adams formula" which he had suggested to the Secretary of State during his negotiation of the Prussian Treaty of 1799 would have restricted that principle, if Prussia had insisted upon retaining it, to a war in which *all* the belligerents agreed to observe it – this was almost the same as abandoning it. After the Louisiana Purchase, when war with Spain seemed likely, Senator John Quincy Adams feared that free ships free goods might let the wealth of the Indies float safely across the Atlantic to Cádiz in neutral British bottoms. "Interest governs nations more than abstract principles," [2] he had told the Senate in tones as arbitrary as Spencer Perceval defending a British order in council. Since then the experience of the United States between the millstones of France and Britain during the Napoleonic wars had convinced him that the best interest of his country – so likely to be neutral in Europe's wars – was to go back to America's birthright, back to the Freedom of the Seas.

Outstanding features of Adams's plan were the prohibition of privateering and the establishment of immunity for private property, belligerent

[1] Above, Ch. II, Section 2.

Carlton Savage has published the most significant articles of the "Plan of 1776" and the "Plan of 1784," with introductory commentary, in his official documentary history of *The Policy of the United States toward Maritime Commerce in War,* I (Washington; Department of State, Publication 331; 1934), 132–4, 157–60.

[2] November 22, 1803. *Plumer's Proceedings U.S. Senate,* p. 35.

as well as neutral, from capture on the seas. The idea of doing away with the capture of private shipping by public cruisers was much more radical, of course, than the mere abolition of privateering. But even in proposing to put an end to privateering Adams was flying in the face of widespread conviction that such an institution was the principal resource of the United States against a superior maritime power like Great Britain. None protested more vigorously than Adams's Massachusetts friend and political confidant Pierre P. F. Degrand, owner or agent for more than a score of these vessels out of Boston and Salem during the recent war with England. Privateers, indeed, were about all that Massachusetts had contributed to the waging of that war.

"A man in his closet," warned Degrand, "thinks that light national vessels can do the whole. I have no objection to their doing their share. Let them burn, sink, and destroy. But who did the enemy dread most? Who most raised the premiums at Lloyds's during the war? Who made the enemy cry *capivi* [*sic*]? Our private armed vessels . . . Great Britain . . . *dreads* our privateers. She knows our merchant service is full of men acquainted with every particular of the course of their trade; and where, and when, to strike for prizes. Sad experience has taught her, that the energies of the mercantile world being hardly awakened, during the late war, the few that dared then to act against them, did more mischief to their vital organs (commerce) than all the navies of America and Europe altogether had done for twenty years. . . . Boston . . . in the event of another war . . . would place a swarm of privateers in India; in the South Seas; on the North West Coast; in the West Indies; in the Mediterranean; in the British Channel, and everywhere else — and would cut off the rich resources which war expenditures drew in England from commerce. She knows all this; she knows that we have great philosophers, philanthropists of pure views, of great *book* knowledge; — she knows that this country is full of men ready to listen to the voice that calls for better morals — and under cover of these finer feelings of human nature, she calls for the destruction of what she most dreads.

"*Destroy that* and she no longer fears to make *war* on you.

"*Keep that weapon* and she dare not awaken your thunder." [3]

It all reminds us of the arguments about the atomic bomb in the years after the Second World War of the twentieth century.

No American statesman could think seriously of giving up the priva-

[3] P. P. F. Degrand to JQA, Boston, August 17, 1819, December 10, 1823. Adams MSS.

The classic study of the late Admiral Mahan on *Sea Power in Its Relations to the War of 1812* has since shown how mistaken was this notion that privateering was a formidable weapon of war against a big naval power. During that conflict the worst American privateers could do was to cause exasperating and expensive annoyance to Great Britain and drive her merchant marine into convoy; meanwhile the British Navy, despite the great war raging in Europe, easily blockaded the whole Atlantic Coast and landed an army of invasion in the United States.

teering weapon pending achievement of an adequate national navy unless the possible maritime enemies of the United States would go a step farther and agree also to renounce the capture of private property by public as well as private armed ships. Otherwise American merchant shipping would be vulnerable to capture by the enemy's overpowering public navy while his shipping would be immune from capture by American privateers. It was to guard against this that John Quincy Adams proposed to Great Britain, the greatest sea power, to do away altogether with the capture of private shipping, in case (which God forbid!) of a war between themselves, as the United States and Prussia once had provided in their first Treaty of 1785–95.

His instructions on neutral rights and maritime war[4] begin with a touch of irony. He appealed to British humanitarian motives so ostentatiously exhibited for the suppression of the slave trade. Let them be turned also to world peace and good will. With his tongue still in his cheek, he next invoked the Christian precepts of the Holy Alliance. The lofty motives of the continental powers had pledged them to the principle, so Adams professed to believe, that it was among the indispensable duties of the rulers of mankind to combine their exertions for the amelioration of the conditions of *war*. Well then, let them take steps to abolish war altogether on this earth. "Nothing could be more congenial to the Government of the United States. It has been a maxim of its foreign policy since its independence."

A first step, the Secretary continued, would be to mitigate the effects of war by confirming neutral rights. In this way the United States and Great Britain would achieve concord by abolishing the principal cause of their own collisions. The next step would be to do away altogether with "private warfare."[5] The immunity would protect enemy vessels as well as neutral vessels and their cargoes. Finally there would be a prohibition of impressment under any circumstances whatever, accompanied by parallel measures of the United States and Great Britain to forbid employment of subjects of either treaty party belligerent in the public navy or private merchant marine of the other party neutral. While Adams was about it, he threw into the Project some humanitarian articles regarding warfare on land similar to those in Jay's Treaty and also an article forbidding either treaty party to use Indian allies in warfare against the other.

The Secretary of State read over to the President the instructions to Rush designed to accompany and explain his draft convention.

[4] JQA to Richard Rush, July 28, 1823. *ASPFR*, V, 529–33.

[5] "I trust you will not take, as I am told some legislative statesmen have done, the proposition mentioned in the Message for abolishing *private war upon the sea* to be a mere offer for abolishing *privateering*. You will understand it as it is meant, a project for the universal exemption of private property upon the ocean from depredation by war." JQA to Robert Walsh, Jr., Washington, December 3, 1823. Adams MSS.

Calhoun came in as he was reading.

"It will not be accepted by Great Britain," said the Secretary of War when his colleague had finished. "Of that I am confident."

"I have no expectation that it will at this time," responded Adams, "but my object is to propose it to Russia and France, and to all the maritime powers of Europe, as well as to Great Britain."

The three men discussed for a while the expediency of making the proposal at all. Adams appealed to the primitive policy of the United States as exemplified in the Treaty of 1785 with Prussia.

"The seed was first sown then," declared the Secretary of State, "and bore a single plant which the fury of the revolutionary tempest has since swept away. I think the present a moment eminently auspicious for sowing the same seed a second time. Although I have no hope it will now take root in England, I have the most cheering confidence that it will ultimately bear a harvest of happiness to mankind and of glory to this Union."[6]

Next day John Quincy Adams read his Project aloud to the Cabinet, article by article. The text, hitherto never fully printed, will be found in the Appendix of this book. At this place it is necessary to list only the salient principles of the Freedom of the Seas as Adams brought them together:

In case of war between the treaty parties:

1. Protection of innocent enemy aliens and private alien property against seizure or molestation; if any private property must be taken for the use of invading armed forces the same should be paid for at a reasonable price.
2. Neither party to authorize its public vessels to capture or destroy merchant vessels, which were to pass free and unmolested.
3. Neither party to commission any private armed vessel empowered to take or destroy any enemy trading vessel or commerce.

In case of war in which one party was neutral and the other belligerent:

1. Free ships make free goods, excepting contraband of war.
2. Neutral property on enemy ships, excepting contraband of war, also to be free.
3. Contraband to be strictly defined by an enumerated list of weapons and military equipment, "and generally all other implements of war," and all else excluded from confiscation.[7]
4. Neutral ships have a right to trade to and between unblockaded ports of a belligerent "whether under the same or several jurisdictions" (that is, colonial ports as well as metropolitan ports – both *grand cabotage* and *petit cabotage*) and between unblockaded belligerent ports and neutral ports.
5. Blockades shall apply "only to a port where there is, by the disposi-

[6] *Memoirs,* VI, 164. July 28, 1823.

[7] In his original draft JQA had included naval stores. See text in Appendix 3.

tion of the power which attacks it with ships stationary or sufficiently near,[8] an evident danger of entering."

6. No natural-born citizen or subject of the one party belligerent shall be employed on board any public or private vessel of the neutral party unless authentically naturalized as a citizen or subject of the neutral party before the commencement of the war.

The purpose of this article, obviously, was to do away with pretexts for impressment.

7. Prohibition of impressment under any plea or pretext whatsoever.

8. No citizens or subjects of either party to accept commissions or instructions from the enemies of the other, under pain of piracy.

9. No privateer to be armed in the ports of the one party against the shipping of the other, nor to sell prizes there, nor enter at all except under stress of weather.

10. Neither party to permit ships of the other to be taken by enemies of the other within the neutral party's territorial jurisdiction (defined as a cannon's range from the shore); if nevertheless taken, the neutral party shall be responsible for reparations.

11. But the ships-of-war and privateers of either party belligerent shall be at liberty to carry their prizes whithersoever they please, even into the ports of the neutral party, without seizure, detention, or taxes.

12. The warships of either party to protect the merchant ships of the other, going the same course, against pirates.

The Secretary finished reading the lengthy Project.

Calhoun still hesitated about proposing it at all, but his doubts were fainter than before.

Crawford thought that Great Britain would never settle the impressment question by treaty. "She will let it die a natural death," he said prophetically, "by abstaining to issue orders to the naval commanders to impress men from our vessels."

Thompson, Secretary of the Navy, declared himself in the most explicit manner in favor of the whole Project.

After the meeting the President directed Adams to forward to the American Minister in London both the instructions and the proposed convention, as they stood, except for one alteration – impossible to identify – proposed by Crawford.[9] The signed documents went forward to London carried personally by Christopher Hughes. The reader has already espied George Canning flirting with Hughes on the steamboat in Liverpool harbor.

Adams restrained his enthusiasm only with great difficulty. If the Proj-

[8] Nothing in the Project indicated how near was "sufficiently near." That question has been the unsettling feature of all blockade law. A belligerent could expand this phrase to include offshore blockades.

[9] *Memoirs,* VI, 164–5. July 29, 1823. For differences between JQA's original draft and the final document, see Appendix 3.

ect succeeded, it would be the greatest achievement of his life. "What a real and solid blessing it will be to the human race," he confided to his Diary. "I feel that I could die for it with joy, and that if my last moments could be cheered with the consciousness of having contributed to it, I could go before the throne of Omnipotence with a plea for mercy, and with a consciousness of not having lived in vain for the world of mankind. It has been for more than thirty years my prayer to God that this might be my lot upon earth, to render signal service to my country and to my species. For the specific object, the end, and the means, I have relied alike upon the goodness of God. What they were, or would be, I knew not. For 'it is not in man that walketh to direct his steps.' I have rendered services to my country, but not such as could satisfy my own ambition. But this offers the specific object which I have desired. And why should not the hearts of the rulers of mankind be turned to approve and establish it? I have opened my soul to the hope, though with trembling." [10]

When John Quincy Adams drew up minutes, in November 1823, for the President's annual message to Congress, on affairs under the direction of the Department of State, there were two subjects uppermost in his mind. One of these was the Non-Colonization Principle, already discussed. The other was the abolition of private warfare upon the sea. Neither one concerned the Canning-Rush conversations of the previous August. But the secret exchanges between George Canning and Richard Rush in London, and the deliberations of the American Cabinet on them, had caused President Monroe to interject a new and dramatic topic into the discussion of his advisers. The resulting Monroe Doctrine has obscured Adams's great Project for the regulation of commercial and maritime neutrality from the history books. He himself regarded it to be as important as his other contributions to the celebrated message of December 2, 1823, if not more important.

2

Rush presented the maritime questions, in the negotiations of 1824, with all the anxiousness that belonged to its deep and permanent connection with the interest and character of the United States, with the recollections that past history called up, and with all the anticipations that concern for the future must awaken. Echoing the words of Adams, he told the British Commissioners, Huskisson and Stratford Canning, that the United States was not less anxious than any of the powers of Europe in desiring to bring about a general improvement in the condition of mankind. "Peace is their invariable desire, as well as policy." But in the case of war it was also their desire to invoke those beneficent principles which would serve to mitigate its evils. The great changes that had taken place in the world had brought in an auspicious time for the

[10] *Memoirs,* VI, 165–7. July 31, 1823.

settlement of questions of belligerent and neutral rights in the broad maritime field. The "impairment" of the European alliance, the independence of Latin America, the impeding revolution in the old colonial system, Britain's neutrality both in the Spanish-American wars and in the more recent hostilities in the Spanish Peninsula, all suggested that she might now be disposed to view neutral doctrines in different and more favorable lights than heretofore.

The American Minister then laid down the traditional argument according to the plans of 1776 and 1784 for the Freedom of the Seas. Of all the problems of neutral rights, he insisted, impressment was the most important.

"But if Great Britain still views [these matters] as hitherto," he declared, "if she still feels herself restrained from treating of them but on her former maritime principles, my government would prefer being so informed with candour in the outset, it being alike due to candour to say, that the principles of the United States remain the same, there having been no equipollent changes in their political, commercial, or maritime position in the world."

"Are you willing to treat of the above class of questions generally," the British plenipotentiaries asked him, "supposing impressment not to be included among the number?"

"I am unwilling to enter at all upon the other points of maritime law," he stated, "unless the question of impressment be received by Great Britain as a part of the negotiation." He was speaking of the principles of neutral rights independently of the proposal to abolish private warfare upon the seas. "But I am perfectly ready to take up impressment by itself," he added.

"Have you any new securities to propose," immediately inquired the British plenipotentiaries, "against the employment of British subjects in the merchant-vessels of the United States?"

"None that differs essentially from those brought forward in former negotiations."

"Great Britain anxiously desires to reconcile the exercise of this established right of impressment with the convenience and feelings of other nations," Stratford Canning and Huskisson assured him. "But the right is essential to her highest interest. . . . She can never abandon such a right; it is impossible. Nor will her duty allow her to waive it, with respect to the United States, but upon . . . ample security that the objects for which it is exercised may be attained by other means."

On the question of impressment, then, the whole subject of neutral rights fell to the ground.

Rush then raised the question of abolishing privateering and the capture of private property at sea, which he presented as a wholly new and separate matter.

"All other questions of a maritime nature having been shut out of the negotiation," rejoined the British representatives, "there would be manifest inconvenience in going into that for abolishing private war upon the ocean. . . . Besides being totally new, as between the two governments, it contemplates a most extensive change in the principles and practice of maritime war, as hitherto sanctioned by all nations."[11]

Since John Quincy Adams had instructed Rush not to communicate the draft Project to the British Government unless they first agreed to negotiate on the subject, he withheld it altogether. It remained until this day in the State Department archives.

George Canning already had forgotten all about Thomas Jefferson and the American principles of neutrality that he had extolled so conspicuously the year before. Instead, the message of President Monroe and the Non-Colonization Principle were smarting in his mind. He had got his slave-trade treaty signed and he had no more immediate need of American co-operation. So there was no further discussion of neutral rights or the abolition of private warfare on the ocean in the negotiations of 1824. Albert Gallatin, in his negotiations of 1826 to 1827, did not conceive himself empowered to make any new proposal on impressment. "The renewal of the practice," he told Canning, "would be considered as a declaration of war."[12] He awaited proposals from the British Government. Therefore he did not get into any discussion of other maritime questions, like neutral rights, much less the abolition of privateering and private warfare upon the ocean. Following Canning's death, August 8, 1827, Gallatin came home, after having signed the convention of September 29, of that year, for arbitration of the northeast boundary dispute.[13]

In truth Adams could hardly expect Canning to give up British sea power any more than the British Foreign Secretary could expect Adams to abandon American demands for the Freedom of the Seas. The British Navy held the balance of power in the world, and Canning was the last man who might be expected to abandon maritime prerogatives that were in his eyes the birthright of Empire. To him it was unthinkable to abolish private warfare on the oceans in a century when Britain controlled the seas. The contest had become all the more hopeless for the United States

[11] These epitomes, in direct discourse, of the diplomatic conversations, are taken word for word from Richard Rush's report to the Secretary of State as printed in *ASPFR*, V, 533–82 (see particularly 549–53), and in Rush's *Residence at the Court of London*, II (London, 1845), 119–323 (see particularly 225–48).

The British set of documents relating to the same negotiation, with George Canning's confidential instructions to William Huskisson and Stratford Canning, are to be found in a "private" official print: *Papers Relating to the Negotiation in London, between the British Plenipotentiaries and the Plenipotentiary on the Part of the United States of America January to August, 1824*, in Huskisson "Papers Relating to the Affairs of America." WRC.

[12] Gallatin to Clay, confidential, London, December 22, 1826. *Writings of Albert Gallatin*, II, 347.

[13] Below, Ch. XXIII.

after the Secretary of State ceased to insist on the Freedom of the Seas and the abolition of impressment as *quid pro quo* for any agreement to a convention for the suppression of the slave trade. But such a stand would have blocked all negotiation. Spurred on by American humanitarian sentiment, as evidenced in the resolutions of the House of Representatives, Adams had to choose between unconditionally accepting a slave-trade convention at the outset of the negotiation, with a hope that this would lead to further progress for American principles, and nothing at all. He yielded to this forlorn hope for perfect Anglo-American amity.

To George Canning, that "implacable and rancorous enemy of the United States," John Quincy Adams attributed the frustration of all his efforts to settle colonial and maritime questions with the "waspish" British Government.[14]

3

Unsuccessful in his long struggle to get Great Britain to agree to the American definition of the Freedom of the Seas, John Quincy Adams had to content himself with writing those principles into treaties with the new states of South America. In these agreements, as in all the other maritime treaties he had negotiated since 1799, he had to introduce the old Adams proviso to allow for British recalcitrance: "Provided, however, that the stipulations in this article contained, declaring that the flag shall cover the property, shall be understood as applying to those powers only who recognize this principle." That is to say, American treaties for the Freedom of the Seas did not amount to much unless Great Britain, the Mistress of the Seas, were a party to them.

A century ago, conscious that his long life was coming to a close, Adams lamented the fact that he had not done more to abolish the two great afflictions of mankind, slavery and war:

"If my intellectual powers had been such as have been sometimes committed by the Creator of man to single individuals of the species, my diary would have been, next to the Holy Scriptures, the most precious and valuable book ever written by human hands and I should have been one of the most precious benefactors of my country and mankind. I would

[14] So Adams characterized George Canning upon hearing of his death: "May this event, in the order of Providence, avert all the evils which he would, if permitted, have drawn down upon us, and all evil counsels formed against our peace and prosperity be baffled and defeated!" *Memoirs,* VII, 328. September 10, 1827. To Richard Rush (then Secretary of the Treasury), President Adams wrote (September 20, 1827) in a more decorous vein: "Mr. Canning's decease has buried in my bosom all the feelings of resentment which his conduct toward us had kindled. I hope that wiser and better men will take his place. But if not we must contend with them as we have with him and 'Trust the Ruler with his skies.'" Adams MSS. To Henry Clay, Secretary of State, the President wrote (September 24, 1827) in a still softer tone: "If anything could warrant *us* in regretting the decease of Mr. Canning, it is that it happened at precisely the moment when he was relaxing from his feelings of hostility to this country, and *beginning* to listen to reason." Adams MSS.

by the irresistible power of genius and the irrepressible energy of will and the favor of Almighty God have banished war and slavery from the face of the earth forever. But the conceptive power of mind was not conferred on me by my Maker, and I have not improved the scanty portion of His gifts as I might and ought to have done."[15]

None of John Quincy Adams's successors has ever succeeded in writing the abolition of private warfare on the seas into another treaty. Only one other Secretary of State has proposed it since.

At the end of the next war in Europe, the Crimean War, which was hardly a maritime war so far as commerce-destroying was concerned, the great powers, including Great Britain, subscribed in the Declaration of Paris of 1856 to some of the American principles that John Quincy Adams had put forward to England in his Project of 1823:

1. Privateering is, and remains, abolished.
2. The neutral flag covers enemy's goods with the exception of contraband of war.
3. Neutral goods, with the exception of contraband of war, are not liable to capture under enemy's flag.
4. Blockades, in order to be binding, must be effective; that is to say, maintained by a force sufficient really to prevent access to the *coast* of the enemy.[16]

Contraband, however, was left undefined. By expanding the definition of contraband any party to the Declaration who controlled the seas could shut off neutral carriage to enemy ports.

Secretary of State Marcy, speaking for the United States, would not accept this limited code of American principles formulated at Paris unless the parties to the Declaration would agree to abolish private warfare altogether as John Adams, Benjamin Franklin, Thomas Jefferson, and John Quincy Adams had tried to do in their time. During the Civil War, Secretary Seward, in order to outlaw the privateers of the Confederacy, tried to accede unconditionally to the Declaration of Paris. John Quincy Adams's son Charles Francis Adams, then Minister to the Court of St. James's, did his best to consummate the accession. Great Britain refused the overture unless it was agreed that the principles should not apply to the existing Civil War in the United States. Such a condition was impossible. To arm Seward in his dealings with Great Britain, Congress

[15] *Memoirs,* XII, 276–7. October 31, 1846.

[16] Italics inserted. This attenuated Adams's criterion of "sufficiently near" the blockaded *port* and was another step in the direction of the offshore blockade. The Declaration of London of 1912 (Article 2) repeated the definition of blockade of the Declaration of Paris, but also stipulated: "A blockade must not be extended beyond the ports and coasts belonging to or occupied by the enemy" (Article 1), and "The question whether a blockade is effective is a question of fact." This phraseology stretched the institution of blockade still farther out to sea. The First World War and the Second World War of the twentieth century, like the Napoleonic wars of a century before, deformed blockade out of all legal shape.

passed a law enabling the President to issue letters of marque to privateers, but the executive branch of the Government never saw fit to resort to this power. Since the Peace of Ghent the United States has never commissioned a privateer.

Following the First and Second World Wars of the twentieth century the Freedom of the Seas sank beneath the oceans. The "real and solid blessings for the human race" for which John Quincy Adams dared to hope and tremble in his soul, the immunity of civilian populations and their property on sea as well as on land in time of war, have not come to pass. International law, so sorely stricken all around the globe, now writhes in dreadful agony. The ocean floors lie strewn with countless loads of human bones in noble gaping ships. In time of war force, and force alone, rules the waves.

CHAPTER XXII
Equality of Commercial Opportunity (1776–1829)

Independence, equal favors, and reciprocity.

JOHN QUINCY ADAMS'S
FORMULA FOR COMMERCIAL TREATIES

LIKE the Freedom of the Seas, freedom of commerce and navigation was a birthright of independence, a twin birthright. By freedom of commerce and navigation, loosely called "commercial reciprocity," the founding fathers meant freedom to sail and trade with foreign countries, including colonial dominions, on terms of entire equality with the subjects of those sovereigns. Such a freedom was one of the impulses of the Revolution itself, a protest against the shackles of the traditional British navigation laws, which had kept the colonies closed to the traffic of alien flags and prohibited American colonial ships from trading unrestricted to foreign ports. The revolting colonists expected that independence would liberate them from the whole web of British mercantilism and bring them free and unfettered trade for their ships and products in all the ports of the world. In return they were ready to grant reciprocal privileges in their own fruitful country. A new and revolutionary idea in the society of nations of the eighteenth century, equality of commercial opportunity has remained ever since a high and constant aim of American policy.

The new Republic had much to gain in matters of commerce and navigation by a liberal dispensation, little to lose. American commercial policy, therefore, was an attack, by force of argument, and by example, and by retaliation in kind against the monopolies and the internal discriminations of European mercantilism and imperialism.[1]

Like so many of the basic issues of American diplomacy — boundaries, fisheries, Freedom of the Seas — which John Quincy Adams had to face during that first half-century in which the foundations of our foreign policy were being laid, commercial reciprocity went back to the mind and times of his patriot father. It had been John Adams who had drafted for the committee of the Continental Congress the famous Plan of 1776,

[1] Vernon G. Setser: *The Commercial Reciprocity Policy of the United States, 1774–1829* (Philadelphia, 1937), p. 3. This excellent monograph has greatly lightened the labor of reviewing the whole mass of diplomatic correspondence relating to this subject during the period of John Quincy Adams's diplomatic career. I have relied on it heavily in this chapter.

which had marched hand in hand with independence itself in the deliberations of that body. The committee's blueprint called for equality of commerce and navigation in time of peace, as well as for juridical freedom of the seas in time of war: reciprocal liberties for the ships and citizens of the United States in all the ports, havens, roadsteads, cities, towns, countries, or islands of the other treaty party on the basis of full equality with nationals.

The perfect reciprocal equality of the Plan of 1776 did not permeate the original treaty structure of the United States. Rather it was the Treaty of Commerce of 1778 with France that served as model for the early treaties of amity, commerce, and navigation. That instrument provided for a reciprocity of treatment of the citizens and subjects of each country and their ships and products in the direct trade between ports of the United States and those of France in Europe, equal to that extended to the nation the most favored in this respect: that is, the *conditional* most-favored-nation formula.[2]

Nobody was more familiar than Adams with the American program for reciprocal freedom of commerce and navigation in time of peace and for the Freedom of the Seas in time of war. From his diplomatic boyhood to his diplomatic manhood he had become thoroughly indoctrinated with the ideal and practice of commercial equality and nondiscrimination. He had come to look upon it as a moral duty of nations toward each other.[3] As Secretary of State it was his task to labor further for that policy in diplomatic controversies with France, the Netherlands, Great Britain, Spain, and other European powers with which, because of the long wars on that Continent, the United States had been unable to conclude treaties of commerce.

[2] This formula meant that either treaty party would extend to the other favors in commerce and navigation equal to those enjoyed by the nation the most favored in that respect unless those favors had been granted in return for a particular equivalent; even then the favor would be extended only in return for the same particular equivalent. It was stated as follows in the Franco-American Treaty of Commerce of 1778:

"Article II. The Most Christian King, and the United States engage mutually not to grant any particular Favour to other Nations in respect of Commerce and Navigation, which shall not immediately become common to the other Party, who shall enjoy the same Favour, freely, if the Concession was freely made, or on allowing the same Compensation, if the Concession was Conditional." Vernon G. Setser, answering the question: "Did Americans Originate the Conditional Most-Favored-Nation Clause?" *Journal of Modern History,* V (1933), 320, suggests that this conditional article was inserted at the initiative of France rather than of the United States. However that may be, it was standard American practice up to 1923 to interpret the most-favored-nation clause conditionally, whether stipulated conditional or not.

[3] See his anonymous article: "The British Colonial and Navigation System," written and published while he was President, in *Quarterly Review,* II (No. 3, September 1827), 267–306.

1

One of the problems was with France, with whom the matrix of American commercial policy had been established originally by the Treaty of 1778. The Convention of Morfontaine of 1800 had superseded that treaty as well as the alliance of 1778 together with the consular convention of 1788. The Convention of 1800 (Articles VI and XI) stipulated that commerce and navigation between any and all parts of the United States and the territories of the French Republic in Europe should "in general" be "free" on the basis of the most favored nation, without saying anything about conditional interpretation. The treaty for the cession of Louisiana in 1803 further provided that the ships of France should be treated "forever" in the ports of Louisiana upon the footing of the most favored nation.

During the Napoleonic wars the British Navy all but swept the French merchant marine from the seas, and the restored Bourbon monarchy endeavored to assist the recovery of its shipping by means of tariff and navigation laws not dissimilar to those of the United States, except that they did not have any provision for reciprocal abatements of discrimination like the American law of 1815. The new French tariff rested on two levels, a higher impost on goods coming to France in foreign bottoms, and a lower tax for articles imported under the French flag. Additional discrimination against imports in foreign vessels existed in the shape of exasperating quarantine charges and ships' brokers' expenses, from which French ships were exempt. Taken together these handicaps more than equaled freight costs on a cargo of goods from the United States to France; if they were continued, French vessels in no distant time would engross completely the Franco-American carrying trade.[4]

The vexatious quarantine and brokerage charges were a violation of the Convention of 1800, and Monroe's Government succeeded in getting temporary removals of them; but the French discriminatory tariffs, which, like the American navigation laws, applied to all foreign nations, did not necessarily violate any treaty; the trouble was that France would not annul them reciprocally, as invited to do by the American reciprocity act of 1815. On the other hand, the French Government maintained that French ships were entitled by the Treaty of 1803 to admission into all the ports of Louisiana on terms equal to those allowed to the nation most favored in this respect – namely, to Great Britain. It seemed useless for John Quincy Adams to point out that British ships and products came in to American ports, including those of the Louisiana Purchase, on the same terms as American ships only because Great Britain, by the Treaty of 1815, admitted American ships into the British Isles on the same terms as British ships: there was a natural condition, Adams insisted, implied in any most-favored-nation arrangement, that prevented one party from

[4] Setser: *Reciprocity Policy*, p. 199.

having favors extended to it *gratuitously,* without giving the same equivalent for which those concessions had been granted by the United States to the favored nation. If France would allow American goods and ships to come in to her ports on the same terms as French ships bearing the same cargoes, then she could enjoy an equality of treatment with American shipping not only in Louisiana but in all the ports of the United States. The fact was that France preferred a *reciprocity of discrimination,* or what French diplomats euphemistically called a "reciprocity of advantages," to a reciprocity of nondiscrimination. Only in this way could she hope to build up her merchant marine, which simply could not compete successfully with the American flag without the aid of special favors. The French Government declined to negotiate any kind of settlement without connecting it with a recognition of the Louisiana trade grievances, and satisfaction of two spoliation claims against the United States. One of these was for the capture of the *Jeune Eugénie,* a ship alleged but not proved to be a slave-trader. The other was for detention in St. Mary's River and libeling in the Federal courts of a merchant ship, the *Apollon,* which with the advice and support of the French Government was attempting to smuggle goods from Florida waters into the United States during the uncertain interval between the signing and ratification of the Transcontinental Treaty, while Florida was still technically Spanish.

The only way to make France listen to reason, advised Albert Gallatin, our Minister in Paris, was for Congress to enact a retaliatory tonnage duty on French vessels equal to the average of the special duties levied on American goods imported into France in American vessels. This he calculated to be about $12.50 per ton on cotton cargoes, and $17 per ton on tobacco shipments. At the behest of the President and the Secretary of State, Congress accordingly, without opposition, levied a special duty of $18 per ton on French bottoms beginning July 1, 1820.[5] The French Chambers replied with a retaliation of their own: an additional tonnage duty of 90 francs a ton on American ships, with a ten-per-cent discount in tariff on cotton when imported into France from any part of America except the United States – this last an attempt to rouse the Southern cotton states against the Administration's resourcefulness. With a commercial war under way between the two nations, to the obvious profit of third parties, the French Government offered to settle the question of commerce and navigation on the basis of a measured reciprocity of discrimination, so fixed as to leave the carrying trade between the United States and France half in French vessels, half in American.

"The French know very well that you have the advantage of them as navigators," Hyde de Neuville said to John Quincy Adams. "It is, therefore, only a nominal reciprocity, to place the duties upon an equal footing in the two countries. We must look to results. Even with the difference in

[5] Act approved May 15, 1820.

duties, which we have in France, our shipping could not stand the competition with yours. . . . When once the balance is restored [with the aid of discriminations in favor of French ships in France], so that the number of French and American vessels engaged in the trade is nearly equal, France will very readily enter into any commercial arrangement to keep them so. There is also [he added] the privilege which France claims in the ports of Louisiana, by the eighth article of that treaty, upon which you have left my last note unanswered." [6]

Hyde de Neuville also wanted a new consular convention similar to the old one of 1788, at that time the most unpopular treaty in American history, which had all but placed French citizens in the United States under extraterritorial protection.

"Our object is amicable arrangement," declared the Secretary of State to the popular French Minister as he departed for his homeland loaded with honors and consideration after four years of service in the United States. "If France will treat, we will readily consider any proposal which she may offer to secure a real reciprocity, but we cannot wait for the full effect of the unequal regulations of France, to take precautionary measures against you. Mr. Gallatin has powers to conclude a treaty of commerce."

From Paris the conciliatory Gallatin had recommended to his Government that the French principle of a reciprocity of discriminations might be accepted; he thought that American vessels could pay as much as $2.30 a ton more than French vessels and still compete. In the Cabinet, Crawford, always opposing Adams when a profitable opportunity presented itself, favored Gallatin's point of view, and the President was inclined to sympathize with their stand. But John Quincy Adams persisted in the fight against any compromise with the original American principles of nondiscrimination. He stood firm for reciprocity of equal treatment. "We have offered to all the world entire reciprocity. Great Britain and several other nations have accepted the proposal. France now calls upon us to agree to be clogged, in order to enable her people to hold competition with us. If we should assent, our own people would first be dissatisfied, and next, all the nations with which we have stood on terms of reciprocity. We should have clamor and discontent from all quarters. As to the consular convention, that, with France, is an affair of State [not of commerce]. She wants, by means of consular jurisdictions, to retain all her power over Frenchmen in this country." [7]

For the moment Adams prevailed. The Cabinet decided unanimously against accepting the principle proposed by France.[8] Gallatin was instructed to go ahead with a negotiation for reciprocal equality and to keep

[6] *Memoirs,* V, 123–4. May 17, 1820. Hyde de Neuville to JQA, May 24, 1820. DS, *Notes from French Legation,* VI.

[7] *Memoirs,* V, 179.

[8] *Memoirs,* V, 195.

the other controversies out of the discussion. In Paris the French Minister of Foreign Affairs, Pasquier, insisted that the treatment of French vessels in Louisiana was inseparable from the main issue – actually it served as a convenient means to postpone any commercial arrangement. Gallatin could not admit such a demand; to have done so would have been to break down a fundamental of American foreign policy now stressed by Adams: the conditional interpretation of the most-favored-nation formula whether so stipulated or not in a treaty. So the controversy voyaged back to Washington, and with it the Baron Hyde de Neuville, assigned to conclude a treaty of commerce with the United States on his way to a new diplomatic post at Rio de Janeiro.

The friendly and skillful but emotional French envoy now faced a situation that threatened to lose all the good will for his country which he had built up on his previous tour of duty in the American capital. During the spring and summer of 1821 [9] the two diplomatists exchanged numerous projects and counterprojects. At length Hyde de Neuville offered to remove one half the new French discriminating duties on imports if the United States would give up its retaliatory tonnage duties; but he held to an unconditional interpretation of the most-favored-nation treaty formula for French vessels in the ports of the Louisiana Purchase, continued to demand satisfaction for the *Apollon* and *Jeune Eugénie,* and asked for a new consular convention like the old one of 1788.

If it had been left entirely to John Quincy Adams to decide, he would not have yielded one bit; but Gallatin's influence for compromise, and Cabinet deliberations, overruled him. He therefore met Hyde de Neuville's proposal by offering to accept a mutually discriminating duty, on American ships in French harbors and French ships in American harbors, of one and one-half per cent of the value of the cargo, or $1.50 a ton of merchandise, and to *discuss* a consular convention. But he would pay little attention to the Louisiana question, or to the *Apollon* and *Jeune Eugénie,* not to mention another French ship, the *Neptune,* captured as a suspected slaver; on the other hand he did not insist on an immediate settlement of the massive spoliation claims that the United States had against France arising out of the Napoleonic wars.

At the end of a long and angry conversation in November 1821, Hyde de Neuville threatened reprisals on American ships in French harbors if reparation were not made for the three captures, "outrages upon the flag and national honor of France." At this point Adams checked him, and led him to acknowledge that all this high talk was only the Minister's "private opinion," not a notification from the French Government.

"I shall report the whole to the President to-morrow," promised the Secretary.

"You may report to the President what you please," Hyde replied. He seemed a little startled, nevertheless.

[9] *ASPFR,* V, 149–214.

"I shall report exactly what has passed between us, and no more; as I first understood you, and as you afterward explained."

This made the Frenchman furious. He jumped up from his seat. He gesticulated vehemently. "Well, Sir," he declared in a loud and peremptory tone, "since you think proper to report to the President what I came to say in a confidential conversation with you, I desire you to tell him from me, as my individual opinion, that if satisfaction is not made to France in the affair of the *Apollon,* the *Neptune,* and the *Eugénie,* France ought to declare war on the United States."

Hyde de Neuville rolled out the word "war" with a long and virulent emphasis: *"la France doit leur déclarer la guer-r-r-r-e."*

Without waiting for a reply, he grabbed his hat and rushed from the room, through the corridors of the State Department, out the front door, into the darkening street. John Quincy Adams followed him "composedly," with a light.

In the entry was the faithful Antoine.

"Monsieur! vous avez oublié votre surtout," he called to the outraged Minister disappearing in the late November dusk.

Hyde de Neuville turned back and thrust himself into his overcoat. He said nothing to the valet. He would not even look at the Secretary, who stood there all kindness in the chill evening patiently holding aloft the light, his bare head glistening under the flickering flame.

It was almost a burlesque, but the next morning between two and three o'clock Adams lay sleepless and anxious. At five he rose and made a record for the President of the "memorable conversation."

Monroe was surprised and indignant. He was on the point of asking Hyde de Neuville's recall. The Secretary suggested laying the whole situation in a friendly way before Congress in the coming annual message, stressing how these three dubious claims prevented any progress. After long Cabinet deliberations, in which Adams and Crawford were mostly at odds, the President decided to mention the French negotiation in a conciliatory manner, but to prepare and hold ready for publication all the relevant diplomatic correspondence.

Adams urged that the statement include a review of the whole commercial system of the United States.

"I understand it is your opinion that it ought to be maintained?" he said to the President, alluding to the reciprocity policy of the United States, after the other gentlemen of the Administration had departed.

"It is," said Monroe.

"Not only do I think the present system ought to be maintained," Adams affirmed, "but it is of the utmost importance to the welfare of the country that it should be maintained. A liberal system of commercial intercourse with foreign nations is, in my view, one of the ingredients of our national independence. It originated with our national existence. It has been established as a fundamental principle of our relations with other powers, deliberately adopted and after full discussion; it was proclaimed to the world in our first treaty with France, in terms certainly inserted by our Ministers [10] – I suppose by Dr. Franklin. That France should have subscribed to them at all is extraordinary; she had never spoken such language in any treaty before. That principle we had invariably maintained until now. Mr. Jefferson reasserted it in his report to Congress in 1793. The act of March 3, 1815 offered it again to the acceptance of all nations. We have departed from it, I believe, for the first time, in this negotiation with France, by acceding to a principle of discriminating duties to operate avowedly against ourselves. We have not satisfied France. She wants more inequality."

"To be candid with you," he went on, "I am glad she has not accepted our offer. I have always been averse to making it, and should have felt inexpressible reluctance in signing any treaty containing it. Now France is giving us notice that she intends to take further measures to force us into her terms. There is a diversity of opinion in Congress, and in the country, upon the policy of persevering in our policy, and I have taken the liberty of making these remarks to you, because I think it not improbable that the decisions of Congress might be what your opinion recommends."

"It will not be withheld upon any proper occasion," said the President, terminating the conversation.[11] In his annual message of December 3, 1821 Monroe reviewed the whole commercial system of the United States, as Adams desired, with a patient explanation of France's uncompromising attitude on the *Apollon* case.

The flurry subsided. Hyde de Neuville must have realized that he had been indiscreet to the point of making a tool of himself and his own Government ridiculous by such empty histrionics. France was in no position to threaten war over trifles. Obviously the French Government must be pushing them, and the Louisiana technicality, for their bargaining effect on the commercial negotiations. Meanwhile three fourths of the carrying trade between the United States and France had fallen to the ships of Great Britain and other competitors.[12]

Gallatin's capable exertions in Paris elicited further compromise. Early in 1822 Hyde de Neuville got new instructions, authorizing him to accept a treaty stipulation for a French tonnage duty as low as twenty francs a ton on American products in American ships – that is, only two ninths of the existing retaliatory levies – and to postpone the Louisiana question to a later discussion. Immediately the Minister agreed with Adams to negotiate on the commercial question alone. He offered a reduction of French tonnage duties to one fourth of their existing amount, with subsequent annual reductions mutually until all discrimination should end.

It was now a question for Monroe's Government to decide whether or

[10] See note 3, above.
[11] *Memoirs,* V, 414–28.
[12] Setser: *Reciprocity Policy,* p. 205.

not to compromise. Adams was against it, but the door had already been opened in the previous proposal that France had rejected. In the Cabinet, Calhoun and Crawford urged acceptance of a reasonable offer, and Monroe decided for it. Meanwhile the suit of the Government against the *Apollon* was dismissed, and the *Eugénie* and *Neptune* were restored to French consuls.[13]

The resulting treaty of June 24, 1822, all but unanimously accepted by the Senate,[14] contained only two provisions: an even balance of discriminating duties, and an article to facilitate the arrest and return of deserting French seamen – this in place of a consular convention. It allowed France to collect during the next two years an additional duty of twenty francs a ton on goods imported in American ships, and permitted the United States to levy a duty not exceeding $3.75 a ton on French articles imported in French ships. After two years the amount of the special duties was to be lowered annually by one fourth until all discriminations disappeared on both sides, or until either party should denounce the treaty.

It was really a face-saving formula for France. The two Governments, which could not agree not to discriminate against each other's flag at all in their direct trade, agreed to discriminate, but equally and not very much! The treaty lived until the discriminations wore out, and thus in the end there was a victory for American reciprocity policy, at least in the direct trade with continental France. Except for the article on seamen, the treaty still lives on today (1949).

Adams did not betray any real dissatisfaction with this good result. The controversy had ended not unsuccessfully, and he had been able to stress another fundamental of American foreign policy. The American spoliation claims and the French Louisiana grievance lingered on through Monroe's Administration and Adams's own Presidency, not to be adjusted until President Andrew Jackson's day, and there is no need in these chapters to follow their dormant life much further. By the treaty signed July 4, 1831 France engaged to pay the United States a lump sum of 25,000,000 francs in six annual installments for quittance of all spoliation claims; and the United States agreed to pay France 1,500,000 francs in six annual installments for complete liberation from all French claims. In return for a lower duty on French wines entering the United States, France abandoned her claim to unconditional most-favored-nation treatment in the ports of Louisiana.

[13] Robert Aubrey McLemore: *Franco-American Diplomatic Relations, 1816–1836,* (University of Louisiana, 1941), pp. 22–3.

[14] The Senate advised and consented unanimously to the treaty and "the first separate article" (providing for a refund of the extra duties levied by either side before the convention's signature); and by a vote of 41 to 3 for the treaty with the second article (stipulating that only excess of importations over exportations was liable to the discriminating duty in the United States). The French Government did not ratify the second separate article and it is not published with the treaty, but for its content see *Memoirs,* VI, 20–1. For technicalities of ratification see Miller: *Treaties,* III, 86–8.

President Jackson's success in making a recalcitrant France actually pay the treaty sums is one of the most virile and refreshing episodes of American diplomatic history. On the other hand the yielding of an equivalent for France's abandonment of her unconditional most-favored-nation claim in the ports of Louisiana was a lesion to the conditional interpretation, a basic tenet of American foreign policy.

2

Most spectacular of all the commercial problems was the colonial question with Great Britain, who refused to allow American ships into the salt-water ports of British North America and the British West Indies. The commerce itself was not so important as with some of the other West India islands, but John Quincy Adams looked upon British exclusion as a veritable challenge to one of America's basic policies. Further, it was canceling out all the advantages of full reciprocity in the direct trade between the United States and Great Britain, because British ships could make double profits in the triangular voyages denied to the American flag – from England to the United States to the colonies to England – and thus undercut the direct trans-Atlantic carriage between the two countries open to American vessels. It made a nullity of real reciprocity.

As United States Minister in London, Adams had argued in vain that the system of colonial monopoly was outmoded and unprofitable. The Tory Government of Lord Liverpool had refused to risk the prejudices of imperial tradition. In the face of obstinate persistence to exclude the American flag from the West Indies and British North America there was only one effective answer: if it was proper for Great Britain to exclude the United States from maritime trade with her colonies it was also unexceptionable for the United States to exclude from its ports British ships engaged in the same commerce, or at least to charge them with additional duties. Castlereagh had his eyes wide open to this alternative when he persisted in a policy of exclusion.[15] The result was a trade war injurious to all concerned, but most damaging to the British West Indies.

Disappointed in not being able to adjust the question satisfactorily in the negotiation of 1818,[16] Adams inspired Congress to pass discriminating legislation of its own.

Acts of 1817, 1818, and 1820 first imposed an extra tonnage duty on British ships coming from ports forbidden to vessels of the United States, and finally excluded them altogether unless bringing products *directly* from the colony in which they were grown. The latter provision was to prevent West Indian commerce getting into the United States by way of a British colonial vestibule in North America. The latest law dealt a sharp blow to colonial prosperity and was one of the reasons for the spectacular downfall of the planter class in the British Islands in contrast to the con-

[15] *Memoirs,* III, 423. [16] Above, Ch. XIV.

temporary prosperity of the French West Indies. It was less injurious to American exporters and importers than to the economy of the British colonies. After all, the United States did not depend for its economic welfare on the British West Indies, or on British North America. It could stand a trade war better than they could. Parliament yielded in 1822. It opened a number of colonial ports to American ships. But it allowed them to bring to British colonial ports only an enumerated list of United States products — carefully classified so as not to compete too much with British North American products — and to take colonial products (except arms or naval stores) directly to the United States, all on the same terms as British ships.

The favors of this act were made contingent on similar privileges being allowed to British ships in American ports. The law carefully reserved complete freedom to levy preferential tariffs on the same articles when imported into the island colonies from British North America instead of from foreign countries. Since American ships could not engage in British intercolonial carriage (any more than British ships could participate in the coastwise traffic of the United States) Monroe's Government could not see a real reciprocity in the British legislation. Already the West Indian triangular trade, forbidden to American ships, was canceling out the equal advantages for the United States of reciprocity in the direct trans-Atlantic commerce secured by the Anglo-American Convention of July 3, 1815. Now the devices of intercolonial preferences and ingenious prohibitions of particular products threatened to frustrate a nominal reciprocity in colonial commerce. In resorting to both of these stratagems Great Britain was completely within her sovereign rights. But the United States could be equally resourceful.

Elated at the British concession of 1822, John Quincy Adams gave the legislative screw another turn before the American electorate. Under his guiding hand Congress responded with the act of March 1, 1823. It opened the ports of the United States again to British ships coming from British colonial ports to which American vessels had been recently admitted, and allowed them to import goods coming *directly* from those colonies. At the same time it gave the President contingent authority — which he promptly executed — to impose a ten-per-cent discriminatory tariff charge on colonial goods imported in British ships, until Great Britain should do away with her intercolonial preferences.

Such was the situation when the Secretary of State drafted his voluminous instruction of June 23, 1823 to Rush on the subject of colonial commerce.[17] Replete with historical details and legislative technicalities it makes a document as long as a chapter of this book. In the sweltering heat of Washington it was difficult enough for the Secretary himself to hold his mind to this "dry and intricate" matter. If John Quincy Adams, who

[17] *ASPFR*, V, 511–20.

grew up with the subject, found it onerous, certainly it would be unkind to inflict too many details upon the reader.[18] The principal object of the instruction was to break down British intercolonial preference, which prevented perfect Anglo-American commercial reciprocity in fact as well as theory. One feature, astray from the general plea for strict reciprocity in fact, should however be noted. That is the navigation of the St. Lawrence River.

The British Government after the War of 1812 had offered to allow reciprocity of inland commerce and navigation, not including the St. Lawrence River, between Canada and the United States. But the United States had refused to reciprocate unless a right to the free navigation of that river was recognized. Adams brought this new subject into discussion as a result of a memorial received from the inhabitants of Franklin County, New York, backed up by a committee report of the House of Representatives,[19] setting forth the hardships of not being able to navigate the river where it passed through British banks, and requesting the President to "obtain by negotiation" the use of the waterway – it did not allege a "right." The Secretary did not like the assumption that it was a concession to be obtained "in a day, or even a year" by negotiation, for which equivalents always had to be paid. He urged the representatives of the northern border states to clamor for it as a right, not a privilege.[20]

The United States had just as good a legal right to the navigation of the St. Lawrence River through British banks to the open sea as it had to the navigation of the Mississippi through Spanish banks to the Gulf of Mexico before Pinckney's Treaty of 1795. That was no right at all. International law recognized only treaty rights on the part of an up-river

[18] The implacable student may explore the complicated subject quite fully in F. Lee Benns's learned and lucid treatise on *The American Struggle for the West Indian Carrying Trade, 1815–1830*, University of Indiana Studies, X, No. 56 (Bloomington, March 1923).

[19] *ASPFR*, V, 518.

[20] "That committee reported no opinion favorable to the *right* of navigating the St. Lawrence. Their report without directly asserting the contrary looked very much that way. Now it is very easy for a Branch of the legislature to request the President to *obtain* by negotiation with a foreign power the removal of all just causes of complaint, but if with this request they couple argument to show that we have no manner of right to that which they request the President to *obtain*, what is actually to be expected of the result of the negotiation?

"I speak explicitly and confidentially upon this subject because it is not an affair likely to be settled in a *day* or even a *year*. A deliberate purpose, a systematic persevering pursuit of it, a profound investigation of the question and of all its bearings in international law, a thorough knowledge of facts and of interests both British colonial and American, and the most harmonious cooperation between the Executive and Congress in all the measures to be adopted will be *indispensable* before we shall obtain the navigation of the St. Lawrence. All the representatives in Congress from the borders of the Lakes should feel that their constituents have a deep and common interest in this concern." JQA to Micah Sterling, Member of the House of Representatives from the Watertown district of New York. July 9, 1823. Adams MSS.

riparian state to navigate waterways through foreign territory to the ocean. Spain, for example, had no right to navigate the Tagus through Portugal to the port of Lisbon.

The inhabitants of Franklin County invoked "natural" right. John Quincy Adams echoed the claim, not only from them but also from the state papers of John Jay, Thomas Jefferson, Thomas Pinckney, John Adams, and all those statesmen of the Revolution who had struggled with Spain for the free navigation of the Mississippi and finally forced her to concede it. The United States was just as much bound, Adams asseverated in the instructions to Rush, to maintain the navigation of the St. Lawrence for the inhabitants of the States of Illinois, Indiana, Ohio, Pennsylvania, New York, and Vermont and the territory of Michigan as it had been in the old days to insist on the free navigation of the Mississippi for the benefit of the Southern and Western states and territories.

The Secretary of State cited to Richard Rush the recent stipulations of Vienna in favor of the free navigation of the Rhine, the Neckar, the Main, the Moselle, the Maas, and the Scheldt. But they were treaty rights, created by mutual agreement, not natural rights. It takes at least two parties to make a treaty. Any recognition of the free navigation of the St. Lawrence would need the agreement of Great Britain. The Secretary did not mention any equivalent that the United States would be prepared to offer.

There was more than a legal flaw in Adams's position on the navigation of the St. Lawrence. It was diplomatically weak as well: the time to have presented such a claim, as British negotiators would be certain to point out, was in the peace negotiations of 1782, or the discussions of Jay in London in 1794, or even at Ghent in 1814; on none of these occasions had the United States claimed the navigation of the St. Lawrence at all. It was certainly very late to bring it up as a right in 1824. But at least he had placed himself on record before the voters of six interested frontier states. It could do no harm to set forth their cause, even if it could do little immediate good so far as the thing itself was concerned. Real determination and preponderating force on the part of the supplicating state, or distressing international predicaments of the possessory sovereign, were necessary to drive home such a "right." The United States did not have that much force and Great Britain was not that much embarrassed.

A separate instruction set forth the claim of the United States for the admission of American consuls into the colonial possessions of Great Britain in the New World.[21] This presupposed, of course, the establishment of a satisfactory commercial relationship.

President Monroe's Cabinet considered and approved, with very little discussion, the instructions on colonial commerce.[22] Really Adams did not expect very much to follow. Nor was he very enthusiastic about con-

[21] *ASPFR*, V, 527–8.

[22] *Memoirs*, VI, 141. June 6, 1823.

tinuing a trade war. One of the first things that the British Government had done in answer to the American tariff discriminations of 1823 was to lay a countervailing duty of four shillings threepence sterling (equal to a dollar) a ton on American vessels arriving in British colonial ports. In February 1824, before the negotiations really had got under way in London, Stratford Canning's successor in Washington, the chargé H. U. Addington, had a general conversation on colonial commerce with the Secretary, occasioned by the refusal of the British Government to grant an exequatur to a United States Consul at Antigua. Addington closed his dispatch describing the talk with a confidential postscript:

"Mr. Adams had entered upon the above subject with much gravity, and even severity, of tone and feature. Before the close of our conversation, however, his brow, from one cause or another, expanded into greater openness, and his countenance assumed an expression of mildness approaching to hilarity; when, upon my asking him distinctly, but frankly and cordially, whether he proposed to take any further measures on the subject, he, by one of those singular impulses which sometimes overtake the most cautious, replied: 'Why, we shall desire Mr. Rush to press the point of strict reciprocity, and to intimate an intention on our part of retaliating, in case that principle is not conceded. Not that we shall retaliate, I suppose,' added Mr. Adams laughing, 'but we must at all events say we will.'"

"I draw no inference from this curious confession," Addington concluded, "but relate it exactly as it dropped from Mr. Adams's mouth." [23]

H. U. Addington may have drawn no inference, but certainly George Canning would not fail to do so!

3

Another subject in the group of instructions to Rush for his guidance in the general negotiations in London was the everlasting fisheries question.[24] It is recalled that one of the American fishing grounds designated by the Convention of 1818 was the west coast of Newfoundland from Cape Ray to the Quirpon Islands.[25] Along the northern reaches of this stretch of coast France had secured fishing rights for her subjects by the Treaty of Utrecht of 1713,[26] renewed in succeeding wars. In the fishing seasons of 1820 and 1821 the commanders of French armed vessels based

[23] H. U. Addington to George Canning, No. 8, Washington, February 2, 1824. PRO, F.O., 5, Vol. CLXXXV.

[24] *ASPFR*, V, 528–9.

[25] See Map 3.

[26] "But it shall be allowed to the subjects of France to catch fish and to dry them on land, in that part only, and in no other part besides that, of the said island of Newfoundland, which stretches from the place called Cape Bonavista to the northern point of the said island, *and thence running down by the western side, reaches as far as the place called Point Riche.*" Article XIII of the Treaty of Utrecht. Italics inserted.

on neighboring St. Pierre and Miquelon Islands proceeded to order several American vessels away from territorial waters lying strictly within the jurisdiction of Newfoundland. Adams protested to the French Government, only to be told that France had an *exclusive* fishing right there in common with British subjects. Instead of appealing to the Franco-American Treaty of 1800,[27] or taking reprisals on French fishermen directly, as would have been indicated, the United States appealed to Great Britain to make France stop interfering with a fishing right guaranteed to American citizens in common with British subjects. Adams directed Rush to call upon the British Government "to maintain at once the faith of their treaty with us and the efficacy of their own territorial jurisdiction, violated by the exercise of force against the fishing vessels of the United States engaged in their lawful occupation under its protection" – or be liable for indemnity.

If Great Britain did once have the duty of protecting American subjects against foreign interference with their fishing rights within British territorial waters, that duty had certainly ceased with the independence of the United States, like the old protection against Barbary pirates. There could be little expectation that the British Government would see fit gratuitously to extend it to foreign citizens exercising a servitude in British jurisdiction, treaty or no treaty. The Secretary's stand on this question is the least impressive of any claim he ever made. It reminds one of the vacationist who gets a privilege to go fishing in a farmer's trout brook and then expects that rural citizen to protect him against bumptious neighbors who have the same permission – or pay damages.

Perhaps Adams expected that once a concert of peace had been erected between the two English-speaking nations, this little police favor would naturally follow. It is interesting to note in this connection that one of the articles of his maritime Project called for protection against pirates of each party's merchant ships by the warships of the other party going the same course. Such an article would have been very one-sided in favor of the United States, because the British Navy was so much bigger than the American Navy. It would have meant for all practical purposes the restoration of the old British naval protection against marauders of the sea all over the globe, something the United States had sorely missed since 1776. This was on a par with Adams's expectation of protection against French intrusion on the fishery coast; or with his contention that

[27] The Franco-American Convention of 1800 stipulated, Article XXVII: "Neither party will intermeddle in the Fisheries of the other on it's [*sic*] coast or disturb the other in the exercise of the rights, which it now holds or may acquire on the coast of Newfoundland, in the Gulph of St. Lawrence, or elsewhere on the American coast, northward of the United States."

Before the Convention of 1800 it might have been argued that the Treaty of Amity and Commerce of 1778 had recognized indirectly an "indefinite and *exclusive*" French fishery right on the coast of Newfoundland (see Article X). Of course that convention had been abrogated by the Convention of 1800.

the independent United States had a right to navigate the St. Lawrence River out through British territory to the ocean while denying to Great Britain the right any longer to navigate the Mississippi River. In short, John Quincy Adams was presuming that the United States could at once be independent of British sovereignty and nevertheless enjoy some of the advantages of British subjects.

4

As soon as the Anglo-American Convention of March 13, 1824 for suppression of the African slave trade was signed, Canning lost interest in the historical issues which Adams, at least softly and faintly, had hoped to reconcile through Richard Rush's negotiations in London. Piqued by the Monroe Doctrine, the British Foreign Minister turned his attention to other affairs, notably to Latin America, and left it to Huskisson and Stratford Canning to wrangle politely over North America, and colonial commerce, and such curious and novel departures as the Freedom of the Seas. Six months of amiable but unprofitable discussion followed. At no point could the affable American Minister budge the British Commissioners from the position that their Government had taken under Canning's directions on all of the other questions so vitally interesting to the United States.[28]

Huskisson refused to give up the intercolonial preferences. They were too much a part of the whole British colonial system.[29] "Each Country reserves to Itself the carrying trade of its own Coasts," George Canning had instructed him.[30] Under his guidance Great Britain built up a scheme of further retaliation against the retaliations of Congress. In 1826, after John Quincy Adams had become President, an act of Parliament excluded American ships altogether from the West Indies until the United States should repeal the special duties on imports from the British colonies. Anticipating some such action, Huskisson and Stratford had refused to consider the admission of American consuls into colonials ports until the larger question of colonial commerce should be settled with the United States.

As to the St. Lawrence River, the British Commissioners refused for one moment to admit that the United States had any right, legal or natural, to the free navigation of that waterway through British territory to Montreal and Quebec, much less out to the sea. Nevertheless they offered to permit such a navigation as part of a compromise settlement of the

[28] George Canning to the British Plenipotentiaries, Foreign Office, May 31, 1824. *Papers relating to the Negotiation in London, between the British Plenipotentiary on the Part of the United States of America* (January to August 1824; "Private," official print not published). Huskisson "Papers Relating to the Affairs of America." WRC.

[29] Anna Lane Lingelbach has analyzed the significance of these negotiations to "Huskisson and the Board of Trade," in *AHR,* XLIII (No. 4, July 1938), 759–75.

[30] Ibid., p. 47.

northeast boundary.[31] Rush would not allow the two questions of navigation and boundary to balance against each other. His British opposites did not insist that this was the only compromise possible: one might be found, they suggested, within the area of the boundary question itself. They asked him if he had any specific compromise to propose. He had to answer no, not until the negotiation on that subject should be planted in Washington, where the maps and documents were.

As to the American demand that Great Britain make France stop interfering with Yankee fishermen on the treaty coast of Newfoundland, the British Commissioners simply would not discuss it. In Rush's words, they "threw it out." [32]

As President, John Quincy Adams sent Albert Gallatin to London to begin the general negotiation all over again. Gallatin found the British Government in no mood for a negotiation. Doubtless the Senate's mutilation of the slave-trade convention contributed to the "waspish" temper in London.[33] All that he could do with the colonial question was to renew, for another ten years, the Commercial Convention of July 3, 1815 [34] — that is to say, nothing more at all. Canning told the American Minister quite tartly that so long as the United States stuck to its stand against interimperial preferences the British Government could not hold itself bound to remove its interdict "as a matter of course" against American ships in British colonial ports "whenever it might happen to suit the convenience of the foreign Government to reconsider the measures by which the application of that interdict was occasioned." [35] As to the St. Lawrence navigation, the unbending attitude of the President, insisting on it as a "right," served only to postpone a final settlement.[36]

To Adams the intercolonial preferences were merely a means of nullifying a paper reciprocity not only in the colonial intercourse but in the direct trade with Great Britain as well. In his eyes they became the very

[31] See Ch. XXIII following.

[32] For Rush's long report of his negotiations, see his *Residence,* II, 119–323, and *ASPFR,* V, 510–82. See also George W. Brown's study of "The Opening of the St. Lawrence River to American Shipping," *Canadian Hist. Rev.,* VII (No. 1, March 1926), 7–8.

[33] "They were undoubtedly in a waspish temper, and Mr. Canning had determined to play off upon us one of his flourishes for effect. He had been laying up a stock of resentments, for which he was hoping to expose us to a public and open humiliation. I believe that which rankled most in his mind was the disappointment of the slave-trade convention, though he said, perhaps, not a word to you about it." JQA to Gallatin, Washington, 1827. *Writings of Gallatin,* II, 398.

[34] Gallatin also negotiated two other separate conventions in other fields of controversy: one arranging for the arbitration of the northeast boundary dispute, the other extending indefinitely the ten-year article of the Convention of October 20, 1818, for the regulation of the territory on the North West Coast of America, west of the Rocky Mountains. See Chapters XXIII and XXV.

[35] Canning to Gallatin, September 11, 1826. *ASPFR,* VI, 253.

[36] Gallatin to JQA, New York, December 5, 1827. *Writings of Gallatin,* II, 395.

symbol of an outworn imperialistic and mercantilistic economy. To influence American opinion and feeling in support of the Administration policy for an "equal and honest reciprocity" of colonial trade the President wrote for Robert Walsh's *Quarterly Review*, anonymously, an article on "The British Colonial and Navigation System." [37] The theme of this piece was that British statesmen, who so long had undertaken to give the law to the United States as to their colonies, in ordaining that the traffic be carried exclusively in British ships, had come to a pretension where they believed that they were conferring a *boon* on the other party by admitting it to any portion of the trade whatever. "Such is the doctrine of colonial monopoly; and such is the theory of the British Navigation Acts." "It becomes not the self respect of the United States," he declared in his annual message of December 4, 1827, "to solicit gratuitous favors or to accept as the grant of a favor that for which an ample equivalent is extended."

There is no question that America's most doughty champion of the Freedom of the Seas in time of war and commercial reciprocity in time of peace had gone too far in expecting the British Empire to yield under the coercion of American retaliatory legislation. He had been more adamant than in the negotiation of his French treaty. There — against his own better judgment, to be sure — he had accepted temporarily something less than perfect reciprocity even in trade between European France and the United States. In the case of the British colonial question Adams had to retreat and to negotiate in vain for a restoration of the reciprocity of 1822, on the basis of intercolonial preferences for the British flag, under which American ships had been rapidly taking over nine tenths of the commerce with the islands before the British cut it off again in 1826. But even then, after 1826, American ships commanded a great deal of the British West Indian commerce with the United States by using the other European islands in the Caribbean as entrepôts.[38] The fact that John Quincy Adams lost his bout with Canning does not prove that he was wrong; but it gave some ammunition to his political opponents in his hopeless presidential campaign of 1828.

5

The other imperialistic powers of Europe did not present any such challenging problem as Great Britain for trading to their American colonies. They had no dominions in the temperate regions of North America capable of complementing the economies of their Caribbean islands. The lumber and foodstuffs of the United States were indispensable to their prosperous existence; moreover, they needed American ships to bring those products to them in sufficient quantity. They also had to have an

[37] Vol. II (No. 2, September 1827), 267–306.

[38] Setser: *Reciprocity Policy*, pp. 238–9.

American market to take care of their surplus sugar, molasses, coffee, and cocoa. So the old colonial monopolies became largely a dead letter.

Cuba, for example, received vessels of the United States flag with no other restrictions than a high tariff. The trade between that Spanish island and the Republic of the North soon surpassed that of all the British sugar islands combined, even during the intervals when the latter were open to the Stars and Stripes. Local regulations of the Dutch islands of St. Eustatius and Curaçao also admitted American ships and products. In the case of the French Antilles, the old ordinance of 1784 still remained the basic law, but a royal decree of 1826 offered to remove all restrictions in Guadeloupe and Martinique on a reciprocal basis; and an act of Congress met this proposal in 1828 by lifting discriminations on French vessels loaded with the produce of those principal French islands. Secretary of State Henry Clay concluded in 1826 under the Administration of President Adams a treaty of commerce with Denmark on terms of reciprocal equality of the citizens and subjects of each party in all the ports of the other, not excluding the West Indian colonies. But none of the colonial powers, except Sweden for her little island of St. Bartholomew, would allow the ships of the United States to engage in the colonial trade between their islands and the mother country, any more than the United States would permit foreign ships to engage in its coastwise traffic.

The revolution of the Spanish and Portuguese colonies of course solved the problem of colonial monopolies in those regions. John Quincy Adams did not try to extract any special favors in return for prior recognition of independence. On the other hand, he strove to eliminate and to prevent the repetition of any particular discrimination against the United States, such as existed in Brazil by virtue of the Anglo-Portuguese treaty of commerce of 1810.[39] What the United States wanted in treaties with the new states was equality of treatment for all powers in those ports – what today we would call the Open Door, preferably on the same footing, reciprocally, as enjoyed by native citizens; if not, then on the most-favored-nation basis. "The only object we shall have much at heart in the negotiation will be the sanction by solemn compact of the broad and liberal principles of independence, equal favors, and reciprocity." [40] The result of these Latin-American negotiations, continued by Henry Clay after Adams became President, was three new treaties of commerce and amity: with Colombia (signed October 3, 1824), and Brazil (December 12, 1828), based on the conditional most-favored-nation formula; and one with the short-lived Central American Federation (December 5,

[39] By this treaty the Brazilian Government admitted British and other European produce (usually carried by British ships) at a duty of fifteen per cent. It taxed the produce of the United States twenty-four per cent.

[40] Initial instructions of JQA to Richard C. Anderson, first American Minister to Colombia, May 27, 1823. See also his instructions to Caesar A. Rodney, first Minister to Buenos Aires, May 17, 1823. *Writings*, VII, 424–89.

1825), first treaty to embody the complete American reciprocity policy in all its fullness: reciprocal treatment on the basis of equality with natives, *regardless of the origin of the cargoes.*[41]

American reciprocity policy had been limited before 1817 to the products of particular countries parties to a reciprocity of equality with native or at least of most-favored-nation treatment. During John Quincy Adams's term as Secretary of State the Netherlands and Sweden, each of them outlets by their shipping for a foreign hinterland either in the Germanies or in the Baltic countries, endeavored to extend reciprocal concessions to the products of foreign regions customarily exported through their own ports or shipping. An act of the United States Congress of April 20, 1818 [42] consummated the extension in the case of the Netherlands, and another act of January 7, 1824 [43] did so for Prussia, the Hanseatic cities of Hamburg and Bremen, Sweden-Norway, Sardinia, Russia, and the Duchy of Oldenburg. The Central American treaty simply carried this policy a step further by including all foreign products. The first treaty with Denmark (April 26, 1826) stipulated that each nation should receive the shipping of the other on the same terms as its own, without regard to the origin of the cargo, excepting however the direct carriage between Denmark and her colonies. Pursuing the same principle an act of Congress of May 24, 1828 authorized the President to remove by proclamation the discriminating duties levied on goods imported in foreign ships, regardless of the origin of the goods, for those countries which would do the same for the United States.[44] A treaty with the Hanseatic cities of Hamburg, Bremen, and Lübeck (December 20, 1827) and a new treaty (the third) with Prussia (May 1, 1828) placed their commerce and shipping on the same full reciprocal privileges.

The Adams Administration was unable to conclude treaties of commerce with Portugal, Russia, and Turkey. In the case of Portugal, claims against the United States for spoliations by Artigan (irregular Uruguayan) privateers alleged to have been fitted out in American harbors stood in the way. With Russia, Adams thought that it was perhaps desirable but not at all necessary to conclude a treaty of commerce: she had no discriminating duties, no colonial monopoly to remove; and both he and

[41] During Adams's Administration, Joel R. Poinsett, first American Minister to Mexico, signed a most-favored-nation treaty of commerce with that Republic on July 10, 1826, and, this failing of ratification by Mexico, a new one on February 14, 1828, which was not fully ratified, because of complications concerned with the extradition of fugitive slaves, and with the parallel boundary negotiations. Trade and boundary treaties were finally ratified in 1831. See below, p. 564. Later the United States concluded treaties embodying the principles of the Freedom of the Seas and most-favored-nation commercial reciprocity with Chile (1832), Venezuela (1836), Ecuador (1839), Peru-Bolivia (1851).

[42] *U.S. Statutes at Large,* III, 464.

[43] Ibid., IV, 2.

[44] Ibid., III, 308.

Monroe were nervous lest commercial negotiations involve the United States in entangling political relationships, for instance, in the Eastern Question.[45] As Secretary of State and as President, John Quincy Adams persisted in secret overtures to the Porte for a treaty of navigation and commerce with the Ottoman Empire that would permit American ships to reach the rich trade of the Black Sea ports through the Bosporus, but widespread sympathy in the United States for the struggling Greeks so antagonized the Sultan that he would not treat.[46] Nevertheless Adams's approaches prepared the way for the later successful negotiations of 1829 and the Turkish Treaty of May 7, 1830.

Adams's stout stand throughout his diplomatic career for reciprocal freedom of commerce with all nations and colonies, in fact as well as in theory, was characteristic of his defense of the interests, dignity, and equality of his country in those decades when it was struggling to establish its peace and respect in the world circle of international politics and economy. Though not immediately successful, his uncompromising attitude had a wholesome effect in the long run in establishing one of the fundamentals of American foreign policy from that day to this.

[45] *Memoirs,* V, 430. November 29, 1821. For the Treaty with Russia of 1824, fixing boundaries and trade with the Indians of the North West Coast of America, see Ch. XXV below.

[46] Correspondence of JQA with George Bethune English, confidential agent to open discussions with Turkey, 1823–8; and with Luther Bradish, superseding English, in 1828. Jacob Radcliff, of New York, to JQA, June 21, 1828; JQA to Samuel L. Southard, Secretary of the Navy, July 23, 1828, April 5, 1829, and allied documents. Adams MSS. See also anonymous articles by JQA on "Greece," "Russia and Turkey," and "Russia," *Annual Register,* LXIX (1827), Ch. XII; LXX (1828), Ch. XI; and LXXI (1829), Ch. XI. Henry M. Wriston has described these missions in his encyclopedic *Executive Agents in American Foreign Relations* (Baltimore, 1929), pp. 321–8.

CHAPTER XXIII
The Northeast Boundary Question[1] (1815–1842)

> Excepting . . . a cession of Territory belonging to any State in the Union, or the abandonment, express or implied, of the right to navigate the St. Lawrence, or the surrender of any territory south of latitude 49° on the North West Coast. . . .
>
> PRESIDENT JOHN QUINCY ADAMS TO HENRY CLAY, WASHINGTON, JULY 5, 1826, FOR THE INSTRUCTION OF ALBERT GALLATIN IN THE LONDON NEGOTIATIONS OF 1826–7

THE NORTHERN boundary that John Adams and his colleagues had written into the Treaty of Peace and Independence of 1783 and had traced on their personal copies of Mitchell's Map of North America was difficult to follow on the actual continental scene. It made its way along water-courses, over hills and dales of untracked wilderness, upstream and down-stream, through forests and swamps, across low divides, then along heights of land and parallels of latitude and by the great inland water-ways from the Bay of Fundy to the "northwesternmost point" of the Lake of the Woods and "due west" – according to the words of the treaty – to the Mississippi River. Nobody had ever surveyed the great irregular trajectory. It is doubtful whether white men had ever yet visited all the woodland nooks and streambeds and highlands mentioned in the treaty. Some of the geographical terminology used on Mitchell's Map, and followed by the treaty-makers, was unknown on the actual terrain: for example, there was no "St. Croix" River at which to begin the boundary. A mixed commission set up by Jay's Treaty had settled the identity of that river in 1798, fixed the boundary up the stream, and placed a stone marker at its source. From there on north and west nothing had ever been done to mark the international frontier to its western terminus.

[1] I have followed the historical inconsistencies of separation in spelling of "north-east" and "northwest" in my references to the Northeast Boundary Question in this chapter, and the North West Coast in the following chapter.

It has already been noted [2] that no line "due west" from the Lake of the Woods could hit the Mississippi anyway.

After the War of 1812 the Convention of 1818, negotiated by Richard Rush and Albert Gallatin in London under John Quincy Adams's direction from Washington, had closed the northwest boundary gap by carrying the line due west to the Rocky Mountains, along the parallel of 49° N.L., leaving the Pacific slope free and open to the occupation of both parties. As we have seen, it was the first step of Adams's transcontinental diplomacy. Meanwhile the mixed commissions set up by the Treaty of Ghent to survey and mark out the several segments of the whole boundary line between the United States and British North America had proceeded with their labors and consumed much of the time of John Quincy Adams and Stratford Canning. It was only the northeastern boundary, where the British wanted a military road across Maine, that produced irreconcilable disputation based on calculated disagreement.

From the beginning it had been the determination if not the instruction of the British Commissioner, Thomas Barclay, to rectify the northeast boundary rather than to locate and survey it according to the plain specifications of the Treaty of Peace and Independence as marked down in 1782 by the negotiators on Mitchell's Map of North America. From the beginning the American Commissioner, Cornelius P. Van Ness, had resisted the stratagem of his British opposite. After years of wrangling, crimination, and recrimination, all recorded in a voluminous and staggering record,[3] the two Commissioners had agreed to disagree. In 1822 the British Commissioner drew up his separate statement and separate map. According to his contention Mars Hill, an elevation forty miles due north of the source of the St. Croix (about 158 miles south of the main stream of the St. Lawrence), was the "North West Angle" of Nova Scotia, designated in the treaty as lying on the "highlands" that divide the rivers that empty themselves into the St. Lawrence from those rivers, *not including the St. John's,* which fall into the Atlantic Ocean. These were the treaty highlands, he declared, along which the line must run to the "Northwesternmost Head of Connecticut River." [4]

[2] See Map 5.

[3] For a list of the books, maps, surveys, and MS. documents see *ASPFR,* VI, 926–7.

[4] "And that all Disputes that might arise in future on the Subject of the Boundaries of the said United States, may be prevented, it is hereby agreed and declared, that the following are and shall be their Boundaries, Viz. From the northwest Angle of Nova Scotia, vizt. That Angle which is form'd by a Line drawn due north from the Source of the St. Croix River to the Highlands along the said Highlands which divide those Rivers that empty themselves into the River St. Lawrence, from those which fall into the Atlantic Ocean, to the Northwesternmost Head of Connecticut River: Thence down along the middle of that River to the forty fifth Degree of North Latitude; From thence by a Line due West on said Latitude until it strikes the River Iroquois or Cataraquy [St. Lawrence]; Thence along the middle of said River into Lake Ontario; through the middle of said Lake . . ." etc., etc. Article 2 of the Definitive Treaty of Peace and Independence of September 3, 1783, which repeats the language

The American Commissioner stuck ingenuously to the plain language of the treaty and to Mitchell's Map. He maintained that the North West Angle was to be found 144 miles north of the St. Croix River (about 52 miles south of the St. Lawrence) on the "highlands" which divide the rivers that empty themselves into the River St. Lawrence from those rivers, *including the St. John's,* which fall into the Atlantic Ocean. He contended that it was along this more northern low-lying watershed that the boundary should proceed to the northwesternmost head of Connecticut River.

There is no longer any doubt that the American location of the North West Angle and the highlands corresponded perfectly to what the negotiators of the peace settlement of 1782–3, American, British, French, and Spanish, had marked on their respective copies of Mitchell's Map to illustrate the Treaty of Peace and Independence.[5] This was the line traced on the section of that map which Benjamin Franklin a few days before his death in 1790 had sent to Secretary of State Thomas Jefferson when first the identity of the St. Croix had been called into question.[6] Unfortunately the negotiators had not attached Mitchell's Map to their treaty or even mentioned it in the articles.

Between the British claim in the State of Maine and the American position there was a north-south gap of over a hundred miles. The area in dispute spread out over 7,697,280 acres. All of it, or even half of it, would have given plenty of room to Great Britain for the much desired all-British military road. If by arbitrarily disputing a large area one can eventually compromise on half of it, something is to be gained for the ingenuity with which the dispute is originally contrived and the obstinacy with which it is advanced and maintained. The British construction of the language of the treaty and understanding of local geography required a dexterity of reasoning that, in the restrained language of John Bassett Moore, did not exceed the requirement of the Commissioner's pretensions.[7] It obliged him to argue that the St. John's River did not flow into the Atlantic Ocean but rather into the Bay of Fundy![8]

Each of the boundary Commissioners of 1822 also had his own conception of which stream at its source marked the northwesternmost head of Connecticut River according to the definitive Treaty of 1783. The British Commissioner located it as far east as possible in order to give the most territory to Great Britain. The American Commissioner located it as far

of the Preliminary Articles of November 30, 1782, except for minor clerical variations. Miller: *Treaties,* II, 97, 152.

[5] Lawrence Martin and Samuel Flagg Bemis showed in 1937 that "Franklin's Red Line Map was a Mitchell," in *N.E. Quarterly,* I (No. 1, March 1937), 105–11.

[6] Benjamin Franklin to Thomas Jefferson, April 8, 1790. Sparks: *Works of Franklin,* X, 447–8.

[7] *Digest of International Arbitrations,* I, 78.

[8] "Compendium of Arguments." MS. in Huskisson "Papers Relating to the Affairs of America," WRC. See Map 5.

west as possible in order to give the most territory to the United States. Here the area in dispute was 100,000 acres of valuable timberland.

During their long disputations the two Commissioners had uncovered and agreed upon the fact that the old survey of the line of 45° north latitude, northern boundary of Vermont and New York westward to the St. Lawrence, was defective. It had arched that parallel too far north by three quarters of a mile where it crossed the outlet of Lake Champlain. To rectify it would be to leave on British soil the expensive fortifications which the United States had constructed at Rouse's Point to guard against any invasion from the north down the historic Champlain Valley. Thus the Northeast Boundary Question came to include a new point of controversy indubitably in Britain's favor. It might make it possible to propose the exchange of one strategical rectification for another.

The United States and Great Britain had pledged themselves by Article V of the Treaty of Ghent [9] to refer to a friendly sovereign or state any differences that their respective Commissioners might record concerning the northeast boundary. They had engaged to consider his decision as "final and conclusive on all the matters so referred."

Stratford Canning was urging Adams to name an arbitrator. The Secretary suggested the Emperor of Russia. The British Minister was not inclined to accede to that. The Emperor had just handed down an award in favor of the United States in the dispute submitted on Britain's liability for the abducted slaves. Stratford then proposed the King of the Netherlands.

"He is your own King's cousin," said Adams. "Let us agree on a compromise line."

"State rights!" cautioned Stratford knowingly: "Maine, Massachusetts, Vermont, New York!" [10]

John Quincy Adams had grown up with the Northeast Boundary Question, so to speak, ever since his boyhood years with his father in Paris. John Adams had repeatedly stated that Mitchell's Map was the only one used by the peacemakers at Paris and that they had delineated the boundaries of the United States upon that map and only upon that map.[11] A Mitchell's Map of 1755, first edition, second impression, exists in the Adams archives, but it has no markings of the northeast boundary controversy between the United States and Great Britain. The younger Adams believed, mistakenly, that he had found in the archives of the Department "the identical copy of Mitchell's Map used by the Ministers who negotiated the peace of 1782 and with the boundary pencil-marked by them." [12] It confirmed the American claim. But President Jefferson and

[9] In reference also to the procedure established in Article IV.

[10] *Memoirs*, VI, 139–40. June 2, 4, 1823.

[11] Miller: *Treaties*, III, 329–30.

[12] *Memoirs*, VI, 15. June 10, 1822. It was not the identical copy of Mitchell's Map used and marked by the negotiators. Rather it was an impression from the same

Secretary of State Madison had made some damaging statements in the earlier years of the controversy. They had admitted, and it was now a matter of public record, that the "highlands" had been impossibly described by the treaty.[13] These careless expressions came home to embarrass every later American negotiator. Once conceded, this point about the uncertainty of the "highlands" was impossible to get rid of. It led to an eventual compromise where none really was necessary.

Adams of course knew perfectly well what the British were after. He had known ever since the negotiations at Ghent in 1814. He could not yet bring himself to leave such a vital American question to the complete disposition of a foreign arbiter. Perhaps it would be safer to compromise it directly.

"Does it seem probable that we can negotiate for a successful adjustment of that line?" he asked Stratford.

Stratford was cautious. "Why, what are you disposed to do?" he asked, to feel Adams out.

"You want a road between your provinces, do you not?"

"Yes," acknowledged the British Minister.

"Well," suggested the Secretary of State, "we will treat on that basis. You shall have the road, and give us an equivalent accommodation of territory." [14]

Stratford seemed well enough pleased with Adams's suggestion – which the Secretary of State had thrown out with the President's approval [15] – even though the two powers stood already pledged to arbitration. The later negotiation was to show that the British Government was not averse to a compromise that would have yielded the desired military route. A little slice of territory along the line of 45°, if that were all the United States asked, was a cheap price to pay for a major strategical rectification that would cut millions of acres from the northern part of the State of Maine. Britain was ready to pay more than that. She would have been willing to allow the navigation of the St. Lawrence.

It did not take Adams long to realize that such an exchange of territory was politically impossible for any candidate for the Presidency in 1824. States' rights did indeed stand in the way. They would have immediately brought down upon his head the wrath of the Maine authorities and of his

plates that had printed the copy of Mitchell's Map that the negotiators used. It was sold to the Department by a British-born American citizen, one William Tatham (see D.A.B.), along with four other documents relating to the northeastern boundary. Tatham himself had traced on his copy of Mitchell "the boundary of the United States as it seems to have been settled by the discussion of our former commissioner." William Tatham to the President of the United States, July 16, 1815; to Richard Rush, March 21, 1816 [?]; to James T. Austin, July 4, 1816; to James Monroe, July 6, 1816; to John Graham, January 20, 1817. DS, *Miscellaneous Letters.*

[13] Moore: *Digest of International Arbitrations,* I, 68.

[14] *Memoirs,* VI, 91. October 28, 1822.

[15] *Memoirs,* V, 407.

own Commonwealth of Massachusetts. In the particular instruction [16] that he drafted for Richard Rush's guidance on this head, in the general negotiations of 1823, for a diplomatic instead of an arbitral settlement of the Northeast Boundary Question, he did not even mention such an exchange, nor any specific compromise at all.

Adams argued indefatigably for Rush's edification that it would be impractical to submit the question to arbitration. The long record of the controversy, including the voluminous journals of the Commissioners, the three collections of conflicting maps, the two disputed maps that the opposing agents had finally presented to the opposing Commissioners as the proper boundary, the five hundred "closely written" pages of the British Commissioner's final report, not to mention the shorter differing statement of the American Commissioner, the complicated proceedings of the geographers and surveyors, the whole comprising thirty volumes of manuscripts "all in the English language," surely this array of labor would overtax the patience and friendship of any foreign prince or even his technical deputy! Besides, it would be embarrassing, almost shameful, for the United States and Great Britain "to uncover their common nakedness to the eyes of a common friend." They would be exhibiting their mutual imputations of bad faith, falsification of documents, *knavery*, and *perfidy* – here the Secretary repeated and underscored words that the British Commissioner had employed. It were better to compromise the controversy. The British Government had given some reason to believe that a direct negotiation would be acceptable. If so the United States Government would present a compromise line. But the negotiation for that purpose would have to be carried on in Washington, where the relevant maps and documents were at hand. And the two parties would have to agree in advance on the map on which the compromise line could be drawn.

What that line was Adams never did reveal. It would be interesting to know how closely it corresponded with the compromise boundary laid down by the King of the Netherlands in the arbitration of 1831 or with the actual treaty line that Secretary of State Daniel Webster settled in the negotiations with Lord Ashburton in 1842, when he gave up 3,207,680 acres belonging to the State of Maine.

The British Government had a right to insist on arbitration according to Article V of the Treaty of Ghent; in that case Adams directed Rush to draw up an agreement of arbitration. Here he went into procedural detail, interesting enough to the student of early arbitral procedure. As to the friendly sovereign or state to be selected, the United States was willing to accept the Emperor of Russia, or the King of Prussia, but not the King of the Netherlands: the relations of this Prince with Great Britain were too intimate and his obligations to the British Government too great

[16] June 25, 1823. *ASPFR*, V, 523–7.

to make him an impartial arbitrator. It was British diplomacy, of course, that had revived the house of Orange and put one of its princelings on the throne of the Netherlands as a buffer state between France and England. Actually, King William had been an honorary general in the British Army ever since 1813.[17]

The Secretary of State took the draft of his paper to the White House for the President's inspection and approval. He also brought along for Monroe's edification the northeast section of the Mitchell's Map on which the negotiators of 1782 had "pencil-marked" the boundary.[18] Following a Cabinet discussion the President approved Adams's instructions to Rush just as he had drafted them.[19]

In the negotiations at London in 1824 Great Britain wanted something she was not entitled to, the northern part of the State of Maine, in order to get an all-British military road out to a warm-water port on the Bay of Fundy. The United States also wanted something it was not entitled to, the navigation of the St. Lawrence River, in order to have unrestricted shipping through British territory to the Gulf of St. Lawrence and the Atlantic Ocean; it also wanted to rectify the boundary at the outlet of Lake Champlain enough to keep its fort there on acknowledged American territory. Therefore a compromise would seem to have been reasonable. Huskisson and Stratford Canning offered to allow the navigation of the St. Lawrence if the United States would accommodate British desires on the northeastern boundary; George Canning was prepared also to allow the old survey at the outlet of Lake Champlain, leaving the new American fort on American soil, and to accept the American claim at the head of Connecticut River.[20] But Rush refused to couple the navigation of the

[17] Major General, December 13, 1813; Lieutenant General, July 8, 1814; General, July 25, 1814. See *List of Officers of the Army and Royal Marines* (London, 1815–30, annually).

[18] This may have been the same square that Franklin had sent to Jefferson back in 1790; or it may have been another copy of Mitchell, still in DS and undoubtedly the one sold to the Department by Tatham (see above, note 12). On this "Tatham" copy of Mitchell's Map, Tatham himself had drawn a faint pencil line, hardly as apparent as the impress of the pencil itself. It begins in the highlands dividing the waters of the St. Lawrence from the streams that flow into the St. John's, namely at the North West Angle of Nova Scotia, according to the American contention, and runs southwesterly along those highlands toward the Connecticut River, northwestern branch. For a description of the various copies of Mitchell's Map in the archives of the Department of State and elsewhere, in the year 1933, see Miller: *Treaties,* III, 326–55, particularly 334, 340; IV, 403–13. Dr. Miller had at his disposal Colonel Lawrence Martin's scholarly notes on Mitchell's Map. Dr. Miller lists the excerpts of Colonel Martin's work that had been already published in ibid., III, 328, n. 1. Dr. Miller kindly afforded me a copy of his unprinted memorandum of February 21, 1949 on "William Tatham and the Northeast Boundary."

[19] *Memoirs,* VI, 141, 151.

[20] Mr. Secretary [George] Canning to the British Commissioners. Foreign Office, May 31, 1824. *Papers Relating to the Negotiations in London, between the British Plenipotentiaries and the Plenipotentiary on the Part of the United States of America,*

St. Lawrence River with the settlement of the Northeast Boundary Question. His chief had insisted on a right to the navigation of the St. Lawrence which ought not to be purchased by yielding another right in the shape of a just title of territory. If John Quincy Adams had yielded, he would have had to cope with the State of Maine, whose officers would be sure to resist any compromise alienating their territory.

Rush's British opposites did not pretend that this was the only compromise possible: perhaps one could be agreed upon within the area of the disputed northeast boundary itself. They asked him to suggest one. But whatever ideas Adams once had about a compromise disappeared under the pressure of states' rights. He had mentioned none for Rush's direction; that Minister therefore had to say that none could be suggested until the negotiation could be shifted to Washington.

Nor were the two sides able to agree in 1824 upon any *compromis* of arbitration. The British Commissioners declared that none was really necessary: it was sufficient to submit to the arbitrator, once he were agreed upon, the *ex parte* statement of the British boundary Commissioner, that carefully prepared report of over five hundred "closely written" pages, against the opposite summary report of his American colleague. Under his instructions from the Secretary of State, to which he adhered most scrupulously all through the laborious negotiation, Rush could not possibly accede to this. Until the field of arbitration could be fenced in, there was not much need to discuss the question of who should be the friendly sovereign or state to be called upon to arbitrate the boundary.

Albert Gallatin took up the Northeast Boundary Question again in the negotiations of 1826–7. His original instructions were to get the settlement of that dispute shifted to Washington; but upon Gallatin's protest to the President against being bound down too rigidly by Henry Clay's instructions, Adams directed his Secretary of State to leave the envoy a large measure of discretion: in short, to propose or accede to anything that he thought would be satisfactory to the people, and be likely to pass the Senate, excepting "cession of Territory belonging to any State in the Union, or the right to navigate the St. Lawrence, or the surrender of any territory south of latitude 49° on the North West Coast."[21] The President had his eye on Governor Enoch Lincoln of Maine, who was ever solicitous, anxious, and vigilant about the boundary negotiation, "querulous, testy, and suspicious," denying the right of the Federal Government to compromise the question at the expense of his state, full of warlike "rhodomontades."[22]

---

endorsed "Private and Confidential for Mr. Huskisson." Huskisson "Papers Relating to Affairs with America." WRC.

[21] JQA to Henry Clay, Washington, July 5, 1826. Adams MSS.

[22] *Memoirs,* VII, 263. April 26, 1827. See also ibid., pp. 267, 327, 383.

After an arduous negotiation with the British Commissioners, H. U. Addington and Charles Grant, Gallatin signed a convention, September 29, 1827, agreeing to submit the "points of difference" of this complex and difficult subject to the arbitration of "some friendly sovereign or state." The rules of procedure followed those laid down by John Quincy Adams in 1823. Instead of assembling the voluminous and complicated mass of documents relating to the controversy the disputants agreed to set their two opposing maps before the arbitrator: the United States, Mitchell's Map, acknowledged to have been used by the negotiators in 1782–3, with the line claimed by the United States; Great Britain, the boundary as fixed on a certain map drawn up by the British agent in 1822, denominated "Map A." [23] Each disputant could then present to the arbitrator a supporting statement, rebuttals allowed.

The Senate advised and consented to the convention by a vote of 35 to 4, without knowing who the arbitrator would be. Among the four opposing votes were the two Senators from Maine, John Chandler and Albion K. Parris, and Senator Levi Woodbridge of New Hampshire.[24]

Gallatin had been particularly worried from the beginning about the arbitrator, where to find in Europe a sufficiently friendly sovereign prince or state. The American preferences had been in this order: the Emperor of Russia, the King of Prussia, the King of Denmark, the King of the Netherlands. First choice of the British Government seems to have been Sardinia or Austria, with the Netherlands as third preference. During a visit to Paris in the autumn of 1826 Gallatin learned from Pozzo di Borgo, the Russian Ambassador to France, who was singularly well acquainted with the Northeast Boundary Question, that the Czar did not want to serve. This corroborated the Minister's earlier report of an "approximation" between Great Britain and Russia [25] following the death of Alexander I of cherished memory, the absolute sovereign whose influence on Adams's life had been so "great and auspicious." [26] Prussia, living in deadly fear of Russia, was too dependent upon Great Britain. The same considerations, in fact, applied with greater or less force to every other European sovereign.[27] Gallatin returned home soon after signing the convention without having agreed upon any arbitrator. Not until the fol-

[23] Map 5.

[24] The fourth was William Smith of South Carolina.

[25] Gallatin to JQA, London, October 18, 1826. *Writings of Gallatin,* II, 331–32.

[26] "The Emperor Alexander was perhaps of all living men the man whose life was most important to the rest of mankind. To what changes his death may lead, conjecture is at fault. From personal motives I ought to cherish his memory, for through my agency he rendered essential good offices to my country. His influence upon the history of my life has been great and auspicious." *Memoirs,* VII, 112. February 5, 1826.

[27] Gallatin to Clay, No. 1, New York, June 29, 1826. *Writings of Gallatin,* II, 309. For the difficulties and details accompanying choice of the arbitrator, see Miller: *Treaties,* III, 357–9.

lowing June did William B. Lawrence, chargé d'affaires, finally agree with Lord Aberdeen, the new Foreign Minister, on the King of the Netherlands, the last choice of each party.[28]

In the ensuing arbitration Gallatin, agent for the United States, bungled the whole affair. The most obvious inquiries would have turned up copies of Mitchell's Map that would have proved the American case completely; for example, King George's own copy, then available in the British Museum. Gallatin, with all his experience in public affairs, neglected to search even that far. Instead, he based the case on the 1755 edition of Mitchell and resorted to the Proclamation of 1763 and the Quebec Act of 1774 to support the American definition of the "highlands." The royal arbitrator naturally could not find these references on a Mitchell's Map of 1755, the edition carelessly placed before him, the document on which the United States had pinned its argument. Gallatin had neglected to point out that it was a later edition of Mitchell, of 1775, that the negotiators had used in 1782!

It was easy for the Dutch monarch to conclude that neither side had proved its case. Instead of pronouncing which was right, the northeast boundary as laid down by the United States according to Mitchell's Map or the boundary as laid down by Great Britain according to "Map A," he took it upon himself to assume the functions of a mediator. In 1831 he awarded to Great Britain the northern half of the disputed territory in Maine, enough for the desired military road. The honorary General in the British Army proved to be no mean strategist.

Both sides agreed that the arbitrator had gone beyond his authority, that they were not bound to split the difference between them; but Great Britain naturally was willing to accept the compromise if the United States would.

Andrew Jackson was now President, and engaged in building up a Democratic party machine in the East as well as in the West and South. Personally inclined to accept the award, he did not want to brook the opposition of the State of Maine or the parent State of Massachusetts, which had reserved proprietorship of lands in the disputed area. So he evaded full responsibility by seeking the advice and consent of the Senate – an interesting precedent which never took root. Since only a small minority of the Senate seemed to be in favor of the fifty-fifty compromise, Jackson refused it. The State of Maine refused to acquiesce in any further treaty negotiation that would alienate her territory. Meanwhile the advent of railroads gave the controversy still greater vitality.[29] The dispute grew and festered malignantly toward war until 1842.

[28] W. B. Lawrence to Henry Clay, No. 45, London, June 22, 1828. Adams MSS.

[29] For Jackson and the Senate, and the opposition of the State of Maine, see Miller: *Treaties*, III, 370–85. Thomas LeDuc has stressed the significance of railroads to "The Maine Frontier and the Northeastern Boundary Controversy," *AHR*, LIII (No. 1, October 1947), 30–41.

By then Daniel Webster had become Secretary of State. Constantly carried by his careless personal economy into impecunious circumstances, he craved to fill a very expensive public post, that of Minister of the United States to the Court of St. James's. A big step toward his ambition might be to clear up the most grievous disputes with England. A settlement of the Northeast Boundary Question would save the peace and make him *persona gratissima* in England. He was ready to use almost any means to get a compromise treaty consummated.

The Secretary of State had picked up from a second-hand dealer a copy of Mitchell's Map with markings on it by some unknown hand that supported the British position. Webster's academic acquaintance Professor Jared Sparks of Harvard College had seen in the French archives a map that he thought might have been the "red-line" map on which Benjamin Franklin had marked "with a strong red line" for the Count de Vergennes the boundary between the United States and British North America agreed upon in 1782. From his notes and memory he marked the line on a map of Maine and sent it to Webster. The drawing confirmed the British northeast boundary claim.[30] Actually Sparks's "red-line map" was not a Mitchell but a map by a French cartographer, d'Anville, 1746, and was not used by Benjamin Franklin or any of the negotiators of the Treaty of Peace and Independence for marking down the boundary. As evidence of the treaty line of 1782 it was therefore worthless. But it was good enough for Webster. These spurious documents were just what he was looking for to overcome native objections to ceding away so much territory in the northeast corner of the United States.

Edward Everett, Minister of the United States to London and former Governor of Massachusetts, knew, *what Sparks knew too,* that there was in the Lansdowne papers good British evidence to show, from the correspondence of Lord Shelburne, Prime Minister in 1782, that the American claim was right. Sparks had worked that private collection in England a few years before and had shown Everett transcripts of his notes, but Sparks – and Everett – considered themselves under pledges to the owner not to use the information to Britain's prejudice in the current boundary question. Nevertheless Everett had kept urging Webster *to look for maps in England.* Webster, with his own specious maps to suit his own peculiar purposes, ordered Everett to desist from any search in London archives.[31]

In Washington the British plenipotentiary, Lord Ashburton, found out about Webster's maps only after he had agreed with the Secretary of State on a new conventional line, based on the award of the King of the

[30] Herbert B. Adams innocently described Sparks's activities, without the revelations of Ashburton's private correspondence with Aberdeen, in *The Life and Writings of Jared Sparks* (2 vols., Boston, 1893), II, 393–418.

[31] Charles Everett: *Life of Edward Everett.* Professor Everett permitted me to read this work while still in MS.

Netherlands, with certain departures for mutual convenience. If he had had this information sooner, he reported, he would have demanded still more territory. As it was, he could only applaud Webster's cartographical aberrations and assist them. He paid somebody, presumably Webster, over fourteen thousand dollars — to be exact, two thousand nine hundred ninety-eight pounds sterling and one shilling — to "compensate" Jared Sparks and enable him to go to Augusta, capital of Maine, and with this "stimulant" help defeat the "schemes" of the Democratic Governor of Maine, John Fairfield, and the "honest" but "obstinate" Maine Commissioner in Washington, William Pitt Preble,[32] to prevent a radical truncation of their state's territory. This large sum was much more than necessary to cover Sparks's traveling expenses from Boston to Augusta and back. A hundred pounds, or four hundred and fifty dollars, would have sufficed for that. Ashburton and his chief, Lord Aberdeen, Minister of Foreign Affairs in the Peel Government, were prepared to employ "the same means to a greater extent in any quarter," but did not have to.[33] The Maine solons accepted the confidential evidence displayed by Sparks and withdrew their opposition to the Treaty of 1842. Webster himself won Massachusetts over to the settlement. It corresponded to what George Canning stood ready to offer in 1824 — except it did not include the navigation of the St. Lawrence River!

Thus did Great Britain finally get her strategic road from Quebec to the Bay of Fundy, now the route of the Canadian National Railroad and of motor highway No. 2. Thus did Daniel Webster willfully relinquish millions of acres of good American territory of the State of Maine in return for retaining the old survey line of 45°, the American fort at the northern outlet of Lake Champlain, and the greater part of the contested territory at the head of Connecticut River. And he never did get the ministerial assignment he hankered for to the Court of St. James's, where he would have been ready to trade away most of the Oregon country in another territorial treaty with Great Britain and Mexico.[34]

After the Webster-Ashburton Treaty of 1842 was safely ratified, debates in Parliament made public the fact that the British Government had possessed all along King George III's own copy of Mitchell's Map and that it completely confirmed the American claim. Lord Aberdeen, who had instructed Ashburton to pay even more money in "any quarter" to accomplish his purpose, told Edward Everett that he had not been aware of the existence of the King George Map, and Ashburton felt constrained to write Webster from London that he had not learned of the "new dis-

[32] One of four Commissioners representing the interests of the State of Maine during the negotiation. Massachusetts, which inherited title to some of the Maine lands in dispute, after the separation of the two states, also had three Commissioners in Washington for the same purpose.

[33] See Appendix 4.

[34] See below, Ch. XXV, Sec. 9.

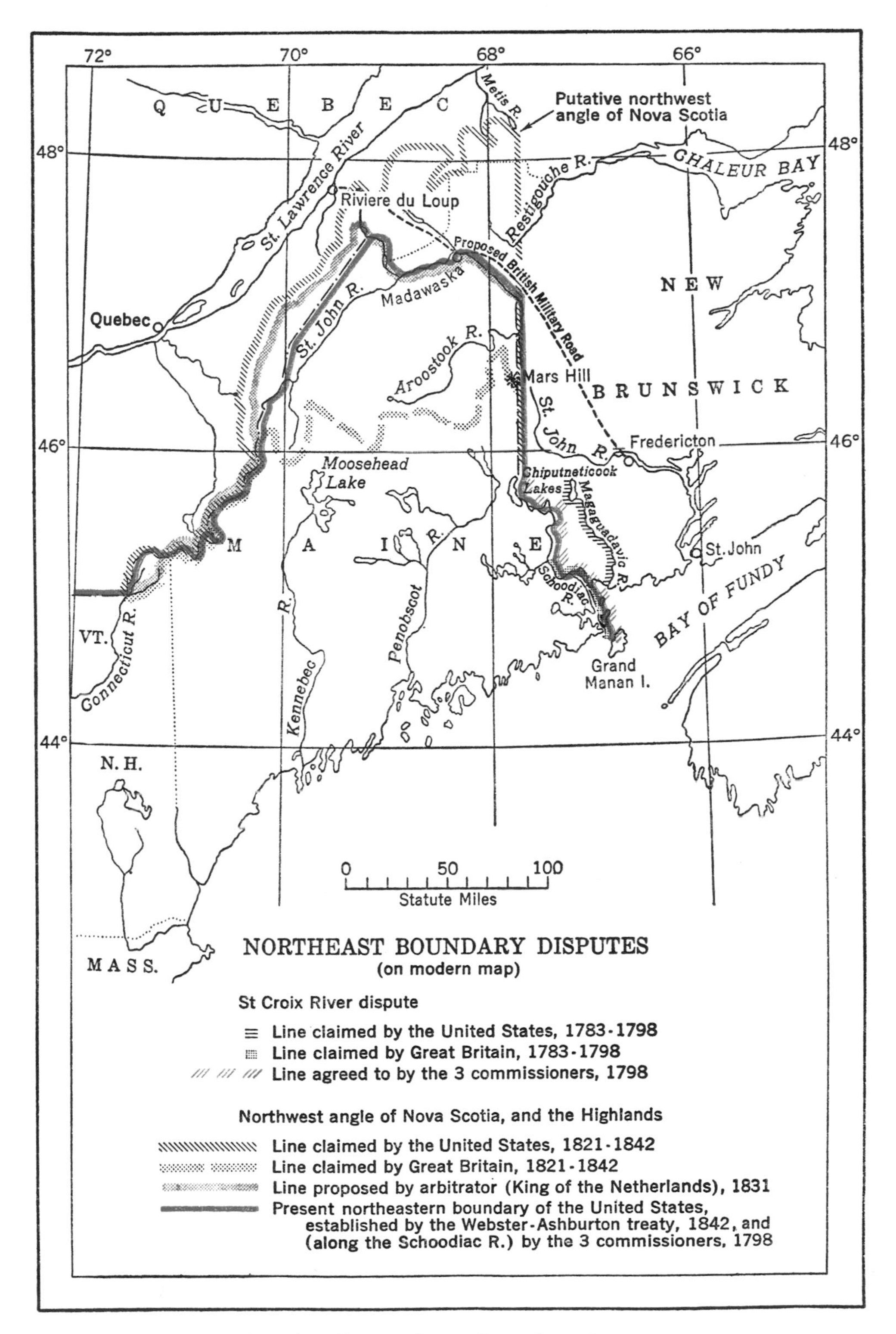

MAP 5 *The Northeast Boundary Disputes*

coveries" until after he got home from Washington; but other British officials, presumably cricket players, certainly knew about the map.[35]

John Quincy Adams, then an old man in the House of Representatives, let his younger friend Webster know in no uncertain terms what he thought about "blowing up Jared Sparks's impostures in mousing among the papers of that old juggler Vergennes." [36]

Even the Old Man Eloquent would have been struck speechless if he had known all about Webster's dealings with Ashburton to clinch the northeast boundary "compromise" in the Treaty of 1842. Sparks had considered himself pledged as a gentleman not to reveal good historical evidence, privately obtained through British hospitality, to help the United States Government. Be that as it properly may. But neither Jared Sparks nor Daniel Webster seems to have considered himself pledged as a patriot not to use evidence, and questionable evidence at that, to the prejudice of his native land. Acting as he did, Webster achieved a diplomatic triumph – against his own country.

[35] Miller: *Treaties,* IV, 408–10.

[36] *Memoirs,* XI, 369. April 24, 1843.

CHAPTER XXIV
The North West Coast
(1818–1822)

There is hardly a passion in the human heart but
that is arrayed against me.

JOHN QUINCY ADAMS
ON HIS FIFTY-FIFTH BIRTHDAY, JULY 11, 1822

A CURIOUS diplomatic triangle had been taking shape in 1823 to distort and perhaps to disrupt the traditional Russian-American equilibrium vis-à-vis Great Britain. The most sensitive point of the triangle rested like a touchy elbow on the North West Coast of America. Before coming to the part which the Coast played in the negotiations of 1823–4 in London and St. Petersburg it is desirable to glance back again to America's growing interest on the other side of the Continent and also at the domestic politics that entered the scene to complicate the international situation, as they have bedeviled the diplomacy of many a Secretary of State before and since John Quincy Adams.

1

"Joint occupancy" is the term that writers almost without exception have used to describe the status of the North West Coast under article three of the Convention of October 20, 1818 between the United States and Great Britain. It is a euphemistic phrase coined by British diplomats in later discussions of 1826–7 and unwittingly repeated by Albert Gallatin in his dispatches to Washington.[1] The deceptive description suggests that any occupation under the treaty was joint. Of course there was no such thing as joint occupancy. What the treaty really stipulated was that any territory claimed by either party on the North West Coast should be "free and open" to the vessels, citizens, or subjects of the two powers without prejudice to the sovereign claims of either for at least ten years. More appropriately it might be called the Free-and-Open Occupation Treaty.

British subjects were on the ground to take prompt advantage of the arrangement. Under the American flag they already possessed Fort George (Astoria) as private property of the North West Company. No American had remained to see whether the Stars and Stripes actually continued to

[1] *ASPFR*, VI, 657, 658, 659.

fly over the post after its restoration to the United States in 1818.[2] Presumably the colors ceased to wave there in the Pacific breezes. Not long after the *Ontario* sailed away the buildings of Fort George burned down.[3]

The North West Company prospered except for its bitter competition with the Hudson's Bay Company, and a merger with the latter organization put an end to that rivalry in 1821. An act of Parliament of the same year confirmed to the Hudson's Bay Company an exclusive trading monopoly, so far as British subjects were concerned, throughout all the territory between Rupert's Land (the Company's original domain – that is, the drainage basin of Hudson's Bay) and the Rocky Mountains, and beyond the mountains as far as the North West Coast. The Hudson's Bay Company held a magnificent position. It could bring its heavy supplies into the River of the West by sea with the protection of the British Navy. No rival, national or foreign, obstructed its overland route by canoe or bateau from the headwaters of the Columbia to the eastward-flowing rivers of Canada down to the Great Lakes and Montreal. All along the way across the Continent there was trade and profit.

To discourage American overland fur-traders and mountain men from entering the Columbia basin the Hudson's Bay Company embarked upon a policy of methodically trapping out the fur country south of the river. They strove to create a sterile belt of territory that would protect their preserves to the north, including the incomparable harbor of Puget Sound.[4] Speedily the Columbia River country was reduced to a condition of economic vassalage to a British corporation.

It was in a state of political vassalage as well. The "Ancient and Honourable Company" retained its old charter privileges of government. That is to say, it had authority and governance over British subjects within its domain including the free-and-open country west of the mountains. It had the right to impose pains and penalties not repugnant to British law. It could administer British justice in all causes civil and criminal according to the laws of the realm of England. Without the force of a single redcoat the benevolent Dr. John McLoughlin, Chief Factor for the Columbia Department of the Company, ruled like a viceroy over British subjects and over the aborigines of that vast unbounded region. In 1825 he abandoned the site of Fort George and moved the Company's Pacific headquarters farther up the river to Fort Vancouver.

The new post was on the north bank just east of where the Willamette flows in from the south, a short distance below the Cascades. Over Fort Vancouver the British flag floated unquestioned. British cannon saluted it

[2] Above, Ch. XIV.

[3] "Slacum's Report on Oregon, 1836–1837," *Ore. Hist. Quar.*, XIII (No. 2, June 1912), 175–224.

[4] Frederick Merk showed how the Company resorted to this device in "The Snake Country Expedition, 1824–1825; an Episode of Fur Trade and Empire." *Mississippi Valley Hist. Rev.*, XXI (1934), 49–62.

from within the stockade. British peace prevailed throughout the valley. Thus did British trade, British settlement, British law, British government quickly extend to the whole region,[5] all in conformity with the Free-and-Open Occupation Treaty.

The United States had just as good a right as Great Britain to create a corporation and give it a monopoly over American trade within the same country. Its citizens had an equal pretension with British subjects to make settlements there, to erect stockades, to put cannon in them, and to hoist the national flag over them. Under the treaty it too could extend its law over American citizens, not to mention the Indians in that area. Thomas Hart Benton of St. Louis went so far as to advocate the immediate incorporation of an American Fur Company powerful enough to cope with the North West and Hudson's Bay Companies and to roll back upon their own heads the thunder that they had directed for forty years against the frontiers of the United States.[6] Secretary of War Calhoun urged that very thing as a means of establishing control over the Indian tribes in the West and excluding foreign adventurers from the trade. "It would speedily destroy all foreign competition," he reported to Congress, "and would, in a few years, push our trade to the Pacific Ocean." [7]

But Congress, much less the executive branch of the Government, was not ready to embark upon such a counteroffensive. The principal object of the Free-and-Open Occupation Treaty was, in its own words, to prevent disputes and differences between the two countries. Actually no treaty could have been better constructed to invite quarrels and collisions had the United States taken advantage of its right actively to contest with Great Britain by assisting and supporting American trade and settlement. Monroe's Administration had no such desire nor intent. The voters were not yet sufficiently interested in the North West Coast. After the Astorians had sold out, there was little expectation that pioneers would soon push in great numbers across the mountains, certainly not for another decade. Because American settlers did not challenge the Hudson's Bay Company, peace and amity prevailed. Therefore the treaty served its peaceful purpose.

American interest in the North West Coast focused on the maritime fur trade and allied trans-Pacific commerce and on the whale fisheries of the North Pacific Ocean rather than on the Columbia River. Those industries operated out of New England round Cape Horn, principally from Massa-

5 Frederick Merk: *Fur Trade and Empire; George Simpson's Journal* (Cambridge, 1931), pp. vii–xxvi.

6 *Selections of Editorial Articles from the St. Louis Enquirer, on the Subject of Oregon and Texas, as Originally Published in that Paper in the Years 1818–19; and Written by the Hon. Thomas Benton, to which is annexed, His Speech in the Senate of the United States, in March, 1825, on the Bill for the Occupation of the Columbia River* (St. Louis: Missourian Office; 1844), p. 8.

7 Report to the House of Representatives, December 5, 1818. *Annals of Congress,* 15th Cong., 2d Sess., 1818–19, II, 2464.

chusetts seaports, Boston, Salem, Newburyport, New Bedford, Nantucket. It was this trade that Minister John Quincy Adams at St. Petersburg in 1810 had protected against Russian exclusion and sovereignty by eluding treaty overtures for its regulation. As long as the maritime fur trade could be protected, as long as American claims to the continental coast could be kept decently alive, Secretary of State Adams had been satisfied to postpone any international controversy over that remote territory.[8] As has been remarked already, there were more immediate if not greater problems pressing to be settled with Great Britain and Spain.

President Monroe was even more anxious to avoid issues in that distant part of the world. He had never been much interested in American claims beyond the mountains. He was not at all sure that the North West Coast could ever be a part of the Union. Only John Jacob Astor's importunities had impelled him, when Secretary of State, to look after the Columbia River in the Ghent negotiations and to see that captured Astoria was restored to the American flag following the peace. Since then John Quincy Adams's continental instincts had kept the territorial title alive under Monroe's Presidency and strengthened it, first in the Free-and-Open Occupation Treaty of October 20, 1818, then in the Transcontinental Treaty with Spain of February 22, 1818 (ratified February 22, 1821), but even Adams was content to keep the Columbia River country in his diplomatic refrigerator. What brought the North West Coast prematurely into controversy following the Treaty of 1818 was the agitation of Dr. John Floyd of Virginia backed by Benton. Primarily for political motives and purposes they accused Adams of neglecting Western interests for the sake of Eastern advantages.

2

John Floyd had been a member of the House of Representatives from Virginia since 1817. He was a frontiersman in heredity, spirit, training, and association. Two weeks before he saw the light of day in 1783 the Indians had killed his father at Floyd's Station in "the Dark and Bloody Ground." As a boy in Kentucky he knew George Rogers Clark. He named two of his sons after the Western hero of the Revolution. Since his early youth he had been a friend of General Clark's younger brother, William Clark, the explorer whose name is linked immortally with that of Meriwether Lewis of Virginia. A cousin of John Floyd was the Sergeant

[8] "It may be proper to observe attentively the movements of Russia with regard to their settlements on the northwestern coast," he wrote to George Washington Campbell, the new Minister setting out for St. Petersburg in June 1818, "but they never can form a subject of serious difference, or jarring interest between that Empire and the United States." *Writings,* VI, 372.

Again in 1820 he wrote to Campbell's successor, Henry Middleton, that while the movements of the Russian-American Company might perhaps occasionally deserve his attention, "they will probably be found less important than they have been imagined." *Writings,* VII, 52.

Charles Floyd who lost his life on Lewis and Clark's expedition to the Columbia. In Congress Dr. Floyd continued to be a Western-minded man. At Brown's Hotel in Washington he met and talked with two old Astorians, Ramsay Crooks of New York and Russel Farnham of Massachusetts. Benton, Senator-elect from the newly admitted State of Missouri, a friend of old Daniel Boone, was a fellow boarder with Dr. Floyd at that popular caravansary. Floyd eagerly read Benton's newspaper writings [9] on the overflowing of the West beyond the Rocky Mountains. He sympathized with the Missourian's attacks on John Quincy Adams's Free-and-Open Occupation Treaty of 1818 and Transcontinental Treaty of 1819. He saturated himself with the famous Westerner's polemics and enthusiasm.[10]

Floyd and Benton were the original protagonists in Congress of American occupation of the Columbia River. In December 1819 Floyd introduced in the House of Representatives a resolution calling for a select committee to inquire into the situation of the settlements upon the Pacific Ocean and the expediency of occupying the Columbia.[11] More out of courtesy to an esteemed member than out of any real interest in the subject the House accepted Floyd's motion. The Speaker appointed him as chairman of the committee, with Thomas Metcalfe of Kentucky and Thomas V. Swearingen of Virginia as fellow members.

Their long, disjointed report, a potpourri of fact and fancy, is a capital document in the history of the North West Coast. Edward Gaylord Bourne, speaking at the Lewis and Clark Centennial Exposition of 1905 at Portland, went so far as to say that it bears the same relation to Oregon that Richard Hakluyt's *Discourse on Western Planting* has to the foundation of the English colonies in America.[12] Historians of the North West Coast and Oregon Question have declared it ought to be in every library of the Pacific North West. Thanks to them it now is. The *Oregon Historical Quarterly* reprinted it in 1907.[13] Few will read it. It is a tremendously overrated document. The style and sentence structure is clumsy, involved, distressing, sometimes unintelligible. Floyd's speeches that defended it were far more effective.

The first sentence of the Report was the essential one. If its wording was involved, its meaning was not obscure. "They [the Committee] have carefully examined the subject referred to them, and, from every consideration which they have been able to bestow on it, [they] believe, from the usage of all nations, previous and subsequent to the discovery of America, the title of the United States to a very large portion of the coast

[9] Benton: *Selections*, op. cit.

[10] Thomas Hart Benton: *Thirty Years' View* (2 vols., New York, 1854), I, 13–15. Charles H. Ambler: *Life and Diary of John Floyd, Governor of Virginia, an Apostle of Secession, and the Father of the Oregon Country* (Richmond, 1918).

[11] December 19, 1820. *Annals of Congress*, 16th Cong., 2d Sess., 1820–1, p. 679.

[12] *Ore. Hist. Quar.*, VI, 263.

[13] Ibid., VIII (March–December 1907), 51–75, 290–4.

of the Pacific Ocean to be well founded; nor have they been able to ascertain that any other government than Spain has made any claim to any part of it, from Cape Horn to the sixtieth degree of North Latitude."

It was absurd thus to wave aside Britain's claim, or Russia's, to any part of the coast below 60° N.L. Historically the report sinned profusely both in commission and in omission. It took great pains to build up France's former title to Texas as far west as the Rio Grande and the "mountains of Mexico." Ostensibly this was to bolster the claim of the United States to adjacent territory beyond the Rocky Mountains, but its real purpose was to attack the Administration and particularly Adams for betraying the West in letting Texas go to Spain. Here appeared the hand but certainly not the pen of Benton.

The unanimity of the Senate in advising and consenting to the treaty with Spain had made no impression on Missouri's first statesman. He attacked John Quincy Adams for giving away Texas. He called down woe on the heads of all those who continued to favor it. "*The Spanish Government* had offered us more than we accepted," he declared; "it was our policy, and not hers, which deprived us of Texas and the large country in addition to Texas, which lay between the Red River and Upper Arkansas." [14] Benton gave Adams no credit whatsoever for opening the way diplomatically to the North West Coast in 1818, nor for strengthening America's claim beyond the mountains by adding Spain's title to it in 1819. Journals all over the country copied from the St. Louis newspapers Benton's denunciation of John Quincy Adams's diplomacy.

Floyd's Report echoed Benton's thoughts. It did not say anything directly about Adams's Spanish treaty, although that was the treaty by which the United States had acquired Spain's title above 42°. Perhaps it did not mention it because Spain had not yet ratified the document. Floyd's committee merely said that the United States possessed a better title to the North West Coast than any other power — as once it had to Texas! The chairman dwelt on Russian enterprise and advances in the North Pacific. He described their menace to the increasing commerce of the United States upon the "Western Ocean." Then he traced the history of the British corporation, the North West Company. He calculated the profits of its overland fur trade. "Your committee are well persuaded," he concluded, "that by a little care and small expense, the citizens of this Republic might reap all the benefits of this trade, not only profitable now, but . . . [to] increase for many years. . . . The Committee cannot doubt that an establishment made on the Pacific . . . would give this country the advantage of all its own treasures, which otherwise must be lost forever, or rather never enjoyed . . . of more profit . . . than the mines of Potosí." [15]

Before bringing in the Report on the floor of the House, Dr. Floyd sub-

[14] *Thirty Years' View*, p. 15.

[15] *Annals of Congress*, 16th Cong., 2d Sess., 1820–1, pp. 945–59.

mitted it, and an accompanying bill, to President Monroe for suggested alterations. Monroe turned the papers over to Adams.

"What do you think of it?" asked the President.

"I can't recommend any alteration," said the Secretary of State. "The paper is a tissue of errors in fact and abortive reasoning, of invidious reflections and rude invectives. Nothing but the fire can purify it."

"The Columbia River settlement project is for Dr. Floyd's brother-in-law," vouchsafed Monroe, explaining that that individual had embezzled thousands of dollars from the State of Virginia and that his friends were preparing a retreat for him on the shores of the Pacific.[16]

Floyd's committee brought in its Report to the House on January 25, 1821. They presented a bill to authorize the occupation of the Columbia River and to regulate intercourse with the Indian tribes within the United States and its territories. The proposed law provided for the extinction of Indian titles along the river, land grants to American settlers, the administration of justice, a port of entry and a customs house as soon as the President should deem it expedient, and salaried Indian agents among the Columbia River tribes. It extended United States administration over the aborigines there and provided for the licensing of fur-traders among them.

Floyd's bill proposed to do little more than the British Government already was doing through the instrumentality of the North West Company. Even so it would have led to collision with British settlers and traders on the grounds. Congress gave it no support or even attention. Both House and Senate were then completely engrossed in the final debates on the admission of Missouri as a slave state into the Union. At least for the time being they forgot about settlements on the remote Columbia River.

3

The British Minister, Stratford Canning, keeping his ear to the ground in Washington, felt the continental tremors. In the gallery of the House of Representatives he listened to the remarks of Hugh Nelson of Virginia implying a design to make some new American settlement on the shores of the South Sea. There was also a communication from Senator Eaton of Tennessee in the *National Intelligencer* of Washington, at this time generally understood to speak for the Administration. It presented William Davis Robinson's plan for a settlement on the Pacific Ocean anywhere between 42° and 49° N.L.[17] At the same time Commodore David Porter

[16] *Memoirs,* V, 238. January 18, 1821. Ambler, op. cit., says: "This was undoubtedly a reference to the defalcation of one of John Preston Floyd's kinsmen. See Richmond *Enquirer,* Jan. 30, 1820."

[17] *National Intelligencer,* January 26, 1821. William Davis Robinson was an American merchant and adventurer who sojourned in Caracas, 1799–1806. In 1816 he embarked from New Orleans on the U.S.S. *Saranac* and was put ashore on the coast of Mexico. He had conferences with the insurrectionary leader Guadalupe Victoria. Later

made public an old letter of his of October 31, 1818 to President Madison urging a naval expedition to the Pacific and North West Coast, to be combined with an overland military expedition. Now, in 1821, three hundred people signed it as a memorial to President Monroe.

Canning hurried to Adams's office.

"What are the intentions of your Government in this respect?" he asked.

"From a prevailing disposition in the country," replied the Secretary, "it is very probable that our settlement at the mouth of the Columbia will at no remote period be increased."

"Am I to understand this as the determination of the American Government?"

"No, sir," denied Adams. "You are to understand nothing as the determination of the Government that I say to you without consultation with and directions from the President. What I have now said to you is merely an opinion of my own."

A spirited dialogue ensued. Canning asserted that an American settlement on the Columbia would be a violation of the Treaty of October 20, 1818. John Quincy Adams rose and got a copy of the treaty. He read the free-and-open occupation article to Canning. "Now, sir," he said, "if you have any charge to make against the American Government for a violation of this article, will you please to make the communication in writing." [18]

The Secretary seemed to consider Stratford's interference respecting the Columbia River as offensive and unwarranted.

Stratford was determined not to let himself be beaten down by "mere violence of tone and assertion."

"Do you suppose that I am to be dictated to in the manner in which I may think proper to communicate with the American Government?" the Minister asked angrily.

Adams was equally resolved not to allow remarks on the floor of Congress to be made the subject of foreign remonstrances. He roundly asserted indisputable right to the territory of the Columbia and utterly denied the right of a British Minister to interfere with the eventual arrangements of the United States on that head.

The two men kept it up, long and vehemently.

"I am responsible for my conduct only to my own Government," said Canning.

"We understand fully the rights and privileges of a foreign Minister,"

---

the Spanish forces captured him and put him in dungeons, first at Fortress San Juan de Ulloa in the harbor of Vera Cruz, then at Ceuta (North Africa). At the instance of the United States Government he was belatedly released. His ideas and experiences appeared in his *Memoirs of the Mexican Revolution* (Philadelphia, 1820), extracts of which appeared in the *National Intelligencer* in January and February 1821.

The Spanish officials at first confused him with another American adventurer, Dr. John Hamilton Robinson.

[18] *Memoirs*, VI, 243–4. January 26, 1821.

Adams assured him, "and mean that you should enjoy them. But we also know the right of every Government receiving a foreign Minister to judge of the propriety of his conduct. . . . My own opinion is that the best mode of treating [the subject] would be in writing."

Canning cooled down. He was in no position to make a written protest. He had no instructions on the matter. "For my part," he finally said, "I am willing to forget all that has now passed."

"I neither ask nor promise to forget," said Adams.

"Do you refuse to confer further on the subject?"

"No."

"Will you appoint a time for that purpose?"

"Now."

Canning was too excited to continue. They agreed to meet the next day at one o'clock. Adams told the President what had passed. Monroe backed him up. "Be perfectly explicit," he directed, "as to our claim of right, and equally so in denying the right of Great Britain to contest it."[19]

Canning's hot temper puzzled the Secretary. Perhaps the British Government, to dissolve dissension at home, was trying to pick a quarrel with the United States on the North West Coast as Pitt had done with Spain at Nootka Sound in 1790.[20]

The following afternoon when Stratford came into the State Department at five minutes to one, he was almost fit to be tied. Adams was busy when the Minister arrived. Presently the Secretary was able to receive him. Stratford tried to keep cool. He took out his watch. "I am forty minutes faster than the clock here," he observed.

The State Department clock struck one.

Adams said nothing.

Canning pulled a copy of the *National Intelligencer* out of his pocket. It contained a full account of Floyd's Report and Floyd's bill.

"This, I presume," he said, controlling himself with obvious effort, "leaves no question of the propriety of my application to you!"

When Adams had discussed Floyd's Report with the President it had seemed a tissue of errors and abortive reasoning. But a protest from the diplomatic representative of a foreign power on something said in Congress evoked a different reaction from the Secretary of State. Promptly and vigorously he defended the Report. The peppery interchange that ensued will remain one of the most quoted passages of John Quincy Adams's imperishable *Memoirs:*

"Suppose, sir," the Secretary assumed, "that Mr. Rush should be present at a debate in the House of Commons, and should hear a member in the course of a speech say something about the expediency of sending a regiment of troops to the Shetland Islands, or a new colony to New South Wales; suppose another member of Parliament should publish in a newspaper a letter recommending the same project; and suppose Mr. Rush

[19] *Memoirs,* V, 248–9. [20] *Memoirs,* V, 184; *Writings,* VII, 67–8.

should then go to Lord Castlereagh and formally allege those two facts as his motives for demanding whether the British Government had any such intentions; and, if answered that very probably they might, he should assume an imperious and tragical tone of surprise and talk about a violation of treaties: how do you think it would be received?"

"*Now* I understand you," replied Canning, "and can account for what has passed. Your answer is perfectly explicit. But do you consider the cases parallel?"

"So far as any question of right is concerned," Adams asserted, "perfectly parallel."

"Have you," replied Canning, "any *claim* to the Shetland Islands or New South Wales?"

"Have you any *claim*," the Secretary inquired, "to the mouth of Columbia River?"

"Why, do you not *know* that we have a claim?"

"I do not *know* what you claim nor what you do not claim. You claim India; you claim Africa; you claim — "

"Perhaps," Canning interposed, "a piece of the moon."

"No," Adams admitted, "I have not heard that you claim exclusively any part of the moon; but there is not a spot on *this* habitable globe that I could affirm you do not claim; and there is none which you may not claim with as much color of right as you can have to Columbia River or its mouth."

"And how far would you consider," asked the British Minister, "this exclusion of right to extend?"

"To all the shores of the South Sea," Adams responded, doubtless thinking of the Antarctic islands. "We know of no right that you have there."

"Suppose," Canning suggested, "Great Britain should undertake to make a settlement there, would you object to it?"

"I have no doubt we should."

"But, surely," said Canning, "proof was made at the negotiation of the Convention of October, 1818, of the claims of Great Britain, and their existence is recognized in it."

"There was no proof," declared Adams, coming back to the Continent of North America, "made of any claim, nor, to my knowledge, any discussion of claim. The boundary to the Stony Mountains was defined; westward of them Great Britain had no settlement whatever. We had one at the mouth of the Columbia, which, having been broken up during the war, was solemnly restored to us by the British Government, in fulfilment of a stipulation in the treaty of peace. We stipulated in the Convention that the ports and places on the Pacific Ocean should be open to both parties for ten years, and, taking all these transactions together, we certainly did suppose that the British Government had come to the conclusion that there would be neither policy nor profit in cavilling with us about territory on this North American continent."

"And in this," Canning asked, "you include our northern provinces on this continent?"

"No," said Adams, "there the boundary is marked, and we have no disposition to encroach upon it. Keep what is yours, but leave the rest of this continent to us."

"But this affects the rights of Russia and of Spain," Canning objected.

"Russia and Spain," replied Adams, "are the guardians of their own rights. Have you, Mr. Canning, any right to speak in their name?"

"Why, sir," the British Minister declared, "I can assure you that Great Britain is in very close alliance with them."

"Yes, sir, Great Britain has strong allies; we know that very well," said Adams, "but they have not authorized you to speak for them."

"And do you wish me," asked Canning, in a tone highly incensed, "*to report to my Government* what you have now said to me?"

"Sir, you may report to your Government just what you please. Report to them, if you think proper, every word that I have said to you, not only now, but at any time, or that I ever shall say, provided you report nothing but the truth, as I have no doubt you will."

"I thank you for the addition of that opinion," replied the British Minister tartly.

"I have no doubt you will report nothing but the truth, and shall not, by anticipation, admit any suspicion to the contrary. . . . If you meant to make a Falkland Island or Nootka Sound affair of it, I thought it best the discussion should be in writing, which would not be liable to misapprehension." [21]

Canning emerged from the interview disturbed, crestfallen, and upset. He had followed assiduously Castlereagh's instructions to cultivate Adams's friendship. He considered himself on intimate and even confidential terms with the redoubtable Secretary, only to meet this "ill humour" and "irascibility." He reported the conversation to the Foreign Office in a dispatch of eighteen pages of official foolscap plus one separate unnumbered ciphered communication and an additional private letter.[22] His account agrees substantially with Adams's version in fact if not in so much detail. Even the characterizations by each diplomat of the other's manner are similar in tone. Canning's description of Adams's vehemence matches Adams's portrayal of Canning's arrogance. Canning thought Adams "determined," "acrimonious," "impatient," and "rude," just as Adams believed Canning to be "vehement," "peremptory," "loud," and "passionate."

Stratford Canning's reluctance to make any written remonstrance had given John Quincy Adams the measure of British policy: "They are anxious to prevent our acquiring a firm footing on the shores of the South Sea,

[21] *Memoirs*, V, 249–53.

[22] Stratford Canning to Castlereagh, No. 3, Washington, January 28, 1821, and separate (in cipher), Washington, January 30, 1821; and private to Joseph Planta, February 6, 1821. PRO, F.O., 5, Vol. CLVII.

and yet they dare not take a fixed, unequivocal stand against it."[23] In other words, it was a bluff.

The British Government wisely allowed this stormy interview to slide into oblivion. It remained there until the publication of Adams's *Memoirs* half a century later. Castlereagh commended Stratford Canning's zeal, but took pains to check it. The Treaty of 1818, he reminded, reserved the rights of both parties for future discussion.[24]

If the dispute over the North West Coast had been left to the United States and Great Britain to settle between them, there would have been no immediate controversy. Great Britain, enjoying the advantage of actual occupation, was willing to let well enough alone. Monroe's Government did not care to challenge the British position until the tide of settlement was ready to flow in sufficient volume over the mountains and down the Columbia River. That seemed a long time off in 1821, probably more so to an Adams than to a Benton. But the United States and Great Britain were not the only powers interested in the region. Floyd's Report and bill stirred another Government into activity and thus touched off the three-cornered controversy on that distant shore of the Continent.

4

Ever since John Quincy Adams's mission to St. Petersburg the Russian-American Company had worried about the competition of American navigators and traders on the North West Coast. In vain Count Rumiantzov had tried to adjust the situation, both with Secretary of State Monroe in Washington and with Minister Adams on the banks of the Neva. It had been impossible to get the United States to agree that its citizens should not trade with the Indians on the coast claimed by Russia. To have done so would have been to recognize Russia's sovereignty there, as Adams had pointed out. Rumiantzov on his part had been unwilling to accept any boundary north of the Columbia. So the matter had rested. The two Governments had too much in common during Napoleon's campaign and afterward to bother about that distant stretch of rock and water.

23 *Memoirs,* V, 261.

24 "It is not the King's intention that you should renew the discussions with the American Govt. relative to the territory bordering upon the Columbia, without His Mj's special instructions. Upon referring to the 3rd. article of the treaty signed in London in 1818, you will perceive that the only arrangement proposed to be effectuated by that instrument was a mutual right of intercourse with the settlement of either state upon the waters of the Pacifick: — The rights of both parties were saved for subsequent adjustment, but no attempt was made either to determine those rights, to define what *might* be regarded as the existing state of occupation, or to preclude either party from forming new settlements within the disputed territory during the period, vizt. 10 years, for which the privilege of mutual intercourse was covenanted." Castlereagh to S. Canning, April 10, 1821. PRO, F.O., 5, Vol. CLVI. See also Katherine B. Judson: "The British Side of the Restoration of Fort Astoria," *Ore. Hist. Quar.,* XX (1919), 329.

Meanwhile American competition continued. The Yankee traders' gunpowder and whisky were ruining Russia's hold on the Indians of the Coast. By 1821 the "Bostonese" had greatly depleted the sea otters below 51°.[25] They were infiltrating into the bays and inlets above that latitude, threatening the extinction of those interesting amphibians, not to mention the fur seals. They were undermining the Russian-American Company and its base on Baranof Island, at New Archangel, or Sitka, N.L. 57° 04′. When the Russian Government heard of the new movement in the American Congress to settle the Columbia River, it took immediate steps to conserve the remaining fur preserves along the still bountiful northern shores.

The Czar issued a ukase of September 4/16, 1821 granting exclusively to Russian subjects the pursuits of commerce, whaling, and fishery, and all other industry on the North West Coast of America from Bering Straits south to 51° N.L., and also from the Aleutian Islands to the eastern coast of Siberia, as well as along the Kurile Islands from Bering Straits to the island of Urup. It shut all foreigners out from those coasts on both sides of the Pacific. Under pain of capture and confiscation it prohibited any foreign ship to approach within less than one hundred Italian miles of the designated coasts and islands "belonging to Russia," except in case of distress from heavy gales or want of provisions. Even in such contingencies the decree forbade all trade and barter between a foreign merchant ship and people in the employ of the Company, or with the natives along the Coast or its islands.[26] To enforce the order against trespassers the Russian Admiralty sent out a ship-of-war. A separate ukase of September 13/25, 1821 renewed the charter and monopoly of the Russian-American Company, extending it south to 51°.[27]

Neither the United States nor Great Britain had ever conceded Russia's right to territorial sovereignty as far south as 51°. For that matter, neither had recognized Russian sovereignty as far south as 55° N.L., southern limit of the hunting and trading monopoly that the Czar "by right of possession by Russia" had granted in 1799 to the Russian-American Company "operating under our highest protection." Citizens and subjects of the United States and Great Britain as well as of Spain and of other nations had been hunting, fishing, and trading on the North West Coast as far as 60° N.L. for years before the charter of the Russian-American Company.

25 William Sturgis to James Lloyd, Boston, May 13, 1820. Monroe Papers, New York Public Library. See also Sturgis's unsigned article in *North American Review,* XV (October 1822), 390. Adele Ogden has published a study of *The California Sea Otter Trade, 1784–1848* in University of California Publications in History, Vol. XXVI (Berkeley, 1941), which shows a small trade still left in Mexican California as late as 1840.

26 *ASPFR,* IV, 851–64. The ukase and accompanying diplomatic correspondence are also printed in *Alaska Boundary Tribunal Proceedings,* 58th Cong., 2d Sess., Sen. Doc. 162, II, 25–93.

27 See Map 6.

John Quincy Adams had never admitted Russia's title to any territory at all on the *Continent* of North America, as distinct from the island trading factories (he closed his eyes to Fort Ross in California, now that it was no longer [since the Transcontinental Treaty] within territory claimed by the United States). Much less could the United States or Great Britain accept the arbitrary expansion of Russian territorial waters a hundred miles out from the mainland. Even Great Britain revolted against such a pretension of flagrant usurpation of the high seas. The ukase confirmed what Prevost's confidential dispatch from the Columbia had suggested in 1818 and Floyd's public Report to Congress had declared in 1821: the danger of Russian enterprise and encroachment. A stroke of the Czar's pen threatened to extinguish one of Massachusetts's most profitable industries.

As soon as Congress convened in December 1821 John Floyd reopened his campaign for the occupation of the Columbia River. He got another special committee appointed to consider the subject, with himself chairman and Francis Baylies of Massachusetts and John Scott of Missouri as the two other members. Then he put a resolution through the House of Representatives requesting the Secretary of the Navy to estimate the cost of transporting artillery to the North West Coast. It would cost $25,000, replied the Secretary of the Navy; actually, Floyd told the House, cannon could go out there in ballast. On January 18, 1822 Floyd's committee brought in the Report of the year before,[28] word for word. They accompanied it with another bill, like that of the previous year, for the occupation of the Columbia River and the reorganization of the United States Indian service.

At the same time Floyd also brought forward personally a resolution requesting the President to communicate to the House all the correspondence relating to the Treaty of Ghent together with the protocol of the negotiations. The bill just reported to the House, he explained, contemplated a very considerable change in intercourse with the Indian tribes of the West. It appeared, by a report of the Secretary of War made the day before on the administration of Indian affairs, that "our European neighbors" exercised a great influence over the natives in that quarter. The correspondence between the Commissioners at Ghent had embraced this subject. It was desirable that the House should have *the whole* of it.[29] The

[28] House Rept. No. 18, 17th Cong., 1st Sess.

[29] January 17, 1822. *Annals of Congress,* 17th Cong., 1st Sess., 1821–2, I, 529, 733, 744. A number of scholars, E. G. Bourne, Lester B. Shippee, and Verne Blue, have reviewed various aspects of Floyd's campaign, in *Ore. Hist. Quar.,* VI (1905), 255–75; XIX (1918), 111–33, 189–214; XXIII (1922), 193–219. Charles H. Carey: *History of Oregon* (Portland, 1922), was the only one to couple Floyd's interest in the North West Coast with his effort to discredit Adams's diplomatic record. Judge Carey would appear to have been mistaken in suggesting that Adams's characterization of Floyd's original Report was due to the latter's call for the remaining papers relating to the Treaty of Ghent. It was on January 18, 1821 that Adams described the first Floyd

House adopted the resolution with an amendment adding the words: "which in his [the President's] opinion, it may not be improper to disclose."

John Quincy Adams saw the implication of the resolution, particularly the addition of words calling for the *protocols* of the conferences at Ghent as well as the diplomatic correspondence describing them. The actual protocols registered word for word all proposals back and forth between the American and British delegations as they drafted the treaty articles. The dispatches of the Commissioners had narrated the progress of the negotiation much more summarily. Only someone intimate with the negotiations at Ghent, presumably a fellow Commissioner, could have been aware of this distinction.

So far Floyd had been directing his aim principally at Great Britain – and at the Secretary of State who had permitted that power to get a lodgment so dangerous to American sovereignty in the West and North West. The Czar's ukase of 1821 brought back into view another target – Russia. On February 16, 1822 Floyd carried a resolution requesting information from the President whether any foreign government had laid claim to any part of the territory of the United States on the Pacific Ocean.[30]

Floyd's agitation and the Czar's ukase made the Monroe Administration take more immediate notice of the North West Coast. They could no longer afford to overlook this direct challenge by Russia to sovereignty over a portion of the high seas, as well as the North American Continent. To let the fur trade perish by default might weaken the political support of New England. To countenance the territorial claims of Britain or of Russia to the Coast might turn the West against Monroe – and Adams. Under the circumstances the Secretary of State was obliged to say something to the Czar's Government right away. What he said was gentle, very gentle. American friendship for Russia could be just as obstinate as Russian friendship for the United States.

The President was surprised, so Adams notified Poletica, at Russia's assertion of a territorial claim as far south as 51° N.L. The relations of the United States with His Imperial Majesty had always been of the most friendly character. It was the earnest desire of the Government to keep them so. But it had been expected that before any such claims were asserted a definition of boundaries "on this Continent" would be arranged by treaty. To exclude the vessels of the United States beyond the ordinary territorial jurisdiction had excited still greater surprise. Mildly Adams asked Poletica whether he could justify the regulations under the laws and usages of nations.

Poletica in a long reply immediately attempted to do so. The United

---

Report as a "tissue of errors, in fact and abortive reasoning." Floyd did not call for the papers relating to the Treaty of Ghent until a year later.

[30] *Annals of Congress,* ibid., I, 1073.

States, he said, had inherited Spain's claim by the Treaty of 1821. It had no better title than that. And Spain never claimed any farther north than 60°. The United States had settled with Spain at 42° N.L. Fifty-one degrees, which Russia now set up as the southern limit of her possessions, was a good "median point" between the two extremes of Spain's old claim. As to the maritime features of the decree, the Russian Government had not been able by pacific means to stop the "illicit" trade of American citizens in arms and ammunition with the natives in the "Russian possessions in America"; now it would have to use more rigorous measures. As a matter of fact, Poletica said, Russia, which held both shores of the North Pacific Ocean, the east as far south as 51°, the west as far south as 45°, would really be entitled to declare the waters of that ocean to be a closed sea north of a line between those two coastal points. But the Czar's Government preferred to assert only its "essential rights," without taking advantage of "localities."

Adams responded temperately. The President was persuaded, he declared, that American citizens would remain unmolested in the prosecution of their lawful commerce and that no effect would be given to an interdiction manifestly incompatible with their right.

It would be "imprudent," Poletica insisted, for American citizens to attempt to trade north of 51° on land or sea. The Russian Government would maintain the rights of the Russian-American Company in their absolute integrity. But any explanation that the United States cared to make to the Emperor would be received in the most friendly and consequently in the most conciliatory disposition.[31]

There was another reason for Adams to talk gently and go slow with Russia. At that moment the Czar was sitting in arbitration on the Anglo-American controversy concerning slaves deported after the Peace of Ghent. It would not be diplomatic to provoke the arbitrator by raising a dispute with him before he had handed down his award. Fortunately the arbitration was out of the way by the time the Secretary of State could bring up the new territorial issue at St. Petersburg. The Czar announced his decision, April 22, 1822, in favor of the United States.

The Secretary of State phrased his protest to the Russian Government so as to appeal to traditional Russian-American collaboration for the Freedom of the Seas. In the Pacific, he suggested, Russia was outstripping the arbitrary doctrines of Britain herself. He directed Middleton to make it distinctly understood, albeit in the most amicable manner possible, that the United States could not for one moment acquiesce in the new imperial regulations. It would never admit that they could in any manner impair its right or those of its citizens.[32]

Middleton's importunities together with similar remonstrance by the

[31] *ASPFR*, IV, 861–4.

[32] JQA to Middleton, No. 12, Washington, May 13, 1822. DS, *Instructions, U.S. Ministers*, IX, 121–3.

British Minister at St. Petersburg, Sir Charles Bagot,[33] induced the Czar's Government to send out naval orders not to apply the hundred-mile rule "too strictly." Speedily the ukase became a dead letter. Responding to the blunt objections of the Duke of Wellington at Verona and Adams's bland insinuations in Washington, Russia separately invited the United States and Great Britain to negotiate at St. Petersburg a final treaty settlement of the controversy.

Floyd's agitation had forced John Quincy Adams to take a stand on the North West Coast before he would have preferred to do so.

5

Certainly there could be no public advantage in raking over the diplomatic correspondence of the Treaty of Ghent and bringing to light differences of opinion that had been expressed within the deliberations of the American delegation before they jointly and unanimously presented their demands to the enemy. The Mississippi Question was ended. The Indian Question had disappeared. The Convention of October 20, 1818 had set the Fishery Question at rest. Time had resolved these controversies favorably to the United States. Therefore why not let them lie forever quiet and peaceful?

Obviously Floyd with his resolution asking for the protocols of Ghent was aiming at more than one bird. Clearly other people had helped him load his Western blunderbuss and had pointed out the game. Ratification of the Transcontinental Treaty accompanied by a complete annulment of the Spanish land grants had dampened the ammunition of John Quincy Adams's adversaries, but now they had found a new charge of political gunpowder. Here was a chance to bring their rival down before he should rise too high. A plot was shaping to show that the Massachusetts diplomatist, who had done more than any statesman since Jefferson to advance his country's boundaries westward, was consistently unfriendly to Western interests.

Certainly somebody who knew very intimately the diplomatic record of Ghent was seeking to prove that John Quincy Adams had been willing to trade away the navigation of the Mississippi in order to secure the fishery liberty for New England, and that he had been willing to let Great Britain get into the Indian country below the northern frontier. That somebody, Adams came to believe, was Henry Clay. Jonathan Russell, Clay's and Adams's old colleague at Ghent, had just entered Congress from Mas-

[33] Middleton to JQA, No. 23, St. Petersburg, August 8, 1822. *Alaska Tribunal,* II, 42–6. "Sir Charles Bagot called a few days since. I inquired what his Government had done in the matter. He said they had *protested,* but there the matter rested. 'I suppose *we* must let the matter die away, provided they will consent to leave the Ukase a dead letter. We need not insist that this man [Alexander I] shall eat his words,' etc. verbatim. Pray burn this scrap." Middleton to JQA, Private. *Most Confidential.* St. Petersburg, 8/20 August 1822. Adams MSS.

sachusetts. It must have been Russell, Adams thought, who inspired Floyd to put through the resolution calling for all the documents leading up to the signature of the Treaty of Ghent.

When the Commissioners had signed the Treaty of Peace at Ghent, they hastily summarized their recent negotiations in their dispatch of the next morning, December 25, 1814. In their understandable hurry to rush the news to Washington they did not take the time to copy the full record of their conversations and protocols since October 31, date of their last dispatch. The Senate relied on their earlier summary correspondence and had ratified the treaty immediately upon receiving it. Thus it was that the last weeks of the full record had never been made public. Among the still unpublished documents in the archives of the Department of State was the separate communication of Jonathan Russell to the Secretary of State (then James Monroe), of December 25, 1814, mentioned in an earlier chapter.[34] This was the letter in which Russell reserved to himself the privilege of a later personal dispatch to explain why he had not favored the proposal made to the British plenipotentiaries, and rejected by them, to continue to British subjects the navigation of the Mississippi in return for the perpetuation of the fishery liberty to American citizens.

When putting together the documents for the President to send in to the House of Representatives in answer to their recent call Secretary Adams wondered whether this letter ought to be communicated. Technically it was not one of the papers *leading to* the treaty, which the resolution had called for. Strictly speaking, Russell had written it *after* the signature of the treaty. Yet most likely it was the very piece that the supporters of the resolution most wanted. If Adams should exclude it, he might be accused of trying to hide something. Therefore he asked Russell, in a conversation at the former's own residence, whether he would prefer to have it submitted.

Russell was not sure. It might be a private letter, he said. He went over to the Department to take a look at it. While there he leafed through the whole record of the Ghent negotiations. His eyes fell on Secretary Monroe's original instructions to the Commissioners of April 15, 1813. They had been put on their guard against renewing Jay's Treaty of 1794,[35] or allowing the North West Company and British traders to carry on trade with the Indian tribes within American limits, as had taken place during the war years, with pernicious effects.

[34] See above, p. 219.

[35] The so-designated permanent articles of Jay's Treaty of 1794 had granted to British subjects the free navigation of the Mississippi "from its source to the sea." Further, it had allowed American citizens and British subjects and Indians dwelling on either side of the boundary freely to pass and repass by land or inland navigation into the respective territories and countries of the two parties (excepting the country within the limits of the Hudson's Bay Company), and to navigate all the lakes, rivers, and waters thereof, and freely to carry on trade and commerce with each other. The War of 1812, of course, had put an end to Jay's Treaty.

Russell asked, and received, permission to make a copy of these early instructions. He paid no attention to later instructions of October 19, 1814 (received at Ghent November 24) which had canceled the original injunction and allowed the Commissioners to accept the *status quo ante bellum*. It had not been until the arrival of those October instructions that Clay and Russell reluctantly put their signatures to the majority's proposal of December 1, 1814 offering the navigation of the Mississippi for the fisheries.

After refreshing his memory at the Department's archives, Russell told Daniel Brent, Chief Clerk, that it was all right, so far as he was concerned, to send in his Christmas 1814 letter to Congress along with the documents leading up to the signature of the treaty. He reminded Brent that there was another, later letter of his to Monroe that he wanted to have sent in too – the one anticipated in that of December 25.

This was the first Adams had known of the existence of the second letter. It was not in the Department files. He told Russell so. Actually Russell had dispatched it from Paris on February 11, 1815, as a private letter to Secretary Monroe.

Having secured Russell's approval for communication of his private letter of December 25, 1814, the Secretary of State had it copied along with the other pieces to be sent in to Congress. The President handed in the papers on February 23, 1822. The House ordered the message and accompanying documents to lie on the table, meanwhile to be printed. Two months later (April 19, 1822) it passed another resolution of Floyd's, suggested by Russell.[36] It requested the President, "if not injurious to the public good," to send in the second Russell letter, of February 11, 1815 – that is, "any letter or communication which may have been received from Jonathan Russell . . . after the signature of that treaty."

Knowing that there was no such letter in the Department files, Daniel Brent, acting on his own initiative and without Adams's instructions, but with his subsequent approval, went to Russell's lodgings and asked him whether he could and would furnish the Department a copy of the letter. Russell said yes, his daughter had recently transmitted him the draft of the letter. He would provide a copy. Mark it a duplicate rather than a copy, suggested Brent, doubtless with an eye to completing the Department files. Russell said he would do so. He would leave it with President Monroe himself, to whom as Secretary of State he had addressed the epistle from Paris on February 11, 1815.

[36] Russell later denied that he "procured" Floyd to bring up this resolution, as Adams charged.

What happened was that Floyd had asked Russell for a copy of the letter and he had refused to give him one. The only way to get it, said Russell, was to call for it specifically. If Russell had not "procured" Floyd to bring in the resolution, he had certainly suggested it in this way. Statements of Daniel Brent and John Bailey, Chief Clerk and Clerk respectively in the Department of State, July 10, 1822. *The Duplicate Letters, the Fisheries and the Mississippi*, post cit., pp. 154–8.

Already Russell had prepared a copy of the letter. Two days later he left at the Department — not with the President — a "duplicate." He had scratched off the word "copy" and marked it "duplicate," as Brent had suggested. This made it look as though he was restoring to the files of the Department of State a letter that had unaccountably disappeared from them. He took pains not to mark the "duplicate" as *private*, as he had labeled the document that Monroe had actually received in 1815.

Adams read carefully through the "duplicate." It was a long, sophistical defense of Clay and Russell's first stand against offering the navigation of the Mississippi for the fisheries. Russell's rebuttal of Adams's argument at Ghent on the indefeasibility of the fishery liberty would have done credit to the enemy negotiators themselves. This was the same Russell who had joined Clay and the other Commissioners December 1, 1814 in a unanimous offer of the Mississippi navigation for the fisheries, fortunately rejected by the British plenipotentiaries.

As John Quincy Adams read over the remarkable paper, his eye hit on some questionable passages that looked as though they had been written since 1815, even since 1818, perhaps in 1822, possibly just a day or two before. Interpolated into the transcript was a copy of the instructions of 1813, which Russell had recently secured from the Department archives. There followed a sentence accusing the Commissioners of having violated those instructions by offering to continue the navigation of the Mississippi in return for continuance of the fisheries. On the other hand there was no mention of the instructions of October 19, 1814, which had released the Commissioners from the earlier injunction. There were also some suspicious paragraphs at the end of the paper. Great Britain, said Russell, writing supposedly on February 11, 1815 from Paris, had expected to reconquer New Orleans and therefore obtain the navigation of the Mississippi for nothing. That is why he had counseled against yielding the Mississippi for the fisheries. "If she [Great Britain] be disappointed in her views on Louisiana," Russell represented himself to have written to Monroe on February 11, 1815, "and *I trust to God and the valour of the West she will be*,[37] I shall not be surprised if, hereafter, she grant us the fishery privilege, which cost her absolutely nothing, without any extravagant equivalent."

It is always easy to express a trust in God, at least rhetorically. Interpolating in 1822, it was also easy for Russell to have a well-justified faith in the valor of the West to protect the Mississippi, since Andrew Jackson's victory over the British invaders was long since a fact of history.[38] Again in his interpolations, Russell had correctly divined *ex post facto* that the United States would confirm the fisheries in the treaty of October 20, 1818 without any extravagant equivalent. All this to prove to his country-

[37] Italics inserted.

[38] Writing from Paris on February 11, 1815, however, Russell could hardly have known, before the days of cable or radio, of the Battle of New Orleans the previous January 8.

men how right he and Clay had been in opposing the proposition of Gallatin, Bayard, and Adams on December 1, 1814 to yield the navigation of the Mississippi for the fisheries. And how the West would have suffered if the British had accepted that careless offer espoused by Adams! Already in 1819 John Quincy Adams had signed away Texas in the Spanish Treaty. In 1822 the same man was still Secretary of State. Now this person was about to let Oregon go by default too. How could such a statesman be relied on to protect the destinies of the West? Such was the impression Russell wished to convey.

"Trust in God and the valour of the West," indeed! With paleographical instinct Adams turned to the President. Perchance Russell's original letter from Paris of February 11, 1815 was a private one, to be located in Monroe's personal files. The President looked and found it. Adams's practiced eye eagerly scanned the original and the "duplicate." Sure enough, Russell had brought these new passages into the 1822 alleged duplicate of his 1815 letter. He had also touched up the latter document in other places to make it favorable to Clay and himself and pejorative to Adams and the majority of the Ghent Commission.

The Secretary of State was an old hand at comparing texts. He had done it many times before signing treaties. He went over the two documents word for word, letter for letter, comma for comma. Including the major interpolations and the prophetic addenda, there were 172 variations!

Except for the extraordinary interpolations, most of the differences were of no significance. They were such as were to be expected in handwritten copies. But amid the understandable variations of punctuation and word order Russell had deliberately introduced at least one important small change – from *I* to *we* – to attribute to the whole Commission, instead of himself alone, a low opinion of the fisheries.

John Quincy Adams must have leaned back in his chair and breathed a sigh of relief. He had found his own defense. As he ran his thumb testingly along the sharp edge of the weapon that his clumsy enemy had placed in his hands he must have mused on the fallibility of human contrivance. Straightway he set about drawing up a report on the "duplicate letter" for the President to communicate to the House of Representatives. He arranged Russell's original and his duplicate of February 11, 1815, side by side, the 172 variations italicized and numbered. He added some not too temperate remarks of his own on the spurious passages, together with sarcastic observations on the author's remarkable gifts of prophecy. From the authentic record of the historic negotiations at Ghent, Adams defended at length the position taken by the majority of the Commissioners on the navigation of the Mississippi and the fisheries. It was easy to point out that Russell himself, the remonstrant of 1822, had signed the offer of December 1, 1814 along with Clay and all the others. Why at this late date was he taking such pains to explain his position and argue the former enemy's case?

Adams personally confronted his former associate with the detected imposture, also with the instructions of October 19, 1814, which had finally permitted the Peace Commissioners to sign a treaty, if necessary, on the basis of the *status quo ante bellum.*

Russell flushed and then turned pale as he realized the significance of the record.

"I have no recollection of the receipt of this letter of October 19, 1814," he asserted. Yet he had just been consulting the archives of the negotiation in the Department of State, including the several instructions to the Commissioners. "Do you think the 'status ante bellum' necessarily included the right of the British to navigate the Mississippi?"

"You are at liberty to make an argument upon that matter," Adams replied. "But it is impossible for me to doubt that the passage you cite [the instructions of April 13, 1813] had been cancelled."

"If you recollect that," admitted Russell, "there can be no question about it. I can assure you," he hastened to add, "I have not acted in this case in concert with your enemies, and I have never written or published a word against you in the newspapers. I have acted from no motive of hostility against you."

It was all too transparent. Russell's words meant nothing.

"Mr. Russell," replied Adams curtly, "I wish not to enquire into your motives. Henceforth, as a public man, if, upon any occasion whatever, I can serve either you or your constituents, it will afford me as much pleasure as if nothing had ever occurred between us; but of private and individual intercourse, the less there is between us from this time forward the more agreeable it will be to me."

"I wish you well," was Russell's only reply as he left the office.[39]

Russell immediately went to the President. He made it apparent to Monroe that he was no longer anxious for the publication of his "duplicate" letter.

The Chief Executive was anxious not to stir up any further commentary on an international issue long since settled so happily. He preferred to keep out of all election squabbles. Looking in Olympian detachment from the White House, he preferred to shelve the whole wretched controversy. He wanted simply to tell the House of Representatives that no such document was to be found in the Department files.

"It is impossible that the fact will not become notorious," the Secretary warned him. "It cannot but appear that it is known to you from my report."

"*Your* report!" retorted Monroe sharply and angrily. "'Tis *my* report. It is no report at all until I have accepted it."

The two men were closest to a quarrel that they ever got in their seven years as President and Secretary of State. Adams insisted. His reputation,

[39] *Memoirs,* V, 505–7. April 29, 1822.

his career were at stake. "I ask no favor," he told Monroe, "nothing but a hearing." [40]

On May 4, 1822 the President transmitted to the House of Representatives a report of the Secretary of State saying that no such letter as requested could be found *in the Department,* but that Mr. Russell had furnished what purported to be a duplicate. Later, said Monroe, he had found the original letter in his own personal papers. Mr. Russell's duplicate, continued the President, communicated a difference of opinion between Mr. Russell and his colleagues at Ghent regarding certain questions since satisfactorily adjusted by treaty. Those colleagues who survived would be entitled to reply. Mr. Adams, in particular, had requested that the letter be sent in to the House, together with some remarks of his own. The President had therefore decided it would be improper to communicate the document, unless the House, aware of all the circumstances, should insist further. Monroe was warning Floyd's friends in Congress that if they still insisted on having the letter they would also get a reply from Adams.

Russell set out for Massachusetts May 5, confident that under the new circumstances Floyd would not renew his call for the letter. On his way home he stopped at Philadelphia long enough to put into the hands of John Quincy Adams's journalist friend Robert Walsh, Jr., still another version of his now famous letter of February 11, 1815. Walsh published it in his *National Gazette,* May 10, 1822, together with supporting editorial remarks obviously furnished by Russell. This "triplicate," as John Quincy Adams called it, was not marked *private* like the original. The author, now knowing that the President had the original in his possession, stripped the "triplicate" of the grosser excrescences that Adams had detected in the "duplicate." It looks as though Russell was trying to publish a putatively authentic text while at the same time desperately hoping that the document altered at Washington would never see the light of day. Even the Philadelphia "triplicate" was not a true copy. Carelessly or designedly, the author left in it some of the smaller interpolations of the "duplicate."

The Seventeenth Congress was now approaching adjournment. As Russell expected, friend Floyd made no move to call for the letter when the House of Representatives received the President's communication of May 4. But the implacable John Quincy Adams would not allow the matter to rest so comfortably for his opponents. He went out of his way to let his acquaintances on Capitol Hill know he thought the letter ought to be published. One of them, Timothy Fuller of Massachusetts, presented a resolution calling upon the President for the document.

Floyd now reversed his position. He opposed the call. It was apparent, he said, that there had been nothing in the Ghent papers about the Columbia River. That was all he had wanted to know. He would not press

[40] *Memoirs,* V, 504–9. April 29–30, 1822.

the President any further. Nevertheless the House passed Fuller's resolution, May 7, without a tallied vote. The President immediately sent in his communication, with John Quincy Adams's Remarks as originally prepared, pruned of three or four harsh expressions. It included the original and "duplicate" letters of February 15, 1815, set in deadly parallel columns.

Next day, May 8, Congress adjourned without the House of Representatives having given orders for the printing of the report. But the whole subject had become public. The *National Intelligencer* printed the documents, doubtless provided by Adams, in its issues of May 21, 22, 23, 1822. Honest Robert Walsh reprinted them in his *National Gazette* of May 25, calling attention to the variation of texts between the "triplicate" and the "duplicate" and between the "duplicate" and the original. "We may remark at once," the editor hastened to add, "that so far as regards the proposal to allow the British the free navigation of the Mississippi, Mr. Adams has placed his conduct and views beyond the reach of calumny and apprehension for the future."

Arrived home in Mendon, Massachusetts, Jonathan Russell tried to climb out of the political pit he had dug for his old colleague. In a long letter to the Boston *Patriot* of June 27, 1822 he endeavored to account for the discrepancies in the several versions of his now notorious private letter to James Monroe. He defended himself against the "infirmities of Mr. Adams's temper," against the "unprovoked and unprincipled attack" upon his character. He complained that Mr. Adams had directed his remarks against the "duplicate" instead of the original, as if he, Russell, had not written both!

As to the Ghent negotiations, he pointed out that a majority of the Commissioners had first voted, as early as November 5, 1814,[41] against Clay and himself, to offer the Mississippi for the fisheries. This was *before* they received (on November 24) their instructions of October 19, 1814, releasing them from the earlier ones of April 15, 1813. Only Henry Clay's refusal to sign such an offer had held back the majority at that earlier moment,[42] when it *would* have violated their instructions. Russell starkly denied that he had ever "procured" Floyd to make a call for his letter of February 11, 1815. He reasserted his contention, in difference with Mr. Adams, that the War of 1812 had destroyed the fishery privilege – the old British argument. He still thought the Mississippi more valuable than the fisheries. If the British had accepted the Commission's offer of December 1, he said, it would have afforded to British smugglers and British emissaries a "pernicious facility" to defraud the United States revenue laws and to excite the Indians, the very thing against which their first instructions had warned the plenipotentiaries.

That was Russell's strongest point. That was what he wanted to impress

[41] See above, p. 213. [42] Ibid.

upon the country: that Henry Clay and he had championed the integrity of the Mississippi, perhaps too feebly, alas, but at least they had championed it; that the majority, led on almost traitorously by John Quincy Adams, had preferred to barter the navigation of the river to the British; that only the ineptitude of the enemy had saved the West from betrayal by Adams, Bayard, and Gallatin. Russell boasted that his larger national patriotism had withstood the narrow bias of local interests in opposing the sell-out of the West.[43]

The defense was just plausible enough, in its turn of phrase and twist of argument, to impress the casual reader. It started a train of newspaper comment in his favor. Two Clay journals in the West, the *Kentucky Reporter* of Lexington and the *Argus of Western America* of Frankfort, promptly belled off a hue and cry against the Secretary of State and pretender to the Presidency. The supporters of Clay, Calhoun, and Crawford were delighted at the spectacle of two eminent citizens of Massachusetts cudgeling each other. The controversy degenerated into a real political fight, no holds barred. It raised so much dust that for the time being most people lost sight of the North West Coast altogether.

Adams still felt that he was on trial for his character before his country. Russell had delivered himself into his opponent's hands securely enough; but the Secretary feared that Clay, for whom Russell had performed the part of "jackal," would profit from the prejudice stirred up in the West and South. "There is hardly a passion in the human heart but that is arrayed against me . . . a single false step would ruin me."[44] So John Quincy Adams brooded on his fifty-fifth birthday as he planned his campaign of self-vindication.

He fell on Russell and smote him hip and thigh. Two articles in the *National Intelligencer* of July 17 and August 7 simply tore apart the treacherous assailant. Floyd now tried to absolve himself from any collusion with Russell. Adams replied effectively to him too.[45]

All through the roasting Washington summer John Quincy Adams labored with his pen, denying himself the usual annual vacation visit to his aged father in Quincy, forgoing even a trip with Louisa on their twenty-fifth wedding anniversary. He prepared three long commentaries on the relative value of the fisheries and the navigation of the Mississippi. These later strictures got to be too voluminous for weary newspaper readers. The indefatigable Secretary therefore put them into a documentary history of the whole controversy, which he privately published in September 1822

[43] "As a citizen of Massachusetts, I believed that justice and sound policy required that we should treat fairly and liberally every other section of the Union, and to do as we would be done by. As a Minister of the United States, it was my duty to act impartially towards the great whole."

[44] *Memoirs,* VI, 43–4.

[45] Richmond *Enquirer,* August 27, 1822. Adams's reply in *National Intelligencer,* August 31, 1822.

under the title of *The Duplicate Letters, the Fisheries and the Mississippi.*[46]

It was the final word on the subject. Russell wilted. He did not reply. He could not. His adversary had finished him. Even Henry Clay expressed regret for the discrepancy in the two versions of Russell's private letter to Monroe. The Kentuckian, in temporary retirement from politics at Lexington, refused to side with his vanquished supporter. He sought rather to give the impression of neutrality in the regrettable controversy between his two colleagues at Ghent over an issue safely dead. Some day, he said, when nobody's motives could be misrepresented, he might publish a work of his own on the Ghent negotiations, to clear up any inaccuracies, no doubt unintentional, in Mr. Adams's publication. This he never did.

As to the Russell letter, Clay said ambiguously: "I had no knowledge of the intentions of the Honorable Mr. Floyd to call for it, nor of the call itself, through the House of Representatives, until I saw it announced in the public prints. Nor had I any knowledge of the subsequent call which was made for the letter of the Honorable Mr. Russell, or the intention to make it, until I derived it through the same channel." [47]

For Clay to say that he had no knowledge of the Honorable Mr. Floyd's "intentions" was not to say that he had not planted the seed in his mind. Floyd had explained that in the winter of 1819–20, when a group of his friends were discussing in his Washington lodgings the Columbia River and the value of the fur trade on our Western rivers, "one of the gentlemen" had remarked that the Mississippi River had been discussed at Ghent, and that from the character of the diplomats engaged in this discussion he might get something useful out of it if he had the correspondence.[48] Who could the gentleman have been but Clay? Russell did not come to Congress until December 1821. Gallatin was in Europe. Bayard was dead.

"Concurring with Mr. Clay that the controversy should never have arisen," Adams answered, "I have only to find consolation in the reflection that from the seedtime of 1814 to the harvest of 1822 the contest was never of my seeking, and that since I have been drawn into it, whatever I have said, or written, or done in it has been *in the face of day and under the responsibility of my name.*" [49]

[46] *The Duplicate Letters, the Fisheries and the Mississippi. Documents Relating to Transactions at the Negotiation of Ghent, Collected and Published by John Quincy Adams, One of the Commissioners of the United States at the Negotiation* (Washington, printed by Davis and Force, Franklin's Head, Pennsylvania Avenue, 1822).

[47] Letter to the *National Intelligencer,* Lexington, Kentucky, November 16, 1822, reprinted in *Memoirs,* VI, 116–18.

[48] Floyd's letter of August 14, 1822, published in the Richmond *Enquirer* of August 27, 1822. *The Duplicate Letters, the Fisheries and the Mississippi,* pp. 243–6.

[49] JQA's letter of December 18, 1822 to the *National Intelligencer. Writings,* VII, 334–5. Italics inserted.

That would hold Clay for a while. Henry Clay would rather be President than right.

Clay's failure to support Russell was the last blow to that unfortunate politician. He was not re-elected to Congress. His embitterment led him to denounce the man whose star he had picked at Ghent to follow. Later, in 1827, Russell allowed a letter of his of October 15, 1815 to Henry Clay, reviling both Gallatin and Adams and their roles at Ghent, to be published as a means of hurting both Clay and Adams.[50]

The joust with the Secretary of State left Russell a broken man. His opponent had little sympathy for him. Upon the death of his onetime colleague Adams noted in his Diary: "He is gone to his account, and was sufficiently punished in this world for his perfidy." [51] For years afterward a new verb lingered in the New England vernacular. To "jonathanrussell" anyone meant to pillory him mercilessly before the bar of public opinion.[52]

Following the publication of *The Duplicate Letters, the Fisheries and the Mississippi,* letters poured in to Adams from all over the Union attesting the complete annihilation of the wretched Russell, expressing contempt for his treachery, both to his colleagues and to his country, and making it clear that no individual, not even a newspaper, North, East, South, or West, would openly support him in his charges. More requests came in for copies of John Quincy Adams's pamphlet than he could supply.

Even old Timothy Pickering, his ancient Essex Junto enemy, most recently hurt when Adams had so sorely twisted the British Lion's tail on the Fourth of July, could not find a good word to say for Russell. "Sir," that worthy exploded at a Philadelphia dinner table, "I regard Mr. Russell as a man fairly *done over*. Mr. Adams will be exalted in the estimation of New England by his Remarks, and ought to be exalted in any part of the world. He has nearly effaced with me the impression of his Fourth of July oration." Pickering pointedly declared that Adams had shown Russell to be "a fool and a rascal." Someone observed: "We must see Russell's defense." "He can make none," the old Essexman retorted, "and if he attempts it, so much the worse for him." [53]

[50] MHS *Proceedings*, XLIV (1910–11), 304–22.

[51] *Memoirs*, IX, 3.

[52] For this controversy see in addition to Adams's own *Memoirs*, V and VI, and his above-mentioned pamphlet on the *Duplicate Letters, the Fisheries and the Mississippi*, the following: Updyke: *Diplomacy of the War of 1812*, pp. 377–82; Stewart Mitchell's sketch of Jonathan Russell in *Dictionary of American Biography*, and *Annals of Congress*, 17th Cong., 1st Sess., 1821–2, I, 722, 733, 734, 1617, 1619, 1790, 1871, 1891, 2057, 2170, 2194, *et passim*. This volume of the *Annals* omits the proceedings of the House of Representatives from March 11 to May 8, 1822. Adams had a great deal of correspondence on the subject at the time. Most of it is printed in his *Writings*, VI.

[53] Robert Walsh to JQA, Philadelphia, June 3, 1822. Walsh was present at the dinner. H. A. S. Dearborn to JQA, Boston, August 13, 1822, reports that a gentleman who also was at the dinner told him about the conversation. Adams MSS.

The insidious electioneering trick, calculated to slay Adams as a presidential candidate, had the opposite effect. It made the public all the more aware of his diplomatic record and the worthiness of his pretensions for still higher office than that of Secretary of State. The attacks upon his public career thus proved to be heaven-sent gifts. They enabled a man who exasperated his friends because he would make no move for the Presidency to keep himself before the people nevertheless as a candidate, while he himself turned to public business, including the Oregon Question.

CHAPTER XXV
The Oregon Question
(1822–1827)

> I think a government by federation will be found practicable upon a territory as extensive as this continent, and that the tendency of our popular sentiment is increasingly toward Union.
>
> JOHN QUINCY ADAMS
> ON OREGON IN THE CABINET, MARCH 9, 1824

RUSSIA had been one of the considerations that had impelled President Monroe to follow John Quincy Adams into an independent expression of the Monroe Doctrine in Washington instead of taking the advice of Thomas Jefferson and James Madison to issue a joint Anglo-American manifesto in London. He hoped that Russia, to prevent any harmony in policy between the United States and Great Britain, might recede from her own desire for legitimacy in the New World.[1] He was anxious to keep Russia in balance against Great Britain. The Czar on his part wanted to continue the United States as an offset against the same power. Nobody could be more aware of this desirable equilibrium than John Quincy Adams with his background of experience in Russia and in England. It is now time to show how he tried to use this balance to protect American sovereignty in Oregon.

1

The dust of the Adams-Russell bout had barely settled when voices rose from New England in defense of American claims to the North West Coast if not to the Columbia River country. First heard was William Sturgis, famous Boston merchant, son-in-law of John Quincy Adams's old friend Judge John Davis. Nobody knew the Coast and the commerce of the Pacific better than Captain "Bill" Sturgis. He had gone out in 1798 as a sixteen-year-old boy in the ship *Eliza,*[2] owned by Thomas Handasyd

[1] "We know that Russia dreads a connection between the United States and Great Britain, or harmony in policy moving on our ground," he wrote to Jefferson, explaining the message of December 2, 1823. "The apprehension that unless she [Russia] retreats, that effect may be produced, may be a motive with her for retreating." *Writings of Monroe,* VI, 345.

[2] Samuel Eliot Morison: *The Maritime History of Massachusetts* (Boston, 1921),

Perkins, one of John Quincy Adams's old cronies of the Crackbrain Club. A member of the firm of Bryant & Sturgis, the captain had made a fortune in the China trade.

Floyd's bill of 1822 for the occupation of the "borders of the Columbia" and a settlement there impelled Sturgis to write a series of articles in the Boston *Daily Advertiser* (January 28, 31, February 6, 20, 1822) stressing the value of the North West Coast as far up as 60° and deprecating the idea of any American "settlement" on the river. The best place for a settlement, said Sturgis, if settlement there must be, was not in the estuary of the Columbia behind a sandbar that excluded all ships of more than four hundred tons, nor for that matter anywhere along any part of the "iron-bound" shore subject to the broad sweep of the Pacific. It was rather at Port Discovery, on Fuca Strait, seventy-five miles in from the open ocean near the entrance to Puget Sound. A settlement there, better a military and naval post, would give access to the beautiful inland waters north and south: to the Gulf of Georgia with its innumerable islands and inlets, and to the protected reaches of Puget Sound and thence south to the Cowlitz River country, back door to the north bank of the Columbia. It was unwise to encourage a settlement of American emigrants, Sturgis concluded, if only because the region was too remote even to form an integral part of the Union. But it was good policy to occupy the North West Coast to prevent it falling into the hands of some other power, Russia or Great Britain.

Sturgis repeated and elaborated his ideas in an unsigned article entitled "Examination of the Russian Claims to the North West Coast" which appeared in the October 1822 number of the *North American Review*.[3] The essay buttressed with a wealth of historical documentation and personal observation the protests that John Quincy Adams had made earlier in the year in his mild expostulations to Poletica against the Russian ukase. The commerce and navigation of the whole Coast, argued this experienced trader, had been the common right of all nations for nearly forty years. Both British [4] and American Governments subsequently made use of this notable article in their respective disputes with Russia.

p. 69. Charles G. Loring: "Memoir on the Hon. William Sturgis," MHS *Proc.*, VII (1863–4), 420–73.

[3] When the Oregon Question was at its climax in 1845 Sturgis worked over his earlier articles and elaborated them into three lectures in 1845–6. See William Sturgis: *The Oregon Question. Substance of a Lecture before the Mercantile Library Association,* delivered January 22, 1845 (Boston: Jordan, Swift & Wiley; 1845). Summaries of these lectures are printed in *Old South Leaflets,* No. 219, and edited by F. W. Howay in *British Columbia Hist. Quar.*, VIII (No. 1, January 1944), 11–27. In his lectures and in a correspondence with George Bancroft, Polk's Secretary of the Navy, in which he urged settlement of the Oregon Question on the basis of 49°, westward to Georgian Bay, Sturgis recommended leaving Vancouver Island to Great Britain.

[4] Stratford Canning to Bathurst, separate, Washington, November 21, 1822. PRO, F.O., 5, Vol. CLXIX.

Boston's entry into the debate quickened the interest of the Secretary of State in the North West Coast while Floyd's campaign kept it fixed also on the Columbia River.

When Congress convened again in December 1822 for the short session, Floyd again introduced his bill for the occupation of the Columbia River, only now he called it the Oregon. By this time the sonorous words of William Cullen Bryant's poem *Thanatopsis* were reverberating across the Continent to those continuous woods where rolled the Oregon and heard no sound save his own dashings. The boy poet had got the name from reading Jonathan Carver's *Travels in the Interior of North America* (London, 1778) and applied it to the Columbia River. Carver in his day had picked up the word – as *Origon* – from Major John Rogers, who had written of the *Ouragon* River beyond the Rocky Mountains.[5] After Bryant's *Thanatopsis* the North West Coast was part of the larger Oregon Question.

The Oregon bill went immediately to the Committee of the Whole. A brisk debate followed. Floyd in an eloquent speech described the American "ball of Empire" rolling westward. He appealed not only to Western expansionist sentiment but also to Eastern commercial and maritime interests, particularly those of John Quincy Adams's own state.

"The settlement on the Oregon as contemplated in this bill," declared the frontier enthusiast, "connecting the trade of that river and coast with the Missouri and Mississippi, is to open a mine of wealth to shipping interests and the Western country surpassing the hopes even of avarice itself. It consists principally of things which will purchase the manufactures and products of China at a better profit than gold or silver, and if that attention is bestowed upon the country to which its value and position entitle it, it will yield a profit, producing more wealth to the nation than all the shipments which have in one year been made to Canton from the United States."

From Boston, he might have said.

But Oregon was more than a matter of local significance to only one section or to one constituency. It concerned the whole Union in the largest way. "All contemplate with joy," Floyd declaimed, "the period when these states shall extend to the Rocky Mountains. Why not then to the Pacific Ocean?"[6]

Francis Baylies, from Taunton, Massachusetts, constituency of New Bedford and Nantucket whalers so dear to the heart of old John Adams,

[5] T. C. Elliott: "The Strange Case of Jonathan Carver and the Name Oregon," "The Origin of the Name Oregon," and "Jonathan Carver's Source for the Name Oregon," in *Oregon Hist. Quar.*, XXI (No. 4, December 1920), 341–68, XXII (No. 2, June 1921), 91–115, XXIII (No. 1, March 1922), 53–69. Elliott suggests plausibly that Rogers may have heard some French *voyageur* speak of *le pays* or *la rivière d'ouragan,* the country or river of the big winds.

[6] *Annals of Congress,* 17th Cong., 2d Sess., 1822–3, p. 408.

seconded Floyd's arguments. He stressed the fishing, the whaling and maritime fur trade, the sea-otters and the sea-elephants, the growing interests of his state on the North West Coast and in the whole Pacific Ocean. He too went farther than local sectional interests. Baylies's speeches on Oregon envisioned a Republic fronting on the two oceans united by an Isthmian canal. His peroration must have warmed the blood of any believer in Manifest Destiny:

"If we reach the Rocky Mountains, we should be unwise did we not pass the narrow space which separates the mountains from the ocean, to secure advantages far greater than the existing advantages of all the country between the Mississippi and the mountains. Gentlemen are talking of natural boundaries. Sir, our natural boundary is the Pacific Ocean. The swelling tide of our population must and will roll on until that mighty ocean interposes its waters, and limits our territorial empire. Then, with two oceans washing our shores, the commercial wealth of the world is ours, and imagination can hardly conceive the greatness, the grandeur, and the power that await us."[7]

From sea to sea, a Continental Republic, divided in the poet's fancy only by the coursing fall of day!

John Quincy Adams could hardly gainsay words like these. Had not he himself said, back in 1811, that the whole of North America appeared to be destined by divine Providence to be peopled by one nation, speaking one language, accustomed to one general system of religious and political principles, leading one way of life, which ought to be associated in one Federal Union?[8] Certainly Oregon was a foothold for Manifest Destiny on the Pacific Coast.

The opposition replied that Oregon was too far away, too distant even to be a part of the Union. It was an "imaginary Eden." It would drain off unprofitably the manpower and economy of the East. They repeated what the Essex Junto once had said about Louisiana when John Quincy Adams entered the Senate.

All of the speakers skirted around the real difficulty: danger of a collision with British establishments already planted in Oregon. From anything said aloud on the floor of the House one would scarcely imagine that Great Britain seriously disputed the claim of the United States to that region.[9] In the final vote representatives of the manufacturing and frontier sections united against commercial and small farming constituencies to defeat the first Oregon bill, 100 to 61.[10] Obviously the nation, in-

[7] *Annals of Congress*, 17th Cong., 2d Sess., 1821–2, pp. 414–22, 682–3.

[8] Above, p. 182.

[9] Stratford Canning to George Canning, No. 25, Washington, February 25, 1823. PRO, F.O., 5, Vol. CLXXV. Senator Benton did not soft-pedal the British issue when he introduced a bill in the upper house to enable the President to take possession of the territories "belonging to the United States on the North West Coast." But Benton's bill never reached a vote in the Senate.

[10] Ambler, op. cit., 69.

cluding the West, was not ready for a show-down with Great Britain in the free-and-open country beyond the mountains.

Benton, Floyd, and Russell had tried to destroy Adams in Western favor by showing that eight years previously at Ghent he had been willing to allow Britain the free navigation of the Mississippi in return for a share in the North Atlantic coastal fisheries. Adams had downed his two lesser adversaries on this dead issue. Now Benton took a new tack. He charged that more recently the Secretary of State had let Britain into the Oregon country south of 49° in return for securing a continuation of the fisheries liberty in the Treaty of 1818, signed at London three years after Ghent.

"The sovereignty of the Columbia," Benton declared to his fellow Senators, "was substituted for the navigation of the Mississippi, as the price of the important privilege of taking and curing fish on the desert shores of Labrador and Newfoundland." [11]

Already Britain had established herself in Oregon, Benton reminded the Senate. She was disputing American sovereignty. If something were not done to undo Adams's diplomatic blunders, she would remain in possession in 1828 when the Treaty of October 20, 1818 would come to the end of its term.

The persistent attacks of Western spokesmen upon his diplomatic record, and the maritime interests of Massachusetts on the North West Coast, were pushing John Quincy Adams into the Oregon Question much earlier than he would have chosen, particularly in reference to Great Britain. More protests against the Russian monopoly came in from his own section. In May 1823 President Monroe received a letter from Senator James Lloyd of Boston [12] — Adams's Federalist successor in 1808, now returned to the Senate again from Massachusetts — appealing for the protection of American rights on the North West Coast. It was a graphic description of the fur trade from that region to China via the Sandwich (Hawaiian) Islands, and of the sea-elephant and whale fisheries of the waters of California and the North Pacific. Lloyd explained how the Yankee traders employed Kodiak Indians to catch the fur-seals and sea-otters in the inlets of the Aleutian Islands and along the North West Coast between 51° and 60° north latitude. He stressed the importance of preserving an access to those coasts and waters for prosecution of the fur trade and refreshment of the whalers. Enclosed was a letter from Captain Sturgis with a reference to his unsigned article in the *North American Review,* on which Lloyd, himself a trader to those parts, had relied heavily in drawing up his statement.

The President turned these papers over to Adams to answer. The Sec-

[11] *Annals of Congress,* 17th Cong., 2d Sess., 1821–2, p. 251. February 17, 1823. See also Benton's *Selections.*

[12] James Lloyd to James Monroe, Boston, May 16, 1823, enclosing William Sturgis to James Lloyd, Boston, May 13, 1823. Monroe Papers, New York Public Library.

retary responded in a letter to Lloyd fully accepting the necessity of an early settlement with Russia and the indispensability of upholding against Great Britain the claims of the United States to the entire Columbia River basin, and a government establishment there, preferably at the mouth of the river. In closing the epistle he took occasion to repeat his Non-Colonization Principle.[13]

Lloyd, old Junto Federalist and anti-Louisiana man that he was, was more interested in the North West Coast than in the interior country of Oregon. He had his eyes on the golden profits of the maritime fur trade, which the Russian ukase threatened to destroy. The "Bostonese" did not care so much about the Columbia River, he wrote back to Adams. It was too difficult for an ocean-going ship to get over the "appalling" bar into the estuary, he explained, quoting Sturgis. Would it not be better to join with England for the time being against Russian pretensions and postpone a costly establishment on the Columbia until the inevitable flood of pio-

[13] "The transactions in which we have been concerned relating to the North West Coast, and the Pacific Ocean, since the close of our late war with Great Britain," Adams continued in this letter to his former senatorial rival, "have led me, some time since, to the conclusion, that we ought to have, without delay, a permanently established post there, adequate to ensure us, by actual possession, the line of coast to which we are entitled. And *I am not aware of any spot, so well suited to that object as the settlement already formed at the mouth of the Columbia River.* According to our most recent maps, the waters of the Columbia extend southward to latitude 41, or 42, and northward, at least, to 50 or 51. Possession, at the mouth of the river, gives the right to a line of coast parallel, or nearly so, to these extremes; and that of the waters through all their interior wanderings, till they almost mingle their sources with those of the Missouri, Platte and Arkansas. I know of no other position upon the coast which promises like advantages, or would afford support so indisputable to our claims. Observing, however, in your letter to the President, a doubt intimated, whether the mouth of the Columbia River offers inducement sufficient for locating the permanent establishment there, I now write principally to request a further development of your views in this respect.

"I am aware that the depth of water at the mouth of the Columbia may not be sufficient to serve as a port for ships of war, perhaps even of the burden of our large frigates [this had been Sturgis's objection to the Columbia]. I think they would not however be excluded from it, and I am not aware of any other place upon that coast which would yield a safer, or more accessible harbour. But the object of occupying the port would not be confined to that purpose. The right of the River, and to all the territories washed by its water would be an object more important, and more urgent for the early adoption of the measure. We know of no other river extending from the Western Ocean far into the interior, the mouth of which is north of the Red River of California [Colorado River of the West.]

"I do not see that the 100 Italian miles of close sea will form a stubborn knot in the negotiation. But what right has Russia to *any* colonial footing on the *continent* of North America? Has she any that we are bound to recognize? And is it not time for the American *Nations* to inform the sovereigns of Europe, that the American continents are no longer open to the settlement of new European colonies?" JQA to James Lloyd, S.U.S. [Senator United States], Boston. Private. Washington, July 15, 1823. Adams MSS. Italics inserted in first paragraph only.

neer settlers poured over the Rocky Mountains into the Columbia Valley to reinforce the title of the United States south of 48°? [14]

The Secretary of State also would have preferred to postpone the question if only the Western politicians, the Bentons and the Floyds, had left him alone. When they forced the issue, he took over their arguments and those of Baylies and made them measures of the Monroe Administration.

2

John Quincy Adams's strategy on the North West Coast was to play Great Britain and Russia against each other to the advantage of the United States. He relied on a sufficient community of Anglo-American interests to resist Russian advances from the north and on the obstinate friendship of Russia to relieve the weight of British pressure on the Columbia River basin. Already he had suggested to Stratford Canning that their two Governments reach a common understanding before negotiating with Russia; perhaps they could then work out a tripartite treaty, if the Foreign Office would but send appropriate instructions to Charles Bagot, British Minister in St. Petersburg. "The United States have no territorial claim *of their own* as high as the 51st degree of latitude," Adams told Stratford, "although we dispute the extent of those advanced by Russia and oppose the right of that power to exclude our citizens from trading with the native inhabitants of those regions over which the sovereignty of Russia has been for the first time asserted by the late edict of the Emperor, and most particularly the extravagant Russian pretension to prohibit the approach of foreign vessels within a hundred Italian miles of the coast." [15]

[14] Cape Flattery, at the entrance of the Strait of Juan de Fuca, leading on to Puget Sound, between 48° and 49°, was the goal post of Lloyd's boundary concepts. He was little interested in the mainland east of Puget Sound.

"If then our title to the extent of territory we claim in the Pacific, and which now has become well defined, and ascertained, is not to be disputed by any other power; and if the appalling, and as they appear to me, immediate disadvantages of the mouth of the Columbia, as a national location, either for a commercial port, or a naval depot, are as great as they are represented, I confess, Sir, I have thought it much better, to await the certain, and not tardy march, of our pioneer settlers, to find its own way, at its own, and not distant period, to the Rocky Mountains, and from thence naturally to progress along the watercourses of the Columbia, to the borders of the Pacific, rather than prematurely to subject the nation, to a heavy expense in forming an establishment, too remote for its speedy and effective controul, where according to the propensities of the human heart, power might for no inconsiderable time supersede right, and which, if it did not eventually, create difficulties, instead of preventing them, might be long a puny, and abortive, rather than a respectable and useful establishment." James Lloyd to JQA, Boston, July 28, 1823. Monroe Papers, New York Public Library.

[15] Stratford Canning to George Canning, No. 47, Washington, May 3, 1823. Received June 12. PRO, F.O., 5, Vol. CLXXVI. Italics inserted. The conversation took place on April 30, 1823. JQA's Diary records merely: "Mr. Canning. Two hours con-

The Secretary of State was hinting that if Great Britain did not co-operate with the United States against the territorial as well as the maritime pretensions of Russia she might get caught in a Russian-American vise closed at 51°, the southern limit of Russian claims. Great Britain, on her part, sought to widen her Pacific frontage at the expense of both the United States and Russia.

It was Britain's design to advance on the north to 58°, southernmost limit of the island posts of the Russian-American Company, and on the south to the Columbia River, location of the Pacific headquarters of the Hudson's Bay Company. It was less important, however, to push northward against Russia than to thrust southward against the United States. To the north lay the bleak fog-bound shores of Unalaska, more convenient to Yankee navigators than to French-Canadian *voyageurs* of the Hudson's Bay Company. To the south lay the rich Oregon country, Fort Vancouver and the interior trading posts of the Company from Lake Windermere to Fort Hall. That vast span of Inland Empire protected the overland communications from the northern headwaters of the Columbia down the Saskatchewan River to the Great Lakes and Montreal, or to York Factory on Hudson's Bay itself.

It did not need a John Quincy Adams to sense the fact that British territorial claims weighed more heavily southward on Oregon than northward on Russian-America. To preserve the maritime fur trade of the North West Coast, Adams had proposed British collaboration against Russia. His next move to save Oregon was by seeking Russian collaboration against Great Britain.

Adams's instructions to Middleton and to Rush on the subject of the Columbia River and the North West Coast, both dated July 22, 1823, attest the degree to which Benton and Floyd on the one hand and Sturgis and Lloyd on the other — that is to say, the West and the East separately acting — had impelled him into diplomatic action against Russia and Great Britain.[16]

To Russia, Adams proposed a ten-year bilateral treaty confirming reciprocally a freedom of navigation and fisheries and trading on the Coast in places not already occupied, and agreeing that no American citizens would henceforth make settlements north of 55°, nor Russian subjects south of that degree.[17] Perhaps, he suggested, these terms could be worked into a tripartite convention, among the United States, Great Britain, and Russia.[18]

versation. Left a minute of several of his notes to be answered, and spoke of the slave trade, of the Piracies, of the Russian North West Coast pretensions, and of the prospects of war in Europe."

16 See note 18 below, as italicized.

17 *Alaska Tribunal,* II, 51–2.

18 "The right of the United States from the forty-second to the forty-ninth parallel of latitude on the Pacific Ocean we consider as unquestionable," Adams advised Middleton, "being founded, first, on the acquisition by the treaty of February 22, 1819, of

The Secretary was disposed to accept the line of 55° as a boundary between American and Russian *pretensions*, provided Russia recognized the right of American traders and fishermen to frequent the unsettled portions of the Coast north of that point. That meant really *the whole mainland itself*, for Russian settlements were still limited to Sitka and Kodiak Island. A reciprocal right of Russian subjects to frequent that part of the Coast claimed by the United States south of 55°, even south of 49°, did not amount to much in fact, as Adams knew. Russia had practically no merchant ships in those waters. To supply the depot at Sitka the Russian-American Company had to charter American ships.[19] This would leave the United States free to delimit its own claims as already established before the announcement of the Non-Colonization Principle, which had prohibited any *further* European colonization on the Continent of North America.

If Russia could be sure of 55°, the old limits of the Russian-American Company's charter, perhaps then she would not crowd Britain too far down against the United States.

Adams hoped that if Great Britain were eased of Russian pressure north of say 55° N.L., she would herself press less heavily south of 51°, at any rate south of 49°. He affected to believe that since the restoration of Fort George in 1818 British diplomacy had abandoned all claims to the Columbia River. He recalled that Stratford Canning had never handed in the written protest against American sovereignty there "intimated" in the provocative "piece-of-the-moon" altercations of January 1822. What he now proposed to Great Britain was a three-power treaty making the unsettled places of the North West Coast free and open to the fishermen and traders of the United States, Great Britain, and Russia, but drawing boundary lines beyond which neither power would permit its citizens or subjects *to make settlements:* Russia, none south of 55°; Great Britain none north of 55° nor south of 51°; the United States none north of 51°.

His reason for fixing on 51° as the most northern claim of the United States was not because that had been the southern boundary of the Czar's latest pretensions; it was also, and principally, because it appeared according to the latest maps available (like Melish's) to embrace the entire Columbia basin and thus would afford a complete communication between all the headwaters of the Missouri and those of the Columbia. Having secured to the United States, at best, the whole Columbia River basin

all the rights of Spain; second, by the discovery of the Columbia River, first from sea at its mouth, and then by land by Lewis and Clark; and third, by the settlement at its mouth in 1811. This territory is to the United States of an importance which no possession in North America can be of to any European nation, *not only as it is but the continuity of their possessions from the Atlantic to the Pacific Ocean, but as it offers their inhabitants the means of establishing hereafter water communications from the one to the other.*" Instructions of JQA to Henry Middleton, No. 16. Department of State, July 22, 1823. *Alaska Tribunal,* II, 47–52. *ASPFR,* V, 436–48. Italics inserted.

[19] See Map 6.

up to 51°, he would leave it to King George IV to keep the Russian bear fenced out north of 55°.

The stipulation of 51° as the northern boundary of the United States left a certain margin for bargaining. As a last recourse to settle the question with England, Adams was willing to extend the British-American boundary line of 49° from the Rocky Mountains straight through to the Pacific Coast.

Reciprocal freedom for citizens and subjects of both powers to fish and trade on all unsettled parts of the Coast, explained the Secretary of State for the benefit of Richard Rush, was nothing more than Great Britain herself had insisted on, vis-à-vis Spain, in the Nootka Sound Convention of 1790. Since then the independence of the Latin-American nations (not yet recognized in London) had put an end to those former rights of Great Britain – and of the United States as well – south of 42° N.L., the northern boundary of Mexico. No foreign nation could any longer have the right of access to the shores of those new states. There might still be claimed a right to frequent the North West Coast, but no system of "colonial exclusion" could prevail there. And the "finger of nature" pointed out that the United States should form establishments there "with views of absolute territorial right and inland communication."

Adams closed his instructions to Rush with a strong statement of the Non-Colonization Principle:

> A necessary consequence of this state of things will be, that the American continents, henceforth, will be no longer subjects of colonization. Occupied by civilized independent nations, they will be accessible to Europeans and to each other on that footing alone, and the Pacific Ocean in every part of it will remain open to the navigation of all nations, in like manner with the Atlantic.
>
> Incidental to the condition of national independence and sovereignty, the rights of interior navigation of their rivers will belong to each of the American nations within its own territories.
>
> The application of colonial principles of exclusion, therefore, cannot be admitted by the United States as lawful upon any part of the North West Coast of America, or as belonging to any European nation. Their own settlements there, when organized as Territorial Governments, will be adapted to the freedom of their own institutions, and, as constituent parts of the Union, be subject to the principles and provisions of their constitution.[20]

Would George Canning accept this new American doctrine, presently to be proclaimed to the world in President Monroe's message of December 2, 1823?

[20] JQA to Richard Rush, No. 70, July 22, 1823. *ASPFR*, V, 447–8.

3

As long as Canning had been seeking American support against any intervention of the Holy Alliance in Latin America – without at the same time recognizing the independence of the new republics – he had been willing to concert with the United States against the excessive maritime pretensions of Russia on the North West Coast. For example, as soon as he heard of John Quincy Adams's suggestion of Anglo-American co-operation in that part of the world, he wrote to Sir Charles Bagot, British Minister in St. Petersburg, what he told Christopher Hughes on the steamboat at Liverpool: such a step would be easy enough; the only question remaining to settle with Russia would be the mode and degree of disavowal necessary to satisfy Great Britain and the United States. As to a territorial demarcation between Great Britain and Russia in North America, Canning declared that he would be satisfied with 57°.[21]

At that moment Britain's Foreign Minister had no notion that Adams, while keeping a British buffer between the United States and Russia on the North West Coast, would presume to set a bound *between Great Britain and Russia* to the north, much less to assert that the whole Continent was no longer to be subject to further colonization. The American Minister in London was prompt to enlighten him on this point at the first opportunity.

Canning summoned Rush to Gloucester House December 17, 1823 to discuss the general negotiations proposed for the settlement of all differences outstanding between the two countries. By then the crisis with France and the Holy Alliance had been ended by the Polignac Memorandum. There was no longer any pressing British need for Anglo-American solidarity.

The Secretary for Foreign Affairs was confined to his room with the gout. Like his predecessor Castlereagh he was wont to receive foreign ministers while lying in bed, after the manner of the Roman Emperor Vespasian or, in a more recent epoch, England's great statesman Lord Chatham.

The first thing he mentioned, deep from the coverlets, was the North West Coast.

"I want to be put in possession of an outline of your views in regard to the North West Coast before preparing my instructions to our Ambassador at St. Petersburg on the same subject."

Rush spread out a map on the bed. Canning raised his head from the pillows. Warily he watched the American Minister trace the territory claimed by the United States.

"Your claim seems much beyond anything England had anticipated," was his only remark. Then they turned to a general conversation. Upon

[21] George Canning to Sir Charles Bagot, July 12, 1823. *Alaska Tribunal*, II, 123–4.

taking his leave Rush left a brief, informal statement of the American claim in writing.

After Rush departed, Canning glanced over the note. It gave him another twinge.

"What is here!" he exclaimed. "Do I read Mr. Rush aright? 'The United States will agree to make no settlement north of 51°, on Great Britain agreeing to make none south of that line.' "

"So far [up to 51°] all is clear," he wrote informally to the American Minister next morning. "The point of contact is touched, and consequently, the point of dispute between the United States and Great Britain; but the memorandum goes on: 'or *north* of 55°.' What can this intend? Our northern question is with Russia, as our southern is with the United States. But do the United States mean to travel *north* to get *between* us and Russia? and do they mean to stipulate against Great Britain, in favour of Russia; or reserve to themselves whatever Russia may not want?"

"It is even so," wrote Rush in reply, carefully following John Quincy Adams's instructions.

To say that it was necessary for the United States to possess the territory up to 51° in order to have all the waters of the Columbia River as well as the North West Coast parallel to it would have made even Castlereagh jump with pain. British pathfinders and fur-traders exclusively had mapped out and exploited the country north of the Columbia-Snake River. British navigators had been the first to discover and enter Puget Sound and to circumnavigate Vancouver Island. The Americans might perhaps have a claim to the lower Columbia and even to the Snake and its tributaries, and to the North West Coast (from their Spanish treaty), but not to the whole Columbia River. Canning was the last man in England to admit that the United States must have all that region just because it wanted it. He had his own eye on the entire course of the Columbia as a minimum boundary for Great Britain.

From his bed of torment Canning wrote another chit to Richard Rush: "Like the wise and wary Dutchman of old times," he said, "I am taking your explanation *ad referendum* and *ad considerandum*."

The gout passed away for the time being, but not the American claims. Meanwhile another blow had fallen on the British Foreign Minister. News of the Monroe Doctrine had reached London.[22]

Canning had an interview with Rush on January 2, 1824. He began the conversation by objecting strongly to any American claim to 51°. "I hope

[22] "On the 12th December Monroe's message was reported in an obscure form, on the 26th and 27th it went broadcast through all Europe." Temperley: *Canning*, p. 121. It is difficult to understand how in the days of sailing ships anything definite about the message could have been known in London only ten days after it was delivered in Washington. Maybe somebody had some previous inside information about the forthcoming message.

you will not urge it," he said to Rush. "Why, it was south of this line that Great Britain had her dispute with Spain about Nootka Sound. How, therefore, can she now yield this point to the United States? I do hope you will not urge it."

Then he turned to the President's message of December 2, 1823, recently arrived in England (December 26), particularly to John Quincy Adams's Non-Colonization Principle. Castlereagh had paid no attention to that extravaganza when Stratford had reported Adams's vehement remarks of January 26, 1821. Canning was another man. "If you have instructions," he observed to Rush, "I wish you would state the precise nature and extent of this principle. I had not been aware of it before. Suppose, for example, that Captain Parry's expedition [in search of the North West Passage from the east, 1819–21] had ended, or that any new British expedition were to end, in the discovery of land proximate to either part of the American continent, north or south, would the United States object to Britain planting a colony there?"

"When such a case arises it may be considered," Rush replied discreetly. "I have no instructions on the principle since it was proclaimed in the message, but I am prepared to support it when the negotiation comes on."

"Well," concluded Canning, "I shall have to address you an official note on the subject before I write to our Ambassador in St. Petersburg; or else I shall have to decline joining with you in the negotiation with Russia on the North West Coast, as you have proposed. I would prefer the latter course, not desiring to bring this part of the Message into discussion at present, as England must necessarily reject it."

A few days later (January 5, 1824) they met again. Canning evidently had been studying President Monroe's message. "As a consequence of the non-colonization principle," he said, "I am still embarrassed in preparing my instructions to Sir Charles Bagot about the North West Coast. I hope you are inclined to let the negotiation proceed separately, without England joining with the United States as your Government contemplated." [23]

The American Minister was entirely willing to let it take that course. He feared Russia would also object to the same Non-Colonization Principle and therefore line up with England against the United States. For this reason he was glad to avoid any preliminary and detailed discussion of so great a principle, against which England had protested *in limine.* He was content to let sleeping dogs lie.

Canning for his part suspected that Adams was trying to gratify Great Britain at the expense of Russia on sea and Russia at the expense of Great Britain on land.[24] This was in large measure true.

[23] Rush's *Residence,* II, 82–8.

[24] G. Canning to C. Bagot, No. 2, Foreign Office, January 15, 1824. See also Canning's "Secret" Memorandum of January 7, 1824, which Bagot, doubtless acting on instructions, showed to Middleton, and which the latter enclosed in his private letter of February 25 (O.S.) to JQA. *Alaska Tribunal,* II, 144–8, 68–9.

4

Negotiations *à deux* proved easy enough in St. Petersburg. Count Nesselrode made no express objection to the Non-Colonization Principle. He got around it by proposing that both parties forgo all discussion of abstract principles and reach a settlement upon the basis of mutual interests. Middleton agreed to do so. The Russian Chancellor then accepted in principle John Quincy Adams's proposed articles, including freedom of the high seas and even the right of American citizens to trade on the *unsettled* parts of the North West Coast north of the line of division, at least for a term of years. These were the principal contentions of the United States.

Nesselrode proposed certain modifications and stipulations on the part of Russia. He readily agreed to the boundary limitation suggested by Adams provided it were drawn at 54° 40′ instead of 55°.[25] This was in order to keep Prince of Wales Island entirely within Russian jurisdiction rather than have the line run across it. The Russian Minister also wanted to prohibit citizens of the United States from trading firearms or firewater to the natives north of 54° 40′. He further sought to alter Article III of Adams's proposed treaty so as to protect Russian claims to Fort Ross in California.[26]

The American proposals having been accepted in principle at the outset, Middleton did the utmost to meet Russian desires. He took it upon himself to take the bound of 54° 40′ instead of 55° as the line beyond which Russia and the United States respectively would not make settlements. In so conceding he could not then know that by leaving all of Prince of Wales Island in the Russian sphere he would be preserving it for the United States later on. Neither Henry Middleton, John Quincy Adams, nor any man then living either in Russia or in North America could look ahead a half-century to the day when Russia would get so tired of Alaska that she would sell it, Aleutian Islands and all, to the United States for almost a song.

Nesselrode in his turn gave up the phraseology designed to protect Russian claims in California: it was not necessary, he decided, since California was not a part of the "North West Coast." Middleton then agreed to prohibit the trade in guns and spirits, provided Russia left *enforcement* of the prohibition to the United States for its own citizens. Finally the American Minister accepted a wording that fixed for ten years the reciprocal right of trade on the unsettled stretches of the whole North West Coast, without unequivocally limiting that right to ten years.

The resulting Convention of April 5/17, 1824, was all that could be desired. Russia gave up her pretension to a *mare clausum* in the North Pacific. She accepted as her boundary with the United States a latitude

[25] See Map 6.

[26] Middleton to JQA, No. 35, St. Petersburg, April 7/19, 1824. *Alaska Tribunal,* II, 52, 73–4, 83, 85.

safely high for the future Continental Republic. She did not insist upon a recognition of Russian sovereignty north of 54° 40′. To use a more recent term, that latitude marked a separation of *spheres of influence* rather than a partition of actual territory. John Quincy Adams could still assert that Russia had no territorial possessions on the Continent of North America. His Non-Colonization Principle was still technically intact.[27]

Russia's concessions to the United States surprised everybody. Bagot had prophesied from St. Petersburg that the Washington Government could never get such a settlement.[28] President Monroe was particularly pleased that Russia, unlike Great Britain, had been willing to sign the treaty despite his promulgation of the Non-Colonization Principle.[29] The Czar's attachment to the United States continued to be "obstinate." John Quincy Adams, with his long Russian experience, had made the most of it.

Although the Russian Government had been in touch with the officials of the Russian-American Company, it signed the convention without finally consulting them. The officers of that corporation after learning of the articles protested because they did not specifically prohibit American vessels from frequenting the Aleutian Islands and the coast of Siberia. They also objected to the American fur trade on the unoccupied coast of America. Baron Tuyll made a perfunctory effort to attach a supplementary note to the pact prohibiting American vessels from frequenting the North West Coast north of 57°.

John Quincy Adams easily talked the Russian Minister out of any such notion. It would have unhinged the whole treaty. If Tuyll insisted on presenting the note, said the Secretary, he would have to reply that the interpretation of treaties lay with the courts and that the executive could not bind the judiciary or the nation. As a matter of fact, Adams added, he intended to send the treaty in to the Senate immediately. It would be a pity to obstruct its ratification with any modification proposed at this late hour. Such a change would really require a new convention. The present one had been an object of great solicitude to both Governments. It had settled a difficult question. It had promoted traditional harmony. It had kept "natural friends" in amity. Let the matter stand, he urged, at least until the treaty got through the Senate, and the time came for the exchange of ratifications. "Then I believe your Court will deem it best that you should not present the note at all. Its apprehensions have been excited by an interest not friendly to the good understanding between the United States and Russia." Adams blandly assured Tuyll that there was really no cause

27 "The Government of Russia has never disputed these positions [Non-Colonization Principle] nor manifested the slightest dissatisfaction at their having been taken." Message of President JQA to the House of Representatives, March 15, 1826.

28 Bagot to G. Canning, No. 48, St. Petersburg, October 17/29, 1823. *Alaska Tribunal,* II, 129–31.

29 *Memoirs,* VI, 403. Monroe to Madison, August 2, October 18, 1824. *Writings of Monroe,* VII, 30–3. Monroe to Samuel Southard, July 31, 1824. Monroe Papers, New York Public Library.

for worry about the article. American merchants would not go to trouble the Russians on the coasts of Siberia, or north of the fifty-seventh parallel of latitude. "*It is wisest not to put such fancies into their heads.*"[30]

Certainly it would not have been wise, since the convention estopped each party from *enforcing*[31] its prohibitions against the citizens or subjects of the other. Tuyll saw the point. He withdrew his representations. The Senate promptly advised and consented to ratification by a vote of 41 to 1.

The lone dissenter was Senator James De Wolf of Rhode Island and Providence Plantations. The reason for his opposition is not known. Senator James Lloyd of Massachusetts privately objected to Adams that prohibition of the liquor trade deprived the Yankee navigators of their "most alluring traffic." He wanted to make ratification contingent upon Great Britain's accepting the same prohibition in a similar treaty with Russia. He also felt that the ten-year term of free trade might be in effect a limitation[32] – as indeed it finally proved to be.[33] But in the end he voted for the convention without reservation. So did Benton of Missouri.

The convention was another Adams victory beyond the reproach of his political adversaries, another forward-looking, western-moving triumph for the veteran diplomatist. When the time came for exchange of ratifications Baron Tuyll signed without further ado.

5

Nesselrode's prompt settlement with the United States at 54° 40′ was advantageous both to Russia and to Great Britain in their contemporaneous but separate negotiations. It enabled Russia to insist more effectively on the point of 54° 40′ as the southernmost limit of her pretensions on the coast against the British demands for 57° 40′, the latitude of Sitka. It made it easy for Great Britain to claim reciprocally for her subjects the right of frequenting the unsettled portions of the whole North West Coast for the purpose of trading with the natives. Before the signature of the Russian-

[30] *Memoirs*, VI, 436–7. Italics inserted. There was an exchange of confidential notes, in French, recording this conversation. Tuyll's is dated December 18/30, 1824. Adams's copy is undated. Adams MSS.

[31] Not until May 19, 1828 did Congress pass a perfunctory law for punishing contraventions of the fifth article of the treaty between the United States and Russia. It provided a penalty of $50 to $200 fine, or 30 days' to six months' imprisonment for selling to the Indians spirituous liquors or firearms or munitions. Jurisdiction over such cases was to be in the Superior Court of the nearest territorial government of the United States. There was at that time no United States territorial government west of the Rocky Mountains.

[32] James Lloyd to JQA, December 25, 1824. Adams MSS.

[33] At the expiration of the ten years the United States maintained that the right still continued, but Russia denied it. The United States maintained its right in theory only. See *Alaska Tribunal*, II, 234–49, and Victor J. Farrar: "The Reopening of the Russian-American Convention of 1824," in *Washington Hist. Quar.*, XI (No. 2, April 1920), 83–8.

American Convention, Canning had been disposed to acknowledge Russia's right to forbid all traffic by foreigners north of her limits once they should be agreed upon. Afterward, however, it could hardly be expected that he would take for British navigators and traders less than what Russia had stipulated for those of any other nation.

Notwithstanding the impulse of the American treaty, Great Britain and Russia were a long time coming to an agreement. The great difficulty, which prolonged the negotiations for a full year, was that of delimiting an overland boundary northward from the latitude of 54° 40′ to the Arctic Ocean.

The Russian negotiators were willing to leave to Great Britain the whole Mackenzie River basin. They did not even insist on extending their claims up to the Rocky Mountains. What they did want was to control all the North West Coast and the myriad islands north of 54° 40′.[34] For this purpose they required a substantial strip or *lisière* of territory on the mainland. The British negotiators on the other hand desired full access to the ocean along the whole coastline of the present Alaska "panhandle." They were willing to leave Prince of Wales Island to Russia, once the United States had done so, but they did not want to see the Hudson's Bay Company's traders excluded from the rich seal rookeries between 54° and 58° N.L. After a long contest the Russian Government secured its modest pretensions in the Treaty of St. Petersburg, February 16/28, 1825, although the *lisière* was not so wide as might have been desired and British subjects secured free navigation of any rivers descending through Russian territory to the Pacific. The Anglo-Russian Convention of 1825 was similar in principle to the Russian-American instrument of the previous year, which paved the way for it – all except for the boundary on the mainland. Here there was a very essential difference: it was a *continental partition.*

The boundary "between the possessions of the high contracting parties upon the coast of the continent and the islands of America to the Northwest" ran north through the channel of Portland Canal "as far as the point on the continent where it strikes the 56th degree of north latitude." From this last mentioned point, the line of demarcation followed the summit of the mountains situated parallel to the coast, as far as the intersection of the 141st degree of west longitude, thence along that meridian to the Frozen Ocean.[35]

The British *possessions,* and the *possessions* which belong to Russia! By

[34] See Map 6.

[35] A separate article provided that whenever the summits of the mountains parallel to the sinuosities of the coast were more than ten marine leagues from the ocean, then the limit between "the British possessions and those which belong to Russia" should "never exceed the distance of ten marine leagues therefrom." Disputes over the interpretation of this article caused the later Alaska boundary controversy between the United States and Great Britain.

The negotiation of the Treaty of St. Petersburg may be followed in the diplomatic documents reproduced from British and Russian archives in *Alaska Tribunal,* I, 13–

MAP 6 *Territorial Claims and Adjustments on the Pacific Coast,* 1818–46

these words Great Britain recognized reciprocally something that the United States had never done: territorial possessions of Russia on the Continent of North America.[36] Between themselves the powers ignored John Quincy Adams's Non-Colonization Principle. It was the first lesion to any of the dicta put forth by President Monroe in his message of December 2, 1823.

Let it be said again that nobody in 1825 by the wildest stretch of imagination ever looked forward to the day, less than half a century away, when these limits would fix the territories not of Russia and Great Britain but rather of the United States and the Dominion of Canada. They remain the present eastern boundary of the Territory of Alaska as determined by the Anglo-American Alaska Boundary Tribunal of 1903.

6

After the Russian treaties of 1824 and 1825 the Oregon Question concerned the United States and Great Britain exclusively. Richard Rush and George Canning had been wrestling with that problem in London following the breakdown of the proposed tripartite negotiations in St. Petersburg. The British Commissioners, Stratford Canning and William Huskisson, took this occasion, on George Canning's express orders,[37] to deny, utterly and explicitly, the validity of the Non-Colonization Principle.[38] They insisted on settling the controversy on the basis of mutual interests, as had the Russians.

Rush had been laboring under serious misapprehension of British intentions. He thought that Canning would not press for anything south of 49° north latitude. He therefore made a stand for 51° while preparing as a last recourse to fall back, under Adams's instructions of July 22, 1823, to 49°. To his surprise his opponents demanded not 49° to the sea but the Columbia River from its mouth to 49°, thence *eastward* along that parallel

231. Stratford Canning, shifted to St. Petersburg after his return from Washington to succeed Bagot, signed for the King; Count Nesselrode and Pierre de Poletica, former Russian Minister to the United States, for the Czar.

[36] Robert Greenhow made this point forcibly in his able *History of Oregon and California* (Boston, 1845), p. 342.

[37] "Adverting to that Declaration [the Non-Colonization Principle, in President Monroe's message of December 2, 1823] . . . it will be advisable for you . . . to give him [the American Plenipotentiary] to understand, that the principle is one which His Majesty's Ministers are prepared to reject in the most unequivocal manner, maintaining, that whatever Right of Colonizing the unappropriated portions of America has hitherto been enjoyed by Great Britain, in common with the other Powers of Europe, may still be exercized in perfect freedom, and without affording the slightest cause of umbrage to the United States." Mr. Secretary [George] Canning to the British Plenipotentiaries [William Huskisson and Stratford Canning], Foreign Office, May 31, 1824. *Papers Relating to the Negotiation in London,* p. 47. Huskisson "Papers Relating to Affairs with America." WRC.

[38] Anna Lane Lingelbach: "Huskisson and the Board of Trade," *AHR,* XLIII (No. 4, July 1938), 769.

to the Rocky Mountains. To accept the American boundary stipulations, Canning told the British Commissioners, would "deprive us in times to come, of the fairest fruits of British enterprise in a region of growing importance." [39] They flatly rejected Rush's counteroffer of extending the line of 49° westward from the Rocky Mountains to the Pacific Ocean. At most Canning was willing to renew the free-and-open occupation article of 1818 for another ten years.[40]

In this first futile round of the negotiations John Quincy Adams and George Canning each had laid down his maximum concession. From then on, the Oregon Question was essentially a dispute for sovereignty over that "triangle" of territory, including Puget Sound, which lies between 49° on the north and the Columbia River on the south and east.[41] One or the other of the powers would have to give ground within that area.

As long as the existing situation continued undisturbed in Oregon, Canning was satisfied. It was all in Britain's favor. But if the United States should take any step to do what Great Britain had already done in the free-and-open country – to organize a rival American fur-trading company, to extend American law over American citizens there, to establish a fortified port – a collision would be imminent. Before this should happen Canning wanted to secure the line of the Columbia. He did not want any real joint occupation. Therefore he invited a renewal of diplomatic discussions, amidst Anglo-American negotiations still lingering on the various other subjects (Freedom of the Seas, impressment, colonial commerce, navigation of the St. Lawrence, northeast boundary, etc.).

7

While the diplomats labored in St. Petersburg and in London to protect American sovereignty over the North West Coast, President Monroe listened to the continued demands of Dr. Floyd for a government settlement on the Columbia River. He showed John Quincy Adams a letter from the Virginia physician to Secretary of War Calhoun asking for the opinion of the Executive on the subject from a military point of view. Now that Oregon had become an Administration measure, as attested by the negotiations on foot in Europe, the President considered the feasibility of sending a special message to Congress recommending the establishment of at least a military post on the Pacific Coast, either at the mouth of the Columbia or on Juan de Fuca Strait, and another on the Yellowstone River as well – the latter project being an old idea of his dating back to 1815. He did not go so far as Rush had urged from London and recommend the stationing of an American frigate out there.

[39] Canning to the British Plenipotentiaries, May 31, 1824, op. cit.

[40] *ASPFR*, V, 553–8. Rush: *Residence*, pp. 250–77.

[41] Frederick Merk: "British Party Politics and the Oregon Question," *AHR*, XXXVII (No. 4, July 1932), 653.

The President read to the Cabinet the draft of his proposed message. It revealed a half-hearted attitude toward the region. While recommending posts for the protection of American claims, it advanced a strong argument against any territorial settlement on the Pacific. Oregon, the President believed, was bound to separate soon from the Union.

"I doubt the expediency or necessity of communicating such an opinion," said John Quincy Adams right away.

Calhoun supported the objection and enlarged upon it.

Southard concurred with them.

Crawford, ill, was not present.

"There will be no separation if we make settlements on the Pacific," said Calhoun.

Adams inclined to the same opinion.

"The passion for aggrandizement is man's paramount law in society," Calhoun went on, "and there is no example in history of the disruption of a nation from itself by voluntary separation."

"There are the tribes of Israel," suggested Adams.

"That is the only exception," the South Carolinian acknowledged.

John C. Calhoun had not yet learned the word *secession.*

Adams recalled Portugal and Spain, Sweden, Denmark, and Norway, but said nothing. His thoughts were fixed on the Union of the United States of America as a Continental Republic stretching from Atlantic to Pacific. He saw the possibility of a group of states out there on the Pacific Coast, states like New England, all in the same Union. At last he spoke out:

"I think a government by federation will be found practicable upon a territory as extensive as this continent, and that the tendency of our popular sentiment is increasingly towards Union."

President Monroe decided not to send in the special message.[42] He waited until his last annual message on the state of the Union, December 7, 1824. Then, after formally announcing the satisfactory treaty with Russia, he submitted to Congress the propriety of establishing a military post at the mouth of the Columbia River, as Adams had urged, together with the maintenance of a frigate there, Rush's recommendation. He said nothing about the doubtful place of that country in the Union.

Floyd immediately brought in his bill again, limited now to the founding of a military post and the creation of a territorial government by the President. This time the House of Representatives passed it, 113 to 57, after striking out the provision for a territorial government; they did not want to entrust that high legislative function to the Executive.[43]

The bill was exactly what the President had called for in his message.

[42] *Memoirs*, VI, 249–51. March 6, 9, 1824.

[43] Shippee, *Oregon Hist. Quar.*, XIX, 124, points out that elimination of this feature was due to reluctance of Congress to endow the Executive with such a power, rather than to fear of international complications.

But the Senate tabled it, 25 to 15, on March 1, 1825. Benton of Missouri, its most eloquent champion, doubted that Oregon would ever be a part of the Union: the "mother Republic" would but plant an infant power beyond the Rockies, strong enough to take care of itself when it reached the age of manhood.[44]

The fact is that since John Quincy Adams had made Oregon an Administration measure the question had lost its immediate efficacy as a political issue. Moreover, the House of Representatives had just elected Adams himself as President of the United States, an Eastern man who believed – in contrast to the Westerner Thomas Hart Benton – that Oregon would one day be a component part of the Union. At this point the organization of this study requires us to anticipate and to follow the Oregon Question through the period of Adams's Presidency, as has been done with the other phases of the general Anglo-American negotiations of 1823–7.

8

President Adams responded readily to Canning's overtures for further discussion of the Oregon Question. An instinctive continentalist, he also needed the political support of the West in order to stay in the White House more than one term. He was anxious to secure Oregon in the northwest and also to buy Texas from Mexico in the southwest. He sent Albert Gallatin to the Court of St. James's to try, among his other tasks, to push the line of 49° – and no less – all the way to the North West Coast. If Great Britain would agree to that line of minimum American continental contentment in the north, John Quincy Adams was willing to concede to British subjects the free navigation of the Columbia from the sea to its source in British territory.[45] He did not really expect Canning to accept 49°. He thought the effect of the offer would be to preserve the peace between the two countries and postpone the issue until the time came when the United States would be able to maintain its claims, if necessary by an appeal to arms.[46]

Before Gallatin reached London, George Canning had perused the report of another "Oregon Committee" of the House of Representatives, presented on May 9, 1825 by Francis Baylies, chairman, in response to President Adams's first annual message. It imputed to Great Britain a studied design to dominate the whole Pacific, future richest ocean of the world's commerce. "What, then, remains to enable her to encompass the

[44] *Register of Debates,* I, 712. March 1, 1825.

[45] Henry Clay to Gallatin, June 19, August 9, 1826, *ASPFR,* VI, 644, 646; Gallatin to Clay, June 29, to JQA, June 30, 1826; JQA to Henry Clay, July 5, 1826. Adams MSS. Greenhow: *Oregon and California,* pp. 346–58; Shippee, op. cit., XIX, 188–214; and Carey, op. cit., pp. 476–81, give full accounts of these negotiations and lead one directly to the sources.

[46] At least so Adams explained twenty years later. *Memoirs,* XII, 221.

globe? Columbia River and De Fuca's Strait! Possessed of these, she will soon plant her standards on every island in the Pacifick Ocean." It all but accused the Adams Administration of negligence. "The indifference of America stimulates the cupidity of Great Britain. Our neglect daily weakens our own claim, and strengthens hers; and the day will soon arrive, when her title to this Territory will be better than ours, unless ours is earnestly and speedily enforced." [47]

The Baylies report was the last sputter in the campaign originally begun by Jonathan Russell and Floyd to alienate the West from supporting John Quincy Adams for President – at least Adams so regarded it.[48]

Canning used the same sort of language to picture American policy that Baylies employed to describe the aims of the British Government.[49] The British Foreign Minister affected to regard the committee report, never adopted by the House of Representatives, as almost tantamount to a declaration of war.[50] "After such language," he informed Lord Liverpool, "it is impossible to suppose that we can tide over the Columbia, or can make to ourselves the illusion that there is any other alternative than either to maintain our claims or to yield them with our eyes wide open." [51]

George Canning seems almost to have fancied that the Americans, particularly John Quincy Adams, had cheated the British Foreign Office by securing from Castlereagh a loyal fulfillment of the plain and simple provision of the Treaty of Ghent. He took it upon himself as a diplomatic tribulation that Castlereagh had allowed Fort George to be surrendered in 1818 without leaving in the written record a producible document to protect British title to the south bank of the Columbia. He regarded it as the first of a series of "compliances with encroachments" pressed on Britain by the "ambitious and overbearing views" of the United States, set on controlling the commerce of the whole Pacific. They had led right up to Adams's extraordinary Non-Colonization Principle, in Monroe's message of December 2, 1823. The duty of British statesmen, Canning had declared to the Prime Minister, was to see that this richest area of gainful enterprise should not be closed to future generations of Englishmen.[52]

It was too late for Canning to rectify his predecessor's alleged blunder. But he instructed Huskisson and Addington, the Commissioners empowered to negotiate with Gallatin, that British interests, and even British honor, required them to stand fast at the Columbia.[53] They summarily rejected Gallatin's final offer of 49° from the Rocky Mountains straight

[47] *House Reports,* No. 213, 19th Cong., 1st Sess., p. 22.

[48] JQA to Gallatin, Washington, March 20, 1827. H. Adams: *Gallatin,* p. 625.

[49] Canning to Liverpool, July 7, 1826. *Official Correspondence of George Canning,* II, 71–5.

[50] Gallatin to H. Clay, No. 30, London, November 27, 1826. *Writings of Gallatin,* II, 343.

[51] July 14, 1826. *Official Correspondence of George Canning,* II, 115.

[52] Canning to Liverpool, July 7, 1826. Ibid., II, 71–5.

[53] Ibid., II, 76–85.

through to the Pacific Ocean. To accept that, they now said, would give up Nootka Sound on Vancouver Island, where Great Britain had risked a war with Spain rather than abandon her claims to the North West Coast.

To secure the line of the Columbia, Canning was willing to make a territorial concession on the Coast north of the river. Gallatin had objected to the Columbia as a boundary for one reason because it would leave the United States without an adequate harbor on the Pacific, because the bar at the mouth of the river made the estuary impracticable as a port. To meet this objection Canning instructed the British Commissioners to offer what is now known as the Olympic Peninsula, west of Admiralty Inlet and Hood's Inlet, including Gray's Harbor on the coast. This would have given to the United States Port Discovery, on Fuca Strait, behind the entrance of Puget Sound, which Sturgis had recommended, and also the waters of the upper part of Hood's Inlet – vermiform appendix to Puget Sound – without any sure way of getting into it. Under Canning's singular proposal Puget Sound proper would have remained entirely British.[54] At the same time a broad belt of British territory north of the Columbia would have separated the proposed enclave from American soil south of the river.

At best Port Discovery could have been only an isolated naval base. There was no overland connection with the United States. It would have been at the mercy of Great Britain by land and sea. It would have been useful only as a port of patrol for the protection and regulation of American fishermen and fur-traders on the North West Coast. As a continental bastion it was worthless, no good even for commerce. Gallatin promptly rejected it. "One inch of ground yielded on the North West Coast," President Adams had warned him, "would be certain to meet the reprobation of the Senate." In the existing temper of the parties all he could do was to adjourn controversies.[55]

Adams could wait, like Canning. The best the diplomats in London could do under the circumstances was to extend indefinitely, by the Convention of August 6, 1827, the free-and-open occupation article of the Convention of 1818, subject to termination at one year's notice. The Senate advised and consented to the ratification of the convention of extension, by a vote of 31 to 7. Benton led a group of Western-minded Senators in opposition. They preferred not to wait. They had wanted to let the Convention of 1818 expire, then negotiate a settlement of the boundaries on the basis of a "separation of interests." [56]

Wisely John Quincy Adams left the Oregon Question to Time the Great Expositor. It seemed scarcely possible to him that any project for the settlement of the North West Coast would get through Congress for at least ten years. Even if it should, the provision for annulment of the conven-

[54] *ASPFR*, VI, 650–76 for the protocols of the conversations, and Gallatin's dispatches describing them.

[55] JQA to Gallatin, Washington, March 20, 1827. H. Adams: *Gallatin*, p. 625.

[56] *Senate Executive Journal*, III, 599, January 15, February 5, 1828.

tion on twelve months' notice made it safe enough to sign in 1827.[57] He could wait for the Oregon pioneers to roll westward in their covered wagons over the Rocky Mountains and down the Columbia Valley.

John Floyd of Virginia came back for a final charge during his last term in Congress. In December 1828 he introduced his last bill for the occupation of the "Oregon River." It provided for extension of American law over American citizens in Oregon, as the act of Parliament of 1821 had put British law over British subjects there, and for the erection of American forts upon the Coast between 42° and 54° 40′. Once more the House of Representatives debated the subject. This time it refused, January 9, 1829, by a vote of 99 to 75, to advance the bill to a third reading. Although there was somewhat of a sectional division, East against West, James K. Polk of Tennessee opposed the bill. The military occupation of Oregon, he said, was sure to provoke a collision with Great Britain.[58]

9

There was no longer much issue in the Oregon Question. Already a Western man had been elected President to succeed Adams. No one could gather political capital by accusing Andrew Jackson of betraying Western interests. Incarnation of the West that he was, Jackson never did a thing for Oregon.

The Oregon Question lay dormant during the Administrations of both Jackson and Van Buren. Then came the Whig President William Henry Harrison, elected in 1840, with his running-mate for Vice President, John Tyler, a Democrat, who succeeded Harrison upon his death to become President of a Whig Administration. Tyler's Secretary of State, Daniel Webster, remained on in the Cabinet after the departure of his Whig colleagues, in order to conclude the British treaty with Lord Ashburton. After attending to that he planned a friendly resignation with the hope of being appointed Minister Plenipotentiary of the United States to the Court of St. James's, *persona grata*. We have seen how in the Webster-Ashburton Treaty of 1842 he let go a large part of the State of Maine, and how with the aid of incorrect cartography and Jared Sparks's spurious historical evidence, not to mention Ashburton's expense money, Webster persuaded Maine to accept the "compromise." Once in England, he was prepared to make another treaty which if successful would certainly make him most acceptable as a successor to the less popular Adamses at that court.

Webster proposed to couple the Oregon Question with the Mexican Question. That Republic owed citizens of the United States $2,026,139.89 of judicial awards of claims for supplies furnished during the revolution

[57] JQA to Henry Clay, Secretary of State. Quincy, September 11, 1827. Adams MSS.

[58] *Register of Debates,* V, 125–43.

against Spain. Other claims of $3,336,837.05 were pending adjudication by a mixed commission. So were large claims of British subjects. At the same time Mexican-American relations were becoming disturbed at the prospect of Texan annexation to the United States, so desired by Western and Southern constituencies, so opposed by antislavery elements in the Northern states. It was Webster's plan to quiet the impending sectional quarrel over Texas by drawing public attention away from the Rio Grande to San Francisco Bay in a tripartite treaty between the United States, Great Britain, and Mexico. The United States would yield to Great Britain the Columbia River as the boundary of Oregon, reserving for itself a detached enclave of territory between Puget Sound and the Pacific – namely, the forest-clad Olympic Peninsula. Mexico would sell to the United States a broad belt of territory six degrees of latitude in width south of 42° N.L., northern boundary of John Quincy Adams's Transcontinental Treaty of 1819 with Spain, and the money would be paid over to Mexico's just creditors in the United States and England.

The Secretary of State had talked his proposal over with President Tyler, described the idea to Edward Everett, Minister of the United States in London, and discussed it informally with Lord Ashburton before that nobleman went home from Washington with the Treaty of 1842 and 3,207,680 acres of the State of Maine in his pocket. Ashburton and Aberdeen seemed very sympathetic to another magnificent territorial compromise. Both Governments were sounding out the Mexican Ministers in their respective capitals as Webster handed in his resignation to Tyler.

John Quincy Adams wormed this proposed contrivance out of Webster in a three-hour interview in the latter's office on March 24, 1843. Now at the height of his second career, as an opponent of slavery expansion, Adams thought Webster's scheme an "outrage" – to accept the line of the Columbia from Great Britain and let the United States stretch out south at the expense of Mexico, all under the "spur" of Western and Southern slavery expansionists. "What an abime of duplicity!" [59]

Fortunately for Oregon and for the United States, Daniel Webster did not get the coveted post as Minister Plenipotentiary to Great Britain. President Tyler turned away from Webster's proposal to a treaty of annexation with Texas instead, something even more hateful to John Quincy Adams than swapping northern Oregon to Great Britain for northern Mexico. With his mind turned to Texas instead of Oregon, Tyler let Edward Everett stay on as Minister in London. Daniel Webster was left without any immediate satisfaction of his ambitions.

It was Andrew Jackson's protégé, President Polk, who gathered the Oregon fruit when the time was ripe. By 1843 American settlers had swarmed over the mountains into the Willamette Valley. Thereafter they

[59] *Memoirs,* XI, 344–7, 351, 355. March 24, 27, April 1, 7, 1843. See also C. A. Duniway, "Daniel Webster," in *American Secretaries of State and Their Diplomacy,* V, 59–64.

outnumbered hopelessly the Hudson's Bay Company establishment across the Columbia from them. The Company was alarmed at the American military potential so close to its Pacific headquarters. Already its *habitants* had trapped out the best fur preserves of the Columbia. In 1844 it decided to abandon the Columbia River country, to change its base from Fort Vancouver on the Columbia to Fort Victoria on Vancouver Island. The British Government prepared to follow suit.[60]

All his life John Quincy Adams remained a champion of Oregon. He supported the memorial of the provisional government of Oregon for the organization by Congress of a territorial government "under the Stars and Stripes forever" which Dr. Elijah White took to Washington in 1845. He advised White that the best way to get it presented would be through some avowed friend of the Administration rather than by himself,[61] none too influential at the White House.

The Old Man Eloquent was greatly pleased when President Polk, in his first annual message, December 2, 1845, came back to the Non-Colonization Principle of Monroe's famous message of 1823 for the protection of the North American Continent.[62] It was Adams's own principle, of course. When Great Britain first refused to accept Polk's "compromise" offer of 49°, Adams supported the President by voting in the House of Representatives for the joint resolution giving the necessary one year's notice for the termination of that free-and-open occupation to which he had agreed as Secretary of State and President in 1818 and 1827.[63] If really necessary he would rather fight Great Britain for the free territory of Oregon than Mexico for the slave state of Texas and the extension of slavery (so he feared) under the American flag into New Mexico and California. But President Polk "flinched" [64] before the prospect of armed conflict over Oregon. Fearful of a double war, with Great Britain as well as Mexico, he submitted to the Senate the latest British offer: the line of 49° through to salt water — John Quincy Adams's minimum line. The resulting Oregon Treaty of 1846 was not a compromise, as historians before Frederick Merk used to depict it. It was a diplomatic victory for the United States. It more than made up for the lavish territorial gift — to use a charitable word — in the Northeast which Daniel Webster had presented to Great Britain in the Webster-Ashburton Treaty of 1842.

John Quincy Adams had made possible the Oregon Treaty of 1846. As a young Senator from Massachusetts, home of the Essex Junto, he had defended the northern boundary of Louisiana against the King-Hawkesbury Convention of 1803, thereby holding to the latitude of the Lake of

[60] Frederick Merk: "The Oregon Pioneers and the Boundary," *AHR*, XXIX (No. 4, July 1924), 681–99.

[61] *Memoirs*, XII, 223.

[62] *Memoirs*, XII, 218.

[63] Benton: *Abridgement of the Debates of Congress*, XV, 372.

[64] *Memoirs*, XII, 239.

the Woods instead of the source of the Mississippi as the future point of departure westward. As Minister to Russia he held the place gained on the North West Coast by American explorers and traders. As Secretary of State he drew the parallel of 49° west to the Rocky Mountains. Next he fixed the Spanish boundary at 42° from the Rocky Mountains to the South Sea, first treaty acknowledgment of American title on the Pacific Coast. He evoked the Non-Colonization Principle and lodged it in the Monroe Doctrine. He put through the Russian Treaty of 1824, narrowing down the Oregon Question to the United States and Great Britain. Then he held the line of forty-nine against Great Britain through the years when it would have been so easy to yield it.

CHAPTER XXVI
President Adams, Henry Clay, and Latin America
1825–1829

Disinterestedness . . . cordial good will . . . fair and equal reciprocity.

PRESIDENT JOHN QUINCY ADAMS'S
FORMULA FOR FUTURE RELATIONS WITH LATIN AMERICA

THE PRESIDENTIAL election of 1824–5 lies beyond the scope of this volume on John Quincy Adams and the foundations of American foreign policy. In that campaign there was no opposition of parties. No political issues dominated the day. It was a contest of personalities within the Republican Party. Three members of Monroe's Cabinet, Adams, Crawford, and Calhoun (who finally dropped out of the race to accept the Vice-Presidency, uncontested), vied with Henry Clay and Andrew Jackson in hot rivalry for the succession. At the ballot boxes the Hero of New Orleans registered the heaviest popular support. In the electoral colleges Jackson received a plurality of votes (99) over Adams (84), Crawford (41), and Clay (37); but he failed to get the required majority. Therefore the choice of President devolved upon the House of Representatives voting by states from among the three highest candidates. Speaker Clay, finding himself out of the race, threw his influence to Adams rather than to his Western rival, General Jackson. Because of this maneuver, and the votes of the Southern states of Maryland and Louisiana, plus the rallying of Illinois's lone representative, Orchard P. Cook, to Adams's cause, the man from Massachusetts ousted Jackson on the first ballot, February 9, 1825.

Politics makes strange bedfellows. John Quincy Adams did what was expected of him: he made Henry Clay Secretary of State. It was the kind of understanding gentlemen frequently find it expedient to have in politics without putting it into words. It was also part of Adams's stratagem, as a minority President, to unite his opponents – Clay, Crawford, and Jackson – into a one-party National Republican Administration that could command the support of Congress and of the whole country, North, South, East, and West. That bold plan failed and with it John Quincy Adams's projects for strengthening the Union by a robust program of internal improvements under national planning and authority.

Political opponents promptly raised the cry of "bargain and corruption" between Adams and Clay. That there was an implicit, unspoken bargain is quite obvious; there was, of course, no corruption. But the charge of corrupt bargain would not down. The facts, so circumstantial, so plausible, seemed to speak for themselves: there was John Quincy Adams in the White House, and there was Henry Clay in the Department of State, traditional stepping-stone to the First Magistracy. Such a spectacle put the Administration on the defensive from the earliest moments of its existence, contributed to an opposition that frustrated all of Adams's worthy national policies, assisted Jackson's election in 1828, and deprived Henry Clay of his cherished goal of the Presidency. It altered the current of American politics for a generation. But it is not our purpose to deal at this place with the final breakdown of the Era of Good Feeling at the expense of John Quincy Adams's imaginative concepts of Union and expansion. We must confine ourselves for the present to those diplomatic problems which in previous chapters have not been carried through his Presidency.

Henry Clay became Secretary of State in order to become President later, if he could. With all his talent, he had been interested in foreign policy primarily as a means to raise issues useful to him in domestic politics. He recognized the ascendancy of Adams in the field of diplomacy, and was content to leave as much as possible to his chief, who had already laid down the fundamental objectives so clearly.

A possible exception to Clay's complaisance was Latin America, where new questions had arisen to arouse the attention and touch the vital interests of the United States: in Cuba and Porto Rico, at the projected Congress of Panama, and in Mexico and Texas.

1

Cuba, in the vernacular of British journalism, was the Turkey of trans-Atlantic politics, tottering to her fall, and kept from falling by those who contended for the right of catching her in her descent.[1] Six nations, American and European, including Spain, the implacable sovereign of the island, were holding Cuba uncertainly in place like big and little players scrambling under a push-ball filled with explosive gas.

France still had her ambitions in Latin America, including Cuba, even though George Canning had set them back with the Polignac Memorandum and James Monroe had put another block in her way with his message of 1823. Great Britain was almost as anxious as the United States, though by no means so vitally interested, to keep France or any other new sovereign out of Cuba. For as long as Cuba continued in Spanish possession it served as a prize hostage to the British Navy for the success of British diplomacy in Europe. When in 1826 a war threatened between Great Britain and Spain over the question of Portugal, Canning

[1] James Morton Callahan: *Cuba and International Relations, an historical study in American diplomacy* (Baltimore, 1899), p. 140.

proposed to strike at Cuba: "It would settle all better than half a dozen Peninsular campaigns." [2]

Cuba libre would cancel off this rich hostage from British diplomatic assets: freed from Spanish control the island might gravitate too readily into the North American Union. Therefore Canning tried to induce the Government of Ferdinand VII to recognize the independence of the new states of the mainland in return for a British guaranty of Spanish sovereignty over the islands.[3] But that ill-willed monarch, Emperor of the Indies, would not listen to reason, even when Mexico and Colombia, more as rivals than as partners, began to make preparations for a descent on Cuba and Porto Rico, last bulwarks of Spain's repressive American policy.[4]

The threat from Latin America of liberation, or conquest – call it whichever one may – of Cuba and Porto Rico was a matter of real alarm in Washington. It presented a new question for American foreign policy at the outset of John Quincy Adams's Administration. He and his predecessors had laid down the dictum that the United States could not regard with indifference the transfer of any colonial dominion on the American Continents from one European power to another. He himself had extended the No-Transfer Principle specifically to the island of Cuba.[5] He had further evoked the second dictum that there could be no further European colonization on the American Continents. President Monroe, after consulting with Adams and his colleagues, had announced to the world that the United States would regard it as the manifestation of an unfriendly disposition to itself for a European power to interfere in any way to control the destiny of the independent nations of the Western Hemisphere. But suppose one of those independent nations themselves, or an alliance of two or more of them, should seek to make a colony or protectorate out of Cuba, or Porto Rico, or actually to extend its sovereignty over them in the course of the war still existing with Spain? What would the United States do in such a case?

Adams and Clay tried to conjure away this question by diplomacy before they might have to meet it head on.

First Clay warned Mexico. "The United States have no desire," he wrote to Joel R. Poinsett, our first Minister to that Republic, "to aggrandize themselves by the acquisition of Cuba. And yet if the island is to be made a dependency of any one of the American states, it is impossible not to allow that the law of its position proclaims that it should be attached to the United States."

[2] Canning to Liverpool, October 6, 1826. *Official Correspondence of George Canning*, II, 144.

[3] Such a guaranty, of course, would disappear in case of war between Great Britain and Spain.

[4] José L. Franco: *Política continental Americana de España en Cuba, 1812–1830. Publicaciones del Archivo Nacional de Cuba,* Vol. XV (La Habana, 1947).

[5] Above, Ch. XVIII.

Next, through Everett in Madrid, Clay reviewed the whole question with Spain: "The United States are satisfied with the present condition of those islands, in the hands of Spain, and with their ports open to our commerce as they are now open. This government desires no change in that condition." The President wanted the war to end, for the sake of Spain, for the sake of humanity, for the repose of the world.

At the end of the century Grover Cleveland and William McKinley were to echo these same expressions to a recalcitrant Spanish Government at a still more critical time for the fate of Cuba and Porto Rico.

Having delivered himself of warnings to Mexico and oral assurances to Spain, President Adams's Secretary of State approached Russia, where Alexander I was still the obstinate friend of the United States. In a note to Middleton (May 10, 1825) for communication to the Russian Government, Clay implored the Czar to enlighten Spain by the wisdom of his counsels, and to influence her Government to make a peace of independence with the new states of the American Continents in order to preserve Cuba and Porto Rico for herself. A copy of this note was furnished to the Colombian Minister, and warnings similar to those to Mexico were conveyed to Colombia through the United States Minister at Bogotá, Richard Anderson.[6] Clay followed this appeal to Russia with instructions to the American Ministers to Great Britain (May 11) and France (May 13) to suggest that those Governments concert together to influence Spain for peace.[7]

In the Old World, Clay's notes produced only a polite and perfunctory response. The Czar's Government leisurely passed on the documents to Spain without much prompting for peace. France did nothing peaceful, on the contrary: she sent a fleet to the West Indies, which excited the apprehension of both the United States and Great Britain, not to mention Colombia and Mexico. Canning, cynical of the whole American suggestion, countered by proposing a tripartite self-denial ordinance for Great Britain, the United States, and France – Britain's favorite diplomatic formula for Cuba, and a real concession for her Government to offer.

President Adams evaded the self-denial proposal in 1825, as he had done in 1823 when Secretary of State. France also declined it. But the

[6] A direct note to the Minister of Colombia in Washington, December 20, 1825, urged suspension of any expedition by Colombia or Mexico against Cuba or Porto Rico. Manning, I, 263. *Memoirs,* VI, 95.

[7] William R. Manning presents an excellent précis of these instructions to Poinsett in Mexico (March 26, 1825), to Everett in Madrid (April 27, 1825), to Middleton in St. Petersburg (May 10, 1825), to King in London (May 11, 1825), to Brown in Paris (May 13, 1825), and other relevant documents from archives of the State Departments of both the United States and Mexico, in his definitive monograph on the *Early Diplomatic Relations between the United States and Mexico* (Baltimore, 1916), pp. 88–165. They are not all printed in full in his *Diplomatic Correspondence of the United States Concerning the Independence of the Latin American Nations.*

separate protests of the United States and Great Britain against any transfer of the island had almost the effect of joint action. They held France back, and in turn the United States and Great Britain stalemated each other in Cuba. All of this tended to keep the Cuban push-ball from falling to the ground among the contestants.

In the New World the attitude of the United States had a restraining effect on Mexico and on Colombia. Both states decided to refer the question of Cuba to the Congress of American States about to assemble on the Isthmus of Panama.

What would the United States have done if thus early in its history some foreign power, say Britain or Mexico, should have actually violated the No-Transfer Principle? President and Secretary of State knew perfectly well that the Executive could not lay down a fundamental of foreign policy and pledge the nation to go to war to maintain it. For this a vote of Congress was necessary. The No-Transfer Policy, older than the Monroe Doctrine, rested on the resolution of Congress of January 15, 1811. But that resolution had applied only to Spanish territories adjacent to the United States. John Quincy Adams had extended it beyond the straits of Florida to Cuba, and from Cuba to Porto Rico. Would Congress follow him across the Gulf Stream if the necessity should arise? Nobody could tell.

In the midst of these problems Henry Clay directed a confidential agent, Judge Thomas B. Robertson of Louisiana, to go to Cuba and report on the resources and ability of Spanish authority there to resist foreign attack or internal commotion. A part of Robertson's instructions was undoubtedly intended for the edification of President Adams's friend, Governor General Vives, formerly Spanish Minister in Washington. Clay declared that the neutrality of the United States fixed its duties with reference to any commotions that might be meditated or might actually arise in Cuba: "if they should happen to be of a character, or take a turn, which would require of the United States, from the relations in which they stand to that island, to interpose their power, it will then be time enough for the Government here to consider and declare the nature of their intervention when the exigency arises." [8] Judge Robertson, however, declined the mission.

If such were the hesitations about committing the United States without a resolution of Congress to resist by force the intervention of Mexico or Colombia in Cuba, as was feared in 1825, they were much greater in regard to the intentions of Great Britain in 1827. When news reached Washington of the Anglo-Spanish crisis over Portugal, and reports were rife of British designs to encourage a revolution in the island and take it in case of war (and this certainly was Canning's plan if war should occur), Clay sent Daniel P. Cook of Illinois, "lame-duck" supporter of the

[8] Clay to Thomas B. Robertson, December 7, 1825. DS, *Instructions, U.S. Ministers,* X, 418.

Adams Administration, to Havana as a secret agent to confer with the Governor General. His instructions were similar to those drawn up for Judge Robertson.[9] In a letter of introduction to Governor General Vives, Clay explained Cook's mission, and said: "it is not necessary to remind you of the explicit and repeated declarations of the wishes *of the Executive* of the United States, that the actual posture of things in Cuba should not be disturbed."[10] That is as far as Clay could go. It was a wish, not a pledge.

In Madrid, Alexander H. Everett, hearing of the same alleged British designs through the Spanish Minister to London (who said he got them from no less a personage than the Duke of Wellington, recently displaced in the British Government), expressed more than a wish. He took upon himself the responsibility[11] of delivering a written statement to the Spanish Government: the United States could not look with indifference upon such British projects in Cuba, "considering it, as they do, as a *settled principle,* that the island of Cuba must in no event, under no pretext, pass into the possession of, or under the protection of, any European power other than Spain."[12]

[9] Henry Clay, Department of State, Washington, March 12, 1827. Adams MSS. Daniel P. Cook completed his secret mission and returned to his home in Illinois mortally ill. He died before he could complete a report. Ninian Edwards sent to the Department of State such memoranda as he left in his papers, but no report can be constructed from them. Copies of Edwards's letter to Clay (undated) and of one memorandum are in the Adams MSS.

[10] Clay to Don Francisco Dionisio Vives, Governor and Captain General of Cuba, Washington, March 14, 1827. Adams MSS. Italics inserted.

[11] During his first year in Spain, Everett personally suggested, on his own initiative and private responsibility, to Zea, the Spanish Secretary of State, that Spain mortgage Cuba to the United States for a large loan ($15,000,000 or $20,000,000 was the sum he had in mind) and put the neutral United States into immediate occupation of the island, thus avoiding any attack on Cuba. After final peace was made, Spain could redeem the island by repaying the loan.

The advantages to the United States of such a transaction, Everett explained in a private letter to JQA, needed not to be enlarged upon. They were:

"1st. Complete security from the danger of any change in the position of the island in consequence of the present troubles.

"Second. *The probability of the eventual acquisition of the entire sovereignty.*"

Alexander H. Everett to JQA, private, ciphered. Madrid, November 30, 1825. Adams MSS. Italics inserted.

The President painstakingly deciphered the letter, but made no reply; at least there is no record of any.

For text, see *The Everett Letters on Cuba* (Boston: G. H. Ellis, printer; 1897), reprinted from *Scribner's Monthly,* XI (April 1876), 876–9.

[12] A. H. Everett to Henry Clay, No. 3, confidential, Madrid, December 12, 1827, enclosing Confidential Memorandum of December 10, 1827, to the Spanish Secretary of State. House Ex. Doc. 121, 32d Cong., 1st Sess., pp. 21–4. Italics inserted. Everett's paraphrase of the note in a private letter to JQA, No. 8, Madrid, July 7, 1828, was still more categorical. After stating that the United States could not look with indifference upon British intrigues in Cuba, he recalled to JQA that he had told the Spanish Secretary of State ad interim, Mr. Salamon, that if the British project was persisted

Our policy it was, yes, as laid down by the executive alone, like the Monroe Doctrine. But only the Senate could ratify such pledges in treaty form. And only the Congress could make good the nation's will. Clay, presumably upon Adams's suggestion, intimated to Everett, through the Minister's brother Edward, that he had been a "little indiscreet."[13]

Thus the diplomacy of President Adams, based on the strategic position of Cuba and Porto Rico for the defense of the United States, and influenced by the slavery problem in the Southern states of the Union, stalled the independence of Cuba. Henry Clay, champion of Latin-American independence, was himself the unreserved spokesman of John Quincy Adams's Cuban policy. Nothing better demonstrates their final meeting of minds concerning the affairs of Latin America.

Consider the history of Cuba in relation to the United States and Spain. From Thomas Jefferson to William McKinley every American President excepting the great Emancipator, Abraham Lincoln, and almost every Secretary of State along the way, expected that some day the island would become a state in the American Union.[14] Yet the Continental Republic has never taken the Pearl of the Antilles to its bosom. The forces of human freedom and of anti-imperialism have proved stronger in American history than the forces of African slavery or of desire for dominion over alien peoples. So ultimately would they prevail in the breast of John Quincy Adams, but not until after he had left the Presidency and the antislavery impulse finally took a real hold on his nation.

2

The idea of a continental confederation or union of Latin-American states like that of the United States in North America dates back to the first stirrings of revolution in the Spanish provinces. It was a favorite concept of the Liberator, Simon Bolívar. He proposed such a combination as a counterweight to the Holy Alliance and the possibility of European intervention in America to restore Spanish sovereignty. He may have had ambitions to preside or even to rule over it. As first steps in the achievement of his grand design he set in motion the negotiation of a series of bi-

in, the United States "would feel called upon to *aid the King* in maintaining the existing state of things in the island." Adams MSS. Italics inserted.

[13] Alexander Everett defended himself, in a private letter to his friend the President, on the ground that he was acting "under special instructions from you [JQA] that the United States could not look on with indifference to see the island of Cuba go into the possession of any European power other than Spain, and that it was our policy to maintain the existing state of things." A. H. Everett to JQA, private, No. 8, Madrid, July 7, 1828. Adams MSS. Everett must have construed such "special instructions" out of something Adams said. No documents establish them.

[14] The eminent Cuban historian Herminio Portell-Vilá has proved this and made annexation the theme of his notable *Historia de Cuba en sus relaciones con los Estados Unidos y España* (4 vols., La Habana, 1938–41).

lateral alliances, signed and ratified in the years 1822–6, between Colombia — Gran Colombia — and Peru, between Colombia and Mexico, and between Colombia and Central America. These treaties of alliance contained mutual guaranties of political independence and territorial integrity, reciprocal rights of citizenship, and pledges to send plenipotentiaries to an "Amphyctionic Assembly" of American states to meet on the Isthmus of Panama — Corinth of the New World — to unite the new nations, under their separate sovereignties, into a perpetual union, league, and confederation. When the preliminary treaties were well advanced, Bolívar issued, in the name of Peru, his famous circular of December 7, 1824 inviting the several independent nations, formerly members of the Spanish Empire, to the Congress of Panama, scheduled to convene on October 1, 1825.

In the midst of these negotiations President Monroe in his equally famous message of December 2, 1823 proclaimed to the world John Quincy Adams's principle of Non-Colonization and recorded the opposition of the United States to any European intervention in the affairs of the independent nations of the Western Hemisphere. Monroe's pronouncement gave high hopes to some Latin-American diplomatists that the Republic of the North might join a "continental confederacy" in common resistance to legitimist Europe.[15] As recalled from a former chapter, Colombia and Mexico promptly sought to write Monroe's dicta into formal alliance with the United States, but Secretary of State Adams declined the proposal.[16]

What the United States would not accept bilaterally it might agree to take in the form of a general inter-American treaty. At least so it appeared to some of the Latin Americans, notably to Don Pedro Gual, Minister of Foreign Affairs of Colombia, where Vice President Santander served as chief executive in the absence of Bolívar on his campaigns in the south. Several weeks before the issue of the Liberator's invitation to the Latin-American Republics, Gual on his own initiative had directed Salazar to sound out the United States Government as to whether it would be disposed to send a plenipotentiary to a Congress of American Republics at Panama. Acting in a parallel way, President Victoria of Mexico similarly instructed his Minister in Washington, Don Pablo Obregón. The Colombian preliminary invitation must be regarded as essentially a proposal to "panamericanize" the Monroe Doctrine, as we might say today.[17]

Gual had represented his country in the United States in the years be-

[15] Reginald F. Arragon: *The Congress of Panama.* I am indebted to Professor Arragon for allowing me to read this scholarly monograph while still in manuscript form.

[16] Above, p. 404.

[17] There is an extensive literature both in published documents and in secondary accounts on the Congress of Panama. For the purpose of this study I have allowed myself to be guided by the late Joseph B. Lockey's account of *Pan-Americanism: Its Beginnings* (New York, 1926), the more recent work of his scholarly disciple Harold A. Bierck, Jr.: *Vida Pública de Don Pedro Gual* (Carácas, 1947), and the long unpublished manuscript of Reginald F. Arragon: *The Congress of Panama.* See also Bemis and Griffin: *Guide to the Diplomatic History of the United States,* pp. 182, 187–8.

fore recognition of Latin-American independence, and thus knew something of the fundamentals of American foreign policy. Very cautiously he approached the Adams Government. In presenting any preliminary invitation to the United States it might be prudent, so ran his instructions to Salazar, to cloak the real object of the Congress with an ostensible purpose, such as the Freedom of the Seas.[18]

According to the tenor of his instructions Salazar, with the collaboration of his Mexican colleague, conferred with the new Secretary of State, Henry Clay, in the early weeks of the Adams Administration. The way was prepared by the appearance in the quasi-official *National Journal*[19] of Washington of a translation of an article from the *Gaceta de Colombia* of February 27, 1825. The publication quite accurately described the agenda of the proposed congress in two categories: subjects relating to the military operations of the belligerents, such as extending the war against Spain to the islands of Cuba and Porto Rico, perhaps even to the Canaries and the Philippines; and subjects relating to belligerents and neutrals "conjointly." Among the latter were: consideration of means of rendering effective the declarations of President Monroe, "in relation to the frustration of any ulterior designs of colonization on this continent, and resisting any interference in our domestic concerns"; establishment of principles of maritime law governing the mutual obligations of belligerents and neutrals; and relations with Haiti. These three points, tactfully commented the article, looked to the future; they did not involve participation in the "present war."

John Quincy Adams, through his diplomatic correspondence public and private, had known ever since 1822 of the movement for a congress of American states and of the possibility that the United States might be in-

[18] Gual to Salazar, October 7, 1824. O'Leary: *Memórias*, XXII, 513–15. Cited by Lockey: *Pan-Americanism*, pp. 326–8.

[19] April 23, 1825. An article by "Mutius Scaevola," extolling the purposes of the Congress of Panama, appeared in the *Democratic Press* of Philadelphia, of March 18, 1825. It urged the United States to take the lead in this movement lest some non-American power do so, and proposed a Pan-American Confederation to wield its united forces in defense of any member nation attacked by a non-American power. The *National Intelligencer* of April 26, 1825 reprinted the article, with an editorial rejoinder protesting, in the name of the traditional foreign policy of the United States, against "the magnificent scheme of the Philadelphia *Mutius*": "We desire, in fine, to be members of no Confederation more comprehensive than that of the United States of America." Lockey: *Pan-Americanism*, p. 204, points out that in the debates in the House of Representatives in April 1826 S. D. Ingham identified "Mutius" as Henry Clay and attributed the rejoinder to John Quincy Adams. I have not been able to find the slightest confirmation of this, in either case. Some of the sentiments of the "Mutius" article resemble those of Speaker Clay in previous years, but the idea of being a part of a hemispheric confederation does not run true to his later instructions to the American plenipotentiaries to Panama. President Adams would not be contributing pieces to the *Intelligencer*, from which he had withdrawn the "countenance" of the Government in 1824, in favor of the *National Journal*. Ingham was doubtless trying to make it seem that Clay and Adams were divided in policy.

vited.[20] As Secretary of State his attitude had been sympathetic but noncommittal: the United States would remain "tranquil but deeply attentive spectators" of the Latin-American revolutions, that "mighty movement in human affairs, mightier far than that of the downfall of the Roman Empire." [21] "If more should be asked of them, the proposition will be received and considered in a friendly spirit, and with a due sense of its importance." [22]

More was asked in 1825. It put another new question of foreign policy to the Adams Administration: should the United States participate in an international congress for the purpose of regulating problems of peace and war? Would this be contrary to the fundamentals of American foreign policy as laid down by George Washington in his Farewell Address? Clay, who had thought so long of placing his country at the head of an American System, was strongly inclined to accept the invitation. Adams saw an opportunity to exercise at least a moral and juridical leadership in the international councils of the World of Columbus. On the other hand there was the danger of an ensnaring entanglement with foreign countries and foreign wars.

"Besides the objects there noticed," the President noted in his Diary, referring to the "paper" in the *National Journal* and to the "great importance" of the Panama project, "that of endeavoring to establish American principles of maritime, belligerent, and neutral law is an additional interest *of infinite magnitude.*" [23]

Perhaps at Panama John Quincy Adams could get written into an American system of international law his most cherished project of a convention for regulating the principles of maritime and commercial neutrality, which recently had received such short shrift at the hands of British diplomacy. Perhaps he could abolish private warfare on the seas by the American nations, as a first step to outlawing it throughout the globe. Nothing could have been better calculated than Gual's stratagem to coax the United States a little farther out of its Washingtonian and Adamsonian isolation toward international co-operation at least in the New World.

At Clay's suggestion the President called a Cabinet meeting to consider the Colombian *démarche.* It was decided to accede to the proposition in principle, *as a neutral,* but to suggest to Salazar and to Obregón that it would be difficult to hold the meeting as soon as October, because time

[20] William Duane to JQA, Bogotá, March 7, 1823. Adams MSS. C. W. Hackett: "The Development of John Quincy Adams's Policy with Respect to an American Confederation and the Panama Congress, 1822–25." *HAHR,* VIII (November 1928), 496–526.

[21] JQA to Richard C. Anderson, Department of State, May 27, 1823. *Writings,* VII, 471.

[22] JQA to Caesar A. Rodney, Minister to Buenos Aires, Department of State, May 17, 1823. *Writings,* VII, 429.

[23] *Memoirs,* VI, 531. April 23, 1825. Italics inserted.

would be necessary to arrange and agree upon the objects of negotiation and methods of procedure.[24] The critical condition of Cuban affairs, discussed at the same meeting, also had an influence on the decision to participate: on later occasions the Colombian Government used the Cuban question as an inducement to bring the United States to the Congress.[25]

Of such transcendent importance did Clay regard the proposed Congress of Panama that he suggested Albert Gallatin, the ablest and most experienced American diplomatist that might be available, to head the proposed mission, jointly with Richard C. Anderson. Anderson himself, then on leave in Washington from his post at Bogotá, mentioned to the President the need of a fellow plenipotentiary. But Adams was doubtful whether the United States Congress, not then in session, would approve the expense of an additional commissioner when it came to footing the bill. Nevertheless he requested Anderson to be ready to leave by September 1 for Bogotá by way of Panama.[26]

There the matter rested while the Colombian and Mexican Ministers referred to their respective Governments the request of the United States for more time and for more specific agenda, as well as the determination of the Republic of the North to remain absolutely neutral in the war between them and Spain. September 1 went by on the calendar and nothing happened. Anderson set out directly for his regular station, there to hold himself in readiness. Adams and Clay decided to make no further movement before hearing from Colombia and Mexico.[27]

The plenipotentiaries of the Colombian Government were already leaving for the Isthmus when the Foreign Office at Bogotá drafted its reply to the United States, delivered by Salazar on November 2, 1825, one day before an analogous note from Obregón, followed by another from the Minister of Central America, Don Antonio José Cañaz. According to the Colombian note there were two classes of subjects to be discussed at the Isthmus: those peculiarly and exclusively concerning the belligerents, and matters relating to both belligerents and neutrals. "Since the United States will not take part in the discussion of the subjects of the first description, we will confine ourselves to the latter." Within this field Gual held forth the following attractions for North American diplomacy:

1. Agreement upon principles of international law, the unsettled state of which had caused much evil to humanity. Presumably the United States Government possessed more light on the subject than the other states of the Hemisphere, "both from its experience during the wars that succeeded the French Revolution and from its negotiations now on foot

[24] *Memoirs,* VI, 542. May 7, 1825. *ASPFR,* V, 835–9. Manning, I, 252–3.

[25] Manning, II, 1293–5.

[26] *Memoirs,* VII, 16. May 27, 1825.

[27] Clay to Anderson, September 16, 1825, Manning, I, 252–4. Clay to Poinsett, September 24, 1825. *ASPFR,* V, 918–19.

with Great Britain and other nations relative to these principles." This seductive language hinted at a Pan-American codification of the Freedom of the Seas, American plan.

2. Confidential parleys anticipating a conditional all-American continental alliance to enforce the Non-Colonization Principle of the Monroe Doctrine.[28]

3. Abolition of the African slave trade. Here the note referred to the convention recently signed between Colombia and the United States, at the instance of the latter, and not yet ratified in Washington.[29] "Would that America, which does not think politic what is unjust, would contribute in union, and with common consent, to the good of Africa!"

4. Determination of a uniform rule of conduct for the treatment of the black Republic of Haiti.

5. Whatever might be considered by the representatives of any government to be for the common good of the Hemisphere.[30]

The Mexican note, of November 3, 1825, said nothing about the African slave trade or mooted points of international law; it emphasized the desirability of a concert of opposition to the interference of any neutral nation in the question and war of independence between the Latin-American states and Spain; and of opposition to colonization in America by the European powers; that is, it invoked the principles of President Monroe's message.[31] In Mexico City, Poinsett had gone so far as to assert, upon no more than his own authority (later disavowed) that the United States had "pledged themselves" not to permit any European power to interfere either with the form of government or with the independence of any of the new American states.[32] He even told the British Minister to Mexico that he hoped personally to go to Panama as a plenipotentiary and that England could not keep the United States excluded from the formation of a general confederation: "the United States were the head of the American powers." [33] No wonder the Mexican Government expected the United States to enter an inter-American alliance to enforce the Monroe Doctrine!

These notes made apparent to Henry Clay and John Quincy Adams the

[28] "The manner in which all colonization of European powers on the American Continent shall be resisted, and their interference in the present contest between Spain and her former colonies prevented are other points of great interest. Were it proper an eventual [i.e., conditional] alliance, in case these events should occur, which is within the range of possibilities; and the treaty, of which no use should be made until the *casus fœderis* should happen, to remain secret; or, if this should seem premature, a convention so anticipated would be a different means to secure the same ends of preventing foreign influence" — all this to be handled *confidentially* for the time being.

[29] Above, p. 435.

[30] *ASPFR,* V, 836–7. The points, although presented in this order in the note, are not numbered.

[31] *ASPFR,* V, 836.

[32] *ASPFR,* VI, 589.

[33] Ward to Canning, Nos. 17, 45. Mexico, July 9, October 17, 1825. Quoted by Arragon: *Congress of Panama,* from PRO, F.O., 50, Vol. XV.

real purpose of the Congress of Panama: to convert the Monroe Doctrine into a conditional multilateral alliance among the states of the Western Hemisphere.

Bolívar himself had not been enthusiastic about bringing the United States into such a pact. The Polignac Memorandum had impressed that Latin-American realist far more than the Monroe Doctrine. It was his opinion that if British diplomacy could be induced to underwrite the prospective treaties of Panama it would fortify the New World much more against the Holy Alliance than anything the United States could do. So the Government of Gran Colombia decided to invite Great Britain to send a representative to the Congress, not as a member but as a guest with club privileges. The British Government was to be assured that any "agent" whom it might think proper to send to Panama would be treated "by the plenipotentiaries" with cordiality and without the least reserve.[34]

Gual caused the subject to be presented somewhat differently in London from what he had caused to be held forth in Washington. The objects of the Congress were twofold. For the allied belligerent members it would be frankly a concert of plans for expanding the sphere of hostilities in their war against Spain in order to compel her to make peace. This really meant, of course, Cuba and Porto Rico, although those islands were not actually mentioned. There would also be formulated some solemn declaration of purposes in combining, such as might remove the prejudicial judgments of European courts about the spirit and institutions of the new states. The neutral states of America (the United States and Brazil) would discuss questions "not opposed to the character of neutrality." The Freedom of the Seas was not mentioned outright to Great Britain, although its principles were carefully set forth in the instructions to tho Colombian plenipotentiaries at Panama, following the precepts of the Armed Neutrality of 1780.[35]

The invitation to London held forth the wondrous opportunity for Britain to grasp the balance between Europe and America [36] as already she held it – or was trying to hold it – on the Continent of Europe. Canning, acting also as a neutral, accepted the invitation.

Gual, on the part of Latin America, was playing off the two great Atlantic rivals for the patronage of Latin-American independence, the republican champion of the Freedom of the Seas against the monarchical

[34] Gual to Hurtado, August 9, 1825. Bierck: *Gual*, p. 468.

[35] Simón B. O'Leary: *Memórias del General* [Daniel Florencio] *publicado por su hijo* (32 vols., Carácas, 1879–88), XXIV, 277–8.

[36] "Great Britain, situated as she is in a certain manner by the nature of her power and her policy between the Old World and the New, perhaps takes greater interest than any other power in the maintenance of equilibrium between the one and the other." Manuel José Hurtado to George Canning, January [11], 1826. Pedro A. Zubieta: *Congresos de Panamá y Tacubaya* (Bogotá, 1926), pp. 30–3. Quotations are from the English translation in Webster: *Britain and the Independence of Latin America*, I, 400–2.

Mistress of the Seas, in order to marshal the support of both against the Holy Alliance.[37]

3

It would be interesting and enlightening to know more about the deliberations that took place in Washington over the formal invitations to attend the Panama Congress, and the topics mentioned, but there is no record.[38] All that can be said is that Secretary Clay formally accepted the invitation. Although the agenda for Panama had not been particularized as precisely as the President desired, Clay declared, the Chief Executive had decided out of "sensibility and friendliness" to appoint commissioners, subject of course to the advice and consent of the Senate. "All unnecessary delay," Clay assured the three inviting Ministers, "will be avoided in the departure of these Commissioners from the United States for the point of their destination." [39]

In his first annual message President Adams referred briefly to the assembly of the Congress of Panama and said that "ministers" would be commissioned to attend and take part in the deliberations upon objects of importance to all the American states in so far as might be compatible with "that neutrality from which it is neither our intention nor the desire of the other American states that we should depart."

Two days later John Forsyth of Georgia called at the White House. He had been chairman of the Senate Committee on Foreign Relations, more recently Minister to Spain, and was now chairman of the House Committee on Foreign Affairs. Although his diplomatic career had left much to be desired, he might have claimed to be the member of Congress most experienced in that realm.

"The intention announced in your message of sending Ministers to Panama," he remarked, "is a change in the policy of the Administration, isn't it?"

[37] "The principal object of the meeting," read the instructions of the Colombian plenipotentiaries to the Congress of Panama, "is to know what part Great Britain and the United States will take with us in case of intervention by Spain's allies in the affairs of the new American powers. The language of President Monroe and of the British Ministers has been so explicit in the matter that there would appear to be no doubt of their disposition to contract a conditional alliance with us. If the fundamental *casus fœderis* of these treaties should never come up, nothing will be lost in having taken the step ahead counseled by foresight and prudence." José R. Revenga to Messrs. Pedro Gual and General Pedro Briceño Méndez, Ministry of Foreign Affairs, Bogotá, September 23, 1825. O'Leary: *Memórias*, XXIV, 278. Bierck, op. cit., makes clear that Gual had already prepared these instructions although Ravenga signed them after Gual resigned to become a plenipotentiary to Panama.

[38] There are no entries in the printed *Memoirs* for the dates between October 27 and November 12, 1825. The Diary is blank, except for line-a-day jottings of visitors, from September 26 to October 25, and October 26 to November 11, 1825.

[39] *ASPFR*, V, 838. The Central American Confederation also joined in the invitation, November 14, 1825, through its Minister in Washington.

"I do not recollect any change in policy," observed the President, "but there has been a great change of circumstances." [40]

Undeterred, Adams went promptly ahead with his plans for Panama. In a special message of December 26, 1825 to the Senate he nominated Richard C. Anderson of Kentucky and John Sergeant of Pennsylvania – Gallatin having declined the mission – to be Envoys Extraordinary and Ministers Plenipotentiary to the Assembly of American Nations, and William B. Rochester of New York to be secretary to the mission. A report from the Secretary of State and copies of the notes exchanged with the Latin-American Governments, explaining the purposes of the assembly, accompanied the message. "It will be seen," the President assured the Senate, "that the United States neither intend nor are expected to take part in any deliberations of a belligerent character; that the motive of their attendance is neither to contract alliances nor to engage in any undertaking or project importing hostility to any other nation."

The objects of the United States in attending the Congress, explained John Quincy Adams, would be to advance certain fundamentals of American foreign policy. They can be summarized as follows:

1. "The principles of a liberal commercial intercourse" – that is, reciprocity and equality of treatment – this he believed to be of "infinite moment."
2. An all-around agreement on the Freedom of the Seas, American plan.
3. An all-American pact to implement the Non-Colonization Principle, each party guarding it by its own means within its own borders.

"In fine," the President concluded, in language that voiced the feelings of Henry Clay, "a decisive inducement with me for acceding to the measure is to show by this token of respect to the southern Republics the interest which we take in their welfare and our disposition to comply with their wishes. Having been the first to recognize their independence, and sympathized with them so far as was compatible with our neutral duties in all their struggles and sufferings to acquire it, we have laid the foundation of our future intercourse with them in the broadest principles of reciprocity and the most cordial feelings of fraternal friendship. To extend those principles to all our commercial relations with them *and to hand down that friendship to future ages* is congenial to the highest policy of the Union as it will be to that of all those nations and their posterity." This was the language of today's Pan-Americanism.

The expectation was that Sergeant and Rochester would set out for Colombia, where they would pick up Anderson, before the middle of January 1826.[41] This required prompt confirmation of the nominations by the Senate. But an unexpected opposition developed in Congress, where consent of the Senate was necessary to confirm the appointment of ministers,

[40] *Memoirs,* VII, 75. December 8, 1825.

[41] Clay to Rochester, November 30, 1825. DS, *Instructions, U.S. Ministers,* X. Cited by Arragon: *Congress of Panama,* p. 273. Italics inserted in message.

and approval of the House was required for appropriations to sustain the mission. The Senate, partly under the influence of Vice President Calhoun, who still controlled the committees, was already hostile to the Administration. On the other hand, Adams's friends dominated the House.

This first specific proposal of the President to the Congress gave the coalescing opposition of Calhounites and Jacksonites, of Southern and Northern "Democrats," as they were now calling themselves in new party terms, something positive to sink their teeth into in an organized attack on the Administration. It was the same coalition in the Senate that had emasculated the slave-trade convention with Great Britain and rejected altogether the one with Colombia. It had resisted the nomination of Henry Clay as Secretary of State. It had spread the propaganda of corrupt bargain. Now, recrudesced in strengthened numbers, it had an opportunity to attack the foreign policy of President Adams and Secretary of State Clay, and to base the attack on principles formally laid down by John Quincy Adams himself.

First expression against the President's proposal came from the Committee on Foreign Relations, which consisted of four Southern Senators and one Northern. Nathaniel Macon of North Carolina, chairman, reported against the nominations, not because of any unfitness on the part of the persons presented for the mission, he said, but rather in opposition to the "novel" measure itself. The Committee easily detected a great and significant discrepancy between President Adams's statement of purposes and reasons for being represented at the Congress and the obvious motives and purposes of the inviting governments. Avowedly the latter wanted to commit the United States to a conditional, even a secret alliance to support the principles of President Monroe's message against future violations by non-American powers at present neutral. Such a treaty would be contrary to the well-established foreign policy of the United States uniformly and happily pursued since George Washington's time, of avoiding political connections with foreign nations, even the most friendly — even, as John Quincy Adams himself was wont to say, with nations struggling for independence and liberty in the North American manner. As for the objectives of the United States set forth by the President, they could be accomplished as well by individual negotiations as by an international congress attended by agents endowed with undefined powers to accomplish undefined objects.

The Committee called attention to the fact that the President in his message to the Senate had passed over the subjects of the slave trade and relations with Haiti, objectionable items set forth explicitly in the notes of invitation. There was also the question of the Spanish islands of the Caribbean, not mentioned by any of the parties: "The very situation of Cuba and Porto Rico furnishes the strongest inducement to the United States not to take a place at the contemplated Congress, since, by so doing, they must be considered as changing the attitude in which they have hitherto stood as impartial spectators of the passing scenes [a phrase from Adams himself] and identifying themselves with the new republics." [42]

The Committee's report was a formidable and exasperating document fortified with arguments, to be fully ventilated in the debates in Congress, out of John Quincy Adams's own armory of American diplomacy – for he had been the greatest isolationist of them all.

Opposition Senators badgered the President with requests for papers, for additional information; they threatened to publish confidential documents, to open the doors of the hitherto secret executive sessions. In both houses the debate on foreign policy tended to assume somewhat of a sectional character reflected in a rather apathetic public opinion.[43] Southern spokesmen revolted at the thought of dealing in any international congress with such inflammatory subjects as the status of Cuba, the abolition of the slave trade, or relations with the Negro Republic of Haiti, all of which touched the tender topic of slavery in the United States. Senator Van Buren of New York doubtless would have defended the Panama mission if President Adams had opposed it. On the other hand Senator Edward Livingston of Louisiana was one of the staunchest supporters of the Panama proposal.

Ugly words came easily to the tongue in those days as now, but often with more serious consequences. John Randolph, referring to Clay's appointment and office, spoke of a "combination of the Puritan with the black-leg" – a "coalition of Blifil and Black George." He insinuated that the Secretary of State himself had procured the invitations for the United States to participate in the Congress of Panama: "this Panama mission is a Kentucky cuckoo's egg, laid in a Spanish-American nest." [44] Randolph's speech led to an immediate challenge and a duel between the Secretary of State and the Senator from Virginia, bloodless, fortunately, but bloodcurdling and embarrassing enough for a President of the United States, opposed to dueling, to be obliged silently to endure while the most conspicuous and brilliant member of his Cabinet, once his most formidable political opponent, risked his life to avenge an insult that applied to his chief as well as himself.

Only after six weeks of debate and delay did the Senate finally confirm

[42] *ASPFR*, V, 857–65. The report and relevant documents are also published in the Historical Appendix of *International American Conference*, Vol. IV (Washington, 1890). See also *The Executive Proceedings of the Senate of the United States on the Subject of the Mission to the Congress at Panama, together with Messages and Documents Relating Thereto*, 19th Cong., 1st Sess., Sen. docs. 68, 73. Printed by order of the Senate of the United States (Washington: Gales & Seaton, 1826).

[43] Arragon: *Congress of Panama*, ch. viii, a detailed analysis of the votes in both houses, and of newspaper comment. Francis L. Reinhold's "New Research on the First Pan-American Congress Held at Panama in 1826," *HAHR*, XVIII (No. 3, August 1938), 342–63, shows merely that on the whole Northern newspapers tended to favor the Congress, using commercial arguments, and Southern journals to oppose it.

[44] *Register of Debates*, 19th Cong., 1st Sess., II, 401–3, March 30, 1826.

the nominations (March 14, 1826) by a vote of 27 to 17 for Anderson, and 26 to 18 for Sergeant.

In the House the battle continued. Acting on Clay's advice,[45] Adams refused to address himself to that body until the Senate had acted favorably. Then he sent in a special message (March 15, 1826) requesting the appropriations, furnishing at the same time documents that the House had particularly asked for. It was one of the most important papers of his diplomatic career, and to it he summoned all the powers of his rhetoric, all the weight of his experience. With great eloquence he replied, one by one, to the objections that had been raised. Even if all these dangers lurked at the Isthmus, which he denied, he would want to have representation there to spy them out and to combat them. He stressed the advantage of kindly and friendly participation in the affairs of the American Continent. He cited as a precedent the commission to John Adams, Benjamin Franklin, and Thomas Jefferson in 1784 to make treaties of amity and commerce, including the Freedom of the Seas and the abolition of private warfare on the oceans, with the nations of Europe; but any informed reader of his message must have recalled that this involved no international congress or diplomatic commitment.

The President's greatest effort was marshaled to meet the most embarrassing argument of all: George Washington's solemn warning against entangling alliances and unnecessary political connections with foreign nations, an admonition stamped in large letters in Adams's own lexicon of foreign policy.

The answer was that times and circumstances had changed, as Washington himself had anticipated in his address – in words too infrequently quoted today.[46] Since Washington's day the United States had trebled its territory, population, wealth, and power physical and moral. It had proclaimed the Non-Colonization Principle and the Monroe Doctrine. Its situation politically, economically, and territorially, in relation to the eight new nations of Latin America – seven of them republics with institutions congenial to our own – was neither detached nor distant.

"Reasoning upon this state of things from the sound and judicious principles of Washington," the President concluded, "must we not say that the period which he predicted as then not far off has arrived; that *America* has a set of primary interests which have none or a remote relation to Europe; [47] that the interference of Europe, therefore, in those

[45] *Memoirs,* VII, 115.

[46] "If we remain one people, under an efficient government, the period is not far off, when we may defy material injury from external annoyance; when we may take such an attitude as will cause the neutrality, we may at any time resolve upon, to be scrupulously respected; when belligerent nations, under the impossibility of making acquisitions upon us, will not lightly hazard the giving us provocation; *when we may choose peace or war, as our interest, guided by justice, shall counsel.*" Italics inserted.

[47] "Europe has a set of primary interests, which to us have none, or a very remote connection." The Farewell Address.

concerns should be spontaneously withheld by her upon the same principles that we have never interfered with hers, and that if she should interfere, as she may, by measures which may have a great and dangerous recoil upon ourselves, we might be called in defense of our own altars and firesides to take an attitude which would cause our neutrality to be respected, *and choose peace or war, as our interest, guided by justice, should counsel.*" [48]

The measure that he proposed, declared the President, responded to the spirit of the Declaration of Independence and to the preambles [49] of our first treaty with France and the first treaty with Prussia consecrating the Freedom of the Seas. Above all, it was perfectly consonant with the Farewell Address and the recently proclaimed Monroe Doctrine.

For his part, Adams would not deny to the New World the hopes of the meeting at Panama. "That the Congress at Panama will accomplish all, or even any, of the transcendent benefits to the human race which warmed the conceptions of its first proposer it were perhaps indulging too sanguine a forecast of events to promise. It is in its nature a measure speculative and experimental. The blessing of Heaven may turn it to the account of human improvement; accidents unforeseen and mischances not to be anticipated may baffle all its high purposes and disappoint its fairest expectations. But the design is great, is benevolent, is humane."

Eye to eye with his old opponent Henry Clay, John Quincy Adams was attempting to adjust American foreign policy to a hemispheric purview at the close of the Age of Emancipation.

The House of Representatives was more tractable than the Senate. The Speaker, who appointed the committees, was John W. Taylor of New York, an Administration man. To be sure, John Forsyth of Georgia, chairman of the Committee on Foreign Affairs, was opposed to Adams and to Panama, but there was a friendly majority. Benjamin W. Crowninshield of Massachusetts handed in a report echoing the arguments of the President's message. After much debate and several more weeks of delay the House passed the necessary appropriation of $40,000 (April 22, 1826) by a vote of 134 to 60.[50]

It was a triumph for John Quincy Adams over sharp and partisan opposition in a historic debate on foreign policy, but the attitude of the Senate was nevertheless a warning that any inter-American alliance to implement the Monroe Doctrine would not be likely to receive the advice and consent of two thirds of the Senators.

It now remains to be seen what little use was made of this, President John Quincy Adams's first and only victory in Congress.

[48] See Note 46.

[49] Both preambles dedicate the treaties to "the most perfect equality and reciprocity."

[50] *Register of Debates*, 19th Cong., 1st Sess., Vol. II, Part 2, p. 2514.

4

Henry Clay already had been drafting, with the close approval of the President,[51] instructions for the guidance of the American plenipotentiaries. A state paper of eighteen thousand words, it is the most important which that diplomatist ever penned, and significant for the history of American foreign policy. The cold caution of official responsibility had already tempered the Kentuckian's warm-hearted sympathy for hemispheric solidarity. The leaning of Congress toward complete isolation had restrained any lingering temptation that he might have felt to put the United States at the head of an American System or "Family" under dangerous international guaranties against the intervention of a European System. It also moderated Adams's desire for a Pan-American agreement to support the Non-Colonization Principle.

The sympathetic tone of the instructions was Henry Clay's; the controlling cleavage to traditional principles was Adams's. The document reveals the real motive of both statesmen in looking to Panama: not so much to implement the Monroe Doctrine by any inter-American defense treaty, all for one and one for all, as to commit the new republics of the south to the fundamental principles of North American foreign policy: abstention from the future wars of Europe; Non-Colonization; No-Transfer; the Freedom of the Seas; the right of expatriation and naturalization; commercial equality and reciprocity, preferably on the basis of reciprocal equality of nationals and foreigners, if not then at least on the conditional most-favored-nation formula; and the abolition of privateering and of private warfare upon the seas according to the provisions of John Quincy Adams's draft Convention for the Regulation of Commercial and Maritime Neutrality. What American diplomacy had not been able to secure from Europe it would at least write into a pact with the nations of the New World.

Clay made plain what the President's messages had already assured Congress, that there was not the slightest intention of altering the policy of neutrality hitherto pursued toward the Latin-American wars for independence. The envoys were to evade all proposals for any alliance to cover the principles of President Monroe; the most they could do was to propose, for moral effect only, a "joint declaration" affirming the Non-Colonization Principle, without commitment to action. As to Cuba and Porto Rico, the Secretary of State reiterated the position of his Government, and added that if Mexico or Colombia should carry hostilities to Cuba it would be a war not of liberation but of "conquest"; in that case the United States might see itself obliged reluctantly to assist the defenders of the island, *be they American or European.*

On the subject of Haiti the Secretary avoided the race question by describing that Republic as only nominally independent, wearing a badge

[51] *Memoirs,* VII, 112.

of "colonial" infeudation to France in the shape of a fifty-per-cent tariff reduction allowed exclusively to her former European sovereign as the price of a sham independence. "The President is not prepared to say that Haiti ought to be recognized as an independent sovereign power." Finally the envoys were to avail themselves of every suitable occasion to urge upon the other American states the propriety of free toleration of religion, as in the United States, to discourage the idea of monarchical institutions, and *to enjoin upon every American nation a solemn duty to reject all foreign dictation in its domestic concerns.*

The instructions also glanced ahead to the future possibility of an Isthmian ship canal on terms of entire equality to all peoples of the Globe; and Clay added to the original items of the Administration's program for Panama a suggestion, taken from the report of the House Committee on Foreign Affairs, that the plenipotentiaries of the United States might serve as arbitrators or umpires of inter-American boundary controversies.[52]

Eye to eye with John Quincy Adams, Henry Clay was endeavoring to adjust his hemispheric concepts to the foundations of American foreign policy as understood and practiced by his chief. He prepared to accomplish this in a series of "good neighborhood" treaties – that was the phrase Clay actually used – to be signed at Panama. A century ahead of their time, Clay's instructions to Anderson and Sergeant anticipated many of the principles of the inter-American system of the twentieth century, including the Doctrine of Nonintervention, but no alliance like that of Havana of 1940, or of Chapultepec of 1945, or of Rio de Janeiro of 1947.

Clay and Adams's blueprint for a Good Neighbor Policy was never presented to the other American Republics because of a series of "accidents unforeseen and mischances not to be anticipated" and the final breakdown of Bolívar's grand design.

Clay signed the instructions on May 8, 1826. Richard Anderson, already at his post in Colombia, had previously been ordered to come down from Bogotá to Porto Bello and wait for a frigate bearing Sergeant from the United States, the two envoys then to proceed together to Panama.[53] But Sergeant refused to set forth for pestilential Panama during the tropical summer season and tendered his resignation.[54] He did well to do so if he valued his life more than the service of his country. Clay hesitated to reopen the whole issue with the Senate by suggesting to the President a fresh nomination. So he allowed the cautious envoy to post-

[52] Henry Clay to Richard C. Anderson and John Sergeant, Esquire, Envoys Extraordinary and Ministers Plenipotentiary to the Congress at Panama, May 8, 1826. *Register of Debates in Congress,* V, Appendix (Washington, 1830), 38–49. See also *International American Conference,* IV, 113–50.

[53] *Memoirs,* VII, 112. February 4, 1826. Clay to Anderson, March 5, 1826. DS, *Instructions, U.S. Ministers,* XI, 16–17. John M. Macpherson to Henry Clay, United States Consulate at Cartagena, July 3, 1826. Copy in Adams MSS.

[54] Clay to Sergeant, May 5, 11, 1826. DS, *Instructions, U.S. Ministers.* Sergeant to Clay, May 8, 13, 1826, ibid. Cited by Arragon: *Congress of Panama,* p. 315.

pone his departure until autumn. The President, who saw much of Sergeant at Philadelphia on his way north to Quincy in July and returning south to Washington in October, recorded no objection.[55]

After the desertion of Sergeant, Anderson received the option of proceeding from the Colombian capital to Panama at once or of sending a note to the meeting explaining his delay and suggesting transfer of the Congress to a more accessible (and healthful) place.[56]

The special messenger bearing these instructions got shipwrecked on Turks Island in June 1826, and they did not arrive at Cartagena until July 22. Anderson then lay dying in the house of the American Consul, too far gone to open dispatches.[57] On his way down from Bogotá to Cartagena he had caught a tropical fever while his steamboat lay grounded on a sandbar in the pestilential Magdalena River. He expired in the American consulate at Cartagena, July 24, 1826.

Thus it was that no representative of the United States was present at the Congress on the Isthmus when, after repeated postponements, that body formally assembled, June 22, in the *Sala Capitular* of the municipality of Panama. The Latin-American plenipotentiaries quickly agreed upon treaties of mutual defense and alliance, union, and confederation, and adjourned July 15, resolved to meet again in the more salubrious location of Tacubaya, Federal District of Mexico, but not until after an envoy from each delegation should have returned to his home government, reported on the Congress, and received powers for exchanging ratifications of the treaties of Panama. This meant that the assembly could not convene again for several months at the earliest.

In Washington it now seemed desirable to fix upon a successor to Anderson before Sergeant finally started out leisurely and comfortably for Tacubaya. At the original suggestion of Congressman Charles F. Mercer of Virginia, strongly advocated also by Secretary of War Bar-

[55] *Memoirs,* VII, 126–7, 160.

[56] Clay to Anderson, May 19, p.s., May 20, 1826. *Instructions, U.S. Ministers,* XI, 72–5. Cited by Arragon: *Congress of Panama,* p. 315. Daniel Brent, Chief Clerk of the Department of State, to JQA, July 18, 1826, referring to Henry Clay's instructions to Richard Anderson of May 20, 1826. Adams MSS.

[57] Ibid. J. M. Macpherson to Henry Clay, United States Consulate, Cartagena, July 26, 1826; Clifton Wharton [the special messenger] to Henry Clay, Cartagena, July 27, 1826. DS, *Despatches Cartagena,* I. Daniel Brent to JQA, August 26, 1826, sending copies from Washington of these papers. Adams MSS. Copies of the sea-blurred papers were sent on from Washington July 17 (DS, *Instructions, U.S. Ministers,* XI, 146–7) only to reach Colombia long after Anderson's death. News of Anderson's death arrived at the Department of State August 26, 1826. Daniel Brent to JQA, Washington, August 26, 1826. Adams MSS.

Referring to the Panama Congress in his second annual message of December 5, 1826, President Adams explained: "The decease of one of our ministers on his way to the Isthmus, and the impediments of the season, which delayed the departure of the other, deprived us of the advantage of being represented at the first meeting of the Congress." He announced his intention of nominating a successor to Anderson as plenipotentiary to the Congress.

bour,[58] John Quincy Adams asked James Monroe, patron of the Latin-American policy of the United States, to "put the seal to his own work" by heading the mission; [59] but the elderly ex-President, citing the ill health of his wife and the necessity of husbanding his own estate (neglected during years of toil in the public service), declined the honor. Thereupon Adams hopefully directed Sergeant to set forth alone, by November, on the U.S. sloop-of-war *Hornet*, ordered around to Philadelphia from Norfolk for the perfect convenience of the envoy.[60] He reached Mexico City in January 1827.[61] When the United States Congress convened, the President nominated the regular Minister in Mexico, Joel Poinsett, to be Sergeant's colleague at Tacubaya, and the Senate confirmed him after six weeks' delay in the Committee on Foreign Relations.

The plenipotentiaries assembled at Panama, who had already waited for months to get a full assembly for themselves, had shown no disposition to delay any longer for the North American envoys, or any concern whether they came or not. It is very doubtful if a representative of the United States, particularly John Sergeant, who knew so little about the Latin-American peoples or their language, could have accomplished much at Panama. He would have come into conflict with the British agent, Edward J. Dawkins, whose instructions were to frustrate any project for putting the United States at the head of an American confederacy against Europe and to block any general subscription to the Freedom of the Seas.[62] Given a free field by the absence of any spokesman of the Republic of the North, Dawkins made the most of his opportunity to increase the prestige of his country at the expense of the United States.[63] Canning thus strengthened his Latin-American policy, which was – much as Gual saw it – to slip in between any formation of the world into two systems, European and monarchical on the one side of the ocean, and American and republican on the other, and to hold the balance between them by preventing the rise of the United States to any ascendancy in the American System.[64]

The signatories of the treaties of Panama – Central America, Colombia, Mexico, and Peru – were never able to assemble fully at Tacubaya. Gual showed up in Mexico City in January 1827, at about the time Sergeant reached that capital; one of the Central American envoys arrived;

[58] C. F. Mercer to JQA, House of Representatives, February 21, 1826. Adams MSS. *Memoirs*, VII, 160. October 25, 1826.

[59] JQA to James Monroe, Loudon County, Virginia, private, Washington, October 21, 1826. Monroe to JQA, Oak Hill, October 24, 1826. Adams MSS.

[60] JQA to John Sergeant, Philadelphia, private, No. 9, Washington, November 21, 1826. Adams MSS.

[61] John Sergeant to JQA, private, Mexico, January 20, 1827. Adams MSS.

[62] Canning to Dawkins, Nos. 1, 4, 5, March 18, 1826. Webster, op. cit., I, 403–9.

[63] Whitaker: *U.S. and the Independence of Latin America*, pp. 582–4. Rippy: *Rivalry of the United States and Great Britain over Latin America*, pp. 227–46.

[64] Temperley: *Canning*, pp. 157–86.

and both Mexican Ministers got home safely from the Isthmus; but none of the Peruvians appeared. "The Ministers will not return 'till the treaties are ratified," Sergeant wrote to John Quincy Adams, "and the Congress will not assemble 'till the Ministers return." Everything, he said, depended on Bolívar.[65]

Although Colombia eventually did uniquely ratify the treaties of Panama, Bolívar had long since given up as impractical the possibility of creating a great confederation of all the American Republics. With the danger of European intervention largely dissipated anyway by the attitude of the United States and Great Britain, he had turned his attention to a new concept, that of uniting the countries liberated by him in the northwestern highlands of South America into one cohesive block under his own rule, a Confederation of the Andes.[66] Even that project broke down under the strain of local jealousies and domestic anarchy in one state after another, and the Liberator fell from power and died, a vastly disillusioned hero, December 17, 1830.

The Congress of Tacubaya never really took place.[67] The Mexican-Colombian project of liberating or conquering Cuba and Porto Rico collapsed under its own light weight, although Mexico continued to be interested in Cuba as late as 1829. Sergeant, already homesick for Philadelphia, returned in July 1827, leaving things in the hands of his colleague, Poinsett.

In the United States the public soon lost any faint interest in a Congress of American Nations awakened by the eloquent messages of President Adams. Clay despaired for the present but not for the future. At his request the President, as the last act of his Administration, on March 3, 1829 communicated to the Senate and House of Representatives the Secretary of State's instructions to Anderson and Sergeant, that they might be published as a manifesto to posterity.

Congress – since 1827 in control of the opposition, for the first time in the nation's history – refused to publish the instructions as a separate government document lest they reflect some glory on the defeated Administration.[68] Not until the close of the century did John Quincy Adams's

[65] John Sergeant to JQA, private, Mexico, January 20, 1827. Adams MSS.

[66] Victor Andrés Belaunde: *Bolívar and the Political Thought of the Spanish American Revolution* (Baltimore, 1938), pp. 271–322.

[67] Gual, the Colombia delegate, Larrizábal of Central America, and the two Mexican Ministers to Panama, Michelena and Domínguez, did hold an informal meeting, October 9, 1827, at Tacubaya, in which Gual reviewed the efforts to date and explained the motives that impelled him to leave the country. Lockey: *Pan-Americanism*, op. cit., p. 350; Bierck: *Gual*, 515–46.

[68] There was hardly time to order a printing before that session expired next day. The special session of the new Democratic Senate, called by President Jackson to confirm appointments, rejected by a vote of 13–18 a motion of Senator Tazewell to print the documents. Benton: *Abridgement of Debates of Congress*, X, Appendix, p. 257, March 16, 1829. They eventually got officially printed obscurely in the Appendix to the *Register of Debates*, in 1830. An English publisher apparently got them from the American newspapers and published them in London in 1829 with anonymous edi-

countrymen hark back to his messages to Congress, and Henry Clay's instructions to the plenipotentiaries, as harbingers of the so-called Pan-American movement of our times, and publish them in the conspicuous historical appendixes to the proceedings of the first International American Conference held at Washington in 1889–90.

The larger Latin-American policy of President John Quincy Adams and Secretary of State Henry Clay was a noble experiment that led to nothing in its day. Ex-President Monroe complained to Richard Rush that our relations with Latin America had been much weakened. "As friendly relations, they cannot have been much weakened," was John Quincy Adams's retort, "for they never were very strong." [69]

The people of the United States had turned their faces toward the West. They were not so much interested in promoting a hemispheric solidarity for liberty throughout the New World as they were in acquiring Texas.

5

President James Monroe had never cared much about Texas. The ominous debates in Congress over the admission of Missouri into the Union convinced him that he had been right in not insisting on Texas at the time of John Quincy Adams's negotiations with Onís, and in not pressing Mexico for the province after she had inherited it from Spain in 1822 as delimited by the Transcontinental Treaty. Texas, in Monroe's mind, would have fatally upset the historical sectional balance upon which the Union had rested ever since independence.[70]

Not so with President John Quincy Adams. We recall that he prided himself on having been the last member of Monroe's Administration to retreat from the Rio Grande to the Colorado, from the Colorado to the Brazos, from the Brazos to the Trinity, to the Sabine. Western protests against the exclusion of Texas had made him nervous,[71] all the more so after the rise of Andrew Jackson as a political power. Neither as Secre-

---

torial comments accusing the United States of ambitions to place itself "at the head of the American family." *Spanish America, Observations on the Instructions given by the President of the United States of America to the Representatives of that Republic, at the Congress to be held in Panama in 1826; on our Relations with Spanish America; with a Copy of the Instructions* (London: Effingham Wilson, Royal Exchange, R. Clay, Printer, Devonshire St., Bishopsgate; 1829). A Spanish translation, with additional commentary, appeared in Philadelphia in 1830 under the title: *Observaciones sobre las instrucciones que dió el Presidente de los Estados Unidos del Norte América a los representantes de aquella república en el Congreso de Panamá en 1826; sobre la conducta del Señor Poinsett, Ministro de los Estados Unidos en México, y sobre nuestras relaciones con la América Española en general, con una cópia de las instrucciones* (Filadelfia: imprenta de Guillermo Stavely; 1830).

[69] JQA to Richard Rush, private, Quincy, August 16, 1827. Adams MSS.

[70] James Monroe to Thomas Jefferson. Washington, May 1820. *Writings of Monroe,* VI, 119.

[71] *Memoirs,* V, 67–9.

tary of State nor as President did he show any disposition to come to a quick agreement with Mexico confirming the Transcontinental Treaty boundary with Spain from the Gulf to the Pacific Ocean.[72] As President he let Secretary Henry Clay have his way about Texas, at least to the point of peaceful negotiations with Mexico for its acquisition.

When Joel Poinsett went to Mexico as our first Minister, Henry Clay advised him that the President considered the United States committed to the boundary line of the recent treaty with Spain, but instructed him to try to rectify that boundary by moving it west from the Sabine to the Brazos River or farther west to the Colorado River of Texas, or to the Snow (Sangre de Cristo) Mountains, or even the Rio Grande. The most plausible reasons that Clay could advance for a gratuitous shift of the line so as to include Texas within the United States were that the Sabine River boundary was too close to "our great western mart," New Orleans, and that such a truncation of Mexico would have the symmetrical effect of leaving her capital city located more nearly in the center of her national territory! [73]

Poinsett sounded out the eminent Mexican Secretary of State, Luís Alemán. The latter politely acquiesced in the idea of boundary rectification to the advantage of both nations, but suggested that it might be the line of Pinckney's Treaty of 1795 – essentially the Mississippi River. He could have pointed out, but did not, that such a shift of the boundary of the United States eastward would have placed the city of Washington closer to the geographical center of the Union.

Poinsett found the "reactionary" Mexican Government of the day inclined to look to Europe rather than to the United States for protection and tutelage, to monarchy rather than republicanism, to clericalism rather than freedom of religion and political expression. He deliberately intervened in Mexican domestic politics to upset the existing regime by organizing the "liberal" elements into secret York-rite lodges, as opposed to the Scottish-rite political Masonry of the aristocratic landowners, clergy, and Spanish elements.[74] Poinsett's almost magic success in peacefully overthrowing the Mexican Government was an unpardonable intrusion of the kind that John Quincy Adams once had been so quick to condemn on the part of the Citizen Genet, when that French Minister had tried to demolish the Government of President Washington by playing upon the Democratic Societies of 1793. It was a violation of the principle of Clay's own instructions to the American delegations to the Congress of Panama rejecting foreign dictation in domestic concerns.

Clay disapproved Poinsett's indiscreet and "unfriendly" conduct and urged the President to remove the Minister forthwith and replace him

[72] Manning: *U.S. and Mexico,* pp. 276–86.

[73] Clay to Poinsett, March 26, 1825. Ibid., 286–8.

[74] Manning: *U.S. and Independence of Latin America,* III, 1649–1706, publishes many of Poinsett's official dispatches from Mexico to the Secretary of State.

with James Barbour, Secretary of War, who wanted the appointment.[75] But Adams, to whom Poinsett in his private letters had frankly avowed and explained his conduct,[76] declined to make a change unless the Mexican Government should officially ask for it.[77] That Government did not formally request Poinsett's recall until October 17, 1829. President Jackson then complied, replacing him with the egregiously offensive Anthony Butler, who kept on trying and intriguing to buy Texas until the Mexican Government also asked for his recall.[78]

The new liberal Government in Mexico, and its successors of various colors, proved no more amenable to the idea of ceding or selling Texas to the United States. But Clay persisted, despite the intimations of Poinsett that it would be better to wait until Texas filled up with recalcitrant Americans.[79] Taking advantage of Mexican uneasiness after the abortive Fredonian Revolt of Hayden Edwards in eastern Texas in December 1826 – expressly discountenanced by the United States – the Secretary of State again suggested to Poinsett a rectification of the boundary, this time in order to enable Mexico to get rid of such disorderly elements! [80] Clay authorized Poinsett to offer a million dollars for Texas up to the line of the Rio Grande and Puercos (Pecos) Rivers, thence due north to the Arkansas River and by that stream to 42° N.L. and through on that latitude to the Pacific as in the Transcontinental Treaty: this would still leave Santa Fe within the limits of Mexico and the navigable portions of the Red and Arkansas Rivers altogether within the limits of the United States. Or, if Mexico would not accept such a boundary, the Minister could offer half a million dollars for the line of the Colorado River of Texas to its source and due north to the Arkansas and the old treaty line. The Secretary of State was willing to turn over to Mexico some old warships as an additional inducement.

Santa Fe, and also all of Texas, were already within Mexican territorial limits. There seemed no good reason why even the politically shaken Republic of Mexico should alienate its fairest province for a paltry sum of dollars as long as it retained any sovereignty at all. Poinsett after feel-

[75] Henry Clay to JQA, Washington, August 17, 23, 1827. Adams MSS. *Memoirs,* VII, 277.

[76] Poinsett to JQA, private, Mexico, April 26, July 18, 1827. Adams MSS.

[77] JQA to Henry Clay, private and confidential, Quincy, August 23, 1827; same to same, October 1, 1827. Adams MSS.

[78] Justin H. Smith defends "Poinsett's Career in Mexico" in *Proc. Am. Antiq. Soc.,* new series, XXIV, Pt. 1 (1914), 77–92, but did not have available Poinsett's private correspondence with Adams, nor the correspondence of Adams and Clay.

[79] "No views, in my opinion, ought to be entertained of acquiring for the United States any territory beyond the line established by you [of the Transcontinental Treaty]. The State of Texas must from the nature of things one day drop off from this confederation; and the policy to be pursued by the United States in such an event ought to be early and deeply meditated." J. R. Poinsett to JQA, private, Mexico, April 26, 1827. Adams MSS.

[80] Clay to Poinsett, March 26, 1827, cited by Manning: *U.S. and Mexico,* p. 286.

ing out the situation refrained from making a formal proposition. The Mexican Government refused to ratify the commercial treaty, which he had signed on July 10, 1826, until the United States agreed to a new boundary convention reaffirming the line of the Spanish treaty. Poinsett yielded this in 1828, but still the constitutional authorities at Chapultepec delayed ratification of both treaties until after President Adams and Secretary Clay went out of office, only to find a tougher customer in Andrew Jackson; the treaties nevertheless went into effect in 1832.

There is no doubt that John Quincy Adams wholeheartedly supported Henry Clay's peaceable efforts to secure Texas. He carefully studied Clay's correspondence with Poinsett. The President noted in his Diary for March 15, 1827: "He [Clay] read his instruction to Poinsett to propose the purchase of Texas. I advised him to leave out the offer of ships of war, and offer only money."[81] When it was obvious that such a proposition would not be entertained, both he and Clay declined to push the matter further despite the demands of Western expansionists in the election year 1828. But he left the White House persuaded that the acquisition of Texas was not far off,[82] little realizing that soon he would turn around, in a new career of his life, most vigorously to oppose it.

6

John Quincy Adams wrote off the Panama Congress, and all the preparations for it, as a diplomatic fiasco. Toward the end of his life, in 1845, Calvin Colton, biographer of Henry Clay and editor of his writings, called at Quincy to talk with the Old Man Eloquent about his former relations with the famous Kentucky politician, still a candidate for the Presidency. Adams was as kind as possible to the reputation of his Secretary of State.

[81] *Memoirs,* VII, 240.

[82] Charles Hammond, antislavery advocate and Administration supporter in Ohio, editor of the Cincinnati *Gazette,* suggested that Mexico's failure to ratify the boundary treaty of 1828 on time gave to the Government an opportunity to please Western and Southwestern expansionists, otherwise Jackson men, by moving the boundary westward to the Trinidad, and added that if the South should get into power later, it would demand the Rio Grande, which would break up the Union. In a second letter he suggested the exchange of Oregon for Texas, an idea he had seen expressed in the Nashville *Republican* for February 12, 1829. Adams did not reply to Hammond until after he had left office. Even then he did not explain how he and Clay had tried to get Texas not only to the Trinidad, but also to the Colorado or even the Rio Grande. "We know," he wrote to Hammond, "that the Mexican Government is tenacious of territory, and will be apt to consider that, between the Sabine and the Rio del Norte, there is a region of human residence, for which nothing beyond the Rocky Mountains is to be offered that may be considered in any way an equivalent exchange for it. Perhaps it may be more tractable hereafter. It is highly probable that the acquisition may be at no distant period of time made." Charles Hammond to JQA, Cincinnati, September 20, 1828, February 22, 1829. JQA to Hammond, Meridian Hill, Washington, March 22, 1829. Adams MSS.

"He was inquisitive concerning the Panama mission," the old man noted in his Diary, referring to Colton's questions, "out of which he expects to weave a magnificent monument to Mr. Clay's statesmanship. But there is not much in it." [83]

There was not much in it, perhaps, to Adams in his day, but Time the Great Expositor has woven a magnificent monument to it in the inter-American peace structure of the twentieth century, Bolívar's noble legacy.

[83] *Memoirs*, XII, 207. August 11, 1845.

CHAPTER XXVII
The Foundations of American Foreign Policy (1776–1826)

A stout heart and a clear conscience, and never despair.

JOHN QUINCY ADAMS TO CHARLES FRANCIS ADAMS. JANUARY 1, 1848[1]

THE AGE of Emancipation had already closed when John Quincy Adams left the White House. The great revolutions of his lifetime had shaken the world for human freedom. The American Revolution had established the independence of the United States on the basis of self-government under written constitutions. The French Revolution had galvanized the peoples of Europe with the spirit of nationalism. The revolutions of the Latin-American peoples had carried the fruits of the American and French Revolutions to that part of the New World, where they took feeble root to survive for greater fullness. In North America there was to be another convulsion in 1861–5, to bring freedom to colored people as well as white. It was an age of violence and of great trial in human affairs, followed by exhaustion and repose during the British Century, happiest century in the annals of men. During those hundred years that followed Waterloo self-government burgeoned forth as never before upon this earth. The Age of Emancipation had tipped the scales of history in favor of the liberties of mankind for a century to come.

Only in such an era of upheaval and conflict could the United States have won its independence, consolidated its nationality under the Constitution of 1787, redeemed its territorial integrity from the garrisons of occupying powers, and doubled its national domain by the lucky Louisiana procurement. It did this by taking advantage instinctively of the wars and revolutions of the Old World. In this almost miraculous achievement it had the blessed endowment of such fathers of American independence as George Washington, Benjamin Franklin, Alexander Hamilton, Thomas Jefferson, and John Adams. Without them it could not have prospered so surely and so mightily on the premises of peace and neutrality, despite the one slip of 1812.

[1] *Memoirs,* XII, 281.

John Quincy Adams, son of the American Revolution, observer on the Continent of Europe of the wars of the French Revolution and Napoleon, later from the new village capital on the Potomac a witness of the remoter wars of Latin America, understood the portents and opportunities of the age. At least as much as any other statesman of those days he realized his country's fortunate place and felt her Manifest Destiny as a continental power greater in potentialities for human freedom than any association of men hitherto seen on this planet. Sensing America's advantage from Europe's distress he peaceably broke through the paper trammels of Old World imperialism in the empty western stretches of North America. Diplomatically he carried the ball of American Empire – to use the wholesome phrase of his opponent Dr. John Floyd – across the boreal plains over the Rocky Mountains down through the continuous woods that veiled the Oregon, to establish republican sovereignty impregnably on the Pacific Coast beyond the reach of further European colonization. More than any other man of his time he was privileged to gather together, formulate, and practice the fundamentals of American foreign policy – self-determination, independence, noncolonization, nonintervention, nonentanglement in European politics, Freedom of the Seas, freedom of commerce – and to set them deep in the soil of the Western Hemisphere. On that solid ground they stood and prospered for a century to come.

It is easy now to lay down these classic principles in historical order and to appraise Adams's relation to them. Clear and simple they stand forth. Let them finally be listed, one by one. The foundations of American foreign policy came to rest in John Quincy Adams's time on the following fourteen fundamentals:

1. Sovereign independence to preserve the rights of English freemen. John Quincy Adams as a son of the American Revolution was completely devoted to its gospel.

2. Freedom of the Seas. John Quincy Adams through successive decades fought a slow but gaining fight for that great birthright of American independence. To enshrine the Freedom of the Seas – not to mention the freedom of international rivers – in international law and to abolish private warfare upon the oceans were the great goals of his life, never realized. No man has striven longer or more gloriously for that ideal.

3. Freedom of commerce and navigation: that is, reciprocal equality without discrimination against foreign subjects or ships, whether in homeland or colonies. John Quincy Adams was a consistent champion of this other birthright of American independence – twin birthright to the Freedom of the Seas. In the twentieth century it developed into the Open Door and the New Reciprocity.

4. Abstention from the "ordinary" vicissitudes and "ordinary" combinations and collisions of European politics and wars, first expressed in Washington's Proclamation of Neutrality in 1793, then in the Farewell Address of 1796, finally in the Monroe Doctrine of 1823. The reader of this volume

knows how John Quincy Adams moved contemporaneously in the spirit and practice of all three of those pronouncements, how he had some small influence on the formulation of the Farewell Address, how he followed Washington's Great Rule of foreign policy all his diplomatic life, how he was personally a power, during the deliberations of President Monroe's Cabinet, in laying down uncompromisingly the three dicta of the Monroe Doctrine, including the principle of Abstention. So far as Europe was concerned, he remained an unwavering isolationist; in 1823 his advice prevailed with President Monroe over that of Thomas Jefferson and James Madison.

5. The No-Transfer Principle: opposition to the transfer of adjacent colonial dominions in North America from one European sovereign to another, in order to prevent a strong imperialistic power from menacing American security and republican self-government by stepping into strategically dangerous parts of the dissolving Spanish Empire. Secretary of State John Quincy Adams extended this policy, first crystallized by the resolution of Congress of January 15, 1811, from contiguous territory like Florida or Texas to the Spanish islands of the Caribbean, from whence later it was to be expanded to all the Western Hemisphere.

6. Continental expansion. John Quincy Adams was certainly one of the great apostles of Manifest Destiny, if he did not coin the actual phrase itself. Born on the shore of Massachusetts Bay, a spot he loved above all others in the world, he did more than any other man diplomatically to push the sovereignty of the United States all the way over the mountains to the fabulous shores of the South Sea. In this his first career he was the greatest continentalist in American history.[2] Later, when continental expansion became identified in Adams's mind and politics with slavery expansion, he would turn about in his second career, one of the greatest personal reversals of the century, and oppose the march of Manifest Destiny into Texas and beyond the Rio Grande to the coast of California — Polk's superb complement to Adams's earlier diplomacy, a continental achievement that none other than John Quincy Adams would work in vain to block!

7. Self-determination of peoples, as evidenced by recognition of the independence of the revolted colonies of Spanish America. John Quincy Adams sensed keenly enough the destiny of independence for the whole Hemisphere from the ties of European imperialism, but he had his eyes and heart set first on the continental expansion of the United States in

[2] Comparison inevitably presents itself with another continentalist, Thomas Jefferson, friend of John Quincy Adams's boyhood years in Paris, author of the Declaration of Independence, and of *Notes on Virginia,* i.e. on North America. But of Jefferson it must always be remembered that during the Louisiana negotiations of 1803 he would have been willing to guarantee to France the whole west bank of the Mississippi — this would have denied to the United States its Manifest Destiny of expansion through to the other ocean.

North America. Not until he had staked that out forever in the triumphant Transcontinental Treaty of 1819 would he let his fixed view waver from North America to South America. His cool-headed calculation of his own country's Manifest Destiny on its own Continent balanced the warm-heartedness and mixed motives of Henry Clay's politics.

8. No further European colonization in the New World, a corollary to the self-determination and independence of the nations of America. This was a policy out of John Quincy Adams's own genius.

9. Nonintervention, as manifested in the Monroe Doctrine: to Europe, Hands Off America; and as next contained in the instructions of Henry Clay, written under the oversight and final responsibility of President John Quincy Adams, to the intended plenipotentiaries of the United States to the Congress of Panama.

10. The right of expatriation and naturalization and the wrong of impressment. No one expressed this doctrine of the immigrant nations of the New World more consistently, vigorously, or eloquently than John Quincy Adams throughout his lifetime.

11. Suppression of the African slave trade. Adams was only a belated convert to this humanitarian British policy, after public opinion in America had persuaded him that it would be politically expedient even at some risk of impressment. Then his political conversion became a moral conversion leading him step by step slowly and cautiously into the road of his second great career – the antislavery crusade, the resulting revolution of the Southern states against the Union, the final triumph of the Nation and the freeing of the slaves. All that, together with his personal and political biography after he left the Department of State for the White House, is a longer story, so big and so dynamic that it would take at least another volume to tell it.

12. Pan-Americanism. After the ratification of the Transcontinental Treaty, ensuring the continental future of the United States, following recognition of the Latin-American Republics, and after pronouncement of what we now call the Monroe Doctrine, John Quincy Adams was willing to follow Henry Clay toward an inter-American treaty structure, without commitment to the use of force, based on the maxim of Good Neighborhood, the Non-Colonization Principle, the No-Transfer Principle, the Monroe Doctrine, Nonintervention, and the other established fundamentals of the foreign policy of the United States; but neither Adams nor Clay, nor any North American statesman before the year 1940, proved willing to write those principles into a hemispheric alliance of the Republics of the New World.

13. International arbitration as practiced in the boundary and other controversies with Great Britain from Jay's Treaty to the Northeastern Boundary Question. John Quincy Adams was always willing to arbitrate justiciable questions – that is, questions relating to a point of interna-

tional law or the interpretation of a treaty — not involving national sovereignty or national honor; but he preferred direct diplomatic settlement to arbitration whenever possible.

14. Anti-imperialism. Implicit in all these fundamentals, which all together we may connect with the name of John Quincy Adams more than with that of any other one man, was a feeling strongly sensed and practiced, but never quite articulate, of anti-imperialism, which may be added as a cardinal principle of American foreign policy. It stemmed from the Anglo-American Revolution and the Latin-American Revolution of the New World. If one defines imperialism as dominion or control over alien peoples, the United States as an exponent of Manifest Destiny in North America can scarcely be said to have been an imperialistic power until the close of the nineteenth century; and even then it was so only temporarily, for a quarter of a century, during the new and dangerous frame of power and politics suddenly ushered in by the simultaneous appearance of Germany and Japan as aggressive world powers. That late-born, unwanted imperialism of the United States which followed the Spanish-American War was liquidated after the First World War just as soon as it seemed safe to do so, and the Republic went back to the classic fundamentals of its foreign policy as laid down in their aggregate by John Quincy Adams.

It is one thing to define the fundamentals of a nation's foreign policy; it is another to make them prevail. John Quincy Adams did not make all these principles prevail in his day, but he stood fast by them so that they lived to predominate in another day of greater national power. What was the secret of Adams's success in defining, defending, and sustaining American foreign policy in the first half-century of our independence? It was the adjustment of his personal qualifications to his country's interests and advantages instinctively grasped and painstakingly pursued.

Personally Adams was a competent, reliable, and agreeable man to do business with. His personal animus and choler he reserved for his political opponents at home who tried to pull him down by attacking the integrity of his diplomatic record. The representatives of foreign powers in Washington had no complaint to make on the score of amenities. But he thought always of his own country first. He did not believe in a global Santa Claus. He always insisted on a diplomatic equivalent for any concession made. He never surrendered an advantage, as Don Luis de Onís could testify, but he always preserved his temper in diplomatic intercourse and maintained a simple-mannered republican urbanity. He would yield in dignity to no one when to do so involved the dignity or prestige of his Government. Let a foreign diplomat near the Government of the United States assume a high tone, and Adams would reply, not in real anger or irascibility, but in kind, if necessary with added measure, as Stratford Canning and his fellows in office might have been able to testify. Let a Minister get angry or make a threat, or bluff, as once the good Frenchman

Hyde de Neuville did in a moment of folly, and Adams could follow his bluster to the door, gently and quizzically, candle in hand. As Secretary of State he towered above the foreign diplomats in Washington. He never lost ground in his handling of personal situations. His diplomatic friends and adversaries, at home and abroad, admired his learning, his sobriety, his self-discipline, his industry, his integrity, and his unwavering patriotic vigilance. They respected him and through him they learned to respect his Government. He has often been called America's greatest diplomatist. Let those who dispute the title suggest a greater.

John Quincy Adams's success as a diplomatist resulted from more than his personal qualities, his vast learning, and his long practical experience in dealing with foreign affairs. It stemmed from taking advantage of the favorable position of the new Republic in world geography and world politics. The detached and distant position of the United States gave it safety for a century and freedom to stretch through to the other ocean while Europe was convulsed by war or exhausted in peace. The only power that could have gainsaid or blocked the United States on this Continent after Adams became Secretary of State was Great Britain, but Britain would never call a categorical halt to the westward-moving Republic if only because of the exposed position of Canada, hostage to Anglo-American amity during the British Century.

Canada the Hostage was not the only reason for Anglo-American amity. In the possession of any other imperialist power Canada would have been not a hostage but a vestibule, for invasion of the United States. Other more friendly reasons, a common heritage of freedom and culture, and common dangers to that heritage, steadily brought the two English-speaking peoples closer and closer after Adams's day, and after the day of his son, as he had striven to bring them together in his time. The resolution of all outstanding controversies with Great Britain toward the end of the century followed the pattern that John Quincy Adams had set for Anglo-American reconciliation in 1823.

Adams grasped the essentials of American policy and the position of the United States in the world more surely than any other man of his time. He availed himself of matchless opportunities to advance the continental future of his country and the fundamental principles for which it stood in the world. Nothing is clearer than that the fourteen fundamentals above reviewed remained the main tenets of American foreign policy during the century following. With two notable exceptions – the Freedom of the Seas, recently stultified, and Isolation, now abandoned – they have persisted constantly throughout our history. This perhaps is a test of their virtue. When the United States became a great naval power, the mightiest in all time, it proceeded to sink the Freedom of the Seas beneath the oceans. John Quincy Adams would never have applauded that. But we may surmise that he, and the fathers of American Independence as well, had they lived to share the troublous times beyond the British

Century in the science-shrunken smallness of the globe, and to experience the *extraordinary* vicissitudes, combinations, and wars of global politics, would have joined the diplomatic revolution rejecting Isolation, and that he would say, as he did say at the time of the Congress of Panama: "I do not recollect any change in policy; but there has been a great change in circumstances."

Even if John Quincy Adams was not to have another great career, as a crusader against the expansion of slavery, this first and mighty achievement, of no less than continental proportions, in laying the foundations of American foreign policy, would have been enough for one lifetime.

APPENDIXES

APPENDIX 1

(NOTE TO CHAPTER VII)

John Quincy Adams's Accounts of His Break with the Federalists

DURING John Quincy Adams's Presidency, and as a prelude to the political campaign of 1828, Governor William Branch Giles of Virginia, Adams's old confidant of 1807, wrote a public letter to the Richmond *Enquirer*, September 7, 1827, attacking the pro-Adams newspapers for asserting that Jefferson had approved the measures of Adams's Administration. To show that this was not so, Giles published a letter of Jefferson to him of December 26, 1825, lamenting the usurpation of states' rights by the Federal Government under Adams, counseling patience, and advocating an amendment to the Constitution to give the Federal Government power to build interstate roads and canals. Publication of this letter drew forth from Jefferson's heirs, at the request of Adams's friends, another letter from Jefferson to Governor Giles, dated December 25, 1825, in which Jefferson did justice to Adams's superiority over all ordinary considerations when the safety of his country was in question. Jefferson further recalled, with confessedly imperfect memory, that it was Senator John Quincy Adams who had sought an interview with him during the embargo and informed him of a negotiation between certain citizens of Massachusetts and agents of the British Government with the object of withdrawing the Eastern states from the "war then going on." Adams's warnings of the dissatisfaction of New England with the embargo, said Jefferson, convinced him of the necessity of abandoning the embargo in order not to break up the Union.

The publication of these two letters of Jefferson led to a statement in the Washington *National Intelligencer* of October 21, 1828, "authorized" (i.e., written) by President Adams, describing (with the aid of his Diary) his interview with Jefferson on March 15, 1808 and clearing up some of the discrepancies of Jefferson's memory and his obvious confusion of embargo days with the War of 1812. The purpose of the correction was to show that the plottings of certain Federalist leaders, unnamed, alluded to by Jefferson, on the authority of his interview with Adams, had not occurred "during the war," as Jefferson said, but in 1808 or before, and were therefore not treasonable.

Adams's statement, instead of relieving the surviving Essexmen, provoked an indignant reply, November 26, 1828, from thirteen signed survivors of the Hartford Convention, or their sons, challenging him to name the "leaders" who for several years prior to 1804 had been plotting a dissolution of the Union. To this Adams replied, December 30, 1828, without naming names, and taking occasion to stress at length his approval of the Louisiana Purchase, which had provoked the Federalist leaders to think of separation. The outraged Massachusetts Federalists then published a lengthy *Appeal of the Citizens of the United States,* January 28, 1829.

As soon as he left the White House, March 4, 1829, Adams began to collect documentary material for a detailed answer, and in fact composed a *Reply to the Appeal of the Massachusetts Federalists.* It is a long and somewhat tautological account of his relation with the Essex Junto and his political position as Senator, and shows very clearly that Timothy Pickering was the leader of the separatist movement in 1804. Reflection, and the advice of friends, persuaded him not to publish the polemic and to let the controversy subside. In 1877 John Quincy Adams's grandson, Henry Adams the historian, published the *Reply* in his *Documents Relating to New England Federalism,* together with the controversial pieces above mentioned.

In the early summer of 1829 John Quincy Adams composed a fragmentary sketch of political parties in the United States, reviewing the struggle between Federalists and Republicans from 1789 to 1812, with a brief review of the disappearance of party issues after the War of 1812 and of the personal politics that preceded the election of 1824. These notes were apparently intended for the assistance of Philip Richard Fendall, who was preparing a history of the United States and the Adams Administration, of which a prospectus appeared in Peter Force's *National Journal* of February 19, 1829.[1] This narrative justifies, most plausibly, the position taken by John Adams and by his son, the author, in the party controversies that attended the foundations of American nationality. It explains John Quincy Adams's split with the Federalists with less tautology and better perspective than does the longer account of 1829 above referred to and printed by Henry Adams in 1877. Curiously enough, Henry Adams made no editorial reference to this manuscript in his *Documents Relating to New England Federalism.* It is not certain whether he even knew about it. Charles True Adams (no direct descendant) obtained a copy of the manuscript from a dealer and printed it in New York (Greenberg, publisher) in 1941, under the title *Parties in the United States.* There is a manuscript draft and a fair copy among the Adams MSS.

[1] Charles M. Wiltse published a scholarly review of this work in *Journal of Politics,* IV (No. 4, August 1940), 407–14, placing the date of composition.

APPENDIX 2

(NOTE TO CHAPTER XIX)

Text of John Quincy Adams's Supplementary Instructions to Richard Rush, No. 1.77 (*secret*), *Washington, December* 8, 1823 [1]

Sir,

Since the date of my last letter, your intermediate despatches Nos. 333 and 335 have been received, and also the numbers 337 and 338. With this you will receive a printed copy of the President's Message to Congress, at the commencement of the present session. Your attention will be particularly called to that part of it, in which the condition of South America is noticed, and to the sentiments therein expressed, with regard to any contingent purpose of one, or more European powers to interfere, by active hostility, in any contest between the Southern Republics of this hemisphere and Spain.

The same sentiments have been explicitly avowed in a confidential correspondence between this Department and the Baron de Tuyll, the Russian Envoy residing here. About the same time that your letters were received reporting the confidential communications between Mr. Secretary Canning and you, Baron de Tuyll addressed to me a Note, declaring that the Emperor Alexander, faithful to the political principles maintained by him and his allies had determined not to receive General Devereux, as Minister from the Government of Colombia, nor any other Agent from any of the recently established Governments de facto, in the New World. With the answer to this note, several other communications, connected with the same general subject, have passed between us, and several conferences have taken place, the result of which is indicated by the manifestation of the political principles of the United States, and of the views of their Executive Government in relation to Spanish and South American affairs in the Message.

The concurrence of these sentiments with those of the British Government as exhibited in the proposals of Mr. Canning, will be obvious to you. It will now remain for Great Britain to make hers equally public. The moral effect upon the councils of the Allies, to deter them from any interposition of force between Spain and America, will be complete. It is hoped that nothing further will be necessary.

By the surrender of Porto Cavello, the last spot of ground within the

[1] Arthur P. Whitaker, op. cit., p. 515, n. 38, had reference to this important document which he found among the papers of Richard Rush now owned by Mr. Benjamin Rush, of Chesteridge, West Chester, Pennsylvania. Manning does not print it, because it does not occur in the letterbook of Instructions of the Department of State. The text here published for the first time is taken from the copy in the Adams MSS.

Republic of Colombia, that was yet in the possession of a Spanish force, has been wrested from them. So totally is the Spanish power there extinguished, that the very imagination of its re-establishment is an absurdity. Were it possible to suppose that a reconquest of the country should be among the contemplations of the European Alliance, it could not be with the view of restoring it to Spain. Whatever the ostensible course of operations might be, the real purpose could only be to transfer the possession of it to another power.

The object, proposed in the confidential letters of Mr. Canning, having been thus accomplished, the consideration of what remains further to be done, will depend upon the definitive movements of the European allies. Among the papers which have passed between the Russian Minister here, and this Department, is one, being an extract of a despatch from his Government to him dated the 30th of August last, containing a full exposition of the *principles* of the Emperor Alexander, and his allies, *Austria, France,* and *Russia* in relation to the affairs of Spain and Portugal. Great Britain is not once mentioned throughout the paper. As its communication here was entirely confidential, no copy of it can now be suffered to go from the Office, but you will perceive the purport of it, in the observations upon the communications recently received from the Russian Minister, which have been delivered to him, and a copy of which is herewith enclosed.

The President is anxiously desirous, that the opening to a cordial harmony, in the policy of the United States and of Britain, offered on this occasion, may be extended to the general relations between the two Countries. While availing yourself, therefore, of the open and explicit declaration of our views, so far as they can be disclosed by the Executive Government, contained in the Message, you will not fail attentively to mark and report the manner, in which they will be received by the British Government. In our own Country, so far as the public sentiment has been discovered, the message and especially that part of it, has been received with universal approbation.

Since the surrender of Cadiz, rumours have been prevalent, that the question of interference in South American affairs had been settled by the European Allies, long *before,* and even that an army of twelve thousand men, was to be despatched immediately to accomplish the re-conquest. There are obvious impediments of execution to such a project, had it really been matured in purpose, which require time for their removal. And that time may yet be employed, if necessary, by Great Britain and the United States, in a further concert of operations to counteract that design, if really entertained. You will communicate freely and cautiously with the British Government with regard to *their* ulterior views. And while adverting to the frank and explicit manner in which *we* have spoken to the world, on this great emergency, you will, in the most conciliatory and friendly manner, lead the mind of Mr. Canning to the necessary inference, that to the end of concert and co-operation, the *intentions* of Great Britain, under all the contingent aspects, which the subject may assume, should be as unequivocally known to us.

Mr. Alexander McRae will be the Bearer of this despatch. He is authorized, under instructions from the Department, to proceed to any place in Europe, where you and Mr. Brown may think his services may be useful, in giving information to this Government, or to you, and will return to the United States when they may be no longer necessary.

APPENDIX 3

(NOTE TO CHAPTER XXI)

John Quincy Adams's Project of a Convention for Regulating the Principles of Commercial and Maritime Neutrality [1]

Article 1st. Neither the debts due from individuals of the one nation to individuals of the other, nor shares, nor moneys which they may have in the public funds, or in the public or private Banks, shall ever in any event of War, or National differences be sequestered or confiscated, it being unjust and impolitic that debts and engagements contracted and made by individuals having confidence in each other and in their respective Governments should ever be destroyed or impaired by national authority on account of national differences, and discontents.

Article 2d. If at any time a rupture should take place between the contracting parties, the Merchants and others of each of the two Nations residing in the dominions of the other shall have the privilege of remaining and continuing their trade so long as they behave peaceably, and commit no offence against the Laws; and in case their conduct should render them suspected, and the respective Governments should think proper to order them to remove, the term of twelve months from the publication of the order, shall be allowed them for that purpose, to remove with their families, effects, and property; but this favour shall not be extended to those who shall act contrary to the established Laws.

Article 3d. Neither of the contracting parties will order or authorize any acts of reprisal against the other, on complaints of injuries or damages until the said party shall first have presented to the other a statement thereof, verified by competent proof, and evidence, and demanded justice, and satisfaction, and the same shall either have been refused, or unreasonably delayed. Nor shall a rupture be deemed to exist, while negotiations for

[1] DS, *Instructions, U.S. Ministers,* X. Mr. Henry Adams, 2d, has compared this document with the original draft in the Adams MSS. Words here italicized do not occur in the original draft. Words here inserted in brackets occur in the original draft but not in the final document.

accomodating differences shall be depending, nor until the respective Ambassadors or Ministers, if such there be, shall be recalled, or sent home on account of such differences, and not on account of personal misconduct, according to the nature and degree of which, both parties retain their rights, either to request the recall, or immediately to send home the Ambassador, or Minister of the other, without prejudice to their mutual friendship and good understanding.

Article 4th. And in the said event of War between the parties, all women and children, scholars of every faculty, cultivators of the earth, artisans, manufacturers, and fishermen, unarmed, and inhabiting unfortified towns, villages, or places, and in general all others whose occupations are for the common subsistence and benefit of mankind, shall be allowed to continue their respective employments, and shall not be molested in their persons, nor shall their houses or goods be burnt, or otherwise destroyed, nor their fields wasted by the armed force of the enemy, into whose power, by the Events of war, they may happen to fall; but if any thing is necessary to be taken from them for the use of such armed force, the same shall be paid for at a reasonable price. And all Merchant and trading vessels employed in exchanging the products of different places, and thereby rendering the necessaries, conveniences, and comforts of human life, more easy to be obtained, and more general, shall be allowed to pass free and unmolested; and neither of the contracting parties shall *authorize their public vessels to capture or destroy them,* or grant or issue any commission to any private armed vessels, empowering them to take or destroy such trading Vessels, or interrupt such commerce.

Article 5th. The two contracting parties agree, by all the means in their power, to restrain the Indians living within their respective dominions from committing hostilities against the territory, citizens, or subjects of the other party. And both powers mutually pledge themselves in the event of War between them, not to employ any Indians, nor to admit of their aid and co-operation in the prosecution of the War against the other party.

Article 6th. No natural born subject or Citizen of either party, shall be compelled or held by any other means than in consequence of his own voluntary engagement or consent to enter or to continue in the Military or Naval service of the other. And if War should break out between the parties, no natural born (or naturalized) subject or Citizen of either party, who may then happen to be in the said Military or Naval service of the other shall be compelled against his will to continue therein. Neither shall any such person be detained or held as a prisoner of War. But every such person shall at his own request; be discharged from the service; his wages till the time of his discharge, shall be paid him, and he shall be furnished with a Passport or safe conduct to return without molestation to his own Country.

Article 7th. If either of the contracting parties should hereafter be engaged in a War against a third Power, to which War the other of the parties shall remain neutral, [it is agreed that] every Vessel of the neutral party sailing for a port or place belonging to the enemy of the belligerent, without knowing that the same is besieged, blockaded, or invested, may be turned away from such port or place, but shall not be detained, nor her Cargo, if not contraband, be confiscated, unless after such notice, she shall again attempt to enter; but she shall be permitted to go to any other port or place not so besieged, blockaded or invested. Nor shall any Vessel or goods of either party which may have entered into such port or place before the same was besieged, blockaded, or invested by the other and be found therein after the reduction or surrender of such place, be liable to confiscation but shall be restored to the proprietors thereof. And in order to determine what characterizes a blockaded port, that denomination is given only to a port where there is, by the disposition of the power which attacks it with Ships stationary or sufficiently near, an evident danger of entering.

Article 8th. It shall be lawful for the Citizens and subjects of either party, to sail with their Ships and Merchandize (contraband goods excepted) from any port whatever to any port of the enemy of the other and to sail and trade with their Ships and Merchandize with perfect security and liberty from the Countries, ports, and places of the enemies of either party without opposition or disturbance, and to pass not only directly from the places and ports of the enemy to neutral ports and places, but also from one place to another, both belonging to an enemy, whether under the same or under several jurisdictions; with the exception of Ports or places actually blockaded, besieged, or invested.

Article 9th. Under the denomination of contraband of War, shall be comprised all arms and implements, serving for the purposes of War, such as Cannon, mortars, muskets, pistols, and other fire arms, petardes, bombs, grenades, carcases, saucissas, rockets, carriages for cannon, firelocks, musket-rests, bandoliers, gunpowder, salt-petre, sulphur, matches, balls, bullets, helmets, or head pieces, cuirasses, swords, pikes, halberts, lances, javilins [javelins], saddles, bridles, and other horse furniture, holsters, pouches, belts, and generally all other implements of War [as also timber for shipbuilding, tar and rozin, copper in sheets, sails, hemp and cordage, and generally whatever may serve directly to the equipment of such vessels, unwrought iron and planks only excepted]. All the above articles, and none others shall be subject to confiscation whenever they are attempted to be carried to an enemy. But no vessel shall be detained on pretence of carrying contraband of War, unless some of the above mentioned articles are found on board of said Vessel at the time when searched.

Article 10th. It is hereby stipulated that free ships shall make free goods, and that every thing found on board the ships, belonging to the Citizens or subjects of either party shall be free and exempt from capture, although the whole lading, or any part thereof should belong to the enemies of either, contraband goods excepted. The same liberty shall be extended to persons on board a free ship, and although enemies to either party they shall not be taken out of said Ship, unless they are soldiers in actual service of the enemy. The property of the subjects or Citizens of either party which may be found laden on any ship belonging to the enemies of the other, shall also be free from confiscation, and on due proof of its being neutral property, shall be restored to its owners.

Article 11th. In all cases where vessels shall be captured, or detained on just suspicion of carrying to the enemy articles which are contraband of War, the said Vessel shall be brought to the nearest, or most convenient port. The contraband Articles only shall be made prize, and the Vessel shall be at liberty to proceed with the remainder of her Cargo without any impediment. All proper measures shall be taken to prevent delay in deciding the cases of ships or cargoes so brought in for adjudication, and in the payment or recovery of any indemnification, adjudged or agreed to be paid to the masters or owners of such ships.

Article 12th. It is agreed that whenever a War shall break out between either of the contracting parties, and a third power, to which War the other party shall be neutral, no natural born subject or citizen of the Belligerent party, being a mariner or sea faring person, unless naturalized as a subject or Citizen of the other party by a public and authentic act before the commencement of the said War, shall, during the continuance of the War, be employed on board any of the Public or private Vessels of the neutral party. The high contracting parties hereby engage themselves to adopt respectively without delay, the most effectual measures for carrying this Article into effect; and such measures when adopted shall be immediately communicated by each party to the other. The commanders of all public Vessels and the masters, owners and officers of all private vessels of said Neutral party shall be forbidden upon adequate penalties, from employing or permitting to be employed, admitting or receiving, or permitting to be admitted or received to such employment any such seaman or sea-faring person, being as aforesaid a subject or Citizen of the belligerent party. No seaman, or seafaring man, being a subject or Citizen as aforesaid of the belligerent party, shall in any port of the said party be admitted or received as a passenger on board any public or private vessel of the neutral party, without permission in writing from the proper officers of the said Port.

Article 13th. It is agreed by the high contracting parties that no commander, or officer in the naval service of either power shall in any event impress or forcibly withdraw, or cause to be impressed, or forcibly withdrawn any person or persons not in the actual military service of the enemy from the vessels of the other power upon the high seas, or anywhere without the ordinary jurisdiction of either power as acknowledged by the Law of Nations on any plea or pretext whatsoever. [Provided always that nothing contained in this article shall be used to impair or affect the rights of either party within its Ports, and ordinary territorial jurisdiction, or the rights of search for contraband, as authorized in time of War by the law of nations.]

Article 14. All commanders of Ships of war and privateers and all others concerned therein, the Citizens or subjects of either party, shall forbear doing any damage to those of the other party, or committing any outrage against them; and for any such outrage they shall be punished, and shall also be bound in their Persons and Estates to make satisfaction and reparation for all damages, and the interest thereof, of whatever nature the said damages may be.

For this cause, all Commanders of Privateers, before they receive their commissions, shall be obliged to give, before a competent Judge, sufficient security by at least two responsible sureties, who have no interest in the said Privateer, each of whom, together with the said Commander, shall be jointly and severally bound in the sum of fifteen hundred pounds sterling, or six thousand, six hundred and sixty six dollars sixty six cents, or if such ships be provided with above one hundred and fifty seamen or soldiers, in the sum of thirteen thousand, three hundred and thirty three dollars, thirty three cents, or three thousand pounds sterling to satisfy all damages and injuries which the said Privateer or her officers or men or any of them may do or commit during their cruise, contrary to the tenor of this treaty, or to the laws and instructions for regulating their conduct; and it is further agreed that, in all cases of aggressions, the said commissions shall be revoked and annulled.

Whenever a Judge of a Court of Admiralty of either of the parties shall pronounce sentence against any vessels or goods or property belonging to the subjects or citizens of the other party, a formal and duly authenticated copy of all the proceedings in the cause, and of the said sentence shall, if required, be delivered to the commander of the said vessel, without delay, he paying all legal fees and demands for the same.

Article 15. The Citizens and subjects of the two nations shall not do any acts of hostility or violence against each other, nor accept commissions or instructions so to act, from any foreign Prince or State, enemies to the other party; [nor shall the enemies of one of the Parties be permitted to enlist in their military service any of the citizens or subjects of the other party] and the laws against all such offences and aggressions shall be punctually executed. And if any citizen or subject of the said parties respectively shall accept any foreign commission or Letters of Marque, for arming any vessel to act as a Privateer against the other party, it is hereby declared to be lawful for the said party to treat and punish the said citizen or subject having such commission or Letters of Marque, as a Pirate.

Article 16. It shall not be lawful for any foreign privateer, whether belonging to the citizens or subjects of either of the contracting parties, or commissioned by any other Prince or State or People in amity with either of the two Nations, to arm their ships in the ports of the neutral party, nor to sell what they have taken, nor in any other manner to exchange the same; nor shall they be allowed to purchase more provisions than shall be necessary for their going to the nearest Port of the Prince, State or People from whom they obtained their commissions. No shelter or refuge shall be given in the Ports of either party, being neutral, to the subjects or citizens of either belligerent party, having made a prize upon the citizens or subjects of the other. But if forced by stress of weather or the dangers of the sea to enter therein, particular care shall be taken to hasten their departure, and to cause them to retire as soon as possible.

Article 17. Neither party shall permit the ships or goods belonging to the citizens or subjects of the other, to be taken within cannon shot of the coast, nor in any of the Bays, Ports or Rivers of their territories by ships of war or others having commission from any Prince, State or People whatever. But, in case it should so happen, the party whose territorial rights shall thus have been violated, shall use his utmost endeavours to obtain from the offending party, full and ample satisfaction for the vessel or vessels so taken, whether vessels of war or merchant vessels. And *the* commanders of all ships of war, public and private, of the contracting parties, shall be strictly forbidden to commit any act of hostility or make any prize within cannon shot of the neutral coast of the other party, or in any of the Bays, Ports or Rivers of the neutral territory; and if, contrary to such prohibition, any such act of hostility should be committed or prize made, by any ship of war of the Belligerent party within the jurisdiction of the neutral party, satisfaction for the same shall be made, on complaint thereof by the neutral to the Belligerent Government, and the property so taken shall be restored or full indemnity therefore be made.

Article 18. The ships of war and Privateers belonging to the said parties respectively shall, nevertheless, be at liberty to carry whithersoever they please, the ships and goods taken from their enemies upon the high seas: nor shall the said prizes when compelled by stress of weather or the danger of the seas to enter a port of the neutral party, be detained or seized, or obliged to pay any fee to the officers of the Admiralty or to any judges whatever: neither shall the searchers or other officers of those places visit such prizes; (except for the purpose of preventing the carrying of any part of the cargo thereof on shore, in any manner contrary to the Laws) nor shall such officers take cognizance of the validity of such prizes; but they shall be at liberty to depart as speedily as may be, and to carry their said prizes, according to the authority in their commissions, which the commanders of the said ships of war or privateers shall be obliged to show.

Article 19. The contracting parties shall not only refuse to receive any Pirates into any of their Ports, Havens, or Towns, or to permit any of their inhabitants to receive, protect, harbour, conceal or assist them in any manner, but will bring to condign punishment all such inhabitants as shall be guilty of such acts or offences. And all their ships, with the goods or merchandizes taken by them, and brought into any port of either of the said parties, shall be seized as far as they can be discovered, and shall be restored to the owners or their factors or agents duly deputed and authorized by them (proper evidence being first given in the Court of Admiralty, for proving the property) even in case such effects should have passed into other hands by sale, if it be proved that the buyers knew, or had good reason to believe or suspect that they had been piratically taken.

Article 20. If any vessel or effects of the Neutral power, be taken by the enemy of the other party, or by a pirate, and re-taken by the Power at war, they shall be [restored to the first proprietor upon the payment of reasonable salvage by sentence of the Admiralty Court of the Recaptor which shall in no case exceed one eighth part of the recaptured property] brought into some port of either of the parties, and delivered into the custody of the officers of the Port and restored to the true proprietor as soon as due proof shall be made concerning the property thereof; — reasonable compensation being allowed by the Court of Admiralty of the said port to the recaptors: or the re-captured vessel may be restored to its master when re-taken; the compensation for re-capture being then settled by agreement between the commander of the re-capturing, and the master of the re-captured vessel.

Article 21. [In the event] The vessels of war of either party shall give protection to the merchant vessels of the other, going the same course, against Pirates, and shall defend such vessels as long as they hold the same course, against all piratical aggression, in the same manner as they ought to protect and defend vessels belonging to their own party.

APPENDIX 4

(NOTE TO CHAPTER XXIII)

Lord Ashburton, Daniel Webster, and Jared Sparks, 1842

THE revelations of Lord Ashburton's use of money to assist Daniel Webster in quieting the opposition of Maine to the treaty line of 1842, by the use of Sparks's faithless cartographical evidence, come from the Aberdeen Papers in the British Museum, Additional MSS. 42123. See also PRO, Declared Accounts, L, 282. The Aberdeen Papers contain exchanges of private letters between Lord Aberdeen, British Foreign Minister, and Lord Ashburton, British Plenipotentiary on special mission to Washington in 1842. Pertinent extracts from this correspondence follow:

Ashburton to Aberdeen, private, Washington, June 14, 1842:

". . . Our great question the Maine Boundary up to this day looks well. It has been ably conducted through Webster during his visit to New England where he defeated the schemes of the Democratic Governor of

Maine. Our only serious difficulty here will be with Preble, a very obstinate, but I believe honest, man, who thinks & dreams of nothing but this boundary and who was appointed to the Commission by the Governor to defeat a settlement. I believe he will ultimately be satisfied. – I have some reason to suspect that Webster has discovered some evidence, known at present to nobody, but favorable to our claim, and that he is using it with the Commissioners. I have some clue to this fact and hope to get at it. . . ."

The confidential postscript to this letter, referred to in the following reply by Lord Aberdeen, of July 2, 1842, is missing from the original document in the British Museum.

Aberdeen to Ashburton, July 2, 1842:

"The postscript to your private letter of the 14th of last month has only been communicated by me to Peel [Prime Minister], under injunctions of the strictest secrecy, and you may rely on our desire to observe the utmost caution with respect to the matter contained in it. But this incident has, I confess, quite taken me by surprise, and opens a new view of measures which perhaps may be followed up with advantage, should there yet be time for you to do so. In order to insure success, you need not be afraid of employing the same means to a greater extent in any quarter where it may be necessary. In what you have done you have been perfectly right; and indeed I look upon the proposal made to you from such a quarter, as the most certain indication we could receive of a determination to bring the negotiation to a happy issue. In any further transactions of the same kind, I have only to desire that it may be made the means of leading to success, as the condition of having recourse to it. If you can command success you need not hesitate. . . ."

Ashburton to Aberdeen, private, Washington, July 28, 1842:

"I am well pleased to see by your private letter of the 2d that you were satisfied with what I communicated to you the 14th of last month. I had no doubt & did not hesitate but I do not think it likely that I shall have more to say to you on the same subject. –

"You will see that I have at last made my important move, and that my Boundary is on the high road to the Senate. The men of Maine were most difficult to deal with, and I was obliged somewhat irregularly to undertake them, for the Secy of State had no influence with them; and for a day or two I was in doubt whether I might not fail altogether, but at last Preble yielded and after signing he went off to his wilds in Maine as sulky as a Bear. – You may rely that no better terms were obtainable, and that if obtained would be decidedly in danger in the Senate. For my own part you are aware that I have been fighting for details to which I do not attach the same importance as my masters. My great wish was that there should be *a* settlement, because I was sure that if this failed we should come very soon to collision, but I am well pleased that we end by driving the enemy off that crest of Highlands so much coveted at the war office.

"There has been no demand of money by anybody during the whole discussion, & I need not add that on this subject I have been cautiously silent. — . . ."

Ashburton to Aberdeen, private and confidential, August 9, 1842:

"Since I communicated to you the very extraordinary information about the Boundary, I have seen Sparkes's letter and the map to which he refers. I made immediately a memorandum of the facts from which I now copy. The letter from Dr. Franklin to the Count de Vergennes is dated 6 December 1782, and is in the following words: 'I have the honor to return to Your Excellency the map you sent me yesterday and I have marked according to your desire with strong red ink the limits of the United States as decided by the preliminaries of peace signed by the British and American Plenipotentiaries.' These preliminaries were signed six days before. — On reading this letter Sparkes went to the topographical department where there were 60000 maps & charts but so well indexed & catalogued that he had no difficulty of finding the map. It is by D'Anville dated 1746 — and of the size of about 18 inches — and has the red ink mark referred to by Dr. Franklin of the exact boundaries of the United States, marked apparently by a hair pencil or a blunt pen. —

"The line marked gives Great Britain more than what is claimed by our line, for beginning at the St. Croix it runs carefully round all the tributaries of the St John so as to throw even the country about Houlton into New Brunswick. It is evident that the division intended was by *rivers* and that, as we always maintained, the waters of the St John throughout were intended to belong to G Britain. —

"This extraordinary evidence places this case beyond all possible doubt, and if I had known it before I *agreed* to sign I should have asked your orders, notwithstanding the manner of my becoming acquainted with it. At the same time the communication to me was strictly confidential and *then* communicated because I *had* agreed to sign, so that taking all things into consideration I could not and did not hesitate. I should certainly, if I had known the secret earlier, have made my stand on the upper St Johns & probably at the Madawaska settlements. But these speculations come now too late. The money I wrote about went to compensate Sparkes & to send him, on my first arrival, to the Governors of Maine & Massachusetts. My informant thinks that without this stimulant Maine would never have yielded, and here it has removed many objections in other quarters. — The secret now is with the President & his Cabinet the Governors of Maine & Massachusetts, seven Commissioners, four Senators, and it has this day been communicated to two more who are leading members of the Senates Committee for foreign affairs. In my house it is known only by Mildmay. This is a large number for keeping so singular a Secret but I must beg it may be strictly kept on your side, as my source of information would be betrayed. I am assured that it is not known by Everett. – There is one consolation to be derived from our tardy acquaintance with this fact. If I had known it before treating, in any way which would have permitted me to use it, we could not well have refrained from maintaining our undoubted right and yet we never should have got the Aroostook without fighting for it. All the evidence of angels would not have moved the Maine lumberers. This is my scrap of consolation. I have drawn on you a bill for £2998 – 1 – 30 days sight for the purpose mentioned in my former private letter and you will find this put into proper form. I am not likely to want anything more. The President is at open war with his Congress & Webster's Whig friends press him strongly to retire when he has finished our treaty. I think he will do so and he has a hankering to go to London & send Everett to Paris in Cass's place. I think this will be so arranged & Cass can now do no mischief here. I think you may now confidently reckon on peace with this country for some time barring very extraordinary accidents & with common care. I now relieve you my dear Ld Aberdeen from a tiresome correspondent.

"ps. It is very singular that among the number of persons who have been busy with this Boundary question nobody should have thought of so very natural an Enquiry at Paris excepting Sparkes."

Since Ashburton did not know of Sparks's map information until near August 9, we may guess that Ashburton had handed the money over to Webster with only a general assurance that it would help out.

The late Clyde A. Duniway called my attention to this intrigue years ago. I first learned of Ashburton's subornation of Professor Sparks in J. R. Baldwin's study of "The Ashburton-Webster Boundary Settlement," *Canadian Historical Association, Report of the Annual Meeting held at Ottawa,* May 23–4, 1938 (University of Toronto, 1938), p. 131. The authorities of the British Museum and Record Office most obligingly allowed a record agent to make photostats for me of the documents that Mr. Baldwin cited.

Professor Charles Everett copied the letter from Aberdeen to Ashburton of July 2, 1842 in the British Museum in July 1948 and kindly afforded me a copy.

INDEX

[Prepared by Charles N. Lurie]

A NOTE ON THE TYPE

The text of this book was set on the Linotype in CALEDONIA, *a type face belonging to the family of printing types known to the printer as "modern face." This term, "modern," was used to mark the change in type-letter style that occurred at the end of the eighteenth century – a radical change in letter shapes evinced in the types designed by Bodoni, Baskerville, Martin, the Didots, and others.*

The book was composed, printed, and bound by The Plimpton Press, Norwood, Massachusetts. The typography and binding design are by W. A. Dwiggins.

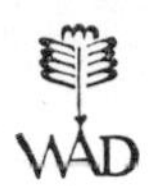

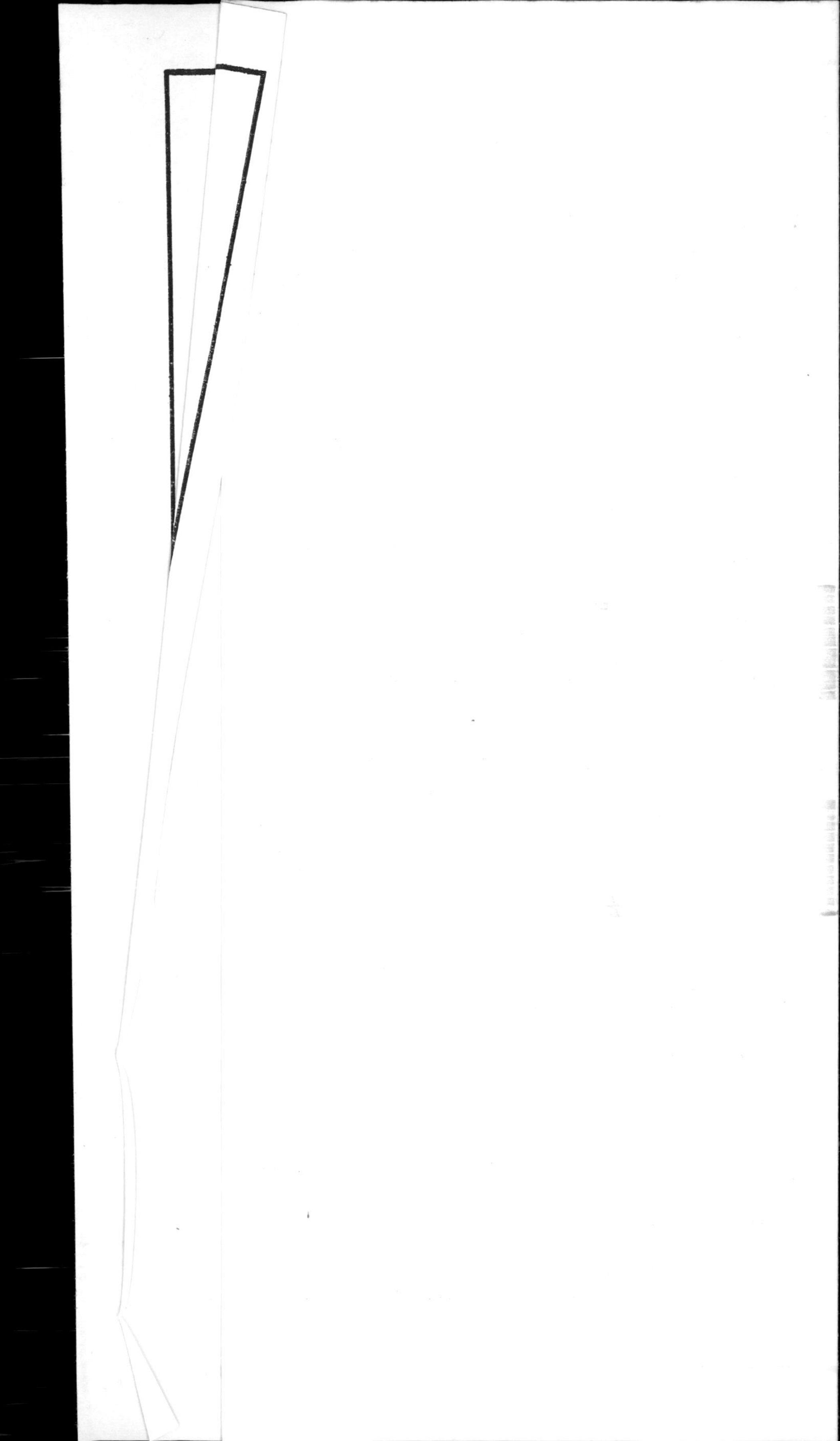